ADVANCES IN COMPUTER SCIENCE AND ENGINEERING

Edited by **Matthias Schmidt**

Advances in Computer Science and Engineering
Edited by Matthias Schmidt

Published by InTech
Janeza Trdine 9, 51000 Rijeka, Croatia

Publishing Process Manager Katarina Lovrecic

Technical Editor Teodora Smiljanic

Cover Designer InTech Design Team

Additional hard copies can be obtained from orders@intechopen.com

Advances in Computer Science and Engineering, Edited by Matthias Schmidt
p. cm.
ISBN 978-953-307-173-2

For EU product safety concerns:
IN TECH d.o.o., Prolaz Marije Krucifikse Kozulić 3, 51000 Rijeka, Croatia,
info@intechopen.com or visit our website at intechopen.com.

Meet the editor

Dr. Matthias Schmidt was born in 1978 in Germany. He studied industrial engineering and economics in Hanover. After his work as a project engineer he finished his doctoral thesis in the field of assembly logistics and received his doctor's decree from the Faculty of Mechanical Engineering of the Leibniz University Hannover. Dr. Schmidt is the author of several international articles and book chapters. He has lectureships in the areas of company management and lean production. Currently, he is the Head of Research and Industry at the Institute of Production Systems and Logistics of the Leibniz University Hannover. He coordinates research activities in the areas factory planning, logistics, production management, lean production and ergonomics as well as industrial consulting projects in the same areas.

Contents

Preface

"Amongst challenges there are potentials."
(Albert Einstein, 1879-1955)

The speed of technological, economical and societal change in the countries all over the world has increased steadily in the last century. This trend continues in the new millennium. Therefore, many challenges arise. To meet these challenges and to realize the resulting potentials, new approaches and solutions have to be developed. Therefore, research activities are becoming more and more important.

This book represents an international platform for scientists to show their advances in research and development and the resulting applications of their work as well as and opportunity to contribute to international scientific discussion.

The book *Advances in Computer Science and Engineering* constitutes the revised selection of 23 chapters written by scientists and researchers from all over the world. The chapters are organized in four sections: Applied Computing Techniques, Innovations in Mechanical Engineering, Electrical Engineering and Applications and Advances in Applied Modeling.

The first section Applied Computing Techniques presents new findings in technical approaches, programming and the transfer of computing techniques to other fields of research. The second and the third section; Innovations in Mechanical Engineering and Electrical Engineering and Applications; show the development, the application and the analysis of selected topics in the field of mechanical and electrical engineering. The fourth section, Advances in Applied Modeling, demonstrates the development and application of models in the areas of logistics, human-factor engineering and problem solutions.

This book could be put together due to the dedication of many people. I would like to thank the authors of this book for presenting their work in a form of interesting, well written chapters, as well as the InTech publishing team and Prof. Lovrecic for their great organizational and technical work.

Dr. Matthias Schmidt,
Institute of Production Systems and Logistics
Leibniz University of Hannover
Produktionstechnisches Zentrum Hannover (PZH)
An der Universität 2
30823 Garbsen
Germany

Part 1

Applied Computing Techniques

1

Next Generation Self-learning Style in Pervasive Computing Environments

Kaoru Ota[1], Mianxiong Dong, Long Zheng,
Jun Ma, Li Li, Daqiang Zhang and Minyi Guo
[1]*School of Computer Science and Engineering, The University of Aizu,*
Department of Computer Science and Engineering, Shanghai Jiao Tong University
Department of Computer Science, Nanjing Normal University
[1]*Japan*
China

1. Introduction

With the great progress of technologies, computers are embedded into everywhere to make our daily life convenient, efficient and comfortable [10-12] in a pervasive computing environment where services necessary for a user can be provided without demanding intentionally. This trend also makes a big influence even on the education field to make support methods for learning more effective than some traditional ways such as WBT (Web-Based Training) and e-learning [13, 14]. For example, some WBT systems for educational using in some universities [1, 2, 9], a system for teacher-learners' interaction in learner oriented education [3], and real e-learning programs for students [7, 8] had succeeded in the field. However, a learner's learning time is more abundant in the real world than in the cyber space, and learning support based on individual situation is insufficient only with WBT and e-learning. In addition, some researches show that it is difficult for almost all learners to adopt a self-directed learning style and few of learners can effectively follow a self-planned schedule [4]. Therefore, support in the real world is necessary for learners to manage a learning schedule to study naturally and actively with a self-learning style. Fortunately, with the rapid development of embedded technology, wireless networks, and individual detecting technology, these pervasive computing technologies make it possible to support a learner anytime and anywhere kindly, flexibly, and appropriately. Moreover, it comes to be able to provide the support more individually as well as comfortable surroundings for each learner through analyzing the context information (e.g. location, time, actions, and so on) which can be acquired in the pervasive computing environment.
In this chapter, we address a next-generation self-learning style with the pervasive computing and focus on two aspects: providing proper learning support to individuals and making learning environments suitable for individuals. Especially, a support method is proposed to encourage a learner to acquire his/her learning habit based on Behavior Analysis through a scheduler system called a Ubiquitous Learning Scheduler (ULS). In our design, the learner's situations are collected by sensors and analyzed by comparing them to his/her learning histories. Based on this information, supports are provided to the learner in order to help him/her forming a good learning style. For providing comfortable

surroundings, we improve the ULS system by utilizing data sensed by environments like room temperature and light for the system, which is called a Pervasive Learning Scheduler (PLS). The PLS system adjusts each parameter automatically for individuals to make a learning environment more comfortable. Our research results revealed that the ULS system not only benefits learners to acquire their learning habits but also improved their self-directed learning styles. In addition, experiment results show the PLS system get better performance than the ULS system.

The rest of the chapter consists as follows. In the section 2, we propose the ULS system and describe the design of the system in detail followed by showing implementation of the system with experimental results. In section 3, the PLS system is proposed and we provide an algorithm to find an optimum parameter to be used in the PLS system. The PLS system is also implemented and evaluated comparing to the ULS system. Finally, section 4 concludes this chapter.

2. The ULS system model

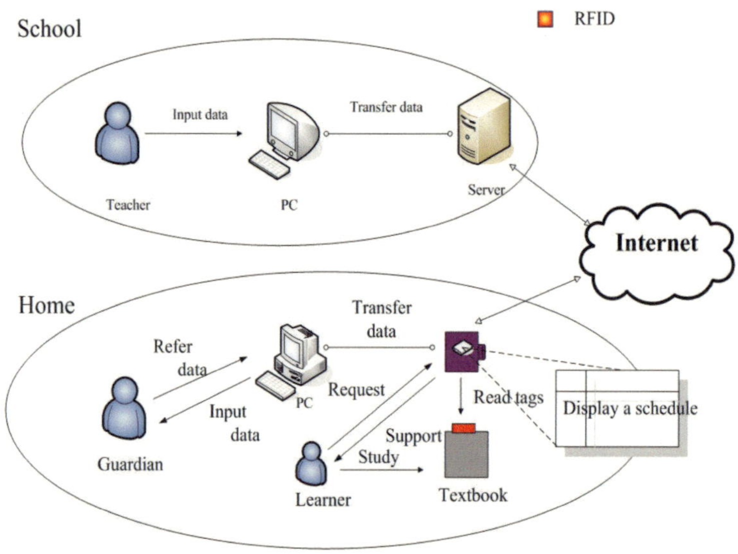

Fig. 1. A model of the ULS system

Figure 1. shows a whole model of a ubiquitous learning environment. The system to manage a learning schedule is embedded in a special kind of desks which can collect learning information, send it as well as receive data if needed, and display a learning schedule. In the future, it will be possible to embed the system in a portable device like a cellular phone. As a result, a learner will be able to study without choosing a place.

In Figure 1., there are two environments. One is a school area. In this area, a teacher inputs a learner's data, test record, course grade, and so forth. This information is transferred to the learner's desk in his/her home through the Internet. The other is a home area. In this area, a guardian inputs data based on his/her demands. This information is also transferred to the desk. When the learner starts to study several textbooks, his/her learning situation is collected by reading RFID tags attached to textbooks with an RFID-reader on the desk. Based on combination of teacher's data, parent's demand, and learner's situation, a learning

schedule is made by the system. A learning schedule chart is displayed on the desk. The learner follows the chart. The chart changes immediately and supports flexibly. The guardian also can see the chart to perceive the learner's state of achievement.
In this paper, we are focusing on the home area, especially learners' self-learning at home. We assume a learning environment is with the condition as same as Figure 1. To achieve the goal, we have the following problems to be solved:

1. How to display an attractive schedule chart to motivate the learner?
2. How to give a support based on Behavior Analysis?
3. When to give a support?
4. How to avoid failure during learning?

In order to solve the above problems, at first, a method which can manage a learning schedule is proposed. Its feature is to manage a learning schedule based on combination of the teacher's needs, the parent's needs, and learner's situation. Its advantage is that the learner can determine what to study at the present time immediately. Secondly, the ULS is implemented based on behavior analyzing method. Because behavioral psychology can offer students more modern and empirically defensible theories to explain the details of everyday life than can the other psychological theories [9].The function of the ULS is to use different colors to advise the learner subjects whether to study or not.

2.1 Ubiquitous Learning Scheduler (ULS)

This paper proposes a system called Ubiquitous Learning Scheduler (ULS) to support learner managing their learning schedule. The ULS is implemented with a managing learning schedule method. It analyses learning situations of the learner and gives advices to the leaner. This method solves the problems we mentioned above. Its details are described in following sections.

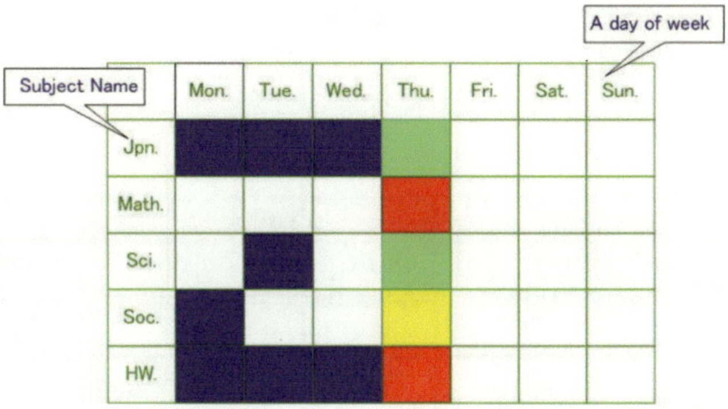

Fig. 2. An example of a scheduling chart

Figure 2. shows how to display a learning schedule chart in the ULS. Its rows indicate names of subjects and its columns indicate days of the week. For instance, a learner studies Japanese on Monday at a grid where Jpn. intersects with Mon. The ULS uses several colors to advise the learner. The learner can customize the colors as he/she like. Grids' colors shown in Figure 2. is an example of the scheduling chart. Each color of grids means as follows.

- Navy blue: The learning subject has been already finished.
- Red: The subject is in an insufficient learning state at the time or the learner has to study the subject as soon as possible at the time.

- Yellow: The subject is in a slightly insufficient learning state at the time.
- Green: The subject is in a sufficient learning state at the time.

As identified above, red grids have the highest learning priority. Therefore, a learner is recommended to study subjects in an ideal order: red→yellow→green.

The indications consider that accomplishments lead to motivations. There are two points. One is that a learner can find out which subjects are necessary to study timely whenever he/she looks at the chart. If a learning target is set specifically, it becomes easy to judge whether it has been achieved. The other is that the learner can grasp at a glance how much he/she has finished learning. It is important for motivating the learner to know attainment of goals accurately.

Basically, the ULS gives a learner supports when he/she is not studying in an ideal order. For example, when the learner tries to study a subject at a green grid though his/her chart has some red grids, the ULS gives a message such as "Please start to study XXX before YYY", where XXX is a subject name at a red grid and YYY is the subject name at the green one.

2.2 Supports to avoid failure during learning

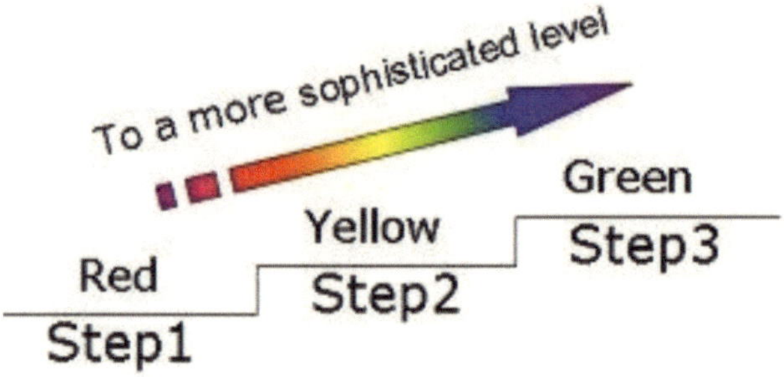

Fig. 3. Model of Shaping

	Red	Yellow	Green
Compliment Examples	Good! You've challenged this subject.	Quite good! You've done basic study for this subject.	Excellent! You've studied this subject quite enough.
Learning Time (Objective Time)	Regard-less of time	More than 10 min.	More than 20 min.

Table 1. Example of complements and learning time

The ULS also aims to lead the learner to a more sophisticated learning style than his/her initial condition. To solve this problem, we used the Shaping principle in Behavior Analysis [9]. When differential reinforcement and response generalization are repeated over and over, behavior can be "shaped" far from its original form [9]. Shaping is a process by which learning incentive is changed in several steps from their initial level to a more sophisticated level [9]. Each step results from the application of a new and higher criterion for differential reinforcement [9]. Each step produces both response differentiation and response generalization [9]. This principle also makes sense in the learning behavior. By referring to Figure 3., this paper considers red grids as step 1, yellow ones as step 2, and green ones as step 3. Step 1 is the lowest level. The ULS gives the learner different compliments based on learning time according to each color. Learning time depends on a learner's situation. Table 1 shows an example of that. Learning time of yellow and green are based on average of elementary students' learning time in home in Japan [4].

2.3 Design of the ULS system

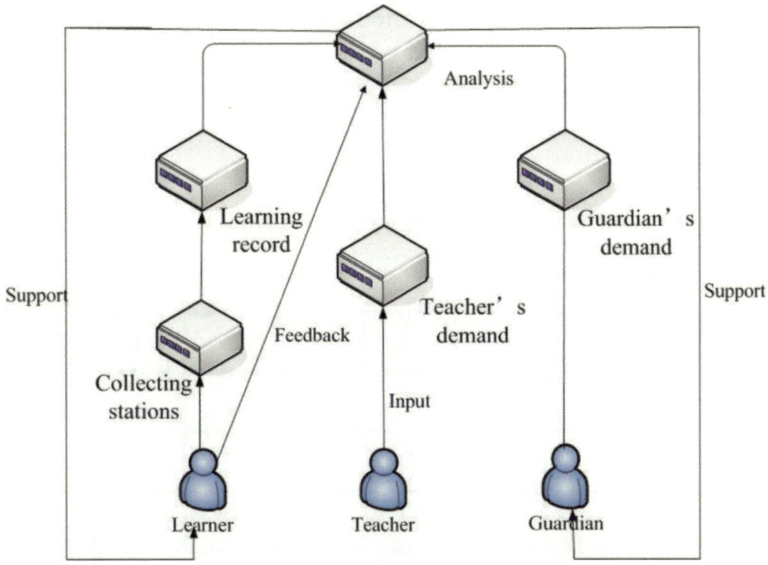

Fig. 4. Model of Shaping

Figure 4. shows a flow chart of the system in this research. A teacher and a guardian register each demand for a learner into each database, a *Teacher's Demand DB* and a *Guardian's Demand DB*. The demands indicate which subject the learner should have emphasis on. Each database consists of learning priorities and subject names. On the other hand, the learner begins to study with some educational materials. At the same time, the ULS collects his/her learning situations and puts them into a *Learning Record DB*. The database consists of date, learning time, and subject names. By comparing and analyzing the information of three databases, the ULS makes a scheduling chart such as Figure 2. and always displays it in learning. The learner pursues its learning schedule. The ULS gives him/her supports, depending on learning situations. The guardian can grasp the learner's progress situation of the schedule by the ULS supports.

Each grid's color is decided with calculating Color Value (CV). We define the following equation for determining CV.

$$CV = CV_0 * LAD + SAD \tag{1}$$

Each notation means as follows.

$$CV[\ 2 \leq CV \leq 4] : Color\ Value \tag{2}$$

CV decides a color of the current grid and has some ranges for three colors such as red, yellow, and green. The green range is from -2 to 0, the yellow one is from 0 to 2, and the red one is from 2 to 4. Also, the value smaller than -2 will be considered as green and bigger than 4 will be considered as red respectively. For example, when CV equals to 0.5, the color is yellow. These ranges are not relative to RGB code and are assumed to be set by the teacher in this research.

$$CV_0[0 \le CV_0 \le 1] : \textit{Initial Color Value} \tag{3}$$

CV_0 is decided with combination of the teacher's demand and the guardian's one. At first, the teacher and the guardian respectively input priority of subjects which they want the learner to self-study. Priority is represented by a value from 1 to 5. 5 is the highest priority and 1 is the lowest one. ULS converts each priority into CV_0. CV_0 is calculated by the following equation.

$$CV_0 = (TP + GP) * 0.1 \tag{4}$$

In the equation (4), TP and GP mean Teacher's Priority and Guardian's Priority respectively.

	Jpn.	Math.	Sci.	Soc.	HW.
Teacher	5	2	3	4	1
Guardian	5	4	2	3	1
Sum.	10	6	5	7	2
CV_0	1.0	0.6	0.5	0.7	0.2

Table 2. An example of a relationship between ranks and CV0

For an example, in Table 2, Math ranks the value as 2 by the teacher and the 4 by the guardian. Therefore the sum of their priority equals to 6 and CV_0 is decided as 0.6.
The learner's situation also affects CV. We express it as Long-term Achievement Degree (LAD) and Short-term Achievement Degree (SAD). Both of their values are fixed at the end of a last studying day.

$$LAD[0 \le LAD \le 100] : \textit{Long-term Achievement Degree} \tag{5}$$

LAD indicates how much the learner has been able to accomplish a goal of a subject for a long term. In this paper, this goal is to acquire his/her learning habit. The default value is 100 percent. We assume that the learner has achieved his/her goal when all grids are green. Then, the LAD value equals to 100 percent. For example, if the number of green grids is 12 where the number of all grids of a subject is 15 at current time, the LAD value equals to 80 percent. The term period is assumed to be set by a teacher. For instance, the term can be a week, or a month. LAD values are initialized when the term is over.

$$SAD[\ 1 \le SAD \le 1] : \textit{Short-term Achievement Degree} \tag{6}$$

SAD indicates how much the learner has been able to accomplish a goal of a subject for a short term. In this paper, this goal is to study a subject for objective time of a day. The default value is 0. SAD has particular three values, -1, 0, and 1. These values means as follows.

1. The learner has studied for no time.
2. The learner has studied for less than objective time.
3. The learner has studied for more than objective time.

Objective time depends on a grid's color. This idea is based on Section 4.4. For example, objective time is 10 minutes for red grids, 20 minutes for yellow ones, and 30 minutes for green ones. At a subject on a red grid, we assume that a learner is not willing to study it. Therefore, to compliment studying is important, even if the learner studies for only a fraction of the time. That is why objective time of red grids is less than one of others. If the learner takes 10 minutes to study a subject on a yellow grid, the SAD value equals to 0. In this paper, objective time is initialized by the teacher based on the learner's ability. Since the learner starts to use the ULS, the ULS automatically has set objective time. The ULS analyzes average learning time of the learner, and decides it as objective time for yellow grids. The ULS also analyzes minimum learning time and maximum one, and decides each them as objective time for red grids and green ones. Therefore, the objective time is flexibly changed with the learner's current ability.

Sometimes there are some relationships between the subjects. If the learner studies the subjects in a meaningful order, it will result a better understanding. Otherwise, the learning efficiency is down. For example, classical literature (Ancient writings or Chinese writing) witch is told in traditional Japanese class might require some pre-knowledge about the history to help learner understanding the contents and meaning well. In this case, it is clear that the priority of study the subject History is higher than the subject Japanese. Also, it is a common sense that rudimentary mathematics might be a prerequisites course before science study. Considering this characteristics, we also define an equation to improve the system,

$$CV'_i = CV_i + (\sum_{j=1}^{n} CV_j) * P_i \tag{7}$$

where, $P_i = \dfrac{X_i}{\sum_{j=1}^{n} X_j}$

We improve the CV' to apply the shaping principle. P means the priority of each subject. In this paper, we take the teacher's priority into this formula. Because teachers are more familiar with the relationships between each courses than guardian and it should has more weighted to influence the learner.

	Jpn.	Math.	Sci.	Soc.	HW.
TP	5	4	1	2	3
CV	1.8	1.2	-0.5	0.4	0.8
CV'	3.03	2.18	-0.25	0.89	1.54

Table 3. An example of relationship between CV and CV'

For example, in Table 3., the teacher set the priorities as (Jpn., Math., Sci., Soc., HW.), (5, 4, 1, 2, 3) respectively. Using the equation (7), we can earn the new priority, for example, Jpn. like:

$$CVJpn.' = 1.8 + (1.8 + 1.2 - 0.5 + 0.4 + 0.8) * \frac{5}{(5+4+1+2+3)} = 3.03$$

$$CVMath.' = 1.2 + (1.8 + 1.2 - 0.5 + 0.4 + 0.8) * \frac{4}{(5+4+1+2+3)} = 2.18$$

and the same to the other subjects.

2.4 Implementation and evaluation of the ULS system

We implemented the ULS system based on a specialized desk using a laptop PC, which is connected to a RFID-READER with RS-232C in this research. We use version 1.01 of DAS-101 of Daiichi Tsushin Kogyo Ltd for RFID-READER and RFID [10]. Programming langrage C# is used to develop the ULS system. We use Microsoft Access for a *Teacher's Demand DB*, a *Guardian's Demand DB*, and a *Learning Record DB*.

In this research, each class has its own textbook with an RFID-tag. The ULS recognizes that a learner is studying a subject of which an RFID is read by the RFID-READER. We assume that as learning time while the RFID-READER reads the RFID.

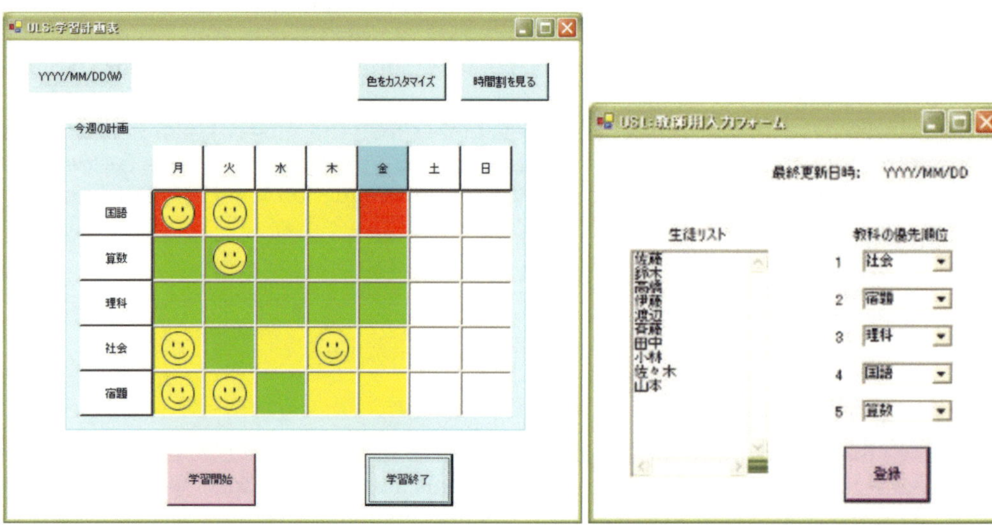

Fig. 5. Screen shot of ULS

Figure 5. is a screen capture of ULS in this research. It shows a learning scheduling chart for a student and his/her guardian. Marks indicate that the learning of the subject has been already finished.

The purpose of the evaluation is as follows:

1. Could the system provide efficient and effective learning style to the learner?
2. Could the system increase the learner's motivation?
3. Could the system improve self-directed learning habit of the learner?

Through verifying these points, we attempted to find several needs to be improved in this system.

The method of this evaluation is a questionnaire survey. 20 examinees studied five subjects with this system for a few hours. Based on their information such as liked or disliked subjects, Color Value of each subject is initialized. After an examining period, they answered some questionnaires for evaluating this system. Contents of the questionnaires are as follows:

Q1: Did you feel this system makes your motivation increase for self-directed learning?
Q2: Did the system provide suitable visible-supports to you?
Q3: Do you think this system helps you to improve your learning habit at home?
Q4: Did you feel this system was easy to use?

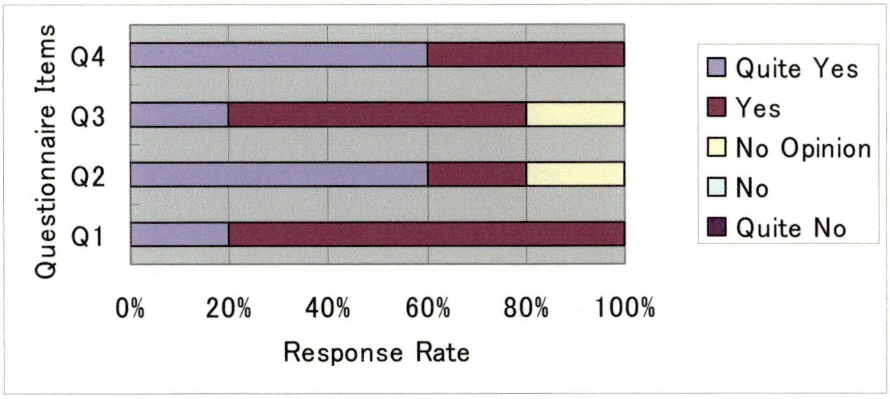

Fig. 6. Result of Questionnaire Survey (1)

Figure 6. shows statistical results of questionnaire survey of only using the equation (1). Positive responses, more than 80 percent of "quite yes" and "yes", were obtained from every questionnaire item. However, some comments were provided in regard to supports of this system. For example, "It will be more suitable if the system can support for a particular period such as days near examination." One of this reasons was the system was designed focused on usual learning-style.

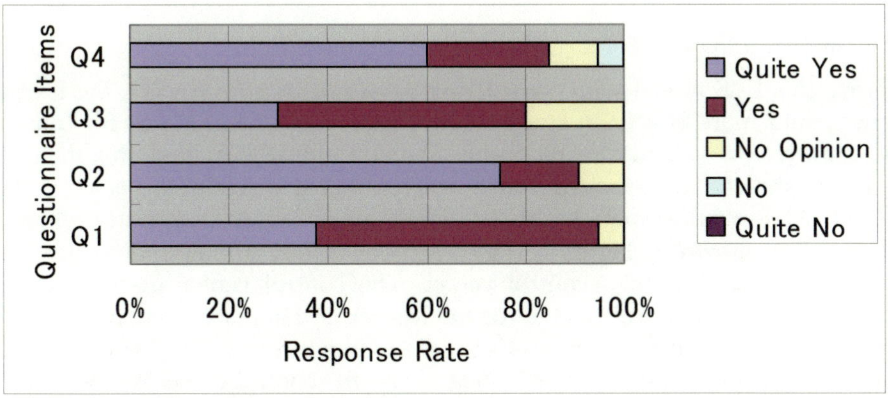

Fig. 7. Result of Questionnaire Survey (2)

Figure 7. shows statistical results of questionnaire survey with the equation (7) implemented in the system. We can see there is a progress especially on the answer "Quite Yes" comparing with the result only using the equation (1).

3. The new model of the ULS system

3.1 Pervasive Learning Scheduler (PLS)

So far, we propose a support method for self-managing learning scheduler using Behavior Analysis in a ubiquitous environment. Based on our method, the ULS is implemented. According to the experiment results, the contribution of the ULS can be summarized as follows: the ULS is effective to motivate a learner at his/her home study, and the ULS helps to improve his/her self-directed learning habit with considering his/her teacher's and his/her guardian's request.

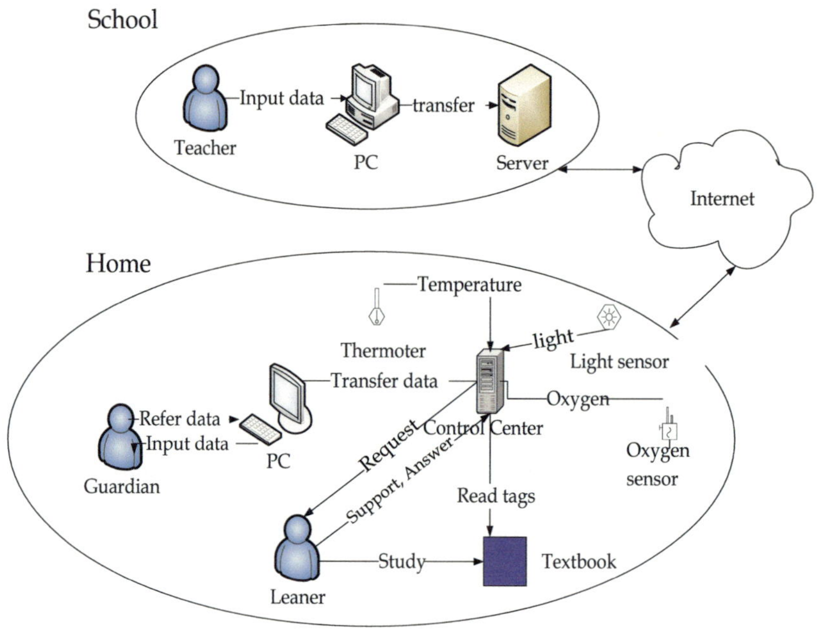

Fig. 8. The improved model: Pervasive Learning Scheduler (PLS)

We improve this ULS model with considering enviroments surrounding the learner since the learner could more effecively study in an environment comfortable for him/her. For example, intuitively it is better for the leaner to study in a well-lighted area than in a dark one. Figure 8. shows the improved model and we call it as called a Pervasive Learning Scheduler (PLS). In this research, we only consider an environment at home where sensors are embedded as shown in Figure 8. These sensors collect corresponding data from the environment and send it to a control center. The control center decides whether the corresponding parameters are suitable for the learner and adjusts them automatically. For example, a learner accustoms himself to a temperature of 26 degree. The current temperature collected by the sensor is 30 degree. As the control center receives this data, it makes a decision on adjusting the temperature. We only show three kinds of sensors in the figure, however; the PLS also can include other several kinds of sensors as users need.

To this end, we have the following problem: how does the control center decide optimum values for each parameter? In order to solve this, we propose a data training method. Its feature is to select adaptive step to approach the optimum value.

3.2 Design of the PLS system

In the PLS system, sensors collect data from an environment and send it to the control center. Based on collected data from a learner's surroundings, the control center adjusts each parameter to the optimal value. A problem is how to decide the optimum values by the control center. As we take a temperature as an example, then the problem can be rephrased as: how does the control center know the suitable temperature for each individual learner.

You may think that a learner can tell the control center a preferred temperature as the optimal value in advance. More precisely, however, the learner can only set an approximate value not exactly optimal one on the system. We solve this problem to train the data based on the following algorithm.

1. A learner sets the current temperature with a preferred value and sets a step value.
2. The system increases the current temperature by the step value while the learner studies.
3. At the end of study, the system compares the studying efficiency with a previous one in a record. If the efficiency ratio increases, go to the phase (2).
4. If the efficiency becomes lower, it shows that the step value is too large, so we should deflate the value. Divide the step value by 2, then go to the phase (2). Stop after the step value is less than a threshold value.
5. After find an optimum temperature with the highest efficiency ratio, reset the step value to the initial one. Repeat the above phases from (1) to (4) except for the phase (2). In the phase (2), the system decreases the current temperature by the step value.
6. After find another optimum temperature by the second round, compare it with the optimum temperature we firstly found, and choose the better one according to their efficiency ratios.

The studying efficiency is derived based on *CV'* obtained by the equation (7) in subsection 2.3. The efficiency *E(t)* is calculated at time *t* of the end of study with the following equation (8).

$$E(t) = \frac{n}{\sum_{j=1}^{n} CV'_j(t)} \tag{8}$$

Then, we can obtain the efficiency ratio comparing *E(t)* with *E(t-1)* which is the efficiency of the previous study at time *t-1* in a record with the following equation (9).

$$Efficiency\ Ratio = \frac{E(t)}{E(t-1)} \tag{9}$$

Temperature	24	25	25.5	26	26.5	27	28
Efficiency ratio	0.8	0.95	1.4	1	1.3	0.96	0.85

Table 2. An example of temperature values and efficiency ratios

Table 2. shows an example of how to decide the optimum temperature value when firstly the learner sets 26 degree as an approximate temperature which makes him/her comfortable. We can assume that the optimum temperature is around the approximate temperature 26 degree, then the optimum temperature can be in [26-*A*, 26+*A*], where *A* is a positive number larger enough to find the optimum value. *A* is the step value and initially set by the learner. We assume the learner sets it as A=2. According to our algorithm, we compare the efficiency ratio of temperature of 28 and 26. We can see that the efficiency ratio of 28 degree is lower than that of 26 degree. We decrease the step value and get a new step value: $A'=A/2=1$. Then, we compare the efficiency ratio of 27 degree with that of 26 degree. The efficiency ratio of 26 degree is still higher, so we decrease the step value again and get another step value: $A''=A'/2=0.5$. The efficiency ratio of 26.5 degree is higher than that of 26 degree. As a result of the first round, we find that the optimum temperature that is 26.5 degree. For simplicity, we generally stop when the step equals to 0.1. Then, we repeat the phases to obtain another optimum temperature. As a result of the second round, we find the optimum temperature that is 25.5 degree. Comparing the efficiency ratio of 25.5 degree to that of 26.5 degree, we finally choose 25.5 degree as the optimum temperature because its efficiency ratio is higher.

Each day, we only modify the temperature once, and we get the corresponding efficiency ratio. After several days, we can finally get the optimum temperature. In the same way, the control center finds an optimum value for each parameter.

3.3 Implementation and evaluation of the PLS system

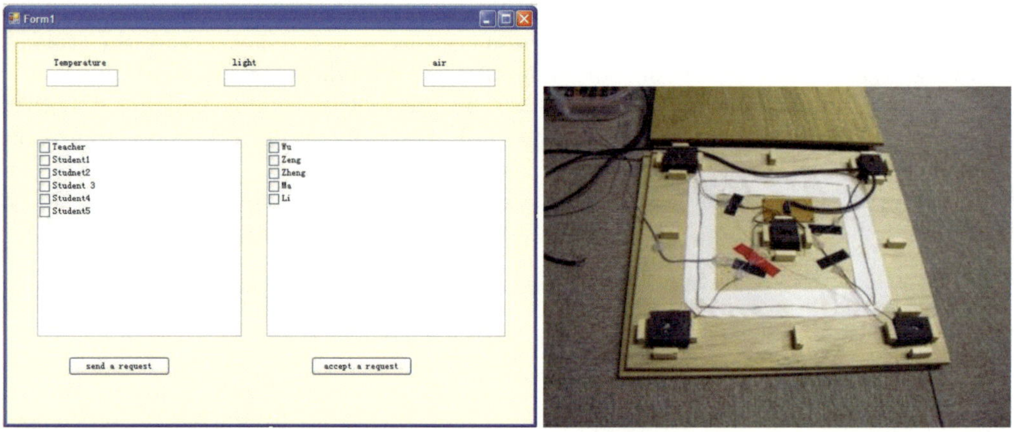

(a) A snapshot of the control center (b) Back side of a special tile

Fig. 8. Implementation of the PLS system

We implement the PLS system based on the ULS system. Figure. 8(a) shows a screen capture of the Control Center in the PLS system.

To improve performance of gathering sensory data, we develop special tiles as shown in Figure. 8(b). The special tiles are embedded with an RFID antenna and pressure sensors, which are spread all over the desk. Each book includes an RFID tag showing text information (e.g., English textbook). The dynamic information of a book put on the tile is acquired by the tile connected to a sensor network. We designed to solve the following problems; passive RFID reader only has a narrow range of operation and sometimes it works not well for gathering data of all books on the desk. We separated the antenna from the reader and created a RF-ID antenna with coil to broad the operation range of it. As the result, with a relay circuit 16 antennas can control by only one reader. The tile also has five pressure sensors. By using the special tile, accuracy of gathering learning information was increased.

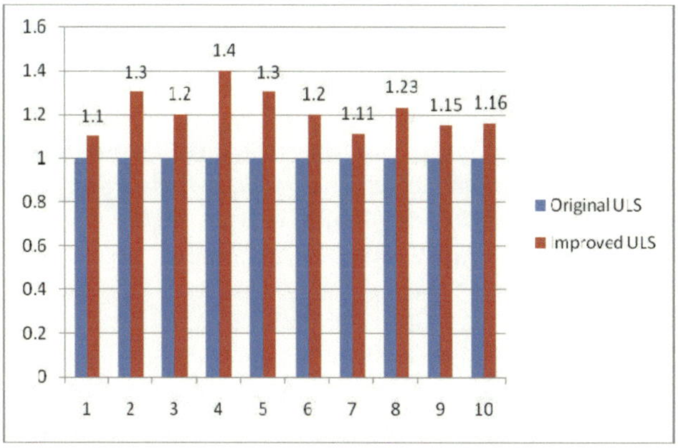

Fig. 9. Efficiency ratio comparison between the ULS and the PLS

We evaluate the PLS by involving 10 subjects of students. In order to evaluate learning effectiveness with considering environmental factors, they answer the following questionnaires, which is the same in subsection 2.4, after using the ULS system as well as the PLS system for some periods respectively.

Q1: Did you feel this system makes your motivation increase for self-directed learning?

Q2: Did the system provide suitable visible-supports to you?

Q3: Do you think this system helps you to improve your learning habit at home?

Q4: Did you feel this system was easy to use?

Then, we compare feedback scores of the PLS system with that of the ULS system and calculate efficiency ratio based on score averages. Figure. 9 shows every subject thinks that the PLS system is more efficient to study than the ULS system. We can conclude PLS system succeeds to provide comfortable learning environments to each learner with pervasive computing technologies, which leads to efficient self-learning style.

4. Conclusion

We address a next-generation self-learning style utilizing pervasive computing technologies for providing proper learning supports as well as comfortable learning environment for individuals. Firstly, a support method for self-managing learning scheduler, called the PLS, is proposed and analyzes context information obtained from sensors by Behavior Analysis. In addition, we have involved the environment factors such as temperature and light into the PLS for making a learner's surroundings efficient for study. The sensory data from environments is sent to a decision center which analyzes the data and makes the best decision for the learner. The PLS has been evaluated by some examinees. According to the results, we have revealed that improved PLS not only benefited learners to acquire their learning habits but also improved their self-directed learning styles than the former one.

5. Acknowledgment

This work is supported in part by Japan Society for the Promotion of Science (JSPS) Research Fellowships for Young Scientists Program, JSPS Excellent Young Researcher Overseas Visit Program, National Natural Science Foundation of China (NSFC) Distinguished Young Scholars Program (No. 60725208) and NSCF Grant No. 60811130528.

6. References

Lima, P.; Bonarini, A. & Mataric, M. (2004). *Application of Machine Learning,* InTech, ISBN 978-953-7619-34-3, Vienna, Austria

Li, B.; Xu, Y. & Choi, J. (1996). Applying Machine Learning Techniques, *Proceedings of ASME 2010 4th International Conference on Energy Sustainability,* pp. 14-17, ISBN 842-6508-23-3, Phoenix, Arizona, USA, May 17-22, 2010

Siegwart, R. (2001). Indirect Manipulation of a Sphere on a Flat Disk Using Force Information. *International Journal of Advanced Robotic Systems,* Vol.6, No.4, (December 2009), pp. 12-16, ISSN 1729-8806

Arai, T. & Kragic, D. (1999). Variability of Wind and Wind Power, In: *Wind Power,* S.M. Muyeen, (Ed.), 289-321, Scyio, ISBN 978-953-7619-81-7, Vukovar, Croatia

Van der Linden, S. (June 2010). Integrating Wind Turbine Generators (WTG's) with Energy Storage, In: *Wind Power,* 17.06.2010, Available from http://sciyo.com/articles/show/title/wind-power-integrating-wind-turbine-generators-wtg-s-with-energy-storage

Taniguchi, R. (2002). Development of a Web-based CAI System for Introductory Visual Basic Programming Course, *Japanese Society for Information and Systems in Education,* Vol.19 No.2, pp. 106-111

Fuwa, Y.; Nakamura, Y.; Yamazaki, H. & Oshita, S. (2003). Improving University Education using a CAI System on the World Wide Web and its Evaluation, *Japanese Society for Information and Systems in Education,* Vol.20 No.1, pp. 27-38

Nakamura, S.; Sato, K.; Fujimori, M.; Koyama, A. & Cheng, Z. (2002). A Support System for Teacher-Learner interaction in Learner-oriented Education, *Information Processing Society of Japan,* Vol.43 No.2, pp.671-682

Benesse Corporation. (2005). Home Educational Information of Grade-school Pupils, Benesse Corporation, Japan

Baldwin, J.D & Baldwin, J.I.; (2001). Behavior Principles in Everyday Life, 4th ed., L. Pearson, (Ed.), Prentice-Hall, Inc., New Jersey

Daiichi Tsushin Kogyo Ltd. (2003). Automatic Recognition System, Daiichi Tsushin Kogyo Ltd., Available from http://zones.co.jp/mezam.html

School of Human Sciences, Waseda University. E-School, Available from http://e-school.human.waseda.ac.jp/

Oklahoma State University. Online Courses, Available from http://oc.okstate.edu/

Barbosa, J.; Hahn, R.; Barbosa, D.N.F. & Geyer, C.F.R. (2007). Mobile and ubiquitous computing in an innovative undergraduate course, *In Proceedings of 38th SIGCSE technical symposium on Computer science education,* pp. 379–383

Satyanarayanan, M. (2001). Pervasive Computing: Vision and Challenges, *IEEE Personal Communication,* pp. 10-17

Ponnekanti, S.R; et al. (2001). Icrafter: A service framework for ubiquitous computing environments, *In Proceedings of Ubicomp 2001,* pp. 56–75

Stanford, V. (2002). Using Pervasive Computing to Deliver Elder Care, *IEEE Pervasive Computing,* pp.10-13

Hinske, S. & Langheinrich, M. (2009). An infrastructure for interactive and playful learning in augmented toy environments, *In Proceedings of IEEE International Conference on Pervasive Computing and Communications (PerCom 2009),* pp. 1-6

Yu, Z.; Nakamura, Y.; Zhang, D.; Kajita, S. & Mase, K. (2008). Content Provisioning for Ubiquitous Learning, *IEEE Pervasive Computing, Vol. 7,* Issue 4, pp. 62-70

2

Automatic Generation of Programs

Ondřej Popelka and Jiří Štastný
Mendel University in Brno
Czech Republic

1. Introduction

Automatic generation of program is definitely an alluring problem. Over the years many approaches emerged, which try to smooth away parts of programmers' work. One approach already widely used today is colloquially known as *code generation* (or code generators). This approach includes many methods and tools, therefore many different terms are used to describe this concept. The very basic tools are included in various available Integrated Development Environments (IDE). These include templates, automatic code completion, macros and other tools. On a higher level, code generation is performed by tools, which create program source code from metadata or data. Again, there are thousands of such tools available both commercial and open source. Generally available are programs for generating source code from relational or object database schema, object or class diagrams, test cases, XML schema, XSD schema, design patterns or various formalized descriptions of the problem domain.

These tools mainly focus on the generation of a template or skeleton for an application or application module, which is then filled with actual algorithms by a programmer. The great advantage of such tools is that they lower the amount of tedious, repetitive and boring (thus error-prone) work. Commonly the output is some form of data access layer (or data access objects) or object relational mapping (ORM) or some kind of skeleton for an application - for example interface for creating, reading, updating and deleting objects in database (CRUD operations). Further, this approach leads to generative programming domain, which includes concepts such as *aspect-oriented programming* (Gunter & Mitchell, 1994), *generic programming*, *meta-programming* etc. (Czarnecki & Eisenecker, 2000). These concepts are now available for general use – for example the AspectJ extension to Java programming language is considered stable since at least 2003 (Ladad, 2009). However, they are not still mainstream form of programming according to TIOBE Index (TIOBE, 2010).

A completely different approach to the problem is an actual generation of algorithms of the program. This is a more complex then *code generation* as described above, since it involves actual creation of algorithms and procedures. This requires either extremely complex tools or artificial intelligence. The former can be probably represented by two most successful (albeit completely different) projects – Lyee project (Poli, 2002) and Specware project (Smith, 1999). Unfortunately, the Lyee project was terminated in 2004 and the latest version of Specware is from 2007.

As mentioned above, another option is to leverage artificial intelligence methods (particularly evolutionary algorithms) and use them to create *code evolution*. We use the term *code evolution* as an opposite concept to *code generation* (as described in previous paragraphs) and later we will describe how these two concepts can be coupled. When using code generation, we let the programmer specify program metadata and automatically generate skeleton for his application, which he then fills with actual algorithms. When using code evolution, we let the programmer specify sample inputs and outputs of the program and automatically generate the actual algorithms fulfilling the requirements. We aim to create a tool which will aid human programmers by generating working algorithms (not optimal algorithms) in programming language of their choice.

In this chapter, we describe evolutionary methods usable for code evolution and results of some experiments with these. Since most of the methods used are based on genetic algorithms, we will first briefly describe this area of artificial intelligence. Then we will move on to the actual algorithms for automatic generation of programs. Furthermore, we will describe how these results can be beneficial to mainstream programming techniques.

2. Methods used for automatic generation of programs

2.1 Genetic algorithms

Genetic algorithms (GA) are a large group of evolutionary algorithms inspired by evolutionary mechanisms of live nature. Evolutionary algorithms are non-deterministic algorithms suitable for solving very complex problems by transforming them into *state space* and searching for optimum state. Although they originate from modelling of natural process, most evolutionary algorithms do not copy the natural processes precisely.

The basic concept of genetic algorithms is based on *natural selection process* and is very generic, leaving space for many different approaches and implementations. The domain of GA is in solving multidimensional optimisation problems, for which analytical solutions are unknown (or extremely complex) and efficient numerical methods are unavailable or their initial conditions are unknown. A genetic algorithm uses three genetic operators – *reproduction*, *crossover* and *mutation* (Goldberg, 2002). Many differences can be observed in the strategy of the parent selection, the form of genes, the realization of crossover operator, the replacement scheme, etc. A basic *steady-state genetic algorithm* involves the following steps.

Initialization. In each step, a genetic algorithm contains a number of solutions (individuals) in one or more populations. Each solution is represented by genome (or chromosome). Initialization creates a starting population and sets all bits of all chromosomes to an initial (usually random) value.

Crossover. The crossover is the main procedure to ensure progress of the genetic algorithm. The crossover operator should be implemented so that by combining several existing chromosomes a new chromosome is created, which is expected to be a better solution to the problem.

Mutation. Mutation operator involves a random distortion of random chromosomes; the purpose of this operation is to overcome the tendency of genetic algorithm in reaching the local optimum instead of global optimum. Simple mutation is implemented so that each gene in each chromosome can be randomly changed with a certain very small probability.

Finalization. The population cycle is repeated until a termination condition is satisfied. There are two basic finalization variations: maximal number of iterations and the quality of the best solution. Since the latter condition may never be satisfied both conditions are usually used.

The critical operation of genetic algorithm is crossover which requires that it is possible to determine what a "better solution" is. This is determined by a *fitness function* (criterion function or objective function). The fitness function is the key feature of genetic algorithm, since the genetic algorithm performs the minimization of this function. The fitness function is actually the transformation of the problem being solved into a state space which is searched using genetic algorithm (Mitchell, 1999).

2.2 Genetic programming

The first successful experiments with automatic generation of algorithms were using Genetic Programming method (Koza, 1992). Genetic programming (GP) is a considerably modified genetic algorithm and is now considered a field on its own. GP itself has proven that evolutionary algorithms are definitely capable of solving complex problems such as automatic generation of programs. However, a number of practical issues were discovered. These later lead to extending GP with (usually context-free) grammars to make this method more suitable to generate program source code (Wong & Leung, 1995) and (Patterson & Livesey, 1997).

Problem number one is the overwhelming complexity of automatic generation of a program code. The most straightforward approach is to split the code into subroutines (functions or methods) the same way as human programmers do. In genetic programming this problem is generally being solved using *Automatically Defined Functions* (ADF) extension to GP. When using automatically defined function each program is split into definitions of one or more functions, an expression and result producing branch. There are several methods to create ADFs, from manual user definition to automatic evolution. Widely recognized approaches include generating ADFs using genetic programing (Koza, 1994), genetic algorithms (Ahluwalia & Bull, 1998), logic grammars (Wong & Leung, 1995) or gene expression programming (Ferreira, 2006a).

Second very difficult problem is actually creating syntactically and semantically correct programs. In genetic programming, the program code itself is represented using a *concrete syntax tree* (*parse tree*). An important feature of GP is that all genetic operations are applied to the tree itself, since GP algorithms generally lack any sort of genome. This leads to problems when applying the crossover or mutation operators since it is possible to create a syntactically invalid structure and since it limits evolutionary variability. A classic example of the former is exchanging (within crossover operation) a function with two parameters for a function with one parameter and vice versa - part of the tree is either missing or superfluous. The latter problem is circumvented using very large initial populations which contain all necessary prime building blocks. In subsequent populations these building blocks are only combined into correct structure (Ferreira, 2006a).

Despite these problems, the achievements of genetic programming are very respectable; as of year 2003 there are 36 human-competitive results known (Koza et al, 2003). These results include various successful specialized algorithms or circuit topologies. However we would like to concentrate on a more mainstream problems and programming languages. Our goal are not algorithms competitive to humans, rather we focus on creating algorithms which are just working. We are also targeting mainstream programming languages.

2.3 Grammatical evolution

The development of Grammatical Evolution (GE) algorithm (O'Neill & Ryan, 2003) can be considered a major breakthrough when solving both problems mentioned in the previous paragraph. This algorithm directly uses a generative context-free grammar (CFG) to generate structures in an arbitrary language defined by that grammar. A genetic algorithm is used to direct the structure generation. The usage of a context-free grammar to generate a solution ensures that a solution is always syntactically correct. It also enables to precisely and flexibly define the form of a solution without the need to alter the algorithm implementation.

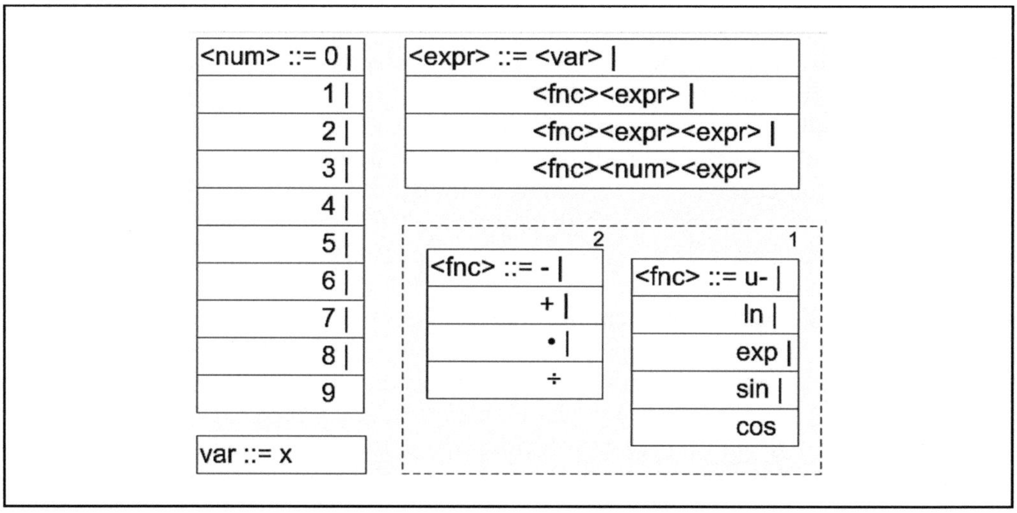

Fig. 1. Production rules of grammar for generating arithmetic expressions

In grammatical evolution each individual in the population is represented by a sequence of rules of a defined (context-free) grammar. The particular solution is then generated by translating the chromosome to a sequence of rules which are then applied in specified order. A context-free grammar G is defined as a tuple G = (Π,Σ,P,S) where Π is set of non-terminals, Σ is set of terminals, S is initial non-terminal and P is table of production rules.

The non-terminals are items, which appear in the individuals' body (the solution) only before or during the translation. After the translation is finished all non-terminals are translated to terminals. Terminals are all symbols which may appear in the generated language, thus they represent the solution. Start symbol is one non-terminal from the non-terminals set, which is used to initialize the translation process. Production rules define the laws under which non-terminals are translated to terminals. Production rules are key part of the grammar definition as they actually define the structure of the generated solution (O'Neill & Ryan, 2003).

We will demonstrate the principle of grammatical evolution and the backward processing algorithm on generating algebraic expressions. The grammar we can use to generate arithmetic expressions is defined by equations (1) – (3); for brevity, the production rules are shown separately in BNF notation on Figure 1 (Ošmera & Popelka, 2006).

$$\Pi = \{expr, fnc, num, var\} \quad (1)$$

$$\Sigma = \{\sin, \cos, +, -, \div, \cdot, x, 0, 1, 2, 3, 4, 5, 6, 7, 8, 9\} \quad (2)$$

$$S = expr \quad (3)$$

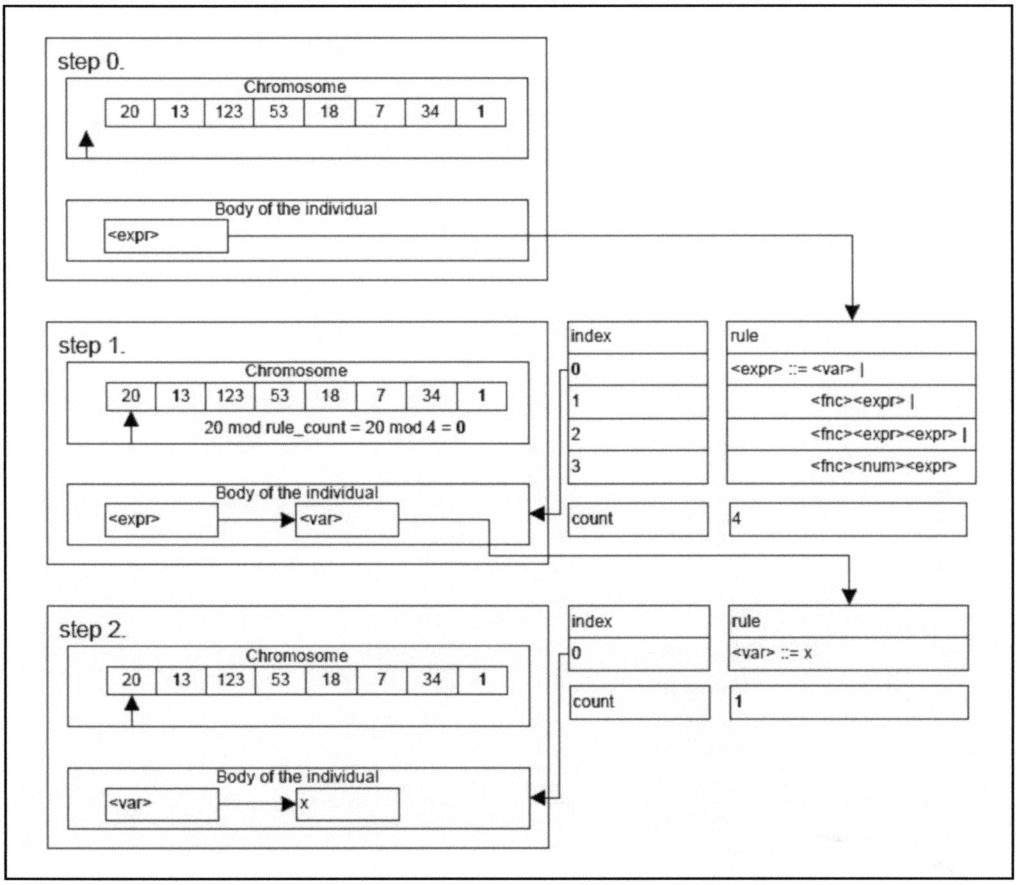

Fig. 2. Process of the translation of the genotype to a solution (phenotype)

The beginning of the process of the translation is shown on Figure 2. At the beginning we have a chromosome which consists of randomly generated integers and a non-terminal <expr> (expression). Then all rules which can rewrite this non-terminal are selected and rule is chosen using modulo operation and current gene value. Non-terminal <expr> is rewritten to non-terminal <var> (variable). Second step shows that if only one rule is available for rewriting the non-terminal, it is not necessary to read a gene and the rule is applied immediately. This illustrates how the genome (chromosome) can control the generation of solutions. This process is repeated for every solution until no non-terminals are left in its' body. Then each solution can be evaluated and a genetic algorithm population cycle can start and determine best solutions and create new chromosomes.

Other non-terminals used in this grammar can be <fnc> (function) and <num> (number). Here we consider standard arithmetic operators as functions, the rules on Figure 1 are divided by the number of arguments for a function ("u-" stands for unary minus).

3. Two-level grammatical evolution

In the previous section, we have described original grammatical evolution algorithm. We have further developed the original grammatical evolution algorithm by extending it with

Backward Processing algorithm (Ošmera, Popelka & Pivoňka, 2006). The backward processing algorithm just uses different order of processing the rules of the context free grammar than the original GE algorithm. Although the change might seem subtle, the consequences are very important. When using the original algorithm, the rules are read left-to-right and so is the body of the individual scanned left-to-right for untranslated non-terminals.

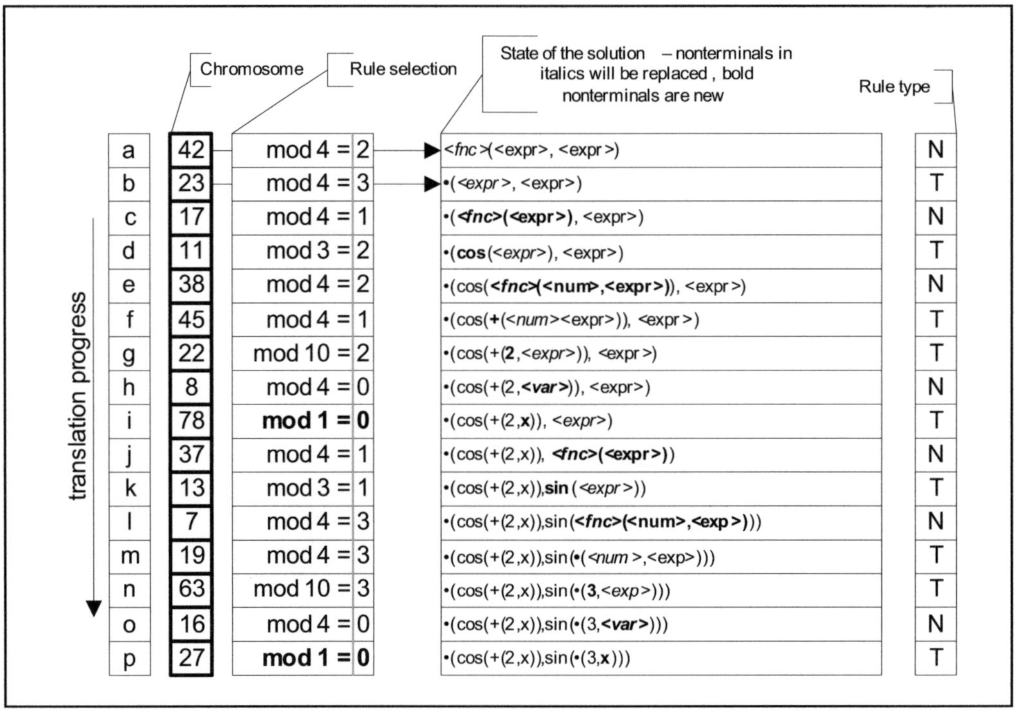

Fig. 3. Translation process of an expression specified by equation (4)

3.1 Backward processing algorithm

The whole process of translating a sample chromosome into an expression (equation 4) is shown on figure 3 []. Rule counts and rule numbers correspond to figure 1, indexes of the rules are zero-based. Rule selected in step a) of the translation is therefore the third rule in table.

$$\cos(2+x)\cdot\sin(3\cdot x) \tag{4}$$

The backward processing algorithm scans the solution string for non-terminals in right-to-left direction. Figure 4 shows the translation process when this mode is used. Note that the genes in the chromosome are the same; they just have been rearranged in order to create same solution, so that the difference between both algorithms can be demonstrated. Figure 4 now contains two additional columns with *rule type* and *gene mark*.

Rule types are determined according to what non-terminals they translate. We define a *T-terminal* as a terminal which can be translated *only* to terminals. By analogy N-terminal is a terminal which can be *translated* only to non-terminals. T-rules (N-rules) are all rules translating a given T-nonterminal (N-nonterminal). Mixed rules (or non-terminals) are not allowed. Given the production rules shown on Figure 1, the only N-nonterminal is <expr>, non-terminals <fnc>, <var> and <num> are all T-nonterminals (Ošmera, Popelka & Pivoňka, 2006).

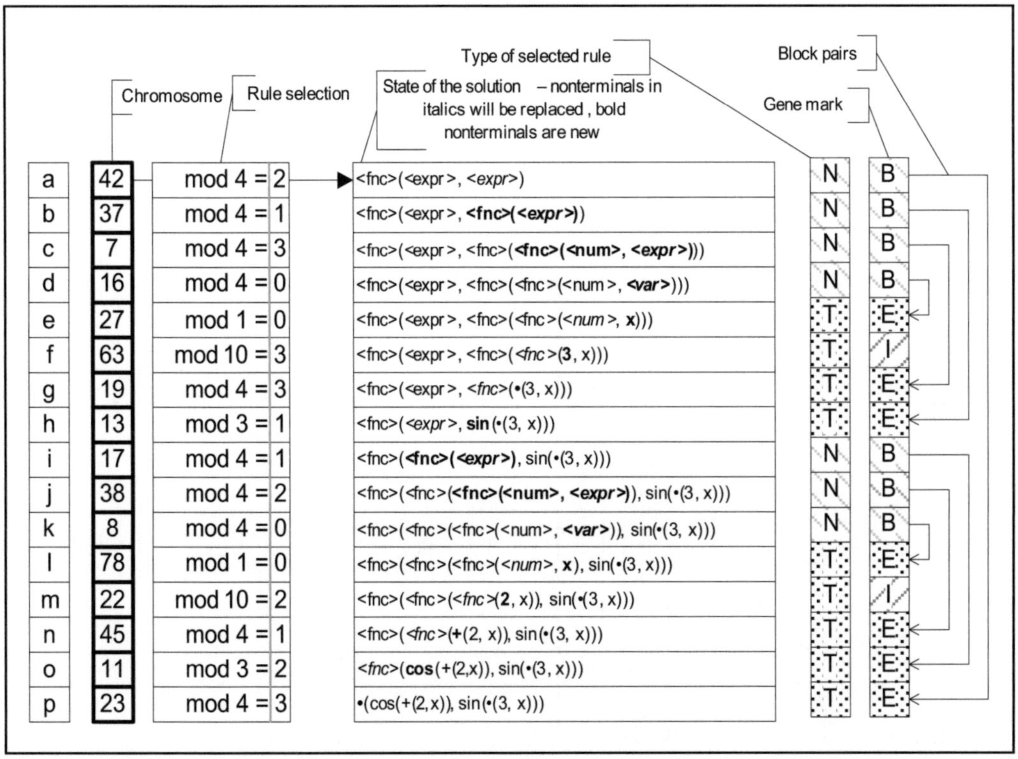

Fig. 4. Translation of an expression (equation (4)) using the backward processing algorithm

Now that we are able to determine type of the rule used, we can define *gene marks*. In step c) at figure 4 a <expr> non-terminal is translated into a <fnc>(<num>, <expr>) expression. This is further translated until step g), where it becomes $3 \cdot x$. In other words – in step c) we knew that the solution will contain a function with two arguments; in step g) we realized that it is multiplication with arguments 3 and *x*. The important feature of backward processing algorithm that all genes which define this sub-expression including all its' parameters are in a single uninterrupted block of genes. To explicitly mark this block we use *Block marking algorithm* which marks:

- all genes used to select N-rule with mark B (Begin)
- all genes used to select T-rule except the last one with mark I (Inside)
- all genes used to select last T-rule of currently processed rule with mark E (End).

The B and E marks determine begin and end of *logical blocks* generated by the grammar. This works independent of the structure generated provided that the grammar consists only of N-nonterminals and T-nonterminals. These logical blocks can then be exchanged the same way as in genetic programming (figure 5) (Francone et al, 1999).

Compared to genetic programing, all the genetic algorithm operations are still performed on the genome (chromosome) and not on the actual solution. This solves the second problem described in section 2.2 – the generation of syntactically incorrect solutions. Also the problem of lowered variability is solved since we can always insert or remove genes in case we need to remove or add parts of the solution. This algorithm also solves analogical problems existing in standard grammatical evolution (O'Neill et al, 2001).

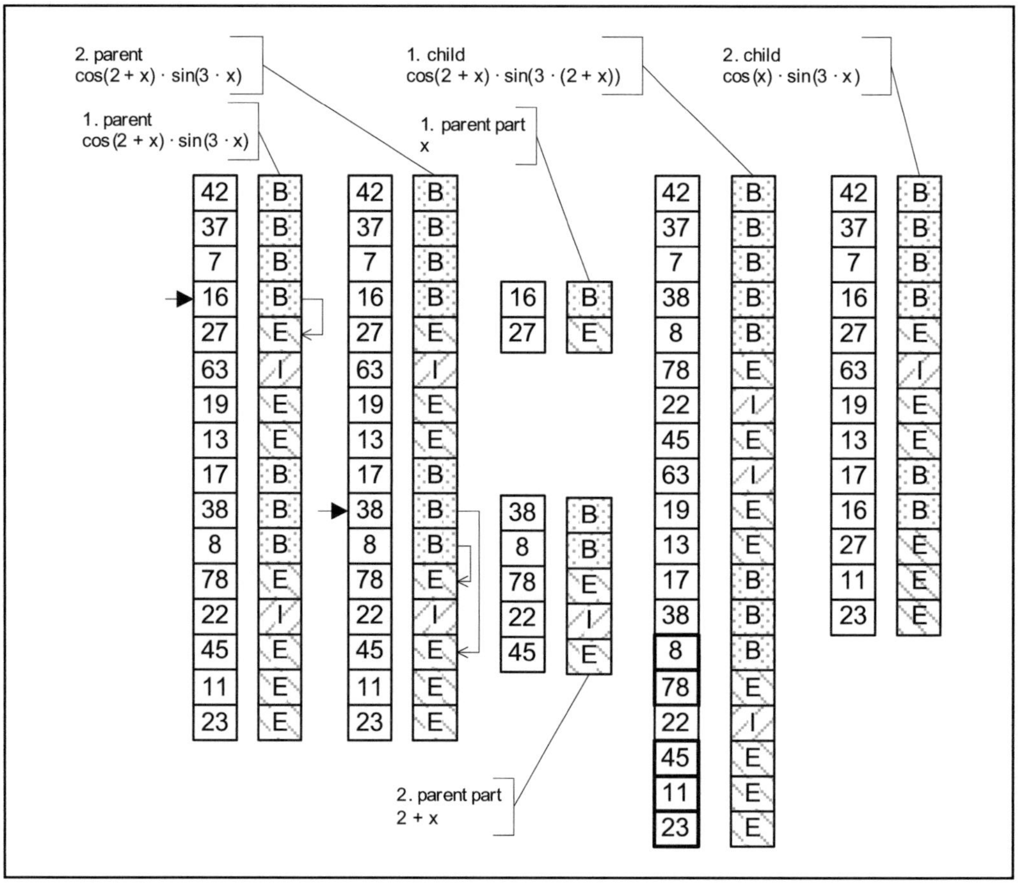

Fig. 5. Example of crossing over two chromosomes with marked genes

The *backward processing algorithm* of *two-level grammatical evolution* provides same results as original grammatical evolution. However in the underlying genetic algorithm, the genes that are involved in processing a single rule of grammar are grouped together. This grouping results in greater stability of solutions during crossover and mutation operations and better performance (Ošmera & Popelka, 2006). An alternative to this algorithm is *Gene expression programming* method (Cândida Ferreira, 2006b) which solves the same problem but is quite limited in the form of grammar which can be used.

3.2 Second level generation in two-level grammatical evolution

Furthermore, we modified grammatical evolution to separate structure generation and parameters optimization (Popelka, 2007). This is motivated by poor performance of grammatical evolution when optimizing parameters, especially real numbers (Dempsey et al., 2007). With this approach, we use grammatical evolution to generate complex structures. Instead of immediately generating the resulting string (as defined by the grammar), we store the parse tree of the structure and use it in second level of optimization. For this second level of optimization, a Differential evolution algorithm (Price, 1999) is used. This greatly improves the performance of GE, especially when real numbers are required (Popelka & Šťastný, 2007)

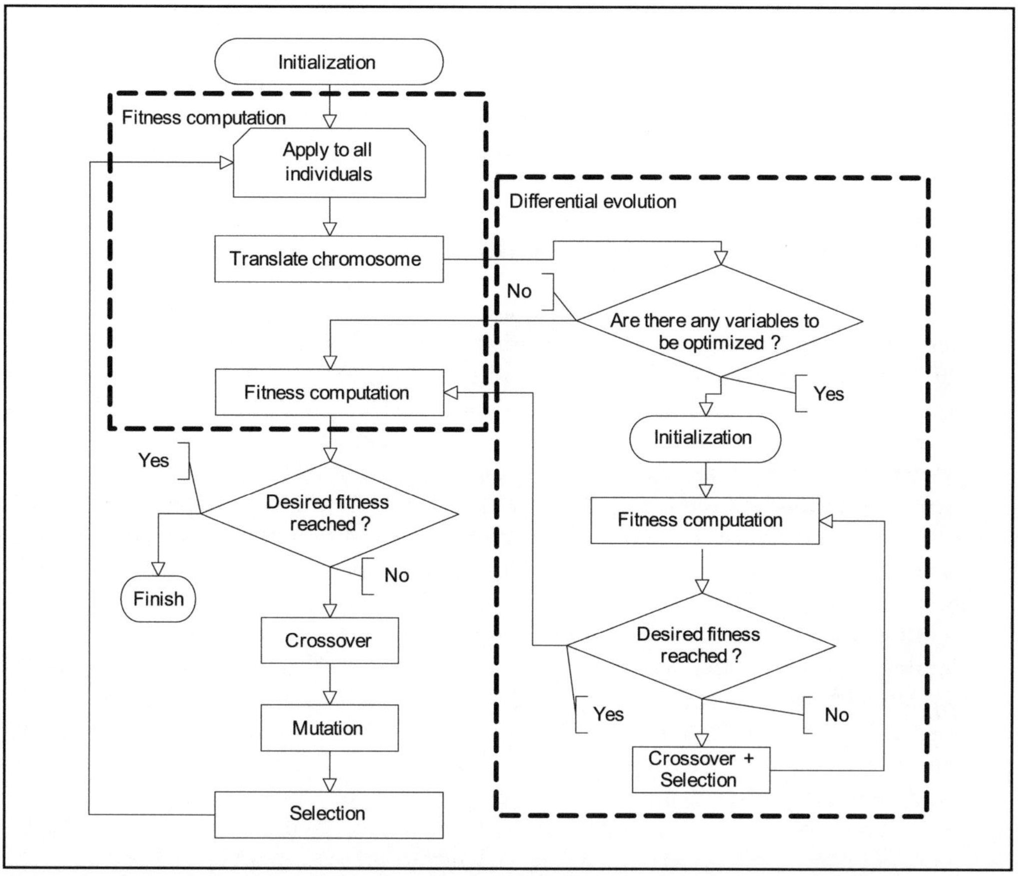

Fig. 6. Flowchart of two-level grammatical evolution

The first level of the optimization is performed using grammatical evolution. According to the grammar, the output can be a function containing variables (*x* in our case); and instead of directly generating numbers using the <num> nonterminal we add several symbolic constants (*a*, *b*, *c*) into to grammar. The solution expression cannot be evaluated and assigned a fitness value since the values of symbolic constants are unknown. In order to evaluate the generated function a secondary optimization has to be performed to find values for constants. Input for the second-level of optimization is the function with symbolic constants which is transformed to a vector of variables. These variables are optimized using the differential evolution and the output is a vector of optimal values for symbolic constants for a given solution. Technically in each grammatical evolution cycle there are hundreds of differential evolution cycles executed. These optimize numeric parameters of each generated individual (Popelka, 2007). Figure 6 shows the schematic flowchart of the two-level grammatical evolution.

3.3 Deformation grammars

Apart from generating the solution we also need to be able to read and interpret the solutions (section 4.2). For this task a syntactic analysis is used. Syntactic analysis is a process which decides if the string belongs to a language generated by a given grammar, this can be used for example for object recognition (Šťastný & Minařík, 2006). It is possible to use:

- *Regular grammar* – Deterministic finite state automaton is sufficient to analyse regular grammar. This automaton is usually very simple in hardware and software realization.
- *Context-free grammar* – To analyse context-free grammar a nondeterministic finite state automaton with stack is generally required.
- *Context grammar* – "Useful and sensible" syntactic analysis can be done with context-free grammar with controlled re-writing.

There are two basic methods of syntactic analysis:

- *Bottom-up parsing* – We begin from analysed string to initial symbol. The analysis begins with empty stack. In case of successful acceptance only initial symbol remains in the stack, e.g. Cocke-Younger-Kasami algorithm (Kasami, 1965), which grants that the time of analysis is proportional to third power of string length;
- *Top-down parsing* – We begin from initial symbol and we are trying to generate analysed string. String generated so far is saved in the stack. Every time a terminal symbol appears on the top of the stack, it is compared to actual input symbol of the analysed string. If symbols are identical, the terminal symbol is removed from the top of the stack. If not, the algorithm returns to a point where a different rule can be chosen (e.g. with help of backtracking). Example of top down parser is Earley's Parser (Aycock & Horspool, 2002), which executes all ways of analysis to combine gained partial results. The time of analysis is proportional to third power of string length; in case of unambiguous grammars the time is only quadratic. This algorithm was used in simulation environment.

When designing a syntactic analyser, it is useful to assume random influences, e.g. image deformation. This can be done in several ways. For example, the rules of given grammar can be created with rules, which generate alternative string, or for object recognition it is possible to use some of the methods for determination of distance between attribute description of images (string metric). Finally, *deformation grammars* can be used.

Methods for determination of distance between attribute descriptions of images (string metric) determine the distance between attribute descriptions of images, i.e. the distance between strings which correspond to the unknown object and the object class patterns. Further, determined distances are analysed and the recognized object belongs to the class from which the string has the shortest distance. Specific methods (Levenshtein distance Ld(s, t), Needleman-Wunsch method) can be used to determine the distance between attribute descriptions of image (Gusfield, 1997).

Results of these methods are mentioned e.g. in (Minařík, Šťastný & Popelka, 2008). If the parameters of these methods are correctly set, these methods provide good rate of successful identified objects with excellent classification speed. However, false object recognition or non-recognized objects can occur.

From the previous paragraphs it is clear that recognition of non-deformed objects with structural method is without problems, it offers excellent speed and 100% classification rate. However, recognition of randomly deformed objects is nearly impossible. If we conduct syntactic analysis of a string which describes a structural deformed object, it will apparently

not be classified into a given class because of its structural deformation. Further, there are some methods which use structural description and are capable of recognizing randomly deformed objects with good rate of classification and speed.
The solution to improve the rate of classification is to enhance the original grammar with rules which describe errors – *deformation rules*, which cover up every possible random deformation of object. Then the task is changed to finding a non-deformed string, which distance from analysed string is minimal. Compared to the previous method, this is more informed method because it uses all available knowledge about the classification targets – it uses grammar. Original grammar may be regular or context-free, enhanced grammar is always context-free and also ambiguous, so the syntactic analysis, according to the enhanced grammar, will be more complex.
Enhanced deformation grammar is designed to reliably generate all possible deformations of strings (objects) which can occur. Input is context-free or regular grammar G = (VN, VT, P, S). Output of the processing is *enhanced deformation grammar* G′ = (VN′, VT′, P′, S′), where P′ is set of weighted rules. The generation process can be described using the following steps:
Step1:

$$V_N' = V_N \cup \{S'\} \cup \{E_B | \; b \in V_T\} \tag{5}$$

$$V_T \subseteq V_T' \tag{6}$$

Step 2:
If holds:

$$A \rightarrow \alpha_0 b_1 \alpha_1 b_2 ... \alpha_{m-1} b_m \alpha_m; \; m \geq 0; \; \alpha_1 \in V_N' \wedge b_i \in V_T'; \; i = 1,2,...,m; \; l = 0,1,...,m \tag{7}$$

Then add new rule into P' with weight 0:

$$A \rightarrow \alpha_0 E_{b1} \alpha_1 E_{b2} ... \alpha_{m-1} E_{bm} \alpha_m \tag{8}$$

Step 3:
Into P'add the rules in table 1 with weight according to chosen metric. In this example Levenshtein distance is used. In the table header L is Levenshtein distance, w is weighted Levenshtein distance and W is weighted metric.

Rule	L	w	W	Rule for
$S' \rightarrow S$	0	0	0	-
$S' \rightarrow Sa$	1	w_I	$I'(a)$	$a \in V_T'$
$E_a \rightarrow a$	0	0	0	$a \in V_T$
$E_a \rightarrow b$	1	w_S	$S(a,b)$	$a \in V_T, b \in V_T', a \neq b$
$E_a \rightarrow \delta$	1	w_D	$D(a)$	$a \in V_T$
$E_a \rightarrow bE_a$	1	w_I	$I(a,b)$	$a \in V_T, b \in V_T'$

Table 1. Rules of enhanced deformation grammar

These types of rules are called deformation rules. Syntactic analyser with error correction works with enhanced deformation grammar. This analyser seeks out such deformation of input string, which is linked with the smallest sum of weight of deformation rules. G' is ambiguous grammar, i.e. its syntactic analysis is more complicated. A modified Earley parser can be used for syntactic analyses with error correction. Moreover, this parser accumulates appropriate weight of rules which were used in deformed string derivation according to the grammar G'.

3.4 Modified Early algorithm

Modified Early parser accumulates weights of rules during the process of analysis so that the deformation grammar is correctly analysed (Minařík, Šťastný & Popelka, 2008). The input of the algorithms is enhanced deformation grammar G' and input string w.

$$w = b_1 b_2 ... b\_m \tag{9}$$

Output of the algorithm is lists $I_0, I_1, ... I_m$ for string w (equation 9) and distance d of input string from a template string defined by the grammar.

Step 1 of the algorithm – create list I_0. For every rule $S' \rightarrow \alpha \in P'$ add into I_0 field:

$$[S' \rightarrow \cdot\alpha, 0, x] \tag{10}$$

Execute until it is possible to add fields into I_0. If

$$[A \rightarrow \cdot B\beta, 0, y] \tag{11}$$

is in I_0 field then add

$$B \overset{z}{\rightarrow} \gamma \text{field} [B \rightarrow \cdot\gamma, 0, z] \tag{12}$$

into I_0.

Step 2: Repeat for $j = 1, 2, ..., m$ the following sub-steps A – C:

a. for every field in I_{j-1} in form of $[B \rightarrow \alpha \cdot a\beta, i, x]$ such that $a = b_j$, add the field

$$[B \rightarrow \alpha a \cdot \beta, i, x] \tag{13}$$

into I_j. Then execute sub-steps B and C until no more fields can be added into I_j.

b. If field $[A \rightarrow \alpha \cdot, i, x]$ is in I_j and field $[B \rightarrow \beta \cdot A\gamma, k, y]$ in I_j, then
   a. If exists a field in form of $[B \rightarrow \beta A \cdot \gamma, k, z]$ in I_j, and then if x+y < z, do replace the value z with value $x + y$ in this field
   b. If such field does not exist, then add new field $[B \rightarrow \beta A \cdot \gamma,\ k,\ x + y]$

c. For every field in form of $[A \rightarrow \alpha \cdot B\beta, i, x]$ in I_j do add a field $[B \rightarrow \cdot\gamma, j, z]$ for every rule

$$B \overset{z}{\rightarrow} \gamma \tag{14}$$

Step 3: If the field

$$[S' \rightarrow \alpha \cdot, 0, x] \tag{15}$$

is in I_m, then string w is accepted with distance weight x. String w (or its derivation tree) is obtained by omitting all deformation rules from derivation of string w.

Designed deformation grammar reliably generates all possible variants of randomly deformed object or string. It enables to use some of the basic methods of syntactic analysis for randomly deformed objects. Compared to methods for computing the distance between attribute descriptions of objects it is more computationally complex. Its effectiveness depends on effectiveness of the used parser or its implementation respectively. This parses is significantly are more complex than the implementation of methods for simple distance measurement between attribute descriptions (such as Levenshtein distance).

However, if it is used correctly, it does not produce false object recognition, which is the greatest advantage of this method. It is only necessary to choose proper length of words describing recognized objects. If the length of words is too short, excessive deformation (by applying only a few deformation rules) may occur, which can lead to occurrence of description of completely different object. If the length is sufficient (approximately 20% of deformed symbols in words longer than 10 symbols), this method gives correct result and false object recognition will not occur at all.

Although deformed grammars were developed mainly for object recognition (where an object is represented by a string of primitives), it has a wider use. The main feature is that it can somehow adapt to new strings and it can be an answer to the problem described in section 4.2.

4. Experiments

The goal of automatic generation of programs is to create a valid source code of a program, which will solve a given problem. Each individual of a genetic algorithm is therefore one variant the program. Evaluation of an individual involves compilation (and building) of the source code, running the program and inputting the test values. Fitness function then compares the actual results of the running program with learning data and returns the fitness value. It is obvious that the evaluation of fitness becomes very time intensive operation. For the tests we have chosen the PHP language for several reasons. Firstly it is an interpreted language which greatly simplifies the evaluation of a program since compiling and building can be skipped. Secondly a PHP code can be interpreted easily as a string using either command line or library API call, which simplified implementation of the fitness function into our system. Last but not least, PHP is a very popular language with many tools available for programmers.

4.1 Generating simple functions

When testing the two-level grammatical evolution algorithm we stared with very simple functions and a very limited grammar:

<statement> ::= <begin><statement><statement> |
<if><condition><statement> |
<function><expression><expression> |
<assign><var><expression>
<expression> ::= <function><expression> |
<const> |
<var> |
<function><expression><expression>
<condition> ::= <operator><expression><expression>
<operator> ::= < | > | != | == | >= | <=

<var> ::= $a | $b | $result
<const> ::= 0 | 1| -1
<function> ::= + | - | * | /
<begin> ::= {}
<if> ::= if {}
<assign> ::= =

This grammar represents a very limited subset of the PHP language grammar (Salsi, 2007) or (Zend, 2010). To further simplify the task, the actual generated source code was only a body of a function. Before the body of the function, a header is inserted, which defines the function name, number and names of its arguments. After the function body, the return command is inserted. After the complete function definition, a few function calls with learning data are inserted. The whole product is then passed to PHP interpreter and the text result is compared with expected results according to given learning data.

The simplest experiment was to generate function to compute absolute value of a number (without using the abs() function). The input for this function is one integer number; output is absolute value of that number. The following set of training patterns was used:

P = {(−3, 3); (43, 43); (3, 3); (123, 123); (−345, 345); (−8, 8); (−11, 11); (0, 0)}.

Fitness function is implemented so that for each pattern it assigns points according to achieved result (result is assigned, result is number, result is not negative, result is equal to training value). Sum of the points then represents the achieved fitness. Following are two selected examples of generated functions:

```
function absge($a) {
        $result = null;
        $result = $a;
        if (($a) <= (((-(-((-($result)) + ((-($a)) - (1))))) - (-1)) - (0))) {
                $result = -($result);
        }
        return $result;
}
function absge($a) {
        $result = null;
        $result =  -($a);
        if ((-($result)) >= (1)) {
                $result =  $a;
        };
return $result;
}
```

While the result looks unintelligible, it must be noted that this piece of source code is correct algorithm. The last line and first two lines are the mandatory header which was added automatically for the fitness evaluation. Apart from that it has not been processed, it is also important to note that it was generated in all 20 runs from only eight sample values in average of 47.6 population cycles (population size was 300 individuals).

Another example is a classic function for comparing two integers. Input values are two integer numbers a and b. Output value is integer c, which meets the conditions $c > 0$, for $a > b$; $c = 0$, for $a = b$; $c < 0$, for $a < b$. Training data is a set of triples (a, b, c):

P = {(−3, 5,−1); (43, 0, 1); (8, 8, 0); (3, 4,−1); (−3,−4, 1);}

The values intentionally do not correspond to the usual implementation of this function: $c = a - b$. Also the fitness function checks only if c satisfies the conditions and not if the actual value is equal, thus the search space is open for many possible solutions. An example solution is:

```
function comparege($a, $b) {
	$result = null;
	if ((($a) - (($b) * (-(($result) / (1))))) <= ($result)) {{
		$result = 0;
		$result = $b;
	}}
	$result = ($b) - ($a);;
	$result = -($result);;
	return $result;
}
```

The environment was the same like in the first example; generation took 75.1 population cycles on average. Although these tests are quite successful, it is obvious, that this is not very practical.

For each simple automatically generated function a programmer would need to specify a very specific test, function header, function footer. Tests for genetic algorithms need to be specific in the values they return. A fitness function which would return just "yes" or "no" is insufficient in navigating the genetic algorithm in the state space - such function cannot be properly optimized. The exact granularity of the fitness function values is unknown, but as little as 5 values can be sufficient if they are evenly distributed (as shown in the first example in this section).

4.2 Generating classes and methods

To make this system described above practical, we had to use standardized tests and not custom made fitness functions. Also we wanted to use object oriented programming, because it is necessary to keep the code complexity very low. Therefore we need to stick with the paradigm of small simple "black box" objects. This is a necessity and sometimes an advantage. Such well-defined objects are more reliable, but it is a bit harder to maintain their connections (Büchi & Weck, 1999).

Writing class tests before the actual source code is already a generally recognized approach - *test-driven development*. In test-driven development, programmers start off by writing tests for the class they are going to create. Once the tests are written, the class is implemented and tested. If all tests pass, a coverage analysis is performed to check whether the tests do cover all the newly written source code (Beck, 2002). An example of a simple test using PHPUnit testing framework:

```
class BankAccountTest extends PHPUnit_Framework_TestCase {
	protected $ba;
	protected function setUp() {
		$this->ba = new BankAccount;
	}
	public function testBalanceIsInitiallyZero() {
		$this->assertEquals(0, $this->ba->getBalance());
	}
```

```
    public function testBalanceCannotBecomeNegative() {
        try {
            $this->ba->withdrawMoney(1);
        }
        catch (BankAccountException $e) {
            $this->assertEquals(0, $this->ba->getBalance());
            return;
        }
        $this->fail();
    }
    ...
}
```

The advantage of modern unit testing framework is that it is possible to create class skeleton (template) from the test. From the above test, the following code can be easily generated:

```
class BankAccount {
    public function depositMoney() {}
    public function getBalance() {}
    public function withdrawMoney() {}
}
```

Now we can use a PHP parser to read the class skeleton and import it as a template grammar rule into grammatical evolution. This task is not as easy as it might seem. The class declaration is incomplete – it is missing function parameters and private members of the class.

Function parameters can be determined from the tests by static code analysis, provided that we refrain from variable function parameters. Function parameter completion can be solved by extending the PHPUnit framework. Private members completion is more problematic, since it should be always unknown to the unit test (per the black box principle). Currently we created grammar rule for grammatical evolution by hand. In future, however, we would like to use deformed grammar (as described in section 3.3) to derive initial rule for grammatical evolution. We use <class_declaration_statement> as starting symbol, then we can define first (and only) rewriting rule for that symbol as (in EBNF notation):

```
<class_declaration_statement> :==
    "class BankAccount {" <class_variable_declarations>
        "public function depositMoney("<variable_without_objects>") {"
            <statement_list>
        "}
        public function getBalance() {"
            <statement_list>
        "}
        public function withdrawMoney("<variable_without_objects>") {"
            <statement_list
        "}
    }"
```

This way we obtain the class declaration generated by the unit test, plus space for private class members (only variables in this case) and function parameters. It is important to note that the grammar used to generate a functional class needs at least about 20 production rules (compared to approximately 10 in the first example). This way we obtain grammar to generate example class *BankAccount*. This can now be fed to the unit test, which will return number of errors and failures.

This experiment was only half successful. We used the concrete grammar described above – that is grammar specifically designed to generate *BankAccount* class with all its' public methods. Within average of 65.6 generations (300 individuals in generation) we were able to create individuals without errors (using only initialized variables, without infinite loops, etc.). Then the algorithm remained in local minimum and failed to find a solution with functionally correct method bodies.

After some investigation, we are confident that the problem lies in the *return* statement of a function. We have analyzed hundreds of solution and found that the correct code is present, but is preceded with return statement which exits from the function. The solution is to use predefined function footer and completely stop using the return statement (as described in section 4.1). This however requires further refinement of the grammar, and again deformation grammars might be the answer. We are also confident that similar problems will occur with other control-flow statements.

We have also tested a very generic production rules, such as:

```
<class_declaration_statement> :== "class BankAccount {" {<class_statement>} "}"
<class_statement> :== <visibility_modifier> "function ("<parameter_list>"){"
                    <statement_list> "}"
                    | <visibility_modifier> <variable_without_objects> ";"
                    ...
```

When such generic rules were used, no solution without errors was found within 150 allowed generations. This was expected as the variability of solutions and state space complexity rises extremely quickly.

5. Conclusion

In this chapter, we have presented several methods and concepts suitable for *code evolution* a fully automated generation of working source code using evolutionary algorithms. In the above paragraphs, we described how code evolution could work together with code generation. Code generation tools can be used to create a skeleton or template for an application, while code evolution can fill in the actual algorithms. This way, the actual generated functions can be kept short enough, so that the code evolution is finished within reasonable time.

Our long term goal is to create a tool which would be capable of generating some code from unit tests. This can have two practical applications – creating application prototypes and crosschecking the tests. This former is the case where the code quality is not an issue. What matters most is that the code is created with as little effort (money) as possible. The latter is the case where a programmer would like to know what additional possible errors might arise from a class.

The method we focused on in this chapter is unique in that its' output is completely controlled by a context-free grammar. Therefore this method is very flexible and without any problems or modifications it can be used to generate programs in mainstream programing languages. We also tried to completely remove the fitness function of the genetic algorithm and replace it with standardized unit-tests. This can then be thought of as an extreme form of test-driven development.

6. Acknowledgement

This work was supported by the grants: MSM 6215648904/03 and IG1100791 Research design of Mendel Univeristy in Brno.

7. References

Ahluwalia, M. & Bull, L. (1998). Co-evolving functions in genetic programming: Dynamic ADF creation using GliB, Proceedings of *Evolutionary Programming VII - 7th International Conference, EP98 San Diego*. LNCS Volume 1447/1998, Springer, ISBN-13: 978-3540648918, USA

Aycock, J. & Horspool, R.N. (2002). Practical Early Parsing, *The Computer Journal*, Vol. 45, No. 6, British Computer Society, pp. 620-630, DOI: 45:6:620-630

Beck, K. (2002). Test Driven Development: By Example, Addison-Wesley Professional, 240 p., ISBN 978-0321146533, USA

Büchi, M., Weck, W. (1999). The Greybox Approach: When Blackbox Specifications Hide Too Much, Technical Report: TUCS-TR-297, Turku Centre for Computer Science, Finland

Cândida Ferreira (2006a). Automatically Defined Functions in Gene Expression Programming in *Genetic Systems Programming: Theory and Experiences, Studies in Computational Intelligence*, Vol. 13, pp. 21-56, Springer, USA

Cândida Ferreira (2006b). *Gene Expression Programming: Mathematical Modelling by an Artificial Intelligence* (Studies in Computational Intelligence), Springer, ISBN 978-3540327967, USA

Czarnecki, K. & Eisenecker, U. (2000). *Generative Programming: Methods, Tools, and Applications*, Addison-Wesley Professional, ISBN 978-0201309775, Canada

Dempsey, I., O'Neill, M. & Brabazon, A. (2007). Constant creation in grammatical evolution, *Innovative Computing and Applications*, Vol. 1, No.1, pp. 23–38

Francone, D. F, Conrads, M., Banzhaf, W. & Nordin, P. (1999). Homologous Crossover in Genetic Programming, *Proceedings of the Genetic and Evolutionary Computation Conference (GECCO)*, pp. 1021–1026. ISBN 1-55860-611-4, Orlando, USA

Goldberg, D. E. (2002). *The Design of Innovation: Lessons from and for Competent Genetic Algorithms*. Kluwer Academic Publishers, 272 p. ISBN 1-4020-7098-5, Boston, USA

Gunter, C. A. & Mitchell, J. C. (1994). *Theoretical Aspects of Object-Oriented Programming: Types, Semantics, and Language Design*, The MIT Press, ISBN 978-0262071550, Cambridge, Massachusetts, USA

Gusfield, D. (1997). Gusfield, Dan (1997). *Algorithms on strings, trees, and sequences: computer science and computational biology*, Cambridge University Press. ISBN 0-521-58519-8. Cambridge, UK

Kasami, T. (1965). An efficient recognition and syntax-analysis algorithm for context-free languages. Scientific report AFCRL-65-758, Air Force Cambridge Research Lab, Bedford, MA, USA

Koza, J. R. (1992). *Genetic Programming: On the Programming of Computers by Means of Natural Selection*, The MIT Press, ISBN 978-0262111706, Cambridge, Massachusetts, USA

Koza, J. R. (1994). Gene Duplication to Enable Genetic Programming to Concurrently Evolve Both the Architecture and Work-Performing Steps of a Computer Program, *IJCAI-*

95 – Proceedings of the Fourteenth International Joint Conference on Artificial Intelligence, Vol. 1, pp. 734-740, Morgan Kaufmann, 20-25 August 1995, USA

Koza, J.R. et al (2003). Genetic Programming IV: Routine Human-Competitive Machine Intelligence. Springer, 624 p., ISBN 978-1402074462, USA

Laddad, R. (2009). *Aspectj in Action: Enterprise AOP with Spring Applications,* Manning Publications, ISBN 978-1933988054, Greenwich, Connecticut, USA

Mitchell, M. (1999). *An Introduction to Genetic Algorithms,* MIT Press, 162 p. ISBN 0-262-63185-7, Cambridge MA, USA

Minařík, M., Šťastný, J. & Popelka, O. (2008). A Brief Introduction to Recognition of Deformed Objects, *Proceedings of International Conference on Soft Computing Applied in Computer and Economic Environment ICSC,* pp.191-198, ISBN 978-80-7314-134-9, Kunovice, Czech Republic

O'Neill, M. & Ryan, C. (2003). *Grammatical Evolution: Evolutionary Automatic Programming in an Arbitrary Language,* Springer, ISBN 978-1402074448, Norwell, Massachusetts, USA

O'Neill, M., Ryan, C., Keijzer, M. & Cattolico, M. (2001). Crossover in Grammatical Evolution: The Search Continues, Proceedings of the European Conference on Genetic Programming (EuroGP), pp. 337–347, ISBN 3-540-41899-7, Lake Como, Italy

Ošmera P. & Popelka O. (2006). The Automatic Generation of Programs with Parallel Grammatical Evolution, *Proceedings of: 13th Zittau Fuzzy Colloquium,* Zittau, Germany, pp. 332-339

Ošmera P., Popelka O. & Pivoňka P. (2006). Parallel Grammatical Evolution with Backward Processing, *Proceedings of ICARCV 2006, 9th International Conference on Control, Automation, Robotics and Vision,* pp. 1889-1894, ISBN 978-1-4244-0341-7, Singapore, December 2006, IEEE Press, Singapore

Patterson, N. & Livesey, M. (1997). Evolving caching algorithms in C by genetic programming, Proceedings of Genetic Programming 1997, pp. 262-267, San Francisco, California, USA, Morgan Kaufmann

Poli, R. (2002). Automatic generation of programs: An overview of Lyee methodology, *Proceedings of 6th world multiconference on systemics, cybernetics and informatics,* vol. I, proceedings - information systems development I, pp. 506-511, Orlando, Florida, USA, July 2002

Popelka O. (2007). Two-level optimization using parallel grammatical evolution and differential evolution. *Proceedings of MENDEL 2007, International Conference on Soft Computing, Praha,* Czech Republic. pp. 88-92. ISBN 978-80-214-3473-8., August 2007

Popelka, O. & Šťastný, J. (2007). Generation of mathematic models for environmental data analysis. *Management si Inginerie Economica.* Vol. 6, No. 2A, 61-66. ISSN 1583-624X.

Price, K. (1999). An Introduction to Differential Evolution. In: New Ideas in Optimization. Corne D., Dorigo, M. & Glover, F. (ed.) McGraw-Hill, London (UK), 79–108, ISBN 007-709506-5.

Salsi, U. (2007). PHP 5.2.0 EBNF Syntax, online: http://www.icosaedro.it/articoli/php-syntax-ebnf.txt

Smith, D. R. (1999). Mechanizing the development of software, In: *Nato Advanced Science Institutes Series,* Broy M. & Steinbruggen R. (Ed.), 251-292, IOS Press, ISBN 90-5199-459-1

Šťastný, J. & Minařík, M. (2006). Object Recognition by Means of New Algorithms, *Proceedings of International Conference on Soft Computing Applied in Computer and Economic Environment ICSC*, pp. 99-104, ISBN 80-7314-084-5, Kunovice, Czech Republic

TIOBE Software (2010). TIOBE Programming Community Index for June 2010, online: http://www.tiobe.com/index.php/content/paperinfo/tpci/

Wong M. L. & Leung K. S. (1995) Applying logic grammars to induce sub-functions in genetic programming, *Proceedings of 1995 IEEE International Conference on Evolutionary Computation (ICEC 95)*, pp. 737-740, ISBN 0-7803-2759-4, Perth, Australia, November 1995, IEEE Press

Zend Technologies (2010). Zend Engine - Zend Language Parser, online: http://svn.php.net/repository/php/php src/trunk/Zend/zend_language_parser.y

3

Application of Computer Algebra into the Analysis of a Malaria Model using MAPLE™

Davinson Castaño Cano
EAFIT University
Colombia

1. Introduction

At the moment, we are at the edge of a possible biological trouble. Some people say that the 19th century was the century of chemistry, the 20th was the century of physics, and they say that the 21st will be the century of biology. If we think, the advances in the biological field in the recent years have been incredible, and like the physics and its atomic bomb, with biology could create global epidemics diseases. Also the climate change could produce a new virus better than the existing virus, creating an atmosphere of panic, such as the influenza A (H1N1) in recent years or Malaria who still killing people. To go a step further, we use computer science in the improvement of disease prevention (Baker, 2007; Magal & Rouen, 2008).

For beginning, we mention quickly some plagues in history such as the Black Death as an example of Bubonic plague, and we present from their basic concepts the most common classical epidemic models.

We present a transmission malaria model with inhomogeneities in a human population, which is proposed in terms of SIR coupled models for human and mosquitoes, which are described by differential equations. The human population is considered divided into several groups depending on genetics profiles, social condition, differentiation between rural or urban people, etc. Within malaria model we consider that mosquitoes bite humans in a differentiated way in accordance with the inhomogeneity. We use an algorithm for the analysis from local stability of the infection-free equilibrium and that algorithm is implemented on Maple™. This algorithm consists on determinate the characteristic polynomial from Jacobian matrix of the model and the analysis of their eigenvalues using Routh-Hurwitz theorem. As a result we obtain the basic reproductive number for malaria (R_o) and the threshold condition for a malaria epidemic triggering (R_o>1). From this result we can derivate effective control measures for avoiding malaria outbreaks and determinate the minimum level of income for a community becomes free of malaria infection. This work pretend to show the symbolic computing potential from CAS (Computer Algebra Systems), in our case Maple™, for analysing automatically complex epidemic models and the usefulness of them for designing and implementing public health politics.

2. Historical survey of epidemiological models

In this first part of the chapter, we are going to mention two aspects to capture your attention, the first one is a little tour for history where we refer to some of the most tragic plagues, but we just pretend to show some examples of diseases for that reason it is not all the history of each plague, and the second one is a presentation of the most common models used in epidemics problems such as SIS, SIR and SEIR models, trying to explain their dynamics. This model models can be used in other sciences such as economics, biology, etc. (Perthame, 2007)

2.1 Epidemic infections

It's true that in our time, every year is more difficult to find an outbreak in the developed countries, but it isn't the same situation in the developing countries, in which the epidemics problems appear frequently (Porta, 2008).

Initially, human diseases began with the change of their way to live, the first change was when humans learnt the agriculture which made possible that more people could live in the same place, this situation produced problems on healthiness and then, the diseases started. The next step in the change of life was domesticating animals, which gave us some disease because of their genetic changes. Some of the diseases that we have thanks to animals are Measles, Tuberculosis, Smallpox, Influenza, Malaria, between others.

We introduce the *Bubonic Plague* who had his biggest spreading with the name *Black Death* in mid-fourteenth century, it received his name because of the black skin that people had when they were dying. This plague is spread by vectors that could be rats and other small mammals, and their fleas. Some cases of this plague were reported in Athens in the Peloponnesian War, and after the 14th century, in the World War II, Japan spread infected fleas over some cities in China (Christakos et al., 2005; Gottfried, 1983).

Now we talk about *Malaria* and *Yellow Fever*, both diseases are transmitted by flies and it for that reason that these diseases are very dangerous because his range of spread could be extremely wide. In the case of the *Malaria* the historians believe that its beginning was in the apes in Africa, this disease is also called *Burning Ague* because of intermittent painful fevers. The *Yellow Fever* is called "*Yellow Jack*", the name yellow is for the colour that people have with this illness. These diseases are described even in the bible, the old testament, Leviticus 26:16, "*then I will do this to you: I will visit you with panic, with wasting disease and fever that consume the eyes and make the heart ache...*" and Deuteronomy 28:22, "*The LORD will strike you with wasting disease and with fever, inflammation and fiery heat...*" And in present days still happen even more in countries near to the equatorial line because the mosquitoes find ideal conditions to survive, temperature between 20°C and 30°C, and humidity over 60%.

As a final example of infections, we bring the *Smallpox* and *Measles*, which are the most severe example of how humans appear the diseases, and these diseases have the highest fatality rate in the history, surpassing even the medieval *Black Death*. The *Smallpox* was widely used in the process of America's conquest with the intension of decimate the native population. With the last phrase we note the human intention to use biological weapons, and it's worrying to think in the biological weapon that we could have with the actual technologies (Bollet, 2004).

2.2 Models used

Now, we talk about some models used to predict the behaviour of the population along an infection. The models we show here are classical in epidemiology and they are differential equations systems (Stewart, 2002). We won't show the equations systems because they depend on the characteristics of the epidemic, but we will show some diagrams. If you want to find the mathematical expressions, you can see the references (Brauer et al., 2008; Capasso, 2008; Ma & Xia, 2009; Daley & Gani, 2005). All these models have been formulated by great researchers who have contributed to the development of the techniques of diseases dynamics treatment, also it's important to note that the difficulty for the accuracy in these models is the obtaining of the parameters (Bellomo, 2008).

- **SIS Model**

This model is the simplest model in epidemiology because it has only two population groups the susceptible and the infected, which are related by λ and γ functions that could depend on time or be just a constant, these functions are named: λ is the infectious rate function and γ is the recovering rate function. Also, it is a model with a boucle or feedback. It could easily model a pneumonia disease (Ma & Xia, 2009).

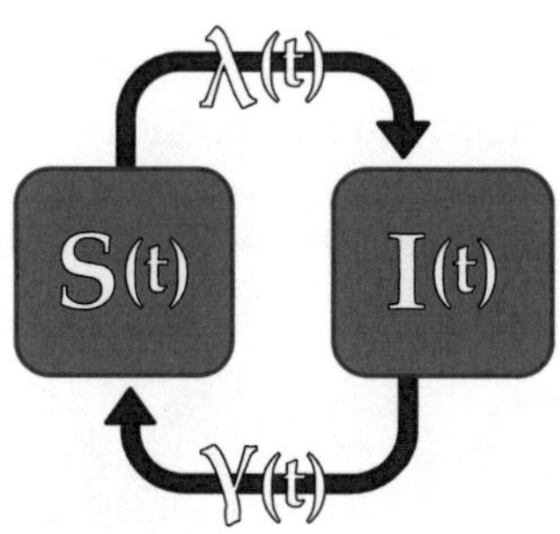

Fig. 1. Representation of the SIS Model

- **SIR Model**

Now, we present a model which has been widely used. In this model is included a new group, the Recovered group which is immune of the infection, in this chapter we are going to use a modified version of this model, with this system we can model a lot of diseases related to viruses such as Malaria, Influenza, Smallpox, Measles, Rubella, Yellow Fever, Dengue Fever, etc. (Castaño C., 2009; Ma & Xia, 2009).

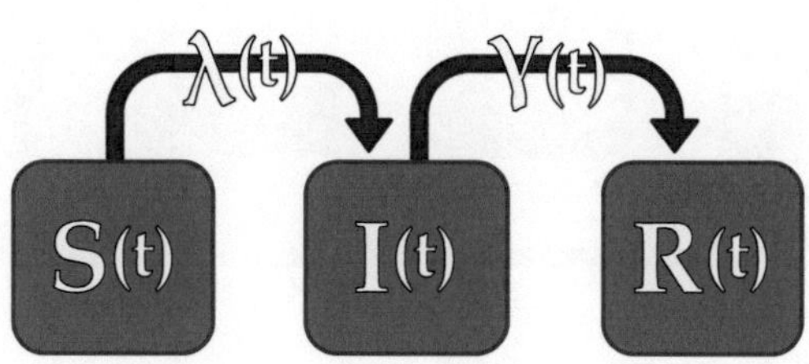

Fig. 2. Representation of the SIR Model

- **SIRS Model**

This model is basically the same SIR model except for the temporal immunity and the recovered people will be susceptible again after a time. In this model apart from the λ and γ functions is included a third relation function ξ which represent the susceptible creation rate. This model is used in the same cases of the SIS model such as Gonorrhoea, Typhoid Fever, Tuberculosis, Cholera, Meningitis, etc. The election depends on the person, if he wants to have in count the immunity time (Capasso, 2008).

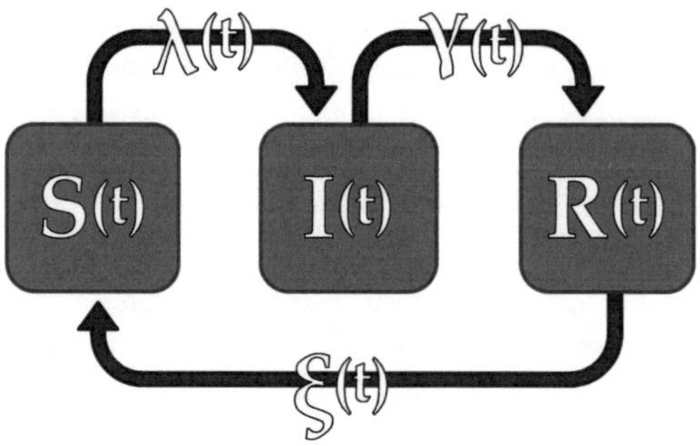

Fig. 3. Representation of the SIRS Model

- **SEIR and SEIRS Models**

These models are more elaborated because they included another group which is called the Exposed group that means; a person who has a contact with an infected person, he become exposed and passed certain time he become infected and start infecting too. The dynamics of the SEIR and SEIRS model is very similar to the SIR and SIRS models, respectively. Also, in these models appear a new function β that is the exposition rate.

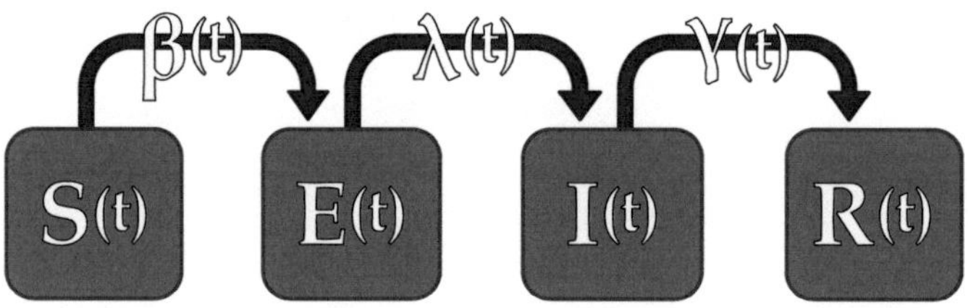

Fig. 4. Representation of the SEIR Model

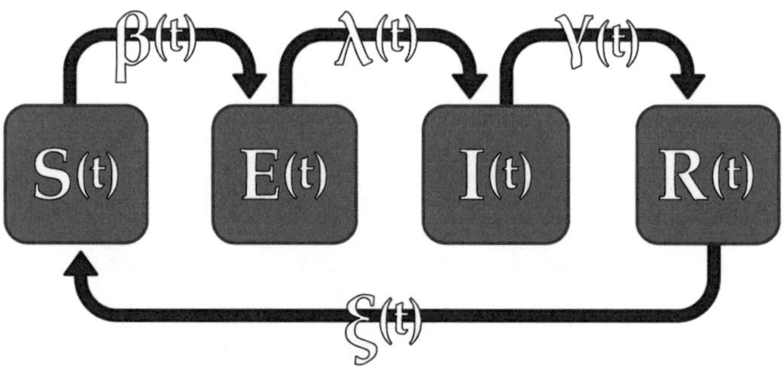

Fig. 5. Representation of the SEIRS Model

Apart from these models there are others like the M-Models which included in the M-group that is for the newborns who have a passive immunity in the moment of birth and after they will be part of the susceptible group (S-Group). If you want to clarify some concept of these models, we recommend reading the book of Basic Epidemiology (Bonita et al., 2006).

3. Malaria SIR coupled model

Now, we present the work we did based in the SIR model, which is coupled with other equal. These coupled models are for the human population and the vectors that allow model the Malaria disease. We begin with a human group without inhomogeneities and after we start to include inhomogeneities for in the humans that are represented with the creation of different groups of humans, we begin with a single group until three groups of humans, and also, we present a generalization for the basic reproductive number. We introduce briefly the concept of Mechanized Reasoning too.

3.1 SIR model for one group of humans

For beginning we introduce the differential equations that describe the dynamics of the Malaria disease, apart from this, we introduce to Maple™ environment and show how to solve the model; showing the given instructions and the results.
We start presenting the differential equation system that describes the human population behaviour; this population is constant in time:

$$\frac{d}{dt}S_h(t) = \mu_h\, N_h - \frac{b\,\beta_{v,h}\,S_h(t)\,I_v(t)}{N_h} - \mu_h\, S_h(t) \tag{1}$$

$$\frac{d}{dt}I_h(t) = \frac{b\,\beta_{v,h}\,S_h(t)\,I_v(t)}{N_h} - (\gamma_h + \mu_h)\,I_h(t) \tag{2}$$

$$\frac{d}{dt}R_h(t) = \gamma_h\, I_h(t) - \mu_h\, R_h(t) \tag{3}$$

For inserting equation on Maple™ we write in a line the expression we want to have, like example for the equation (1), we write (note that *diff()* is the command for differential):

*diff(S[h](t),t)=mu[h]*N[h]-b*beta[v,h]*S[h](t)*I[v](t)/N[h]-mu[h]*S[h](t);*

The variables that appear in the equation system are:
μ_h : Natural death rate which is the same birth rate for keeping a constant population.
N_h : Total population of humans.
b : Susceptibility of the susceptible individuals.
$\beta_{v,h}$: Infection rate from the infected vectors to the susceptible humans.
γ_h : Recovering rate or Immunisation rate.
The subscript h is for referring to humans and the v is for the vectors.
Now, we introduce the analogue equations for the vector system:

$$\frac{d}{dt}S_v(t) = \mu_v\, N_v - \frac{b\,\beta_{h,v}\,S_v(t)\,I_h(t)}{N_h} - \mu_v S_v(t) \tag{4}$$

$$\frac{d}{dt}I_v(t) = \frac{b\,\beta_{h,v}\,S_v(t)\,I_h(t)}{N_h} - (\gamma_v + \mu_v)\,I_v(t) \tag{5}$$

$$\frac{d}{dt}R_v(t) = \gamma_v\, I_v(t) - \mu_v\, R_v(t) \tag{6}$$

For using the algorithm and obtaining an algebraic system, we exclude the time dependence in the functions:

$$S_h(t) = S_h \quad I_h(t) = I_h \quad R_h(t) = R_h \quad S_v(t) = S_v \quad I_v(t) = I_v \quad R_v(t) = R_v \tag{7}$$

These expressions, we introduce them:

S[h](t)=S[h],I[h](t)=I[h],R[h](t)=R[h],S[v](t)=S[v],I[v](t)=I[v],R[v](t)=R[v];

Taking the right hand side of the equation from (1) to (6), and replacing in them (7), we obtain a group of expressions:

$$\begin{gathered}
\mu_h N_h - \frac{b\,\beta_{v,h} S_h I_v}{N_h} - \mu_h S_h \\
\frac{b\,\beta_{v,h} S_h I_v}{N_h} - (\gamma_h + \mu_h) I_h \\
\gamma_h I_h - \mu_h R_h \\
\mu_v N_v - \frac{b\,\beta_{h,v} S_v I_h}{N_h} - \mu_v S_v \\
\frac{b\,\beta_{h,v} S_v I_h}{N_h} - (\gamma_v + \mu_v) I_v \\
\gamma_v I_v - \mu_v R_v
\end{gathered} \tag{8}$$

For taking the right hand side in Maple™ we use command *rhs()* and write as follow for obtaining the vector (command *Vector()*) of relations:

*Vector(subs(**(7)**,[rhs(**(1)**),rhs(**(2)**),rhs(**(3)**),rhs(**(4)**),rhs(**(5)**),rhs(**(6)**)]));*

In this command appears some number in bold, which indicate the reference, for making a link with the references we use *Ctrl+L*. For solving (8), we use the command *solve()* like the following line:

*solve(**(8)**,[S[h],I[h],R[h],S[v],I[v],R[v]]);*

Solving this group we find in the first place the trivial solution:

$$S_h(t) = N_h \quad I_h(t) = 0 \quad R_h(t) = 0 \quad S_v(t) = N_v \quad I_v(t) = 0 \quad S_v(t) = 0 \tag{9}$$

Continuing with the algorithm for finding the basic reproductive number, we build the Jacobian, for that we use the commands *Matrix()* and *jacobian()*, and also, we use (8):

*Matrix(jacobian(**(8)**,[S[h],I[h],R[h],S[v],I[v],R[v]]));*

We obtain the follow matrix:

$$\begin{bmatrix}
-\frac{b\beta_{v,h} I_v}{N_h} - \mu_h & 0 & 0 & 0 & -\frac{b\beta_{v,h} S_h}{N_h} & 0 \\
\frac{b\beta_{v,h} I_v}{N_h} & -\gamma_h - \mu_h & 0 & 0 & \frac{b\beta_{v,h} S_h}{N_h} & 0 \\
0 & \gamma_h & -\mu_h & 0 & 0 & 0 \\
0 & -\frac{b\beta_{h,v} S_v}{N_h} & 0 & -\frac{b\beta_{h,v} I_h}{N_h} - \mu_v & 0 & 0 \\
0 & \frac{b\beta_{h,v} S_v}{N_h} & 0 & \frac{b\beta_{h,v} I_h}{N_h} & -\gamma_v - \mu_v & 0 \\
0 & 0 & 0 & 0 & \gamma_v & -\mu_v
\end{bmatrix} \tag{10}$$

However, we replace (9) in (10), for that we use the command *subs()*:

*subs(**(9)**,**(10)**);*

Obtaining the simplified matrix:

$$\begin{bmatrix} -\mu_h & 0 & 0 & 0 & -b\beta_{v,h} & 0 \\ 0 & -\gamma_h - \mu_h & 0 & 0 & b\beta_{v,h} & 0 \\ 0 & \gamma_h & -\mu_h & 0 & 0 & 0 \\ 0 & -\frac{b\beta_{h,v}\, N_v}{N_h} & 0 & 0-\mu_v & 0 & 0 \\ 0 & \frac{b\beta_{h,v}\, N_v}{N_h} & 0 & 0 & -\gamma_v - \mu_v & 0 \\ 0 & 0 & 0 & 0 & \gamma_v & -\mu_v \end{bmatrix} \quad (11)$$

From (11) we generate the characteristic polynomial (command *charpoly()*):

*factor(charpoly(**(11)**,lambda));*

We find:

$$(\lambda + \mu_v)^2(\lambda + \mu_h)^2\left(\lambda^2 + (\gamma_h + \mu_h + \gamma_v + \mu_v)\lambda + (\mu_h + \gamma_h)(\mu_v + \gamma_v) - b^2\beta_{v,h}\beta_{h,v}\frac{N_v}{N_h}\right) \quad (12)$$

Now we take the larger term:

$$\lambda^2 + (\gamma_h + \mu_h + \gamma_v + \mu_v)\lambda + (\mu_h + \gamma_h)(\mu_v + \gamma_v) - b^2\beta_{v,h}\beta_{h,v}\frac{N_v}{N_h} \quad (13)$$

From (13), we catch the lambda non-dependent term. For the infection-free equilibrium, this term should be major than zero.

$$0 < (\mu_h + \gamma_h)(\mu_v + \gamma_v) - b^2\beta_{v,h}\beta_{h,v}\frac{N_v}{N_h} \quad (14)$$

Isolating N_v, we obtain (command *isolate()*):

$$N_v < \frac{(\mu_h + \gamma_h)(\mu_v + \gamma_v)N_h}{b^2\beta_{v,h}\beta_{h,v}} \quad (15)$$

Ordering (15), we define the basic reproductive number (Chowell et al., 2009):

$$R_0 = \frac{b^2\beta_{v,h}\beta_{h,v}}{(\mu_h + \gamma_h)(\mu_v + \gamma_v)}\frac{N_v}{N_h} \qquad R_0 < 1 \quad (16)$$

Here we have obtained the condition for the infection-free equilibrium, if we have a system that satisfy $R_0 < 1$, then the population will be free of infection when the time lay to infinity (Ma et al., 2009).

For recapitulating the lines we put in Maple™, we present all the commands we used for obtain each equation presented before:

```
(1) diff(S[h](t),t)=mu[h]*N[h]-b*beta[v,h]*S[h](t)*I[v](t)/N[h]-mu[h]*S[h](t);
(2) diff(I[h](t),t)=b*beta[v,h]*S[h](t)*I[v](t)/N[h]-gamma[h]*I[h](t)-mu[h]*I[h](t);
(3) diff(R[h](t),t)=gamma[h]*I[h](t)-mu[h]*R[h](t);
(4) diff(S[v](t),t)=mu[v]*N[v]-b*beta[h,v]*S[v](t)*I[h](t)/N[h]-mu[v]*S[v](t);
(5) diff(I[v](t),t)=b*beta[h,v]*S[v](t)*I[h](t)/N[h]-gamma[v]*I[v](t)-mu[v]*I[v](t);
(6) diff(R[v](t),t)=gamma[v]*I[v](t)-mu[v]*R[v](t);
(7) S[h](t)=S[h],I[h](t)=I[h],R[h](t)=R[h],S[v](t)=S[v],I[v](t)=I[v],R[v](t)=R[v];
(8) Vector(subs((7),[rhs((1)),rhs((2)),rhs((3)),rhs((4)),rhs((5)),rhs((6))]));
(9) solve((8),[S[h],I[h],R[h],S[v],I[v],R[v]]);
(10) Matrix(jacobian((8),[S[h],I[h],R[h],S[v],I[v],R[v]]));
(11) subs((9),(10));
(12) factor(charpoly((11),lambda));
(13) collect(expand(subs(lambda+mu[v]=1,lambda+mu[h]=1,(12))),lambda);
(14) coeff((13),lambda,0)>0;
(15) solve((14),N[v]) assuming b>0,beta[h,v]>0,N[h]>0,beta[v,h]>0:%[1][1];
(16) R[0]=factor(lhs((15))*denom(rhs((15)))/numer(rhs((15))));
```

It is vital to charge the package of linear algebra:

with(linalg);

For more information about this software, we recommend to you to see the reference that we have utilised for some command (Maplesoft, 2007).

3.2 SIR model for two groups of humans

Now we are concerned to a system that has an inhomogeneity in the humans, this could be thought as two different resistances against the infection or two different races. We present the constitutive equations, for the first group of humans we have:

$$\frac{d}{dt}S_{h,1}(t) = \mu_{h,1}\,N_{h,1} - \frac{b\,\beta_{v,h,1}\,S_{h,1}(t)\,I_v(t)}{N_{h,1}} - \mu_{h,1}\,S_{h,1}(t) \tag{17}$$

$$\frac{d}{dt}I_{h,1}(t) = \frac{b\,\beta_{v,h,1}\,S_{h,1}(t)\,I_v(t)}{N_{h,1}} - \left(\gamma_{h,1} + \mu_{h,1}\right) I_{h,1}(t) \tag{18}$$

$$\frac{d}{dt}R_{h,1}(t) = \gamma_{h,1}\,I_{h,1}(t) - \mu_{h,1}\,R_{h,1}(t) \tag{19}$$

For the second we have:

$$\frac{d}{dt}S_{h,2}(t) = \mu_{h,2}\,N_{h,2} - \frac{b\,\beta_{v,h,2}\,S_{h,2}(t)\,I_v(t)}{N_{h,2}} - \mu_{h,2}\,S_{h,2}(t) \tag{20}$$

$$\frac{d}{dt}I_{h,2}(t) = \frac{b\,\beta_{v,h,2}\,S_{h,2}(t)\,I_v(t)}{N_{h,2}} - \left(\gamma_{h,2} + \mu_{h,2}\right) I_{h,2}(t) \tag{21}$$

$$\frac{d}{dt} R_{h,2}(t) = \gamma_{h,2}\, I_{h,2}(t) - \mu_{h,2}\, R_{h,2}(t) \tag{22}$$

And for the vector or group of mosquitoes, we have:

$$\frac{d}{dt} S_v(t) = \mu_v\, N_v - \left(\frac{b_1 \beta_{h,v,1}\, I_{h,1}(t)}{N_{h,1}} + \frac{b_2 \beta_{h,v,2}\, I_{h,2}(t)}{N_{h,2}}\right) S_v(t) - \mu_v S_v(t) \tag{23}$$

$$\frac{d}{dt} I_v(t) = \left(\frac{b_1 \beta_{h,v,1}\, I_{h,1}(t)}{N_{h,1}} + \frac{b_2 \beta_{h,v,2}\, I_{h,2}(t)}{N_{h,2}}\right) S_v(t) - (\gamma_v + \mu_v)\, I_v(t) \tag{24}$$

$$\frac{d}{dt} R_v(t) = \gamma_v\, I_v(t) - \mu_v\, R_v(t) \tag{25}$$

Now, we need to change the notation from differential equation to algebraic expressions, we have to change the equations (17) to (25), following the next terms:

$$\begin{array}{ccc} S_{h,1}(t) = S_{h,1} & I_{h,1}(t) = I_{h,1} & R_{h,1}(t) = R_{h,1} \\ S_{h,2}(t) = S_{h,2} & I_{h,2}(t) = I_{h,2} & R_{h,2}(t) = R_{h,2} \\ S_v(t) = S_v & I_v(t) = I_v & R_v(t) = R_v \end{array} \tag{26}$$

With (26), and the right hand side of the equations (17) to (25), we make the change to algebraic expression, after that, we generate the Jacobian matrix which allow us analysing the stability of the system, in other words, seeing if the system will be free of infection. We continue showing the Jacobian we have made:

$$\begin{bmatrix}
-\frac{b_1\beta_{v,h,1}I_v}{N_{h,1}} - \mu_{h,1} & 0 & 0 & 0 & 0 & 0 & 0 & -\frac{b_1\beta_{v,h,1}S_{h,1}}{N_{h,1}} & 0 \\
\frac{b_1\beta_{v,h,1}I_v}{N_{h,1}} & -\gamma_{h,1} - \mu_{h,1} & 0 & 0 & 0 & 0 & 0 & \frac{b_1\beta_{v,h,1}S_{h,1}}{N_{h,1}} & 0 \\
0 & \gamma_{h,1} & -\mu_{h,1} & 0 & 0 & 0 & 0 & 0 & 0 \\
0 & 0 & 0 & -\frac{b_2\beta_{v,h,2}I_v}{N_{h,2}} - \mu_{h,2} & 0 & 0 & 0 & -\frac{b_2\beta_{v,h,2}S_{h,2}}{N_{h,2}} & 0 \\
0 & 0 & 0 & \frac{b_2\beta_{v,h,2}I_v}{N_{h,2}} & -\gamma_{h,2} - \mu_{h,2} & 0 & 0 & \frac{b_2\beta_{v,h,2}S_{h,2}}{N_{h,2}} & 0 \\
0 & 0 & 0 & 0 & \gamma_{h,2} & -\mu_{h,2} & 0 & 0 & 0 \\
0 & -\frac{b_1\beta_{h,v,1}S_v}{N_{h,1}} & 0 & 0 & -\frac{b_2\beta_{h,v,2}S_v}{N_{h,2}} & 0 & A & 0 & 0 \\
0 & \frac{b_1\beta_{h,v,1}S_v}{N_{h,1}} & 0 & 0 & \frac{b_2\beta_{h,v,2}S_v}{N_{h,2}} & 0 & B & -\gamma_v - \mu_v & 0 \\
0 & 0 & 0 & 0 & 0 & 0 & 0 & \gamma_v & -\mu_v
\end{bmatrix} \tag{27}$$

Where A and B are:

$$A = -\frac{b_1\beta_{h,v,1}I_v}{N_{h,1}} - \frac{b_2\beta_{h,v,2}I_v}{N_{h,2}} - \mu_v \tag{28}$$

$$B = \frac{b_1\beta_{h,v,1}I_v}{N_{h,1}} + \frac{b_2\beta_{h,v,2}I_v}{N_{h,2}} \tag{29}$$

As the first model, we find that the trivial solution is:

$$\begin{array}{ccc} S_{h,1}(t) = N_{h,1} & I_{h,1}(t) = 0 & R_{h,1}(t) = 0 \\ S_{h,2}(t) = N_{h,2} & I_{h,2}(t) = 0 & R_{h,2}(t) = 0 \\ S_v(t) = N_v & I_v(t) = 0 & R_v(t) = 0 \end{array} \tag{30}$$

Replacing the found results in the trivial solution (30) in (27), we find the simplified matrix which let us find the basic reproductive number.

$$\begin{bmatrix} -\mu_{h,1} & 0 & 0 & 0 & 0 & 0 & 0 & -b_1\beta_{v,h,1} & 0 \\ 0 & -\gamma_{h,1}-\mu_{h,1} & 0 & 0 & 0 & 0 & 0 & b_1\beta_{v,h,1} & 0 \\ 0 & \gamma_{h,1} & -\mu_{h,1} & 0 & 0 & 0 & 0 & 0 & 0 \\ 0 & 0 & 0 & -\mu_{h,2} & 0 & 0 & 0 & -b_2\beta_{v,h,2} & 0 \\ 0 & 0 & 0 & 0 & -\gamma_{h,2}-\mu_{h,2} & 0 & 0 & b_2\beta_{v,h,2} & 0 \\ 0 & 0 & 0 & 0 & \gamma_{h,2} & -\mu_{h,2} & 0 & 0 & 0 \\ 0 & -\dfrac{b_1\beta_{h,v,1}N_v}{N_{h,1}} & 0 & 0 & -\dfrac{b_2\beta_{h,v,2}N_v}{N_{h,2}} & 0 & -\mu_v & 0 & 0 \\ 0 & \dfrac{b_1\beta_{h,v,1}N_v}{N_{h,1}} & 0 & 0 & \dfrac{b_2\beta_{h,v,2}N_v}{N_{h,2}} & 0 & 0 & -\gamma_v-\mu_v & 0 \\ 0 & 0 & 0 & 0 & 0 & 0 & 0 & \gamma_v & -\mu_v \end{bmatrix} \tag{31}$$

With the matrix we find the characteristic polynomial,

$$(\lambda+\mu_{h,2})^2(\lambda+\mu_{h,1})^2(\lambda+\mu_v)^2(\lambda^3+C\lambda^2+D\lambda+E) \tag{32}$$

Where C, D and E:

$$C = \gamma_{h,1}+\mu_{h,1}+\gamma_{h,2}+\mu_{h,2}+\gamma_v+\mu_v \tag{33}$$

$$D = (\gamma_{h,1}+\mu_{h,1})(\gamma_{h,2}+\mu_{h,2}) + (\gamma_{h,1}+\mu_{h,1})(\gamma_v+\mu_v) + (\gamma_{h,2}+\mu_{h,2})(\gamma_v+\mu_v) - \left(\frac{b_1^2\beta_{h,v,1}\beta_{v,h,1}}{N_{h,1}} + \frac{b_2^2\beta_{h,v,2}\beta_{v,h,2}}{N_{h,2}}\right)N_v \tag{34}$$

$$E = (\gamma_{h,1}+\mu_{h,1})(\gamma_{h,2}+\mu_{h,2})(\gamma_v+\mu_v) - \left(\frac{b_1^2\beta_{h,v,1}\beta_{v,h,1}}{N_{h,1}}(\gamma_{h,2}+\mu_{h,2}) + \frac{b_2^2\beta_{h,v,2}\beta_{v,h,2}}{N_{h,2}}(\gamma_{h,1}+\mu_{h,1})\right)N_v \tag{35}$$

From (32) we substrate the larger term:

$$\lambda^3+C\lambda^2+D\lambda+E \tag{36}$$

Here, we take the term lambda non-dependent, which should be major than zero, for accomplish the free-equilibrium condition:

$$0 < (\gamma_{h,1} + \mu_{h,1})(\gamma_{h,2} + \mu_{h,2})(\gamma_v + \mu_v) - \left(\frac{b_1^2 \beta_{h,v,1} \beta_{v,h,1}}{N_{h,1}} (\gamma_{h,2} + \mu_{h,2}) + \frac{b_2^2 \beta_{h,v,2} \beta_{v,h,2}}{N_{h,2}} (\gamma_{h,1} + \mu_{h,1})\right) N_v \tag{37}$$

For the free-equilibrium, the population of mosquitoes should be:

$$N_v < \frac{(\gamma_{h,1} + \mu_{h,1})(\gamma_{h,2} + \mu_{h,2})(\gamma_v + \mu_v)}{\left(\frac{b_1^2 \beta_{h,v,1} \beta_{v,h,1}}{N_{h,1}} (\gamma_{h,2} + \mu_{h,2}) + \frac{b_2^2 \beta_{h,v,2} \beta_{v,h,2}}{N_{h,2}} (\gamma_{h,1} + \mu_{h,1})\right)} \tag{38}$$

Where the basic reproductive number R_0 is:

$$R_0 = \frac{b_1^2 \beta_{h,v,1} \beta_{v,h,1}}{(\gamma_{h,1} + \mu_{h,1})(\gamma_v + \mu_v)} \frac{N_v}{N_{h,1}} + \frac{b_2^2 \beta_{h,v,2} \beta_{v,h,2}}{(\gamma_{h,2} + \mu_{h,2})(\gamma_v + \mu_v)} \frac{N_v}{N_{h,2}} \tag{39}$$

If you notice the equation (16) and (39) are similar in their structure.

3.3 SIR model for three groups of humans

In this subsection we just present another model where it's included a third inhomogeneity, so we have now three groups of humans. We commence with the systems of humans, which are represented by nine equations, every group with three equations, for the first group:

$$\frac{d}{dt} S_{h,1}(t) = \mu_{h,1}\, N_{h,1} - \frac{b\, \beta_{v,h,1}\, S_{h,1}(t)\, I_v(t)}{N_{h,1}} - \mu_{h,1}\, S_{h,1}(t) \tag{40}$$

$$\frac{d}{dt} I_{h,1}(t) = \frac{b\, \beta_{v,h,1}\, S_{h,1}(t)\, I_v(t)}{N_{h,1}} - (\gamma_{h,1} + \mu_{h,1})\, I_{h,1}(t) \tag{41}$$

$$\frac{d}{dt} R_{h,1}(t) = \gamma_{h,1}\, I_{h,1}(t) - \mu_{h,1}\, R_{h,1}(t) \tag{42}$$

For the second one:

$$\frac{d}{dt} S_{h,2}(t) = \mu_{h,2}\, N_{h,2} - \frac{b\, \beta_{v,h,2}\, S_{h,2}(t)\, I_v(t)}{N_{h,2}} - \mu_{h,2} S_{h,2}(t) \tag{43}$$

$$\frac{d}{dt} I_{h,2}(t) = \frac{b\, \beta_{v,h,2}\, S_{h,2}(t)\, I_v(t)}{N_{h,2}} - (\gamma_{h,2} + \mu_{h,2})\, I_{h,2}(t) \tag{44}$$

$$\frac{d}{dt} R_{h,2}(t) = \gamma_{h,2}\, I_{h,2}(t) - \mu_{h,2}\, R_{h,2}(t) \tag{45}$$

And for the third system:

$$\frac{d}{dt}S_{h,3}(t) = \mu_{h,3}\,N_{h,3} - \frac{b\,\beta_{v,h,3}\,S_{h,3}(t)\,I_v(t)}{N_{h,3}} - \mu_{h,3}S_{h,3}(t) \tag{46}$$

$$\frac{d}{dt}I_{h,3}(t) = \frac{b\,\beta_{v,h,3}\,S_{h,3}(t)\,I_v(t)}{N_{h,3}} - (\gamma_{h,3} + \mu_{h,3})\,I_{h,3}(t) \tag{47}$$

$$\frac{d}{dt}R_{h,3}(t) = \gamma_{h,3}\,I_{h,3}(t) - \mu_{h,3}\,R_{h,3}(t) \tag{48}$$

Now we show in the same direction, the system for the vectors:

$$\frac{d}{dt}S_v(t) = \mu_v\,N_v - \left(\sum_{i=1}^{3}\frac{b_i\beta_{h,v,i}\,I_{h,i}(t)}{N_{h,i}}\right)S_v(t) - \mu_v S_v(t) \tag{49}$$

$$\frac{d}{dt}I_v(t) = \left(\sum_{i=1}^{3}\frac{b_i\beta_{h,v,i}\,I_{h,i}(t)}{N_{h,i}}\right)S_v(t) - (\gamma_v + \mu_v)\,I_v(t) \tag{50}$$

$$\frac{d}{dt}R_v(t) = \gamma_v\,I_v(t) - \mu_v\,R_v(t) \tag{51}$$

Now, with all the equations from our system we can start replacing the time dependent functions for variables:

$$\begin{matrix} S_{h,1}(t) = S_{h,1} & I_{h,1}(t) = I_{h,1} & R_{h,1}(t) = R_{h,1} \\ S_{h,2}(t) = S_{h,2} & I_{h,2}(t) = I_{h,2} & R_{h,2}(t) = R_{h,2} \\ S_{h,3}(t) = S_{h,3} & I_{h,2}(t) = I_{h,3} & R_{h,2}(t) = R_{h,3} \\ S_v(t) = S_v & I_v(t) = I_v & R_v(t) = R_v \end{matrix} \tag{52}$$

Where the trivial solution is:

$$\begin{matrix} S_{h,1}(t) = N_{h,1} & I_{h,1}(t) = 0 & R_{h,1}(t) = 0 \\ S_{h,2}(t) = N_{h,2} & I_{h,2}(t) = 0 & R_{h,2}(t) = 0 \\ S_{h,3}(t) = N_{h,3} & I_{h,2}(t) = 0 & R_{h,2}(t) = 0 \\ S_v(t) = N_v & I_v(t) = 0 & R_v(t) = 0 \end{matrix} \tag{53}$$

With this information and following the algorithm that we have been following in this section, we build the Jacobian matrix:

$$\begin{bmatrix} 12\ x\ 12\ Matrix \\ Data\ Type{:}\ anything \\ Storage{:}\ rectangular \\ Order{:}\ Fortran\_order \end{bmatrix} \tag{54}$$

We just put in (54) the information that Maple™ give us about the matrix, and also, we just put this because the matrix is too big for the paper size.

If the matrix is big, you can imagine the characteristic polynomial, for that reason for this model, we just write the basic reproductive number.

$$R_0 = \frac{b_1^2 \beta_{h,v,1} \beta_{v,h,1}}{(\gamma_{h,1} + \mu_{h,1})(\gamma_v + \mu_v)} \frac{N_v}{N_{h,1}} + \frac{b_2^2 \beta_{h,v,2} \beta_{v,h,2}}{(\gamma_{h,2} + \mu_{h,2})(\gamma_v + \mu_v)} \frac{N_v}{N_{h,2}} + \frac{b_3^2 \beta_{h,v,3} \beta_{v,h,3}}{(\gamma_{h,3} + \mu_{h,3})(\gamma_v + \mu_v)} \frac{N_v}{N_{h,3}} \tag{55}$$

Again, we can see that this result is similar to the others (16) and (39). With that it's easy to introduce the next section.

4. Generalized malaria SIR coupled model

As we will show in this section, it is possible in an intuitive way to start generalizing some part of the model, we start resuming the equation for the n groups of humans:

$$\frac{d}{dt} S_{h,i}(t) = \mu_{h,i}\, N_{h,i} - \frac{b\, \beta_{v,h,i}\, S_{h,i}(t)\, I_v(t)}{N_{h,i}} - \mu_{h,i} S_{h,i}(t) \tag{56}$$

$$\frac{d}{dt} I_{h,i}(t) = \frac{b\, \beta_{v,h,i}\, S_{h,i}(t)\, I_v(t)}{N_{h,i}} - (\gamma_{h,i} + \mu_{h,i})\, I_{h,i}(t) \tag{57}$$

$$\frac{d}{dt} R_{h,i}(t) = \gamma_{h,i}\, I_{h,i}(t) - \mu_{h,i}\, R_{h,i}(t) \tag{58}$$

And the group of vectors or mosquitoes:

$$\frac{d}{dt} S_v(t) = \mu_v\, N_v - \left(\sum_{i=1}^{n} \frac{b_i \beta_{h,v,i}\, I_{h,i}(t)}{N_{h,i}} \right) S_v(t) - \mu_v S_v(t) \tag{59}$$

$$\frac{d}{dt} I_v(t) = \left(\sum_{i=1}^{n} \frac{b_i \beta_{h,v,i}\, I_{h,i}(t)}{N_{h,i}} \right) S_v(t) - (\gamma_v + \mu_v)\, I_v(t) \tag{60}$$

$$\frac{d}{dt} R_v(t) = \gamma_v\, I_v(t) - \mu_v\, R_v(t) \tag{61}$$

The complete system is described for $3(n+1)$ equations, which is condensed in the last six expressions. For solving these systems for large values of n, it becomes in a computational problem; for that reason the idea of a computer that with the simplest forms of the problem could obtain generalized results. This foundation is called Mechanized Reasoning and in this direction is thought this section (Castaño C, 2009).

With the results that we have obtained in the three studied cases, we could intuitively try to discover de general rule or expression for our generalized system.

Could see the results (16), (39) and (55), with this results we can build a logical general result, it's important to note that we rewrite the basic reproductive number with the intension to show easily the behaviour of the result between the different values for n. We note $R_{0,n}$ for each model where n is the number of the groups of humans.

$$R_{0,1} = \frac{b^2 \beta_{v,h} \beta_{h,v}}{(\mu_h + \gamma_h)(\mu_v + \gamma_v)} \frac{N_v}{N_h} \tag{62}$$

$$R_{0,2} = \frac{b_1^2 \beta_{h,v,1} \beta_{v,h,1}}{(\gamma_{h,1} + \mu_{h,1})(\gamma_v + \mu_v)} \frac{N_v}{N_{h,1}} + \frac{b_2^2 \beta_{h,v,2} \beta_{v,h,2}}{(\gamma_{h,2} + \mu_{h,2})(\gamma_v + \mu_v)} \frac{N_v}{N_{h,2}} \tag{63}$$

$$R_{0,3} = \frac{b_1^2 \beta_{h,v,1} \beta_{v,h,1}}{(\gamma_{h,1} + \mu_{h,1})(\gamma_v + \mu_v)} \frac{N_v}{N_{h,1}} + \frac{b_2^2 \beta_{h,v,2} \beta_{v,h,2}}{(\gamma_{h,2} + \mu_{h,2})(\gamma_v + \mu_v)} \frac{N_v}{N_{h,2}} + \frac{b_3^2 \beta_{h,v,3} \beta_{v,h,3}}{(\gamma_{h,3} + \mu_{h,3})(\gamma_v + \mu_v)} \frac{N_v}{N_{h,3}} \tag{64}$$

$$\vdots$$

$$R_{0,n} = \sum_{i=1}^{n} \frac{b_i^2 \beta_{h,v,i} \beta_{v,h,i}}{(\gamma_{h,i} + \mu_{h,i})(\gamma_v + \mu_v)} \frac{N_v}{N_{h,i}} \tag{65}$$

This is how we have found the generalized result, which could be used in lot of cases in where the Malaria is the main actor, with this generalization we can find the basic reproductive number for whatever inhomogeneities we have or whatever information we obtain in the real world.

5. Future work

The work in epidemiology never ends because every day there is the possibility that a new virus or infective form could appear in the society, for that reason we have to be prepared for finding the way to remain alive. Also, there are a lot of difficulties in the sense of recovering the information of the world and adapting to the models that exist. In first place, it is necessary to think in a new form to obtain this information, and for the other side it is important to find models that can used the information that exist until now.

If we talk to the generated models in this chapter, there is other thing we can improve and that is to create a mosquito's population with inhomogeneities, in other words, to generate a model with n-groups of humans and m-groups of vectors, and finding the basic reproductive number for this new general model. This could be used without the restriction of grouping the people and the varieties of mosquitoes in some. However, we consider that the mechanized reasons foundation should be developed for the benefit of all scientific community.

6. Acknowledgements

The authors would like to thank Prof. Dr. Eng. Andrés Sicard and Prof. Mario Elkin Vélez for keeping company in this work in the Logic and Computation group. They are also especially grateful for Prof. Juan Fernando Ospina Giraldo for his support during the reviewing process. This research was support by the Logic and Computation group at EAFIT University.

7. References

Baker, Robert (2007). *EPIDEMIC: The Past, Present and Future of the Diseases that Made Us.* Satin Publications Ltd, ISBN 978-1-905745-08-1, London.

Bellomo, Nicola (2008). *Mathematical Modeling of Biological Systems, Volume II.* Birkhäuser, ISBN 978-0-8176-4555-7, Berlin.

Bollet, Alfred J. (2004). *Plagues & Poxes: The Impact of Human History on Epidemic Disease.* Demos, ISBN 1-888799-79-X, New York.

Bonita, Ruth; Beaglehole, Robert & Kjellström, Tord (2006). *Basic Epidemiology 2ed.* World Health Organization, ISBN 978-92-4-154707-9, Geneva.

Brauer, Fred; Wu, Jianhong & van den Driessche, Pauline (2008). *Mathematical Epidemiology.* Springer, ISBN 978-3-540-78910-9, Berlin.

Capasso, Vincenzo (2008). *Mathematical Structures of Epidemic Systems.* Springer, ISBN 978-3-540-56526-0, Berlin.

Castaño C., Davinson (2009). World Congress on Engineering and Computer Science. *Proceedings of the World Congress on Engineering and Computer Science 2009 Vol I.* pp. 36-40, ISBN 978-988-17012-6-8, San Francisco USA, October 2009.

Chowell, Gerardo; Hyman, James M.; Bettencourt, Luis M. A. & Castillo-Chavez, Carlos (2009). *Mathematical and Statistical Estimation Approaches in Epidemiology.* Springer, ISBN 978-90-481-2312-4, London.

Christakos, George; Olea, Ricardo A.; Serre, Marc L.; Yu, Hwa-Lung & Wang, Lin-lin (2005). *Interdisciplinary Public Health Reasoning and Epidemic Modelling: The Case of Black Death.* Springer, ISBN 3-540-25794-2, New York.

Daley, D.J. & Gani, J. (2005). *Epidemic Modelling: An Introduction.* Cambridge University Press, ISBN 978-0-521-64079-4, New York.

Gottfried, Robert S. (1983). *The Black Death: Natural and Human Disaster in Medieval Europe.* Fress Press, ISBN 978-0029123706, New York.

Ma, Stefan & Xia, Yingcun (2009).*Mathematical Understanding of Infectious Disease Dynamics.* World Scientific, ISBN 978-981-283-482-9, London.

Ma, Zhien; Zhou, Yicang; Wu, Jianhong (2009). *Modeling and Dynamics of Infectious Diseases.* World Scientific, ISBN 978-7-04-024757-2, China.

Magal, Pierre & Ruan Shigui (2008). *Structured Population Models in Biology and Epidemiology.* Springer-Verlag, ISBN 978-3-540-78272-8, Berlin.

Maplesoft (2007). *Maple User Manual.* Maplesoft, ISBN 978-1-897310-20-5, Canada.

Perthame, Benoît (2007).*Transport Equations in Biology.* Birkhäuser Verlag, ISBN 978-3-7643-7841-7, Berlin.

Porta, Miquel (2008). *A Dictionary of Epidemiology.* Oxford University Press, ISBN 978–0-19–531449–6, New York.

Stewart, Antony (2002). *Basic Statistics and Epidemiology: A practical guide*. Radcliffe Medical Press, ISBN 1-85775-589-8.

4

Understanding Virtual Reality Technology: Advances and Applications

Moses Okechukwu Onyesolu[1] and Felista Udoka Eze[2]
[1]*Nnamdi Azikiwe University, Awka, Anambra State.*
[2]*Federal University of Technology, Owerri, Imo State, Nigeria*

1. Introduction

Virtual Reality (VR) is not an entirely new concept; it has existed in various forms since the late 1960s. It has been known by names such as synthetic environment, cyberspace, artificial reality, simulator technology and so on and so forth before VR was eventually adopted. The latest manifestation of VR is desktop VR. Desktop VR is also known by other names such as Window on World (WoW) or non-immersive VR (Onyesolu, 2006). As a result of proliferation of desktop VR, the technology has continued to develop applications that are less than fully immersive. These non-immersive VR applications are far less expensive and technically daunting and have made inroads into industry training and development. VR has perhaps at last come within the realm of possibility for general creation and use most especially in education where computer-based virtual learning environments (VLE) are packaged as desktop VR. This, in turn, points the way for its inclusion in educational programs (Ausburn & Ausburn, 2004). These computer-based virtual learning environments (VLEs) have opened new realms in the teaching, learning, and practice of medicine, physical sciences and engineering among others. VLEs provide students with the opportunity to achieve learning goals. VLE-based applications have thus emerged in mainstream education in schools and universities as successful tools to supplement traditional teaching methods. These learning environments have been discovered to have greater pedagogical effectiveness on learners. Virtual learning environments provide three-dimensional (3D) insights into the structures and functions of any system desired. Students can thereby learn the principles of such system in a fast, effective and pleasurable way by interacting with and navigating through the environment created for such system (Onyesolu, 2009a; Onyesolu, 2009b). It is known that VR can make the artificial as realistic as, and even more realistic than, the real (Negroponte, 1995).

2. The technology: Virtual Reality

There are some people to whom VR is a specific collection of technologies; that is, headset, glove and walker (Haag et al., 1998; Williams & Sawyer, 2001; Isdale, 1993). VR is defined as a highly interactive, computer-based multimedia environment in which the user becomes the participant in a computer-generated world (Kim et al., 2000; Onyesolu, 2009a; Onyesolu & Akpado, 2009). It is the simulation of a real or imagined environment that can be

experienced visually in the three dimensions of width, height, and depth and that may additionally provide an interactive experience visually in full real-time motion with sound and possibly with tactile and other forms of feedback. VR is a way for humans to visualize, manipulate and interact with computers and extremely complex data (Isdale, 1998). It is an artificial environment created with computer hardware and software and presented to the user in such a way that it appears and feels like a real environment (Baieier, 1993). VR is a computer-synthesized, three-dimensional environment in which a plurality of human participants, appropriately interfaced, may engage and manipulate simulated physical elements in the environment and, in some forms, may engage and interact with representations of other humans, past, present or fictional, or with invented creatures. It is a computer-based technology for simulating visual auditory and other sensory aspects of complex environments (Onyesolu, 2009b). VR incorporates 3D technologies that give a real-life illusion. VR creates a simulation of real-life situation (Haag et al., 1998).
Therefore, VR refers to an immersive, interactive, multi-sensory, viewer-centered, 3D computer-generated environment and the combination of technologies required to build such an environment (Aukstakalnis & Blatner, 1992; Cruz-Niera, 1993). By immersing viewers in a computer-generated stereoscopic environment, VR technology breaks down barriers between humans and computers. VR technology simulates natural stereoscopic viewing processes by using computer technology to create right-eye and left-eye images of a given 3D object or scene. The viewer's brain integrates the information from these two perspectives to create the perception of 3D space. Thus, VR technology creates the illusion that on-screen objects have depth and presence beyond the flat image projected onto the screen. With VR technology, viewers can perceive distance and spatial relationships between different object components more realistically and accurately than with conventional visualization tools (such as traditional CAD tools).

3. Virtual Reality components

The components necessary for building and experiencing VR are divided into two main components-the hardware components and the software components.

3.1 Hardware components

The hardware components are divided into five sub-components: computer workstation, sensory displays, process acceleration cards, tracking system and input devices.

3.1.1 Computer workstation

A computer workstation is a high-end microcomputer designed for technical or scientific applications. Intended primarily to be used by one person at a time, workstations are commonly connected to a local area network and run multi-user operating systems. The term workstation has also been used to refer to a mainframe computer terminal or a personal computer (PC) connected to a network.
Workstations had offered higher performance than personal computers, especially with respect to CPU and graphics, memory capacity and multitasking capability. They are optimized for the visualization and manipulation of different types of complex data such as 3D mechanical design, engineering simulation animation and rendering of images, and mathematical plots. Workstations are the first segment of the computer market to present advanced accessories and collaboration tools. Presently, the workstation market is highly

commoditized and is dominated by large PC vendors, such as Dell and HP, selling Microsoft Windows/Linux running on Intel Xeon/AMD Opteron. Alternative UNIX based platforms are provided by Apple Inc., Sun Microsystems, and Silicon Graphics International (SGI) (http://en.wikipedia.org/wiki/Workstation). Computer workstation is used to control several sensory display devices to immerse you in 3D virtual environment.

3.1.2 Sensory displays

Sensory displays are used to display the simulated virtual worlds to the user. The most common sensory displays are the computer visual display unit, the head-mounted display (HMD) for 3D visual and headphones for 3D audio.

3.1.2.1 Head mounted displays

Head mounted displays place a screen in front of each of the viewer's eyes at all times. The view, the segment of the virtual environment generated and displayed, is controlled by orientation sensors mounted on the "helmet". Head movement is recognized by the computer, and a new perspective of the scene is generated. In most cases, a set of optical lens and mirrors are used to enlarge the view to fill the field of view and to direct the scene to the eyes (Lane, 1993).

Fig. 1. Visette 45 SXGA Head Mounted Display (HMD)

3.1.2.2 Binocular Omni-Orientation Monitor (BOOM)

The BOOM is mounted on a jointed mechanical arm with tracking sensors located at the joints. A counterbalance is used to stabilize the monitor, so that when the user releases the monitor, it remains in place. To view the virtual environment, the user must take hold of the monitor and put her face up to it. The computer will generate an appropriate scene based on the position and orientation of the joints on the mechanical arm (Aukstakalnis & Blatner,

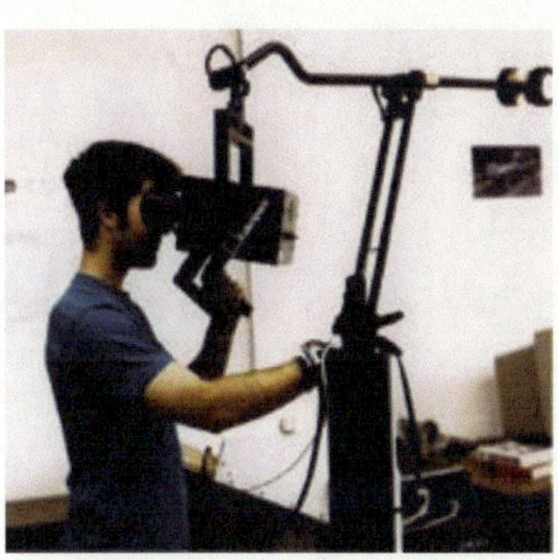

Fig. 2. A Binocular Omni-Orientation Monitor (BOOM)

1992). Some of the problems associated with HMDs can be solved by using a BOOM display. The user does not have to wear a BOOM display as in the case of an HMD. This means that crossing the boundary between a virtual world and the real world is simply a matter of moving your eyes away from the BOOM.

3.1.2.3 Visual Display Unit (VDU) or monitors

There are two types of computer visual display unit. The CRT monitors and the LCD monitors. The distinguishing characteristics of the two types are beyond the scope of this piece.

3.1.3 Process acceleration cards

These cards help to update the display with new sensory information. Examples are 3D graphic cards and 3D sound cards.

3.1.4 Tracking system

This system tracks the position and orientation of a user in the virtual environment. This system is divided into: mechanical, electromagnetic, ultrasonic and infrared trackers.

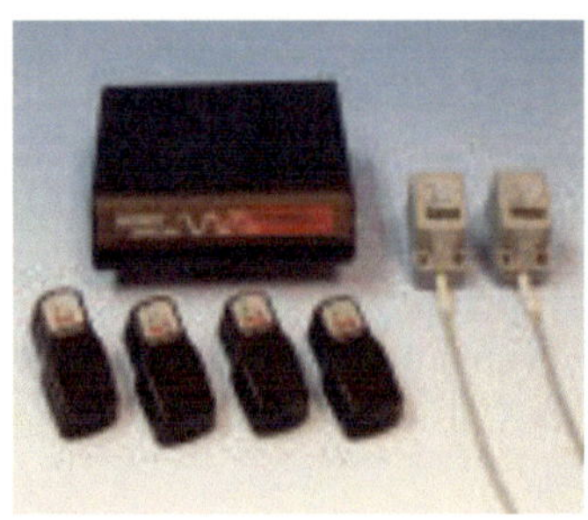

Fig. 3. Patriot wireless electromagnetic tracker

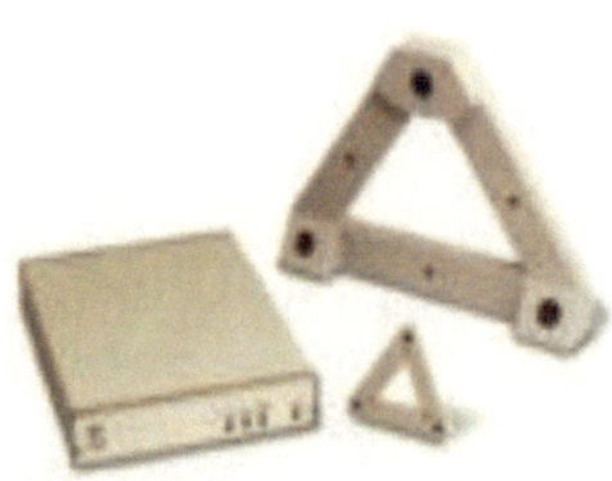

Fig. 4. Logitech ultrasonic tracker

3.1.5 Input devices

They are used to interact with the virtual environment and objects within the virtual environment. Examples are joystick (wand), instrumented glove, keyboard, voice recognition etc.

3.2 Software components

The software components are divided into four sub-components: 3D modeling software, 2D graphics software, digital sound editing software and VR simulation software.

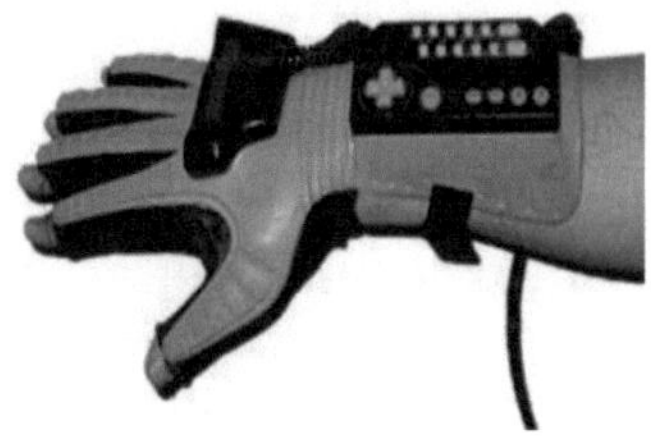

Fig. 5. An instrumented glove (Nintendo power glove)

3.2.1 3D modeling software

3D modeling software is used in constructing the geometry of the objects in a virtual world and specifies the visual properties of these objects.

3.2.2 2D graphics software

2D graphics software is used to manipulate texture to be applied to the objects which enhance their visual details.

3.2.3 Digital sound editing software

Digital sound editing software is used to mix and edit sounds that objects make within the virtual environment.

3.2.3 VR simulation software

Simulation software brings the components together. It is used to program how these objects behave and set the rules that the virtual world follows.

4. Classification of Virtual Reality systems

VR is classified into three major types: (a) Non-Immersive VR Systems, (b) Semi-Immersive VR Systems and (c) Immersive (Fully Immersive) VR systems. Other forms of classification are levels of VR and methods of VR. Levels of VR deals with efforts employed to develop VR technology. Under this classification we have entry level, basic level, advanced level, immersive systems and big-time systems. Methods of VR classification deals with methods employed in developing VR system. Under this class we have simulation based systems, projector based systems, avatar-image based systems and desktop based system.

4.1 Non-immersive VR systems

As the name suggests, are the least implementation of VR techniques. It involves implementing VR on a desktop computer. This class is also known as Window on World (WoW) (Onyesolu, 2006). Using the desktop system, the virtual environment is viewed through a portal or window by utilizing a standard high resolution monitor. Interaction with the virtual environment can occur by conventional means such as keyboard, mouse or trackball

4.2 Semi-immersive VR systems

A semi immersive VR system comprise of a relatively high performance graphics computing system which can be coupled with either a large screen monitor; a large screen projection system or multiple television projection system. Using a wide field of view, these systems increase the feeling of immersion or presence experienced by the user and stereographic imaging can be achieved using some type of shutter glasses.

4.3 Immersive (fully immersive) VR systems

An Immersive VR system is the most direct experience of virtual environments. Here the user either wears an head mounted display (HMD) or uses some form of head-coupled display such as a Binocular Omni-Orientation Monitor (BOOM) to view the virtual environment, in addition to some tracking devices and haptic devices. An HMD or BOOM uses small monitors placed in front of each eye which provide stereo, bi-ocular or monocular images.

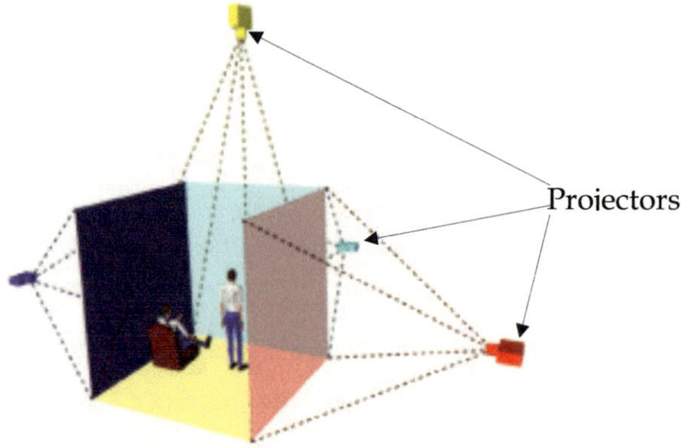

Fig. 6. Schematic representation of a CAVE

5. Low-cost VR technology

Low-cost VR, also called personal computer (PC)-based VR, uses inexpensive devices such as PC workstations and VR glasses, combined with VR-enabled software applications or playstations and projectors, to partially immerse viewers in a virtual scene (Fang et al., n.d.). Fig 5 is a low-cost VR system developed with three playstations, a network switch and two projectors.

Fig. 7. PlayStation2 VR system

The benefits of low cost virtual reality hardware are obvious; high performance systems which were previously exclusive to research institutions with well funded budget can now be constructed relatively cheaper. The reduced price/performance ratio has positive implications for hospitals, educational institutions, museums and other organizations where funding of new technologies are often limited. Previously disadvantaged communities can also benefit from this new technology. In education, cheap VR can provide massive quality education through the interactive learning environment; in medicine, cheap virtual environment has been shown to provide promising results in the field of exposure therapy (Fang et al., n.d.).

6. How Virtual Reality works

The idea behind VR is to deliver a sense of being there by giving at least the eye what it would have received if it were there and, more important to have the image change instantly as the point of view is changed (Smith & Lee, 2004). The perception of spatial reality is driven by various visual cues, like relative size, brightness and angular movement. One of the strongest is perspective, which is particularly powerful in its binocular form in that the right and left eyes see different images. Fusing these images into one 3D perception is the basis of stereovision.

The perception of depth provided by each eye seeing a slightly different image, eye parallax, is most effective for objects very near you. Objects farther away essentially cast the same image on each eye. The typical dress code for VR is a helmet with goggle-like displays, one for each eye. Each display delivers a slightly different perspective image of what you would see if you were there. As you move your head, the image rapidly updates so that you feel you are making these changes by moving your head (versus the computer actually following your movement, which it is). You feel you are the cause not the effect.

7. VR development tools and resources

There are many VR development tools and resources. Some of these tools and resources are free (open source to use), some are proprietary (closed source) (Wang & Canon, 1996). VR related development is in progress regarding the availability, usability and capability of customization for existing development tools and resources. VR development tools and resources are quite numerous; some examples are presented:

7.1 Virtual Heroes Inc. (VHI)

This is an "Advanced Learning Technology Company" that creates collaborative interactive learning solutions for Federal Systems, Healthcare and Corporate Training markets (http://www.virtualheroes.com/about.asp). VHI applications facilitate highly interactive, self-paced learning and instructor-led, distributed team training on its Advanced Learning Technology (ALT) platform. Major components of this platform include the Unreal® Engine 3 by Epic Games, and Dynamic Virtual Human Technology (DVHT). ALT leverages simulation learning and digital game-based learning paradigms to accelerate learning, increase proficiency and reduce costs. DVHT combines best-in-class electronic computer game technology with a digital human physiology engine, digital pharmacokinetic drug models, accurate biomechanical parameters and artificial intelligence subroutines for the most realistic virtual humans available anywhere.

7.2 On-Line Interactive Virtual Environment (OLIVE)

This is a product of Forterra Systems Inc. Forterra Systems Inc. builds distributed virtual world technology and turnkey applications for defense, homeland security, medical, corporate training, and entertainment industries (http://company.mmosite.com/forterra /index.shtml). Using the On-Line Interactive Virtual Environment (OLIVE) technology platform, customers can rapidly generate realistic three-dimensional virtual environments that easily scale from single user applications to large scale simulated environments supporting many thousands of concurrent users. Forterra's technology and services enable organizations to train, plan, rehearse, and collaborate in ways previously considered impossible or impractical.

OLIVE combines multimedia, scalable computing and network enabled connectivity to provide a complete IT-ready platform for developing and supporting truly collaborative, multiplayer interactive virtual environments. It is a 3D client-server virtual world platform using PC clients connected to a central server via a network. The architecture scales from a Windows based development environment to large scale Linux clusters. This architecture supports many thousands of concurrent, geographically distributed users (http://www.webbuyersguide.com/product/brief.aspx?src=rss&kc=rss&id=52841)

7.3 Icarus Studios Inc.

The company offers tools and products for creating massively multi-player online (MMO) environments, virtual worlds, and serious games for major entertainment, corporate, and government clients (Mousa, n.d). Icarus provides next generation technology, tools and production services enabling publishers and marketers to develop immersive environments to create new revenue streams and branding opportunities (http://www.icarusstudios.com/). Icarus Studios products include compatibility with industry standard tools such as 3D Max, Collada, and other 3D applications with simple editors.

7.4 OpenSimulator (OpenSim)

OpenSimulator is a 3D application server. It can be used to create a virtual environment (world) which can be accessed through a variety of clients, on multiple protocols (Mousa, n.d). OpenSimulator allows you to develop your environment using technologies you feel work best. OpenSimulator has numerous advantages which among other things are:

i. OpenSimulator is released under BSD license, making it both open source, and commercially friendly to embed in products.
ii. It has many tools for developers to build various applications (chat application, buildings, and avatars among others).
iii. OpenSimulator can be extended via modules to build completely custom configuration.
iv. It is a world building tools for creating content real time in the environment.
v. Supports many programming languages for application development such as Linden Scripting Language / OpenSimulator Scripting Language (LSL/OSSL), C#, and/or Jscript and VB.NET
vi. It incorporates rich and handy documentations and tutorials.

7.5 Croquet

Croquet is an open source 3D graphical platform that is used by experienced software developers to create and deploy deeply collaborative multi-user online virtual world applications on and across multiple operating systems and devices (http://www.opencroquet.org/index.php/Main_Page). Croquet is a next generation virtual operating system (OS) written in Squeak. Squeak is a modern variant of Smalltalk. Squeak runs mathematically identical on all machines. Croquet system features a peer-based messaging protocol that dramatically reduces the need for server infrastructures to support virtual world deployment and makes it easy for software developers to create deeply collaborative applications. Croquet provides rich tutorials, resources and videos as educational materials for developers.

7.6 Ogoglio

Ogoglio is an open source 3D graphical platform like Croquet. The main goal of the Ogoglio is to build an online urban style space for creative collaboration. Ogoglio platform is built from the languages and protocols of the web. Therefore, it's scripting language is javascript; it's main data transfer protocol is hypertext transfer protocol (HTTP), it's 2D layout is hypertext markup language (HTML) and cascading style sheet (CSS), and it has lightwave object geometry format for its 3D (http://foo.secondlifeherald.com/slh/2007/01/interview_with_.html). Ogoglio is very different from the other virtual reality world development platforms because it uses Windows, Linux, Solaris operating system platforms and runs on web browsers such as Internet Explorer, Firefox, and Safari.

7.7 QuickDraw 3D (QD3D)

QuickDraw 3D is a 3D graphics API developed by Apple Inc. in 1995. It was delivered as a cross-platform system, though originally developed for their Macintosh computers. QD3D provides a high-level API with a rich set of 3D primitives that is generally much more full-featured and easier to develop than low-level APIs such as OpenGL or Direct3D.

7.8 Autodesk 3d Max (3D Studio MAX)

Autodesk 3d Max (formerly known as 3D Studio MAX) is a modeling, animation and rendering package developed by Autodesk Media and entertainment. 3d Max is the third most widely-used off the shelf 3D animation program by content creation professionals. It has strong modeling capabilities, a flexible plugin architecture and a long heritage on the Microsoft Windows platform. It is mostly used by video game developers, television commercial studios and architectural visualization studios. It is also used for movie effects and movie pre-visualization.

7.9 Blink 3D Builder

Blink 3D Builder is a proprietary authoring tool for creating immersive 3D environments. The 3D environments can be viewed using the Blink 3D Viewer on the Web or locally.

8. Applications and advancements in VR technology

There are a lot of applications and advancements in VR technology. VR is being applied in all areas of human endeavour and many VR applications have been developed for manufacturing, training in a variety of areas (military, medical, equipment operation, etc.), education, simulation, design evaluation (virtual prototyping), architectural walk-through, ergonomic studies, simulation of assembly sequences and maintenance tasks, assistance for the handicapped, study and treatment of phobias (e.g., fear of height), entertainment, rapid prototyping and much more (Onyesolu, 2006). This has been made possible due to the power of VR in transporting customers to a virtual environment and convincing them of their presence in it (Wittenberg, 1993).

In industry, VR has proven to be an effective tool for helping workers evaluates product designs. In 1999, BMW explored the capability of VR for verifying product designs (Gomes de Sa & Zachmann, 1999). They concluded that VR has the potential to reduce the number of physical mockups needed to improve overall product quality, and to obtain quick answers in an intuitive way during the concept phase of a product. In addition, Motorola developed a VR system for training workers to run a pager assembly line (Wittenberg, 1995). They found that VR can be used to successfully train manufacturing personnel, and that participants trained in VR environments perform better on the job than those trained for the same time in real environments.

In 1998, GE Corporate Research developed two VR software applications, Product Vision and Galileo, which allowed engineers to interactively fly through a virtual jet engine (Abshire, & Barron, 1998). They reported that the two applications were used successfully to enhance design communication and to solve maintenance problems early, with minimal cost, delays, and effort. They also reported that using the VR applications helped make maintenance an integral part of their product design process.

The success stories from industry show that VR-technology-literate professionals are a present and future industry need. However, most students currently do not have an opportunity to experience VR technologies while they are in school. Therefore, introducing VR into design and graphics curricula is imperative, to keep pace with the changing needs of industry.

Boeing (the largest aircraft manufacturers in the world) developed the Virtual Space eXperiment (VSX). VSX is a demonstration of how virtual environment systems can be applied to the design of aircraft and other complex systems involving human interactions (Kalawsky, 1993). It is a 3D virtual model of the interior and exterior of a tilt-rotor aircraft in virtual space that allows persons to interact with various items such as maintenance hatch, cargo ramp. McDonnell Douglas uses a ProVision 100 VPX system to evaluate how a virtual environment can aid the design of new engine types. The system is utilized to explore the processes for installing and removing engines, especially for detecting the potential interface with other devices. The automotive industry starts to use the VR technology to design and build cars. It can take two years or more to advance from the development of an initial concept for a new type of car to the moment that a production version rolls off the assembly line.

A virtual reality-based point-and-direct (VR-PAD) system was developed to improve the flexibility in passive robot inspection (Wang & Cannon, 1996). An operator in a remote control room monitors the real working environment through live video views displayed on the screen and uses the virtual gripper to indicate desirable picking and placing locations. The robot in the inspection system completes material handling as specified so that the system can achieve flaw identification. The CERN, European Laboratory for Particle Physics, performed the pilot project that evaluated and promoted the use of virtual environment technology to help design, building and maintaining the Large Hedron Collider (LHC) premises and equipment (Balaguer & Gennaro, 1996). The project consists of several applications, such as network design and integration, territory impact study, and assembly planning and control to respond to the needs of LHC engineers.

Virtual Reality is a powerful tool for education since people comprehend images much faster than they grasp lines of text or columns of numbers. VR offers multisensory immersive environments that engage students and allow them visualize information (Eslinger, 1993). Mathematics and science teachers have used VR for explaining abstract spatial data. Winn and Bricken (1992) used VR to help students learn elementary algebra. They used three-dimensional space to express algebraic concepts and to interact with spatial representations in a virtual environment. They concluded that VR has the potential for making a significant improvement in the way students learn mathematics. Haufmann et al (2000) used VR in mathematics and geometry education, especially in vector analysis and descriptive geometry. Their survey showed that all participants (10 students) rated VR as a very good playground for experiments, and all participants wanted to experience VR again. Students also thought it was easier to view a 3D world in VR rather than on a flat screen.

VR was used to demonstrate molecular mechanisms in chemical engineering courses (Bell, 1996; Bell & Fogler, 1998). Though no statistical analysis was provided, some evidence of enhanced learning in some cases was reported. At the University of Michigan, Vicher (Virtual Chemical Reactors) was developed in the department of Chemical Engineering to teach students catalyst decay, non-isothermal effects in kinetics and reactor design and chemical plant safety (Bell & Fogler, 1996a; Bell & Fogler, 1996b). The developers believed that humans retain up to 90% of what they learn through active participation. The most exciting possibilities in terms of education and VR are found as it is implemented in the education of the disabled.

Sulbaran and Baker (2000) created an online learning system to study the effectiveness of VR in engineering education. They used VR to train participants on how to operate a lock and to identify construction machines. They found that 82% of learners thought learning with VR was more engaging than learning from reading books and listening to lectures using overheads containing graphics or pictures. They also found, in their first survey, that 69% of the students thought they had learned how a lock operates, and 57% thought they had learned how to identify construction machines. 7 to 21 days later, 92% of the students were still able to operate a lock and identify construction machines. Finally, in their second survey, 91% of the learners strongly agreed or agreed that the learning experience benefits from the use of VR.

VR technology promises to shorten a product development cycle greatly by skipping the need for physical mockups (Vince, 1995). The Ford's Alpha simultaneous engineering team developed a VR system for evaluating process installation feasibility in automotive assembly. In Japan, customers bring the architectural layout of their home kitchen to the Matsushita store and plug it into the computer system to generate its virtual copy (Newquist III, 1993). They can install appliances and cabinets, and change colors and sizes to see what their complete kitchen will look like without ever installing a single item in the actual location. Similarly, Mike Rosen and Associates has been using an interactive and immersive VR technology to assist its building industry clients in the design, visualization, marketing, and sales (Neil, 1996). The applications let the customers become actively involved in the visualization process, such as making changes of colors, textures, materials, lighting, and furniture on the fly.

Researchers at NASA Johnson Space Center in Texas have developed an impressive virtual learning environment for high school students--a virtual physics laboratory which enables students to explore such concepts as gravity, friction, and drag in an interactive, virtual environment. Students have several balls and a pendulum with which to work. They also have several investigative tools, such as a distance measuring device and a digital stopwatch. In addition, the computer provides several interesting capabilities such as the ability to view dynamic events in slow motion or to show trails on objects to better show their movements (Dedula, 1997).

9. The impact of VR

There has been increasing interest in the potential social impact of VR. VR will lead to a number of important changes in human life and activity (Cline, 2005). Cline (2005) argued that: VR will be integrated into daily life and activity and it will be used in various human ways; techniques will be developed to influence human behavior, interpersonal communication, and cognition (i.e., virtual genetics); as we spend more and more time in virtual space, there will be a gradual "migration to virtual space," resulting in important changes in economics, worldview, and culture and the design of virtual environments may be used to extend basic human rights into virtual space, to promote human freedom and well-being, and to promote social stability as we move from one stage in socio-political development to the next. VR has had and is still having impact in heritage and archeology, mass media, fiction books, television, motion pictures, music videos, games, fine arts, marketing, health care, therapeutic uses, real estates and others numerous to mention.

9.1 Heritage and archaeology

The first use of a VR presentation in a Heritage application was in 1994 when a museum visitor interpretation provided an interactive "walk-through" of a 3D reconstruction of Dudley Castle in England as it was in 1550 (Colin, 2006). This comprised of a computer controlled laser disc based system designed by British-based engineer Colin Johnson. The use of VR in Heritage and Archaeology has enormous potential in museum and visitor centre applications. There have been many historic reconstructions. These reconstructions are presented in a pre-rendered format to a shared video display, thus allowing more than one person to view a computer generated world, but limiting the interaction that full-scale VR can provide.

9.2 Mass media

Mass media has been a great advocate and perhaps a great hindrance to the development of VR over the years. In 1980s and 1990s the news media's prognostication on the potential of VR built up the expectations of the technology so high as to be impossible to achieve under the technology then or any technology to date. Entertainment media reinforced these concepts with futuristic imagery many generations beyond contemporary capabilities (http://en.wikipedia.org/wiki/virtual reality).

9.3 Fiction books

There are many science fiction books which described VR. One of the first modern works to use this idea was Daniel F. Galouye's novel "Simulacron-3". The Piers Anthony's novel "Killobyte" follows the story of a paralysed cop trapped in a VR game by a hacker, whom he must stop to save a fellow trapped player with diabetes slowly succumbing to insulin shock. The first fictional work to fully describe VR was included in the 1951 book-"The Illustrated Man". The "Otherland" series of novels by Tad Williams shows a world where the Internet has become accessible via VR. It has become so popular and somewhat commonplace that, with the help of surgical implants, people can connect directly into this future VR environment. Some other popular fictional works that use the concept of VR include William Gibson's "Neuromancer" which defined the concept of cyberspace, Neal Stephenson's "Snow Crash", in which he made extensive reference to the term avatar to describe one's representation in a virtual world, and Rudy Rucker's "The Hacker and the Ants", in which programmer Jerzy Rugby uses VR for robot design and testing.

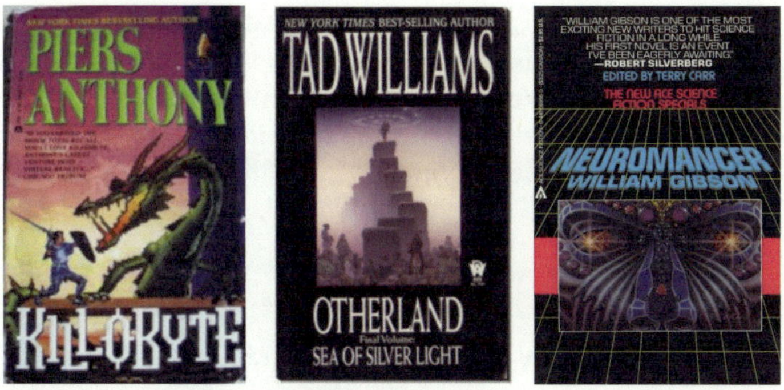

Fig. 8. Fiction books that described Virtual Reality

9.4 Television

Perhaps the earliest example of VR on television is a Doctor Who serial "The Deadly Assassin". This story introduced a dream-like computer-generated reality known as the Matrix. The first major television series to showcase VR was "Star Trek: the Next Generation". They featured the holodeck, a VR facility on starships that enabled its users to recreate and experience anything they wanted. One difference from current VR technology, however, was that replicators, force fields, holograms, and transporters were used to actually recreate and place objects in the holodeck, rather than relying solely on the illusion of physical objects, as is done today.

9.5 Motion pictures

There are a lot of motion pictures that explored and used the idea of VR. Steven Lisberger's film "TRON" was the first motion picture to explore the idea. This idea was popularized by the Wachowski brothers in 1999's motion picture "The Matrix". The Matrix was significant in that it presented VR and reality as often overlapping, and sometimes indistinguishable. Total Recall and David Cronenberg's film "ExistenZ" dealt with the danger of confusion between reality and VR in computer games. Cyberspace became something that most movies completely misunderstood, as seen in "The Lawnmower Man". Also, the British comedy "Red Dwarf" used in several episodes the idea that life is a VR game. This idea was also used in "Spy Kids 3D: Game Over". Another movie that has a bizarre theme is "Brainscan", where the point of the game is to be a virtual killer. A more artistic and philosophical perspective on the subject can be seen in Avalon. There is also a film from 1995 called "Virtuosity" with Denzel Washington and Russell Crowe that dealt with the creation of a serial killer, used to train law enforcement personnel, that escapes his VR into the real world.

9.6 Music videos

The lengthy video for hard rock band Aerosmith's 1993 single "Amazing" depicted VR, going so far as to show two young people participating in VR simultaneously from their separate personal computers (while not knowing the other was also participating in it) in which the two engage in a steamy makeout session, sky-dive, and embark on a motorcycle journey together.

9.7 Games

A lot of industries sprang up and started developing VR games. In 1991, the W Industries released a VR gaming system called the 1000CS. This was a stand-up immersive HMD platform with a tracked 3D joystick. The system featured several VR games including "Dactyl Nightmare", "Legend Quest", "Hero", and "Grid Busters". There were other games developed such as "VR World 3D Color Ninja", "VR Wireless TV Tennis Game", "Mage: the Ascension", "Kingdom Hearts II", "System Shock", "System Shock2", and "VR 3D Drangonflight" among others.

9.8 Fine art

Fine art is also influenced by VR. Artists stated to create impressions using VR. David Em was the first fine artist to create navigable virtual worlds. Jeffrey Shaw explored the potential of VR in fine arts with early works like "Legible City", "Virtual Museum", and "Golden Calf". Char Davies created immersive VR art pieces in "Osmose" and "Ephémère". Works such as "Is God Flat", The "Tunnel under the Atlantic ", and "World Skin", by Maurice Benayoun introduced metaphorical, philosophical or political content, combining VR, network, generation and intelligent agents. There are other pioneering artists working in VR.

9.9 Marketing

Advertising and merchandise have been associated with VR. There are a lot of television commercials using VR. TV commercials featuring VR have been made products, such as Nike's "Virtual Andre". This commercial features a teenager playing tennis using a goggle and gloves system against a computer generated Andre Agassi. There are some others commercials as seen in most English premier league commercials.

9.10 Health care

VR is finding its way into the training of health care professionals. Use ranges from anatomy instruction to surgery simulation. VR also has numerous applications that can be directly related to health care. In a white paper on the use of Virtual Environments for Health Care, Moline (1995) indicated several areas where patient care can be assisted by VR techniques. These include the use of VR for remote tele-surgery; the use of VR techniques in local surgery such as endoscopy, where the surgeon manipulates instruments by viewing a TV monitor; the use of virtual environments as surgical simulators or trainers; the use of virtual environments as therapy devices to reduce anxiety or fear. One example is dentists using 3D eyeglasses to divert a patient's attention during dental operations and the use of virtual environments to reduce phobias such as agoraphobia and vertigo. North et al (1996) provided an overview of current work in the use of VR techniques to reduce phobias in their book VR Therapy.

9.11 Therapeutic uses

The primary use of VR in a therapeutic role is its application to various forms of exposure therapy, ranging from phobia treatments, to newer approaches to treating Post Traumatic Stress Disorder (PTSD) (Goslin & Morie, 1996; Krijn, 2005; Schuemie, 2003; Schuemie et al., 2001). A very basic VR simulation with simple sight and sound models has been shown to be invaluable in phobia treatment as a step between basic exposure therapy such as the use of simulacra and true exposure (North et al., 1996). A much more recent application is being piloted by the U.S. Navy to use a much more complex simulation to immerse veterans (specifically of Iraq) suffering from PTSD in simulations of urban combat settings. Much as in phobia treatment, exposure to the subject of the trauma or fear seems to lead to desensitization, and a significant reduction in symptoms.

9.12 Real estate

The real estate sector has used the term VR for websites that offer panoramic images laced into a viewer such as QuickTime player in which the viewer can rotate to see all 360 degrees of the image.

10. Advantages and uses of VR

Researchers in the field have generally agreed that VR technology is exciting and can provide a unique and effective way to learn and that VR projects are highly motivating to learners (Mantovani et al., 2003). From research, several specific situations have emerged in which VR has strong benefits or advantages. For example, VR has great value in situations where exploration of environments or interactions with objects or people is impossible or inconvenient, or where an environment can only exist in computer-generated form. VR is also valuable when the experience of actually creating a simulated environment is important to learning. Creating their own virtual worlds has been shown to enable some students to master content and to project their understanding of what they have learned (Ausburn & Ausburn, 2004).

One of the beneficial uses of VR occurs when visualization, manipulation, and interaction with information are critical for its understanding; it is, in fact, its capacity for allowing learners to display and interact with information and environment that some believe is VR's greatest advantage. Finally, VR is a very valuable instructional and practice alternative when the real thing is hazardous to learners, instructors, equipment, or the environment. This advantage of the technology has been cited by developers and researchers from such diverse fields as firefighting, anti-terrorism training, nuclear decommissioning, crane driving and safety, aircraft inspection and maintenance, automotive spray painting and pedestrian safety for children (Ausburn & Ausburn, 2004).

11. Disadvantages and limitations of VR

One important issue in the use of VR is the high level of skill and cost required to develop and implement VR, particularly immersive systems. Very high levels of programming and graphics expertise and very expensive hardware and software are necessary to develop immersive VR, and considerable skill is needed to use it effectively in instruction. While desktop VR technology has dramatically reduced the skill and cost requirement of virtual environments, it still demands some investment of money and time.

Another set of limitations of VR environments stems from the nature of the equipment they require. A long-standing problem with immersive VR has been health and safety concerns for its users. The early literature was top-heavy with studies of headaches, nausea, balance upsets, and other physical effects of HMD systems. While these problems have largely disappeared from current VR research as the equipment has improved, and appear to be completely absent in the new desktop systems, little is known about long-term physical or psychological effects of VR usage. A second equipment limitation of VR arises from the fact that it is computer-based and requires high-end hardware for successful presentation. Inadequate computing gear can dramatically limit the response time for navigation and interaction in a virtual environment, possibly destroying its sense of presence for users and damaging or destroying its usefulness as a simulation of reality. This response situation sometimes referred to as the "latency problem" of VR, can also arise from bandwidth limitations when VR is distributed over a network or the Internet.

12. Conclusion

A lot of advancements have been made using VR and VR technology. VR has cut across all facets of human endeavours-manufacturing/business, exploration, defense, leisure activities, and medicine among others. The exciting field of VR has the potential to change our lives in many ways. There are many applications of VR presently and there will be many more in the future. Many VR applications have been developed for manufacturing, education, simulation, design evaluation, architectural walk-through, ergonomic studies, simulation of assembly sequences and maintenance tasks, assistance for the handicapped, study and treatment of phobias, entertainment, rapid prototyping and much more. VR technology is now widely recognized as a major break through in the technological advance of science.

13. References

Abshire, K. J. & Barron, M. K. (1998). Virtual maintenance: Real-world applications within virtual environments, *IEEE Proceedings Annual Reliability and Maintainability Symposium*, 132-137.

Aukstakalnis, S. & Blatner, D. (1992). *Silicon mirage: The art and science of virtual reality.* Peachpit Press, Berkley.

Ausburn, L. J. & Ausburn, F. B. (2004). Desktop virtual reality: A powerful new technology for teaching and research in industrial teacher education. *Journal of Industrial Technical Education*, Vol. 41, No.4, [Online], Available: http://scholar.lib.vt.edu/ejournals/JITE/v41n4/ausburn.html

Baieier, K.P. (1993). *Virtual reality: Short introduction.* [Online]. Available: http://www-vrl.umich.edu/intro.html/

Balaguer, J. & Gennaro, S. (1996). VENUS: A virtual reality project at CERN. *Computer Graphics, 30*, 40-43.

Bell, J.T. (1996). Introducing virtual reality into the engineering curriculum, *Proc. of University Programs in Computer Aided Engineering and Design Manufacturing*, Charlottesville, VA. [Online]. Available: http://www.vrupl.evl.uic.edu/vrichel/.

Bell, J.T. &. Fogler, H.S. (1998). Virtual Reality in the Chemical Engineering Classroom, *Proc. of American Society for Engineering Education Annual Conference*, Seattle, WA.

Bell, J.T. &. Fogler, H.S. (1996a). Vicher: A prototype virtual reality based educational module for chemical reaction engineering, *Computer Applications in Engineering Education, 4*(4).

Bell, J.T. &. Fogler, H.S. (1996b). Recent developments in virtual reality based education, *Proc. of the American Society for Engineering Education Annual Conference,* Washington, DC.

Cline, M. S. (2005). *Power, madness, and immortality: The future of virtual reality.* [Online]. Available: http://virtualreality.universityvillagepress.com/index.php

Colin, J. (2006). Computer Visualization of Dudley Castle. [Online]. Available: http://www.extrenda.net/dudley/index.htm

Croquet. [Online]. Available: http://www.opencroquet.org/index.php/Main_Page

Cruz-Niera, C. (1993). Virtual reality overview. *Proceeding of ACM SISGRAPH 93 Conference on Applied Virtual Reality,* Anaheim, California.

Dedula, W. T. (1997). *About virtual reality and its use in the mobile aeronautics education laboratory (MAEL).* [Online]. Available: http://www.grc.nasa.gov/WWW/MAELVRSTATION/news_info.html

Eslinger, C. (1993). Education. *Encyclopedia of Virtual Environments.* World Wide Web URL: http://www.hitl.washington.edu/scivw/EVE/I.A.1.Displays.html

Fang, K.P., Feng, F.K. & Wai , K.K. (n.d). Low Cost Virtual Reality System: PlayStation 2 VR system: Technical Report No. CS031900. [Online]. http://cs.uct.ac.za

Forterra System Inc. [Online]. Available: http://company.mmosite.com/forterra/index.shtml

Gomes de Sa, A. & Zachmann, G. (1999). Virtual reality as a tool for verification of assembly and maintenance processes, *Computers and Graphics, 23,* 389-403.

Goslin, M. & Morie, J. F. (1996). Virtopia: Emotional experiences in virtual environments. *Leonardo,* 29(2), 95-100.

Haag, S.; Cummings, M., & Dawkins, J. (1998). *Management Information Systems for the Information Age.* Irwin/McGraw Hill, ISBN 0-07-025465-6, New York.

Haufmann, H., Schmalstieg, D. & Wagner, M. (2000). Construct3D: A Virtual Reality Application for Mathematics and Geometry Education, *Education and Information Technologies, 5* (4), 263-276.

Icarus Studio :Worlds Beyond Reality. [Online]. Available: http://www.icarusstudios.com/

Isdale, J. (1998). *What is virtual reality? A web-based introduction.* Retrieved November 12, 2005. [Online]. Available: http://whatis.techtarget.com/definition//0.sid9_gci213303,00.html

Isdale, J. (1993). *What is virtual reality? A homebrew introduction.* Retrieved November 12, 2005. [Online]. Available: http://whatis.techtarget.com

Kalawsky, R. S. (1993). *The Science of Virtual Reality and Virtual Environments.* Wokingham: Addison-Wesley

Kim, J., Park, S., Yuk, K., Lee, H. and Lee, H. (2000). Virtual reality simulations in physics education. *Interactive Multimedia Electronic Journal of Computer-Enhanced Learning* [Online]. Available: http://imej.wfu.edu/articles/2001/2/02/index.asp

Krijn, M. (2005). Virtual reality and specific phobias: Welcome to the real world. Retrieved September 20, 2007 from http://graphics.tudelft.nl/~vrphobia/Thesis_Krijn_DRUKKER.pdf

Lane, C. (1993). Display Technologies. *Encyclopedia of Virtual Environments.* World Wide Web URL: http://www.hitl.washington.edu/scivw/EVE/I.A.1.Displays.html

Mantovani, F., Gaggiolo, A., Castelnuovo, G. & Riva, G. (2003). Virtual reality training for health-care professionals. *CyberPsychology and Behavior, 6*(4), 389-395.

Moline, J. (1995). Virtual environments for health care. White paper for the advanced technology program (ATP). National Institute of Standards and Technology.

Mousa, H. E. (n.d.). Alternative Virtual reality and virtual worlds development tools and Health care! [Online], Available: http://www.goomedic.com/alternative-virtual-reality-and-virtual-worlds-development-tools-and-health-care.html

Negroponte, N. (1995). *Being Digital*. Vintage Books, New York, USA.

Neil, M. J. (1996). Architectural Virtual Reality Applications, Computer *Graphics, 30*, 53-54.

Newquist III, H. P. (1993). Virtual Reality Special Report. *AI Expert.*

North, M., North, S. & Coble, J. (1996). *Virtual Reality Therapy*. IPI Press, Colorado Springs, CO, USA.

Onyesolu, M.O. (2009a). Virtual reality laboratories: The pedagogical effectiveness and use in obtaining cheap laboratories using the computer laboratory, *Journal of Science Engineering and Technology,* Vol. 16, No.1, (March 2009) 8679-8689, ISSN 1117-4196.

Onyesolu, M.O. (2009b). Virtual reality laboratories: An ideal solution to the problems facing laboratory setup and management, *Proceedings of world congress on engineering and computer science 2009*, pp. 291-295, ISBN: 978-988-17012-6-8, San Francisco, USA, October 2009, Newswood Limited, Hong Kong.

Onyesolu, M.O. & Akpado, K.A. (2009). Virtual reality simulations in computer engineering education. *International Journal of Electrical and Telecommunication Systems Research,* Vol. 3, No.3, (July 2009) 56-61, ISSN 0795-2260.

Onyesolu, M.O. (2006). Virtual reality: An emerging computer technology of the 21st century. *International Journal of Electrical and Telecommunication Systems Research,* Vol. 1, No.1, (August 2006) 36-40, ISSN 0795-2260.

Schuemie, M.J. (2003). Human-Computer Interaction and Presence in Virtual Reality Exposure Therapy. Retrieved September 23, 2006 from http://graphics.tudelft.nl/~vrphobia/dissertation.pdf

Schuemie, M.J., Van Der Straaten, P., Krijn, M. & Van Der Mast, C.A.P.G. (2001). Research on presence in virtual reality: A survey. *Cyberpsychology and Behavior, 4*(2).

Smith, S. &. Lee, S. (2004). A pilot study for integrating virtual reality into an introductory design and graphics course. *Journal of Industrial Technology. 20*(4).

Sulbaran, T. & Baker, N. C. (2000). Enhancing engineering education through distributed virtual reality, *30th ASEE/IEEE frontiers in Education Conference*, October 18-21, Kansas City, MO, S1D-13 - S1D-18.

The Alphaville Herald: Interview with Ogoglio's Trevor Smith. [Online]. Available: http://foo.secondlifeherald.com/slh/2007/01/interview_with_.html

Vince, J. (1995). *Virtual Reality Systems.* (Reading, Massachusetts: Addison-Wesley).

Wang, C. & Cannon, D. J. (1996). Virtual-Reality-Based Point-and-Direct robotic inspection in manufacturing. *IEEE Trans.*

We are virtual heroes. [Online]. Available: http://www.virtualheroes.com /about.asp

Williams, B.K., & Sawyer, S.C. (2001). *Using Information Technology: A Practical Introduction to Computers and Communications*. McGraw Hill, ISBN 0-07-239803-5, New York.

Winn, W. & Bricken, W. (1992). Designing virtual worlds for use in mathematics education: The example of experiential algebra, *Educational Technology, 32* (12), 12-19.

Wittenberg, G. (1995). Training with virtual reality, *Assembly Automation, 15* (3), 12-14.

Wittenberg, G. (1993). Virtual reality in engineering, *The Industrial Robot, 20,* 21-22.

Ziff Davis enterprise web buyer's guide. [Online]. Available: http://www.webbuyersguide.com/product/brief.aspx?src=rss&kc=rss&id=52841

5

Real-Time Cross-Layer Routing Protocol for Ad Hoc Wireless Sensor Networks

Khaled Daabaj[1] and Shubat Ahmeda[2]
[1]*Murdoch University*
[2]*Alfateh University*
[1]*Australia*
[2]*Libya*

1. Introduction

Reliable and energy efficient routing is a critical issue in Wireless Sensor Networks (WSNs) deployments. Many approaches have been proposed for WSN routing, but sensor field implementations, compared to computer simulations and fully-controlled testbeds, tend to be lacking in the literature and not fully documented. Typically, WSNs provide the ability to gather information cheaply, accurately and reliably over both small and vast physical regions. Unlike other large data network forms, where the ultimate input/output interface is a human being, WSNs are about collecting data from unattended physical environments. Although WSNs are being studied on a global scale, the major current research is still focusing on simulations experiments. In particular for sensor networks, which have to deal with very stringent resource limitations and that are exposed to severe physical conditions, real experiments with real applications are essential. In addition, the effectiveness of simulation studies is severely limited in terms of the difficulty in modeling the complexities of the radio environment, power consumption on sensor devices, and the interactions between the physical, network and application layers. The routing problem in ad hoc WSNs is nontrivial issue because of sensor node failures due to restricted recourses. Thus, the routing protocols of WSNs encounter two conflicting issue: on the one hand, in order to optimise routes, frequent topology updates are required, while on the other hand, frequent topology updates result in imbalanced energy dissipation and higher message overhead.

In the literature, such as in (Rahul et al., 2002), (Woo et al., 2003), (TinyOS, 2004), (Gnawali et al., 2009) and (Burri et al., 2007) several authors have presented routing algorithms for WSNs that consider purely one or two metrics at most in attempting to optimise routes while attempting to keep small message overhead and balanced energy dissipation. Recent studies on energy efficient routing in multihop WSNs have shown a great reliance on radio link quality in the path selection process. If sensor nodes along the routing path and closer to the base station advertise a high quality link to forwarding upstream packets, these sensor nodes will experience a faster depletion rate in their residual energy. This results in a topological routing hole or network partitioning as stated and resolved in and (Daabaj 2010).

This chapter presents an empirical study on how to improve energy efficiency for reliable multihop communication by developing a real-time cross-layer lifetime-oriented routing protocol and integrating useful routing information from different layers to examine their joint benefit on the lifetime of individual sensor nodes and the entire sensor network. The proposed approach aims to balance the workload and energy usage among relay nodes to achieve balanced energy dissipation, thereby maximizing the functional network lifetime. The obtained experimental results are presented from prototype real-network experiments based on Crossbow's sensor motes (Crossbow, 2010), i.e., Mica2 low-power wireless sensor platforms (Crossbow, 2010). The distributed real-time routing protocol which is proposed in this chapter aims to face the dynamics of the real world sensor networks and also to discover multiple paths between the base station and source sensor nodes. The proposed routing protocol is compared experimentally with a reliability-oriented collection-tree protocol, i.e., the TinyOS MintRoute protocol (Woo et al., 2003). The experimental results show that our proposed protocol has a higher node energy efficiency, lower control overhead, and fair average delay.

2. Motivations

While the majority of WSN-related research activities have used open-source network simulators such as ns-2 (ISI, 2010) and OMNeT++ (Omnetpp, 2010), others have used well-controlled indoor remote access testbeds such as Motelab (Werner-Allen, 2005) to demonstrate the benefits of employing various routing algorithms' scalable performance. However, simulations and remote access testbeds have limitations in fully emulating real-world low power WSN characteristics. In addition, sensor nodes are prone to failure and various adverse factors that are unpredictable and difficult to capture in simulations. Therefore the work done in this chapter has been conducted on a real-world WSN by taking in account the asymmetrical behaviour of wireless signal propagation, and how it changes spatially, temporally, or with certain environmental conditions; and how the real sensor device's inconsistent or erroneous behaviour affects a routing protocol's performance or even a device's rate of energy consumption. In low power WSNs, the unreliability of the links and the limitations of all resources bring considerable complications to the routing scheme. Even in the presence of static topology of fixed sensor nodes, the channel conditions may vary due to many factors such as the irregularity of radio transmission range, antenna orientations, and multipath fading effects. Furthermore, sensor nodes are typically battery-powered, and ongoing maintenance may not be feasible; thereby the progressive reduction of the available residual power needs to be considered as a crucial factor in the route selection process to control nodes' energy drain for the extension of the lifetime of the individual nodes and for the achievement of energy balancing in the entire network.

In this chapter, the above points will be addressed by describing the proposed protocol, and presenting a detailed analysis of the protocol's performance using a physical WSN platform. In the proposed protocol, the decision where to forward data packets depends on many potential factors from different layers. The implementation section will include a detailed discussion of the performance of the proposed protocol which is benchmarked against the baselines in an indoor using wireless platform. Standalone evaluation of routing efficiency is impracticable, as temporal dynamics prevent knowing what the optimal route would be for data dissemination. Therefore, routing efficiency is evaluated as a comparative measure. The proposed protocol is benchmarked with the updated version of TinyOS MintRoute (Woo et al., 2003) implementation using Crossbow's Mica2 sensor motes. Since MintRoute protocol (Woo et al., 2003) has been used in recent WSNs deployments, it is considered a reasonable evaluation. The testbed environment is conducted indoor using Crossbow's

Mica2 868/916MHz (Crossbow, 2010). Currently, Mica2 motes represent the lowest cost wireless sensor platform based on commercial off-the-shelf hardware components for low power sensor networks. Mica2 platform is running with the TinyOS (TinyOS, 2004) development environment.

3. Related work

In the literature, many reliability-based routing protocols have been proposed. However, the main disadvantages of the existing TinyOS collection routing protocols based on link quality are that they are unaware of the energy status of nodes and do not explicitly pursue balanced energy usage in their routing schemes; thereby diverting load to sensor nodes with low energy capacity. As a result, this chapter focuses on balanced energy dissipation scheme for lifetime maximisation by taking the advantage from reliability-oriented routing schemes, i.e., MintRoute (Woo et al., 2003), MultihopLQI (TinyOS, 2004) and CTP (Gnawali et al., 2009) collection protocols, and traditional energy-aware routing schemes, i.e., Energy-Aware Routing (EAR) protocol (Rahul et al., 2002). Although the main objective of load balancing routing is the efficient utilization of network resources, none of the studies reviewed above takes jointly link reliability and energy-wise metrics into account with load balancing. There is no doubt that a better distribution of load leads to the more efficient use of bandwidth, which means that there is less contention and consequently less energy is consumed, but it is not self-contained for achieving complete energy efficiency. WSNs are not necessarily energy-homogeneous, and there is thus insufficient information about the sensor nodes' load tasks to enable the energy-wise selection of the paths. The current load of a given sensor node can be used to estimate the future dissipation of energy but it does not contain a record of past activities and the residual energy level of the sensor node remains hidden. The proposed routing algorithm allows a child sensor node dynamically searches for a new reliable parent node with more residual energy and takes in account the tradeoffs between latency and energy. This dynamic adaptation strategy can alleviate the energy hole problem. The chapter aims to improve the performance evaluation of the proposed routing scheme by extending the experiments to indoor, outdoor, and simulations on larger networks.

4. Description of the real-time cross-layer routing protocol

4.1 Overview

Since the communications overheads are the major energy consumer during a sensor node's operation, the proposed routing protocol, a simple but reliable routing algorithm, aims to cause minimal communication overheads for network configuration and multi-hop data dissemination. As shown in figure 1, the proposed protocol uses Channel State Information (CSI) and residual energy capacity with other overheard parameters, e.g., aggregation load, sensor node-*id*, and tree-level, to form a cost function for selecting the most reliable and energy-efficient route towards the base station. In low power sensor networks, the unreliability of the links and the limitations of all resources bring considerable complications to routing. Even though most deployed sensor networks use stationary nodes or have low mobility, the channel conditions vary because of various effects such as asymmetrical radio performance, or multipath fading effects which modify the patterns of radio wave reflections. Since sensor nodes are typically battery-powered, and ongoing maintenance may be impracticable, the progressive reduction of the available residual power needs to be considered jointly with other factors as a crucial factor in the parent selection process to control nodes' energy drain for the extension of the lifetime of the individual nodes and for the achievement of load balancing and consistent energy usage within the entire network. The proposed protocol is a hybrid, reactive and proactive, routing algorithm designed to adaptively provide enhanced balanced energy usage on reliable routes and to employ ready-to-use neighbourhood routing tables in order to allow sensor nodes to quickly find a new parent upon parent loss due to link degradation or run-out of energy. In the proposed protocol, the remaining energy capacity in the forwarding sensor nodes and the link or channel quality between communicating sensor nodes are the key factors that shape the network topology: the hardware-based Channel State Information (CSI) can be measured directly from the radio hardware circuitry of the wireless platform in form of signal quality or computed by software at the receiver based on the successfully received packets; the residual energy capacity is estimated after deducting the estimated dissipated energy based on the current consumption model of the mote system (processor and radio) during its operations. These parameters with other overheard local information are used to form a cost function for the selection of the most efficient route. Moreover, the presence of a time constraint requires the network to favour routes over a short path with minimum number of hops at network layer and delay-sensitive data aggregation at application layer in order to minimize the average end-to-end data transfer latency. The proposed protocol is a tree-based routing protocol where a child sensor node forms a routing tree to its parent towards the perimeter base station and is also address-free in that a sensor node does not send a packet to a particular sensor node; instead, it implicitly chooses a parent sensor nodes by choosing a next hop based on the selection parameters.

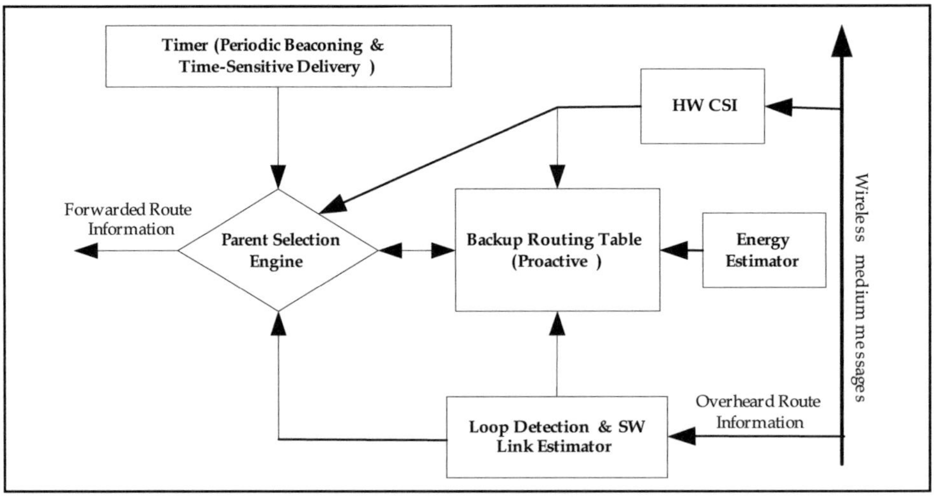

Fig. 1. Routing protocol framework

The proposed protocol mutually employs hardware-based Channel State Information (CSI) such as the Received Signal Strength Indicator (RSSI) and the Link Quality Indicator (LQI), to evaluate the signal quality of the wireless link and software-based link quality estimates of set of adjacent neighbours such as the Packet Reception Ratio (PRR), to provide an estimate of the number of transmissions and retransmissions it takes for the sensor node to successfully receive a unicast packet. This improves delivery reliability and keeps the proposed protocol adaptive to unforeseen traffic changes. The proposed protocol does also exploit the benefit from in-network processing mechanisms in term data aggregation, which can pack multiple small packets into a single data packet with the aim of minimising energy consumed for communications while considering the time-sensitive amount of aggregation load. The proposed protocol requires each sensor node to switch among multiple parents for load-balancing purposes. Taking the load-balancing optimization into consideration at the MAC layer will significantly complicate the design and implementation of MAC protocols. Therefore, the proposed protocol is designed to perform the dynamic adaptation at the network or routing layer.

Although the main objective of load balancing routing is the efficient utilization of WSN resources, the load balancing is advantageous technique for evening out the distribution of loads in terms of efficient energy consumption. As a result, maximising lifetime of each sensor node can be achieved with fair battery usage. The cost function takes into account not only the current energy capacity of the sensor nodes and the channel state but also considering other factors like deployment pattern, event patterns. In other words, the proposed protocol considers the overall distribution of the delay-sensitive aggregation load along the routes by means of load balancing benefits for ensuring the even distribution of traffic, which translate into more efficient energy utilization reliable packet delivery.

Sensor nodes with the best link quality average values are considered first in the initial stages of parent selection process, while sensor nodes with the highest residual energy capacity levels are considered afterwards. Thus, a parent is selected if it offers a reliable route, but when the traffic load, e.g., aggregation load, increases, the remaining battery capacity of each sensor node is also accounted as the second prime metric in the parent/route selection process to choose the routes along which all sensor nodes have the actual available battery capacity levels exceeding a given threshold. The cost function selects the route that requires the lowest energy per bit. If there is no such route, then it picks that route which maximises the minimum battery level by utilizing the principle of max-min cost function as explained in Conditional Max-Min Battery Capacity Routing. To ensure a longer network lifetime, the strategy of minimising the variance in energy levels is employed to dissipate up all batteries powers uniformly to avoid some nodes suddenly running out of energy and disrupting the network. Hence, routes should be chosen such that the variance in battery levels between different routes is reduced.

From energy cost point of view, the residual energy capacity defines the refusal or readiness of intermediate sensor nodes to respond to route requests and forward data traffic. The maximum lifetime of a given route is determined by the weakest intermediate sensor node, which is that with the highest cost.

4.2 Routing tree formation

The routing tree is a directed non-cyclical graph which relays packets towards the base station over multiple paths. The routing tree is built by assigning a *level number* to each sensor node depending on its distance (e.g., number of hops) to the base station, and delivers sensing data packets from higher-level to lower-level sensor nodes. The base station is at *level* 0. Each sensor node at level *i* can select a valid parent from its level *i* or from lower level *i*-1 towards the base station as shown in figure 2. The valid parent is elected by the routing metrics used in the routing cost function, i.e., link quality, residual energy, hop-count, aggregation load or latency. Obviously, any path from source sensor nodes to the base station is the most efficient path in the resulting routing tree. The routing tree starts with the easily-constructed shortest path tree (SPT), and then allows each sensor node to pick a new parent node if it appears to provide better routing cost with a higher link quality. Using the broadcast nature of the contention-based wireless medium, a sensor node can easily observe its neighbourhood by receiving and overhearing periodic beacon packets which initially originate by the base station.

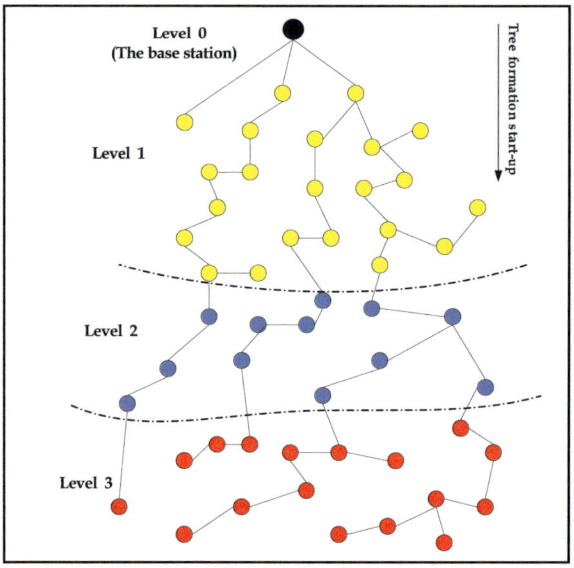

Fig. 2. Routing tree formation

4.3 Routing tree construction phases

The construction of the routing tree is performed in three overlapped phases: *Tree setup*, *Data transmission*, and *Route maintenance*.

In the *tree setup phase*, the base station acts as a tree root which initially disseminates a route setup message into the network to find all possible routes and to measure their costs back from the source sensor nodes to base station. The routes costs are kept updated by using the periodic beaconing during the *reactive* route maintenance phase in order to adapt with link dynamics. Therefore, the receiving sensor nodes determine all routes with their updated cost parameters to be used in parent selection process. The base station is assigned with a tree level or depth equal to *zero*, it is also set with the cost parameters to *zero* before sending the setup message. The intermediate sensor nodes at level one, for example, one-hop from the base station, that can receive the route setup message from the base station, forward the route setup packets to the reachable sensor nodes at level two, for example, two-hops from the base station. Sensor nodes that have a higher cost compared with other peer sensor nodes, for example, lower residual energy level or lossy link, are discarded from the routing table. Sensor nodes at level three repeat the previous steps and all information travels until it reaches the leaf nodes and all nodes know their depth and the tree is fully defined.

In the *data transmission phase*, the source sensor nodes start to transmit data packets towards the base station through the preselected least-cost route based on the parent selection parameters. Consecutively, intermediate sensor nodes aggregate and relay the data packets to the upstream parents toward the base station. This process continues until the data

packets of interest reach the base station. More challenging is the case when the time it takes a sensor node to deliver its local measurements or its own aggregates to its parent in the tree and there is also other costs involved in the waiting time decision according to topology changes and time-sensitive application. *Data aggregation load* is considered in this phase in order to maintain delay-sensitive data delivery. Hence, each sensor node must decide when to stop waiting for more data to be aggregated based on a preset maximum waiting time. For example, at the start-up time, an aggregating parent sensor node starts aggregating data from its own, if any, and from its children that have participated in aggregation. Later this aggregator node will forward the so far aggregated data to its parent. The amount of aggregated data is a function increasing in participating sensor nodes and decreasing in the waiting time. Moreover, sensor node within its communication range can exploit unavoidable overhearing or eavesdropping on neighbouring nodes' traffic to improve the selection of parent nodes and data aggregation. This feature is kept optional and application-specific in the proposed routing scheme as it can be enabled or disabled based on the application. Since this distributed parent selection process is performed dynamically whenever there is a packet to send, this approach can adaptively change the topology of aggregation according to different situations based on the aggregation load.
Route maintenance is the most important phase, which is performed using periodic beacons to handle link dynamics and disconnection failures and all valid routes are *reactively* kept on-demand available before any data packet transmissions. Hence, the routing tree is sustained and the neighbour routing tables are also kept updated to avoid relays with lower energy and unreliable links. To achieve reliable data packets delivery and parent selection process, each sensor node maintains a neighbour routing table indicating one hop sensor nodes it can reach. This table contains the links quality to such sensor nodes, their residual energy, depth or node *id*, and other helpful routing information. The rationale behind maintaining neighbour table is to proactively keep track of possible efficient routes to the base station and be able to order them on the basis of a joint metric favouring high-quality links, relays with good energy resources above predetermined threshold, and low number of hops. By keeping track reactively and proactively of the channels with minimum link quality and the sensor nodes with the lowest residual energy, overloaded relays "bottlenecks" can be promptly identified and avoided during network operations.

4.4 Avoidance of routing loops

During routing tree formation, specifically, in tree setup phase, a sensor node can only pick its parent in the same level or lower according to its communication range and routing metrics. Routing loops are prevented at the same level using a tiebreaker i.e., sensor node *id*. Choosing a parent node from the same level gives the routing scheme more flexibility and unrestricted membership of parent candidates in the parent selection process. To prevent the formation of possible loops in the whole routing tree, the parent selection of a sensor node is restricted to neighbours which are not farther away than its level. For instance, if a source sensor node and its parent candidate are in the same level, sensor node's *id* is used as a *tiebreaker* to prevent loop at this level. Without the tiebreaker, two sensor nodes in the same level may pick each other as their parents and form a routing loop at this level. In figure 2 shown earlier, sensor nodes can select parents from sensor nodes in the same level and one level downwards and no upward selection is allowed. As sensor node *id* is used as a *tiebreaker*, sensor nodes in the same level have an *ascending* ordering in the priority of being selected as parents, i.e., sensor node with larger *id* is selected as a parent for sensor nodes with smaller *id*. Therefore, no loop can be formed within the same level. As a result, this prevents the routing scheme from creating loops within the entire network.

4.5 Neighbourhood participation policy

The high-level algorithm shown below describes how a sensor node selects its valid parent. To perform the algorithm, routing information can be easily acquired through periodic beaconing or packet overhearing to be maintained in the routing tables. While the information maintained in the routing tables is used for the *proactive* quick rerouting, the periodic broadcasting packets are also necessary for updating routing tables and the *reactive* routing to be used for route dynamics. The routing information required for the routing tree of the proposed algorithm is added into the original beacon packets' headers, so that sensor nodes can have the necessary neighbour information to modify the routing path up on request. In network start-up, the network is initially considered as fully identified and the values of route metrics are initially obtained in the routing table and ready for route maintenance.

High-Level Algorithm:

```
Initialization: network start-up
For Each Node
    If (ParentLossTime < WaitingTime) then
       For Beacon_recieved
            Update Route_infomation
            Send in next beacon
       End loop
    Else
       If (linkQuality & EnergyCapacity > Threshold) then
          If (ParentLevel <= NodeLevel) & (Parent_id > Node_id) then
             Set Parent
          End if
       End if
    End if
End loop
```

5. Experimental methodology

5.1 Overview

This section describes in details the indoor experimental testbed platform, and performance parameters used to evaluate the operation of the sensor network by means of the proposed routing protocol. The experimental approach considers a many-to-one real-time event-driven sensor network where sensing nodes deliver their sensing measurements to a single base station under a time constraint and with the overall target of reliable communications and minimised energy consumption of the forwarding sensor nodes.

The wireless sensor testbed comprises a wireless platform of Mica2 a link layer of B-MAC (Polastre, 2004) in indoor channels. The proposed protocol is compared with the official TinyOS implementation of MintRoute collection protocol on Mica2 motes. In the conducted indoor experiments, all sensor nodes are homogeneous with fixed low transmission powers in each run, and commence with the same residual power capacity. Mica2 sensor nodes

(Crossbow, 2010) are equipped with Omni-directional whip antennas. On Mica2 sensor nodes, the standard TinyOS B-MAC MAC layer (Polastre, 2004) is used for CC1000 radio. B-MAC is a contention-based MAC protocols. Since the TinyOS-1.x version has several differences from its newer version TinyOS-2.x, the TinyOS-2.x version is not fully backward compatible with version TinyOS-1.x. Hence, the official stable release TinyOS-2.0.2 that supports different platforms is used for all indoor and outdoor experiments.

5.2 Implementation platform

To develop an understanding of sensor nodes' indoor communications performance, this section investigates the implementation challenges in the tiny wireless sensors by means of the proposed routing scheme. The implementation was done indoor using the low-power Mica2 (MPR400CB) wireless sensor network platform (Crossbow, 2010) with the component-based operating system TinyOS (TinyOS, 2004) which is written in an event-driven language called network embedded systems C-like language (nesC). The implementation is based on a real world testbed of wireless sensor nodes, specifically, the Berkeley's Mica2 motes which are popular due to their simple architecture, open source development and commercially available from Crossbow® Technology. UC Berkeley Mica2 Motes utilise a powerful Atmel® ATmega128L microcontroller and a frequency tuneable radio with extendable range. The UC Berkeley Mica2 Mote Module is a third generation tiny, wireless platform for smart sensors designed specifically for deeply embedded low power sensor networks. Table 1 reveals the specifications of a typical radio/processor platform Mica2 (MPR400CB) (Crossbow, 2010) which is powered by AA batteries. Mica2 is built with an 8-bit, 7.3828MHz Atmel® ATmega 128L processor, 128Kbytes of in-system program memory, 4Kbytes of in-system data memory, and 512Kbytes of external flash (serial) memory for measurements storage. Figure 3 shows the overall block diagram of Mica2 mote (Crossbow, 2010). A sensor node can be configured as a base station to route over standard serial port interface by attaching the interface board MIB520. The base station serves as the traffic sink.

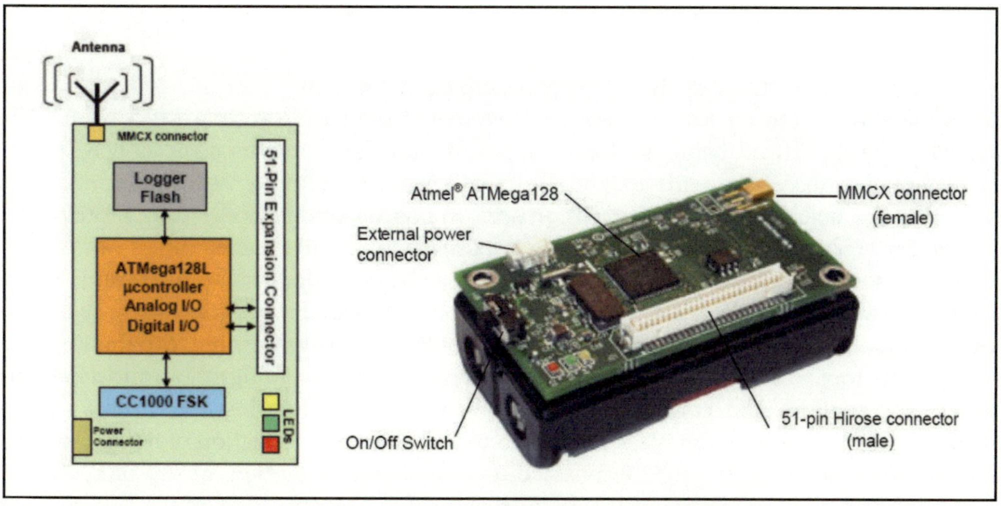

Fig. 3. Crossbow Mica2 868/916MHz Mote (MPR400CB) (Crossbow, 2010)

These resources seem unfit for computationally expensive or power-intensive operations. Explicit energy saving techniques are necessary to extend battery lifetime as much as possible. Communication is much more expensive than computation on wireless sensor devices. For instance, the Mica2 radio component when transmitting draws 30% more current than the CPU when it is active. Low-power radio operation is necessary to carry out long-term monitoring with sensor network deployments. If the radio and CPU are constantly active, battery power will be consumed in less than a week.

Component	Feature
Processor	8-bit Atmel® ATmega128L Processor (7.3828 MHz)
In-System Program Memory	128 Kbytes
In-System Data memory	4 Kbytes
External Serial Flash Measurements Memory	512 Kbytes
Radio Chip Transceiver	Chipcon CC1000 Radio with receive sensitivity of -98dBm
Centre Frequency	868/916 MHz, 4 channels
Modulation Format	FSK modulation
Effective Data Rate	38.4 Kbps
Hardware Encoding	Manchester encoded [2:1]
Antenna Type	Omni-directional whip
Transmission Power Range	-20dBm to 5dBm
Max. Packets Rate (100% Duty Cycle)	42.93 Packets/Sec

Table 1. Crossbow Mica2 mote (MPR400CB) specifications (Crossbow, 2010)

5.3 Experimental features of the deployed wireless platform

The Mica2 Mote features several new improvements over the original Mica Mote. These features make the Mica2 better suited to experimental deployments such as 868/916MHz multi-channel transceiver with extended range, wireless remote reprogramming, wide range of sensor boards and data acquisition add-on boards, and supported by MoteWorks™ platform for WSN applications. MoteWorks™ (Crossbow, 2010) enables the development of custom sensor applications and is specifically optimised for low-power and battery-operated networks. MoteWorks™ is based on the open-source TinyOS operating system and provides reliable, ad-hoc mesh networking, over-the-air-programming capabilities, cross development tools, server middleware for enterprise network integration and client user interface for analysis and configuration. MoteWorks™ 2.0 provides a complete software development environment for WSN applications. Included is a collection of flexible software packages that enables both quick-and-easy out-of-the-box deployment of sensor systems for monitoring and alerting, to powerful tools to empower custom development of pervasive sensory networks (Crossbow, 2010).

Mica2 contains a processor and radio Platform (MPR400CB) which is based on the Atmel ATmega128L. The ATmega128L is a low-power microcontroller which runs MoteWorks™ 2.0 platform from its internal flash memory. A single processor board (MPR400CB) can be configured to run sensor application/processing and the network/radio communications stack simultaneously. The Mica2 51-pin expansion connector supports Analog Inputs, Digital I/O, I2C, SPI and UART interfaces. These interfaces make it easy to connect to a wide variety of external peripherals (Crossbow, 2010). Any Mica2 Mote can function as a base station when it is connected to a standard PC interface or gateway board. A mote interface board allows the aggregation of sensor network data onto a PC or other computer platform and allows for motes programming. There are different modules of serial or USB interface boards. MIB520 supports USB for the Mica2 Motes for both communication and in-system programming. Finally, Mica2 Motes can be integrated with sensing board or data acquisition board that supports a variety of sensor modalities that support environmental monitoring (e.g., Ambient light, humidity, temperature, 2-axis accelerometer, and barometric pressure) for Mica2 with built-in sensors and an optional GPS (Crossbow, 2010).

5.4 Programming environment (TinyOS)

The firmware of sensor nodes and the base station is based on TinyOS (TinyOS, 2004) which is the de-facto operating system and programming environments for sensor motes. The experimental implementations use various API and libraries provided by TinyOS-2.0.2. TinyOS-2.0.2 is implemented using the nesC-1.2.8 (networked embedded systems-C) event-programming language. Typically, TinyOS is an open source component-based operating system specifically designed for embedded WSNs, which was initially released in 2000 under Berkeley Software Distribution (BSD) licenses. It is supported by nesC's component-based programming model. TinyOS applications are a collection of components, where each component has three computational abstractions: *commands, events and tasks.* TinyOS deals with limited resources of severe energy constraints, very small and efficient code in memory storage of kilobytes, and CPU speed of less 10 MHz. The nesC is a static programming language where applications are made by writing and assembling components which reduces the used memory footprint. The nesC is an extension of C language, a new event-driven programming environment developed for networked embedded systems such as sensor networks. The nesC supports a programming model that integrates reactivity to environment, concurrency and communication. TinyOS defines a number of concepts that are expressed in nesC. First, nesC applications are built out of components with well defined bidirectional interfaces. Second, nesC defines a concurrency model, based on tasks and hardware event handlers and detects data races at compile time. *The nesC application* consists of one or more components linked together to form an executable. *Components* are the basic building blocks for nesC applications and classified as provides and uses interfaces components. A provide interface is a set of methods calls the upper layers while uses interface is a set of methods calls the lower layer components. An interface declares a set of functions called *commands* that the interface provider must implement, and another set of functions called *events* that the interface user must implement. There are two types of components in nesC *modules and configurations*: *A Module* is a nesC component consisting of application code written in a C-like syntax. A *Configuration* is a component that wires other components together. Every application has a single top-level configuration that specifies the set of components in the application and how they invoke another by connecting interfaces of existing components.

6. Underlying layers

6.1 Physical layer

At the Physical Layer, Mica2 mote uses a low powered radio "Chipcon CC1000 RF transceiver" which is a single chip, very low-power, Multichannel radio frequency transceiver supporting 23 different power levels and operates in frequency range 300 to 1000MHz (Crossbow, 2010). Mica2 (MPR400CB) has a digitally programmable/tuneable output radio power levels ranges from -20dBm to +5dBm centred at the 868/916MHz setting within two frequency regions: (868-870MHz) and (902-928MHz). However, CC1000 power levels are not distributed evenly across this range and the default output power is 1mW (0 dBm) at level 14. CC1000 radio uses Frequency Shift Keying (FSK) modulation with an effective data rate or throughput of 38.4Kbps. CC1000 radio has an integrated bit-synchroniser and uses a hardware-based Manchester encoding scheme to encode the transmitted data. It also uses the linear received signal strength indicator (RSSI) to measure the strength of the received signal (Crossbow, 2010).

6.2 Mac layer

TinyOS operating system provides a variety of tools, including a programming environment and a complete network stack on wireless sensor node platform. This stack contains a basic radio driver: physical and link layer protocols, and an adjustable energy efficient MAC layer, e.g., B-MAC with low-power listening (LPL) scheme, the default TinyOS MAC protocol developed at the UC Berkeley (Polastre, 2004). TinyOS CC1000 has 128bytes maximum MAC frame size and employs Frequency Shift Keying (FSK) modulation Scheme. Due to the highly dynamic and untethered nature of WSNs, the inherent advantages of contention-based protocols, i.e., B-MAC (Polastre, 2004), makes them the preferred choice, and they have been widely adopted in WSNs. B-MAC was preferred for the MAC layer for the implementation of the proposed routing scheme. Although B-MAC protocol is not as energy-efficient as schedule-based protocols, it has several advantages as well as most CSMA/CA. First, B-MAC scales more easily across changes in sensor node density or traffic load. Second, it is more flexible as topologies change, because there is no requirement to form communication clusters as in cluster-based routing protocols. Third, it totally asynchronous and does not require fine-grained time-synchronisation. Instead, each packet is transmitted with a long enough preamble so that the receiver is guaranteed to wakeup during the preamble transmission time. It also employs an adaptive preamble sampling scheme to reduce duty cycle and minimise idle listening without overhearing avoidance. Before a sender sends out a packet to a receiver, it will first send a preamble long enough for all its neighbours to wake up, detect activity on the channel, receive the preamble, and then receive the packet. Therefore, in addition to the receiver, all the other neighbours of the sender will receive the packet, even the packet is not addressed to them, e.g., overhearing. In this situation, the helpful information used (e.g., link quality estimations and node *id*) for routing decisions in the proposed scheme is being imbedded in the packet header. When a sensor node receives a packet not addressed to itself, it can retrieve this helpful information from the packet header before dropping the packet. Finally, B-MAC is aware to the protocols that run above it and offers control to the protocols that sit on top of it, allowing to the routing and application layers to change parameters like the low-power listening duration or the number and type of retransmissions used. Thus, B-MAC allows each sensor node to overhear packets transmitted by its neighbours; this allows high layer network protocols, i.e., routing protocols, to employ snooping for the sake of link quality estimation, and in-network processing and data aggregation. B-MAC also provides an interface by which the application can adjust the sleep schedule to adapt to changing traffic loads which is very important MAC feature for time-sensitive data aggregation provided by the proposed routing scheme. The method of adaptation is an application-dependent. B-MAC does not perform link-level retransmission or hidden terminal avoidance using RTS/CTS schemes as it has been assumed that such schemes will be implemented at higher layers if necessary. On Mica2 sensor nodes with CC1000 radios, B-MAC supports synchronous acknowledgments that require only a few extra bit times on the end of each packet to transmit. This depends on the ability of the sender and receiver to quickly switch roles at the end of a packet transmission and remain synchronized before any additional sender can sense an idle channel and begin transmitting (Polastre, 2004).

Moreover, B-MAC uses the energy detect indicator as a carrier sense mechanism which is common to many existing radios. It is based on RSSI readings obtained from the radio front end. B-MAC is a packet-collision avoidance scheme and integrates a power management scheme within the MAC protocol that utilizes low power listening and an extended preamble to achieve low power communication. B-MAC was originally developed for bit streaming radios like Mica2's Chipcon CC1000 radio, which provides low-level access to the individual bits received by the radio. Hence, B-MAC can generate long preambles with CC1000 radio but the recommended preamble length in B-MAC is 100ms, which is used in the deployed WSN experiment. Even though the official version of B-MAC suffers from the inevitable overhearing, and the long preamble dominates the energy usage, the modified version of B-MAC, provided by TinyOS, has been shown to outperform other MAC protocols, and has been carefully tuned for the CC1000 radio used on Mica2 motes. It has been claimed by the authors of B-MAC that, B-MAC performs well by surpassing existing MAC protocols in terms of throughput (consistently delivers 98.5% of packets), latency, and for most cases energy consumption (Polastre, 2004).

8. Experimental performance evaluation

8.1 Performance metrics and observed entities

The real WSN is evaluated considering different performance metrics that are observed by the base station, relayed to the attached laptop, and saved in log files for later analysis using Matlab scripts. Particularly, the results show how the *link quality measurements* in the considered scenarios and the network behaviour was characterized in terms of: *packet delivery performance* to assess the significance of wireless link reliability on packet loss probability; *average dissipated energy* to figure out how sensor nodes deplete their energy to achieve multihop communication; and *average end-to-end delay* to evaluate the multihop data aggregation and hop count effect on data delivery time.

Received Signal Strength Indicator (RSSI): RSSI represents the amount of signal energy received by the sensor node. It can be measured by either Chipcon radio chips, CC100 on Mica2. RSSI readings 1000 have a range from -100 dBm to 0 dBm and the maximum error (accuracy) is 6 dBm. It is calculated over 8 symbol periods.

Packet Delivery Performance: One of the basic metrics used for evaluating packet delivery performance and to measure link quality is *Packet Reception ratio* (PRR) (also know as *packet delivery fraction*) which is the percentage of successfully received packets to packets transmitted. In other words, the PRR is the ratio of the total number of packets received by the base station that successfully passes the Cyclic Redundancy Check (CRC) to the total number of packets originally sent (considered) by the source sensor nodes as expressed in equation 1.

$$PRR = \frac{Successfully\ received\ packets}{Sent\ packets} \times 100 \quad (1)$$

Average Dissipated Energy measures the ratio of total dissipated energy per sensor node in the network to the number of distinct events received by the base station. This metric computes the average work done by a participating sensor node in delivering data of interest to the base station. This metric also indicates the overall lifetime of sensor nodes. During sensor node's operation, the estimation of average dissipated energy is computed per sensor node using equation 2 and used in the cost function in favour of the most efficient route. Where V_{batt} is the battery voltage of the sensor mote, and I_{drawn} is the current consumed by the mote system. The time spent per *CPU cycle* depends on the type of the mote system, for example, (1/7.3828) µs for Mica2. The number of *CPU cycles* spent during mote's tasks is counted based on the *average dissipated energy profile* of mote system.

$$Energy = V_{batt} \times I_{Drawn} \times CycleTime \times Cycles\ Count \quad (2)$$

Average End-to-End Delay: measures the average one-way latency observed between transmitting a packet form the source sensor node and receiving it at the base station including propagation time.

Cyclic Redundancy Check (CRC) *field*: CRC indicates whether the packet received pass the CRC checking as TinyOS has a CRC field in its radio packet. Chipcon radio chip (CC1000 or CC2420) has an automatic CRC checking capability and the CRC scheme used in is CRC-16.

8.2 Experimental testbed

In order to evaluate the suitability of the proposed routing scheme for indoor WSN, a set of indoor experiments are run on the testbed network for a particular topology. This small indoor testbed consists of 20 Mica2 motes deployed on paved floor inside roofed showground-like building as shown in figure 4. The surrounding conditions and Mica2's antenna orientation have a significant impact on radio performance. To minimize this effect, for a given topology, testing scenarios were performed many times and the average of these runs was recorded. Data packets were set with fixed size to maintain the same transmission and receiving time for each data packet. The motes are organised and the radio power is configured such that the maximum network diameter is three to five hops. While the operating radio frequency is digitally programmable, external hardware attached to the CC1000 is set to operate in one frequency band. That is, a board set to operate in 868/916MHz bands will not operate at the 433MHz band. The operating frequency range of a Mica2 mote is labelled on the mote. Mica2 (MPR400CB) motes are built to operate in the 868/916MHz bands, i.e., 868–870MHz (up to 4 channels) and 902–928MHz (up to 54 channels). Thus, these Mica2 motes are unlikely to create interfere particularly with 802.11 devices that operate in 2.4GHz ISM band. The actual number of possible channels is higher for all the Mica2 motes (Crossbow, 2010). However, the adjacent channel spacing is to be at least 0.5MHz to avoid adjacent channel interference thereby reducing the number of available channels. The sensor node that acts as the base station is connected to MIB520 programmer, and a RS-232 to USB converter is used to connect the laptop and MIB520 to collect messages sent within the network. Sensor nodes are placed indoor in the way they can only communicate with adjacent neighbours with low transmission powers; however, there is still a probability of opportunistic connections for longer distances (Crossbow, 2010).

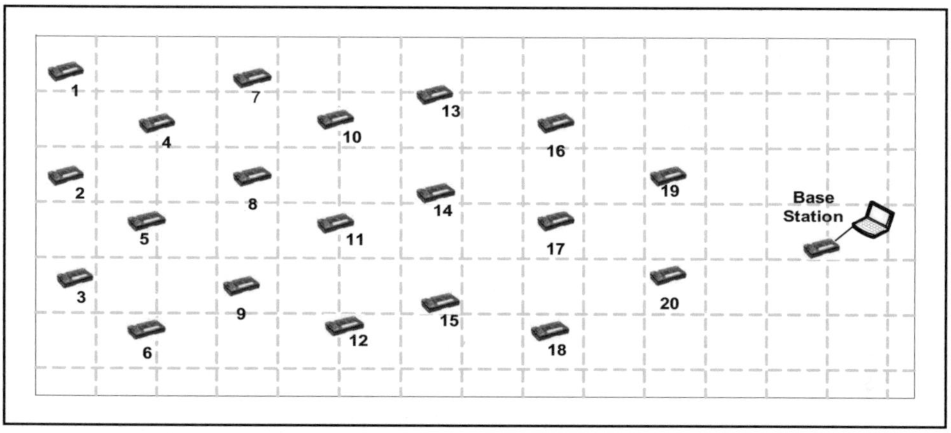

Fig. 4. Indoor testbed topology with perimeter base station

The source sensor nodes broadcast generated data packets towards the base station. The base station acts as a bridging device between sensor nodes and the laptop, relaying the data packets from the sensor nodes to the laptop and the route setup packets from the laptop to the sensor nodes. Also the base station acts as a logging device for various metrics and measurements such as RSSI, CRC, time-stamp, sequence number, and appending them to each received packet. Then, the packet logger/parser program in the laptop processes these received packets, and save them to a log file for thorough analysis using Matlab scripts. TinyOS-2.0.2 is used as the Mica2 CC1000 radio library for earlier TinyOS-1.x releases doesn't support the time-stamping interface. If the local clocks on sensor nodes had the exact frequency and, hence, the offset of the local times were constant, a single synchronisation point would be sufficient to synchronise two sensor nodes. However, the frequency differences of the crystals used in Mica2 motes introduce drifts up to 40μs per second. This would mandate continuous re-synchronisation with a period of less than one second to keep the error in the microsecond range, which is a significant overhead in terms of bandwidth and energy consumption. Therefore, estimation of the drift of the receiver clock with respect to the sender clock is considered.

To limit the radios transmission range, the motes were placed directly on the floor and to determine the distance which provides a reliable delivery performance but minimises the possibility of a mote transmitting further than to adjacent motes; motes were placed at varied distance and the delivery rate recorded. Then, the distance that provided the most reliable packet delivery performance, e.g., PRR is greater than %90, is used. In indoor environment, where space is more limited, the transmitting power of the sensor nodes is initially set to be at the lowest output power level of -20dBm (10μW) and then increased to -15, -10, -5 and 0 dBm and variable in-between spaces are been allowed to provide a reliable delivery performance within 1, 2, or 3 hops and to minimise opportunistic reception. However, it is still likely that some reliable long distance links will form. The Chipcon CC1000 can select a minimum output power level using a variable power radio such that messages are transmitted successfully to their destination, possibly using less power than the default setting. With variable separating spaces between adjacent nodes, adjacent nodes are within the transmission range of each other to allow multi-hop communications. As transmission distance has to be exceeded to make multi-hop more energy efficient than direct transmission. While the network is operating, the source nodes are transmitting packets periodically; the number of packets received by the base station is recorded for each run and the average of these runs is taken. The proposed routing scheme sets up a spanning tree towards the base station and is configured to operate with packet sending rate of one packet apiece 100 ms per source sensor node.

Due to the jitter in the testbed network, transmission start times vary with a mean of few milliseconds. Further, obtaining reliable signal strength measurements for link state indicator can take up to 7ms as this is not a controllable parameter in the CC1000 radios. Therefore, the times at which the signal strength is measured need to be carefully chosen at the receiver to ensure any intended collision. Mica2 motes use CSMA-based MAC protocol, i.e., TinyOS B-MAC that perform Clear Channel Assessment (CCA) and then start transmitting. The automatic ACK feature as well as the retransmissions of the automatic repeat request (ARQ) is disabled, while the link layer functionality is provided using Implicit Acknowledgement. This is to avoid MAC layer overhead and to focus on the routing layer performance. Signal strength measurements are taken in the middle of long packet transmission periods so substantial jitter can be tolerated. In Mica2 CC1000 radio implementation; the data path does not implement software Manchester encoding but it is provided by the CC1000 hardware. The data path interfaces to the radio at the byte level. The CC1000 hardware takes care of bit-synchronization and clocking. The bytes coming off the radio, however, are not necessarily aligned with the data packet. The data path determines and executes the necessary bit shifts on the incoming stream. The CRC computations are running on the received data packet at the base station.

Finally, Mica2 motes are labelled with numbers and placed in predetermined locations on the ground. The base station mote is placed on the MIB520 Mote Interface Board which powered by an AC power supply and attached to a laptop to collect the data of interest. The residual battery capacity is measured and calculated instantaneously and fed into the software in order to be used in the routing cost function in favour of the most energy efficient route. For the initial set of the experiments, all sensor nodes begin with equal battery power levels, roughly 3Volts. The rates at which the data packets are transferred tracked, and the amount of energy required to get the data packets to the base station is monitored.

9. Results and empirical observations

The results obtained experimentally in this section have been worked out based on a real sensor network field which is more important and effective than pure simulation-based approach. Also performance analysis of scenarios in areal sensor field is valuable, satisfactory and possesses academic and practical values on WSN field. Observations and results obtained from the experimental testing are presented and thoroughly analysed using Matlab scripts. This empirical research in the context of WSNs has given a good understanding of the complex irregular behaviour of low-power wireless links in WSNs.

Although the WSN is positioned in indoor environment with very limited ambient noise, multihop WSN has several challenges which represent in: the wireless link limits the number of data packets that can be in flight concurrently from source to destination due to unreliable wireless transmission at each hop and MAC protocol contention problems from hidden nodes and/or exposed nodes; the physical-layer properties that may constrain the throughput achievable over a multihop route; end-to-end reliable delivery of data requires each packet to traverse one or more intermediate hops from the source sensor node towards the base station.

9.1 Link reliability

The RSSI readings are measured at the receiver sensor node based on forward channel. The RSSI is measured indoor within different distances and mote's antenna orientations, then the averaged results are recorded. Figure 5 (a) shows the overall tendency of RSSI measurements as a function of transmission distance and mote/antenna orientation at the highest transmission power. As an overall, it has been observed that in the indoor environment the wireless link reliability estimations based on RSSI doesn't vary significantly with sensor node placement or density within the same space as the hardware-based RSSI provided by CC1000 radio may be inadequate for predicting the link reliability and connectivity. However, different deployment topologies and node density have an observable effect on the overall link reliability of the sensor nodes.

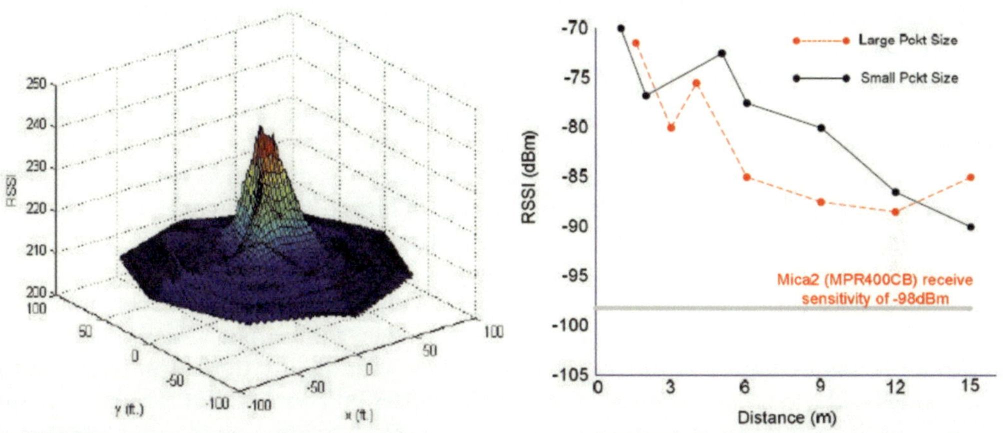

a) RSSI vs. Distance and Orientation

b) RSSI vs. Node Spacing

Fig. 5. RSSI readings measured indoor

The RSSI values decrease as the distance between sensor nodes increase with various packet sizes. Although the indoor experiment is performed with stationary sensor nodes, the RSSI values have a tendency to fluctuate as shown in Figure 5 (b) where the values presented are average values from the packets that are received and do not imply a steady link with various packet sizes. It was observed that within short distances of few meters, the RSSI of small size packets were generally stronger than with the larger size packets with a small packet loss. For longer distances, longer than 13 meters, the larger size packets tend to have stronger RSSI readings. However, the RSSI readings follow an exponential diminishing while the successful packet reception ratio is high; after approximately 20 meters, the signal is noisier and its strength deteriorates to the minimum sensitivity of the CC100 transceiver.

Mica2 (MPR400CB) radio has a receive sensitivity of -98dBm. This extreme sensitivity can be interfered by another oscillator from an adjacent Mica2 node. A distance of at least 65cm should be maintained between adjacent mica2 nodes to avoid local oscillator interference. However, at low transmission power levels, the sensor nodes are still able to communicate with each other.

Using CC1000 RF chip's RSSI independently may not be adequate for predicting the link quality for reliable connectivity. Therefore, for better understanding of low-power wireless link reliability, a newer hardware-based link quality indicator (known as LQI) is used with RSSI for improved link quality estimations in the next experimental outdoor deployment using TelosB's Radio CC2420 that supports LQI measurements as LQI is not supported by Mica2's CC1000 radio.

The experience with the experimental work done has revealed several underlying issues that stem from the properties of the reliability-oriented cost-based routing layers, specifically, MintRoute combined with the resource constraints of the mote platform. Those issues include energy efficiency, long-term link estimations, count-to-infinity and routing loops. The proposed routing scheme considers the suitable countermeasures to address these issues. During the parent selection process, MintRoute uses the link quality estimations with the surrounding neighbours together with cumulated route quality estimation to the base station, and the hop count metric included in the route updates is completely ignored. This can lead to undesirable results in MintRoute, when a sensor node has optimal routes with two or more neighbours with the same best link quality. MintRoute will then arbitrarily choose one of them as its new parent node using its default MT metric, which results suboptimal route that could be in some direction faraway from the base station and in the worst case in the opposite direction of where the base station is located. This results in an undesirable routing problem, e.g., routing hole. The natural occurrence of suboptimal routes is taken into account by the proposed scheme when performing parent selection by adopting, for instance, the least number of hops as a tier breaker; this advantage does not apply for MintRoute, also the proposed protocol is further enhanced in chapter four to avoid routing holes using large-scale simulations. In MintRoute, only next packets transmission may probably reduce the already perceived link quality, which makes the selective forwarder look less attractive. In other words, the parent selection process in MintRoute is merely based on link quality. When the link quality degrades, neighbouring sensor nodes will choose other sensor nodes with a better link quality. For example, creating routing holes in MintRoute is straightforward due to purely relying on the best link quality. When a sensor node has the base station as one of its neighbours, the sensor node will not automatically choose it as its parent. Instead, it will choose the neighbour with the best link quality. To be selected, a sensor node must have both a good send and receive quality. To get a high send quality, the high value must be included in a route update sent by the relay sensor node that caused a routing hole. To get a high receive value, this relay sensor node will have to keep sending packets to prevent the decaying of the receive value by the sensor node. The number of packets that might be lost also lowers the receive quality. Figure 6 (a) shows an example of how routing in MintRoute picks sensor node 2 as a parent for node 5 instead of node 8 and constructs the suboptimal route from sensor node 5 to through sensor node 2 even though node 2 is in the opposite direction of where the base station is located. In figure 6 (b), sensor nodes 11, 13 and 16 select node 14 as their parent with best ink quality using suboptimal routes that purely based on link quality estimations using MT metric. This leads MintRoute to cause a routing hole to the downstream nodes at node 14.

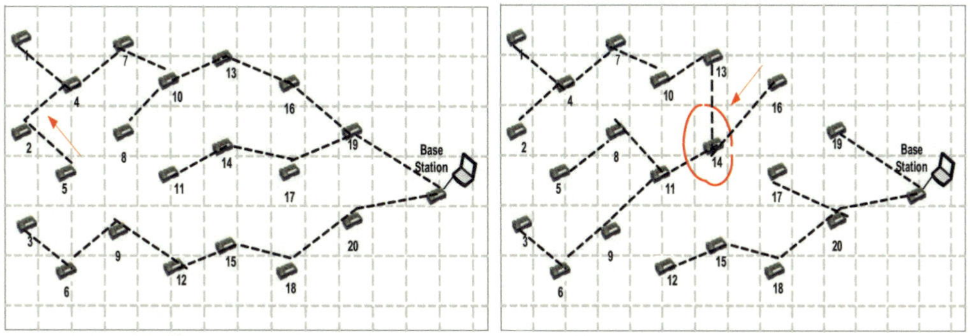

a. Status of fully-connected routing tree b. Status of routing hole problem

Fig. 6. Routing in mintroute protocol

9.2 Average dissipated energy

In the indoor environment, the transmission power of sensor nodes is kept to the lower levels in order to keep the power consumption minimised as possible but the transmission power is increased gradually to maintain reliable multihop connectivity within a limited indoor space. It can be observed from Figure 7 that the average dissipated power by the sensor nodes for transmission and receiving during their operation instantaneously increases faster in MintRoute than in the proposed protocol as the in-between spacing between nodes increases. In terms of energy dissipation cost, since the rate of route message exchanges is low in MintRoute, its energy dissipation in can be minimised. However, MintRoute is more expensive than the proposed protocol at higher message exchange rates and spends a longer time to convey the topological changes to the entire network; during this time, most forwarded packets are routed through optimal paths based on link quality, this leads to additional energy consumption and thus offsets the benefit of energy balancing.

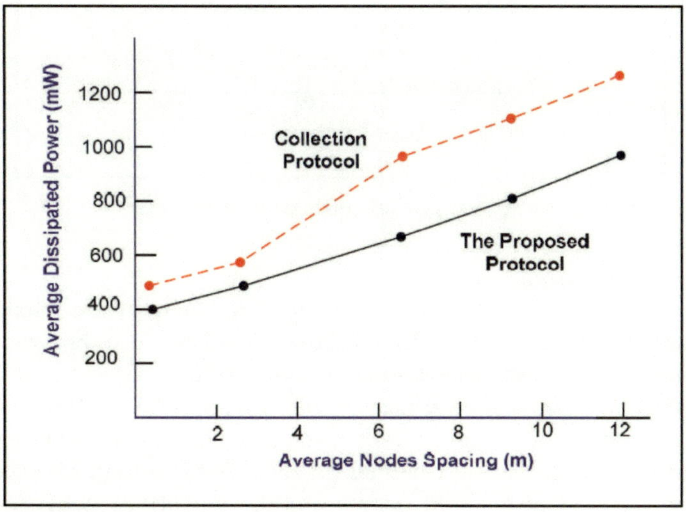

Fig. 7. Average dissipated power vs. inter-nodes spacing

Hence, the proposed routing scheme considers the acceleration of route message exchange rate for reactively adapting the topological changes. Although MintRoute protocol balances the traffic load with unintentional parent switching based on its default Minimum Transmissions (MT) metric, MintRoute protocol does not clearly apply a metric that considers workload balancing in its routing scheme.

The total network-wide energy expenditure is due to: the *parent selection process*; packet transmission; packet overhearing/receiving; failed packet reception, and updating routing table. In B-MAC, overhearing a packet consumes the same energy as receiving a packet because B-MAC requires sensor nodes to receive the whole packet before discarding failed ones. Failed packets reception that may result from packet collision or link failure requires packet retransmission to be successfully received at the destined recipient. Figure 8 shows the total dissipated energy consumption required for retransmissions due to packet loss or link failures. Since the proposed routing scheme has the feature of employing the implicit acknowledgements strategy for less communication overhead, packet transmission is less than that in MintRoute. The fewer packets sent results the less energy consumed for packet receiving, overhearing, and failed packet retransmission. In addition, the total dissipated energy for packet transmission is still much lower in the proposed protocol than in MintRoute even though the proposed protocol requires only 0.48% of computation overhead for parent selection overhead. On average, the proposed protocol saves around 65% on energy consumption for communication less than MintRoute.

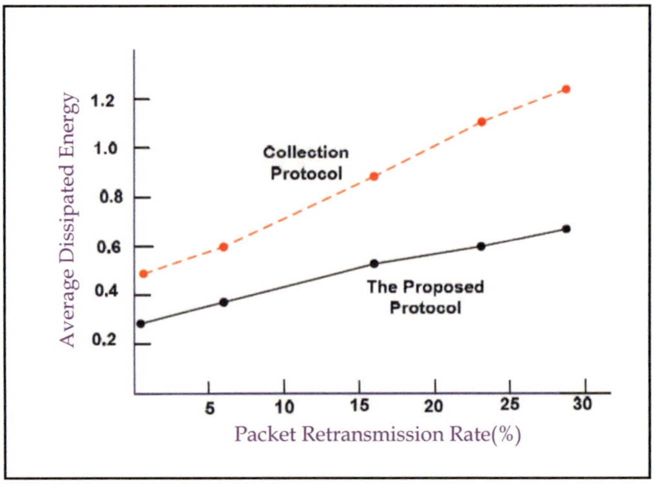

Fig. 8. Average dissipated energy vs. packet retransmissions rate

9.3 Packet delivery performance

In multihop WSN, the achieved throughput may be lower than the maximum achievable throughput for several reasons such as CSMA-based MAC protocol backoff waiting times at each wireless sensor node and packet retransmissions after detected collisions or packet loss. At the physical layer, indoor environment has unconstructive effect on packet delivery performance, especially when a higher transmission power is used, conceivably due to the effect of Multipath Rayleigh Fading Channel (MRFC). Besides that, Manchester coding has much more overhead and also has a negative effect on packet delivery performance in multihop settings, as shown per node transmission and reception overhead in Figure 9. In addition, high signal strength is a necessary but not a sufficient condition for good packet reception ratio. Packet error cannot be distinguished if it was due to physical layer packet error or due to MAC layer collisions. At the MAC layer, about 50-75% of the energy is spent for repairing lost transmissions and the established links has over 50% link asymmetry problem in packet delivery ratio due to surrounding environmental conditions, and mote and antenna orientation.

Typically, there are many different ways for a packet to be corrupted in wireless communication and thereby packet is to be considered lost at the destined recipient. Firstly, a packet may be lost due to errors in the wireless transmission which results in an unsuccessful CRC or not received at all. The second possibility is that two sensor nodes send their packets at times so that the transmissions overlap in time which cases packet collision due to the hidden node problem; thereby resulting in two lost packets. Finally, a packet may be lost before it has been transmitted if a sensor node senses a channel as busy a maximum number of times. In this situation, the sensor node will simply discard the packet and move on to the next packet. As a result, predicting the source of the packet loss is complicated and unclear in terms of the hardware. In addition, previous experimental studies have indicated that radio connectivity is imperfect and non-uniform, even in ideal settings. Furthermore, a packet loss due to link failures is the most common in WSN channels. When data aggregation is enabled, a single link failure will result in an sub-trees of aggregated values being lost, The influence is significant If the failure is close to the base station.

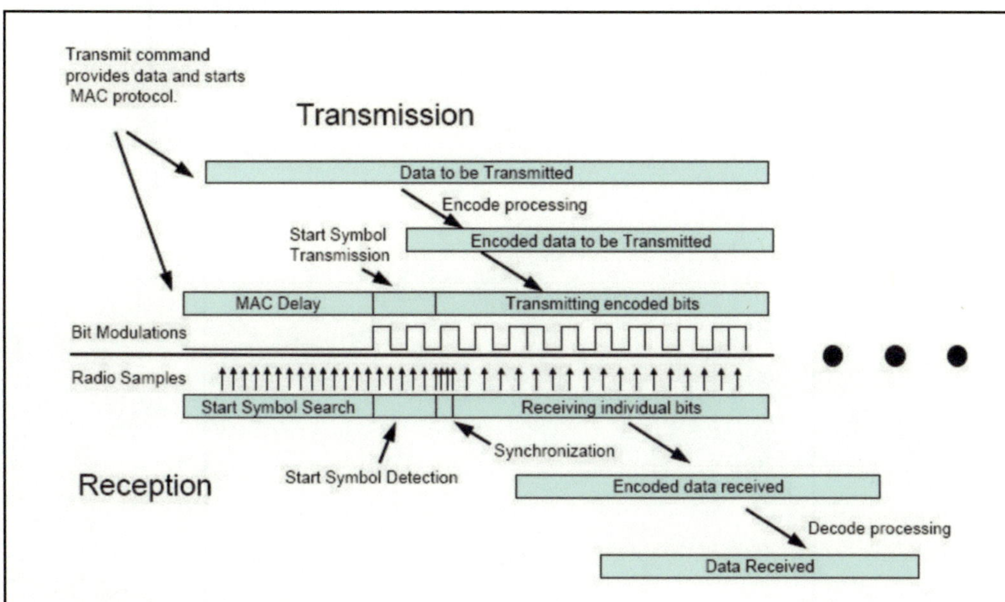

Fig. 9. Wireless communication phases per relay

9.4 Average end-to-end delay

Average end-to-end delivery delay is evaluated in terms of packet transfer rate between the transmitter and the receiver. The transmission rate at the source sensor node has been programmed prior to the experiment and the average of multiple runs with different sending rates is considered. Figure 10 demonstrates how the proposed routing scheme outperforms MintRoute as the packets transfer rate changes through few hops from the source sensor node to the base station. In addition, figure 11 shows how that the packet reception rate for both protocols decreases as the number of hops increases by changing transmission range of the sensor nodes for a constant transmission rate of 7Kbitsps. MintRoute performs poorly in the deployed testbed topology due to the limitation of its route searching and maintenance phases compared to the proposed routing protocol.

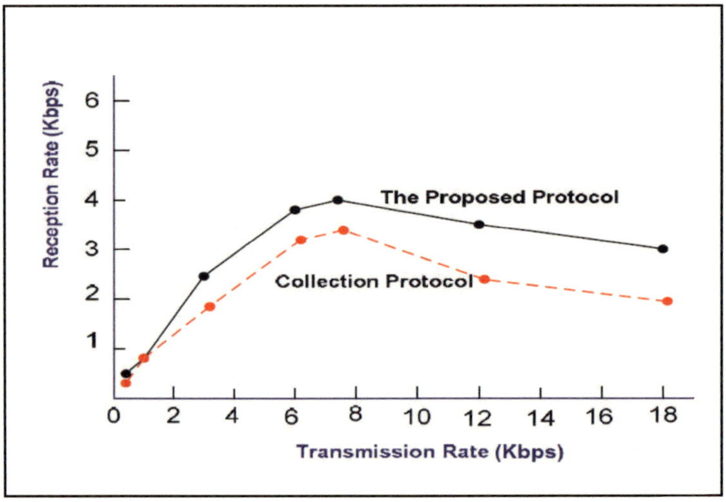

Fig. 10. Reception rate vs. transmission rate

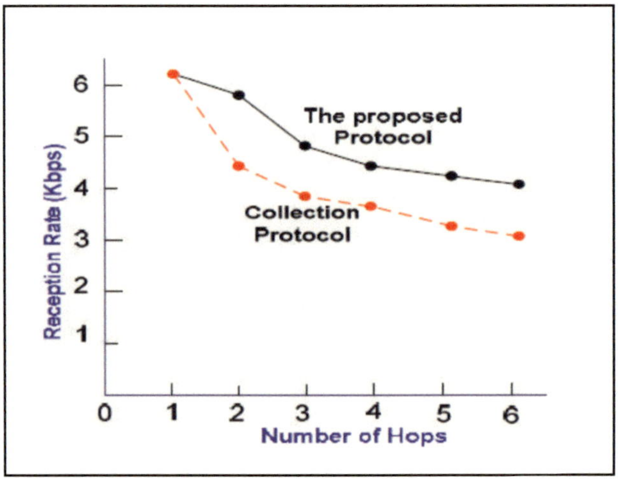

Fig. 11. Reception rate vs. number of traversed hops

10. Conclusion and future work

Some of these observations are well-known phenomena in low power wireless communications. These experiments allow to understanding the irregular behaviour of wireless channel such as asymmetry. A series of experiments were carried with different node spacing. In link asymmetry, there is a noticeable variance in the corresponding packet delivery rate because of a fluctuation in the RSSI below the sensitivity threshold of the receiver due to interference, fading, or shadowing state or due to the fact that the channel is sampled at different times for forward and reverse link estimations. In the most cases, the packet delivery rate for the reverse link is different from its counterpart for the forward link as a consequence of the time-varying nature of the wireless communication channel.

Although the indoor experiment was performed with stationary sensor nodes, the Received Signal Strength Indicator (RSSI) values have a tendency to fluctuate, and do not imply a steady link with various packet sizes. RSSI could yield a routing tree with additional number of hops and extra messages being sent and overheard at the same time as lower transmission power does not mean that the link quality is that such poor. As a result of an irregular low power radio neighborhood, the packet transfer rate is probabilistic and time-varying. Packet transfer rate also changes accordingly with number of hops passed toward the base station. In a multihop sensor network, if the number of hops increases the transfer or reception rate decreases for constant transmission rate due to packet process per relay (e.g., encoding and/or decoding) and wireless signal propagation delay. Moreover, since the radio communication cost is a function of the distance transmitted, it can be observed that the average power dissipated by the sensor nodes during their operation increases as the inter-nodes spacing increases. Since the motes do not constantly communicate, it is optimal to reduce the time the radio spends in active mode and decreasing radio duty cycle is invaluable as an energy saving technique. However, the ability to use the sleep or idle modes depends on network and application behaviour and reducing the cost of each transmission by means of data aggregation is equally important to minimise the current used to power an active radio. Losing packets before reaching the base station not only wastes energy and network resources, but also degrades the quality of application. Another subtle issue is fairness where sensor nodes far-away from the base station are likely to have a lower end-to-end success rate than sensor nodes that are closer. The fall down of success rate by hops or distance verifies this behaviour. Finally, the performance achieved in the real environment is heavily affected by the number of hops that a packet needs to travel to reach the destination and directly affected by the surrounding environment. Finally, While the experiments conducted here have highlighted the substantial performance gains of the proposed scheme, more detailed experiments are needed under different topologies using the new generation of sensor motes such as IRIS 2.4GHz, TelosB that use Chipcon CC2420 and are IEEE802.15.4 compliant. In order to confirm the experiments, analytical and simulation results are also derived. Comparisons using simulations will be addressed against existing stat-of-the art routing protocols for WSNs.

11. References

Burri, N., Rickenbach, P. & Wattenhofer, R. (2007). Dozer: ultra-low power data gathering in sensor networks, *Proceedings of the 6th International Conference on Information Processing in Sensor Networks* (IPSN'07), pp. 450–459, New York, NY, USA, 2007.

Crossbow Technology, Inc. [Online]. Available: http://www.xbow.com (Accessed Sep. '10).

Daabaj, K., (2010). Energy-Aware Reliability-Oriented Scheme to Deliver Time-Sensitive Data in Sensor Networks, *Proceedings of the IEEE International Conference on Service-*

Oriented Computing and Applications (SOCA'10), December 13-15, 2010, Perth, WA, Australia.

Gnawali, O., Fonseca, R., Jamieson, K., Moss, D. & Levis, P. Collection Tree Protocol. *Proceedings of the 7th ACM Conference on Embedded Networked Sensor Systems* (SenSys'09), Berkeley, California, USA, 2009.

ISI, the Network Simulator. ns-2. [Online]. Available: http://www.isi.edu/nsnam/ns/index.html

Omnetpp, OMNeT++ Simulation Framework. [Online]. Available: http://www.omnetpp.org

Polastre, J., Hill, J. & Culler, D. (2004). Versatile Low-Power Media Access for Wireless Sensor Networks, *Proceedings of the Second ACM Conference on Embedded Networked Sensor Systems* (SenSys'04), pp. 95–107, November 2004, Baltimore, MD, USA.

Rahul, S., Jan R. (2002). Energy Aware Routing for Low Energy Ad Hoc Sensor Networks, *Proceedings of IEEE Wireless Communications and Networking Conference (WCNC'02),* pp. 350-355, Orlando, Florida, USA, March 2002.

TinyOS. (2004). MultihopLQI collection protocol, [Online]. Available: http://www.tinyos.net/tinyos-1.x/tos/lib/MultiHopLQI/

Werner-Allen, G., Swieskowski, P. & M. Welsh. (2005). Motelab: A wireless sensor network testbed, *Proceedings of the Fourth International Conference on Information Processing in Sensor Networks* (IPSN'05), Special Track on Platform Tools and Design Methods for Network Embedded Sensors (SPOTS), 2005.

Woo, A., Tong, T. & Culler, D., Taming the Underlying Challenges of Reliable Multihop Routing in Sensor Networks. *Proceedings of the 1st International Conference on Embedded Networked Sensor Systems* (SenSys'03), Los Angeles, CA, USA, Nov. 2003.

Part 2

Innovations in Mechanical Engineering

6

Experimental Implementation of Lyapunov based MRAC for Small Biped Robot Mimicking Human Gait

Pavan K. Vempaty, Ka C. Cheok, and Robert N. K. Loh
Oakland University
USA

1. Introduction

The chapter presents an approach to control the biped humanoid robot to ambulate through human imitation. For this purpose a human body motion capturing system is developed using tri-axis accelerometers (attached to human legs and torso). The tilt angle patterns information from the human is transformed to control and teach various ambulatory skills for humanoid robot bipedalism. Lyapunov stability based model reference adaptive controller (MRAC) technique is implemented to address unpredictable variations of the biped system.

1.1 Background

The biped humanoid robot is one of the accelerated interests in many ongoing research projects. Biped walking is a flexible mechanism that can do dynamic maneuvers in any terrain. Yet, the walking dynamics is non-linear, has many degrees of freedom and requires the development of a complicated model to describe its walking behavior. Existing biped walking methods and control techniques based on Zero moment Point (Babkovic et al., 2007; Kim et al., 2005; Montes et al., 2005; Park, 2003; Kajita et al., 2003; Sughara et al., 2002) give precise stability control for walking robots. However these methods require precise biped walking dynamics and the biped is required to have its feet flat on the ground. Also, these methods may not guarantee a human like walking behavior.

CPG is one biologically inspired method (Kajita et al., 2002; Lee & Oh, 2007; Nakanishi et al., 2004; Righeti & Ijspeert, 2006; Ha et al., 2008; Tomoyuki et al., 2009) defined as the neurons of the nervous system that can generate rhythmic signals in different systems (ex: motors). CPG's are applied to produce several rhythmic patterns or trajectories for biped walking. In these approaches, it is challenging to find appropriate parameters to achieve a stable gait. Most of the CPG's are to be tailor made for specific applications. Moreover it is also important to develop an appropriate controller to meet with disturbances occurring in real-time.

Reinforcement learning (Benbrahim, 1996; Lee & Oh, 2007; Morimoto et al., 2004; Takanobu et al., 2005; Tomoyuki et al., 2009) is a method of learning in which the system will try to map situations to actions, so as to maximize a numerical reward signal. The system is not given any set of actions to perform or a goal to achieve; rather it should discover which

actions yield a maximum reward. Reinforcement learning provides a good approach when the robot is subject to environmental changes, but since this method learns through trial and error, it is difficult to test the performance on a real time robot.
Virtual Model control technique uses simulations of virtual mechanical components to generate actuator torques (or forces) thereby creating the illusion that the simulated components are connected to the real robot (Hu et al., 1999; Pratt et al., 2001). Even so, this method still requires other controllers in conjunction to make the Biped stability reliable.
Intelligent control techniques such as Fuzzy Logic, Neural Networks, Genetic algorithm, and other intuitive controls are useful in making intelligent decisions based on their pre existing data patterns (Benbrahim, 1996; Kun & Miller, 1996; Lee & Oh, 2007; Manoonpong et al., 2007; Miller, 1997; Morimoto et al., 2004; Park, 2003; Takanobu et al., 2005; Tomoyuki et al., 2009; Wolff & Nordin, 2003; Zhou & Meng, 2003). Since these controllers may not guarantee robustness under parameter uncertainties, these methods are useful when combined with conventional control techniques.
In recent years, biped walking through human gait imitation has been a promising approach (Calinon & Billard, 2004; Chalodnan et al., 2007; Grimes et al., 2006; Hu, 1998; Loken, 2006), since it avoids developing complex kinematics and dynamics for the human walking balance and trajectories and gives the biped humanoid robot a human like walking behavior. However, these methods along with the conventional control techniques cannot adapt their behavior when the dynamic environment around the robot changes. Therefore adaptive controllers are useful to handle the changes with respect to the dynamics of the process and the character of the disturbances (Bobasu & Popescu, 2006; Chen et al., 2006, Hu et al., 1999; Kun & Miller, 1996; Siqueira & Terra, 2006; Miller, 1997).

1.2 Current work

In this chapter we show an approach to teach the biped humanoid robot to ambulate through human imitation. For this purpose a human body motion capturing system is developed using tri-axis accelerometers (attached to human legs and torso). The tilt angle patterns information is transformed to control and teach various ambulatory skills for humanoid robot bipedalism. Lyapunov stability based model reference adaptive controller *(MRAC)* technique is implemented to address the dynamic characteristics and unpredictable variations of the biped system (Vempaty et al., 2007, 2009, 2010).
An Adaptive Control system is any physical system that has been designed with an adaptive viewpoint, in which a controller is designed with adjustable parameters and a mechanism for adjusting those parameters. Basically, the controller has two loops. One loop is a normal feedback with the process and the controller. The other loop is the parameter adjustment loop. Due to this ability of changing its parameters dynamically, adaptive control is a more precise technique for biped walking and stability (Section 2).
In MRAC the presence of the reference model specifies the plants desired performance. The plant (biped humanoid robot) adapts to the reference model (desired dynamics). The reference model represents the desired walking behavior of the biped robot, which is derived from the human gait, which is obtained from the human motion capturing system
This chapter shows the design and development methods of controlling the walking motion of a biped robot which mimics a human gait. This process of robot learning through imitation is achieved by a human motion capturing system. In this work, a human motion capturing suit is developed using tri-axis accelerometers that are appended to a human body (Section 4).

In order to ensure precise control and stability, adaptive controller technique is applied. The control system applied for this process is based on Model Reference Adaptive Control (MRAC) with Lyapunov stability criterion. The process of learning to walk, through imitation with MRAC is applied to a real time Humanoid Robot (Robonova) with multiple servo motors (Section 5). This process is carried out by instructing the robot to follow human walking gait with the help of the human body motion capturing system and MRAC schemes (Section 6).

2. MRAC approach for biped walking

Consider the objective of controlling a biped robot so that it imitates the movements of a person. Fig. 1 shows the basic idea where the human movement is represented by $\mathbf{y}_d$ and the biped movement by $\mathbf{y}$. The biped motion is determined by the servo motors which are controlled by the inputs $\mathbf{u}_a$.
In the present problem, we will consider the case where the servo motor has uncertainties including nonlinearities, and unknown parameter values. The overall objective is to find the adaptive $\mathbf{u}_a$ such that $\mathbf{y} \to \mathbf{y}_d$.
In this chapter, we will focus on the adaptation scheme a servo motors (Ehsani, 2007).
Fig. 2 shows the adaptive the objective where the servo motor output angular displacement θ is made to follow a required θ_d, which will be computed from the desired requirement that $\mathbf{y}$ tracks $\mathbf{y}_d$.
Servo motor dynamics including nonlinearities and delays, which have not been widely addressed. The study presented in this chapter deals with the formulation and real-time implementation aspects of the MRAC for Biped imitating human walking motion.

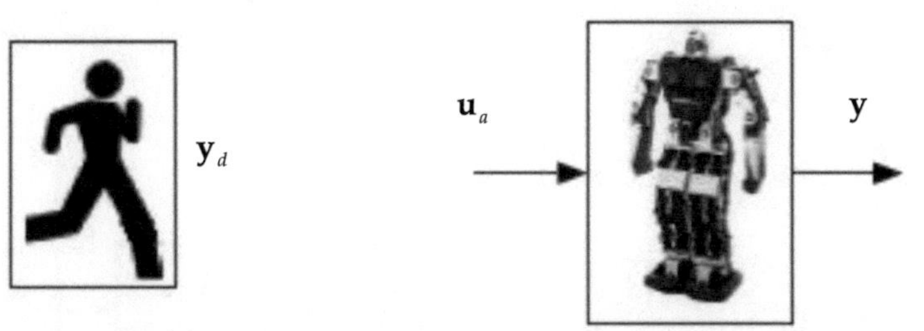

Fig. 1. Human-Robot movements interaction

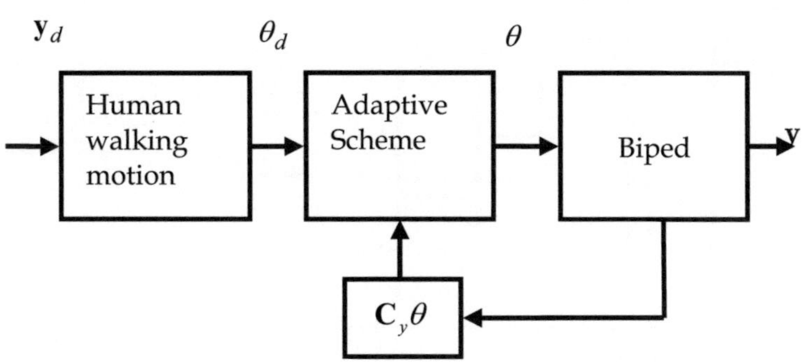

Fig. 2. MRAC for biped mimicking human gait

3. MRAC formulation

3.1 Biped servo model

The biped servo motor model is considered as a 2nd order system with 2 poles, no zero, 1 input, and 2 states described by

$$\dot{\mathbf{x}}_a = \mathbf{A}_a\mathbf{x}_a + \mathbf{B}_a\mathbf{u}_a \tag{1}$$

3.2 Reference model

The adaptive controller scheme for MRAC is shown in Fig. 3, where the reference model for the servo motor is specified by

$$\dot{\mathbf{x}}_m = \mathbf{A}_m\mathbf{x}_m + \mathbf{B}_m\mathbf{u}_m \tag{2}$$

The controller $\mathbf{u}_a$ comprises of a state feedback and a command feedforward terms, given as

$$\mathbf{u}_a = -\mathbf{L}\mathbf{x}_a + \mathbf{N}\mathbf{u}_m \tag{3}$$

The adaptation algorithm in the MRAC will adjust the gains **L** and **N** based on Lyapunov stability criteria as follows.

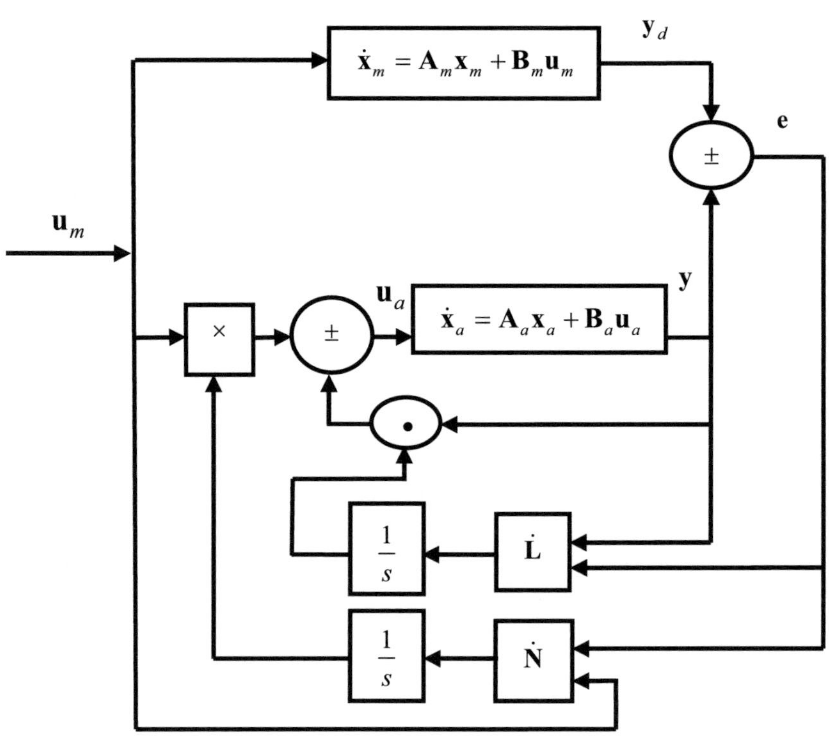

Fig. 3. Lyapunov Stability based MRAC Scheme

3.3 Error equation

Define the errors $\mathbf{e}$ between the biped servo motor states and the desired reference human motion output states as

$$\mathbf{e} = \mathbf{x}_m - \mathbf{x}_a \tag{4}$$

$$\dot{\mathbf{e}} = \mathbf{A}_m\mathbf{e} + \left[\mathbf{A}_a - \mathbf{B}_a\mathbf{L} - \mathbf{A}_m\right]\mathbf{x}_a + \left[\mathbf{B}_a\mathbf{N} - \mathbf{B}_m\right]\mathbf{u}_m \tag{5}$$

3.4 Lyapunov stability analysis

We define the Lyapunov candidate function as

$$\begin{aligned} v = {} & \mathbf{e}^T\mathbf{P}\mathbf{e} + trace\left(\mathbf{A}_m - \mathbf{A}_a - \mathbf{B}_a\mathbf{L}\right)^T \mathbf{Q}\left(\mathbf{A}_m - \mathbf{A}_a - \mathbf{B}_a\mathbf{L}\right) + \\ & trace\left(\mathbf{B}_m - \mathbf{B}_a\mathbf{N}\right)^T \mathbf{R}\left(\mathbf{B}_m - \mathbf{B}_a\mathbf{N}\right) \end{aligned} \tag{6}$$

where $\mathbf{P} = \mathbf{P}^T > 0$, $\mathbf{Q} = \mathbf{Q}^T > 0$ and $\mathbf{R} = \mathbf{R}^T > 0$ are positive definite matrices.

$$\begin{aligned} \dot{v} = {} & \dot{\mathbf{e}}^T\mathbf{P}\mathbf{e} + \mathbf{e}^T\mathbf{P}\dot{\mathbf{e}} \\ & +2\left(trace\left(\mathbf{A}_m - \mathbf{A}_a - \mathbf{B}_a\mathbf{L}\right)^T \mathbf{Q}\left(\mathbf{B}_a\dot{\mathbf{L}}\right)\right) + 2\left(trace\left(\mathbf{B}_m - \mathbf{B}_a\mathbf{N}\right)^T \mathbf{R}\left(-\mathbf{B}_a\dot{\mathbf{N}}\right)\right) \\ = {} & \mathbf{e}^T\left[\mathbf{P}\mathbf{A}_m + \mathbf{A}_m^T\mathbf{P}\right]\mathbf{e} + \\ & 2\left(trace\left(\mathbf{A}_m - \mathbf{A}_a - \mathbf{B}_a\mathbf{L}\right)^T \left(\mathbf{P}\mathbf{e}\mathbf{x}_a^T + \mathbf{Q}\left(\mathbf{B}_a\dot{\mathbf{L}}\right)\right)\right) \\ & +2\left(trace\left(\mathbf{B}_m - \mathbf{B}_a\mathbf{N}\right)^T \left(\mathbf{P}\mathbf{e}\mathbf{u}_m^T + \mathbf{R}\left(-\mathbf{B}_a\dot{\mathbf{N}}\right)\right)\right) \end{aligned} \tag{7}$$

From inspection, we choose

$$\begin{aligned} \mathbf{B}_a\dot{\mathbf{L}} &= \mathbf{Q}^{-1}\mathbf{P}\mathbf{e}\mathbf{x}_a^T \\ \mathbf{B}_a\dot{\mathbf{N}} &= -\mathbf{R}^{-1}\mathbf{P}\mathbf{e}\mathbf{u}_m^T \end{aligned} \tag{8}$$

So that,

$$\dot{v} = \mathbf{e}^T\left[\mathbf{P}\mathbf{A}_m + \mathbf{A}_m^T\mathbf{P}\right]\mathbf{e} \tag{9}$$

Next, choose $\mathbf{S} = \mathbf{S}^T > 0$ and solve $\mathbf{P}$ from

$$\mathbf{P}\mathbf{A}_m + \mathbf{A}_m^T\mathbf{P} = -\mathbf{S} < 0 \tag{10}$$

We now arrive at

$$\dot{v} = -\mathbf{e}^T\mathbf{S}\mathbf{e} \tag{11}$$

It is desirable to then ensure that $\mathbf{P}\mathbf{A}_m + \mathbf{A}_m^T\mathbf{P} = -\mathbf{S} < 0$ (negative definite) where $\mathbf{S} > 0$ (positive definite). $\mathbf{P}$ is solved from the Lyapunov equation (10).
Lyapunov stability theory ensures that the solution $\mathbf{P} > 0$ because $\mathbf{A}_m$ is stable.

4. Human motion sensing

4.1 Human gait acquisition setup

A low cost human motion capturing system is developed using Nintendo Wii remotes (Wiimote). A Wiimote is a Bluetooth based wireless joystick with an ADXL330 tri-axis accelerometer embedded in it. An ADXL330 tri-axis accelerometer can measure acceleration with a full scale range of $\pm 3g$, and can be used to measure the tilt angles when appended to a human body. Fig. 4, shows basic human motion capturing system with Wiimotes attached to the human body. For controlling and instructing the robot on bipedalism, a minimum of five accelerometers are required, two on each leg (attached to thigh and the calf muscles), and one on the torso.

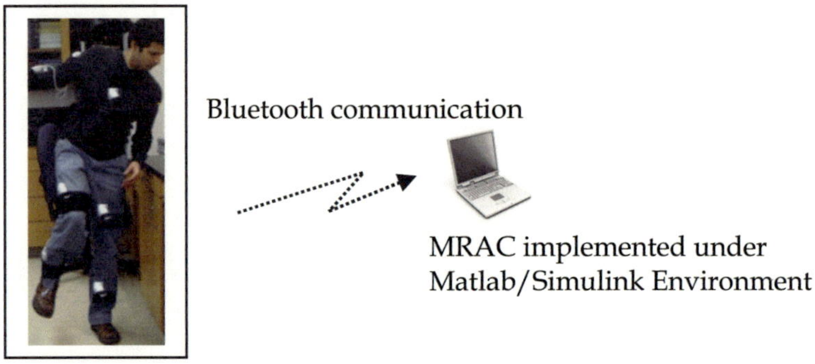

Fig. 4. Nintendo Wiimotes based human motion capturing system

4.2 Human motion data filter

Human motion data is sampled for every 300ms. The raw data captured has noise, redundancy and sensitivity. Due to this the biped may respond for every redundant movement of the human. Therefore in order to reduce this effect, a filter is designed to remove the unwanted human motion data. Fig. 5, shows the human gait data filter algorithm.

The filter basically takes the human motion data and calculates the difference of the first value $\mathbf{u}_m(i)$, with its subsequent value $\mathbf{u}_m(j)$.

The difference $Diff_{\mathbf{u}_m}$ is compared with the threshold values set as 8 degrees and 6 degrees for $PosThresUpper$ and $PosThresLower$. If the difference is satisfied by the condition, then that position data value is sent as the input command $\mathbf{u}_m$, else process is repeated. Fig. 6 shows the filtered data from the raw human gait data acquisition from all the 5 Wii sensors.

It is clearly seen from the plots that the data that is redundant and noisy are ignored. Data is collected and processed only when there is a significant amount of change. This method also helps in sending only the useful information to the biped as well as in saving computer memory storage.

5. Real-Time Implementation

5.1 Robonova biped robot

Robonova is controlled by an Atmel ATMEGA128 8bit RISC processor, and has the capability of simultaneously controlling up to 24 servo motors. In this work, commands for the servo motors are sent from the computer under a Matlab/Simulink environment.

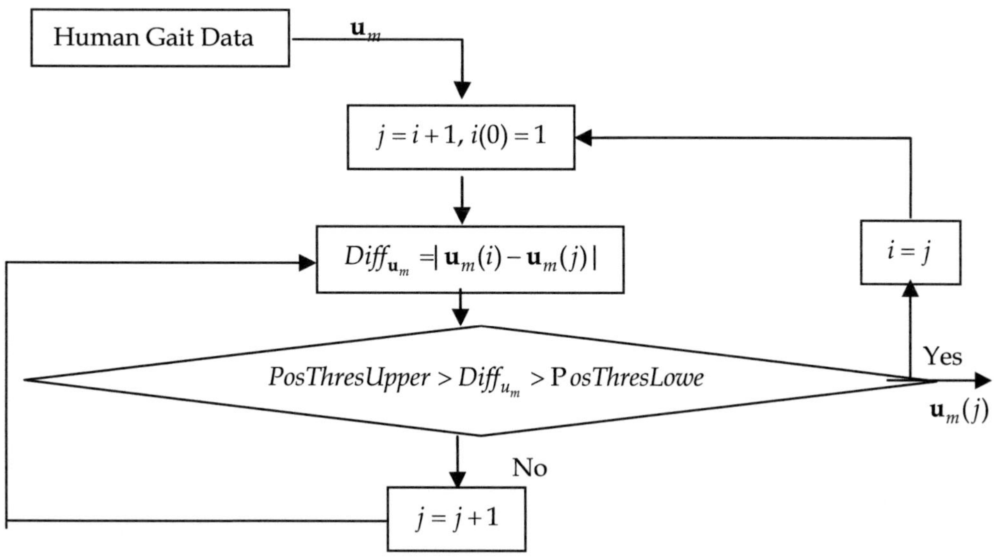

Fig. 5. Filter algorithm for human motion data

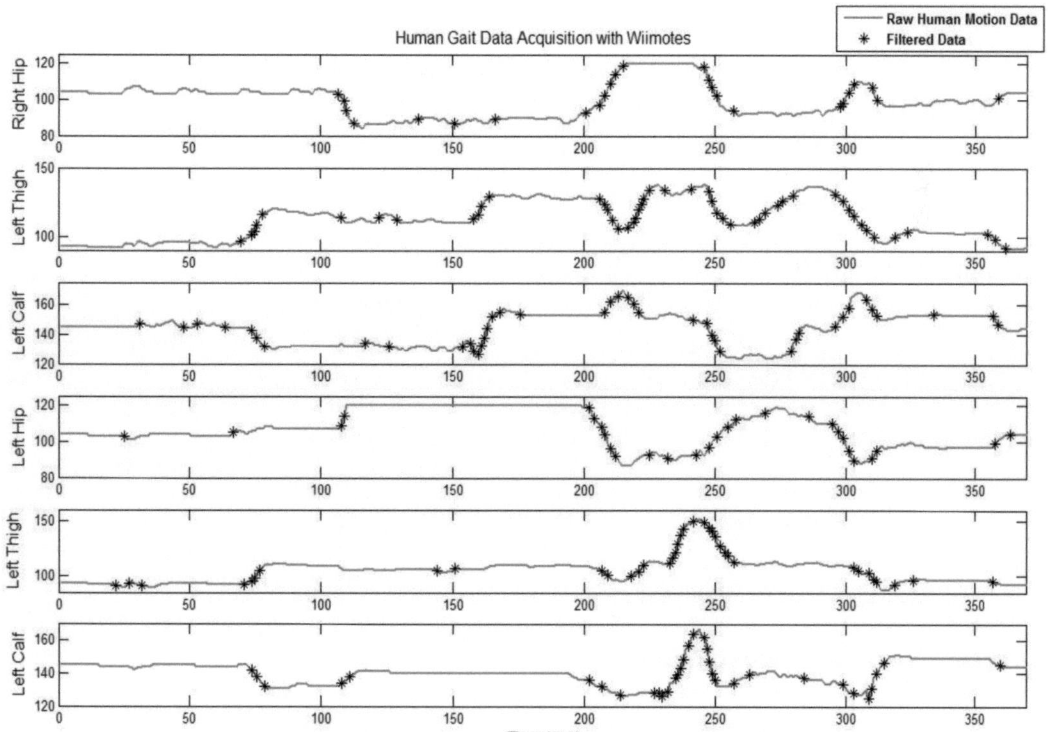

Fig. 6. Ouput of the human motion data filter

Commands for 16 servo motors are issued to the ATMEGA processor via RS232 interface. Five tri-axis ADXL335 ($\pm 3g$ acceleration) accelerometers appended on to its legs (thigh and calf muscles) and onto its torso for position feedback. Fig. 7, shows the basic control and communication setup for Robonova-Computer interaction (Zannatha &Limon, 2009).

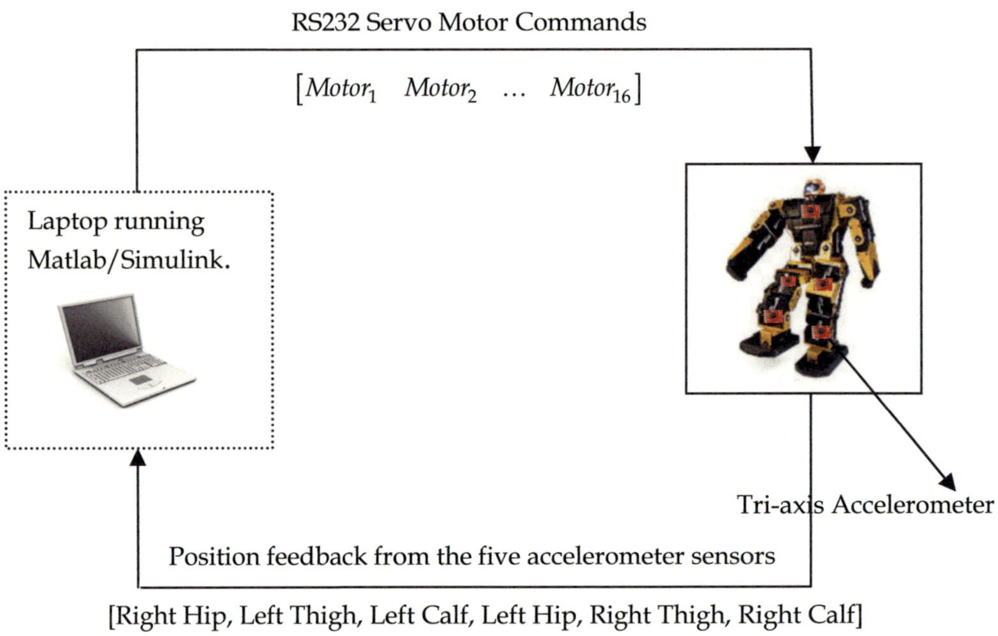

Fig. 7. Biped-Computer Interaction and Interface setup

5.2 Computation of the human movements

Desired human motion data from the Wii device is represented as

$$\mathbf{y}_d = \begin{bmatrix} \theta_{Thigh\,Right} & \theta_{Calf\,Right} & \theta_{Thigh\,Left} & \theta_{Calf\,Left} & \theta_{Torso} \end{bmatrix}_{Human}^{T} \quad (12)$$

Output $\mathbf{y}$ is constructed from the biped's accelerometer sensors as,

$$\mathbf{y} = \begin{bmatrix} \theta_{Thigh\,Right} & \theta_{Calf\,Right} & \theta_{Thigh\,Left} & \theta_{Calf\,Left} & \theta_{Torso} \end{bmatrix}_{biped}^{T} = C_y\theta \quad (13)$$

The desired output will be to have $\mathbf{y} \to \mathbf{y}_d$.

5.2.1 Dynamics of the servo motors

The biped output states $\mathbf{x}_a = \boldsymbol{\theta}$ are the biped servomotor angular displacements. The objective is to derive $\mathbf{u}_a$ which will drive $\boldsymbol{\theta} \to \boldsymbol{\theta}_d$.

It follows that (1) can be decoupled into individual motors represented by the second order dynamics given as

$$\mathbf{x}_a = \begin{bmatrix} x_{a1} & x_{a2} & x_{a3} & x_{a4} & x_{a5} & x_{a6} & x_{a7} & x_{a8} \end{bmatrix}^T$$
$$\mathbf{u}_a = \begin{bmatrix} u_{a1} & u_{a2} & u_{a3} & u_{a4} & u_{a5} & u_{a6} & u_{a7} & u_{a8} \end{bmatrix}^T$$
$$\mathbf{A}_a = diag\{a_{a1} \quad a_{a2} \quad a_{a3} \quad a_{a4} \quad a_{a5} \quad a_{a6} \quad a_{a7} \quad a_{a8}\}$$
$$\mathbf{B}_a = diag\{b_{a1} \quad b_{a2} \quad b_{a3} \quad b_{a4} \quad b_{a5} \quad b_{a6} \quad b_{a7} \quad b_{a8}\}$$

$\mathbf{A}_a$ and $\mathbf{B}_a$ are the uncertain parameter vectors and the states $\mathbf{x}_a$ and the control $\mathbf{u}_a$ are accessible.

5.2.2 Configuration of MRAC for biped servo motors

From (3), the controller $\mathbf{u}_a$ comprises a state feedback and a command feedforward terms Where,

$$\begin{aligned} \mathbf{L} &= diag\{l_1 \quad l_2 \quad l_3 \quad l_4 \quad l_5 \quad l_6 \quad l_7 \quad l_8\} \\ \mathbf{N} &= diag\{n_1 \quad n_2 \quad n_3 \quad n_4\} \end{aligned} \tag{14}$$

Where $\mathbf{u}_m$ is the command input to the MRAC system. The controller gains $\mathbf{L}$ and $\mathbf{N}$ are to be tuned, so that the closed-loop system

$$\dot{\mathbf{x}}_a = (\mathbf{A}_a - \mathbf{B}_a\mathbf{L})\mathbf{x}_a + \mathbf{B}_a\mathbf{N}\mathbf{u}_m \tag{15}$$

behaves with the characteristics of the reference model defined by (2).
From the Lyapunov design 3.1.3, the gains (14) are adjusted according to

$$\begin{aligned} \dot{l}_i &= \frac{1}{b_{ai}q_i} p_i(\theta_{di} - x_{ai})x_{ai} \\ \dot{n}_i &= -\frac{1}{b_{ai}r_i} p_i(\theta_{di} - x_{ai})u_{mi} \end{aligned} \tag{16}$$

The convergence analysis for tuning p,q and r is discussed by (Vempaty et al., 2010).

5.3 Simulation of biped servo motor model

Consider one of the biped servo motor models, derived based on the system identification analysis. The corresponding model is given from (1)

$$\mathbf{A}_a = \begin{bmatrix} 0 & 1 \\ -a_{a2} & -a_{a1} \end{bmatrix}, \mathbf{B}_a = \begin{bmatrix} 0 \\ b_{a1} \end{bmatrix}, \mathbf{x}_a = \begin{bmatrix} x_{a1} \\ x_{a2} \end{bmatrix}, \mathbf{C}_a = \begin{bmatrix} 1 & 0 \\ 0 & 1 \end{bmatrix} \tag{17}$$

Where, $a_{a1} = -4, a_{a2} = -2,$ and $\mathrm{b}_{a1} = 2.28$.
We would like (17) to behave with characteristics of the reference model (2) defined as

$$\mathbf{A}_m = \begin{bmatrix} 0 & 1 \\ -a_{m2} & -a_{m1} \end{bmatrix}, \mathbf{B}_m = \begin{bmatrix} 0 \\ b_{m1} \end{bmatrix}, \mathbf{x}_m = \begin{bmatrix} x_{m1} \\ x_{m2} \end{bmatrix}, \mathbf{C}_m = \begin{bmatrix} 1 & 0 \\ 0 & 1 \end{bmatrix} \tag{18}$$

Where, $a_{m1} = -4, a_{a2} = -8,$ and $\mathrm{b}_{a1} = 8$.

The adaptation of the biped servo model to the reference model is shown in Fig. 8.

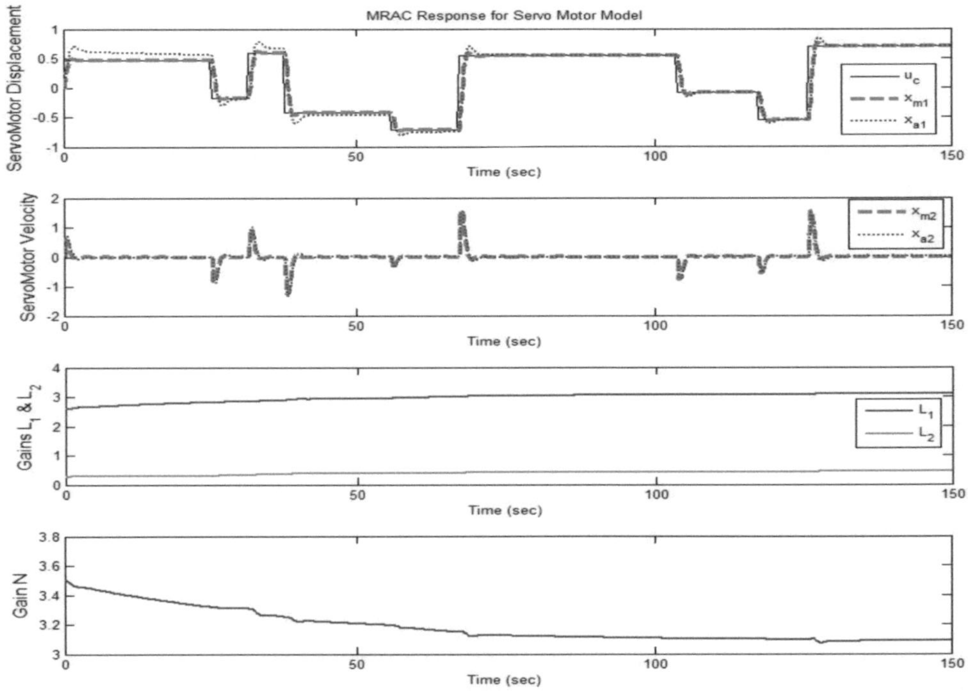

Fig. 8. MRAC response of the biped servo motor model

The coefficients a_{m1}, a_{m2}, and b_m represent the desirable characteristics for the model. It is clear from Fig. 8 that l_1, l_2, and n_1 are tuned so that, from (2), (15) and (4) we infer,

$$\mathbf{A}_a - \mathbf{B}_a\mathbf{L} \rightarrow \mathbf{A}_m,\ \mathbf{B}_a\mathbf{N} \rightarrow \mathbf{B}_m, \text{and } \mathbf{e} \rightarrow 0$$

6. Experiment and results

6.1 Closed-loop setup

The process of a robot learning to walk by mimicking human gait is discussed in this section. Fig. 9, shows the human-robot interaction setup with MRAC scheme. Human movements from the Wiimotes are transferred to Matlab/Simulink; these angles are transformed and calibrated with the accelerometer feedback angles coming from the Robonova.

The angles coming from the human motion change from 10 to 190; these signals are scaled between -1 and 1 to avoid singularities in the computation of MRAC.

The five angles derived from the human movements are sent to the MRAC as the command input signals. In this experiment $\theta_{Torso_{Human}}$ and $\theta_{Torso_{Biped}}$ are set to be constant.

The output of the MRAC with the five control signals is transformed to the corresponding individual servo signals to the Robonova via serial port, and the position of the biped feedback to the controller is transformed via a Kalman filter to reduce the sensor noise.

MRAC is implemented individually to the servo motors defined by (12). The tracking responses of each servo motor are monitored with ±5 % tolerance limit. After the tracking

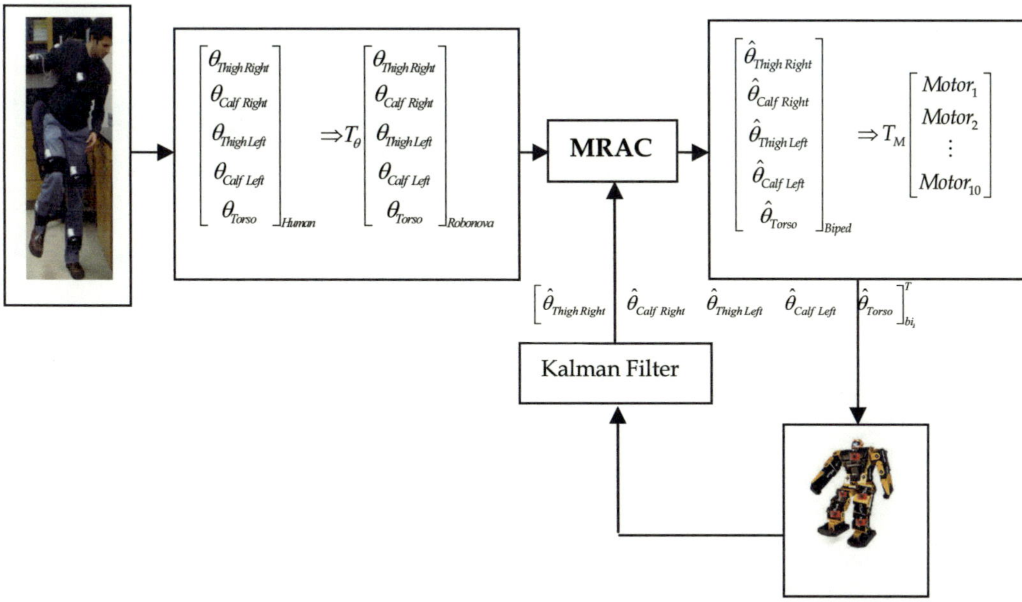

Fig. 9. Closed-loop setup for biped walker imitating human gait with MRAC

requirement is reached, the next input command is issued to the controller and the process repeats.

Although Lyapunov guarantees stability of the system under control, it never guarantees a precise tracking performance. For this, Lyapunov based MRAC schemes should be incorporated with other control schemes.

In this experiment, in order for the biped to meet the real-time response, an integrator is implemented at the command input $\mathbf{u}_a$.

This approach is used in instructing the robot in walking. Here, the robot derives its dynamic and kinematic movements from the human dynamic and kinematic movements.

6.2 Output results of the MRAC based biped walker imitating human gait

Following are the results of the MRAC for a 2-step walking cycle of the biped imitating human gait. Fig. 10-13 show the MRAC outputs when the biped responds to the human gait data.

7. Conclusion

The experimental results verify the MRAC approach for the biped walker imitating the human gait under a real-time environment. The model reference adaptive control system for the servo motor control is derived and successfully implemented with Matlab/Simulink. It has been shown that the application of MRAC for biped walking indeed makes the humanoid robot adapt to whatever reference that is provided.

Therefore, it can be concluded that the use of MRAC for biped walking makes it easy to develop and control a biped system. Tracking performance and learning based on neural networks shall be included in future research.

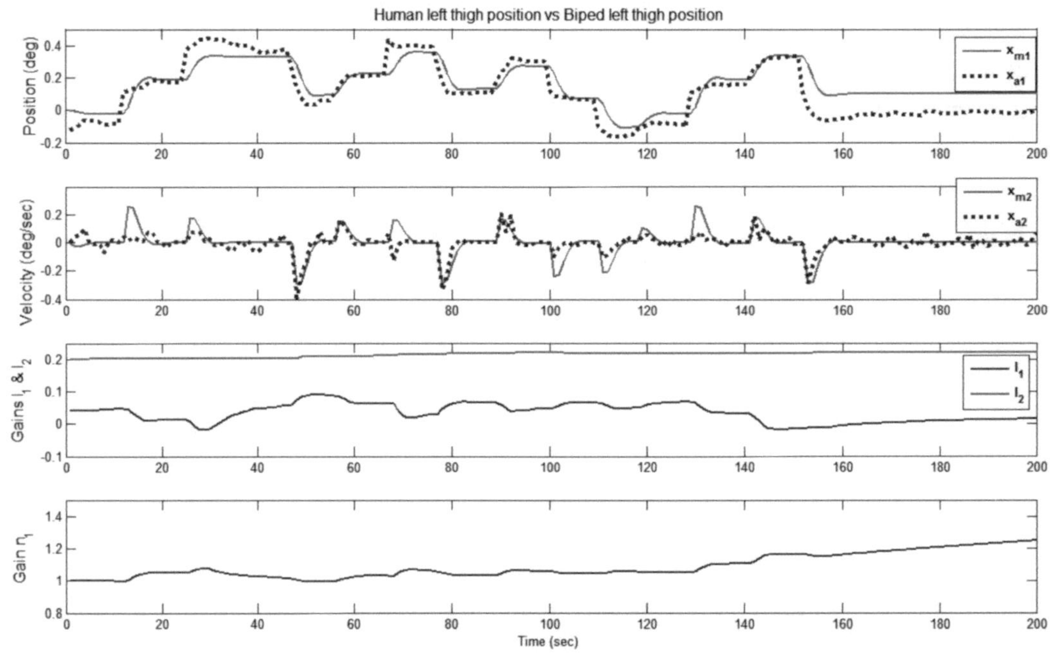

Fig. 10. Closed-loop MRAC biped response to human left thigh motion

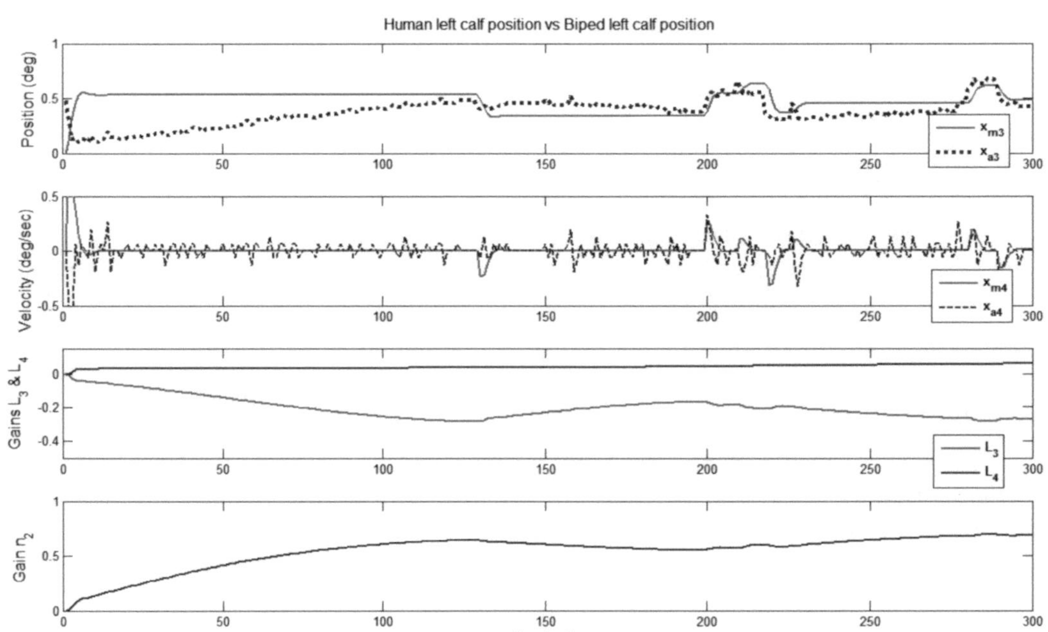

Fig. 11. Closed-loop MRAC biped response to human left calf motion

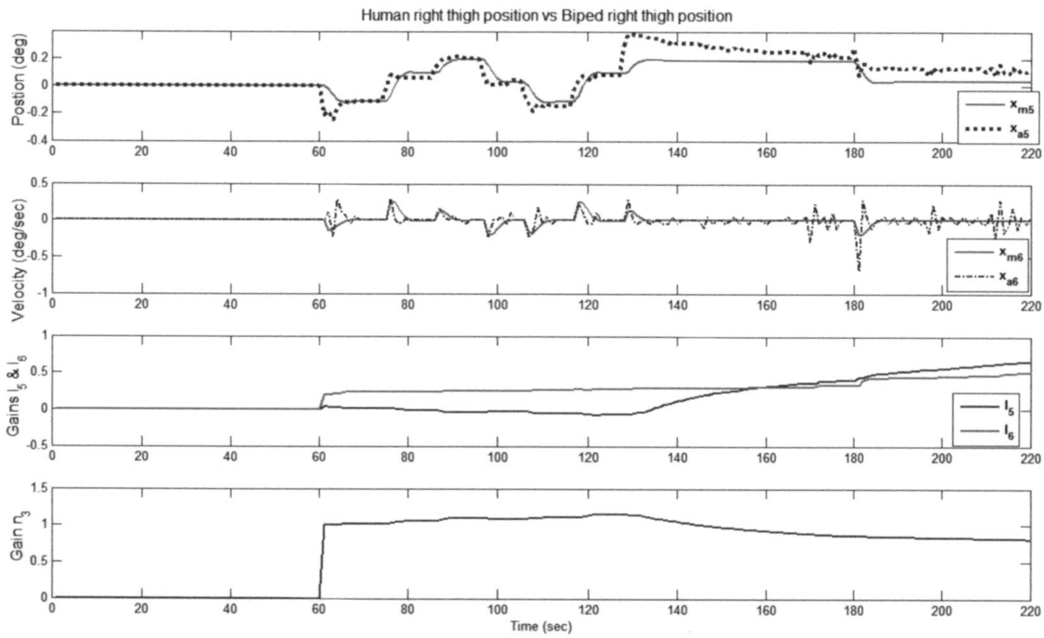

Fig. 12. Closed-loop MRAC biped response to human right thigh motion

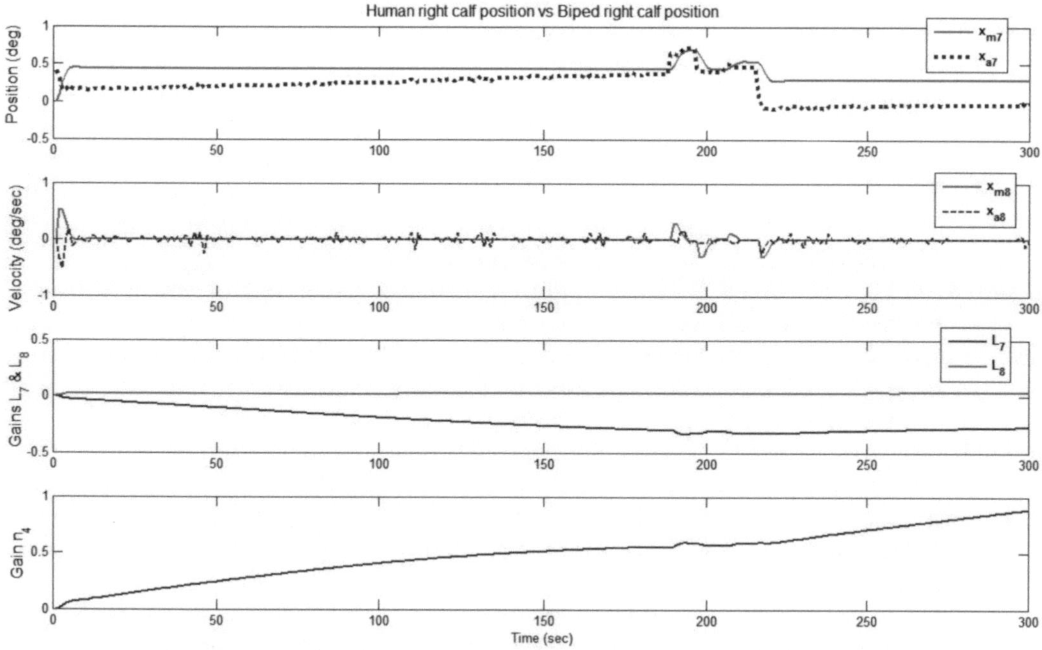

Fig. 13. Closed-loop MRAC biped response to human right calf motion

8. References

A. A. G. Siqueira & M. H. Terra, "Nonlinear H_∞ control applied to biped robots," Proceedings of IEEE Intl. Conf. on Control Applications, pp. 2190-2195, 2006.

A. L. Kun & W. Miller, "Adaptive dynamic balance of a biped robot using neural networks," *Proceedings of IEEE Intl. Conference on Robotics and Automation*, 1996.

Asai Takanobu, Sakuma Jun, & Kobayashi Shigenobu, "Reinforcement learning for biped walking using human demonstration towards the human like walking of biped robot," *Chino Shisutemu Shinpojiumu Shiryo*, vol. 32, pp. 393-398, 2005.

Changjiu Zhou & Qingchun Meng, "Dynamic balance of a biped robot using fuzzy reinforcement learning agents," *Fuzzy sets and systems archive*, vol. 134, issue 1, pp. 169-187, 2003.

D B. Grimes, R. Chalodhorn, & P. N. Rao, "Dynamic imitation in a humanoid robot through nonparametric probabilistic inference," Proceedings of Robotics: Science and Systems, 2006.

D. Kim, S.-J. Seo, & G.-T. Park, "Zero-moment point trajectory modeling of a biped walking robot using an adaptive neuro-fuzzy system," *Proceedings of IEE Int. Conf. on Control Theory Appl.*, vol.152, No.4, July 2005.

Eugen Bobasu & Dan Popescu, "Adaptive nonlinear control algorithms of robotic manipulators," *Proceedings of the 7th WSEAS International Conference on Automation & Information*, pp. 83-88, 2006.

Hamid Benbrahim, "Biped dynamic walking using reinforcement learning,"Doctoral Thesis, University of New Hampshire, Manchester, USA. 1996.

H. Montes, S. Nabulsi, & M. Armada, "Detecting Zero-Moment Point in Legged Robot," *Proceedings of the 7th Int. Conf. CLAWAR*, ISBN 978-3-540-29461-0, pp. 229-236, 2005.

Jerry Pratt, Chee-Meng Chew, Ann Torres, Peter Dilworth, & Gill Pratt, "Virtual model control: an intuitive approach for bipedal locomotion," *Proceedings of the International Journal of Robotics Research*, vol. 20, no. 2, pp. 129-143, 2001.

Jianjuen Hu, "Learning control of bipedal dynamic walking robots with neural networks," Doctoral Thesis, Massachusetts Institute of Technology, Cambridge, USA, 1998.

Jianjuen Hu, Jerry Pratt, Chee-Meng Chew, Hugh Herr, & Gill Pratt, "Adaptive virtual model control of a bipedal walking robot," *Proceedings of the International Journal on Artificial Intelligence Tools*, vol. 8, no. 3, pp. 337-348, 1999.

J. Lee & J. H. Oh, "Biped walking pattern generation using reinforcement learning," *Proceedings of IEEE-RAS Intl. on Humanoid Robots*, pp. 416-421, 2007.

J.M. Zannatha & R.C. Limon, "Forward and inverse kinematics for a small-sized humanoid robot," *Proceedings of IEEE Intl. Conf. on Electric, Communications, and Computers*, pp. 111-118, 2009.

Jong Hyeon Park, "Fuzzy-Logic zero-moment-point trajectory generation of reduced trunk motions of biped robot," *Fuzzy Sets Syst.* 134, pp 189-203, 2003.

Jun Morimoto, Gordan Cheng, Chirstopher G. Atkeson, & Grath Zeglen, "A simple reinforcement learning algorithm for biped walking," *Proceedings of the IEEE Conference on Robotics and Automation*, vol. 3, pp. 3030-3035, 2004.

Jun Nakanishi, Jun Morimoto, Gen Endo, Gordon Cheng, Stefen Schaal, & Mitsuo Kawato, "Learning from demonstration and adaptation of biped locomotion with dynamical movement primitives," *Proceedings of the 4th IEEE /RAS International Conference on Humanoid Robotics*, vol. 2, pp. 925-940, 2004.

K. Babkovic, L. Nagy, D. Krkljes, & B. Borovac, "Inverted Pendulum with a Sensored Foot," *Proceedings of IEEE Intl. Symposium on Intelligent Systems and Informatics*, pp. 183-187, 2007.

Kevin Loken, "Imitation-based learning of bipedal walking using locally weighted learning," MS Thesis, The university of British Columbia, Vancouver, Canada, 2006.

Kristen Wolff & Peter Nordin, "Evolutionary learning from first principles of biped walking on a simulated humanoid robot," *Proceedings of the business and Industry Symposium of the Simulation Technologies Conference ASTC'03*, pp. 31-36, March 30th - April 3rd 2003.

L. Righeti & A. Ijspeert, "Programming central pattern generators: an application to biped locomotion control,"*Proceedings of IEEE Intl. Conf. on Robotics and Automation,*" pp 1585-1590, 2006.

M. S. Ehsani, "Adaptive control of servo motor by MRAC method," *Proceedings of IEEE Intl. Conf. on Vehicle Power and Propulsion*, pp. 78-83, 2007.

Pavan K. Vempaty, Ka C. Cheok, & Robert N. K. Loh, "Model Reference Adaptive Control for Actuators of a Biped Robot Locomotion," *Proceedings of the World Congress on Engineering and Computer Science* (WCECS), vol II, pp. 983-988, San Francisco, USA, Oct 20-22, 2009.

Poramate Manoonpong, Tao Geng, Toman Kulvicius, Bernd Porr, & Florentin Worgotter, "Adaptive, Fast Walking in a Biped robot under neuronal control and learning," *PLos Computational Biology*, 2007.

Rawichote Chalodnan, David B. Grimes, & Rajesh P. N. Rao, "Learning to walk through imitation," *Proceedings to the 20th International Joint Conference on Artificial Intelligence*, pp. 2084-2090, 2007.

S. Calinon & A. Billard, " Stochastic gesture production and recognition model for a humanoid robot," Proceedings of IEEE Intl. Conf. on Intelligent Robots and Systems, pp. 2769-2774, 2004.

Seungsuk Ha, Youngjoon Han, & Hernsoo Hahn, "Adaptive gait pattern generation of biped robot based on human's gait pattern analysis,"*Proceedings of the International Journals of Mechanical System Science and Engineering*, vol. 1, no. 2, pp. 80-85, 2008.

Shuuji Kajita, Fumio Kanehiro, Kenhi Kaneko, Kiyoshi Fijiwara, Kazuhito Yokoi, & Hirohisa Hirukawa, "A realtime pattern generator for biped walking," *Proc. of IEEE Int. Conf. on Robotics & Automation*, vol. 1, pp. 31-37, 2002.

Shuuji Kajita, Fumio Kanehiro, Kenji Kaneko, Kiyoshi Fujiwara, Kensuke Harada, Kazuhito Yokoi & Hirohisa Hirukawa, "Biped walking pattern generation by using preview control of zero-moment point," *Proc. of IEEE Int. Conf. on Robotics & Automation*, vol. 2, pp. 1620-1626, 2003.

T. Sughara, Y. Nakamura, & H. Inoue, "Realtime humanoid motion generation through ZMP manipulation based on inverted pendulum control," *Proceedings of the Intl. Conf. on Robotics and Automation, ICRA*, pp. 1404-1409, 2002.

T. Tomoyuki, Y. Azuma, & T. Shibata, "Acquisition of energy-efficient bipedal walking using CPG-based reinforcement learning,"*Proceedings of IEEE/RSJ Intl. Conf. on Intelligent Robots and Systems*, pp, 827-832, 2009.

W. Miller, "Dynamic balance of a biped walking robot: Adaptive gait modulation using CMAC neural networks," Neural Systems for Robotics, Academic Press, 1997.

Y. Chen, Z. Han, & H. Tang, "Direct adaptive control for nonlinear uncertain system based on control Lyapunov function method," Journal of Systems Engineering and Electronics, vol. 17, pp. 619-623, 2006.

7

Performance Assessment of Multi-State Systems with Critical Failure Modes: Application to the Flotation Metallic Arsenic Circuit

Seraphin C. Abou
Mechanical and Industrial Engineering Department, University of Minnesota Duluth, 1305 Ordean Court, Duluth, MN 55812, USA

1. Introduction

Conventional reliability theory assumes that sub-systems and the system itself usually have two different states: on (*good, operating*) or off (*down, failed*). Owing to this assumption, the structural function of the system is a binary function of binary variables, and the respective model is usually referred to as binary reliability system. However, for many engineering systems, the binary assumption may not be appropriate for describing the possible states that each of the components may experience throughout its life cycle [3], [6], [7], [8].
Precise evaluation of the state probability and performance rate of an element in some multi-state systems is difficult. Some reasons come from inaccuracy and insufficiency of data. In a broad sense, if an event or a kind of behavior of these components meets a predetermined criterion, whatever the criterion is, then we say it is a success. If the criterion is violated, then a failure occurs. Indeed, the accident literature is replete with examples, including the space shuttle Challenger (Vaughan, 1996), Three Mile Island (Chiles, 2002), the London Paddington train crash (Cullen, 2000) and Gulf of Mexico oil disaster among many others. In practice, nonlinearities may be present that are capable of significantly affecting systems performance. Typical phenomena resulting from the presence of nonlinearities include the onset of stable limit cycle oscillations determined by linear theory, or the existence of unstable limit cycles within the linear flutter boundary associated with a sub-critical Hopf bifurcation.
Our motivation in this study is to carry out a theoretical study with practical relevance of nonlinear systems behavior and provide the performance analysis not in the time domain. Thus we assume that the function of safety is to locate and define the operational errors that allow accidents to occur. This function can be carried out in two ways: *i.*) by asking why accidents happen - searching for their root causes - and *ii.*) by assessing the performance levels of certain known effective engineering controls that are being utilized.
Causes of failure are diverse. They can be physical, human and logical or even financial [8]. Evidently, various kinds of criteria and factors can be taken into account to define what a failure means: structure, performance, cost and even subjective intention. However whatever a failure is, if effect of it tends to be critical, research on it becomes essential. In

traditional reliability theory, the components of a system and the system itself are usually assumed to have two different states: on (*good, operating*) or off (*down, failed*). [10], [21], [23], [26].

For instance, in fluid control networks, a defective valve may be either "*stuck-open*" or "*stuck-closed*", in safety monitoring systems, a device will malfunction if it "*fails to detect breakdown*" or "*initiates a false alarm*" etc. A structure whose components experience two different modes of failure is usually referred to as three-state device. A natural extension of the three-state devices is easily developed by assigning to each component $m \geq 2$ failure modes. The resulting structure will then be called *multistate system* (MSS), [14], [16].

In complex MSSs consisting of n elements, any element j, $1 \leq j \leq n$ can have k_j different states with corresponding performance rates (levels), which can be represented by the ordering set as follows, [13], [15]:

$$g_j = \left\{ g_{j,1}, \ldots, g_{j,i}, \ldots, g_{j,k_j} \right\} \tag{1}$$

where $g_{j,i}$ is the performance rate (level) of the element j in the state i; $i \in \left\{1, 2, \ldots, k_j\right\}$.

The performance rate $G_j(t)$ of element j at any instant $t \geq 0$ is a random variable that takes its values from $g_j : G_j(t) \in g_j$. Thus, the probabilities associated with different states for the element j can be represented by a set: $p_j = \left\{ p_{j,1}, \ldots, p_{j,i}, \ldots, p_{j,k_j} \right\}$

The mapping $g_{j,i} \rightarrow p_{j,i}$ is usually called the probability mass function, [13], [14], [16].

There are two fundamental assumptions in the conventional multi-state system reliability theory: *i.*) each state probability of an element, which composed a multi-state system, can be fully characterized by probability measures; and *ii.*) the state performance rate (level) of an element, which composed a multi-state system, can be precisely determined.

One approach to carry out a theoretical study of nonlinear systems behavior is to perform the analysis in the time domain. However, in the literature review, a drawback with this is that though it can yield a complete picture of system behavior for a particular set of initial conditions, it may be inefficient in providing an overall picture of multi-state systems characteristics even for a single set of sub-system parameters. System availability is represented by a multi-state availability/stability function, which extends the binary-state availability. In fact, because modern systems are large scale systems with complex interactions between their elements, precipitating incidents and accidents may have long incubation periods, making identification of a leading error chain difficult. To satisfy the required multi-state system availability, the redundancy principle for each component or universal generating function has been used in [14], [19]. Tavakkoli et al. (2008) assumed a predetermined and fixed redundancy strategy for each subsystem which became an additional decision variable.

In this paper the procedures for the reliability estimation of a flotation circuit is based on the universal generating function (u-function) technique, which was introduced in [21], and proved to be very effective for the reliability evaluation of different types of multistate systems [17], [9] and high dimension combinatorial problems. The u-function extends the widely known ordinary moment generating function [18]. As a result, the concepts of relevancy, availability, coherency, and equivalence defined in this paper are used to characterize the properties of the MSSs. Without loss of the generality, in the former case we assumed that for the MSSs, these properties are strongly related to the stability concept depicted in fig.1. This assumption makes it the unique exception that has been disregarded in the literature review [7], [20], [26] for the MSSs performance assessment.

Billinton R. & Allan R., (*Reliability evaluation of power systems*, 1990) have developed a comparison between four different methods of the assessment of the large scale MSSs reliability and highlighted that the technique is fast enough to be used in complex problems where the search space is sizeable. Throughout, the states which obey the operational constraints and are located inside the *polytope* (i.e., the *recovery zone*) are called *admissible states*. This constitutes a tradeoff between software performance and reliability (particularly with regard to computational time). Moreover in this study, for practical importance, we paid particular attention to the system state's future trajectory so that, after a switch, it stays within the set of the admissible states and converge to the set point.

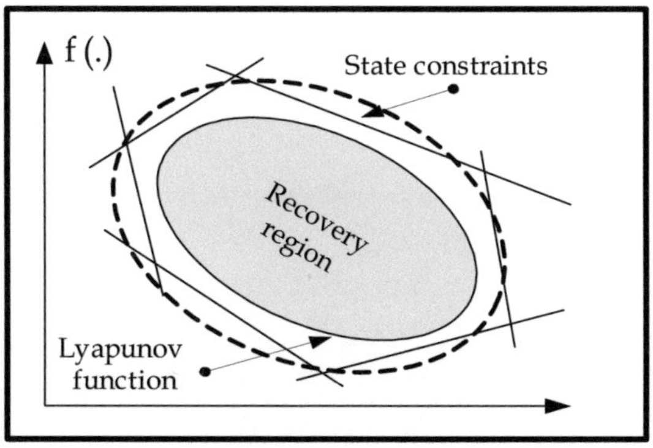

Fig. 1. State constraints and switching rule (*Lyapunov function*)

2. Method for estimating system performance

Performance is a key criterion in design, procurement, and usability of engineering system. In order to get the highest performance for the cost of a given system, an engineer needs, at least, a basic knowledge of performance evaluation terminology and techniques. An important problem in reliability theory is to determine the reliability of a complex system given the reliabilities of its components.
In real life the system and its components are capable of being in a whole range of states, varying from a perfect functioning state to states related to various levels of performance degradation to complete failure. Thus, the binary models are an oversimplification of the actual reality. This paper presents models and their applications in terms of reliability analysis to situations where the system can have whole range of states and all its components can also have whole range of multiple states. Generally a system has various levels of operational performance and hence the total system effectiveness measures should reflect all of these performance levels and their reliabilities. Evaluating design alternatives for linear systems, a number of methodologies are being used.

2.1 Transmitted flow model of linear systems

Let an expression of considerable importance of the design of a linear system be presented by the following block diagram, Fig. 2. *R* is the referential input and *C* is the output of the system.
Due to linear measurement characteristic of this system, the closed-loop block diagram, Fig. 2a.), could be reduced and replaced by an open loop block diagram, Fig. 2b.), with a new

transfer function G which gives the necessary and sufficient condition for stability in the frequency domain of the system.

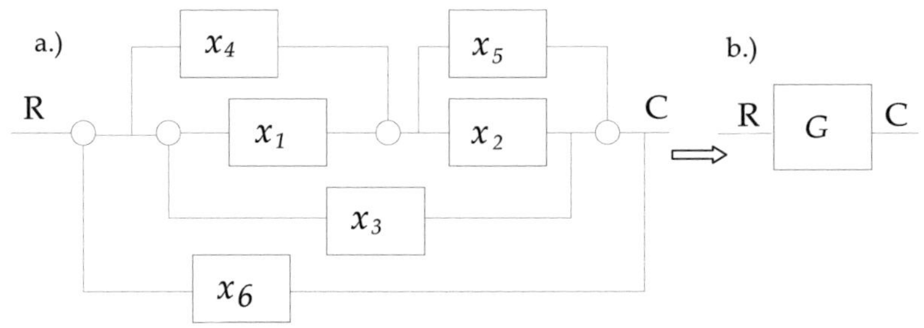

Fig. 2. Block diagram: a) Closed-loop representation b) Reduced block diagram in open-loop representation

The new function transfer G is defined as follows:

$$G = \frac{\left(1+\frac{x_4}{x_1}\right)\left(1+\frac{x_1 x_2}{x_1 x_2 x_3}\right)\left(1+\frac{x_5}{x_1}\right)}{1+\left(1+\frac{x_4}{x_1}\right)\left(1+\frac{x_1 x_2}{x_1 x_2 x_3}\right)\left(1+\frac{x_5}{x_1}\right)x_6} \tag{2}$$

After some involved mathematical manipulations, the function $\wp(s)$ which defines an autonomous system whose characteristic equation maps the dynamics of the open loop system is obtained based on Nyquist stability criterion:

$$\wp(s) = x_1^3 x_2 x_3 + (x_1 + x_4)(x_1 x_2 x_3 + x_1 x_2)(x_1 + x_5)x_6 \tag{3}$$

Hence, performance levels of the given linear system could be assessed upon the response of $\wp(s)$ to a step stimulus. However, nonlinear systems don't offer such simple deductive analysis without losing information while involving simplest assumptions to facilitate their linearization. In the following section, we describe the technique used for evaluating complex systems availability and statistically expected performance while the nominal performance level and availability of their elements are given for open and closed modes.

2.2 System structure and assumptions

Nonlinear system control architectures can include static and dynamic feedback components as well as logic-based switching or discrete event elements. Such complex structures may arise as a matter of design choice or due to intrinsic constraints on the class of controllers that can be implemented.

The system under consideration is a mineral process shown in fig. 3. A wet grinding model has been analyzed with the objective of evaluating the effects of many variables on particle size reduction in continuous grinding processes.

Detailed phenomenological model that describes the charge behaviour has been developed and validated against real data [1]. Indeed, mineral processes present nonlinear/chaotic dynamics. The circuit consists of three variable velocity feeders, a main fixed velocity feeder, a ball mill, a sump, a variable velocity pump and a battery of hydro-cyclones.

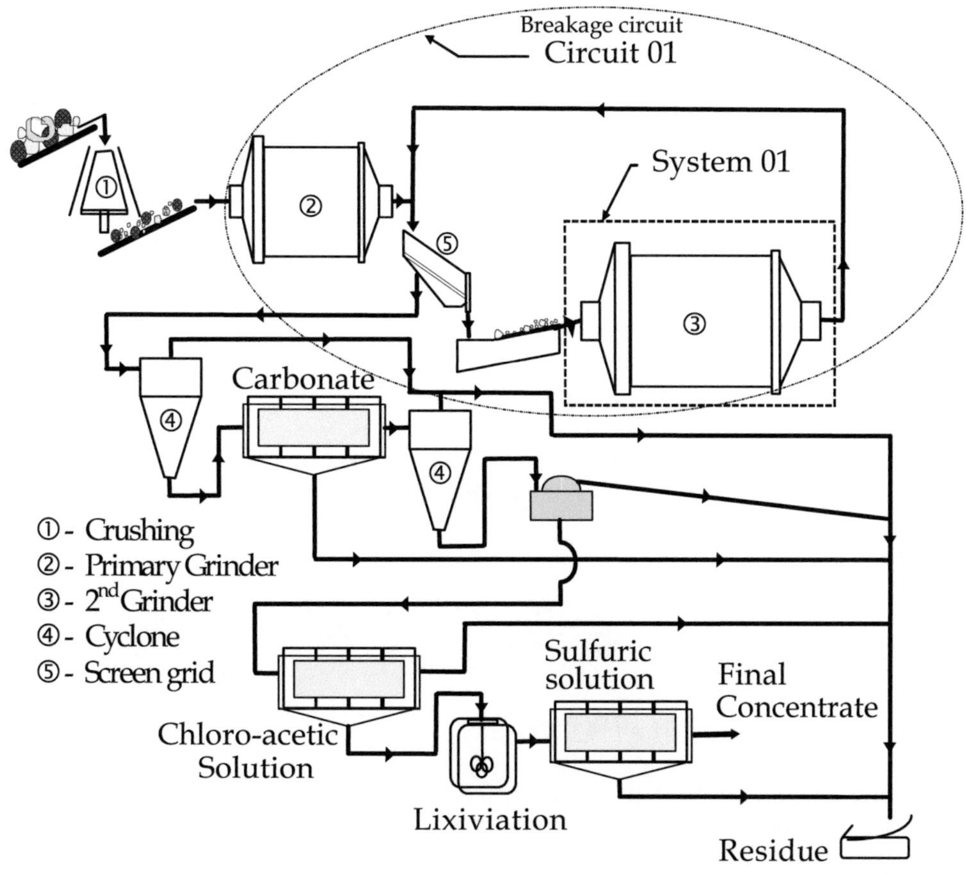

Fig. 3. Mineral processing

The fresh ore is transported towards the main feeder by the variable velocity feeders. Then it continues to the mill where water and the recirculated pulp are added. High performance level of the whole system determines the quality of the final product (the fineness of the grinded ore). This paper suggests reliability measures for complex systems. An important problem in reliability theory is to determine the reliability of a complex system given the reliabilities of its components. In real life, systems as shown in fig.3 and their components are capable of being in a whole range of states, varying from a perfect functioning state to states related to various levels of performance degradation to complete failure.

2.3 Interdependent systems

Reliability theory distinguishes between independent and dependent systems. For dependent systems "*component failures are in some way dependent*" [13]. The term interdependent system has emerged, which we consider to be a subclass of dependent systems. For a system to be interdependent, mutual dependence in the sense of two-way causation among at least two components must be present. For example, if a "*single failure*" component fails and affects the second component, the system is dependent, but if the second component does not affect the main component, the system is not interdependent. Examples occur within aircraft systems, computer networks, fire protection, biological systems, etc... In [11] an airline baggage checking system example was illustrated. It is costly for the airline, but has limited impact if luggage transferred from other airlines is not checked.

Since the expected damage could not be precisely determined, assume d_e as the expected damage and d_r as the real impact on an interdependent system. The utility of a system of n interdependent components are:

$$d_e = \sum_{i=1}^{n} \omega_i p_i ; \quad u = -\sum_{i=1}^{n} (\omega_i p_i + \kappa_i t_i) \tag{4}$$

$$d_r = \sum_{i=1}^{n} \varpi_i p_i ; \quad \mathrm{u_r} = \sum_{i=1}^{n} (\varpi_i p_i - \delta_i T_i) \tag{5}$$

An event may have a cumulative effect on the damage and the utility function. To account for interdependence between systems i and j the unreliable probability p_i is generalized as follow:

$$p_i = \left(\sum_{j=1}^{n} \ell_{ij} \left(t_j^{m_j} + T_j^{m_j} \right) \right)^{-1} \sum_{j=1}^{n} \ell_{ij} T_j^{m_j}$$
$$\begin{cases} i = j \rightarrow \ell_{ij} = 1 \\ i \neq j \rightarrow 0 \leq \ell_{ij} \leq 1 \end{cases} \tag{6}$$

where t_i is the expected time at unit cost κ_i for the component $\boldsymbol{i}$; ω_i is the value of the component $\boldsymbol{i}$; T_i is the duration of the damage at unit cost δ_i; ϖ_i is the damage value; p_i the probability the system becomes dysfunctional; ℓ_{ij} interdependence between systems i and j. Without interdependence $\ell_{ij} = 0$ for all $i \neq j$

2.3.1 Example of two interdependent systems

As illustrated in Fig. 2, assume components 1 and 3 are interdependent. Then (6) becomes:

$$p_1 = \left(T_1^{m_1} + \ell T_3^{m_3} \right) \left(t_1^{m_1} + T_1^{m_1} + \ell \left(t_3^{m_3} + T_3^{m_3} \right) \right)^{-1} \tag{7}$$

$$p_3 = \left(T_3^{m_3} + \ell T_1^{m_1} \right) \left(t_3^{m_3} + T_3^{m_3} + \ell \left(t_1^{m_1} + T_1^{m_1} \right) \right)^{-1} \tag{8}$$

$\ell_{31} = \ell_{13} = \ell$; and (4) and (5) becomes:

$$d_{e13} = \omega_1 p_1 + \omega_3 p_3 ; \; u_{13} = -\omega_1 p_1 - \omega_3 p_3 - \kappa_1 t_1 - \kappa_3 t_3$$

$$d_{r13} = \varpi_1 p_1 + \varpi_3 p_3 ; \; u_{r13} = \varpi_1 p_1 + \varpi_3 p_3 - \delta_1 T_1 - \delta_3 T_3$$

Appendix **A** solves the optimization problem when $m_i = 1$, and $\ell_{31} = \ell_{13} = \ell$ to yield:

$$t_1 = \omega_1^2 \varpi_1 (\delta_1 - \ell \delta_3) \left(\omega_1 \delta_1 + \varpi_1 \kappa_1 - \ell (\omega_1 \delta_3 + \varpi_1 \kappa_3) \right)^{-2} +$$

$$-\ell\omega_3^2\varpi_3\left(\delta_3-\ell\delta_1\right)\left(\omega_3\delta_3+\varpi_3\kappa_3-\ell\left(\omega_3\delta_1+\varpi_3\kappa_1\right)\right)^{-2}$$

$$p_1=\varpi_1\left(\kappa_1-\ell\kappa_3\right)\left(\omega_1\delta_1+\varpi_1\kappa_1-\ell\left(\omega_1\delta_3+\varpi_1\kappa_3\right)\right)^{-1} \tag{9}$$

In case $\omega_1=\omega_3$; $\varpi_1=\varpi_3$; $\kappa_1=\kappa_3$ and $\delta_1=\delta_3$

$$\begin{cases} t_1=t_3=\omega_1^2\varpi_1\delta_1\left(\omega_1\delta_1+\varpi_1\kappa_1\right)^{-2} \\ p_1=p_3=\varpi_1\kappa_1\left(\omega_1\delta_1+\varpi_1\kappa_1\right)^{-1} \end{cases} \tag{10}$$

To illustrate how the framework in this chapter can be used to analyze a specific system performance, consider the mineral processing plant in fig.3. In mineral processing, electrochemical potential and related engineering control (e.g. flow control valves) is considered as an important parameter for controlling the recovery and selectivity of sulphide minerals during flotation. Consider, as an example, the flotation circuit of the process shown in fig.3. Flotation circuit illustrated in fig.4 has been used in solid/solid separation applications using stable froths to recover the mineral particles. Flotation can be incorporated with wastewater-treatment schemes in the following ways: As a unit process for removing contaminants not separated by other processes or as a unit process for sludge thickening.

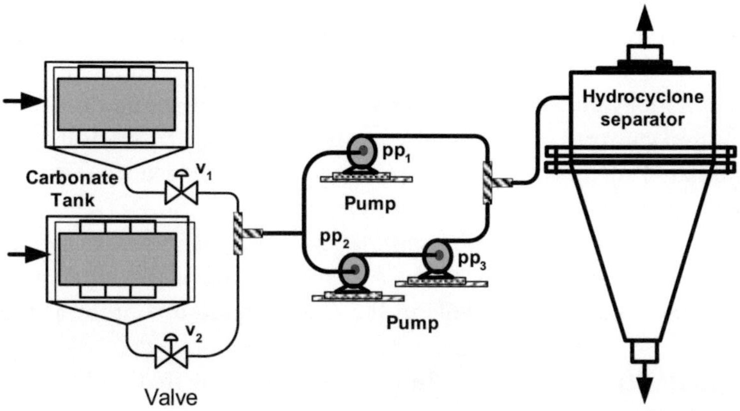

Fig. 4. Flotation circuit

The operating condition of the circuit in fig.4 is as follows: The minimum flow required for successful operation corresponds to the full capacity of one tank or one pump or one pipe. Any elementary component of the system (a tank, a pump or a pipe) is considered to have the following two states: *i.) No flow; ii.) Full flow.* These same states are considered to apply also for any subsystem. Each of the three pump-pipe subsystems can be modeled as two states homogeneous coherent (HC) system. We assume that these systems are multi-state systems *with two failure modes* (S2FM).
In the proposed technique applied to reliability analysis, components are characterized by two states: an up-state and a down-state (failure). We explore the possibility of studying system reliability, by modeling each component with a multi-state system approach, [13], [25]. Hence we focus on S2FM. The procedure of the reliability measures is based on the use

of a *universal generation function* (UGF), [22]. *Systems with two failure modes* consist of devices, which can fail in either of two modes. For instance, servo-valves in the flotation circuit, Fig. 4, can not only *fail to close* when commanded to close but can also *fail to open* when commanded to open. In this circuit, we consider components consisting of different elements characterized by nominal performance level in each mode.

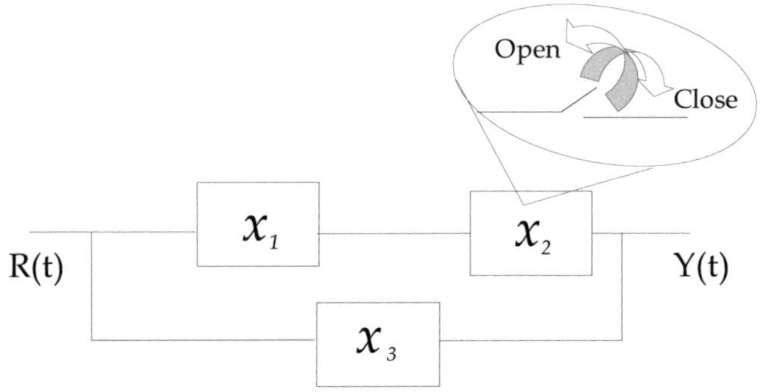

Fig. 5. Block diagram of switching element

Fig. 5 shows a switching element. For instance, a fluid flow valve and an electronic diode are two typical switching devices. Such components are multi-state because they have multiple performance levels in both modes, depending on the combination of elements available at the moment. As a result, the availability of the circuit could be defined as the probability of satisfaction of given constraints imposed on system performance in both modes (open and closed).

In this study, system availability $\varsigma_a(t)$ is considered to be a measure of its ability to meet the (demand) required performance level at each mode. Let $y_{p,m}(t)$ be output performances in mode m of the S2FM at time t. Thus $y_{p,c}(t)$ and $y_{p,o}(t)$ become output performances of the system at time t in its closed and open modes respectively.

Let $f_m(y_{p,m}(t),\eta_m)$ be function representing the desired relation between the system performance level and demand in mode m. The system fails in open mode if condition $f_o(y_{p,o}(t),\eta_o)\geq 0$ is not satisfied; it fails in the closed mode if condition $f_c(y_{p,c}(t),\eta_c)\geq 0$ is not satisfied.

Consider $P_r\left\{f_m(y_{p,m}(t),\eta_m)\right\}$ system failure in mode m. Note that, in the situation presented in Fig. 4, the occurrence probability of the failures in open and closed modes is the same for each component. This is a specific characteristic of homogeneous multi-state systems. Mathematically, a system is homogeneous when it obeys the commutative and the associative laws. As a result, because the failures in open and closed modes, which have probabilities:

$$\begin{cases} \vartheta_o(t,\eta_o) = P_r\left\{f_o(y_{p,o}(t),\eta_o)\right\} < 0 \\ \vartheta_c(t,\eta_c) = P_r\left\{f_c(y_{p,c}(t),\eta_c)\right\} < 0 \end{cases} \tag{11}$$

respectively are mutually exclusive events, and the probabilities of both modes are 0.5 (each command to close is followed by command to open and vice versa), the entire system availability $\varsigma_a(t)$ is defined as:

$$\varsigma_a(t,\eta_c,\eta_o) = 1 - 0.5\left(\vartheta_c(t,\eta_c) + \vartheta_o(t,\eta_o)\right) \tag{12}$$

where, η_c and η_o are required (demand) system output performances in the system's closed and open modes respectively.

While the application of design constraints and engineering relations can occasionally yield analytical relationships which can be exploited for system safety monitoring purposes, there are no global relationships which are able to transform complex measures of performance, like cost and usability, into analytical design relations. There are no such global analytical relationships because, by their very nature, they cannot incorporate the essence of the design process, which is the use of engineering judgment to develop strategies for solving multi-objective problems.

3. The u-function representation of system/ element performance distribution

The system depicted in Fig. 3 is a multi-state system and the capacity or productivity of its elements is the performance measure. The problem posed by this system is one of combinational optimization. The state of the system is determined by the states of its elements. Therefore, the performance rates (levels) of the system are determined by the performance levels of its elements. As a result, the independence of the evidence to be combined would obviously be satisfied if all components' models were completely different, that is, had no overlapping equations.

A conventional controller design procedure does not guarantee those requirements and it may not even be possible to develop such a set of models. Note that the overlapping equations exist in a different environment in each model. This is sufficient for the independence of evidence, in the sense that noise and modeling errors will cause different distortions to the probability assignments in the different models.

Assume the probability distribution σ_d of performance rates for all of the system elements at any instant $t \geq 0$ and system structure function as follows:

$$\begin{cases} g_j,\ p_j \rightarrow 1 \leq j \leq n \\ \phi(G_1(t) \ldots G_n) \end{cases} \tag{13}$$

In general, the total number of possible states or performance rates of the system is:

$$\pi = \prod_{j=1}^{n} k_j \tag{14}$$

Let $L_n = \prod_{j=1}^{n} \{x_{m,1}, \ldots, x_{m,k}\}$ be the space of possible combinations of performance rates for all system elements and $M = \left\{x_{m,1}, \ldots, x_{m,\pi_p}\right\}$ be the space of possible values of entire system performance levels.

The transform $\phi(G_1(t) \ldots G_n(t)) : L_n \rightarrow M$ which maps the space of performance rates of system elements into the space of system's performance rates, is the system structure function, [23].

The probability of the system to be in a given mode can be obtained as: $\sigma = \prod_{j=1}^{n} \sigma_{j,i}$; the performance rate for state i is:

$$g_i = \phi(x_{m,1}, \ldots, x_{m,i}) \tag{15}$$

The function $\phi(.)$ is strictly defined by the type of connection between elements in the reliability logic-diagram sense, i.e. on the structure of the logic-diagram representing the system/subsystem. Despite the fact that the universal generating function resembles a polynomial, it is not a polynomial because: *i.*) its exponents are not necessary scalar variables, but can be arbitrary mathematical objects (e.g. vectors); *ii.*) the operator defined over the universal generating function can differ from the operator of the polynomial product (unlike the ordinary generating function technique, only the product of polynomials is defined) [24].

For instance, consider a flow transmission system (e.g., ore, fluid, energy) shown in Fig.4, which consist of three elements. The system performance rate which is defined by its transmission capacity can have several discrete values depending on the state of control equipments. For instance, the element 1 has three states with the performance rates $g_{1,1}$ = 1.5, $g_{1,2}$ = 1, $g_{1,3}$ = 0 and the corresponding probabilities are $\sigma_{1,1}$ = 0.8, $\sigma_{1,2}$ = 0.1 and $\sigma_{1,3}$ = 0.1. The element 2 has three states with the performance rates $g_{2,1}$ = 2, $g_{2,2}$ = 1.5, $g_{2,3}$= 0 and the corresponding probabilities $\sigma_{2,1}$= 0.7, $\sigma_{2,2}$ = 0.22 and $\sigma_{2,3}$ = 0.08. The element 3 has two states with the performance rates $g_{3,1}$ = 4, $g_{3,2}$ = 0 and the corresponding probabilities $\sigma_{3,1}$ = 0.98 and $\sigma_{3,2}$ = 0.02. According to (9) the total number of the possible combinations of the states of elements is $\pi = 3\times 3\times 2 = 18$.

In order to obtain the output performance for the entire system with the arbitrary structure function $\phi(.)$, a general composition operator ∂_ϕ over individual universal z-transform representations of n system elements is defined as follows:

$$\begin{cases} U(z) = \partial_\phi\left(u_1(z), \ldots, u_n(z)\right) \\ u(z) = \sum_{i=1}^{k_j} \sigma_{j,i} . z^{g_{j,i}} \end{cases}$$
$$U(z) = \sum_{i}^{k_1}\sum_{i}^{k_2}\ldots\sum_{i}^{k_n}\left(z^{\phi(x_{m,1},\ldots,x_{m,n})} . \prod_{j=1}^{n} \sigma_j \right) \tag{16}$$

where $U(z)$ is z-transform representation of output performance distribution for the entire system; $u(z)$ is a polynomial u-function of a multi-state stationary output performance.

Note that, each term of the polynomials relates probability of a certain combination of states of the subsystems to the performance level of the entire system corresponding to the combination of states defined by $\phi(x_{m,1}, ..x_{m,i}.., x_{m,n})$.

Hence for a single element ***i*** in mode m, the individual u-function is:

$$u_{m,i}(z) = \varsigma_{am,i} . z^{x_{m,i}} + (1 - \varsigma_{am,i}) . z^{\tilde{x}_{m,i}} \tag{17}$$

where, $x_{m,i}$ is a nominal performance level; $\tilde{x}_{m,i}$ is fault state performance level; $\varsigma_{am,i}$ is the availability.

Moreover, the definition of $\phi(.)$ also depends on the physical nature of system-performance level and on the nature of the interaction between elements. The system performance distributions in open and closed modes can be defined as follows:

$$\begin{cases} u_o(z) = \sum_{i=1}^{k_j} \sigma_{o,i} . z^{y_{p0,i}} \\ u_c(z) = \sum_{i=1}^{k_j} \sigma_{c,i} . z^{y_{pc,i}} \end{cases} \tag{18}$$

The probability that the conditions stated in (4) are met is determined as follows:

$$\begin{cases} \vartheta_o(t,\eta_o) = P_r\left\{ \mathrm{f}_o(y_{p,o}(t),\eta_o) \right\} < 0 \\ \qquad = \sum_{i=1}^{k_j} \sigma_{o,i} \mathrm{f}_o(y_{p,o}(t),\eta_o) < 0 \end{cases}$$
$$\begin{cases} \vartheta_c(t,\eta_c) = P_r\left\{ \mathrm{f}_c(y_{p,c}(t),\eta_c) \right\} < 0 \\ \qquad = \sum_{i=1}^{k_j} \sigma_{c,i} \mathrm{f}_c(y_{p,c}(t),\eta_c) < 0 \end{cases} \tag{19}$$

Thus, we could determine the anticipated performance of the system in mode m. Using the system's output performance distribution, the statistically expected performance in mode m can be determined as:

$$E_m = \sum_{i=1}^{k_j} \sigma_{m,i} \cdot y_{pm,i} \tag{20}$$

It is very important to point out that, in the worst case, the operation time of the entire system goes to infinity. As a result, the determination of the statistically expected performance E_m using (12) makes no sense. Therefore, the more reasonable way of evaluating the statistically expected performance is by using the *statistically expected operation time* in the range of its finite values (i.e., the conditional statistically expected performance, given the operation time, is finite). In this case, (12) becomes:

$$E_{m,op} = \frac{\sum_{i=1}^{k_j} \left(\sigma_{m,i} \cdot y_{pm,i} \right)}{\sum_{i=1}^{k_j} \sigma_{m,i}} \tag{21}$$

4. Algorithms for determining system reliability in failure modes

In order to estimate both, systems' statistically expected operation time and its performance, different measures can be used depending on the application. The froth phase is extremely important in the operation of a flotation cell shown in fig.4, because, it is critical in determining the amount of unwanted gangue collected in the concentrate which, in turn, affects the purity of the product. Since the execution time of each task is of critical importance in this process, the system reliability is defined (according to performability concept) as a probability that the correct output is produced in less time than its maximal finite realization time allowed.

The above functions can be used for defining the operator for verity of configurations: series, parallel, and bridge connection of multi-state subsystems and the -functions of individual switching elements for two different types of system with two failure modes. These systems are distinguished by their specific performance measures which are: transmitted flow that characterizes performance of flow valves, and operation time that characterizes performance of electronic switches.

In general, failures reduce element performance and therefore, different performance degradation levels should be considered. This algorithm is developed to evaluate the *transmitted flow* and the *operation time models.*

To assess performance of multi-state systems when subsystems are not bridged, one should consider composition operators over pairs of u-functions corresponding to the elements connected in series and parallel and use a recursive procedure to determine the u-function of the entire series-parallel system. The following section presents algorithms for determining performance distributions and the distribution of the total execution time.

4.1 Operation time model

The operation time is the time between '*the instant when a command arrives to the system*' and '*the instant when the command fulfillment is completed*'.

In Fig. 5, systems are presented by multi-state systems for which the performance measure is characterized by the operation time. The availability assessment of this category includes control systems, and data processing systems without regard to computation time efficiency.

Consider for instance, proportional valves v_1 and v_2 connected in parallel within the flotation circuit. The command to open is fulfilled by the system only when it is fulfilled by both subsystems (valves). Therefore, the system operation time in the open mode is the greatest of the operation times of the subsystems. The composition operator $\phi(.)$ for the open mode $(m = 0)$ is obtained as follows:

$$\phi_0\left(\eta_{o,v1}, \eta_{o,v2}\right) = \max\left(\eta_{o,v1}, \eta_{o,v2}\right) \tag{22}$$

On the other hand, for pumps pp_1 and pp_2 connected in series the first disconnected pump disconnects the entire piping in the open mode $(m = 0)$. In this case, operator $\phi_s(.)$ for the open mode is:

$$\phi_{s,o}\left(\eta_{o,pp1}, \eta_{o,pp2}\right) = \min\left(\eta_{o,pp1}, \eta_{o,pp2}\right) \tag{23}$$

where the performance $\eta_{m,i}$ in mode m of an element i is defined as its operation time.

In closed mode $(m = c)$, the operation time of the system is the shortest of the operation times of the subsystems in parallel. Therefore, the composition operator $\phi_p(.)$ is defined for valves v_1 and v_2 in parallel as follows:

$$\phi_{p,c}\left(\eta_{c,v1}, \eta_{c,v2}\right) = \min\left(\eta_{c,v1}, \eta_{c,v2}\right) \tag{24}$$

However, for pumps pp_1 and pp_2 connected in series, both of them should fulfill the command to close in order to make the system closed $(m = c)$.

$$\phi_{s,c}\left(\eta_{c,v1},\eta_{c,v2}\right) = \max\left(\eta_{c,v1},\eta_{c,v2}\right) \tag{25}$$

Consider a system with n elements with total failures in open and closed modes. Assume the element operates in times τ_o and τ_c in open and closed modes respectively. If the element fails to operate, its operation time goes to infinity: $\tau \to \infty$. In parallel configuration, we have:

$$\begin{cases} u_{p,c}(z) = (1-(1-\varepsilon_c)^n).z^{\tau_c} + (1-\varepsilon_c)^n.z^{\infty} \\ u_{p,o}(z) = \varepsilon_o^n.z^{\tau_o} + (1-\varepsilon_o)^n.z^{\infty} \end{cases} \tag{26}$$

where ε_o and ε_c are probabilities in open and closed modes respectively.
In series configuration, the u-function is given as:

$$\begin{cases} u_{s,c}(z) = \varepsilon_c^n.z^{\tau_c} + (1-\varepsilon_c)^n.z^{\infty} \\ u_{s,o}(z) = (1-(1-\varepsilon_o)^n).z^{\tau_o} + (1-\varepsilon_o)^n.z^{\infty} \end{cases} \tag{27}$$

Despite composition operators are implemented for the operation time, another paradigm in multi-state system assessment is based on transmitted flow model. This is achieved according to the following stages.

4.2 Transmitted flow model

Transmitted flow is the amount of flow that passes through the system during each time unit. That flow is equal to the sum capacity of each subsystem:

$$\phi_{m,k}\left(\eta_{m,1},\ldots\ldots,\eta_{m,n}\right) = \sum_{k=1}^{n}\eta_{m,k} \tag{28}$$

The composition operator for the entire system is:

$$U_{m,k}(z) = \sum_{k}^{n_1}\sum_{k}^{n_2}\ldots\sum_{k}^{n_n}\sigma_{m,1}\bullet\bullet\bullet\sigma_{m,k}\bullet z^{\sum\eta_{m,1},\ldots\ldots,\eta_{m,n}} \tag{29}$$

In series configuration, (18) becomes:

$$\phi_{s,m}\left(\eta_{m,1},\ldots\ldots,\eta_{m,n}\right) = \min\left(\eta_{m,1},\ldots\ldots,\eta_{m,n}\right) \tag{30}$$

where the random performance $\eta_{m,i}$ in mode m of an element i is defined as its transmitting capacity, τ_m. In the failure state it will fail to transmit any flow, $\tau_m = 0$.
The u-function of an individual flow transmitting element in open and closed mode is defined as follows:

$$\begin{cases} u_o(z) = \varepsilon_o.z^0 + (1-\varepsilon_o)z^{\tau_o} \\ u_c(z) = \varepsilon_c.z^{\tau_o} + (1-\varepsilon_c).z^0 \end{cases} \tag{31}$$

where τ_o is the nominal flow transmitted.

An individual flow transmitting element with total failures in the closed mode, $(m = c)$, and operational state with probability ε_c, transmits nominal flow τ_o. In general, failures reduce system performance and, therefore, different performance degradation should be considered.

4.3 Control valve processing speed distribution

The electro-hydraulic valves in use in metallurgy require a reliable servo valve system tailored to provide high reliability within permissible weight and space-volume parameters. Specifically, the servo valve system includes a control system, an actuator and a main spool. If a pilot valve sticks at any position, the main stage spool of the valve could stroke unpredictably to either endpoint.

Hardware–software components are failure-prone. Their performance with regard to computation time constitutes a tradeoff between software performance and reliability. The distribution of task execution time of a control valve, such as in Fig. 4, was not explicitly determined in the above procedures.

Since the performance of the control valve depends on hardware processing speed (which in its turn depends on availability of computational resources), the impact of hardware availability should be taken into account when the system performance and availability are evaluated. Different measures are appropriate to different application areas. The reliability index we generate for control valve processing analysis can be referred to as $R(\infty)=Pr(T_t< \infty)$ (which is equal to the probability that the random execution time, T_t, is not greater than its maximal finite realization). As a result, the *conditional expected system execution time,* T_E(given the system produces correct output) is considered to be a measure of its performance. This index determines the expected execution time of the system given that the system does not fail. It can be obtained as:

$$\begin{cases} \tau_E = \dfrac{\sum_{i=1}^{n}\sum_{j=1}^{n} Q_{i,j} t_{ij}}{R(\infty)} \\ t_{ij} = \dfrac{h_j}{s_i} = \dfrac{h_{j-1} + (n-j+1)(c_j - c_{j-1})}{s_i} \end{cases} \tag{32}$$

where c_j is the computational complexity of the jth version; Q_{ij} is the probability that the task terminates after stage i; t_{ij} is the total time of task execution.

More importantly, note that software can have small unnoticeable errors or drifts that can culminate into a disaster. Fixing problems may not necessarily make the software more reliable. On the contrary, new serious problems may arise. Different from traditional hardware reliability, software reliability is not a direct function of time. Therefore, the distribution of the number of correct outputs after the execution of a group of first ***j*** versions is given as follows:

$$\begin{cases} \xi_j(z) = \prod_{j=1}^{k} \upsilon_j(z) = \sum_{j=1}^{k} \alpha_j z^j \\ \quad = \xi_{j-1}(z)\upsilon_j(z) \\ \upsilon_j(z) = a_j z^1 + (1-a_j) z^0 \end{cases} \tag{33}$$

The u-function which defines the performance of the processing units is:

$$u_i(z) = b_i z^{\beta_i} + (1-b_i)z^0 \tag{34}$$

where β_i is the performance of the ith PU with probability b_i
The composition operator which defines the performance distribution of a pair of PUs is the product of the corresponding polynomials:

$$\begin{cases} U(z) = u_i(z) \otimes u_j(z) \\ \quad = \left[b_i z^{\beta_i} + (1-b_i)z^0\right]\left[b_j z^{\beta_j} + (1-b_j)z^0\right] \end{cases} \tag{35}$$

Using the probability mass function, $f_m = \sum_{j}^{n} a_j z^{t_{ij}}$ one could determine the task execution time distribution:

$$\tau_d = f_m(z) \underset{\sim}{\otimes} U(z) = \sum_{i=1}^{n}\sum_{j=1}^{n} Q_{i,j} z^{t_{ij}} \tag{36}$$

To use composition operators, one should find the u-function of the entire multi-state system. To do this, first determine the individual u-functions of each element. The following algorithm is used to formulate the composition operators and determine the performance of multi-state systems.

1. Determine the u-function of each subsystem
2. Define the initial value $\xi_0(z) = 1$ (for software reliability only)
3. Find u-function of the entire parallel-series pair of components
4. For all versions of the software involved determine $\xi_j(z)$ and assign the coefficient in $\xi_j(z)$ to the probability, a_j, that the set of k version produce exactly ***j*** correct outputs

Despite the operator's expertise and knowledge of the inference states of all subsystems, it is noteworthy that the reliability of the presented multi-state system is dependent on the efficiency and performance of the valves and controls involved in operating the mineral processing. Specifically, servo valves form a critical link in flow transmitting mode and a malfunction of these components is detrimental to the smooth operation of the flotation mechanism.

We had to work with the expected conditional distributions of variables associated to a specific failure mode m, given the values of variables associated to the preceding failure modes ($m-1$). A direct consequence of this observation is that, one could probably improve on the reliability value by considering all $m!$ (*m factorial*) possible modes and choosing the one that successfully address users needs. It is however unclear that the slight improvement achieved by that compensates for the additional computational effort is needed.

5. Numerical example

As above pointed out, several configurations of multiple failure mode systems could be constructed by placing the conventional single failure mode systems in a multi-state environment. For example, considering a relay circuit with a bridge structure topology and assuming that each of the components can be either *"failed-open"* or *"failed-closed"* gives birth to a typical multiple failure mode systems. In this sense, the well known *k-out-of-n*, *consecutive k-out-of-n* systems and their generalization (the interested reader may refer to the monograph by Kuo (2003)) can be effortlessly adjusted to a multi-state environment.

In this section we shall proceed to the numerical evaluation of the proposed algorithm for dual failure mode system (S2FM). It is a series-parallel flow transmission switching system with the configuration shown in fig.4. The system is characterized by its availability and performance-level in open and close modes. For a flow transmission system, the performance of an element is its transmitting capacity, τ . For a system of electronic switches, the performance of an element is determined by its operation times in open mode, τ_0 , and in closed mode, τ_c .

In order to determine the system-performance distribution in the open and closed modes, one has to obtain the u-function of the entire system using composition operators over u-functions of individual elements. Consider a control hardware system consists of two PUs; software with k = 3, n = 6 (number of versions that may produce correct result and the total number of software versions, respectively). The availability, computing reliability, computational complexity of the software, speed, and parameters of the system elements are presented in Table 1. Due to operational conditions, sensors produce large amount of data to account for specific experiments, hence connectivity to computational resources is provided well in excess of normal throughput rates. Moreover, modularity is accomplished on a stage basis such that a large number of sensors are accommodated at modest overhead for scalability.

Version : *i*	**1**	**2**	**3**	**4**	**5**	**6**
c_i	7	8	13	15	18	19
a_i	0.68	0.82	0.71	0.9	0.84	0.92
b_i	0.93	0.82	Parameters of PUs			
β_i	4	7				

Table 1. Parameter of system elements and the control software

The distribution of the system cumulative processing speed using u-function (25) is as follows:

$$\begin{cases} U(z) = u_i(z) \otimes u_k(z) = u_1(z) \times u_2(z) \\ \quad = (0.93z^4 + 0.07z^0)(0.82z^7 + 0.18z^0) \\ \quad = 0.76z^{11} + 0.06z^7 + 0.17z^4 + 0.01z^0 \end{cases} \tag{37}$$

After we removed terms corresponding to total hardware failure:

$$U(z) = 0.76z^{11} + 0.06z^7 + 0.17z^4$$

The number of computations till termination of each stage $\boldsymbol{h_j}$ is:

$$h_j = h_{j-1} + (n - j + 1)(c_j - c_{j-1})$$

$$h_0 = 0\,;\; h_1 = 0 + 6(7-0) = 42\,;\; h_2 = 42 + 5(8-7) = 47$$

Successive iteration gives: $h_3 = 67$; $h_4 = 73$; $h_5 = 79$; $h_6 = 80$;
We could use the algorithm to determine $\xi_j(z)$, and then define the probability a_j. Based on data provided in Table 1, we have:

$$\begin{aligned} &V_0(z) = 1;\; \upsilon_1(z) = 0.68z^1 + 0.32z^0;\; V_1(z) = V_0(z).\upsilon_1(z) \\ &V_2(z) = V_1(z).\upsilon_2(z) = 0.61z^2 + 0.36z^1 + 0.03z^0 \\ &V_3(z) = V_2(z).\upsilon_3(z) = 0.5z^3 + 0.40z^2 + 0.09z^1 + 0.006z^0 \end{aligned} \tag{38}$$

Remove the term $0.5z^3$ from $V_3(z)$ and obtain: $a_3 = 0.5$

$$V_4(z) = V_3(z).\upsilon_4(z) = (0.40z^2 + 0.09z^1 + 0.006z^0)\upsilon_4(z) \tag{39}$$

$$V_4(z) = 0.36z^3 + 0.08z^2 + 0.06z^1 + 0.1z^0$$

Remove the term $0.36z^3$ from $V_4(z)$ and obtain: $a_4 = 0.36$; thus

$$V_4(z) = 0.08z^2 + 0.06z^1 + 0.1z^0$$

Continuously we have:

$$V_5(z) = V_4(z).\upsilon_5(z) = 0.07z^3 + 0.064z^2 + 0.09z^1 + 0.016z^0\,;\quad a_5 = 0.07\,;$$

$$V_6(z) = V_5(z).\upsilon_6(z) = 0.06z^3 + 0.09z^2 + 0.022z^1 + 0.001z^0\;;\quad a_6 = 0.06\,;$$

Finally the probability mass distribution, f_m, is given using a_j and h_j:

$$f_m = 0.5z^{67} + 0.36z^{73} + 0.07z^{79} + 0.06z^{80} \tag{40}$$

The u-function representing the task execution time distribution, T_s, is calculated using (26):

$$\tau_s = (0.5z^{67} + 0.36z^{73} + 0.07z^{79} + 0.06z^{80}) \underset{\sim}{\otimes} (0.76z^{11} + 0.06z^7 + 0.17z^4) \tag{41}$$

$$\begin{aligned} \tau_s = {} & 0.38z^{6.09} + 0.274z^{6.64} + 0.0532z^{7.18} + 0.0456z^{7.27} + \\ & + 0.03z^{9.57} + 0.0216z^{10.43} + 0.0042z^{11.29} + 0.0036z^{11.43} + \\ & + 0.085z^{16.75} + 0.0612z^{18.25} + 0.012z^{19.75} + 0.0102z^{20} \end{aligned} \tag{42}$$

As a result, the probability, $R(\infty)$ the system will provide a correct output is: $R(\infty) = 98\%$
Using the above result, we determine the probability the system will produce a correct output in time less than 9 seconds is: $R(9)$ = 75.2%
Note that $R(\infty)$ is determined without respect to the task execution time. Using (22), we determine the conditional expected system time, $\tau_E = 8.6$ For practical engineering situation presented in figure 2, the system failure is defined as its inability to provide at least the required level of flow, in its closed mode, m_c, and to prevent the flow exceeding the setting point, in its open mode, m_o. The failure of the servo-valve is defined as its incapability to switch within required time, η.

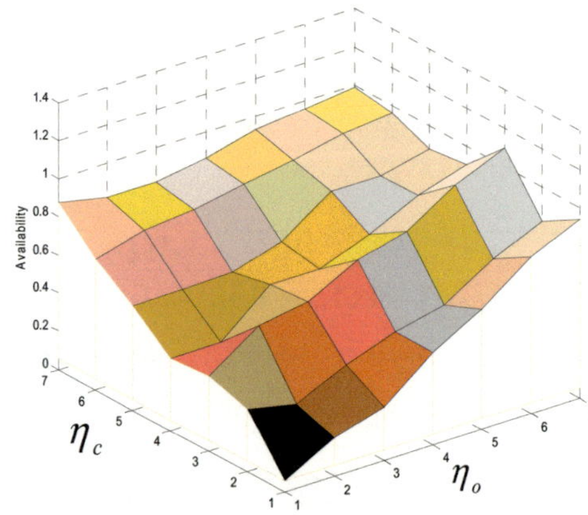

Fig. 6. Electro-valve availability *vs* demands in open and closed modes

Fig. 6 illustrates the availability of the electro-valves as a function of required switching times, $\varsigma_a(\eta_c,\eta_o)$, in the open, m_o, and closed, m_c modes. It maps the performance of the electro-valves according to their switching modes. Due to the inertia of the valves, more than 50% of their availability is reached in time ≥ 3seconds in either one (open or closed) mode.

The above example determined the probability that the system can produce truthful output, both without respect to the task execution time, and with task execution time less than 9 seconds respectively $R(\infty)$ and $R(9)$. Figure 7 depicts the corresponding reliability function $R(t^*)$ of the system to successfully execute its task in time less than t^* for a given value of ***m*** (number of versions that should produce exact results).

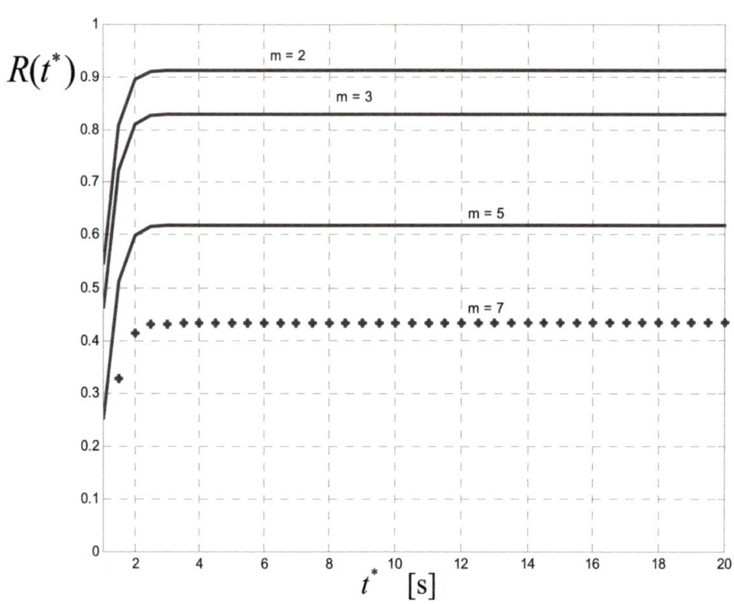

Fig. 7. Reliability function $R(t^{\circ})$ for different values of m

6. Conclusion

The failure concept used in this paper is suitable for hardware and software components. It primarily deals with a broader spectrum of failures, many of which cannot be directly traced to a part failure or to any physical failure mechanism. The assumptions ignore variations in maintenance practices, load changes or additions, changing environmental conditions, circuit alterations, etc.

The developed approach can also be applied to fast evaluation of the upper bound of system performance, which is important when different system designs are compared or when system configuration optimization problems are solved in which approximate estimates of system performance should be obtained for large number of different solutions.

Although the approach does not take into consideration imperfect software task parallelization and existence of common cause failures in both hardware and software, it can be useful as a theoretical framework for in dept development of more sophisticated models.

We provided some approximate distributions for sample estimators of the measures, and approximate tests of hypotheses. Our major concerns are that, the measures of performance used by an empirical investigator should not be blindly chosen because of tradition and convention only, although these factors may properly be given some weight, but should be constructed in a manner having operational meaning within the context of the particular problem.

Appendix A: Solving the optimization problem in section 2.3

Differentiating the utilities in (6) - (8) with respect to the free choice variables when $\ell_{31} = \ell_{13} = \ell$ and $m_k = 1$ gives the first order conditions:

$$\begin{aligned}
\frac{\partial u_{13}}{\partial t_1} &= \omega_1 (T_1 + \ell T_3)(t_1 + T_1 + \ell(t_3 + T_3))^{-2} + \ell\omega_3 (T_3 + \ell T_1)(t_3 + T_3 + \ell(t_1 + T_1))^{-2} - \kappa_1 = 0 \\
\frac{\partial u_{13}}{\partial t_3} &= \omega_3 (T_3 + \ell T_1)(t_3 + T_3 + \ell(t_1 + T_1))^{-2} + \ell\omega_1 (T_1 + \ell T_3)(t_1 + T_1 + \ell(t_3 + T_3))^{-2} - \kappa_3 = 0 \\
\frac{\partial u_{r13}}{\partial T_1} &= \varpi_1 (t_1 + \ell t_3)(t_1 + T_1 + \ell(t_3 + T_3))^{-2} + \ell\varpi_3 (t_3 + \ell t_1)(t_3 + T_3 + \ell(t_1 + T_1))^{-2} - \delta_1 = 0 \\
\frac{\partial u_{r13}}{\partial T_3} &= \varpi_3 (t_3 + \ell t_1)(t_3 + T_3 + \ell(t_1 + T_1))^{-2} + \ell\varpi_1 (t_1 + \ell t_3)(t_1 + T_1 + \ell(t_3 + T_3))^{-2} - \delta_3 = 0
\end{aligned} \tag{A1}$$

Since are two possible decision variables, we consider the Hessian matrices. Maximum utilities exist when matrices are negative semi-define, which occurs when $|H_{11}| \le 0$, which is satisfied, and $\begin{vmatrix} H_{11} & H_{12} \\ H_{21} & H_{22} \end{vmatrix} \ge 0$.

$$H = \begin{vmatrix} \dfrac{\partial^2 u_{13}}{\partial t_1^2} & \dfrac{\partial^2 u_{13}}{\partial t_1 \partial t_3} \\ \dfrac{\partial^2 u_{13}}{\partial t_3 \partial t_1} & \dfrac{\partial^2 u_{13}}{\partial t_3^2} \end{vmatrix}; \quad H_r = \begin{vmatrix} \dfrac{\partial^2 u_{r13}}{\partial T_1^2} & \dfrac{\partial^2 u_{r13}}{\partial T_1 \partial T_3} \\ \dfrac{\partial^2 u_{r13}}{\partial T_3 \partial T_1} & \dfrac{\partial^2 u_{r13}}{\partial T_3^2} \end{vmatrix}$$

Note that: $\frac{\partial^2 u_{13}}{\partial t_3 \partial t_1} = \frac{\partial^2 u_{13}}{\partial t_1 \partial t_3}$ and $\frac{\partial^2 u_{r13}}{\partial T_3 \partial T_1} = \frac{\partial^2 u_{r13}}{\partial T_1 \partial T_3}$

$$\frac{\partial^2 u_{13}}{\partial t_1^2} = -2\omega_1 (T_1 + \ell T_3)(t_1 + T_1 + \ell(t_3 + T_3))^{-3} - 2\ell^2 \omega_3 (T_3 + \ell T_1)(t_3 + T_3 + \ell(t_1 + T_1))^{-3} \leq 0 \quad (A2)$$

$$\frac{\partial^2 u_{13}}{\partial t_3^2} = -2\omega_3 (T_3 + \ell T_1)(t_3 + T_3 + \ell(t_1 + T_1))^{-3} - 2\ell^2 \omega_1 (T_1 + \ell T_3)(t_1 + T_1 + \ell(t_3 + T_3))^{-3} \leq 0 \quad (A3)$$

$$\frac{\partial^2 u_{13}}{\partial t_1 \partial t_3} = -2\omega_1 (T_1 + \ell T_3)(t_1 + T_1 + \ell(t_3 + T_3))^{-3} - 2\ell \omega_3 (T_3 + \ell T_1)(t_3 + T_3 + \ell(t_1 + T_1))^{-3} \leq 0 \quad (A4)$$

$$\frac{\partial^2 u_{r13}}{\partial T_1^2} = -2\varpi_1 (t_1 + \ell t_3)(t_1 + T_1 + \ell(t_3 + T_3))^{-3} - 2\ell^2 \varpi_3 (t_3 + \ell t_1)(t_3 + T_3 + \ell(t_1 + T_1))^{-3} \leq 0 \quad (A5)$$

$$\frac{\partial^2 u_{r13}}{\partial T_3^2} = -2\varpi_3 (t_3 + \ell t_1)(t_3 + T_3 + \ell(t_1 + T_1))^{-3} - 2\ell^2 \varpi_3 (t_1 + \ell t_3)(t_1 + T_1 + \ell(t_3 + T_3))^{-3} \leq 0 \quad (A6)$$

$$\frac{\partial^2 u_{r13}}{\partial T_1 \partial T_3} = -2\ell \varpi_1 (t_1 + \ell t_3)(t_1 + T_1 + \ell(t_3 + T_3))^{-3} - 2\ell \varpi_3 (t_3 + \ell t_1)(t_3 + T_3 + \ell(t_1 + T_1))^{-3} \leq 0 \quad (A7)$$

In order to protect the system, the approach strategically satisfies the following:

$$\begin{vmatrix} H_{11} & H_{12} \\ H_{21} & H_{22} \end{vmatrix} = 4\omega_1\omega_3 (1 - \ell^2)^2 (T_3 + \ell T_1)(t_1 + T_1 + \ell(t_3 + T_3))^{-3} (t_3 + T_3 + \ell(t_1 + T_1))^{-3} \geq 0 \quad (A8)$$

Mathematical manipulation of (A1) we get:

$$\begin{cases} \omega_1 (T_1 + \ell T_3)(t_1 + T_1 + \ell(t_3 + T_3))^{-2} = (\kappa_1 - \ell\kappa_3)(1 - \ell^2)^{-1} \\ \varpi_1 (t_1 + \ell t_3)(t_1 + T_1 + \ell(t_3 + T_3))^{-2} = (\delta_1 - \ell\delta_3)(1 - \ell^2)^{-1} \end{cases}$$

The above system of equation is simplified as follows:

$$t_1 + \ell t_3 = \omega_1 (\delta_1 - \ell\delta_3)(T_1 + \ell T_3)\left[\varpi_1 (\kappa_1 - \ell\kappa_3)\right]^{-1}$$

$$T_1 + \ell T_3 = \omega_1 \varpi_1^2 (\kappa_1 - \ell\kappa_3)(1 - \ell^2) \times (\omega_1\delta_1 + \kappa_1\varpi_1 - \ell(\omega_1\delta_3 + \kappa_3\varpi_1))^{-2} \quad (A9)$$

Combining the above equations yields:

$$t_1 + \ell t_3 = \omega_1^2 \varpi_1 (\delta_1 - \ell\delta_1)(1 - \ell^2) \times (\omega_1\delta_1 + \kappa_1\varpi_1 - \ell(\omega_1\delta_3 + \kappa_3\varpi_1))^{-2} \quad (A10)$$

Repeating the procedure above gives:

$$T_3 + \ell T_1 = \omega_3 \varpi_3^2 (\kappa_3 - \ell\kappa_1)(1-\ell^2) \times (\omega_3\delta_3 + \kappa_3\varpi_3 - \ell(\omega_3\delta_1 + \kappa_1\varpi_3))^{-2} \quad \text{(A11)}$$

$$t_3 + \ell t_1 = \omega_3^2 \varpi_3 (\delta_3 - \ell\delta_1)(1-\ell^2) \times (\omega_3\delta_3 + \kappa_3\varpi_3 - \ell(\omega_3\delta_1 + \kappa_1\varpi_3))^{-2} \quad \text{(A12)}$$

Equations (A10) and (A12) are two equations with two unknown which are solved to yield (9). Analogously, equations (A9) and (A11) are solved to yield:

$$\begin{aligned} T_1 = {} & \omega_1 \varpi_1^2 (\kappa_1 - \ell\kappa_3)(\omega_1\delta_1 + \varpi_1\kappa_1 - \ell(\omega_1\delta_3 + \varpi_1\kappa_3))^{-2} - \\ & -\ell\omega_3\varpi_3^2(\kappa_3 - \ell\kappa_1)(\omega_3\delta_3 + \varpi_3\kappa_3 - \ell(\omega_3\delta_1 + \varpi_3\kappa_1))^{-2} \end{aligned} \quad \text{(A13)}$$

$$\begin{aligned} T_3 = {} & \omega_3 \varpi_3^2 (\kappa_3 - \ell\kappa_1)(\omega_3\delta_3 + \varpi_3\kappa_3 - \ell(\omega_3\delta_1 + \varpi_3\kappa_1))^{-2} - \\ & -\ell\omega_1\varpi_1^2(\kappa_1 - \ell\kappa_3)(\omega_1\delta_1 + \varpi_1\kappa_1 - \ell(\omega_1\delta_3 + \varpi_1\kappa_3))^{-2} \end{aligned} \quad \text{(A14)}$$

7. References

Abou S. C. "*Grinding process modeling for automatic control: application to mineral and cement industries*". Engineering Foundation Conferences, Delft, the Netherlands, 1997

BEA (Bureau d'enquetes et d'anlayses pour le securite de l'aviation civile). Accident on 25 July 2000 at "La Patte d'Oie" in Gonesse (95), to the Concorde, registered F-BTSC operated by Air France. Paris: Ministere de l'equipment des transportes et du logement. http://www.bea-fr.org/docspa/2000/f-sc000725pa/pdf/f-sc000725pa.pdf, retrieved 07/ 2009

Billinton, R., Fotuhi-Firuzabad, M., Aboreshaid, S., "*Power System Health Analysis*". Reliability Engineering and System Safety, Vol. 55, Issue 1, pp.1-8,1997

Chiles, J.R., "*Inviting Disaster: Lessons from the Edge of Technology*". Harper Collins, New York, 2002

DeJoy, D.M., Gerson, R.R.M., Schaffer, B.S., "*Safety climate: assessing management and organizational influences on safety*", Professional Safety, 49 (7), 2004, pp.50–57

Guan J., Wu Y., "*Repairable consecutive-k-out-of-n: F system with fuzzy states*". Fuzzy Sets and Systems, vol.157, pp.121-142, 2006

Hoang Pham."*Reliability analysis for dynamic configurations of systems with three failure modes*". Reliability Engineering & System Safety, Vol.63, Issue 1, pp.13-23, 1999

Huang J., Zuo M.J., Wu Y., "*Generalized multi-state k-out-of-n: G systems*", IEEE Trans. Reliability vol.49, no.1, pp.105-111, 2000

Jose E. Ramirez-Marquez, David W. Coit. "*Optimization of system reliability in the presence of common cause failures*". Reliability Engineering & System Safety, Vol. 92, Issue 10, pp.1421-1434, 2007

Jussi K. Vaurio. "*Uncertainties and quantification of common cause failure rates and probabilities for system analyses*". Reliability Engineering & System Safety, Vol.90, Issues 2-3, pp.186-195, 2005

Kunreuther H, Heal G. "*Interdependent security*". Journal of Risk and Uncertainty, vol.26 (2/3), pp.231–49, 2003

Kuo W. and Zuo M. J., *Optimal Reliability Modeling Principles and Applications*: John Wiley & Sons, 2003
Levitin G., "*Universal Generating Function and its Applications*", Springer, Berlin, 2005
Levitin G., Suprasad V. A. "*Multi-state systems with multi-fault coverage*". Reliability Engineering & System Safety, Vol.93, Issue 11, pp. 1730-1739, 2008
Levitin G., Universal Generating Function in Reliability Analysis and Optimization, Springer-Verlag, London, 2005.
Levitin, G., Lisnianski, A. Optimizing survivability of vulnerable series-parallel multi-state systems. Reliability Engineering and System Safety 79, pp. 319–331, 2003
Lisnianski A. and Levitin G., *Multi-State System Reliability Assessment, Optimization, Applications*: World Scientific, 2003.
Ross S.M., "*Introduction to Probability Models*", Academic Press, 1993
Tavakkoli-Moghaddam R., Safari J., Sassani F. ``*Reliability optimization of series-parallel systems with a choice of redundancy strategies using a genetic algorithm*``. Reliability Engineering & System Safety, Vol.93, Issue 4, pp.550-556, 2008
Terje Aven. "*On performance measures for multistate monotone systems*". Reliability Engineering & System Safety, Vol.41, Issue 3, pp.259-266, 1993
Turner, B.M., Pidgeon, N., "*Man-Made Disasters*", 2nd edition, Butterworth-Heinemann, London, 1997
Ushakov L.A., "*Universal generating function*", Sov. J. Comp. System Science, vol.24, no.5, pp.118-129, 1986
Vaughan, D. "*The Challenger Launch Decision: Risky Technology Culture and Deviance at NASA*", University of Chicago Press, Chicago, 1996
Xue J., Yang K., "Symmetric relations in multi-state", IEEE Trans. on reliability, vol.44, no.4, pp.689-693, 1995
Zaitseva E. "*Dynamic reliability indices for multi-state system*", J. of dynamic system & geometric theories, vol.1, no.2, pp.213-222, 2003,
Zhigang Tian, Gregory Levitin, Ming J. Zuo . "*A joint reliability-redundancy optimization approach for multi-state series-parallel systems*". Reliability Engineering & System Safety, Vol.94, Issue 10, pp.1568-1576, 2009

8

Object Oriented Modeling of Rotating Electrical Machines

Christian Kral and Anton Haumer
AIT Austrian Institute of Technology GmbH
Austria

1. Introduction

The simulation of electric machines is required in many fields of applications. For the simulation of electric vehicles or hybrid electric vehicles it is often important to take multi physical effects into account. Only the full coupling of different physical domains allows a systemic analysis of the entire power train. The electric energy storage, power electronics, control and electric machines may have some kind of forced air or liquid cooling. The cooling circuits of each of the electric devices may be coupled or not. Depending on the complexity of the vehicle, the mutual coupling of thermal, mechanical and electrical effects may be crucial when the entire electric power train shall be designed. A flexible and open environment for modeling the electric energy storage, the power electronics, the electric machines, gears and clutches is thus very beneficial in the design phase.
In this book chapter object oriented models of rotating electric three phase machines will be presented. To these machines will be referred with the general term *induction machines*. Particular machines handled in this paper are

- asynchronous induction machines with squirrel cage,
- asynchronous induction machines with slip rings,
- synchronous reluctance machines,
- electrical excited synchronous machines and
- permanent magnet synchronous machines.

For modeling the machines the language Modelica is used. The presented models are summarized in a library, which is available open source. This library takes the following loss mechanisms into account: temperature dependent copper (ohmic) losses, core losses, friction losses, stray load losses and brush losses which is certainly suitable for most applications. However, the motivation for developing the presented electric machines library is also the expandability of the library, being very powerful for a wide range of advanced drive applications. The expandability of the library enables an extension by considering additional effects, e.g., saturation, deep bar effects, thermal behavior, etc.

2. Modelica

The Modelica Association is a non-profit and non-government association which is developing and maintaining the Modelica language, see Fritzson (2004). Modelica is an object

oriented equation based language for modeling multi physical systems, e.g., analog electrical, digital, mechanical, thermal, magnetic, hydraulic, pneumatic, control, etc.
A Modelica library is a very convenient and reliable way to summarize and maintain developed and tested Modelica models (classes). The most prominent model library is the Modelica Standard Library, which contains a huge set of models (classes) out of many scientific fields. This library is also maintained by the Modelica Association. The entire Modelica Standard Library is open source and can be freely used, distributed and modified. The authors of the proposed book chapter are members of the Modelica Association and contributed to the control, thermal, mechanical, electrical multiphase, and electric machines packages of the Modelica Standard Library.
Modelica allows the modeling of multi physical systems in an object oriented way. Most models (classes) define interfaces and the model equations only refer to the interfaces and internal variables. The interfaces may either be signal connectors as they are used in control, or physical connectors as they are used for physical models. These connectors consist of pairs of potential and flow variables, e.g., the electric potential and the electric current in case of an electric connector. A more complex model can be accomplished by connecting the connectors of different objects to a a more complex object. The potential variables of connected interfaces are set equal as implied by Kirchhoff's voltage law. According to Kirchhoff's current law the sum of flow variables of the connected connectors is set to zero.
The relations between connector variables—describing the behavior of the component—are formulated in an acausal way, i.e., independent of the later usage of the component. Instead of using assignments,

```
  v:=R*i; // assign resistance multiplied by current to voltage drop
```

as in most programming languages, equations are used:

```
  v/R=i;  // voltage drop divided by resistance equals current
```

A software tool gathers all (ordinary) differential and algebraic equations, simplifies the set of equations (e.g. solving some of the algebraic equations analytically), and numerically integrates and solves the simplified set of equations. Thus the formulation of e.g. Ohm's law (for a resistor model) is independent on whether current flowing through the component or voltage applied to its terminals is prescribed by the system.
The advantage of the object oriented approach is that redundant model code can be avoided. This increases the maintainability and reduces the fault liability of the code. In Modelica the generalization of the term model is a class, which may be, e.g., a model, a function or a package—which is a container for additional classes, like, e.g., a directory in a file structure. A tested class can be re-used in other models through inheritances. Modelica supports two different kinds of inheritance. First, the extension of code, i.e., the inserting (extending) of code or code fragments in classes. The second kind of inheritance is instantiation which creates instances of classes which can be accessed through their instance names. For example, when modeling an electrical network of concentrated elements, different instances of, e.g., resistors and inductors may be used.

```
model Network
  Modelica.Electrical.Analog.Basic.Resistor R1(R=1);
  Modelica.Electrical.Analog.Basic.Resistor R2(R=10);
  Modelica.Electrical.Analog.Basic.Inductor L1(L=0.01);
  ...
end Network;
```

The class names starting with `Modelica.Electrical.Analog.Basic.` refer to standard components of the Modelica Standard Library. The dots in the name nomenclature separate different hierarchical levels. The class definitions of the resistor and inductor inherit code through extension from the partial model `OnePort`, which contains the interface connectors and basic variable definitions.

```
partial model OnePort
  Modelica.SIunits.Voltage v;
  Modelica.SIunits.Current i;
  Modelica.Electrical.Analog.Interfaces.PositivePin p;
  Modelica.Electrical.Analog.Interfaces.NegativePin n;
equation
  v = p.v - n.v;
  0 = p.i + n.i;
  i = p.i;
end OnePort;
```

The keyword **`partial`** in this model indicates that the number of variables and equations is not balanced. Different models and partial models may be recursively access code through extension. A non-partial model extending from one or more partial models needs to provide additional equations (and variables) such that the numbers of variables and equations are balanced.
In Modelica physical dimensions of parameters and variables can be assigned. In the Modelica package `Modelica.SIunits` all the base SI units and many derived SI units are provided. When translating a model for the simulation of a particular problem, a unit check of all of the involved equations is performed. This way it can be ensured, that consistency problems of physical equations can be avoided.

3. Electric machine components

An electric machine is an electro mechanical energy converter. The object interfaces are the (electrical) terminal connections of the windings, the (rotational) shaft end and housing, as well as a thermal connector incorporating the significant thermal regions and loss sources of the machine. With reference to asynchronous and synchronous induction machines two different implementations of electric machine models are included in the Modelica Standard Library. The first implementation relies on space phasor theory and this is the library that is presented in this book chapter. The second implementation is based on magnetic fundamental wave models—with respect to the spatial electro magnetic field. The space phasor based machines library was originally released in 2004 and was heavily improved over the last years. The other machines library is included in the Modelica Standard Library since version 3.2, which has been released in 2010. Both machine implementations are fully compatible and model the transient behavior of induction machines in the time domain. For DC machines and transformers a time transient (and an electrically stationary) implementation is also included in the Modelica Standard Library, which will, however, not be addressed in this book chapter. The basic idea of the object oriented modeling in electric machines is that each effect which can be separated from others is encapsulated in an object. Typical machine specific objects are winding resistances, winding stray inductances, cage models and the air gap model, which takes the electro mechanical power conversion and the magnetic main field into account. Other objects are the inertia, and loss models related to mechanical friction, eddy currents in the core, stray load effects and brush contact. Each loss model takes a consistent power balance into account, such that all dissipated losses are always considered in a respective thermal connector. The loss models have been presented and validated against measurements in Haumer et al. (2009). For the mechanical components *actio et reactio* applies. For each torque acting on the stator and rotor side of, e.g., the air gap and friction model, the torques have the same numeric values, but different signs. Different machines, such as asynchronous induction machines with squirrel cage and slip ring rotor, and synchronous machines with permanent magnets, electrical excitation, etc., are modeled out of a minimal subset of components. This way the object oriented Modelica models of electric machines become code and run-time efficient and certainly very robust.

3.1 Assumptions

The induction machine models are summarized in the package `Modelica.Electrical.Machines` of the Modelica Standard Library. For these machine models the following assumptions apply:

- the number of phases is restricted to three
- the phase windings are fully symmetrical
- the inductances are constant and thus the relationships between flux linkages and currents are linear
- saliency effects, represented by different inductances of the d- and q-axis are considered for the synchronous machines models
- cross coupling of inductances is not modeled
- deep bar effects are not taken into account
- only (spatial) fundamental wave effects of the magnetic field are taken into account
- time transients of electrical, mechanical and thermal quantities are not restricted

3.2 Electrical concept

The interface definition of the electric pin in `Modelica.Electrical.Analog.Interfaces.Pin` consists of the electric potential and the current being a flow quantity.

```
connector Pin
  Modelica.SIunits.Voltage v;
  flow Modelica.SIunits.Current i;
end Pin;
```

In order to model multi phase machines an electric plug is defined in `Modelica.Electrical.MulitiPhase.Interfaces.Plug`. This plug contains `m=3` pins by default:

```
connector Plug
  parameter Integer m=3;
  Modelica.Electrical.Analog.Interfaces.Pin pin[m];
end Plug;
```

In all instances of the plug, `m` is finally set to three when applied in the machines package, since only three phase machines are modeled.

3.3 Mechanical concept

For the rotating electric machine models only rotating one dimensional effects need to be taken into account. The rotational interfaces definitions of `Modelica.Mechanics.Rotational.Interfaces.Flange_a` are:

```
connector Flange_a
  Modelica.SIunits.Angle phi;
  flow Modelica.SIunits.Torque tau;
end Flange_a
```

In the rotational package the rotational angle `phi` servers as potential quantity and torque `tau` is the flow quantity.

3.4 Thermal concept

Each loss component is equipped with a heat port which carries the heat flow as flow variable and the accessory operating temperature as potential quantity. The connector definition of `Modelica.Thermal.HeatTransfer.Interfaces.HeatPort` is:

```
connector HeatPort
  Modelica.SIunits.Temperature T;
  flow Modelica.SIunits.HeatFlowRate Q_flow;
end HeatPort;
```

Each machine model has a conditional super heat port, which consists of as many heat ports as loss effects are considered. If the super heat port of a machine is enabled, the heat ports of the loss components are connected with this super heat port. This way the machine model can be coupled with an external thermal model. If the heat port of a machine is disabled the loss components are thermally connected to internal temperature sources representing fixed (operating) temperatures. In this case, the losses are entirely dissipated in internal temperature sources. The concept of coupling an external thermal model with the electro-mechanical model is presented in detail in Haumer et al. (2010).

3.5 Resistance

The resistor objects applied in the machine models are directly taken from the Modelica package `Modelica.Electrical.Analog.Basic.Resistor`, see resistor in tab. 1. This model consists of two electrical pins and one thermal connector. This resistance is modeled temperature dependent

```
R = RRef*(1+alphaRef*(T-TRef));
```

where `RRef` is the reference resistance at the reference temperature `TRef` and `alphaRef` is the linear temperature coefficient at `TRef`. The actual resistance `R` is dependent on the operating temperature `T` which is obtained from the thermal connector of this model.

Three phase resistors are directly taken from the Modelica package `Modelica.Electrical.MultiPhase.Basic.Resistor`, see resistor in tab. 1. This model consists of two electrical three phase plugs, one thermal connector and three single phase resistors. Since the machine models are assumed to have symmetrical phase windings the individual reference resistances for each phase are set to equal values in the machine models.

Icon	Class name	Comment
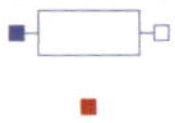	Resistor	Temperature dependent single phase resistor with heat port
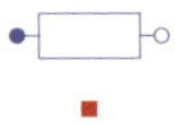	Resistor	Temperature dependent three phase resistor with heat port
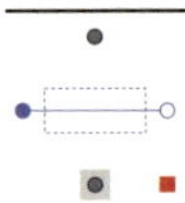	StrayLoad	Stray load losses with heat port and rotor and stator rotational flange
	Friction	Friction losses
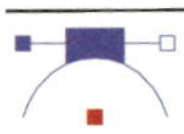	Brushes	Carbon brush losses
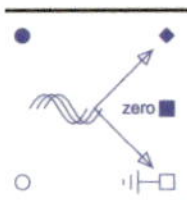	SpacePhasor	Transforms multi phase quantities to space phasors and zero sequence components
	Inductor	Linear single phase inductor
	Inductor	Linear space phasor inductor
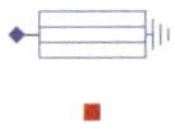	Core	Core losses (without hysteresis losses)
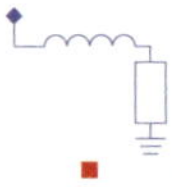	SquirrelCage	Symmetrical squirrel cage with heat port
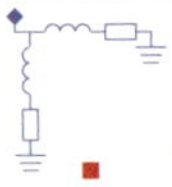	DamperCage	Salient damper cage with heat port
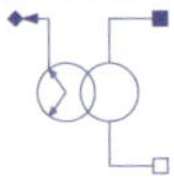	ElectricalExcitation	Transforms excitation voltage and current to space phasors
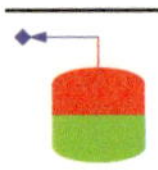	PermanentMagnet	Transforms permanent magnet excitation to an equivalent space phasor
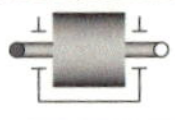	Inertia	Rotating mass

Table 1. Components of the electric machines library

3.6 Stray load losses

The stray load loss model applied to all the induction machine models is originally inspired by the standard 60034-2 (1998) and extended by a thesis of Lang (1984). The stray load losses are modeled to be proportional to the square of the root mean square (RMS) current and to a particular power of speed. In order to consistently cover the loss balance in the machine, stray load losses are considered as an equivalent torque, acting on the rotor (and stator housing, respectively).

```
tau = tauRef*(I/IRef)^2*(w/wRef)^power_w;
```

The term `wRef*tauRef` represents the reference stray load losses at rated current `IRef` and rated angular speed `wRef`. The parameter `power_w` is a positive real quantity in this model.
The stray load loss model consists of two plugs and two mechanical flanges. One mechanical flange is supposed to be connected with the rotor and the other one shall be connected with the stator (housing). The torques of the two mechanical flanges have the same numeric values but different signs. The electrical connectors are part of the stator (winding) circuit. The RMS value of the current is actually computed from the instantaneous values of the phase currents. The actual losses dissipated by this model are equal to the heat flow of thermal connector:

```
heatPort.Q_flow = tau*w;
```

The heat flow and losses, respectively, are independent of the temperature of the heat port. Yet for operating this model an (arbitrary) operating temperature has to be provided at the heat port (see tab. 1).

3.7 Friction losses

The friction losses are modeled by:

```
tau = tauRef*(w/wRef)^power_w;
```

In this equation `wRef*tauRef` represent the reference friction losses at reference angular velocity `wRef`. The exponent `power_w` is a positive real quantity.
In order to avoid numerical problems the torque speed relationship is approximated as a linear curve around the zero crossing. The linear speed region is, however, much smaller than the reference reference speed.

```
tau = if w >= +wLinear then
        +tauRef*(+w/wRef)^power_w
      else if w <= -wLinear then
        -tauRef*(-w/wRef)^power_w
      else
        tauLinear*(w/wLinear);
```

This model requires two mechanical flanges to be connected with the rotor and stator (housing), respectively. The thermal connector dissipates the losses

```
heatPort.Q_flow = tau*w;
```

independent of the actual operating temperature, which has to be provided externally due to consistency reasons, see tab. 1.

3.8 Brush losses

In the induction machine models carbon brush losses (see tab. 1) are currently taken into account only for the excitation circuit of the electrical excited synchronous machine model. The brush model considers three regions. For large positive currents `i>ILinear` the voltage drop is constant and equal to `V`. For currents less than `-ILinear` the voltage drop is equal to `-V`. In between these regions the voltage versus current characteristic is linear.

```
v = if (i>+ILinear) then
      +V
    else if (i<-ILinear) then
      -V
    else
      V*i/ILinear;
```

The brush loss model has only two electrical connectors and one thermal connector. The heat dissipated by the brushes is:

```
heatPort.Q_flow = -v*i;
```

independent of the actual operating temperature.

3.9 Space phasor transformation

The machine models presented in this book chapter rely on the space phasor equations. In literature—instead of space phasor—also the terms space vector or Park's vectors are used. The reason for applying space phasor theory is that the equations are simpler compared to the individual phase equations. When the model equations refer to the rotating reference frame, time transients have lower characteristic frequencies which gives also rise to significant simulation speed advantages.

Space phasor transformation is used to transform the phase voltages and currents of the three plug connectors into voltage and current space phasor—and the zero sequence voltage and current, according to Kleinrath (1980):

$$\underline{v} = \frac{2}{3}\left(v_1 + \underline{a}v_2 + \underline{a}^2 v_3\right)$$

$$\underline{a} = e^{j\frac{2}{3}\pi} = -\frac{1}{2} + j\frac{\sqrt{3}}{2}$$

$$v_0 = \frac{1}{3}\left(v_1 + v_2 + v_3\right)$$

In the presented machines package the space phasor is implemented as an array of two elements, representing real and imaginary part, respectively. The space phasor connector is thus defined by:

```
connector SpacePhasor
  // First component [1] represents real part,
  // second component [2] represents imaginary part
  Modelica.SIunits.Voltage v_[2];
  flow Modelica.SIunits.Current i_[2];
end SpacePhasor;
```

In the space phasor transformation model the following equations apply for the voltages:

```
v_[1] = (2/3)*(v[1]-v[2]/2-v[3]/2);
v_[2] = (1/sqrt(3))*(v[2]-v[3]);
```

The zero sequence connector `zero` is modeled as a regular electrical pin. The respective zero sequence voltage is determined by the following acausal relationship:

```
3*zero.v = v[1]+v[2]+v[3];
```

The same relationships also apply for the space phasor currents and the zero sequence current. In each of the presented machines the zero sequence inductance of the respective (stator or rotor) winding is then connected to the zero sequence connector of the space phasor transformation model, see section 4 and tab. 1.

3.10 Zero inductance

In the presented machines package the zero inductances are modeled by means of single phase inductors which are taken directly from the Modelica package `Modelica.Electrical.Analog.Basic.Inductor` (see inductor model in tab. 1). The same inductor model is used for the stray inductance of single phase excitation windings.

3.11 Stray inductance

In the presented machines package stray inductances are modeled by means of inductors with space phasor connectors and components (see inductor model in tab. 1).

```
v_[1] = L[1]*der(i_[1]);
v_[2] = L[2]*der(i_[2]);
```

The operator **`der()`** represents the time derivative and the inductances `L[1]` and `L[2]` are the inductances in the two axes of the actual space phasor reference frame.

3.12 Core losses

In the current implementation of the core loss model only eddy current losses are taken into account (tab. 1). Therefore, the actual core conductance `Gc` is assumed to be constant, calculated from reference core losses at given reference voltage. The electrical interfaces of the model are space phasor connectors. The space phasor relationship between voltages and currents is simply

```
i_ = Gc*v_;
```

and dissipated losses are:

```
heatPort.Q_flow = -3/2*(+v_[1]*i_[1]+v_[2]*i_[2]);
```

Hysteresis losses are not considered in the actual implementation, since hysteresis losses are usually modeled in the frequency domain as presented by Lin et al. (2003), but the presented model is strictly a time domain approach.

3.13 Air gap, magnetizing inductance and torque

The air gap model takes the magnetizing inductance and the electro mechanical power conversion into account. The stator and rotor side of the model have space phasor connectors representing the voltage and current phasors with respect to the stator and rotor fixed reference frame. Additionally the air gap model has one rotor and one stator (housing) related rotational flange.

In the proposed machine models the entire magnetic circuits are represented by equivalent air gap inductances. In order to express the relationship between stator and rotor currents and magnetizing inductance, the stator and rotor space phasors have to refer to one common reference frame. It is thus required to either

1. transform the stator space phasors to the rotor fixed reference frame or
2. transform the rotor space phasors to the stator fixed reference frame.

For both cases an air gap model is available in the presented machines library. In the following only the first implementation will be discussed, as this represents the more general approach. In the following the rotor fixed rotor current space phasor is referred to as `i_rr`. The first letter after the underscore represents the rotor side and the second letter indicates the reference frame—in this case the rotor fixed reference frame. The stator fixed stator current space phasor `i_ss` is transformed to the rotor fixed reference frame by means of a rotation by the negative angle `gamma`. This quantity is the difference of angular position of the stator and rotor rotation flange, multiplied by the number of pole pairs. The rotor fixed stator current space phasor `i_sr` and the rotor current space phasor `i_rr` add up the magnetizing current phasor:

```
i_mr = i_sr+i_rr;
```

The main flux linkage phasor `psi_mr` of the air gap is thus determined by

```
psi_mr[1] = Lmd*i_mr[1];
psi_mr[2] = Lmq*i_mr[2];
```

where `Lmd` and `Lmq` are the magnetizing inductances in the direct (d) and quadrature (q) axis of the rotor. The different inductances in both axis allow the consideration of saliency effects of the magnetic reluctance of the rotor.
The inner (electrical) torque of the air gap model is determined by the vector product of the magnetizing flux and the stator current space phasor:

```
tauElectrical = 3/2*p*(i_sr[2]*psi_mr[1] - i_sr[1]*psi_mr[2]);
```

In this equation `p` represents the number of pole pairs. As for all mechanically interacting models, the torque at rotor shaft and the stator (housing) have the same numeric quantities but different signs to correctly consider *actio et reactio*; see tab. 1.

3.14 Squirrel and damper cage

For asynchronous induction machines symmetrical squirrel cages are used, whereas synchronous machines use damper cages with different equivalent resistances and stray inductances in direct (d) and quadrature (q) axis. In this sense, the symmetrical squirrel cage is a restricted damper cage with equal parameters in the two axis; see tab. 1. The relationship between the two axis components of the voltages and current spaces phasors are:

```
v_[1] = Rrd * i_[1] + Lrsigmad * der(i_[1]);
v_[2] = Rrq * i_[2] + Lrsigmaq * der(i_[2]);
```

The resistances `Rrd` and `Rrq` are again temperature dependent, and the model is equipped with a heat port. The constant inductances `Lrsigmad` and `Lrsigmaq` are the stray inductances of the cages in the direct (d) and quadrature (q) axis.

3.15 Electrical excitation

For electrically excited synchronous machines, excitation voltage and current have to be transformed to equivalent space phasors (direct axis components), taking the conversion factor between rotor and stator into account:

```
ve = v_[1]*turnsRatio*3/2;
i_[1] = -ie*turnsRatio;
i_[2] = 0;
```

With given main field inductance in d-axis `Lmd`, the `turnsRatio` can be calculated from no-load voltage at given speed (frequency) and excitation current `IeOpenCircuit`:

```
sqrt(2)*VsNominal = 2*pi*fsNominal*Lmd*IeOpenCircuit*turnsRatio
```

3.16 Permanent magnet

For permanent magnet synchronous machines, the effect of the permanent magnet can be considered like a constant DC excitation current (providing a constant remanent flux, neglecting the detailed B-H-characteristic of the magnet material):

```
i_[1] = -Ie;
i_[2] = 0;
```

3.17 Inertia

Inertia models are required to model the rotor and stator (housing) inertia effects with respect to one rotational axis. The relationship between torque `tau` and angular position `phi` of the flange is:

```
phi = flange_a.phi;
phi = flange_b.phi;
w = der(phi);
a = der(w);
J*a = flange_a.tau + flange_b.tau;
```

The inertia model has two flanges, `flange_a` and `flange_b` which are rigidly connected. From a modeling point of view the two different connectors are not required, but are used for convenience reasons when graphically connecting components, see tab. 1.

4. Induction machine models

4.1 Partial induction machine model

The partial induction machine model (see Fig. 1) comprises all components that are common to all induction machines models:

- electrical three phase plugs `plug_sp` and `plug_sn` representing the beginning and end of the stator three phase windings; star or delta connection has to be provided outside of the machine model
- stray load losses `strayLoad`: see sec. 3.6
- resistances `rs` of the three phase stator windings: see sec. 3.5
- space phasor transformation `spacePhasorS` of stator voltages and currents: see sec. 3.9
- stator zero sequence inductor `lszero`: see sec. 3.10; the inductance is set equal to the stray inductance by default, but can be parametrized differently
- stray inductance `lssigma` of the three phase stator windings: see sec. 3.11
- stator core losses `statorCore`: see sec. 3.12
- friction losses `friction`: see sec. 3.7
- rotor moment of inertia `inertiaRotor` (see sec. 3.17) and a rotational flange, representing the shaft end

- stator moment of inertia `inertiaStator` (see sec. 3.17) and an optional rotational flange, representing the housing
- a replaceable internal heat port `internalHeatPort`, an optional replaceable thermal ambient `thermalAmbient` and an optional replaceable thermal port `thermalPort` (see sec. 3.4)

For the user's convenience, a boolean parameter `useSupport` determines whether the stator flange of the air gap model is connected to an internal mechanically fixed point `fixed`), or to the stator moment of inertia and the rotational flange `support`. If the user chooses `useSupport = **true**`, the flange `support` has to be connected to an external mechanical circuit, e.g., representing an elastic mounting.
All induction machine models extend from this partial model, i.e., they inherit all common components, replacing the thermal ports and thermal ambient by machine specific components and add all other specific components (e.g. air gap model).

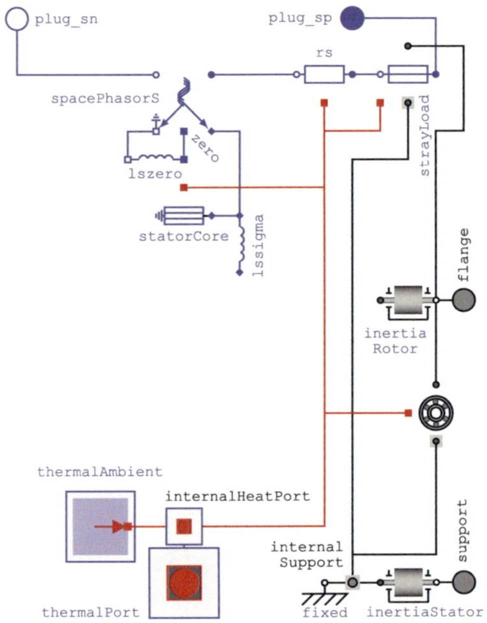

Fig. 1. Partial model of induction machines

4.2 Asynchronous induction machine with squirrel cage

The asynchronous induction machine with squirrel cage (see fig. 2) inherits from the partial induction machine model (see sec. 4.1) and adds the following machine specific components:

- air gap model `airGapS` in the stator fixed reference frame: see sec. 3.13
- squirrel cage `squirrelCageR` in rotor fixed reference frame: see sec. 3.14

4.3 Asynchronous induction machine with slip ring rotor

The asynchronous induction machine with slip ring rotor (see fig. 3) inherits from the partial induction machine model (see sec. 4.1) and adds the following machine specific components:

- air gap model `airGapS` in the stator fixed reference frame: see sec. 3.13

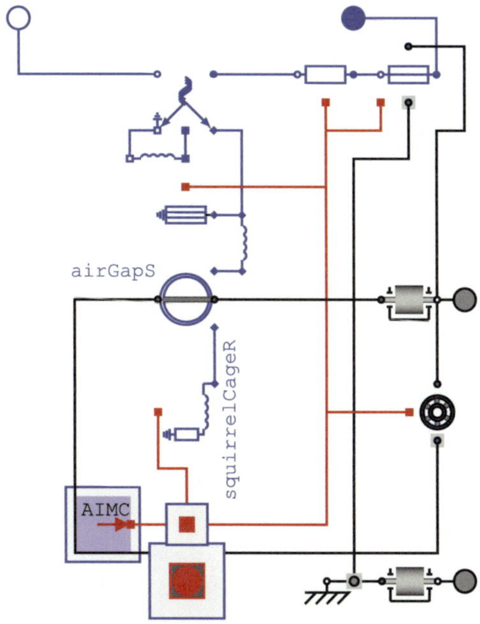

Fig. 2. Asynchronous induction machine with squirrel cage

- electrical threephase plugs `plug_rp` and `plug_rn` for beginning and end of the rotor three phase windings; star or delta connection has to be provided outside of the machine model
- resistances `rr` of the three phase rotor windings: see sec. 3.5
- space phasor transformation `spacePhasorR` of rotor voltages and currents: see sec. 3.9
- rotor zero sequence inductor `lrzero`: see sec. 3.10; the inductance is set equal to the rotor stray inductance by default, but can be parametrized differently
- stray inductance `lrsigma` of the three phase rotor windings: see sec. 3.11
- rotor core losses `rotorCore`: see sec. 3.12
- brush losses (see sec. 3.8) are neglected, since standards consider brush voltage drop dependent on root mean square of current; during transient operation RMS current cannot be calculated; the dependency of brush voltage drop on instantaneous current will be investigated

The space phasor transformation of rotor voltages and currents has to take into account additionally the turns ratio between stator and rotor winding:

$$\frac{v_r'}{v_r} = \frac{\text{effective number of stator turns}}{\text{effective number of rotor turns}}$$

This parameter can either be determined from a pre-processing calculation of the machine, or calculated from the measured locked-rotor voltage v_{r0}:

$$\frac{v_{r0}'}{v_{r0}} = \frac{v_s}{v_{r0}} \cdot \frac{|j\omega_s L_m|}{|r_s + j\omega_s L_s|}$$

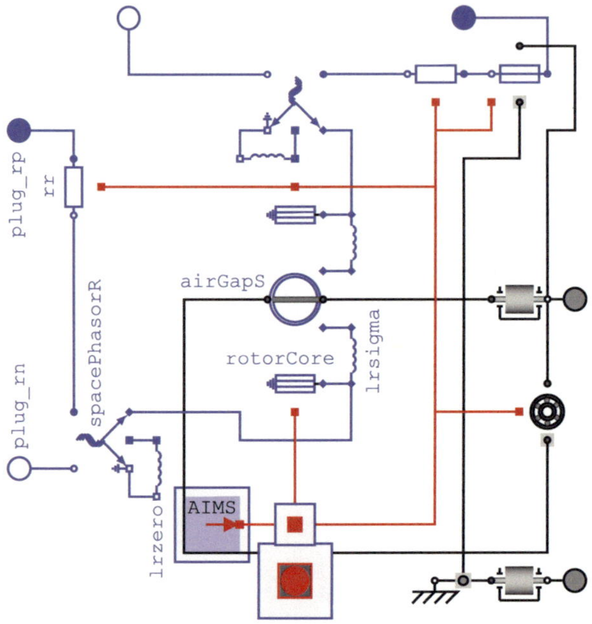

Fig. 3. Asynchronous induction machine with slip ring rotor

4.4 Synchronous reluctance machine

The synchronous reluctance machine (see fig. 4) inherits from the partial induction machine model (see sec. 4.1) and adds the following machine specific components:

- air gap model `airGapR` in the rotor fixed reference frame (see sec. 3.13), since saliency of the rotor has to be taken into account
- optional damper cage model (see sec. 3.14) which can be enabled/disabled by means of the boolean parameter `useDamperCage`; since the damper cage can be disabled (machine without damper cage), an auxiliary heat flow sensor has to be used for connection to the thermal port

4.5 Electrical excited synchronous machine

The electrical excited synchronous machine (see fig. 5) inherits from the partial induction machine model (see sec. 4.1) and adds the following machine specific components:

- air gap model `airGapR` in the rotor fixed reference frame (see sec. 3.13), since saliency of the rotor has to be taken into account
- optional damper cage model (see sec. 3.14) which can be enabled/disabled by means of the boolean parameter `useDamperCage`; since the damper cage can be disabled (machine without damper cage), an auxiliary heat flow sensor has to be used for connection to the thermal port
- electrical single-phase pins `pin_ep` and `pin_en` for beginning and end of the excitation winding
- brush losses `brush` (see sec. 3.8) for modeling losses and the voltage drop due to brushes; if a brushless excitation system is considered, the brush loss equations can be disabled by setting the reference voltage drop to zero

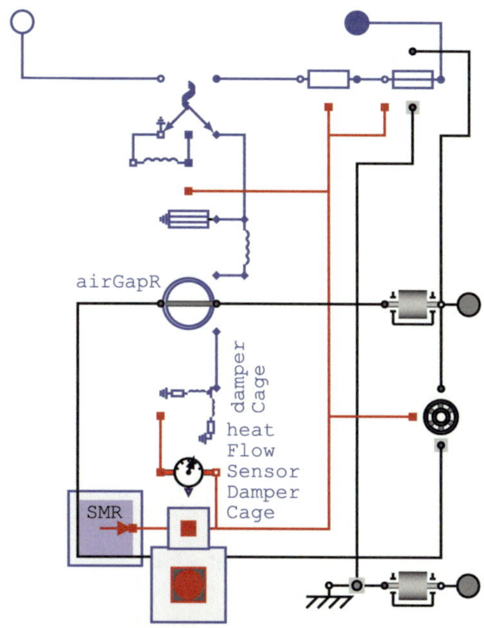

Fig. 4. Synchronous machine with reluctance rotor and optional damper cage

- resistance `re` (see sec. 3.5) of the excitation winding
- stray inductance `lesigma` (see sec. 3.10) of the excitation winding
- electrical excitation: see sec. 3.15

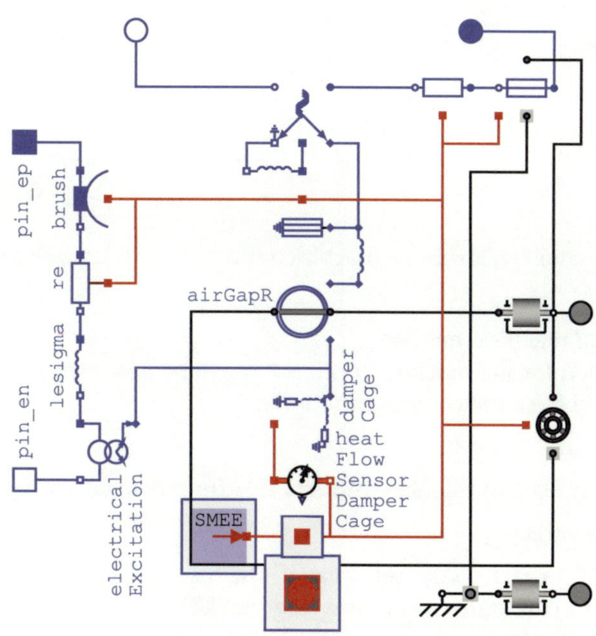

Fig. 5. Electrical excited synchronous machine with optional damper cage

4.6 Permanent magnet synchronous machine

The permanent magnet synchronous machine (see fig. 4.6) inherits from the partial induction machine model (see sec. 4.1) and adds the following machine specific components:

- air gap model `airGapR` in the rotor fixed reference frame (see sec. 3.13), since saliency of the rotor has to be taken into account
- optional damper cage model (see sec. 3.14) which can be enabled/disabled by means of the boolean parameter `useDamperCage`; since the damper cage can be disabled (machine without damper cage), an auxiliary heat flow sensor has to be used for connection to the thermal port
- permanent magnet (see sec. 3.16): the equivalent excitation current `Ie` is calculated from the given no-load voltage at given speed

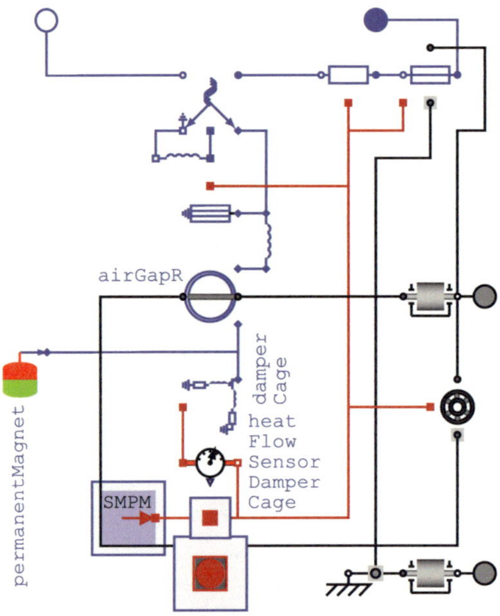

Fig. 6. Permanent magnet synchronous machine with optional damper cage

4.7 Parametrization of machine models

The parameters needed for the machine models have to be taken from pre-processing design software, or calculated from measurement reports:

- number of pole pairs
- nominal frequency: used to calculate inductances from reactances
- rotor moment of inertia
- stator moment of inertia: only relevant if the user chooses to connect an external mechanical circuit to the stator mounting (see sec. 4.1)
- winding resistances (see sec. 3.5):
  - reference resistance at reference temperature

  - reference temperature
  - temperature coefficient at reference temperature
  - operational temperature: only relevant if the user chooses to dissipate the losses to an internal thermal temperature source instead of connecting an external thermal circuit (see sec. 3.4)
- stray inductance
- zero inductance of three phase windings
- magnetizing inductance (see sec. 3.13)
- stray load losses (see sec. 3.6):
  - reference loss power at reference current and reference speed
  - reference current
  - reference speed
  - exponent of stray load torque with respect to speed
- friction losses (see sec. 3.7):
  - reference loss power at reference speed
  - reference speed
  - exponent of friction torque with respect to speed
- brush losses (see sec. 3.8):
  - voltage drop
  - current limit (linear changeover around current = 0)
- core losses (see sec. 3.12):
  - reference loss power at reference voltage and reference frequency
  - reference voltage
  - reference frequency

If it is desired to neglect losses, the reference loss power (stray load losses, friction losses, core losses) respectively the voltage drop (brush losses) can be set to zero.
Resistances and inductances have to be specified per phase as they are accessible for measurements at the respective winding terminals, except squirrel cage and damper cage. Cage parameters (see sec. 3.14) have to be specified with respect to an equivalent three phase stator winding. If temperature dependency shall be neglected, either the temperature coefficient can be set to zero or—in case the heat port shall not be connected to an external thermal model (see sec. 3.4)—the operational temperature can be set equal to the reference temperature.
Additional machine specific parameters are:

- for asynchronous induction machines with slip ring rotor (see sec. 4.3), `turnsRatio` between stator and rotor winding is calculated out of the parameters
  - nominal stator voltage
  - locked-rotor voltage
- for electrical excited synchronous machines (see sec. 4.5 and sec. 3.15), `turnsRatio` between stator and excitation winding as well as excitation stray inductance require the parameters

  - nominal stator voltage
  - open circuit excitation current for nominal stator voltage at nominal frequency
  - stray fraction of total excitation inductance
- for permanent magnet synchronous machines (see sec. 4.6 and sec. 3.16), the calculation of the equivalent excitation current requires the
  - open circuit stator voltage at nominal speed

5. Examples

5.1 Asynchronous induction machine with squirrel cage, started direct on line

The stator windings of an asynchronous induction machine with squirrel cage (`aimc` in fig. 7) is connected in delta, using the auxiliary model `terminalBox` which allows the selection of either star or delta connection. The `terminalBox` is series connected to an RMS current sensor (which determines the length of the current space phasor) and a switch (which is closed at `time = 0.1 s`). The stiff voltage supply is represented by a purely sinusoidal voltage source (`sineVoltage`). The machine's shaft end is connected to the `loadInertia` and a quadratic speed dependent `loadTorque`. The parameters of the load are selected such way that the machine load torque equals the nominal torque at nominal speed. A summary of the machine parameters is listed in tab. 2. Parameters which are not needed for parametrizing the machine model are listed without parameter name. In the presented example, for simplicity reasons, the temperature dependence of the resistances is neglected. All other than ohmic losses are also not taken into account.

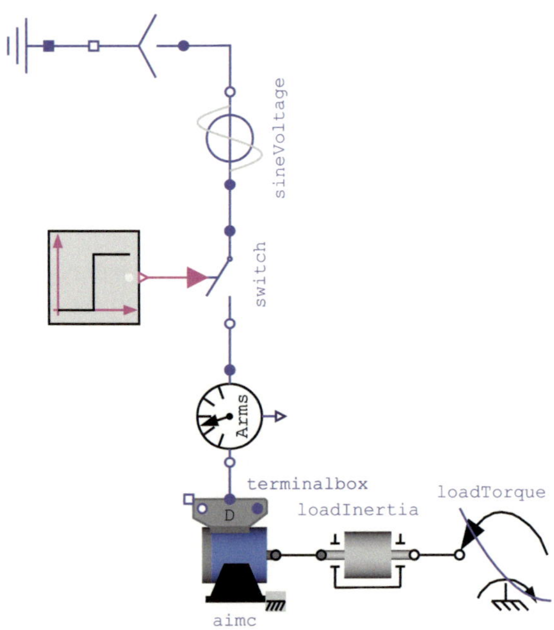

Fig. 7. Asynchronous induction machine with squirrel cage, started direct on line

The line current shown in fig. 8 represents the length of the current space phasor divided by $\sqrt{2}$, which can be interpreted as equivalent RMS value for stationary operation. The current waveform reflects an electro-magnetic transient when the `switch` is closed. Due to

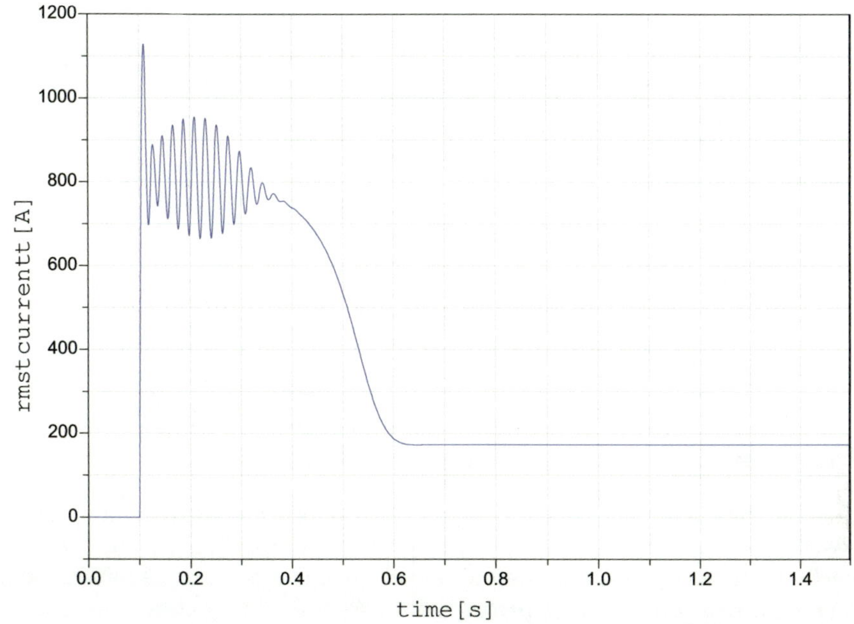

Fig. 8. Line current of asynchronous induction machine with squirrel cage

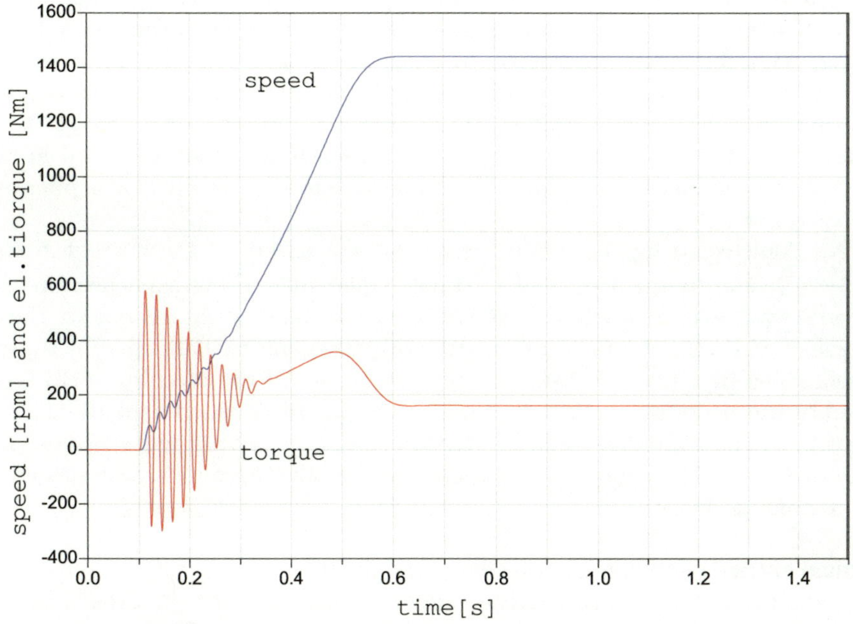

Fig. 9. Speed and electrical torque of asynchronous induction machine with squirrel cage

Comment	Parameter name	Value	Unit
number of pole pairs	`p`	4	
rotor's moment of inertia	`Jr`	0.29	$kg \cdot m^2$
nominal RMS voltage per phase		100	V
nominal RMS current per phase		100	A
nominal frequency	`fsNominal`	50	Hz
nominal torque		161.4	Nm
nominal speed		1440.45	rpm
stator resistance	`Rs`	0.03	Ω
stator stray inductance	`Lssigma`	0.3239	mH
stator zero sequence inductance	`Lszero`	0.3239	mH
main field inductance	`Lm`	9.2253	mH
rotor stray inductance	`Lrsigma`	0.3239	mH
rotor resistance	`Rr`	0.04	Ω

Table 2. Parameters of the asynchronous induction machine with squirrel cage

the electro-magnetic transients the electrical torque developed by the machine also starts with transient oscillations, which causes a speed ripple accordingly (fig. 9). The total moment of inertia (machine plus load) is accelerated by the electromagnetic torque minus the quadratic speed dependent load torque. At approximately 0.6 s the drive reaches nominal operating conditions.

5.2 Asynchronous induction machine with slip ring rotor, started with rheostat

The stator windings of an asynchronous induction machine with slip ring rotor (`aims` in fig. 10) is connected in delta. The stator starting `switch` is closed at `time = 0.1 s`. The machine's shaft end is connected to a `loadInertia` and a quadratic speed dependent `loadTorque` with the same parameters settings as in sec. 5.1. The rotor terminals are connected to a `rheostat`, i.e., an external additional resistor with resistance parameters equal to four times the rotor resistance. This rheostat is shorted during the start procedure after `time = 1 s`. The parameters of the simulated machine are summarized in tab. 3. For simplicity reasons neither temperature dependent resistances nor other loss phenomena are taken into account.

The current depicted in fig. 11, again, represents the length of the current space phasor divided by $\sqrt{2}$. The transient current is smaller than that of the asynchronous induction machine with squirrel cage due to the external rotor resistance of the `rheostat`. The electrical torque developed by the machine also starts with transient oscillations, which give rise to speed oscillations (fig. 12). The total moment of inertia of the machine including load is accelerated by the electromagnetic torque minus the quadratic speed dependent load torque. At approximately 0.7 s the drive reaches stationary operation with the `rheostat` still being switched on. After shorting the rheostat at `time = 1 s`, the machine accelerates with a short transient to nominal speed.

5.3 Electrical excited synchronous machine, load dump

The stator windings of an electrical excited synchronous induction machine (`smee` in fig. 13) is connected in star, using the auxiliary model `terminalBox`. The machine is operated as generator connected to a three-phase resistor and inductor by means of a `switch`. The electrical load has a nominal power factor of 0.8. At `time = 2 s` the open circuit

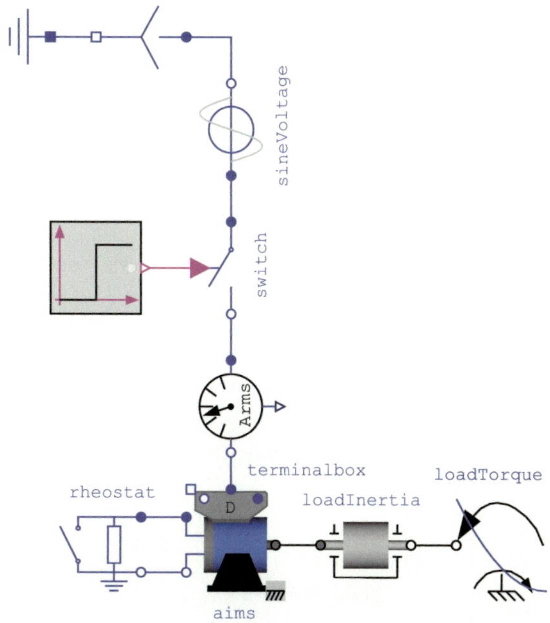

Fig. 10. Asynchronous induction machine with slip ring rotor, started with rheostat

Comment	Parameter	Value	Unit
number of pole pairs	p	4	
rotor's moment of inertia	Jr	0.29	$kg \cdot m^2$
nominal RMS voltage per phase	VsNominal	100	V
nominal RMS current per phase		100	A
nominal frequency	fsNominal	50	Hz
locked rotor RMS voltage per phase	VrLockedRotor	96.603	V
nominal torque		161.4	Nm
nominal speed		1440.45	rpm
stator resistance	Rs	0.03	Ω
stator stray inductance	Lssigma	0.3239	mH
stator zero sequence inductance	Lszero	0.3239	mH
main field inductance	Lm	9.2253	mH
rotor stray inductance	Lrsigma	0.3239	mH
rotor zero sequence inductance	Lrzero	0.3239	mH
rotor resistance	Rr	0.04	Ω

Table 3. Parameters of the asynchronous induction machine with slip ring rotor

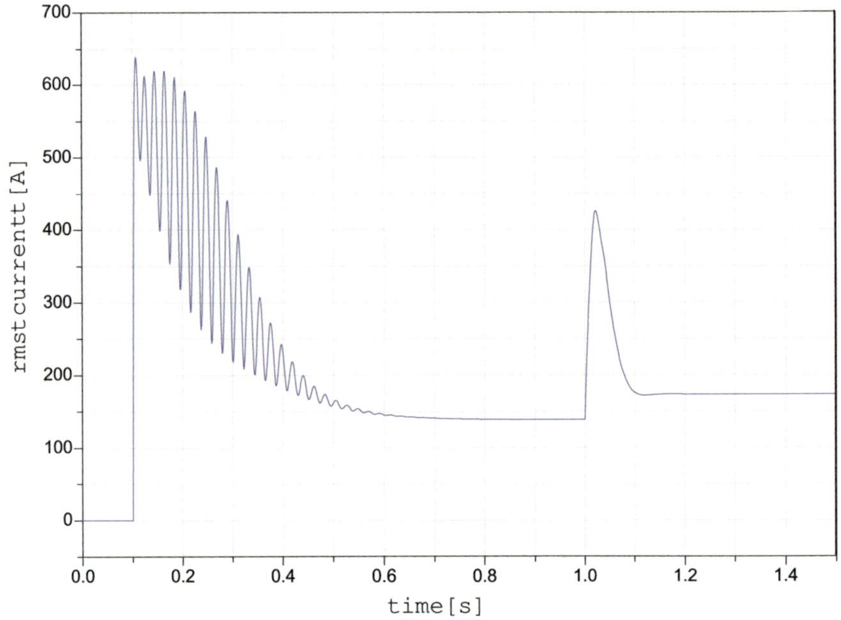

Fig. 11. Line current of asynchronous induction machine with slip ring rotor and rheostat

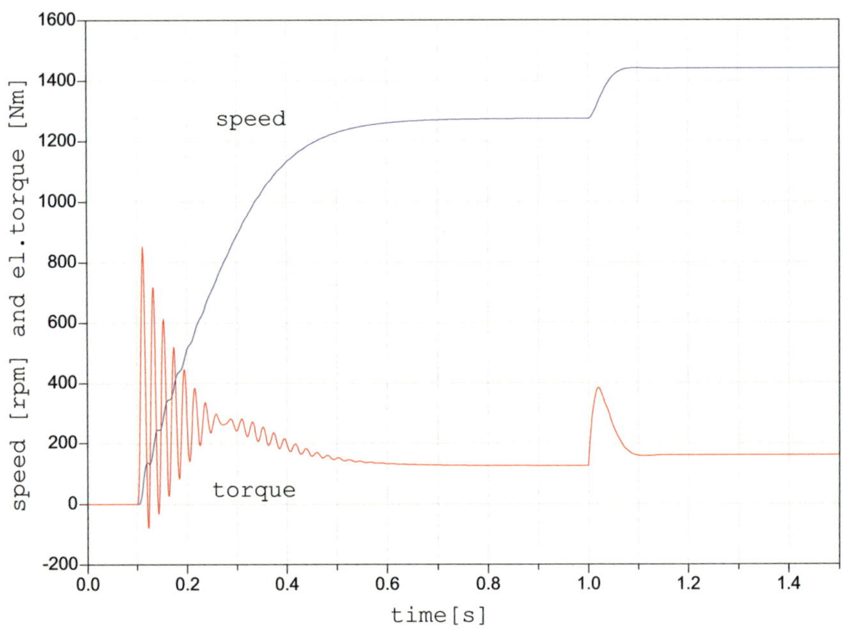

Fig. 12. Speed and electrical torque of asynchronous induction machine with slip ring rotor

of the generator is connected to the load which again is dumped at `time = 4 s`. This procedure is repeated periodically. The machine's shaft end is driven by a prescribed speed representing an ideal turbine. The turbine accelerates the machine within 1 s from standstill to nominal speed. For the remaining simulation time the speed is considered to be constant. The machine excitation is fed by a voltage source, which is controlled by a PI-controller (`voltageController`). The controller reference voltage is defined proportional to speed, the actual RMS voltage of the generator is determined from a voltmeter. The utility record `machineData` calculates the machine parameters (resistances and inductances) from given parameters (transient and subtransient reactances) according to the standard 60034-4 (1998). The parameters of the simulated machine are summarized in tab. 4. In order to simplify the simulation, first, the temperature dependencies of the resistances and, second, all other losses phenomena are not taken into account.

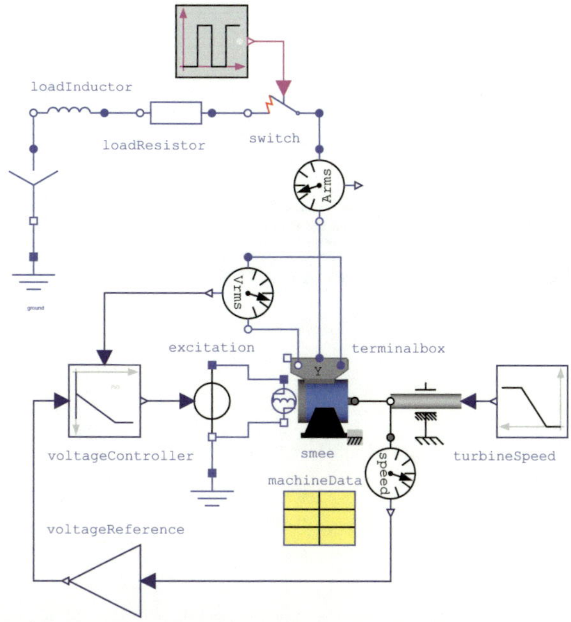

Fig. 13. Electrical excited synchronous machine, behavior during load dump

During starting the generator with `turbineSpeed` the excitation voltage and current as well as the machine terminal voltage increase to no-load operation at nominal voltage. The overshots are due to the settings of the voltage controller. Figure 14 shows the transient changes of line current between no-load and nominal current due to loading and load dump. The terminal voltage—see fig. 15—shows dips during loading and overshots during load dump. The voltage controller increases respectively decreases excitation voltage as shown in fig. 16. The excitation current follows the excitation voltage with a time constant according to total excitation inductance and excitation resistance.

6. Conclusions

The presented electric machines library, which it is part of the Modelica Standard Library, provides comprehensive three phase induction machine models. All relevant loss mechanisms are implemented and encapsulated in Modelica objects. The parametrized machine models

Comment	Parameter	Value	Unit
number of pole pairs	p	4	
rotor's moment of inertia	Jr	0.29	$kg \cdot m^2$
nominal RMS voltage per phase	VsNominal	100	V
nominal RMS current per phase		100	A
nominal frequency	fsNominal	50	Hz
stator resistance	Rs	0.03	Ω
stator stray inductance	Lssigma	0.3183	mH
stator zero sequence inductance	Lszero	0.3183	mH
main field inductance, d-axis	Lmd	4.7746	mH
main field inductance, q-axis	Lmq	4.7746	mH
damper stray inductance, d-axis	Lrsigmad	0.1592	mH
damper stray inductance, d-axis	Lrsigmaq	0.1592	mH
damper resistance, d-axis	Rrd	0.04	Ω
damper resistance, q-axis	Rrq	0.04	Ω
no-load excitation current	IeOpenCircuit	10	A
excitation resistance	Re	2.5	Ω
stray frac. of total exc. inductance	sigmae	2.5	%

Table 4. Parameters of the electrical excited synchronous machine

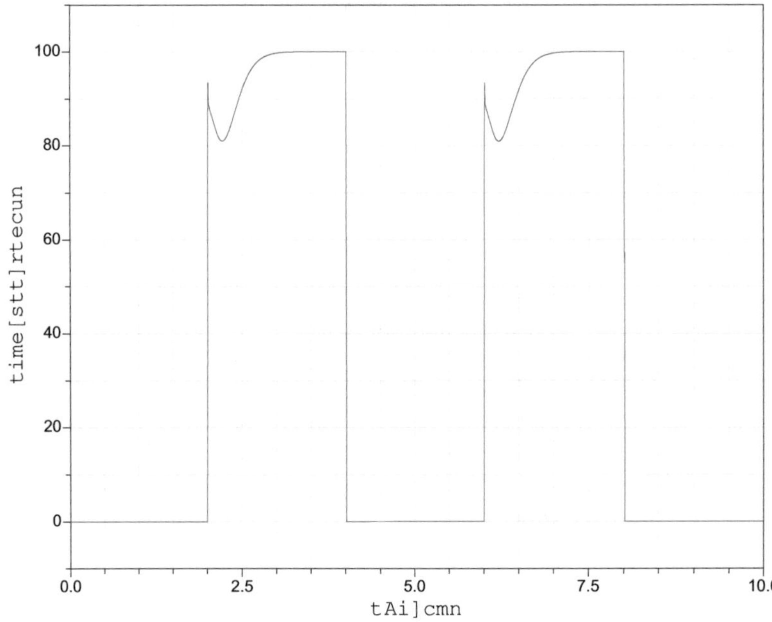

Fig. 14. Current of electrical excited synchronous machine

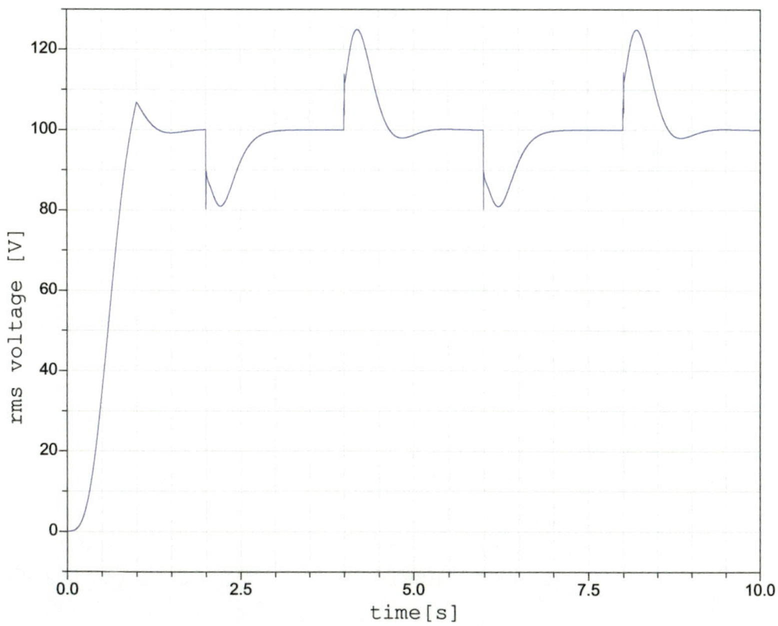

Fig. 15. Stator voltage of the electrical excited synchronous machine

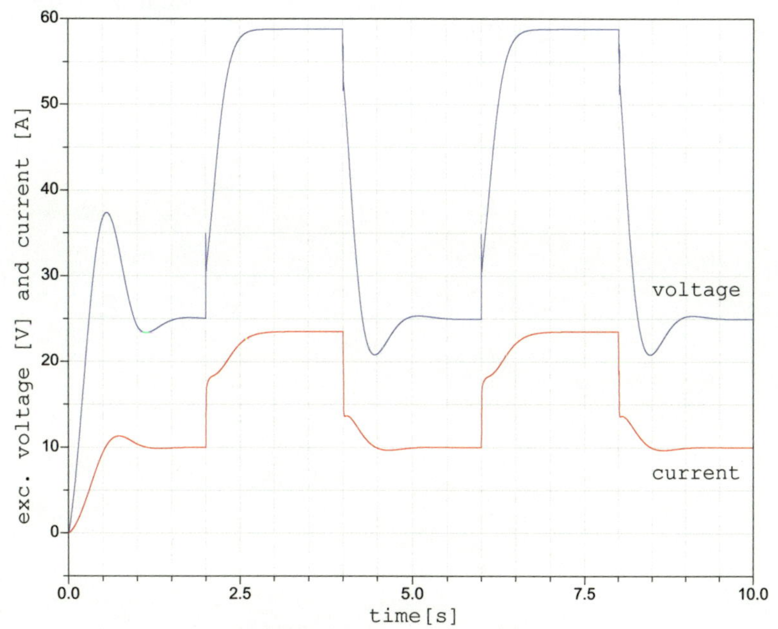

Fig. 16. Excitation of electrical excited synchronous machine

can be used together with other models from the Modelica Standard Library for various investigations; examples are presented in sec. 5. Due to the object oriented implementation all machine models can be used as a basis to implement additional phenomena, such as magnetic saturation or deep bar effects. Since the physical connectors are standardized in the Modelica Standard Library, the machine models have the potential to be used together with power electronic circuits, controll models and thermal models.

7. References

60034-2, D. E. (1998). Drehende elektrische Maschinen – Teil 2: Verfahren zur Bestimmung der Verluste und des Wirkungsgrades von drehenden elektrischen Maschinen aus Prüfungen (ausgenommen Maschinen für Schienen- und Straßenfahrzeuge.

60034-4, D. E. (1998). Drehende elektrische Maschinen – Teil 4: Verfahren zur Ermittlung der Kenngrößen von Synchronmaschinen durch Messung.

Fritzson, P. (2004). *Principles of Object-Oriented Modeling and Simulation with Modelica 2.1*, IEEE Press, Piscataway, NJ.

Haumer, A., Bäuml, T. & Kral, C. (2010). Multiphysical simulation improves engineering of electric drives, *7th EUROSIM Congress on Modelling and Simulation* .

Haumer, A., Kral, C., Kapeller, H., Bäuml, T. & Gragger, J. V. (2009). The AdvancedMachines library: Loss models for electric machines, *Proceedings of the 7th Modelica Conference* pp. 847–854.

Kleinrath, H. (1980). *Stromrichtergespeiste Drehfeldmaschinen*, Springer Verlag, Wien.

Lang, W. (1984) *Über die Bemessung verlustarmer Asynchronmotoren mit Kä□gläufer für Pulsumrichterspeisung*, PhD thesis, Technische Universität Wien.

Lin, D., Zhou, P., Fu, W., Badics, Z. & Cendes, Z. (2003). A dynamic core loss model for soft ferromagnetic and power ferrite materials in transient finite element analysis, *Conference Proceedings COMPUMAG* .

9

Mathematical Modelling and Simulation of Pneumatic Systems

Dr. Djordje Dihovicni and Dr. Miroslav Medenica
Visoka tehnicka skola, Bulevar Zorana Djindjica 152 a, 11070
Serbia

1. Introduction

Program support, simulation and the animation of dual action pneumatic actuators controlled with proportional spool valves are developed. Various factors are involved, such as time delay in the pneumatic lines, leakage between chambers, and air compressibility in cylinder chambers as well as non-linear flow through the valve. Taking into account the complexity of the model, and the fact that it is described by partial different equations, it is important to develop the program support based on numerical methods for solving this kind of problems. Simulation and program support in Maple and Matlab programming languages are conducted, and it is shown the efficiency of the results, from engineering view of point.

These pneumatic systems have a lot of advantages if we compare them with the same hydraulic types; they are suitable for clean environments, and much safer. In accordance with project and space conditions, valves are positioned at relatively large distance from pneumatic cylinder.

Considering real pneumatic systems, it is crucial to describe them with time delay, nonlinearities, with attempt of not creating only academic model. Despite of these problems, development of fast algorithms and using the numerical methods for solving partial different equations, as well as enhanced simulation and animation techniques become the necessity. Various practical stability approaches, for solving complex partial equations, used similar algorithms, (Dihovicni, 2006).

In the third part it is described special group of distributed parameter systems, with distributed control, where control depends of one space and one time coordinate. It has been presented mathematical model of pneumatic cylinder system. The stability on finite space interval is analyzed and efficient program support is developed.

Solving problem of constructing knowledge database of a decision making in process safety is shown in fourth part. It is provided analyses of the requirements as well the analyses of the system incidents caused by specification, design and the implementation of the project. Main focus of this part is highlighted on practical stability problem and conditions for optimal performance of pneumatic systems. Algorithm of decision making in safety of pneumatic systems is developed, and the system has been realized taking into account C# approach in Windows environment.

2. Representation of pneumatic cylinder-valve system

Deatiled mathematical model of dual action pneumatic actuator system, controlled by proportional spool valves, is shown in paper (Richer, 2000), and it is carefully considered effects of non-linear flow through the valve, leakage between chambers, time delay, attenuation and other effects.
These pneumatic systems have a lot of advantages if we compare them with the same hydraulic types, they are suitable for clean environments, and much safer. In accordance with project and space conditions, valves are positioned at relatively large distance from pneumatic cylinder.
Typical pneumatic system includes pneumatic cylinder, command device, force, position and pressure sensors, and as well as connecting tubes.

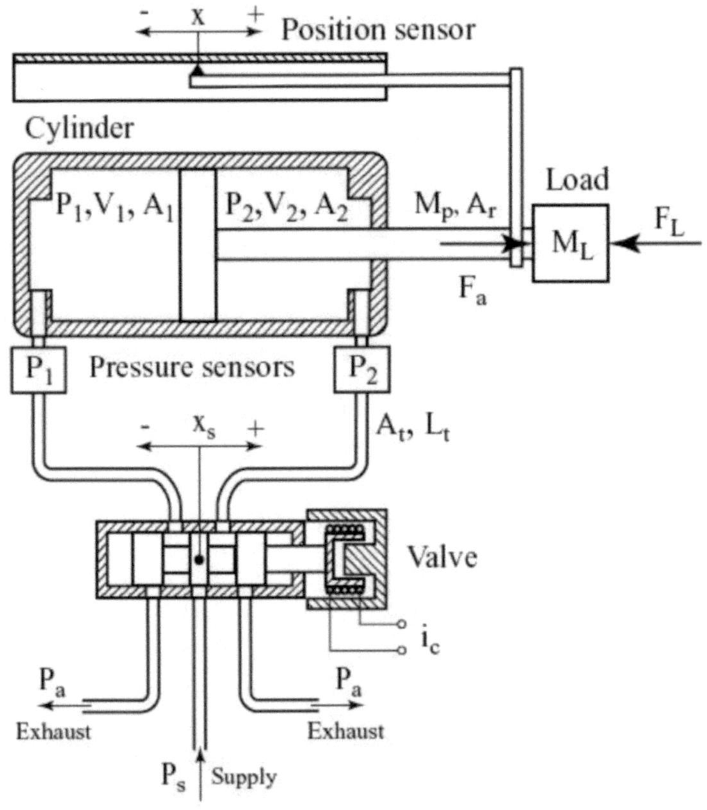

Fig. 1. Schematic representation of the pneumatic actuator system

The motion equation for the piston- road assembly is described as:

$$\left(M_L + M_p\right) \cdot \frac{d}{dt}\dot{x} + \beta \cdot \dot{x} + F_f + F_L = P_1 \bullet A_1 - P_2 \bullet A_2 - P_a \bullet A_r \tag{1}$$

where M_L is the external mass, M_p is the piston and rod assembly mass, x represents the piston position, β is the viscous friction coefficient, F_f is the Coulomb friction force, F_L is the external force, P_1 and P_2 are the absolute pressures in actuator's chambers, P_a is the absolute ambient pressure, A_1 and A_2 are the piston effective areas, and A_r is the rod cross sectional area.

The general model for a volume of gas consists of state equation, the concervation of mass, and the energy equation. Using the assumptions that the gas is ideal, the pressures and temperature within the chambre are homogeneous, and kinetic and potential energy terms are negligible, it should be written the equation for each chamber. Taking into account that control volume V, density ρ, mass m, pressure P, and temperature T, equation for ideal gas is described as:

$$P = \rho \bullet R \bullet T \tag{2}$$

where, R is gas constant. Mass flow is given with:

$$\dot{m} = \frac{d}{dt} \bullet (\rho \bullet V) \tag{3}$$

and it can be expressed as:

$$\dot{m}_{ul} - \dot{m}_{iz} = \dot{\rho} \bullet V + \rho \bullet \dot{V} \tag{4}$$

where, $\dot{m}_{ul}, \dot{m}_{iz}$ are input and output mass flow. Energy equation is described with:

$$q_{ul} - q_{iz} + k \bullet C_v \bullet (\dot{m}_{ul} \bullet T_{in} - \dot{m}_{iz} \bullet T) - W = \dot{U} \tag{5}$$

where q_{ul} and q_{iz} are the heat transfer terms, k is the specific heat ratio, C_v is the specific heat at constant volume, T_{in} is the temperature of the incoming gas flow, W is the rate of change in the work, and $\dot{U}$ is the change of the internal energy. The total change of the internal is given:

$$\dot{U} = \frac{d}{dt}(C_v \bullet m \bullet T) = \frac{1}{k-1} \bullet \frac{d}{dt}(P \bullet V) = \frac{1}{k \cdot 1}(V \bullet \dot{P} + P \bullet \dot{V}) \tag{6}$$

and it is used the expression, $C_v = R/(k-1)$. If we use the term $\dot{U} = P \bullet \dot{V}$ and supstitute the equation (6) into equation (5), it yields:

$$q_{ul} - q_{iz} + \frac{k}{k-1} \cdot \frac{P}{\rho \bullet T}(\dot{m}_{ul} \bullet T_{ul} - \dot{m}_{iz} \bullet T) - \frac{k}{k-1} \bullet P \bullet \dot{V} = \frac{1}{k-1} \bullet V \bullet \dot{P} \tag{7}$$

If we assume that input flow is on the gas temperature in the chambre, which is considered for analyze, then we have:

$$\frac{k}{k-1} \bullet (q_{ul} - q_{iz}) + \frac{1}{\rho} \bullet (\dot{m}_{ul} - \dot{m}_{iz}) - \dot{V} = \frac{V}{k \bullet P} \bullet \dot{P} \tag{8}$$

Further simplification may be developed by analysing the terms of heat transfer in the equation (8). If we consider that the process is adiabatic (q_{ul}-q_{iz}=0), the derivation of the pressure in the chamber is:

$$\dot{P} = k \bullet \frac{P}{\rho \bullet V} \bullet (\dot{m}_{ul} - \dot{m}_{iz}) - k \bullet \frac{P}{V} \bullet \dot{V} \tag{9}$$

and if we substitute ρ from the equation (2), then it yields:

$$\dot{P} = k \bullet \frac{R \cdot T}{V} \bullet \left(\dot{m}_{ul} - \dot{m}_{iz}\right) - k \bullet \frac{P}{V} \bullet \dot{V} \tag{10}$$

and if we consider that the process is isothermal (*T=constant),* then the change of the internal energy can be written as:

$$\dot{U} = C_v \bullet \dot{m} \bullet T \tag{11}$$

and the equation (8) can be written as:

$$q_{in} - q_{out} = P \bullet \dot{V} - \frac{P}{\rho} \bullet \left(\dot{m}_{in} - \dot{m}_{out}\right) \tag{12}$$

and then:

$$\dot{P} = \frac{R \cdot T}{V} \bullet \left(\dot{m}_{in} - \dot{m}_{out}\right) - \frac{P}{V} \bullet \dot{V} \tag{13}$$

Comparing the equation (10) and the equation (13), it can be shown that the only difference is in heat transfer factor term *k*. Then both equations are given:

$$\dot{P} = \frac{R \cdot T}{V} \bullet \left(a_{ul} \bullet \dot{m}_{in} - a_{iz} \bullet \dot{m}_{out}\right) - a \bullet \frac{P}{V} \bullet \dot{V} \tag{14}$$

where a, a_{ul}, and a_{iz} can take values between 1 i k, in accordance with heat transfer during the time of the process .
If we choose the origin of piston displacement at the middle of the stroke, the volume equation can be expressed as:

$$V_i = V_{0i} + A_i \bullet \left(\left(\left(\frac{1}{2}L \pm x\right)\right)\right) \tag{15}$$

where i=1,2 is cylinder chambers, index V_{0i} is non active volume at the end of the stroke, A_i is effective piston area, L is the piston stroke, and x is the position of the piston. If we change the equation (15) into equation (14), and pressure time derivation in pneumatic cylinder chambers, then it yields:

$$\dot{P}_i = \frac{R \cdot T}{V_{oi} + A_i \cdot \left(\frac{1}{2} \cdot L \pm x\right)} \cdot \bullet \left(a_{ul} \bullet \dot{m}_{ul} - a_{iz} \bullet \dot{m}_{iz}\right) - a \bullet \frac{P \bullet A_i}{V_{oi} + A_i \bullet \left(\left(\frac{1}{2} \bullet L \pm x\right)\right)} \bullet \dot{x} \tag{16}$$

2.1 Mathematical model valve-cylinder

In the literature, (Andersen, 1967), two basic equations which consider the flow change in pneumatic systems, are:

$$\frac{\partial P}{\partial s} = -R_i \bullet u - \rho \bullet \frac{\partial w}{\partial t} \tag{17}$$

$$\frac{\partial u}{\partial s} = -\frac{1}{\rho \bullet c^2} \bullet \frac{\partial P}{\partial t} \tag{18}$$

where P is the pressure through the tube, u is the velocity, ρ is the air density, c is the sound speed, s is the tube axis coordinate, and R_t is the tube resistance. If we use mass flow through the tube, $\dot{m}_t = \rho \bullet A_t \bullet w$, where A_t is cross sectional area., finally it yields:

$$\frac{\partial P}{\partial s} = -\frac{1}{A_t} \bullet \frac{\partial \dot{m}_t}{\partial t} - \frac{R_t}{\rho \bullet A_t} \bullet \dot{m}_t \tag{19}$$

$$\frac{\partial \dot{m}_t}{\partial s} = -\frac{A_t}{c^2} \bullet \frac{\partial P}{\partial t} \tag{20}$$

The overall analysis is based on turbulent flow in the tube, which is presented in figure 2.

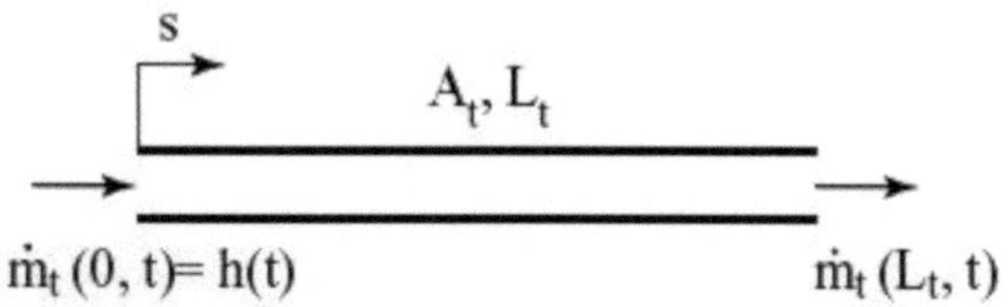

Fig. 2. Turbulent flow in the tube

Differentiating the equation (19), and the equation (20) with respect s, it is given the equation of mass flow through the tube:

$$\frac{\partial^2 \dot{m}_i}{\partial t^2} - c^2 \bullet \frac{\partial^2 \dot{m}_i}{\partial s^2} + \frac{R_i}{\rho} \bullet \frac{\partial \dot{m}_i}{\partial t} = 0 \tag{21}$$

The equation represents generalized wave equation, with new terms, and can be solved by using the form (Richer, 2000), like:

$$\dot{m}_t(s,t) = \varphi(t) \bullet \xi(s,t) \tag{22}$$

where $\xi(s,t)$ and $\varphi(t)$ are new functions. Supstituing equation (22) into equation (21) it yields:

$$\frac{\partial^2 \xi}{\partial t^2} - c^2 \bullet \varphi \bullet \frac{\partial^2 \xi}{\partial s^2} + \left((\varphi \bullet \frac{R_t}{\rho} + 2 \bullet \varphi') \right) \bullet \frac{\partial \xi}{\partial t} + \left((\varphi' \bullet \frac{R_t}{\rho} + \varphi'') \right) \bullet \xi = 0 \tag{23}$$

Simplifying the equation for ξ, it is determined $\varphi(t)$, so after the supstitution in equation (23), remaining of the equation ξ, doesn't contain the terms of firt order, so:

$$2 \bullet \varphi' + \varphi \bullet \frac{R_t}{\rho} = 0 \tag{24}$$

and that yields to:

$$\varphi(t) = e^{\frac{R_t}{2 \bullet \rho} \bullet t} \tag{25}$$

The result equation for ξ, will be in that case:

$$\frac{\partial^2 \xi}{\partial t^2} - c^2 \bullet \varphi \frac{\partial^2 \xi}{\partial s^2} + \frac{R_t^2}{4 \cdot \rho^2} \bullet \xi = 0 \tag{26}$$

which represents dispersive hyperbolic equation. Tubes are usually not so long, so it might be assumpted that the dispersion is small, and it can't be neglected. Using that assumption it yields:

$$\frac{\partial^2 \xi}{\partial t^2} - c^2 \bullet \varphi \frac{\partial^2 w}{\partial s^2} = 0 \tag{27}$$

which represents the classical one-dimension wave equation, which can be solved by using specific boundary and initial conditions:

$$\begin{cases} \xi(s,0) = 0 \\ \dfrac{\partial \xi}{\partial t}(s,0) = 0 \\ \xi(0,t) = h(t) \end{cases} \tag{28}$$

The solution for the problem of boundary-initial values is given in the literature, (Richer, 2000), and can be expressed as:

$$\xi(s,t) = \begin{cases} 0 & if\ t < s/c \\ h \bullet \left((t - \dfrac{s}{c}) \right) & if\ t > s/c \end{cases} \tag{29}$$

The input wave will reach the end of the tube in time interval $\tau = L_t/c$. Supstituing t with Lt/c in the equation (24), and ρ from the state equation, it is given:

$$\varphi = e^{\frac{R_T \cdot R \cdot T}{2 \cdot P} \bullet \frac{L_T}{c}} \tag{30}$$

where P is the pressure. Mass flow at the end of the tube, when $s=L_t$ is given with:

$$\dot{m}_t(L_t,t) = \begin{cases} 0 & if\ t < \dfrac{L_t}{c} \\ e^{\frac{R_T \cdot R \cdot T}{2 \cdot P} \cdot \frac{L_T}{c}} \bullet h\left(t - \dfrac{L_t}{c} \right) & if\ t > \dfrac{L_t}{c} \end{cases} \tag{31}$$

The tube resistance R_t, can be calculated, (Richer, 2000/, and it is shown by following equation:

$$\Delta p = f \bullet \frac{L_t}{D} \bullet \frac{\rho \cdot w^2}{2} = R_t \bullet w \bullet L_t \tag{32}$$

where f is the friction factor, and D is inner diameter of the tube. For laminar flow, $f=64/Re$, where Re, is Reynolds number. The resistance of the tube then becomes:

$$R_t = \frac{32 \bullet \mu}{D^2} \tag{33}$$

where μ is dynamic viscosity of the air. If the Blasius formula is used, then it yields:

$$f = \frac{0.316}{\mathrm{Re}^{1/4}} \tag{34}$$

so the flow resistance for the turbulent flow then becomes:

$$R_t = 0.158 \bullet \frac{\mu}{D^2} \bullet \mathrm{Re}^{3/4} \tag{35}$$

2.2 Program support

Program support is developed in Maple programing language.

```
#
# File for simulation
# the disperzive hyperbolic equation
# Definition the number of precision
Digits: =3:
# Definition of the disperse hyperbolic equation
pdeq : = diff(ξ, t)^2-c^2*φ*diff(ω,s)^2;
# Definition of initial conditions
init1:= ξ(s,0)=0:
init2:= diff(ξ, t)=0
init3:= ξ(0,t)=Heaviside(t)
# Creating the procedure for numeric solving
pdsol :=pdsolve(pdeq,init1, init2,init3):
#Activating the function for graphic display
# the solutions of the equation
plot (i(t), t=0.. 10, i=0.04...008, axes=boxed, ytickmarks=6);
```

2.3 Animation

The animation is created in Matlab programming language, (Dihovicni, 2008).

% Solving the disperse equation

% $\frac{\partial^2 \xi}{\partial t^2} \bullet c^2 - \varphi \frac{\partial^2 w}{\partial s^2} = 0$

%

```
%       Problem definition
g='squareg'; %
b='squareb3'; % 0 o
%           0
c=1;
a=0;
f=0;
d=1;
```

```
%    Mesh
[p,e,t]=initmesh('squareg');

%    Initial coditions:
```
$$\% \quad \xi(s,0)=0$$
$$\% \quad \frac{\partial \xi}{\partial t}(s,0)=0$$
$$\% \quad \xi(0,t)=h(t)$$
```
%    using higher program modes
%    time definition
x=p(1,:)';
y=p(2,:)';
u0=atan(cos(pi/2*x));
ut0=3*sin(pi*x).*exp(sin(pi/2*y));
%    Desired solution in 43 points between 0 and 10.
n=43;
tlist=linspace(0,10,n);
%    Solving of hyperbolic equation
uu=hyperbolic(u0,ut0,tlist,b,p,e,t,c,a,f,d);
%    Interpolation of rectangular mesh
delta=-1:0.1:1;
[uxy,tn,a2,a3]=tri2grid(p,t,uu(:,1),delta,delta);
gp=[tn;a2;a3];
%    Creating the animation
newplot;
M=moviein(n);
umax=max(max(uu));
umin=min(min(uu));
for i=1:n,...
 if rem(i,10)==0,...
 end,...
 pdeplot(p,e,t,'xydata',uu(:,i),'zdata',uu(:,i),'zstyle','continuous',...
      'mesh','off','xygrid','on','gridparam',gp,'colorbar','off');...
 axis([-1 1 -1 1 umin umax]); caxis([umin umax]);...
 M(:,i)=getframe;...
 if i==n,...
 if rem(i,10)==0,...
 end,...
 pdeplot(p,e,t,'xydata',uu(:,i),'zdata',uu(:,i),'zstyle','continuous',...
      'mesh','off','xygrid','on','gridparam',gp,'colorbar','off');...
 axis([-1 1 -1 1 umin umax]); caxis([umin umax]);...
 M(:,i)=getframe;...
 if i==n,...
 if rem(i,10)==0,...
 end,...
```

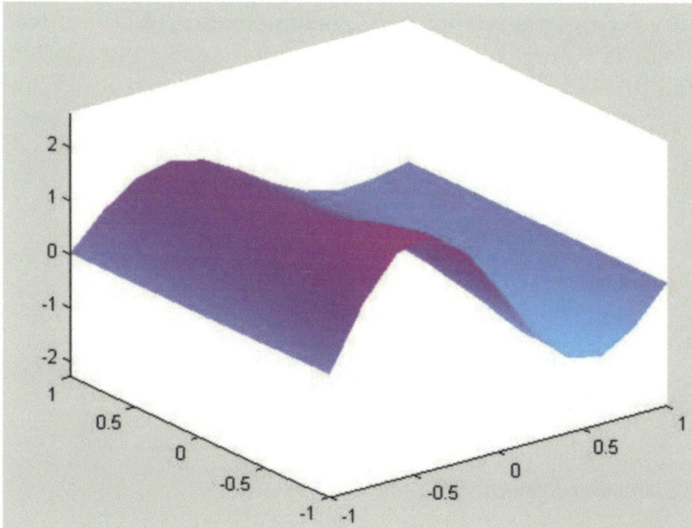

Fig. 3. Animation of the disperse equation

2.4 Conclusions

The complex mathematical model of dual action pneumatic actuators controlled with proportional spool valves (Richer, 2000) is presented. It is shown the adequate program support in *Maple* language, based on numerical methods. The simulation and animation is developed in *Matlab* programming language. The simplicity of solving the partial different equations, by using this approach and even the partial equations of higher order, is crucial in future development directions.

3. Program support for distributed control systems on finite space interval

Pneumatic cylinder systems significantly depend of behavior of pneumatic pipes, thus it is very important to analyze the characteristics of the pipes connected to a cylinder. Mathematical model of this system is described by partial different equations, and it is well known fact that it is distributed parameter system. These systems appear in various areas of engineering, and one of the special types is distributed parameter system with distributed control.

3.1 Mathematical model of pneumatic cylinder system

The Figure 4 shows a schematic diagram of pneumatic cylinder system. The system consists of cylinder, inlet and outlet pipes and two speed control valves at the charge and discharge sides. Detailed procedure of creating this mathematical model is described in, (Tokashiki, 1996).

For describing behavior of pneumatic cylinder, the basic equations that are used are: state equation of gases, energy equation and motion equation, (Al Ibrahim, 1992).

$$\frac{dP}{dt}=\frac{1}{V}\bullet\left(\frac{P\bullet V}{\theta}\frac{d\theta}{dt}+R\bullet\theta\bullet G-P\bullet\frac{dV_d}{dt}\right) \tag{36}$$

where P is pressure (kPa), V- is volume (m^3), θ - temperature (K), R- universal gas constant (J/kgK), and V_d- is dead volume (m^3).

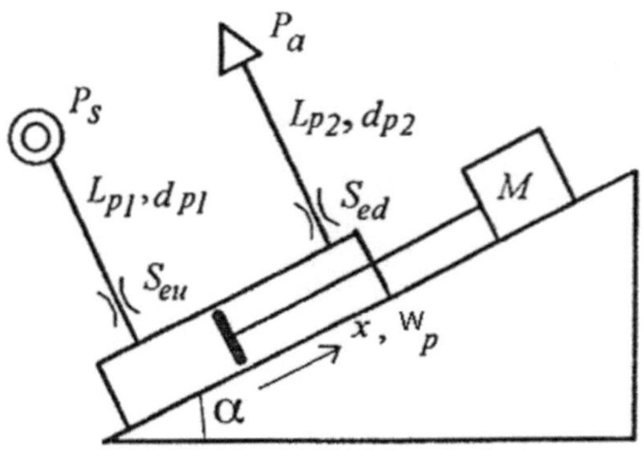

Fig. 4. Schematic diagram of pneumatic cylinder system

The temperature change of the air in each cylinder chamber, from the first law of thermodynamics, can be written as:

$$\frac{d\theta_d}{dt} = \frac{1}{C_v \bullet m_d} \cdot \left\{ S_{hd} \bullet h_d (\theta_a - \theta_d) + R \bullet \dot{m}_d \bullet \theta_d - P_d \bullet \frac{dV_d}{dt} \right\} \tag{37}$$

$$\frac{d\theta_u}{dt} = \frac{1}{C_v \bullet m_u} \cdot \left\{ S_{hu} \bullet h_u (\theta_a - \theta_u) + C_p \bullet \dot{m}_u \bullet T_1 - C_v \bullet \dot{m}_u \bullet \theta_u - P_u \bullet \frac{dV_u}{dt} \right\} \tag{38}$$

where C_v- is specific heat at constant volume (J/kgK), m- mass of the air (kg), S_h –heat transfer area (m^2), $\dot{m}$ - mass flow rate (kg/s), and subscript d denotes downstream side, and subscript u denotes upstream side.

Taking into account that thermal conductivity and the heat capacity of the cylinder are sufficiently large compared with them of the air, the wall temperature is considered to be constant.

In equation of motion, the friction force is considered as sum of the Coulomb and viscous friction, and force of viscous friction is considered as linear function of piston velocity, and other parameters have constant effect to friction force of cylinder. Then, equation of motion may be presented in following form:

$$M \bullet \frac{dw_p}{dt} = P_u \bullet S_u - P_d \bullet S_d + P_a \bullet (S_d - S_u) - M \bullet g \bullet \sin a - c \bullet w_p \bullet F_q \tag{39}$$

where S- cylinder piston area (m^2), w_p- piston velocity (m/s), M- load mass (kg), c-cylinder viscous friction (Ns/m), P_a- atmospheric pressure (kPa), F_q- Coulomb friction (N), g-acceleration of gravity (m/s^2).

By using the finite difference method, it can be possible to calculate the airflow through the pneumatic pipe. The pipe is divided into n partitions.
Applying the continuity equation, and using relation for mass of the air $m = \rho \bullet A \bullet \partial z$ and mass flow $\dot{m} = \rho \bullet A \bullet w$, it can be obtained:

$$\frac{\partial m_i}{\partial t} = \dot{m}_{i-1} - \dot{m}_i \tag{40}$$

Starting from the gas equation, and assuming that the volume of each part is constant, deriving the state equation it follows, (Kagawa, 1994):

$$\frac{dP_i}{dt} = \frac{R \bullet \theta_i}{V}\left(\dot{m}_{i-1} - \dot{m}_i\right) + \frac{R \bullet m_i}{V} \bullet \frac{d\theta_i}{dt} \tag{41}$$

The motion equation of the air, is derived from Newton's second law of motion and is described as:

$$\frac{\partial w}{\partial t} = \frac{P_i - P_{i+q}}{\rho_i \bullet \delta\, z} \bullet \frac{\lambda}{2d} \bullet w_i \bullet |w_i| - |w_i| \bullet \frac{\partial w_i}{\partial z} \tag{42}$$

where λ is pipe viscous friction coefficient and is calculated as a function of the Reynolds number:

$$\lambda = \frac{64}{\text{Re}}, \quad \text{Re} < 2.5x10^3 \tag{43}$$

$$\lambda = 0.3164\ \text{Re}^{0.25}, \quad \text{Re} \geq 2.5x10^3 \tag{44}$$

The respective energy can be written as:

$$\Delta E_{st} = E_{1i} - E_{2i} + L_{1i} - L_{2i} + Q_i \tag{45}$$

where E_{1i} is input energy, E_{2i} is output energy, L_{1i} is cylinder stroke in downstream side, and L_{2i} is cylinder stroke in upstream side of pipe model, and the total energy is calculated as sum of kinematic and potential energy.
Deriving the total energy ΔE_{st} , it is obtained the energy change ΔE_{st}:

$$\Delta E_{st} = \frac{d}{dt}\left\{\left((C_v \bullet m_i \bullet \theta_i + \frac{1}{2} \bullet m_i \bullet \left((\frac{w_{i-1} + w_i}{2}\right)^2)\right)\right\} \tag{46}$$

In equation (45), the inflow and outflow energy as well as the work made by the inflow and outflow air can be presented :
From the following equation the heat energy Q can be calculated:

$$Q = h_i \bullet S_h \bullet \left(\theta_a - \theta_i\right) \tag{47}$$

where h is is heat transfer coefficient which can be easily calculated from the Nusselt number Nu, and thermal conductivity k:

$$h_i = \frac{2Nu_i \bullet k_i}{d_p} \tag{48}$$

where d_p is pipe diameter.
Nusselt number can be calculated from Ditus and Boelter formula for smooth tubes, and for fully developed turbulent flow:

$$Nu_i = 0.023 \bullet \mathrm{Re}_i^{0.8} \bullet \mathrm{Pr}^{0.4} \tag{49}$$

and thermal conductivity k can be calculated as a linear function of temperature:

$$k_i = 7.95 \bullet 10^5 \bullet \theta_i + 2.0465 \bullet 10^3 \tag{50}$$

3.2 Distributed parameter systems

During analyzes and synthesis of control systems, fundamental question which arises is determination of stability. In accordance with engineer needs, we can roughly divide stability definitions into: Ljapunov and non-Ljapunov concept. The most useful approach of control systems is Ljapunov approach, when we observe system on infinite interval, and that in real circumstances has only academic significance.
Let us consider n- dimensional non-linear vector equation:

$$\frac{d\underline{x}}{dt} = f(\underline{x}) \tag{51}$$

for $\frac{d\underline{x}}{dt} = 0$ solution of this equation is $\underline{x}_s$=0 and we can denote it as equilibrium state. Equilibrium state $\underline{x}_r$=0 is stable in sense of Ljapunov if and only if for every constant and real number ε, exists δ(ε)>0 and the following equation is fulfilled, (Gilles, 1973):

$$\|\underline{x}_0\| = \|\underline{x}\|_{t=0} \le \delta \tag{52}$$

for every t ≥0

$$\|\underline{x}\| < \varepsilon \tag{53}$$

If following equation exists:

$$\|\underline{x}_0\| \to 0 \text{ for } t \to \infty \tag{54}$$

then system equilibrium state is asymptotic stable.
System equilibrium state is stable, if and only if exists scalar, real function V($\underline{x}$), Ljapunov function, which for $\|\underline{x}\| < r, r = const > 0$, has following features:

a. $V(\underline{x})$ is positively defined
b. $\frac{dV(\underline{x})}{dt}$ is negatively semi defined for t≥0

System equilibrium state is asymptotic stable, if and only if exists:

$\frac{dV(\underline{x})}{dt}$ is negatively defined for t≥0

Derivation of function V(x) , $\frac{dV(\underline{x})}{dt}$ can be expressed:

$$\frac{dV(x)}{dt} = \nabla_x{}^T \bullet V(\underline{x}) \bullet \frac{d\underline{x}}{dt} = \nabla_x{}^T V(\underline{x}) \bullet \underline{f}(\underline{x}) \tag{55}$$

and

$$\nabla_x = \begin{bmatrix} \begin{bmatrix} \frac{\partial}{\partial x_1} \\ \cdot \\ \cdot \\ \cdot \\ \cdot \\ \frac{\partial}{\partial x_n} \end{bmatrix} \end{bmatrix} \tag{56}$$

By using Ljapunov function successfully is solved problem of asymptotic stability of system equilibrium state on infinite interval.

From strictly engineering point of view it is very important to know the boundaries where system trajectory comes during there's motion in state space. The practice technical needs are responsible for non- Ljapunov definitions, and among them is extremely important behaving on finite time interval- practical stability. Taking into account that system can be stabile in classic way but also can posses not appropriate quality of dynamic behavior, and because that it is not applicable, it is important to take system in consideration in relation with sets of permitted states in phase space which are defined for such a problem. In theory of control systems there are demands for stability on finite time interval that for strictly engineering view of point has tremendous importance. The basic difference between Ljapunov and practical stability is set of initial states of system (S_α) and set of permitted disturbance (S_ε). Ljapunov concept of stability, demands existence of sets S_α and S_ε in state space, for every opened set S_β permitted states and it is supplied that equilibrium point of that system will be totally stable, instead of principle of practical stability where are sets (S_α and S_ε) and set S_β which is closed, determined and known in advance.

Taking into account principle of practical stability, the following conditions must be satisfied:

- determine set S_β - find the borders for system motion
- determine set S_ε - find maximum amplitudes of possible disturbance
- determine set S_α of all initial state values

In case that this conditions are regularly determined it is possible to analyze system stability from practical stability view of point.

3.2 Practical stability

Problem of asymptotic stability of system equilibrium state can be solved for distributed parameter systems, which are described by equation:

$$\frac{\partial \underline{x}}{\partial z} = \underline{f}\left((t, \underline{x}, \frac{\partial \underline{x}}{\partial t}, \frac{\partial^2 \underline{x}}{\partial t^2} ...) \right) \quad t \in (0, T) \tag{57}$$

with following initial conditions:

$$\underline{x}(t,0) = \underline{x}_0(t) \tag{58}$$

To satisfy equation (57), space coordinate z cannot be explicitly defined. The solution of equation (23) is $\frac{\partial \underline{x}}{\partial z} = \underline{0}$, and let the following equation exists:

$$\frac{\partial \underline{x}}{\partial z} = \underline{x}(t,z) - \underline{x}_r(t) \tag{59}$$

Assumption 1: Space coordinate z on time interval $t \in (0,T)$ is constant.

Accepting previous assumption, and equation (58), we have equation for equilibrium state for system described by equation (57):

$$\underline{x}_r(t) = 0 \tag{60}$$

For defining asymptotic stability of equilibrium state the functional V is used:

$$V(x) = \int_0^l W(\underline{x})\, dt \tag{61}$$

where W is scalar of vector $\underline{x}$.

We choose functional V like:

$$V(x) = \frac{1}{2} \bullet \int_0^T \underline{x^T x} \bullet dt \tag{62}$$

when it is used expression for norm:

$$\|\underline{x}\| = \sqrt{\int_0^T \underline{x}^T \bullet \underline{x} dt} \tag{63}$$

For asymptotic stability of distributed parameter systems described by equation (7), we use Ljapunov theorems, applied for functional V:

$$\frac{dV(\underline{x})}{dz} = \int_0^l \nabla^T{}_x \bullet W(\underline{x}) \bullet f\left((t, \underline{x}, \frac{\partial \underline{x}}{\partial t}, \frac{\partial^2 x}{\partial t^2} ...) \right) \bullet dt \tag{64}$$

where W is scalar function of $\underline{x}$.
Let consider distributed parameter system described by following equation:

$$\frac{\partial^3 x}{\partial t^3} = \frac{\partial x}{\partial t} \tag{65}$$

and initial conditions:

$$x(0,z) = \frac{K}{2} \bullet x(T,z) \tag{66}$$

We use the assumption that equation (61) and initial conditions (62) are not explicit functions of space coordinate *z*, so stationary state of system (61) with appropriate border conditions is represented by following equation:

$$x_r(z) = 0, \text{ with} \frac{\partial^3 x}{\partial z^3} = 0 \tag{67}$$

For determination of asymptotic stability of equilibrium system state, we use functional V which is expressed:

$$V(x) = \int_0^l W(\underline{x}) dt \tag{69}$$

where W is scalar function of $\underline{x}$.
Functional V is described by :

$$V = \frac{1}{4} \bullet \int [x(t,z)]^4 \bullet dt \tag{70}$$

and the following condition V(x)>0 is fulfilled.
Derivation of functional V is given by following equation:

$$\begin{gathered} \frac{dV(x)}{dz} = \int_0^L x^3 \bullet \frac{\partial^3 x}{\partial z^3} \bullet dt = \int_0^L x^3 \bullet \frac{\partial x}{\partial t} \bullet dt = \\ \frac{1}{4}\left([x(T,z)]^4 \bullet [x(0,z)]^4 \right) \end{gathered} \tag{71}$$

By using equation (65) and by including it in equation (71) it is obtained:

$$\frac{dV(x)}{dz} = (\left(1 - \frac{K^4}{4}) \right) \bullet ([x(T,z)]^4) \tag{72}$$

and it yields:

$$\frac{dV(x)}{dt} < 0 \text{ when } K^4 < 1/4,\ |K| < 0.7 \tag{73}$$

which is necessary and sufficient condition for asymptotic stability of equilibrium state for system described by equations (61) and (62).

3.3 Distributed control

Control of distributed parameter systems, which depends of time and space coordinate is called distributed control. If we choose control *U*, for pressure difference in two close parts of pneumatic pipe, and for state *X*, if we choose air velocity through the pneumatic pipe, with assumptions that are shown during derivation of mathematical model of pneumatic pipe, finally it is obtained:

$$\frac{\partial X}{\partial t}+|X|\bullet\frac{\partial X}{\partial z}+a\bullet X\bullet|X|=b\bullet U,\ z\in[0,L] \tag{74}$$

where $a=\frac{\lambda}{2\bullet d}$, $b=\frac{1}{\rho\bullet\delta z}$.

Nominal distributed control can be solved by using procedure which is described in (Novakovic, 1989), and result of that control is nominal state $w_N(t,z)$ of chosen system. In that case it yields:

$$\begin{aligned}L(X_N(t,z))=&\frac{1}{b}\bullet\frac{\partial X_N}{\partial t}+\frac{1}{b}\bullet|X|\bullet\frac{\partial X}{\partial z}\\&+\frac{1}{b}\bullet a\bullet X\bullet|X|=U(t,z)\end{aligned} \tag{75}$$

where *L* is appropriate operator.

System (73) is exposed to many disturbances, so the real dynamic must be different from nominal. It is applied deviation from nominal system state, then the nominal system state can be realized as:

$$x(t,z)=X(t,z)-X_N(t,z),\ 0<z\cdot L. \tag{76}$$

Time derivation of deviation from nominal system state, can be presented by following equation:

$$\frac{\partial x(t,z)}{\partial t}=\frac{\partial X(t,z)}{\partial t}-\frac{\partial X_N(t,z)}{\partial t} \tag{77}$$

and from equations (74), it yields:

$$\frac{\partial x(t,z)}{\partial t}=r(t,z)+|X|\bullet\frac{\partial X}{\partial z}+a\bullet X\bullet|X|-b\bullet U \tag{78}$$

where $r=\frac{\partial X_N}{\partial t}$

3.4 Application

Using the concept of extern linearization, which is described in, (Meyer, 1983), we can include distributed control in the following form:

$$U(t,z)=\left[(a-k)\bullet X\bullet|X|+k\bullet X_N\bullet|X|+|X|\bullet\frac{\partial X}{\partial z}+r\right]/b,\quad 0\leq z\leq L \tag{79}$$

Including the equation (79) in the equation (78), it yields:

$$\frac{\partial x(t,z)}{\partial t}=-k\bullet x(t,z),\, 0\leq z\leq L \tag{80}$$

Functional V is chosen in the form:

$$V(x)=\frac{1}{2}\bullet\int_0^L[x(t,z)]^2\bullet dz=\frac{1}{2}\bullet\|x(t,z)\|^2 \tag{81}$$

Derivation of functional V is given as:

$$\begin{aligned}\frac{dV(x)}{dt}&=\int_0^L x\bullet\frac{\partial x}{\partial t}\bullet dz\\&=k\bullet\int_0^L[x(t,z)]^2\bullet dz=2\bullet k\bullet V(x)\end{aligned} \tag{82}$$

Taking into account that *V(x)* is positive defined functional, time derivation of functional given by equation (82) will be negative defined function for *k>0,* and in that way all necessary conditions from Ljapunov theorem applied to functional V, are fulfilled.

$$\nabla_x=\begin{bmatrix}\frac{\partial}{\partial x_1}\\ \cdot\\ \cdot\\ \cdot\\ \cdot\\ \frac{\partial}{\partial x_n}\end{bmatrix} \tag{83}$$

3.5 Program support

For this kind of symbolically presented problems, the most elegant solution can be achieved by using program language Maple.

\#

\# Program support for determination of stability of

\# distributed parameter systems on finite space interval

\# described by equation

\# $\frac{\partial x}{\partial z^3}=f\bullet\left(\frac{\partial x}{\partial t}\right)$

\#

```
# Definition of  procedure dpst
dpst:=proc(ulaz3)
# Read input values
read ulaz3;
# Determination of functional  V
V:=1/4*int[x(t,z)∧2,z]=norm[x(t,z)];
# Determination of functional V derivation
 dV/dz:=int[x(t,z)*diff(x,t),t]
# Applying partial integration on equation dV/dt
with(student)
intpart[Int(x*diff(x∧2,z∧2), x)]
# Presentation of equation dV/dt
dV/dt;
# Calculation of values for parameter K for which the system is stable
result:= solve(dV/dt,K)
#
```

If the procedure dpst would be operational for determination the values of parameter K for which the system is stable, it is necessary to create files with input parameters for current procedure. For case that is analytically calculated, it is created file *input3* with following input data:

```
dx/dt=diff(x∧3,z∧3)
 x(0,z)= =K/2*x(T,z)
```

```
# Program support for distributed parameter systems with distributed control
#
# Definition of procedure dpsdc
dpsdc:=proc(input 1)
# Reading of input parameter values
read input1;
# Determination of functional V
V:=1/2*int[x(t,z)^2,z]=norm[x(t,z)];
# Determinatation of time derivation of functional V
dV/dt:=int[x(t,z)*diff(x,t),z];
# Calculation of time derivation of functional V
derivationfunctional:=solve(dV/dt, z=0..1);
# Calculation the values of parameter K  for which the system is stable
solution:=solve(derivationfunctional,K);
```

For using the procedure *dpsdc* for determination the values of parameter K it is necessary to create files that contain input parameters for given procedure. In case, which is calculated, the file *input 1* with input data:

```
dx/dt=-k*(x,z);
```

By using task *read* it yields to reading procedure *dpsdc.* Specification of input1 as argument of the procedure *dpsdc* starts the process of calculation the values of parameter K for which this distributed parameter system is stable on finite space interval.

It is developed, program support for other types of distributed parameter systems.

```
#
# Program support for determination of stability of
#  distributed parameter systems on finite space interval
# described by equation
```

$$\# \ \frac{\partial x}{\partial t} = f\left(\bullet \frac{\partial x}{\partial z}\right)$$

```
#
# Definition of  procedure srppr
srppr:=proc(ulaz1)
# Read input values
read ulaz1;
# Determination of functional  V
V:=1/2*int[x(t,z)^2,z]=norm[x(t,z)];
#Determinatation of time derivation of functional V
dV/dt:=int[x(t,z)*diff(x,t),z];
#Solving the functional V
derivationfunctional:=solve(dV/dt, z=0..1);
# Calculation the solution for parameter K for which is
# the system stable
solution:=solve(derfunctional,K);
```

If the procedure *srppr* would be operational for determination of value of parameter K for which the system is stable, it is necessary to create files with input parameters for current procedure. It is created file *input1* with following data :

```
dx/dt=-vz*diff(x,z);
x(t,0)=-K*x(t,l)
# Program support for determination of stability of
# distributed parameter diffusion systems on finite space
# interval
# Definition of  procedure srppr
srpdp:=proc(ulaz2)
# Read input values
read input1;
# Determination of functional  V
V:=1/2*int[exp(2*γ*z)*x(t,z)^2, z=0..1];
# Determinatation of time derivation of functional V
dV/dt:=diff(V,t);
# Applying partial integration on equation dV/dt
intpart[Int(exp(2*γ*z)*diff(x,z)^2,z=0..1)]=( γ^2+π^2/1^2)*int[exp(2* γ*z)*x^2, z=0..1);
# Calculation of values for parameter K for which the system is stable
resenje:=solve(dV/dt,K);
```

If the procedure *spdsr* would be operational for determination of value of parameter K for which the system is stable, it is necessary to create files with input parameters for current procedure. It is created file *ula2* with following data:

```
dx/dt=diff(x^2,z^2)+2*a*diff(x,z)-b*x
x(t,0)=x(t,l)=0
```

3.6 Conclusion

Special class of control systems is focus of our scientific paper. Our main idea is to present a practical stability solution for this type of systems with distributed control. From practical view of point, it is crucial to find intervals on which the system is stable, and it is achieved by using this unique approach. Concerning on one-dimensional problem, where mathematical model of distributed parameter system is presented by equations which are dependable of time and only one space coordinate, successfully is applied new method for determination of stability on finite space interval for distributed parameter systems of higher order. The program support proved the efficiency of the theory, and it is developed for various types of distributed parameter systems.

4. Decision making in safety of pneumatic systems

One of the most important tasks in the safety engineering lays in the construction of a knowledge database of decision support for the pneumatic systems, and on that way to ensure optimal conditions, improve quality and boost efficiency. Methods of analysis of control systems and simulation methods, which are used for observing dynamic behavior of linear systems with time delay, and distributed parameter systems, based on linear algebra, operation calculus, functional analyse, integral differential equations and linear matrix non-equations has shown long ago that modern electronic components can be used to achieve more consistent quality at lower cost in safety engineering. The main idea to do so is that the quality service is maintained and controlled. Applying the Fuzzy theory in decision making has given very good results, and provided a flexible framework and over the years numerous mathematical models have been developed.

There are two basic problems to solve in decision making situations: obtaining alternative, and achieving consensus about solution from group of experts. First problem takes into account individual information which existed in collective information units. The later usually means an agreement of all individual opinions. Usually it is considered two approaches for developing a choice process in solving of decision making problems: a direct approach where solution is derived on the basis of the individual relations and as well indirect approach where solution is based on a collective preference relation. In safe engineering technical and economic benefits over hard-wired, discrete components has shown PLC. Main problem in process engineering is practical stability of the system. Chosen system should be stable in required period of time, and this important task is obtained by using practical stability theory for distributed parameter systems. Most pneumatic systems for instance, are described by partial different equations and they belong to group of distributed parameter systems.

4.1 Definitions and conditions of practical stability

Let us consider first order hyperbolic distributed parameter system, which is decribed by the following state- space equation:

$$\frac{\partial \underline{x}(t,z)}{\partial t} = A_0 \bullet \underline{x}(t,z) + A_1 \frac{\partial \underline{x}}{\partial z} \tag{84}$$

with appropriate function of initial state

$$\underline{x}_0(t,z)=\underline{\psi}_x(t,z) \quad 0\le t\le \tau, 0\le z\le \zeta \tag{85}$$

where $\underline{x}(t,z)$ is n-component real vector of system state, A is matrix appropriate dimension, t is time and z is space coordinate.

Definition 1: Distributed parameter system described by equation (84) that satisfies initial condition (85) is stable on finite time interval in relation to [ξ(t,z), β, T, Z] if and only if:

$$\underline{\psi}_x^T(t,z)\bullet\underline{\psi}_x(t,z)<\xi(t,z) \quad \forall t\in[0,\tau],\forall z\in[0,\varsigma] \tag{86}$$

then it follows

$$\underline{x}^T(t,z))\bullet\underline{x}(t,z)<\beta, \quad \forall t\in[0,T]\forall z\in[0,Z] \tag{87}$$

where ξ(t,z) is scalar function with feature $0<\xi(t,z)\le a, 0\le t\le \tau, 0\le z\le \zeta$ where α is real number, β € R and β > α.

Let calculate the fundamental matrix for this class of system:

$$\frac{d\Phi(s,\sigma)}{d\sigma}=A_1\bullet(sI-A)\bullet\Phi(s,\sigma) \tag{88}$$

where after double Laplace transformation, and necessary approximation finally it is obtained, (Dihovicni, 2007):

$$\Phi(t,z)=\exp(A\cdot t\cdot z) \tag{89}$$

where $A=\frac{I-A_0\cdot A_1}{A_1}$.

Theorem1: Distributed parameter system described by equation (84) that satisfies internal condition (85) is stable on finite time interval in relation to [ξ(t,z), β, T, Z] if it is satisfied following condition:

$$e^{2\mu(A)\bullet t\bullet z}<\frac{\beta}{a} \tag{90}$$

Proof: Solution of equation (84) with initial condition (85) is possible to describe as:

$$\underline{x}(t,z)=\Phi(t,z)\cdot\underline{\psi}(0,0) \tag{91}$$

By using upper equation it follows:

$$\underline{x}^T(t,z)\bullet\underline{x}^T(t,z)=\left[\underline{\psi}_x{}^T(0,0)\bullet\Phi(t,z)\right]\cdot\left[\underline{\psi}_x{}^T(0,0)\bullet\Phi(t,z)\right] \tag{92}$$

By using well-known ineqality

$$\left\|\Phi(t,z)\right\| = \left\|\exp[A \bullet t \bullet z]\right\| \leq \exp\{\mu(A) \bullet t \bullet z\} \tag{93}$$

and taking into account that:

$$\begin{gathered} \underline{\psi}_x^T(0,0) \bullet \underline{\psi}_x(0,0) < a \\ \left(\left\|\underline{\psi}_x^T(0,0)\right\| = \left\|\underline{\psi}_x^T(0,0)\right\| < a \right) \end{gathered} \tag{94}$$

then it follows:

$$\underline{x}^T(t,z) \bullet \underline{x}(t,z) \leq e^{2\mu(A \bullet t \bullet z)} \bullet a \tag{95}$$

Applying the basic condition of theorem 1 by using equation (91) to further inequality it is obtained, (Dihovicni, 2007):

$$\underline{x}^T(t,z) \bullet \underline{x}(t,z) < \left(\frac{\beta}{a}\right) \bullet a < \beta \tag{96}$$

Theorem 2: Distributed parameter system described by equation (84) that satisfied initial condition (85) is stable on finite time interval in relation to [ξ(t,z), β, T, Z] if it is satisfied following condition:

$$\begin{gathered} e^{\mu(A) \bullet t \bullet z} < \frac{\sqrt{\beta / a}}{1 + \tau \bullet \zeta \left\|A\right\|} \\ \forall t \in [0, \tau] \forall z \in [0, \varsigma] \end{gathered} \tag{97}$$

The proof of this theorem is given in (Dihovicni, 2006).
Let $|\underline{x}|_{(.)}$ is any vector norm and any matrix norm $\|\cdot\|_2$ which originated from this vector. Following expresions are used:

$$|\underline{x}|_2 = \left(\underline{x}^T \bullet \underline{x}\right)^{1/2} \text{ and } \|\cdot\|_2 = \lambda^{1/2}\left(A^* \bullet A\right)$$

where * and T are transpose-conjugate and transport matrixes.
It is important to define matrix measure as:

$$\mu(A) = \lim_{\varepsilon \to 0} \frac{\left\|1 + \varepsilon \bullet A\right\| - 1}{\varepsilon} \tag{98}$$

The matrix measure μ may be defined in three different forms according to the norm which is used:

$$\begin{gathered} \mu_1(A) = \max\left(\operatorname{Re}(a_{kk}) + \sum_{i=1, i \neq k}^{n} |a_{ik}| \right) \\ \mu_2(A) = \frac{1}{2} \max \lambda_i \left(A^T + A\right) \\ \mu_\infty(A) = \max\left(\operatorname{Re}(a_{ii}) + \sum_{k=1}^{n} |a_{ki}| \right) \end{gathered} \tag{99}$$

Definition 2: Distributed parameter system described by equation (84) that satisfies initial condition (85) is stable on finite time interval in relation to [ξ(t,z), β, T, Z] if and only if, (Dihovicni, 2007):

$$\left|\underline{\psi}_x(t,z)\right|_2 < \xi(t,z) \tag{100}$$

then follows

$$\left|\underline{x}(t)\right|_2 < \beta \tag{101}$$

where ξ(t,z) is scalar function with feature $0 < \xi(t,z) \le a, 0 \le t \le \tau, 0 \le z \le \zeta)$ α is real number, β € R and β > α.

Theorem 3: Distributed parameter system described by equation (84) that satisfies initial condition (85) is stable on finite time interval in relation to [α, β, T, Z] if it is satisfied following condition:

$$\begin{gathered} e^{\mu_2(A)\cdot t\cdot z} < \frac{\sqrt{\beta / a}}{1+\mu^{-1}{}_2(A)} \\ \forall t \in [0,T] \forall z \in [0,Z] \end{gathered} \tag{102}$$

Proof: Solution of equation (1) with initial condition (2) is possible to describe by using fundamental matrix as:

$$\underline{x}(t,z) = \Phi(t,z) \bullet \underline{\psi}_x(0,0) \tag{103}$$

By using the norms of left and right side of the equation (103) it follows:

$$\underline{x}^T(t,z)\cdot\underline{x}(t,z) \le e^{2\mu(A\cdot t\cdot z)}\cdot a \tag{104}$$

and by using well-known inequality

$$\begin{gathered} \left\|\exp(A\bullet t\bullet z)\right\|_2 \le \exp\{\mu(A\bullet t\bullet z)\} \\ t \ge 0, \quad z \ge 0 \end{gathered} \tag{105}$$

it follows:

$$\left|\underline{x}(t,z)\right|_2 \le e^{\mu_2(A)\cdot t\cdot z} \bullet \left|\underline{\psi}_x(0,0)\right|_2 \tag{106}$$

and by using equation (100) it is obtained:

$$\left|\underline{x}(t,z)\right|_2 \le a \bullet e^{\mu_2(A)\bullet t\bullet z} \tag{107}$$

so finally it is obtained:

$$\left|\underline{x}(t,z)\right|_2 \le a\cdot e^{\mu_2(A)t\bullet z}\left\{1+\mu_2{}^1(A)\right\} \tag{108}$$

Applying the basic condition of theorem 3 by using equation (19) it is obtained:

$$\begin{gathered} \left\|\underline{x}(t)\right\|_2 < \beta \\ \forall t \in [0,T], \forall z \in [0,Z] \end{gathered} \tag{109}$$

Theorem 4: Distributed parameter system described by equation (85) that satisfies initial condition (86) is stable on finite time interval in relation to [α, β, T, Z], if it is satisfied following condition, (Dihovicni, 2007):

$$\begin{gathered} e^{\mu(A\bullet t\bullet z)} < \frac{\beta}{a} \\ \forall t \in [0,T], \forall z \in [0,Z] \end{gathered} \tag{110}$$

Theorem 5: Distributed parameter system described by equation (84) that satisfies initial condition (85) is stable on finite time interval in relation to [t_0, J, α, β, Z], if it is satisfied following condition:

$$\begin{gathered} \left[1+(t-t_0)\bullet\sigma_{\max}\right]^2 \bullet e^{2(t-t_0)\cdot z\bullet\sigma_{\max}} < \frac{\beta}{a}, \\ \forall t \in [0,J]\ \forall z \in [0,Z] \end{gathered} \tag{111}$$

where σ_{max} represents maximum singular value of matrix. The proof of this theorem is given in (Dihovicni, 2007).

4.2 Architecture

There are few well known stages in developing computer decision support systems based on knowledge which include choosing suitable mathematical tools, formalization of the subject area, and development of the corresponding software. In the first phase the problem lays in making right diagnosis and in analyses of the requirements and as well the analyses of the system incidents caused by specification, design and the implementation of the project, (Bergmans, 1996). The problem of diagnostics may be stated such as finite number of subsets, or it should be applied classical investigation methods, (Thayse, 1996).

System architecture consists of the following modules:

- Stability checking module. This module is designed as program for checking the practical stability of the system. If the system passes this check it goes further to other modules.
- Analysis module of safe fault-tolerant controllers, I/O, engineering and pressure transmitters.
- Diagnostics module
- Knowledge Module of all possible situations and impacts to pneumatic systems
- Optimal solution- decision making module
- Presentation module

For system realization an object oriented programming approach has been used, and the program has been developed using the C# language. Each module has a supportive library, and the logical structure is based on the classes, which are described down below for ilustrating purpose.

- Main classes are:
- Analyses group which has a primary task of collecting necessary facts about system.
- Practical stability group which determines if the system is stable or not. If the system is unstable in view of practical stability, then it is automaticly rejected.
- **Diagnosis group** describes all possible casualities for not required results, or potencial casualities for not optimal costs.
- Performance group is used for the optimal performance.
- Cost group is used for the optimal cost effect.
- Decision making algorithm for optimal performance and cost consists of two phases:
- Phase 1 is used for input Analyses class, Practical stability class and diagnosis class.
- Phase 2 is used for output Performance and Cost group.

4.3 Conclusion

By analysing process systems from safety and optimal cost perspective, it is important to recognize which systems are not stable in real conditions. From engineering state of view we are interested in such a systems which are stable in finite periods of time, so our first concern should be to maintain stable and safe systems. Our knowledge database is created in DB2, and it involved all possible reasons for non adequate performanse. Key modules for obtaining best performance, safety and the low cost are a good base for the program support in C# programming language and the UML representation.

5. References

Al-Ibrahim, A.M., and Otis, D.R., *Transient Air Temperature and Pressure Measurements During the Charging and Discharging Processes of an Actuating Pneumatic Cylinder,* Proceedings of the 45th National Conference on Fluid Power, 1992

Andersen, B..; Wiley, J. (1967), *The Analysis and Design of Pneumatic Systems,* INC. New York-London-Sydney, 1967

Bergmans J., Gutnikov S., Krasnoproshin V., Popok S. and Vissia H., *Computer-Base Support to Decision-Making in Orthopaedics,* International Conference on Intelligent Technologies in Human related Sciences, vol. 2: Leon, Spain, (1996) pp 217-223

Dihovicni, Dj.; Nedic, N. (2006), *Stability of Distributed Parameter Systems on Finite Space Interval,* 32-end Yupiter Conference, Zlatibor, September 2006, pp 306-312

Dihovicni, Dj.; Nedic, N. (2007), *Practical Stability of Linear Systems with Delay in State,* AMSE, Association for the Advancement of Modelling & Simulation Techniques in Enterprises, Tassin La-Demi-Lune, France, Vol 62 n^0 2 (2007) pp 98-104

Dihovicni, Dj.; Nedic, N., "*Simulation, Animation and Program Support for a High Performance Pneumatic Force Actuator System*", Mathematical and Computer Modelling 48 (2008), Elsevier, Washington, pp. 761–768

Gilles, E; *Systeme mit verteilten Parametern,* Wien 1973

Kagawa T Fujita T, Takeuchi M. *Dynamic Response and Simulation Model of Pneumatic Pipe Systems,* Proc 7th Bath International Fluid Power Workshop 1994

Novakovic, B.; *Metode vodjenja tehnickih sistema,* Skolska knjiga, Zagreb 1989

Richer, E.; Hurmuzlu, Y., *A High Performance Pneumatic Force Actuator System,* ASME Journal of Dynamic Systems Measurement and Control, September 2000, pp 416-425

Thayse A., Gribont P, *Approche Logique de LIInteligence Artificielle l De la Logique,* Bordas, (1997).

Tokashiki, L.; Fujita, T. ; Kogawa T., Pan W., *Dynamic, Characteristics of Pneumatic Cylinders Including pipes,* 9th Bath International Fluid Power Workshop, September 1996, pp 1-14

10

Longitudinal Vibration of Isotropic Solid Rods: From Classical to Modern Theories

Michael Shatalov[1,2], Julian Marais[2],
Igor Fedotov[2] and Michel Djouosseu Tenkam[2]
[1]*Council for Scientific and Industrial Research*
[2]*Tshwane University of Technology*
South Africa

1. Introduction

Longitudinal waves are broadly used for the purposes of non-destructive evaluation of materials and for generation and sensing of acoustic vibration of surrounding medium by means of transducers. Many mathematical models describing longitudinal wave propagation in solids have been derived in order to analyse the effects of different materials and geometries on vibration characteristics without the need for costly experimental studies. The propagation of elastic waves in solids has seen particular interest since the end of the 19th century. The solution for three dimensional wave propagation in solids was derived independently by L. Pochhammer in 1876 and by C. Chree in 1889. The solution describes torsional, longitudinal and flexural wave propagation in cylindrical rods of infinite length and is known as the Pochhammer-Chree solution (Achenbach, 1999:242-246; Graff, 1991:470-473). The Pochhammer-Chree solution is valid for an infinite bar with simple cylindrical geometry only. For even slightly more complex geometry, such as conical, exponential or catenoidal, no exact analytical solution exists. The need for useful analytical results for bars with more complex geometries fuelled the development of one dimensional approximate theories during the 20th century. The exact Pochhammer-Chree solution has typically been used as a reference result in order to make deductions regarding the accuracy of the approximate theories and the limits of their application (Fedotov et al., 2009).

The classical approximate theory of longitudinal vibration of rods was developed during the 18th century by J. D'Alembert, D. Bernoulli, L. Euler and J. Lagrange. This theory is based on the analysis of the one dimensional wave equation and is applicable for long and relatively thin rods vibrating at low frequencies. Lateral effects and corresponding lateral and axial shear modes are fully neglected in the frames of this theory. The classical theory gained universal acceptance due to its simplicity, especially for engineering applications. It is broadly used for design of low frequency mechanical waveguides such as ultrasonic transducers, mechanical filters, multi-stepped vibrating structures, etc.

J. Rayleigh was the first who recognised the importance of the lateral effects and analysed the influence of the lateral inertia on longitudinal vibration of rods. This result was briefly exposed in Rayleigh's famous book "The Theory of Sound", first published in 1877 (Rayleigh, 1945:251-252). A. Love in his "Treatise on the Mathematical Theory of Elasticity", first published in 1892 (Love, 2009:408-409), further developed this theory, which is now referred to as the Rayleigh-Love theory. The lateral inertia effects are important in the case of non-thin cross sections of multi-stepped vibrating structures. From the view point of this theory the governing equation contains a mixed x - t derivative of fourth order which leads to the appearance of a limiting point in the frequency spectrum of the system. Furthermore, the boundary and continuity conditions are modified to take into consideration the lateral inertia effects. From the view point of engineering applications the Rayleigh-Love theory is not difficult and it helps to substantially improve the accuracy of the frequency spectrum predictions in comparison with results based on the classical theory.

R. Bishop (Bishop, 1952) further modified the Rayleigh-Love theory in 1952 by taking into account the lateral shear effects. The theory is referred to as the Rayleigh-Bishop theory. The governing equation of this theory contains a fourth order x derivative together with a mixed fourth order x - t derivative. This eliminates the limiting point of the frequency spectrum of the system, but adds an additional boundary condition on shear stress. An interesting aspect of the Rayleigh-Bishop theory is that, when applied to multi-stepped structures, it is necessary to guarantee zero shear continuity conditions at the junctions of neighbouring sections. From the view point of engineering applications this theory is slightly more complicated than the Rayleigh-Love theory. This theory predicts better resonance frequencies than the classical theory but is also limited by its application to low frequency vibrations.

The classical, Rayleigh-Love and Rayleigh-Bishop theories are based on the fundamental assumption of unimodality, which means that the dynamics of the rod is described by a single unknown function and hence, a single partial differential equation. Another fundamental assumption is that the above mentioned theories are plane cross sectional theories, i.e. displacements in the longitudinal direction preserve their plane and are not functions of distance from the neutral longitudinal axis of the rod. The boundary conditions on the outer cylindrical surface of the rod are fully ignored in the classical theory. In the Rayleigh-Love theory these boundary conditions are implicitly taken into consideration because the radial component of the surface stress is zero (and moreover it is always zero inside the rod) and the shear stress is neglected. In the Rayleigh-Bishop theory the radial component of the surface stress is zero inside and on the outer surface of the rod but the shear stress is taken to consideration inside the rod and hence, it is non-zero on the outer surface of the rod. Therefore these theories are limited to low frequency applications and cannot be used for description of high frequency effects such as the propagation of surface waves.

At higher excitation frequencies, the higher order modes of vibration can be activated and waves with the same frequencies but different wave number will propagate through the bar. The unimodal theories cannot be used to describe this phenomenon, which led to the development of the first multimodal theory by R. Mindlin and G. Herrmann in 1950, now referred to as the Mindlin-Herrmann theory (Graff, 1991:510-521). The Mindlin-Herrmann theory is a two modal plane cross sectional theory, where the lateral displacement mode is defined by a function that is independent of the longitudinal displacement mode of the rod. The dynamics of a rod modelled by the Mindlin-Herrmann theory is therefore described by a system of two coupled partial differential equation.

Investigation of the Pochhammer-Chree frequency equation shows that the frequency of the lateral mode depends on the Poisson ratio η in such a way that the frequency increases with increasing η. When $\eta > 0.2833$, the frequency of the lateral mode is higher than the frequency of the lowest axial shear mode, which is not dependent on η. This means that the Mindlin-

Herrmann (two mode) theory is not well suited for analysis of higher frequency effects, due to the absence of the third (lowest axial shear) mode. This led to the development of a multimodal non plane cross sectional theory by R. Mindlin and H. McNiven in 1960, now referred to as the Mindlin-McNiven theory (Mindlin & McNiven, 1960). In the Mindlin-McNiven theory the number of modes is not restricted and every individual mode is proportional to a Jacobi function of radius of the rod. Mindlin and McNiven further considered a three mode "second order approximation" of their theory, in which the coupling of the longitudinal, lateral and lowest axial shear modes was analysed. The dependence of the frequency spectrum of the lateral mode on the Poisson ratio was also exposed. The main advantage of this approach is in the simplicity of the orthogonality conditions. The main drawback of the theory is that the property of the smallness of the cross section with respect to the length of the rod could not be explicitly formulated because the high order Jacobi functions contain terms linearly proportional to the radius of the rod. The trade-off between simplicity of the boundary conditions and clarity of the physical formulation of the problem was one of the most important features of the subsequent development of the theory of longitudinal vibrations of finite rods. It is important to mention that the boundary conditions on the outer cylindrical surface of the rod are ignored by both of Mindlin's theories.

Modern theory of longitudinal vibration of rods is developing in two different directions. In both cases, the displacement fields are expressed as a power series expansion with respect to the distance from the neutral longitudinal axis of the rod (the radial coordinate r).

The first branch is focussed on the development of unimodal non plane cross sectional theories where either the radial or shear stress boundary conditions (or both) on the outer cylindrical surface are taken into consideration. By equating either the radial or shear stress component to zero throughout the entire thickness (and hence, also on the outer surface) of the rod, all the lateral and axial shear modes can be defined in terms of the longitudinal mode and its derivatives. Hence, the unimodal theories are each described by a single partial differential equation in the longitudinal mode. This theory is taken as the basis for nonlinear generalisation of the linear effects for analysis of soliton propagation in solid rods (Porubov, 2003:66-72). The Rayleigh-Love and Rayleigh-Bishop models are also defined within the frames of this theory.

Second, the theory of longitudinal vibrations of the rod is generalised by means of creation of multimodal approaches where the longitudinal, lateral and axial shear modes are assumed to be independent of one another, as in the case the Mindlin-McNiven theory. In this case, it is possible to take into consideration radial and shear boundary conditions or part of them on the outer cylindrical surface of the rod. One of the recent attempts of development of this approach was presented as the Zachmanoglou-Volterra theory (Grigoljuk & Selezov, 1973: 106-107; Zachmanoglou & Volterra, 1958). This is a four mode non plane cross section theory where the fourth mode is specially matched so to satisfy the zero radial stress boundary condition on the outer cylindrical surface of the rod (the shear stress is non-zero in this theory). Hence, the dynamics of the rod is described by a system of three coupled partial differential equations.

In the above mentioned publications the authors considered mainly longitudinal wave propagation in infinite and semi-infinite rods. This paper will focus on the general methods of solution of the problem of longitudinal vibration of finite length rods for all of the above mentioned theories. The main approach is based on formulation of the equations of motion and boundary conditions using energy methods (Hamilton's principle), finding two orthogonality conditions (Fedotov et al., 2010) and obtaining the general solution of the problems in terms of Green functions. Most of the results obtained by the method of two orthogonalities for derivation of the Green functions are published in this paper for the first time.

The term multimodal theory has been introduced to describe theories in which the longitudinal and lateral displacements described by more than one independent function, where the number of modes is equivalent to the number of independent functions. Theories in which the longitudinal and lateral displacements are described by a single function have been given the term unimode theory. The terms plane cross sectional and non-plane cross sectional theories will also be used in this article. A plane cross sectional theory is based on the assumption that each point x on the longitudinal axis of the rod represents a plane cross section of the bar (orthogonal to the x axis) and that, during deformation, the plane cross sections remain plane. This assumption was first made during the derivation of the classical wave equation. In a non plane cross sectional theory, axial shear modes are introduced and each point x no longer represent a plane cross section of the bar. For example, if the lowest axial shear mode is defined by the term $r^2u(x,t)$, then a point x, located on the x-axis, no longer represents displacement of a plane cross section, but rather that of a circular paraboloid section. This concept was first introduced by Mindlin and McNiven (Mindlin & McNiven, 1960).

2. Derivation of the system of equations of motion

Consider a solid cylindrical bar with radius R and length l which experiences longitudinal vibration along the x-axis and lateral shear vibrations, transverse to the x-axis in the direction of the r-axis and in the tangential direction. Consider an axisymmetric problem and suppose that the axial and lateral wave displacements can be written as a power series expansion in the radial coordinate r of the form

$$u = u(x,r,t) = u_0(x,t) + r^2 u_2(x,t) + \ldots + r^{2m} u_{2m}(x,t) \quad (1)$$

and

$$w = w(x,r,t) = r u_1(x,t) + r^3 u_3(x,t) + \ldots + r^{2n+1} u_{2n+1}(x,t) \quad (2)$$

respectively. The displacements in the tangential direction are assumed to be negligible ($v(x,r,\varphi,t) = 0$). That is, no torsional vibrations are present. The longitudinal and lateral displacements defined in (1)-(2) are similar to those proposed by Mindlin and McNiven. Mindlin and McNiven, however, represented the expansion of u and w in series of Jacobi polynomials in the radial coordinate r (Mindlin & McNiven, 1960). A representation based on the power series expansion in (1)-(2) was first introduced by Mindlin and Herrmann in 1950 to describe their two mode theory (Graff, 1991:510-521), and later by Zachmanoglou and Volterra to describe their four mode theory (Grigoljuk & Selezov, 1973: 106-107; Zachmanoglou & Volterra, 1958). According to choice of m and n in (1)-(2), different models of longitudinal vibration of bars can be obtained, including the well-known models such as those of Rayleigh-Love, Rayleigh-Bishop, Mindlin-Hermann and a three-mode model analogous to the Mindlin-McNiven "second order approximation".

The geometrical characteristics of deformation of the bar are defined by the following linear elastic strain tensor field:

$$\varepsilon_{xx} = \partial_x u, \qquad \varepsilon_{rr} = \partial_r w, \qquad \varepsilon_{\varphi\varphi} = \frac{\partial_\varphi v}{r} + \frac{w}{r} = \frac{w}{r},$$
$$\varepsilon_{xr} = \partial_r u + \partial_x w, \quad \varepsilon_{\varphi x} = \frac{\partial_\varphi u}{r} + \partial_x v = 0, \quad \varepsilon_{\varphi r} = \partial_r v - \frac{v}{r} + \frac{\partial_\varphi w}{r} = 0. \tag{3}$$

The compact notation $\partial_\alpha = \partial/\partial\alpha$ is used. Due to axial symmetry, it follows that $\varepsilon_{\varphi r} = \varepsilon_{\varphi x} = 0$. The stress tensor due to the isotropic properties of the bar is calculated from Hook's Law as follows:

$$\begin{aligned}
\sigma_{xx} &= (\lambda + 2\mu)\varepsilon_{xx} + \lambda(\varepsilon_{rr} + \varepsilon_{\varphi\varphi}),\\
\sigma_{\varphi r} &= \mu\varepsilon_{\varphi r} = 0,\\
\sigma_{rr} &= (\lambda + 2\mu)\varepsilon_{rr} + \lambda(\varepsilon_{xx} + \varepsilon_{\varphi\varphi}),\\
\sigma_{xr} &= \mu\varepsilon_{xr},\\
\sigma_{\varphi\varphi} &= (\lambda + 2\mu)\varepsilon_{\varphi\varphi} + \lambda(\varepsilon_{xx} + \varepsilon_{rr}),\\
\sigma_{\varphi x} &= \mu\varepsilon_{\varphi x} = 0.
\end{aligned} \tag{4}$$

λ and μ are Lame's constants, defined as (Fung & Tong, 2001:141)

$$\mu = \frac{E}{2(1+\eta)} \quad \text{and} \quad \lambda = \frac{E\eta}{(1-2\eta)(1+\eta)}, \tag{5}$$

where η and E are the Poisson ratio and Young's modulus of elasticity respectively.
The equations of motion (and associated boundary conditions) can be derived using Hamilton's variational principle. The Lagrangian is defined as $L = T - P$, where

$$T = \frac{\rho}{2}\int_0^l \int_S \left(\dot{u}^2 + \dot{w}^2\right) ds dx \tag{6}$$

is the kinetic energy of the system, representing the energy yielded (supplied) by the displacement of the disturbances (vibrations),

$$P = \frac{1}{2}\int_0^l \int_S \left(\sigma_{xx}\varepsilon_{xx} + \sigma_{rr}\varepsilon_{rr} + \sigma_{\varphi\varphi}\varepsilon_{\varphi\varphi} + \sigma_{xr}\varepsilon_{xr}\right) ds dx \tag{7}$$

is the strain energy of the system, representing the potential energy stored in the bar by elastic straining, $S = \int_S ds = \int_0^{2\pi}\int_0^R r dr d\varphi = \pi R^2$ is the cross sectional area and ρ is the mass density of the rod.
Exact solutions of the boundary value (or mixed) problems resulting from the application of Hamilton's principle can be found using the method of separation of variables, by assuming that the solution can be written in the form of a generalised Fourier series

$$u_j(x,t) = \sum_{m=1}^{\infty} y_{jm}(x)\Phi(t), \qquad j = 0,1,2,\dots,n-1 \tag{8}$$

where the set of functions $\{y_{jm}(x)\}$, $j = 0,1,2,\dots,n-1$ are the eigenfunctions of the corresponding Sturm-Liouville problem and n is the number of independent functions chosen to represent the longitudinal and lateral displacements in (1)-(2). It is possible to prove that the eigenfunctions satisfy two orthogonality conditions:

$$(y_m, y_n)_1 = \|y_n\|_1^2 \delta_{nm} \quad \text{and} \quad (y_m, y_n)_2 = \|y_n\|_2^2 \delta_{nm} \tag{9}$$

where y_m refers to the set of eigenfunctions $\{y_{jm}(x)\}$, $j = 0,1,2,\ldots,n-1$ corresponding to a particular eigenvalue ω_m and δ_{nm} is the Kronecker-Delta function. The unkown function in time $\Phi(t)$ can be found by substituting (8) into the Lagrangian of the system and making use of the orthogonality conditions (9).

3.1 Unimodal theories

The unimodal theories are derived by establishing a linear dependence of all the displacement modes in (1) and (2) on the first longitudinal displacement mode $u_0(x,t)$ and its derivates. This dependence is obtained by substituting (1) and (2) into the equations for the radial and axial shear stress components σ_{rr} and σ_{xr} and equating all terms at equal powers of the radial coordinate r to zero. By introducing these constraints, either the radial stress (when an even number of terms are considered) or the axial shear stress (when an uneven number of terms are considered) will be equal to zero, not only on the free outer surface, but throughout the entire thickness of the rod. That is, at least one of the classical boundary conditions for the free outer surface of a multidimensional bar, σ_{rr} = 0 and σ_{xr} = 0 at r = R, will be satisfied.

It is further possible to artificially ensure that the remaining non-zero boundary condition term (σ_{rr} for an uneven number of terms and σ_{xr} for an even number of terms) is also equal to zero throughout the entire thickness of the bar by neglecting its effect (that is, assuming this term is zero) when computing the potential energy function (7). This assumption was first introduced independently by both Rayleigh and Love in deriving the well known Rayleigh-Love (two term, unimode) theory. For this reason, all unimode theories where this assumption is made will subsequently be referred to as Rayleigh-Love type theories. Unimode theories in which this assumption is not made will be referred to as Rayleigh-Bishop type theories.

Substituting the resulting kinetic and potential energy functions, given by (6) and (7), into the Lagrangian yields

$$L = T - P = \int_0^l \Lambda\left(\dot{u}_0^{(j-1)}, u_0^{(j)}\right) dx, \qquad j = 1,2,\ldots,n \tag{10}$$

where Λ is known as the Lagrangian density and n is number of terms chosen to represent longitudinal and lateral displacements in (1)-(2). The upper dot denotes the derivative with respect to time t and $u_0^{(j)}$ is the jth derivative of $u_0(x,t)$ with respect to the axial coordinate x. Hamilton's Principle shows that the Lagrangian density Λ satisfies a Euler-Lagrange partial differential equation (typically) of the form:

$$\sum_{j=1}^{n} \left\{ (-1)^{j-1} \frac{\partial^j}{\partial x^{j-1} \partial t} \left(\frac{\partial \Lambda}{\partial \dot{u}_0^{(j-1)}} \right) + (-1)^{j-1} \frac{\partial^j}{\partial x^j} \left(\frac{\partial \Lambda}{\partial u_0^{(j)}} \right) \right\} = 0 \tag{11}$$

where n is the number of dependent terms in (1)-(2).

a) The classical theory

The classical theory is the simplest of the models discussed in this article. The longitudinal displacement is represented by

$$u = u(x,t) = u_0(x,t) \tag{12}$$

and lateral displacements are assumed negligible ($w = 0$). Since, for the classical model, $\eta = 0$ (a fortiori $\lambda = 0$) and $E = 2\mu$, the Lagrangian density of the system is given by

$$\Lambda(\dot{u}_0, u_0') = \frac{1}{2}\left(\rho S\dot{u}_0^2 - ESu_0'^2\right) \tag{13}$$

which satisfies the Euler-Lagrange differential equation

$$\frac{\partial}{\partial t}\left(\frac{\partial \Lambda}{\partial \dot{u}_0}\right) + \frac{\partial}{\partial x}\left(\frac{\partial \Lambda}{\partial u_0'}\right) = 0 \tag{14}$$

The prime denotes the derivate with respect to the axial coordinate x. Substituting (13) into (14) leads to the familiar classical wave equation

$$\rho\partial_t^2 u_0 - E\partial_x^2 u_0 = 0 \tag{15}$$

The associated natural (free end) $u_0'(x,t)\big|_{x=0,l} = 0$ or essential (fixed end) $u_0(x,t)\big|_{x=0,l} = 0$ boundary conditions are derived directly from Hamilton's principle.
The eigenfunctions $\{y_{0n}(x)\}$ of the corresponding Sturm-Liouville problem satisfy the two orthogonality conditions (9) where

$$\left(y_m, y_n\right)_1 = \int_0^l y_{0m}(x)y_{0n}(x)dx, \qquad \left(y_m, y_n\right)_2 = \int_0^l y_{0m}'(x)y_{0n}'(x)dx \tag{16}$$

b) The Rayleigh-Bishop theory

In the Rayleigh-Bishop theory, the longitudinal and lateral displacements are represented by the two term expansion

$$\begin{aligned} u(x,t) &= u_0(x,t) \\ w(x,r,t) &= ru_1(x,t) \end{aligned} \tag{17}$$

Substituting (17) into the equation for the radial stress component σ_{rr} and equating all terms at r^0 to zero yields $u_1(x,t) = -\eta u_0'(x,t)$. That is, the lateral displacement of a particle distant r from the axis is assumed to be proportional to the longitudinal strain:

$$w(x,r,t) = -\eta r\partial_x u(x,t) = -\eta r u_0'(x,t) \tag{18}$$

Applying this constraint to the lateral displacement means that $\sigma_{rr} = 0$ throughout the entire thickness of the bar. The Rayleigh-Bishop model is categorised as a unimode, plane cross section model, since both longitudinal and lateral displacements are defined in terms of a single mode of displacement, u_0, and the term $-\eta r u_0'(x,t)$ in (18) implies that lateral deformation occurs in plane and hence all plane cross sections remain plane during deformation. Substituting (17) and (18) into (6) and (7) results in

$$T = \frac{1}{2}\int_0^l \left(\rho S\dot{u}_0^2 + \rho\eta I_2\dot{u}_0'^2\right)dx \tag{19}$$

and

$$P = \frac{1}{2}\int_0^l \left(SEu_0'^2 + \mu\eta^2 I_2 u_0''^2\right)dx \tag{20}$$

where $I_2 = \int_S r^2 ds = \pi R^4 / 2$ is the polar moment of inertia of the cross section. The Lagrangian density of the system is given by

$$\Lambda(\dot{u}_0, u_0', \dot{u}_0', u_0'') = \frac{1}{2}\left(\rho S\dot{u}_0^2 + \rho\eta^2 I_2\dot{u}_0'^2 - SEu_0'^2 - \eta^2\mu I_2 u_0''\right) \tag{21}$$

which satisfies the Euler-Lagrange differential equation

$$\frac{\partial}{\partial t}\left(\frac{\partial\Lambda}{\partial\dot{u}_0}\right) + \frac{\partial}{\partial x}\left(\frac{\partial\Lambda}{\partial u_0'}\right) - \frac{\partial^2}{\partial x\partial t}\left(\frac{\partial\Lambda}{\partial\dot{u}_0'}\right) - \frac{\partial^2}{\partial x^2}\left(\frac{\partial\Lambda}{\partial u_0''}\right) = 0 \tag{22}$$

The Rayleigh-Bishop equation (Gai et al., 2007) is thus obtained

$$S\left(\rho\partial_t^2 u_0 - E\partial_x^2 u_0\right) - \eta^2 I_2 \partial_x^2\left(\rho\partial_t^2 u_0 - \mu\partial_x^2 u_0\right) = 0 \tag{23}$$

A combination of the natural (free ends)

$$\left.\left[SEu_0'(x,t) + \rho\eta^2 I_2\ddot{u}_0'(x,t) - \eta^2 I_2\mu u_0'''(x,t)\right]\right|_{x=0,l} = 0, \quad \text{and} \qquad u_0''(x,t)\big|_{x=0,l} = 0 \tag{24}$$

or the essential (fixed ends)

$$u_0(x,t)\big|_{x=0,l} = 0 \quad \text{and} \quad u_0'(x,t)\big|_{x=0,l} = 0 \tag{25}$$

boundary conditions can be used at the end points $x = 0$ and $x = l$.
It is possible to prove that the eigenfunctions $\{y_{0n}(x)\}$ of the corresponding Sturm-Liouville problem satisfy the two orthogonality conditions (9) where

$$\begin{aligned}(y_m, y_n)_1 &= \int_0^l \left[Sy_{0m}(x)y_{0n}(x) + \eta^2 I_2 y_{0m}'(x)y_{0n}'(x)\right]dx \\ (y_m, y_n)_2 &= \int_0^l \left[SEy_{0m}'(x)y_{0n}'(x) + \mu\eta^2 I_2 y_{0m}''(x)y_{0n}''(x)\right]dx\end{aligned} \tag{26}$$

c) The Rayleigh-Love theory

As in the case of the Rayleigh-Bishop theory, the longitudinal and lateral displacements for the Rayleigh-Love theory are defined by (17) and (18). It is clear that the Rayleigh-Love theory is a unimode, plane cross sectional theory, for the same reasons as discussed above for the Rayleigh-Bishop case.

In contrast to the Rayleigh-Bishop theory, Rayleigh and Love made the additional assumption that only the inertial effect of the lateral displacements are taken into consideration and the effect of stiffness on shear stress is neglected when computing the potential energy function. That is, $\varepsilon_{xr} = \partial_x w \neq 0$ and $\sigma_{xr} \approx 0$. Under these assumptions, the kinetic energy function is given by (19) and the potential energy function is reduced to

$$P = \frac{1}{2}\int_0^l SEu_0'^2 dx \tag{27}$$

The Langrangian density of the system

$$\Lambda(\dot{u}_0, u_0', \dot{u}_0') = \frac{1}{2}\left(\rho S\dot{u}_0^2 + \rho\eta^2 I_2 \dot{u}_0'^2 - SEu_0'^2\right) \tag{28}$$

satisfies the Euler-Lagrange differential equation:

$$\frac{\partial}{\partial t}\left(\frac{\partial\Lambda}{\partial\dot{u}_0}\right) + \frac{\partial}{\partial x}\left(\frac{\partial\Lambda}{\partial u_0'}\right) - \frac{\partial^2}{\partial x\partial t}\left(\frac{\partial\Lambda}{\partial\dot{u}_0'}\right) = 0 \tag{29}$$

Substituting (28) into (29) leads to the Rayleigh-Love equation of motion (Fedotov et al., 2007):

$$S\left(\rho\partial_t^2 u_0 - E\partial_x^2 u_0\right) - \eta^2 I_2 \rho\partial_x^2\left(\partial_t^2 u_0\right) = 0 \tag{30}$$

A combination of the natural (free ends)

$$\left[SEu_0'(x,t) + \rho\eta^2 I_2 \ddot{u}_0'(x,t)\right]\Big|_{x=0,l} = 0 \tag{31}$$

or the essential (fixed ends)

$$u_0(x,t)\big|_{x=0,l} = 0 \tag{32}$$

boundary conditions can be used at the end points $x = 0$ and $x = l$. Neglecting the shear stress term σ_{xr} in the potential energy function has resulted in the absence of the term with fourth order x derivative in (23). This will result in a supremum (limit point) for the set of eigenvalues ω_n. Note also that, due to the absence of the fourth order x derivative, the number of boundary conditions at each end have been reduced from two to only one.
It is possible to prove that the eigenfunctions $\{y_{0n}(x)\}$ of the corresponding Sturm-Liouville problem satisfy the two orthogonality conditions (9) where

$$\begin{aligned}(y_m, y_n)_1 &= \int_0^l\left[Sy_{0m}(x)y_{0n}(x) + \eta^2 I_2 y_{0m}'(x)y_{0n}'(x)\right]dx \\ (y_m, y_n)_2 &= \int_0^l y_{0m}'(x)y_{0n}'(x)dx\end{aligned} \tag{33}$$

d) Three term Rayleigh-Bishop type theory

Consider the case where the longitudinal and lateral displacements are defined by the three term expansion

$$\begin{aligned} u(x,r,t) &= u_0(x,t) + r^2 u_2(x,t) \\ w(x,r,t) &= r u_1(x,t) \end{aligned} \tag{34}$$

This is a non plane cross sectional theory due to the presence of the axial shear term $r^2u_2(x,t)$. Substituting (34) into the equations for radial and axial shear stress and equating the terms at r^0 and r^1 yields

$$u_1(x,t) = -\eta u_0'(x,t) \quad \text{and} \quad u_2(x,t) = -\frac{1}{2}u_1'(x,t) = \frac{\eta}{2}u_0''(x,t) \tag{35}$$

It follows that the axial shear stress $\sigma_{xr} = 0$ throughout the entire thickness of the bar. Making use of the relations $\lambda + 2\mu - 2\lambda\eta = E$ and $2\eta(\lambda + \mu) = \lambda$, the Lagrangian density of the system can be represented as

$$\begin{aligned} \Lambda &= \Lambda(\dot{u}_0, u_0', \dot{u}_0', \dot{u}_0'', u_0''') \\ &= \frac{1}{2}\left(\rho S \dot{u}_0^2 + \rho\eta I_2 \dot{u}_0 \dot{u}_0'' + \rho\frac{\eta^2}{4} I_4 \dot{u}_0''^2 + \rho\eta^2 I_2 \dot{u}_0'^2 - SEu_0'^2 - \eta I_2 E u_0' u_0''' - \frac{\eta^2}{4} I_4 (\lambda + 2\mu) u_0'''^2 \right) \end{aligned} \tag{36}$$

where $I_4 = \int_S r^4 ds = \pi R^6 / 3$ is a property of the cross section of the rod. The Lagrangian density (36) satisfies the Euler-Lagrange differential equation

$$\frac{\partial}{\partial t}\left(\frac{\partial \Lambda}{\partial \dot{u}_0}\right) + \frac{\partial}{\partial x}\left(\frac{\partial \Lambda}{\partial u_0'}\right) - \frac{\partial^2}{\partial x \partial t}\left(\frac{\partial \Lambda}{\partial \dot{u}_0'}\right) + \frac{\partial^3}{\partial x^2 \partial t}\left(\frac{\partial \Lambda}{\partial \dot{u}_0''}\right) + \frac{\partial^3}{\partial x^3}\left(\frac{\partial \Lambda}{\partial u_0'''}\right) = 0 \tag{37}$$

which leads to the equation of motion for the three term Rayleigh-Bishop type model

$$S(\rho\ddot{u}_0 - Eu_0'') + \eta I_2 \partial_x^2(\rho\ddot{u}_0 - Eu_0'') + \frac{\eta^2}{4} I_4 \partial_x^4\left[\rho\ddot{u}_0 - (\lambda + 2\mu)u_0''\right] - \rho\eta^2 I_2 \ddot{u}_0'' = 0 \tag{38}$$

with the corresponding natural (free ends)

$$\begin{aligned} &\left[-SEu_0' - \eta I_2 E u_0''' - \rho\eta^2 I_2 \ddot{u}_0' + \rho\frac{\eta}{2} I_2 \ddot{u}_0' + \rho\frac{\eta^2}{4} I_4 \ddot{u}_0''' - \frac{\eta^2}{4} I_4 (\lambda + 2\mu) u_0^{(v)} \right]\Bigg|_{x=0,l} = 0, \quad \text{and} \\ &\left[-\rho\frac{\eta}{2} I_2 \ddot{u}_0 - \rho\frac{\eta^2}{4} I_4 \ddot{u}_0'' + \frac{\eta}{2} I_2 E u_0'' + \frac{\eta^2}{4} I_4 (\lambda + 2\mu) u_0^{(iv)} \right]\Bigg|_{x=0,l} = 0, \quad \text{and} \\ &\left[-\frac{\eta}{2} I_2 E u_0' - \frac{\eta^2}{4} I_4 (\lambda + 2\mu) u_0''' \right]\Bigg|_{x=0,l} = 0. \end{aligned} \tag{39}$$

or essential (fixed ends)

$$u_0\big|_{x=0,l} = 0 \quad \text{and} \quad u_0'\big|_{x=0,l} = 0 \quad \text{and} \quad u_0''\big|_{x=0,l} = 0 \tag{40}$$

boundary conditions at the end points $x = 0$ and $x = l$.
It is possible to prove that the eigenfunctions $\{y_{0n}(x)\}$ of the corresponding Sturm-Liouville problem satisfy the two orthogonality conditions (9) where

$$(y_m, y_n)_1 = \int_0^l \left(S y_n y_m + \frac{\eta}{2} I_2 y_n'' y_m + \frac{\eta}{2} I_2 y_n y_m'' + \frac{\eta^2}{4} I_4 y_n'' y_m'' + \eta^2 I_2 y_n' y_m' \right) dx$$
$$(y_m, y_n)_2 = \int_0^l \left(S E y_n' y_m' + \frac{\eta}{2} I_2 E y_n''' y_m' + \frac{\eta}{2} I_2 E y_n' y_m''' + \frac{\eta^2}{4} I_4 (\lambda + 2\mu) y_n''' y_m''' \right) dx \quad (41)$$

e) Three term Rayleigh-Love type theory

As in the case of the three term Rayleigh-Bishop type theory, the longitudinal and lateral displacements for the three term Rayleigh-Love type theory are given by (34) and (35). In this theory, an additional Rayleigh-Love type assumption is made to neglect the radial stress component, which is non-zero in this case, when calculating the potential energy of the system. That is, $\varepsilon_{rr} = \partial_r w \neq 0$ and $\sigma_{rr} \approx 0$. Under these assumptions, the Lagrangian density of the system becomes

$$\begin{aligned}\Lambda &= \Lambda(\dot{u}_0, u_0', \dot{u}_0', \dot{u}_0'', u_0''') \\ &= \frac{1}{2}\Big[\rho S \dot{u}_0^2 + \rho \eta^2 I_2 \dot{u}_0'^2 + \rho \eta I_2 \dot{u}_0 \dot{u}_0'' + \rho \frac{\eta^2}{4} I_4 \dot{u}_0''^2 - S E u_0'^2 - \eta I_2 E u_0' u_0''' - \frac{\eta^2}{2} I_2 \lambda u_0' u_0''' - \\ &\quad - \frac{\eta^2}{4} I_4 (\lambda + 2\mu) u_0'''^2 \Big]\end{aligned} \quad (42)$$

The Lagrangian density (42) satisfies the Euler-Lagrange differential equation

$$\frac{\partial}{\partial t}\left(\frac{\partial \Lambda}{\partial \dot{u}_0}\right) + \frac{\partial}{\partial x}\left(\frac{\partial \Lambda}{\partial u_0'}\right) - \frac{\partial^2}{\partial x \partial t}\left(\frac{\partial \Lambda}{\partial \dot{u}_0'}\right) + \frac{\partial^3}{\partial x^2 \partial t}\left(\frac{\partial \Lambda}{\partial \dot{u}_0''}\right) + \frac{\partial^3}{\partial x^3}\left(\frac{\partial \Lambda}{\partial u_0'''}\right) = 0 \quad (43)$$

which leads to the equation of motion for the three term Rayleigh-Love type model:

$$S(\rho \ddot{u}_0 - E u_0'') + \eta I_2 \partial_x^2 (\rho \ddot{u}_0 - E u_0'') + \frac{\eta^2}{4} I_4 \partial_x^4 \left[\rho \ddot{u}_0 - (\lambda + 2\mu) u_0'' \right] - \rho \eta^2 I_2 \ddot{u}_0'' - \frac{\eta^2}{2} I_2 \lambda \partial_x^4 (u_0) = 0 \quad (44)$$

with the corresponding natural (free ends)

$$\left[-S E u_0' - \eta I_2 E u_0''' - \frac{\eta^2}{2} I_2 \lambda u_0''' - \rho \eta^2 I_2 \ddot{u}_0' + \rho \frac{\eta}{2} I_2 \ddot{u}_0' + \rho \frac{\eta^2}{4} I_4 \ddot{u}_0''' - \frac{\eta^2}{4} I_4 (\lambda + 2\mu) u_0^{(v)} \right]_{x=0,l} = 0, \text{ and}$$
$$\left[-\rho \frac{\eta}{2} I_2 \ddot{u}_0 - \rho \frac{\eta^2}{4} I_4 \ddot{u}_0'' + \frac{\eta}{2} I_2 E u_0'' + \frac{\eta^2}{4} I_4 (\lambda + 2\mu) u_0^{(iv)} + \frac{\eta^2}{4} I_2 \lambda u_0'' \right]_{x=0,l} = 0, \text{ and} \quad (45)$$
$$\left[-\frac{\eta}{2} I_2 E u_0' - \frac{\eta^2}{4} I_4 (\lambda + 2\mu) u_0''' - \frac{\eta^2}{4} I_2 \lambda u_0' \right]_{x=0,l} = 0.$$

or the essential (fixed ends)

$$u_0\big|_{x=0,l} = 0 \text{ and } u_0'\big|_{x=0,l} = 0 \text{ and } u_0''\big|_{x=0,l} = 0 \quad (46)$$

boundary conditions at the end points $x = 0$ and $x = l$. It should be noted that in this case, the Rayleigh-Love type assumption that $\sigma_{rr} = 0$ did not result in a simplification of the equation

of motion or boundary conditions as was the case in the two term theories discussed above. This is true for all unimode theories in which an uneven number of terms have been considered to represent longitudinal and lateral displacements.
It is possible to prove that the eigenfunctions $\{y_{0n}(x)\}$ of the corresponding Sturm-Liouville problem satisfy the two orthogonality conditions (9) where

$$\begin{aligned}(y_m, y_n)_1 &= \int_0^l \left\{ S y_n y_m + \frac{\eta}{2} I_2 y_n'' y_m + \frac{\eta}{2} I_2 y_n y_m'' + \frac{\eta^2}{4} I_4 y_n'' y_m'' + \eta^2 I_2 y_n' y_m' \right\} dx \\ (y_m, y_n)_2 &= \int_0^l \left\{ SEy_n' y_m' + \frac{\eta}{2} I_2 E y_n''' y_m' + \frac{\eta}{2} I_2 E y_n' y_m''' + \frac{\eta^2}{4} I_4 (\lambda + 2\mu) y_n''' y''' + \right. \\ &\left. + \frac{\eta^2}{4} I_2 \lambda y_n''' y_m' + \frac{\eta^2}{4} I_2 \lambda y_n' y_m''' \right\} dx\end{aligned} \tag{47}$$

f) Four term Rayleigh-Bishop type theory

Consider the case where the longitudinal and lateral displacements are defined by the three term expansion

$$\begin{aligned} u(x,r,t) &= u_0(x,t) + r^2 u_2(x,t) \\ w(x,r,t) &= r u_1(x,t) + r^3 u_3(x,t) \end{aligned} \tag{48}$$

Substituting (48) into the equations for radial and axial shear stress and equating the terms at r^0, r^1 and r^2 yields

$$u_1 = -\eta u_0', \quad u_2 = -\frac{1}{2} u_1' = \frac{\eta}{2} u_0'' \quad \text{and} \quad u_3 = -\frac{\eta}{3-2\eta} u_2' = -\frac{\eta^2}{2(3-2\eta)} u_0''' \tag{49}$$

It follows that the radial stress σ_{rr} is zero throughout the entire thickness of the bar. Making use of the relations $\lambda + 2\mu - 2\lambda\eta = E$, $2\eta(\lambda + \mu) = \lambda$ and $2\mu\eta = \lambda(1 - 2\eta)$, the Lagrangian density of the system can be given by

$$\begin{aligned}\Lambda = \frac{1}{2} \Bigg[& \rho S \dot{u}_0^2 + \rho \eta I_2 \dot{u}_0 \dot{u}_0'' + \rho \frac{\eta^2}{4} I_4 \dot{u}_0''^2 + \rho \eta^2 I_2 \dot{u}_0'^2 + \rho \frac{\eta^3}{(3-2\eta)} I_4 \dot{u}_0' \dot{u}_0''' + \rho \frac{\eta^4}{4(3-2\eta)^2} I_6 \dot{u}_0'''^2 - \\ & - SE u_0'^2 - \eta I_2 E u_0' u_0''' - \frac{\eta^2}{4} I_4 (\lambda + 2\mu) u_0'''^2 - \frac{\eta^4}{4(3-2\eta)^2} I_6 \mu \left(u_0^{(iv)} \right)^2 + \frac{\eta^3}{(3-2\eta)} I_4 \lambda u_0'''^2 + \\ & + \frac{\eta^4}{(3-2\eta)^2} I_4 \mu u_0'''^2 \Bigg]\end{aligned} \tag{50}$$

where $I_6 = \int_S r^6 ds = \pi R^8 / 4$ is a property of the cross section of the rod. The Langrangian density of the system satisfies the Euler-Lagrange partial differential equation

$$\frac{\partial}{\partial t}\left(\frac{\partial \Lambda}{\partial \dot{u}_0}\right) + \frac{\partial}{\partial x}\left(\frac{\partial \Lambda}{\partial u_0'}\right) - \frac{\partial^2}{\partial x \partial t}\left(\frac{\partial \Lambda}{\partial \dot{u}_0'}\right) + \frac{\partial^3}{\partial x^2 \partial t}\left(\frac{\partial \Lambda}{\partial \dot{u}_0''}\right) + \frac{\partial^3}{\partial x^3}\left(\frac{\partial \Lambda}{\partial u_0'''}\right) - \frac{\partial^4}{\partial x^3 \partial t}\left(\frac{\partial \Lambda}{\partial \dot{u}_0'''}\right) - \frac{\partial^4}{\partial x^4}\left(\frac{\partial \Lambda}{\partial u_0^{(iv)}}\right) = 0 \tag{51}$$

which leads to the equation of motion for the four term Rayleigh-Bishop type model

$$
\begin{aligned}
&S\left(\rho\ddot{u}_0 - Eu_0''\right) + \eta I_2 \partial_x^2\left(\rho\ddot{u}_0 - Eu_0''\right) + \frac{\eta^2}{4} I_4 \partial_x^4\left[\rho\ddot{u}_0 - (\lambda + 2\mu)u_0''\right] - \frac{\eta^4}{4(3-2\eta)^2} I_6 \partial_x^6\left(\rho\ddot{u}_0 - \mu u_0''\right) - \\
&- \rho\eta^2 I_2 \ddot{u}_0'' - \frac{\eta^3}{(3-2\eta)} I_4 \partial_x^4\left(\rho\ddot{u}_0\right) + \frac{\eta^3}{(3-2\eta)} I_4 \partial_x^6\left(\lambda u_0\right) + \frac{\eta^4}{(3-2\eta)^2} I_4 \partial_x^6\left(\mu u_0\right) = 0
\end{aligned}
\tag{52}
$$

with the corresponding natural (free ends)

$$
\begin{aligned}
&\left[\frac{\partial\Lambda}{\partial u_0'} - \frac{\partial}{\partial t}\left(\frac{\partial\Lambda}{\partial \dot{u}_0'}\right) + \frac{\partial^2}{\partial x\partial t}\left(\frac{\partial\Lambda}{\partial \dot{u}_0''}\right) + \frac{\partial^2}{\partial x^2}\left(\frac{\partial\Lambda}{\partial u_0'''}\right) - \frac{\partial^3}{\partial x^2\partial t}\left(\frac{\partial\Lambda}{\partial \dot{u}_0'''}\right) - \frac{\partial^3}{\partial x^3}\left(\frac{\partial\Lambda}{\partial u_0^{(\mathrm{iv})}}\right)\right]\Bigg|_{x=0,l} = 0 \quad \text{and} \\
&\left[-\frac{\partial}{\partial t}\left(\frac{\partial\Lambda}{\partial \dot{u}_0''}\right) - \frac{\partial}{\partial x}\left(\frac{\partial\Lambda}{\partial u_0'''}\right) + \frac{\partial^2}{\partial x\partial t}\left(\frac{\partial\Lambda}{\partial \dot{u}_0'''}\right) + \frac{\partial^2}{\partial x^2}\left(\frac{\partial\Lambda}{\partial u_0^{(\mathrm{iv})}}\right)\right]\Bigg|_{x=0,l} = 0 \quad \text{and} \\
&\left[\frac{\partial\Lambda}{\partial u_0'''} - \frac{\partial}{\partial t}\left(\frac{\partial\Lambda}{\partial \dot{u}_0'''}\right) - \frac{\partial}{\partial x}\left(\frac{\partial\Lambda}{\partial u_0^{(\mathrm{iv})}}\right)\right]\Bigg|_{x=0,l} = 0 \quad \text{and} \\
&\left[\frac{\partial\Lambda}{\partial u_0^{(\mathrm{iv})}}\right]\Bigg|_{x=0,l} = 0
\end{aligned}
\tag{53}
$$

or essential (fixed ends)

$$
u_0\big|_{x=0,l} = 0 \quad \text{and} \quad u_0'\big|_{x=0,l} = 0 \quad \text{and} \quad u_0''\big|_{x=0,l} = 0 \quad \text{and} \quad u_0'''\big|_{x=0,l} = 0 \tag{54}
$$

boundary conditions at the end points $x = 0$ and $x = l$. The explicit form of the boundary conditions (53) can be determined using the Lagrangian density (50).

g) Four term Rayleigh-Love type theory

As in the case of the three term Rayleigh-Bishop type theory, the longitudinal and lateral displacements for this theory are given by (48) and (49). The constraints (49) result in $\sigma_{rr} = 0$ and $\sigma_{xr} \neq 0$ throughout the entire thickness of the bar. An additional Rayleigh-Love type assumption is made to neglect the axial shear stress component when calculating the potential energy of the system. Under these assumptions, the Lagrangian density of the system reduces to

$$
\begin{aligned}
\Lambda = \frac{1}{2}\Bigg[&\rho S\dot{u}_0^2 + \rho\eta I_2 \dot{u}_0 \dot{u}_0'' + \rho\frac{\eta^2}{4} I_4 \dot{u}_0''^2 + \rho\eta^2 I_2 \dot{u}_0'^2 + \rho\frac{\eta^3}{(3-2\eta)} I_4 \dot{u}_0' \dot{u}_0''' + \rho\frac{\eta^4}{4(3-2\eta)^2} I_6 \dot{u}_0'''^2 - \\
&-SEu_0'^2 - \eta I_2 E u_0' u_0''' - \frac{\eta^2}{4} I_4 (\lambda + 2\mu) u_0''^2 + \frac{\eta^3}{(3-2\eta)} I_4 \lambda u_0''^2 + \frac{\eta^4}{(3-2\eta)^2} I_4 \mu u_0''^2\Bigg]
\end{aligned}
\tag{55}
$$

The Langrangian density of the system satisfies the Euler-Lagrange differential equation

$$
\frac{\partial}{\partial t}\left(\frac{\partial\Lambda}{\partial \dot{u}_0}\right) + \frac{\partial}{\partial x}\left(\frac{\partial\Lambda}{\partial u_0'}\right) - \frac{\partial^2}{\partial x\partial t}\left(\frac{\partial\Lambda}{\partial \dot{u}_0'}\right) + \frac{\partial^3}{\partial x^2\partial t}\left(\frac{\partial\Lambda}{\partial \dot{u}_0''}\right) + \frac{\partial^3}{\partial x^3}\left(\frac{\partial\Lambda}{\partial u_0'''}\right) - \frac{\partial^4}{\partial x^3\partial t}\left(\frac{\partial\Lambda}{\partial \dot{u}_0'''}\right) = 0 \tag{56}
$$

which leads to the equation of motion for the three mode Rayleigh-Love type model:

$$S(\rho\ddot{u}_0 - Eu_0'') + \eta I_2\partial_x^2(\rho\ddot{u}_0 - Eu_0'') + \frac{\eta^2}{4}I_4\partial_x^4\left[\rho\ddot{u}_0 - (\lambda+2\mu)u_0''\right] - \frac{\eta^4}{4(3-2\eta)^2}I_6\partial_x^6(\rho\ddot{u}_0) -$$
$$-\rho\eta^2 I_2\ddot{u}_0'' - \frac{\eta^3}{(3-2\eta)}I_4\partial_x^4(\rho\ddot{u}_0) + \frac{\eta^3}{(3-2\eta)}I_4\partial_x^6(\lambda u_0) + \frac{\eta^4}{(3-2\eta)^2}I_4\partial_x^6(\mu u_0) = 0 \quad (57)$$

A combination of the natural (free ends)

$$\left[\frac{\partial\Lambda}{\partial u_0'} - \frac{\partial}{\partial t}\left(\frac{\partial\Lambda}{\partial\dot{u}_0'}\right) + \frac{\partial^2}{\partial x\partial t}\left(\frac{\partial\Lambda}{\partial\dot{u}_0''}\right) + \frac{\partial^2}{\partial x^2}\left(\frac{\partial\Lambda}{\partial u_0'''}\right) - \frac{\partial^3}{\partial x^2\partial t}\left(\frac{\partial\Lambda}{\partial\dot{u}_0'''}\right)\right]\Bigg|_{x=0,l} = 0 \quad \text{and}$$
$$\left[-\frac{\partial}{\partial t}\left(\frac{\partial\Lambda}{\partial\dot{u}_0''}\right) - \frac{\partial}{\partial x}\left(\frac{\partial\Lambda}{\partial u_0'''}\right) + \frac{\partial^2}{\partial x\partial t}\left(\frac{\partial\Lambda}{\partial\dot{u}_0'''}\right)\right]\Bigg|_{x=0,l} = 0 \quad \text{and} \quad (58)$$
$$\left[\frac{\partial\Lambda}{\partial u_0'''} - \frac{\partial}{\partial t}\left(\frac{\partial\Lambda}{\partial\dot{u}_0'''}\right)\right]\Bigg|_{x=0,l} = 0$$

or the essential (fixed ends)

$$u_0\big|_{x=0,l} = 0, \quad \text{and} \quad u_0'\big|_{x=0,l} = 0, \quad \text{and} \quad u_0''\big|_{x=0,l} = 0. \quad (59)$$

boundary conditions can be used at the end points $x = 0$ and $x = l$. The explicit form of the boundary conditions (58) can be determined from the Lagrangian density (55). Once again, neglecting the shear stress term σ_{xr} in the potential energy function has simplified the equation of motion and boundary conditions. The highest order x derivative (in this case, eighth order) does not appear in the equation of motion (57) and the number of boundary conditions at each end has been reduced from four to three. The absence of the eighth order x derivative, together with the presence of the mixed eighth order x-t derivate will also result in a limit point for the set of eigenvalues ω_n. This simplification of the equation of motion and boundary conditions is true for all unimode theories in which an even number of terms have been considered to represent longitudinal and lateral displacements.

3.2 Multimodal theories

The multimodal theories are derived from the representation of longitudinal and lateral displacements (1)-(2), where all the terms are assumed to be independent of one another. Substituting the resulting kinetic and potential energy functions, given by (6) and (7), into the Lagrangian yields

$$L = T - P = \int_0^l \Lambda\left(u_j, \dot{u}_j, u_j'\right)dx \quad (60)$$

where j depends on the choice of n and m in (1)-(2). Hamilton's Principle shows that the Lagrangian density Λ satisfies a system of Euler-Lagrange differential equations (typically) of the form:

$$\frac{\partial}{\partial t}\left(\frac{\partial \Lambda}{\partial \dot{u}_0}\right)+\frac{\partial}{\partial x}\left(\frac{\partial \Lambda}{\partial u_0'}\right)=0$$
$$\frac{\partial}{\partial t}\left(\frac{\partial \Lambda}{\partial \dot{u}_j}\right)+\frac{\partial}{\partial x}\left(\frac{\partial \Lambda}{\partial u_j'}\right)-\frac{\partial \Lambda}{\partial u_j}=0, \quad j=1,2,\ldots,n-1 \tag{61}$$

where n is the number of displacement modes (independent functions) chosen in (1)-(2). The upper dot and prime denote derivatives with respect to time t and axial coordinate x respectively.

a) Two mode (Mindlin-Herrmann) theory

In the case of the Mindlin-Herrmann theory, the longitudinal and lateral wave displacements are defined as

$$u(x,t)=u_0(x,t)$$
$$w(x,r,t)=ru_1(x,t) \tag{62}$$

The Mindlin-Herrmann theory is the first (and the simplest) of the "multimode" theories, since two independent modes of displacement, $u_0(x,t)$ and $u_1(x,t)$, have been considered. The Mindlin-Herrmann theory is also a plane cross section theory, since the term $ru_1(x,t)$ in (62) implies that all plane cross sections remain plane during lateral (and longitudinal) deformation. It should be noted that both the Rayleigh-Love and Rayleigh-Bishop theories are special cases of the Mindlin-Herrmann theory and can be obtained from the Mindlin-Herrmann theory by introducing a constraint of the form $u_1+\eta u_0'=0$ (that is, a constrained extremum).

Substituting (62) into (6) and (7) results in the following Lagrangian density of the system

$$\Lambda=\Lambda(\dot{u}_0,\dot{u}_1,u_0',u_1',u_1)$$
$$=\frac{1}{2}\left[\rho S\dot{u}_0^2+\rho I_2\dot{u}_1^2-S(\lambda+2\mu)u_0'^2-4S\lambda u_0'u_1-4S(\lambda+\mu)u_1^2-I_2\mu u_1'^2\right] \tag{63}$$

which satisfies the following system of Euler-Lagrange differential equations:

$$\frac{\partial}{\partial t}\left(\frac{\partial \Lambda}{\partial \dot{u}_0}\right)+\frac{\partial}{\partial x}\left(\frac{\partial \Lambda}{\partial u_0'}\right)=0$$
$$\frac{\partial}{\partial t}\left(\frac{\partial \Lambda}{\partial \dot{u}_1}\right)+\frac{\partial}{\partial x}\left(\frac{\partial \Lambda}{\partial u_1'}\right)-\frac{\partial \Lambda}{\partial u_1}=0 \tag{64}$$

Substituting (63) into (64) leads to the system of equations of motion:

$$S\left[\rho\partial_t^2u_0-(\lambda+2\mu)\partial_x^2u_0\right]-2\lambda S\partial_x u_1=0$$
$$2\lambda S\partial_x u_0+I_2\left(\rho\partial_t^2u_1-\mu\partial_x^2u_1\right)+4S(\lambda+\mu)u_1=0 \tag{65}$$

A combination of the natural

$$\left[(\lambda+2\mu)u_0'(x,t)+2\lambda u_1(x,t)\right]\Big|_{x=0,l}=0, \quad \text{and} \quad u_1'(x,t)\Big|_{x=0,l}=0 \tag{66}$$

or the essential

$$u_0(x,t)\big|_{x=0,l} = 0 \quad \text{and} \quad u_1(x,t)\big|_{x=0,l} = 0 \tag{67}$$

boundary conditions can be used at the end points $x = 0$ and $x = l$.
It is possible to prove that the eigenfunctions $\{y_{0n}(x)\}$ and $\{y_{1n}(x)\}$ of the corresponding Sturm-Liouville problem satisfy the two orthogonality conditions (9) where

$$\begin{aligned}(y_m, y_n)_1 &= \int_0^l \left[S y_{0m}(x) y_{0n}(x) + I_2 y_{1m}(x) y_{1n}(x)\right] dx \\ (y_m, y_n)_2 &= \int_0^l \left[4S(\lambda+\mu) y_{1m}(x) y_{1n}(x) + S(\lambda+2\mu) y'_{0m}(x) y'_{0n}(x) + \right. \\ &\quad \left. + I_2 \mu y'_{1m}(x) y'_{1n}(x) + 2S\lambda\left(y'_{0m}(x) y_{1n}(x) + y'_{0n}(x) y_{1m}(x)\right)\right] dx\end{aligned} \tag{68}$$

b) Three mode theory

Consider the case where the longitudinal and lateral displacements are defined by three modes of displacement as follows:

$$\begin{aligned}u(x,r,t) &= u_0(x,t) + r^2 u_2(x,t) \\ w(x,r,t) &= r u_1(x,t)\end{aligned} \tag{69}$$

The longitudinal and lateral displacements defined in (69) are similar to those proposed by Mindlin and McNiven as a "second approximation" of their general theory.
The Lagrangian density of the system is given by

$$\begin{aligned}\Lambda &= \Lambda(\dot{u}_0, \dot{u}_1, \dot{u}_2, u'_0, u'_1, u'_2, u_1, u_2) \\ &= \frac{1}{2}\Big[\left(S\rho\dot{u}_0^2 + 2I_2\rho\dot{u}_0\dot{u}_2 + I_2\rho\dot{u}_1^2 + I_4\rho\dot{u}_2^2\right) - (\lambda+2\mu)S u_0'^2 - \mu I_2 u_1'^2 - (\lambda+2\mu) I_4 u_2'^2 - \\ &\quad -4\lambda S u'_0 u_1 - 4\mu I_2 u'_1 u_2 - 2(\lambda+2\mu) I_2 u'_0 u'_2 - 4\lambda I_2 u'_2 u_1 - 4(\lambda+\mu) S u_1^2 - 4\mu I_2 u_2^2\Big]\end{aligned} \tag{70}$$

which satisfies the following system of Euler-Lagrange differential equations

$$\begin{aligned}&\frac{\partial}{\partial t}\left(\frac{\partial \Lambda}{\partial \dot{u}_0}\right) + \frac{\partial}{\partial x}\left(\frac{\partial \Lambda}{\partial u'_0}\right) = 0 \\ &\frac{\partial}{\partial t}\left(\frac{\partial \Lambda}{\partial \dot{u}_1}\right) + \frac{\partial}{\partial x}\left(\frac{\partial \Lambda}{\partial u'_1}\right) - \frac{\partial \Lambda}{\partial u_1} = 0 \\ &\frac{\partial}{\partial t}\left(\frac{\partial \Lambda}{\partial \dot{u}_2}\right) + \frac{\partial}{\partial x}\left(\frac{\partial \Lambda}{\partial u'_2}\right) - \frac{\partial \Lambda}{\partial u_2} = 0\end{aligned} \tag{71}$$

Substituting (70) into (71) yields the system of equations of motion:

$$\begin{aligned}&S\left[\rho\partial_t^2 u_0 - (\lambda+2\mu)\partial_x^2 u_0\right] - 2\lambda S \partial_x u_1 + I_2\left[\rho\partial_t^2 u_2 - (\lambda+2\mu)\partial_x^2 u_2\right] = 0 \\ &2\lambda S \partial_x u_0 + I_2\left(\rho\partial_t^2 u_1 - \mu\partial_x^2 u_1\right) + 4S(\lambda+\mu) u_1 + 2(\lambda-\mu) I_2 \partial_x u_2 = 0 \\ &I_2\left[\rho\partial_t^2 u_0 - (\lambda+2\mu)\partial_x^2 u_0\right] - 2(\lambda-\mu) I_2 \partial_x u_1 + I_4\left[\rho\partial_t^2 u_2 - (\lambda+2\mu)\partial_x^2 u_2\right] + 4\mu I_2 u_2 = 0\end{aligned} \tag{72}$$

A combination of the natural

$$\begin{aligned}&\left[S(\lambda+2\mu)u_0'(x,t)+2S\lambda u_1(x,t)+I_2(\lambda+2\mu)u_2'(x,t)\right]\Big|_{x=0,l}=0, \quad \text{and}\\&\left[I_2\mu u_1'(x,t)+2I_2\mu u_2(x,t)\right]\Big|_{x=0,l}=0 \quad \text{and}\\&\left[I_2(\lambda+2\mu)u_0'(x,t)+2I_2\lambda u_1(x,t)+I_4(\lambda+2\mu)u_2'(x,t)\right]\Big|_{x=0,l}=0\end{aligned} \tag{73}$$

or essential

$$u_0(x,t)\big|_{x=0,l}=0 \quad \text{and} \quad u_1(x,t)\big|_{x=0,l}=0 \quad \text{and} \quad u_2(x,t)\big|_{x=0,l}=0 \tag{74}$$

boundary conditions can be used at the end points $x = 0$ and $x = l$.

It is possible to prove that the eigenfunctions $\{y_{0n}(x)\}$, $\{y_{1n}(x)\}$ and $\{y_{2n}(x)\}$ of the corresponding Sturm-Liouville problem satisfy the two orthogonality conditions (9) where

$$\begin{aligned}(y_m,y_n)_1=&\int_0^l\big[Sy_{0m}(x)y_{0n}(x)+I_2y_{1m}(x)y_{1n}(x)+I_4y_{2m}(x)y_{2n}(x)+\\&+I_2\left(y_{0m}(x)y_{2n}(x)+y_{0n}(x)y_{2m}(x)\right)\big]dx\\(y_m,y_n)_2=&\int_0^l\big[4S(\lambda+\mu)y_{1m}(x)y_{1n}(x)+4I_2\mu y_{2m}(x)y_{2n}(x)+S(\lambda+2\mu)y_{0m}'(x)y_{0n}'(x)+\\&+I_2\mu y_{1m}'(x)y_{1n}'(x)+I_4(\lambda+2\mu)y_{2m}'(x)y_{2n}'(x)+\\&+2S\lambda\left(y_{0m}'(x)y_{1n}(x)+y_{0n}'(x)y_{1m}(x)\right)+I_2(\lambda+2\mu)\left(y_{0m}'(x)y_{2n}'(x)+y_{0n}'(x)y_{2m}'(x)\right)+\\&+2I_2\lambda\left(y_{1m}(x)y_{2n}'(x)+y_{1n}(x)y_{2m}'(x)\right)+2I_2\mu\left(y_{1m}'(x)y_{2n}(x)+y_{1n}'(x)y_{2m}(x)\right)\big]dx\end{aligned} \tag{75}$$

c) Four mode theory

Consider the case where the longitudinal and lateral displacements are defined by four modes of displacement as follows

$$\begin{aligned}u(x,r,t)&=u_0(x,t)+r^2u_2(x,t)\\w(x,r,t)&=ru_1(x,t)\ +\ r^3u_3(x,t)\end{aligned} \tag{76}$$

In a similar fashion as was described for the three mode theory above, the system of equations resulting from (76) may be written as

$$\begin{aligned}&S\left[\rho\partial_t^2u_0-(\lambda+2\mu)\partial_x^2u_0\right]-d_{12}u_1+I_2\left[\rho\partial_t^2u_2-(\lambda+2\mu)\partial_x^2u_2\right]-d_{14}u_3=0\\&d_{12}u_0+I_2\left(\rho\partial_t^2u_1-\mu\partial_x^2u_1\right)+b_{22}u_1+d_{23}u_2+I_4\left(\rho\partial_t^2u_3-\mu\partial_x^2u_3\right)+b_{24}u_3=0\\&I_2\left[\rho\partial_t^2u_0-(\lambda+2\mu)\partial_x^2u_0\right]-d_{23}u_1+I_4\left[\rho\partial_t^2u_2-(\lambda+2\mu)\partial_x^2u_2\right]+b_{33}u_2-d_{34}u_3=0\\&d_{14}u_0+I_4\left(\rho\partial_t^2u_1-\mu\partial_x^2u_1\right)+b_{24}u_1+d_{34}u_2+I_6\left(\rho\partial_t^2u_3-\mu\partial_x^2u_3\right)+b_{44}u_3=0\end{aligned} \tag{77}$$

where $d_{12} = 2\lambda\partial S_x$, $d_{14} = 4\lambda I_2\partial_x$, $d_{23} = 2I_2(\lambda - \mu)\partial_x$ and $d_{34} = 2I_4(2\lambda - \mu)\partial_x$ are first order differential operators and $b_{22} = 4S(\lambda + \mu)$, $b_{33} = 4I_2\mu$, $b_{24} = 8I_2(\lambda + \mu)$ and $b_{44} = 4I_4(4\lambda + 5\mu)$ are numbers depending on λ, μ, S, I_2 and I_4.

A combination of the natural

$$\begin{aligned} \left[S(\lambda+2\mu)u_0'(x,t)+2S\lambda u_1(x,t)+I_2(\lambda+2\mu)u_2'(x,t)+4I_2\lambda u_3(x,t)\right]\Big|_{x=0,l}&=0, \quad \text{and} \\ \left[I_2\mu u_1'(x,t)+2I_2\mu u_2(x,t)+I_4\mu u_3'(x,t)\right]\Big|_{x=0,l}&=0, \quad \text{and} \\ \left[I_2(\lambda+2\mu)u_0'(x,t)+2I_2\lambda u_1(x,t)+I_4(\lambda+2\mu)u_2'(x,t)+4I_4\lambda u_3(x,t)\right]\Big|_{x=0,l}&=0, \quad \text{and} \\ \left[I_4\mu u_1'(x,t)+2I_4\mu u_2(x,t)+I_6\mu u_3'(x,t)\right]\Big|_{x=0,l}&=0, \end{aligned} \tag{78}$$

or essential

$$u_0(x,t)\big|_{x=0,l}=0 \quad \text{and} \quad u_1(x,t)\big|_{x=0,l}=0 \quad \text{and} \quad u_2(x,t)\big|_{x=0,l}=0 \quad \text{and} \quad u_3(x,t)\big|_{x=0,l}=0 \tag{79}$$

boundary conditions can be used at the end points $x = 0$ and $x = l$.

d) Zachmanoglou-Volterra theory

In the Zachmanoglou-Volterra theory, the longitudinal and lateral displacements are defined by four modes of displacement as

$$u=u_0(x,t)+r^2u_2(x,t) \tag{80}$$

and

$$w=ru_1(x,t)+r^3u_3(x,t) \tag{81}$$

Zachmanoglou and Volterra also considered the additional condition that the radial stress component must be zero on the outer cylindrical surface of the bar, $\sigma_{rr} = 0$ at $r = R$. From this condition, it follows that

$$u_3(x,t)=\frac{1}{R^2(2\eta-3)}\left[u_1(x,t)+\eta\left(u_0'+R^2u_2'\right)\right] \tag{82}$$

That is, $u_3(x,t)$ is defined in terms of $u_0(x,t)$, $u_1(x,t)$ and $u_2(x,t)$, and so the number of independent modes describing the vibration dynamics for the Zachmanoglou-Volterra theory has been reduced from four to three. The reduction of independent displacement modes results in a simplification of the four mode theory, without having an impact on model accuracy. The Lagrangian density of the system is given by

$$\begin{aligned} \Lambda &= \Lambda(\dot{u}_0,\dot{u}_1,\dot{u}_2,\dot{u}_0',\dot{u}_2',u_0',u_1',u_2',u_0'',u_2'',u_1,u_2) \\ &=\frac{1}{2}\left\{S\rho\dot{u}_0^2+I_2\rho\dot{u}_1^2+2I_2\rho\dot{u}_0\dot{u}_2+I_4\rho\dot{u}_2^2+\frac{2I_4\rho}{R^2(2\eta-3)}\left(\dot{u}_1^2+\eta\dot{u}_0'\dot{u}_1+R^2\eta\dot{u}_1\dot{u}_2'\right)+\right. \\ &+\frac{I_6\rho}{R^4(2\eta-3)^2}\left(\dot{u}_1^2+2\eta\dot{u}_0'\dot{u}_1+\eta^2\dot{u}_0'^2+2R^2\eta\dot{u}_1\dot{u}_2'+2R^2\eta^2\dot{u}_0'\dot{u}_2'+R^4\eta^2\dot{u}_2'^2\right)- \\ &-S(\lambda+2\mu)u_0'^2-I_2\mu u_1'^2-2I_2(\lambda+2\mu)u_0'u_2'-I_4(\lambda+2\mu)u_2'^2-\frac{2I_4}{R^2(2\eta-3)}\left(\mu u_1'^2+\right. \\ &\left.+\eta\mu u_0''u_1'+R^2\eta\mu u_1'u_2''\right)-\frac{I_6}{R^4(2\eta-3)^2}\left(\mu u_1'^2+2\eta\mu u_0''u_1'+\eta^2\mu u_0''^2+2R^2\eta\mu u_1'u_2''+\right. \end{aligned} \tag{83a}$$

$$+2R^2\eta^2\mu u_0'' u_2'' + R^4\eta^2\mu u_2''^2\big) - 4S(\lambda+\mu)u_1^2 - 4S\lambda u_0' u_1 - 4I_2\mu u_2^2 - 4I_2\lambda u_1 u_2' -$$
$$-4I_2\mu u_1' u_2 - \frac{I_2}{R^2(2\eta-3)}\Big[16(\lambda+\mu)u_1^2 + 8\eta\lambda u_0'^2 + 16\lambda u_0' u_1 + 8R^2\eta\lambda u_0' u_2' +$$
$$+8R^2\lambda u_1 u_2'\Big] - \frac{I_4}{R^4(2\eta-3)^2}\Big[8\eta(4\lambda+5\mu)u_0' u_1 + 4\eta^2(4\lambda+5\mu)u_0'^2 - 8R^2\eta\mu u_1 u_2' - \tag{83b}$$
$$-8R^2\eta^2\mu u_0' u_2' + 4R^4\eta^2(4\lambda+5\mu)u_2'^2 + 4(4\lambda+5\mu)u_1^2 -\Big]$$
$$-\frac{I_4}{R^2(2\eta-3)}\left(8R^2\eta\lambda u_2'^2 + 4\eta\mu u_0'' u_2 + 4R^2\eta\mu u_2 u_2'' + 4\mu u_1' u_2\right)\Bigg\}$$

The Lagrangian density satisfies the system of three Euler-Lagrange differential equations

$$\begin{aligned}
&\frac{\partial}{\partial t}\left(\frac{\partial\Lambda}{\partial \dot u_0}\right) + \frac{\partial}{\partial x}\left(\frac{\partial\Lambda}{\partial u_0'}\right) - \frac{\partial^2}{\partial x\partial t}\left(\frac{\partial\Lambda}{\partial \dot u_0'}\right) - \frac{\partial^2}{\partial x^2}\left(\frac{\partial\Lambda}{\partial u_0''}\right) = 0\\
&\frac{\partial}{\partial t}\left(\frac{\partial\Lambda}{\partial \dot u_1}\right) + \frac{\partial}{\partial x}\left(\frac{\partial\Lambda}{\partial u_1'}\right) - \frac{\partial\Lambda}{\partial u_1} = 0\\
&\frac{\partial}{\partial t}\left(\frac{\partial\Lambda}{\partial \dot u_2}\right) + \frac{\partial}{\partial x}\left(\frac{\partial\Lambda}{\partial u_2'}\right) - \frac{\partial^2}{\partial x\partial t}\left(\frac{\partial\Lambda}{\partial \dot u_2'}\right) - \frac{\partial^2}{\partial x^2}\left(\frac{\partial\Lambda}{\partial u_2''}\right) - \frac{\partial\Lambda}{\partial u_2} = 0
\end{aligned} \tag{84}$$

with the corresponding the natural

$$\begin{aligned}
&\left[-\frac{\partial\Lambda}{\partial u_0'} - \frac{\partial}{\partial t}\left(\frac{\partial\Lambda}{\partial \dot u_0'}\right) - \frac{\partial}{\partial x}\left(\frac{\partial\Lambda}{\partial u_0''}\right)\right]\Bigg|_{x=0,l} = 0, \text{ and } \left[\frac{\partial\Lambda}{\partial u_0''}\right]\Bigg|_{x=0,l} = 0, \text{ and}\\
&\left[\frac{\partial\Lambda}{\partial u_1'}\right]\Bigg|_{x=0,l} = 0, \text{ and}\\
&\left[-\frac{\partial\Lambda}{\partial u_2'} - \frac{\partial}{\partial t}\left(\frac{\partial\Lambda}{\partial \dot u_2'}\right) - \frac{\partial}{\partial x}\left(\frac{\partial\Lambda}{\partial u_2''}\right)\right]\Bigg|_{x=0,l} = 0, \text{ and } \left[\frac{\partial\Lambda}{\partial u_2''}\right]\Bigg|_{x=0,l} = 0
\end{aligned} \tag{85}$$

or essential

$$u_0\big|_{x=0,l} = 0 \text{ and } u_0'\big|_{x=0,l} = 0 \text{ and } u_1\big|_{x=0,l} = 0 \text{ and } u_2\big|_{x=0,l} = 0 \text{ and } u_2'\big|_{x=0,l} = 0 \tag{86}$$

boundary conditions at the end points $x = 0$ and $x = l$. The explicit form of the equations of motion and boundary conditions (84)-(85) can be determined from the Lagrangian density (83).

4. Exact solution of the two mode (Mindlin-Herrmann) problem

In what follows, the solution of one of the models considered in this article, namely that of the mixed Mindlin-Herrmann problem (65), (66), with initial conditions given by

$$\begin{aligned}
u_0(x,t)\big|_{t=0} &= g(x), \quad \dot u_0(x,t)\big|_{t=0} = h(x)\\
u_1(x,t)\big|_{t=0} &= \varphi(x), \quad \dot u_1(x,t)\big|_{t=0} = q(x)
\end{aligned} \tag{87}$$

is presented. Note that the boundary conditions (66) represent a bar with both ends free (natural boundary conditions).
Applying the method of eigenfunction orthogonalities for vibration problems (Fedotov et al., 2010) to problem (65), (66), (87), two types of orthogonality conditions are proved for the eigenfunctions. Assume the solution of the system (65) is of the form

$$u_0(x,t) = y_0(x)e^{iwt} \qquad u_1(x,t) = y_1(x)e^{iwt} \tag{88}$$

where $i^2 = -1$. After substituting (88) into (65) and the boundary conditions (66) the following Sturm-Liouville problem is obtained

$$\begin{gathered} S\left[-\omega^2 \rho y_0 - (\lambda + 2\mu)\frac{d^2}{dx^2} y_0\right] - 2\lambda S \frac{d}{dx} y_1 = 0 \\ 2\lambda S \frac{d}{dx} y_0 + I_2\left(-\omega^2 \rho y_1 - \mu \frac{d^2}{dx^2} y_1\right) + 4S(\lambda + \mu) y_1 = 0 \end{gathered} \tag{89}$$

with the corresponding boundary conditions. Let $\{y_{0m}(x)\}$ and $\{y_{1m}(x)\}$ be the eigenfunctions of the Sturm-Liouville problem (89), which satisfy the two orthogonality conditions given by (9) and (68). The solution of the problem (65), (66), (87) can therefore be written as

$$u_0(x,t) = S\int_0^l \left[g(\xi)\frac{\partial G_1(x,\xi,t)}{\partial t} + h(\xi)G_1(x,\xi,t)\right]d\xi + I_2\int_0^l \left[\varphi(\xi)\frac{\partial G_2(x,\xi,t)}{\partial t} + q(\xi)G_2(x,\xi,t)\right]d\xi$$

and

$$u_1(x,t) = S\int_0^l \left[g(\xi)\frac{\partial G_3(x,\xi,t)}{\partial t} + h(\xi)G_3(x,\xi,t)\right]d\xi + I_2\int_0^l \left[\varphi(\xi)\frac{\partial G_4(x,\xi,t)}{\partial t} + q(\xi)G_4(x,\xi,t)\right]d\xi$$

where

$$\begin{aligned} G_1(x,\xi,t) &= \sum_{n=1}^{\infty}\left(\frac{y_{0n}(x)y_{0n}(\xi)\sin\omega_n t}{\omega_n \|y_n\|_1^2}\right) & G_2(x,\xi,t) &= \sum_{n=1}^{\infty}\left(\frac{y_{0n}(x)y_{1n}(\xi)\sin\omega_n t}{\omega_n \|y_n\|_1^2}\right) \\ G_3(x,\xi,t) &= \sum_{n=1}^{\infty}\left(\frac{y_{1n}(x)y_{0n}(\xi)\sin\omega_n t}{\omega_n \|y_n\|_1^2}\right) & G_4(x,\xi,t) &= \sum_{n=1}^{\infty}\left(\frac{y_{1n}(x)y_{1n}(\xi)\sin\omega_n t}{\omega_n \|y_n\|_1^2}\right) \end{aligned} \tag{90}$$

are the Green functions, and

$$\omega_n = \frac{\|y_n\|_2}{\sqrt{\rho}\|y_n\|_1}, \qquad n = 1, 2, \ldots \tag{91}$$

are the eigenvalues (eigenfrequencies) of the problem. The solution of all other problems presented in this article can be obtained in a similar manner. The solution of the three mode problem, for example, can be obtained with six Green functions.

5. Predicting the accuracy of the approximate theories

Two forms of graphical display are typically used to analyse the factors governing wave propagation for mathematical models describing the vibration of continuous systems. These are called the frequency spectrum and phase velocity dispersion curves and are obtained from the so-called frequency equation (Achenbach, 2005:206, 217-218; Graff, 1991:54), which shows the relation between frequency ω, wave number k and phase velocity c for a particular model. In the "k - ω" plane the frequency equation for each model yields a number of continuous curves, called branches. The number of branches corresponds to the number of independent functions chosen to represent u and w in (1)-(2). Each branch shows the relationship between frequency ω and wave number k for a particular mode of propagation. The collection of branches plotted in the "k - ω" plane is called the frequency spectrum of the system. Dispersion curves represent phase velocity c versus wave number k and can be obtained from the frequency equation by using the relation $\omega = ck$.

The different approximate models of longitudinal vibrations of rods can be analysed and deductions can be made regarding their accuracy by plotting their frequency spectra (or dispersion curves) and comparing them with the frequency spectrum (or dispersion curve) of the exact Pochhammer-Chree frequency equation for the axisymmetric problem of a cylindrical rod with free outer surface (longitudinal modes of vibration).

In order to find the frequency equation, it is assumed that each independent function can be represented as $u_j(x,t) = U_j e^{i(kx-\omega t)}$, where $j = 0,1,2...n - 1$ and n corresponds to the number of independent functions chosen in (1)-(2). These representations for $u_j(x,t)$ are substituted into the equation(s) of motion, yielding the frequency equation. The frequency equation thus obtained for the classical theory is given by

$$-\omega^2 + c_0^2 k^2 = 0, \tag{92}$$

which gives a single straight line with gradient $c_0 = \sqrt{E/\rho}$, the speed of propagation of waves in an infinite rod described by the classical wave equation. The frequency equations for the Rayleigh-Love and Rayleigh-Bishop theories are given by

$$-\omega^2 S + k^2 c_0^2 S - \omega^2 k^2 \eta^2 I_2 = 0 \tag{93}$$

and

$$-\omega^2 S + k^2 c_0^2 S - \omega^2 k^2 \eta^2 I_2 + k^4 \eta^2 I_2 c_2^2 = 0 \tag{94}$$

respectively, where $c_2 = \sqrt{\mu/\rho}$ is the speed of propagation of shear waves in an infinite rod.

Since the classical, Rayleigh-Love and Rayleigh-Bishop theories are unimodal theories, their frequency equations yield a single branch in the "k - ω" domain That is, the frequency equations (92), (93) and (94) have a single solution for positive ω. The Rayleigh-Love and Rayleigh-Bishop theories, however, do not yield straight lines as in the classical theory. That is, the Rayleigh-Love and Rayleigh-Bishop theories represent dispersive systems (the phase velocity c depends on the wave number k). For the multimodal theories, the substitution results in a system of equations with unknowns U_j. The frequency equation is found by equating the determinant of the coefficient matrix to zero. The frequency equation for the Mindlin-Herrmann (two mode) theory, for example, can be thus obtained as

$$\omega^4 I_2 - \omega^2 k^2 I_2 \left(c_1^2 + c_2^2\right) - 4S\left(\omega^2 - c_0^2 k^2\right)\left(c_1^2 - c_2^2\right) + k^4 c_1^2 c_2^2 I_2 = 0, \tag{95}$$

where $c_1 = \sqrt{(\lambda + 2\mu)/\rho}$ is the speed of propagation of pressure (dilatational) waves in an infinite rod. The well known Pochhammer-Chree frequency equation (Achenbach, 2005:242-246; Graff, 1991:464-473) is given by

$$\frac{2\alpha}{R}\left(\beta^2 + k^2\right) J_1(\alpha R) J_1(\beta R) - \left(\beta^2 - k^2\right) J_0(\alpha R) J_1(\beta R) - 4k^2 \alpha\beta J_1(\alpha R) J_1(\beta R) = 0 \tag{96}$$

where $J_n(x)$ is the Bessel function of the first kind of order n,

$$\alpha^2 = \frac{\omega^2}{c_1^2} - k^2, \qquad \beta^2 = \frac{\omega^2}{c_2^2} - k^2, \tag{97}$$

and R is the outer radius of the cylinder. The Pochhammer-Chree frequency equation yields infinitely many branches the "k - ω" and "k - c" planes.

The figures that follow in this section have been generated for a cylindrical rod made from an Aluminium alloy with Young's modulus E = 70 GPa, mass density ρ = 2700 kg.m^{-3}, and Poisson ratio η = 0.33. It is not necessary to define the radius R of the cylinder, since all frequency spectra and dispersion curves have been generated using the normalized, dimensionless parameters

$$\Omega = \frac{\omega R}{\pi c_2}, \qquad \bar{c} = \frac{c}{c_0}, \qquad \xi = \frac{kR}{\pi} \tag{98}$$

that are independent of the choice of R.

Figure 1a shows the frequency spectra for the classical, Rayleigh-Love and Rayleigh-Bishop theories, as well as the first branch of the two mode theory and the first branch of the exact Pochhammer-Chree frequency spectrum.

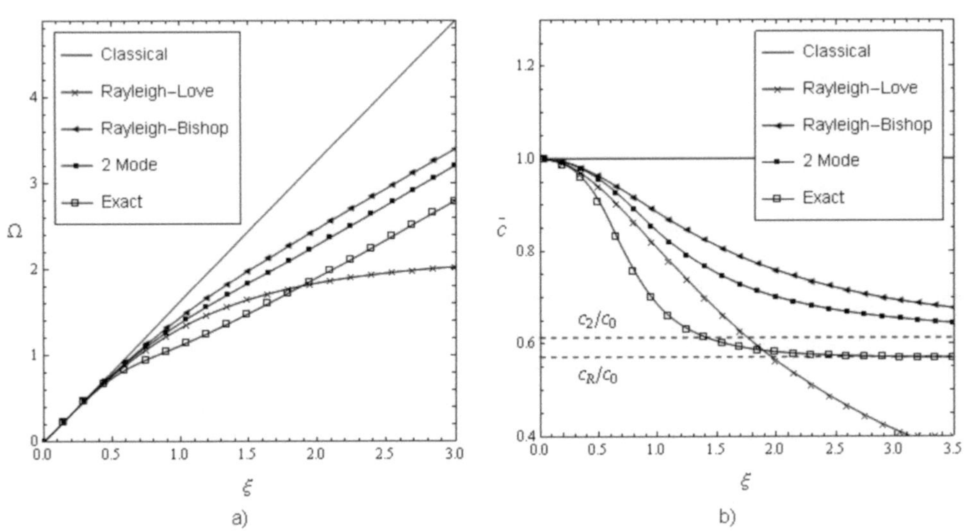

Fig. 1. Comparison of a) frequency spectra and b) dispersion curves of the classical, Rayleigh-Love, Rayleigh-Bishop, two mode (first branch) and exact (first branch) theories.

All the theories (including classical theory) approximately describe the first branch of the exact solution in a restricted "k - ω" domain. The Rayleigh-Love approximation is initially more accurate than the Rayleigh-Bishop and Mindlin-Herrmann approximations, but the values fall away rapidly for values of ξ greater than 2 (approximately). The Rayleigh-Bishop and Mindlin-Herrmann approximations are reasonably accurate over a larger "k - ω"-domain, but the branches asymptotically tend toward the shear wave solution, while the exact solution tends to the (Rayleigh) surface waves mode. The shear wave mode is given by the straight line $\omega(k) = c_2 k$ and the surface wave mode is given by the straight line $\omega(k) = c_R k$, where $c_R \approx 0.9320 c_2$ is the speed of propagation of surface waves in the rod. The factor 0.9320 is dependent on the Poisson ratio $\eta = 0.33$ (Achenbach, 2005:187-194; Graff, 1991:323-328). The phenomenon described above is illustrated in figure 1b, which shows the phase velocity dispersion curves for the first branches of the exact solution and the Mindlin-Herrmann approximation, as well as the phase velocity dispersion curves for the Rayleigh-Love and Rayleigh-Bishop approximations.

The frequency spectra for some of the higher order unimode theories are given in figures 2a (Rayleigh-Bishop type theories) and 2b (Rayleigh-Love type theories), together with the first branch of the exact Pochhammer-Chree frequency equation.

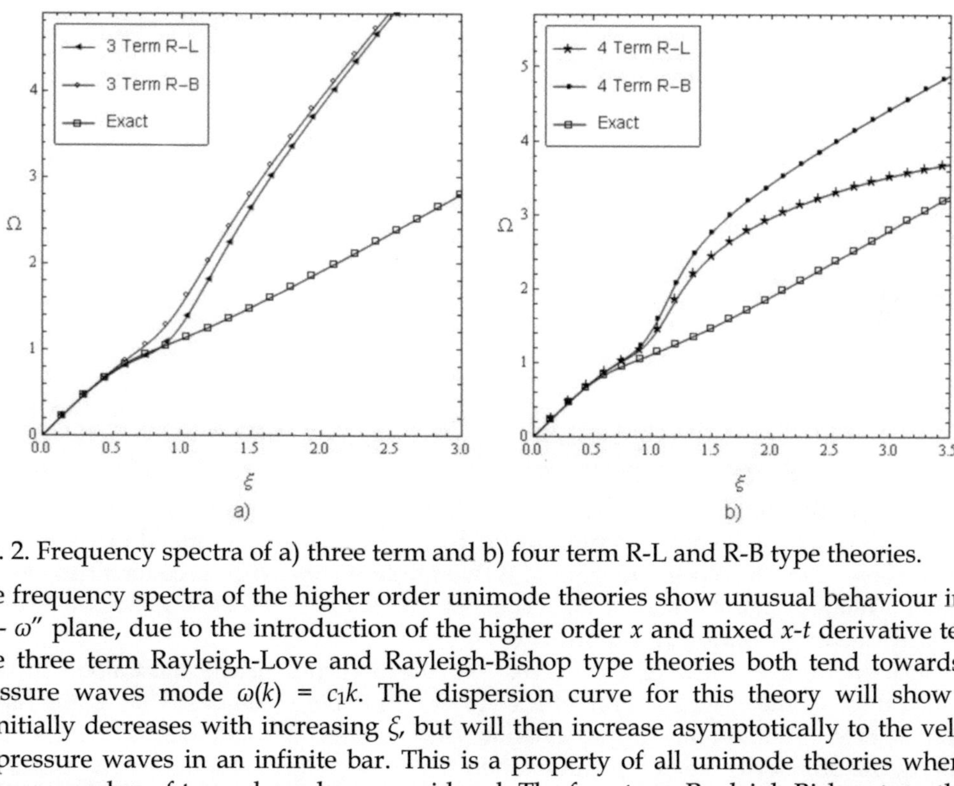

Fig. 2. Frequency spectra of a) three term and b) four term R-L and R-B type theories.

The frequency spectra of the higher order unimode theories show unusual behaviour in the "k - ω" plane, due to the introduction of the higher order x and mixed x-t derivative terms. The three term Rayleigh-Love and Rayleigh-Bishop type theories both tend towards the pressure waves mode $\omega(k) = c_1 k$. The dispersion curve for this theory will show that $\bar{c}$ initially decreases with increasing ξ, but will then increase asymptotically to the velocity of pressure waves in an infinite bar. This is a property of all unimode theories where an uneven number of terms have been considered. The four term Rayleigh-Bishop type theory tends towards the shear wave solution. It is evident from the shape of the frequency spectrum that $\bar{c}$ will initially decrease with increasing ξ, but will then increase again before decreasing to the horizontal asymptote c_2/c_0. All Rayleigh-Bishop type theories where an even number of terms has been considered will tend towards the shear waves mode. The four term Rayleigh-Love type model, as discussed in section 3.1g above, has a limit point in its frequency spectrum, and the phase velocities of waves described by this theory will tend to zero as $\xi \to \infty$. The higher order unimode theories have been applied successfully in the analysis of propagation of solitons (solitary waves) in non-linear elastic solids. However, since the higher order theories are substantially more complicated than the (two term) Rayleigh-Love and Rayleigh-Bishop theories and due to the lack of physical clarity of the higher order derivative terms present in the equations of motion and boundary conditions, these theories are of little value for analysis of wave propagation in linear elastic solids.

Frequency spectra for a selection of multimode theories are presented in figures 3 through 7. The exact Pochhammer-Chree frequency spectrum is shown by dashed lines on all the frequency spectrum plots shown for the multimode models. The imaginary branches (imaginary ξ) represent evanescent waves and describe exponential decay with respect to wave number. Figure 3 shows the frequency spectrum of the two mode (Mindlin-Herrmann) theory described in section 3.2a.

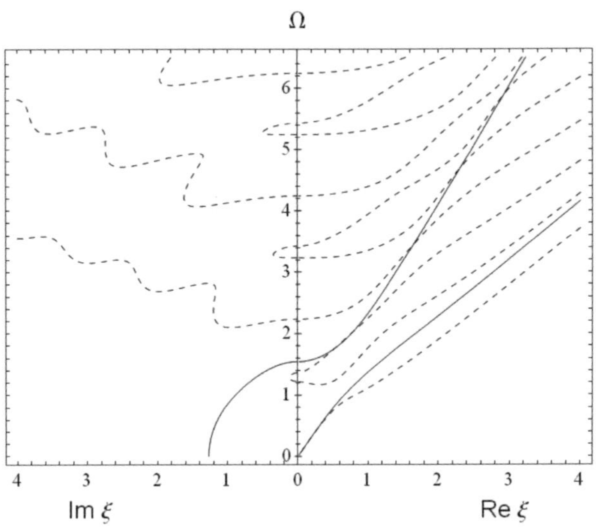

Fig. 3. Frequency spectrum of a two mode model (solid line), exact solution (dashed line).

Figure 4 shows the frequency spectrum of the three mode theory discussed in section 3.2b. Figure 5 shows the frequency spectrum of the four mode theory discussed in section 3.2c. Figure 6 shows the frequency spectrum of a five mode theory with three longitudinal and two lateral modes. Figure 7 shows the frequency spectrum of the Zachmanoglou-Volterra three mode theory discussed in section 3.2d.

It is apparent from analysis of the curves that the branches of the multimode theories approach those of the exact solution with increasing number of modes. That is, the higher the order of the multimode approximation (the greater the number of independent functions) the broader is the "k - ω"- domain in which the effects of longitudinal vibrations of the rods could be analysed. To offset the error introduced by the omission of the higher order modes, Mindlin & McNiven (1960) modified the kinetic and potential energy functions (in their three mode "second order approximation") by introducing four compensating factors that were chosen in such a way as to match the behaviour of the first three branches of the Pochhammer-Chree frequency spectrum at long wavelengths. This methodology could also be applied to the models presented here to obtain similar results. It should be noted that, regardless of the number of independent functions chosen, some of the branches will tend towards the shear wave solution $\omega(k) = c_2k$, while the remaining branches will tend towards the pressure wave solution $\omega(k) = c_1k$ as $k \to \infty$. None of the branches will tend towards the surface waves mode. This is because all the approximate theories discussed in this article are one dimensional theories (since $u_k = u_k(x,t)$), and can therefore not predict the effect of vibration on the outer cylindrical surface of the rod.

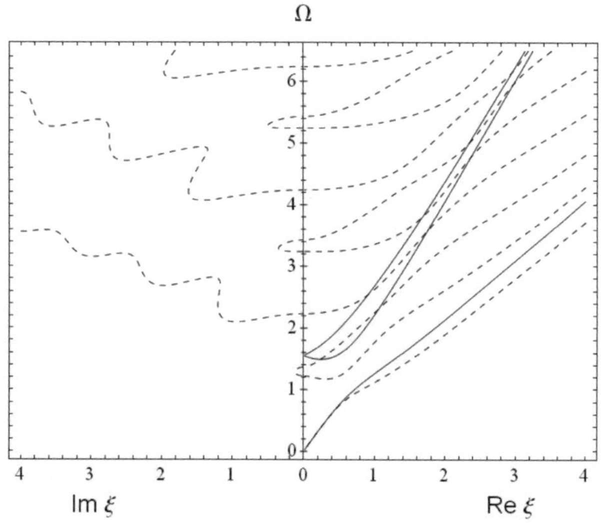

Fig. 4. Frequency spectrum of a three mode model (solid line), exact solution (dashed line).

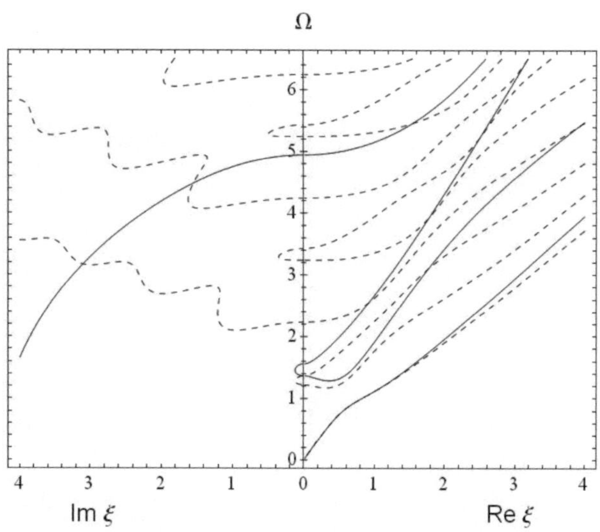

Fig. 5. Frequency spectrum of a three mode model (solid line), exact solution (dashed line).

Comparison of the frequency spectrum shown in figure 6 with figure 4 shows that the accuracy of the three branches in the Zachmanoglou-Volterra theory matches that of the first three branches of the four mode theory. That is, Zachmanoglou and Volterra simplified the four mode theory by reducing the number of partial differential equations and boundary conditions and the simplification did not have a negative impact on accuracy.

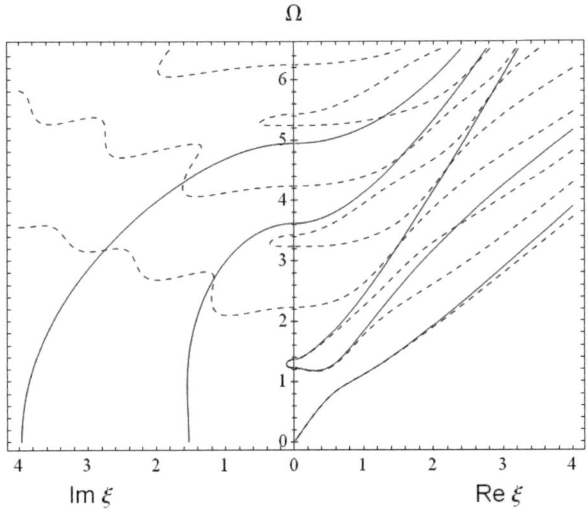

Fig. 6. Frequency spectrum of a five mode model (solid line), exact solution (dashed line).

The nature of the first branches of the multimode theories with increasing number of modes is of particular interest in the design of low frequency ultrasonic transducers and waveguides.

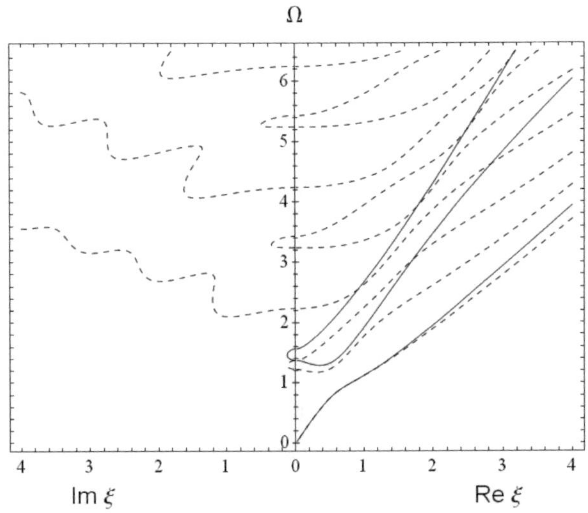

Fig. 7. Frequency spectrum of the Zachmanoglou-Volterra model (solid line), exact solution (dashed line).

Figure 8 shows the first branches of the spectral curves for the two mode, three mode and four mode models, together with the first branch of the exact Pochhammer-Chree solution. It is clear from this figure that the first branch of the approximate multimode theories approaches that of the exact Pochhammer-Chree solution with an increasing number of modes. The first branch of the five mode theory has not been included in figure 8 because it is too close to that of the four mode theory them to be easily distinguished from each other in the selected region for ξ.

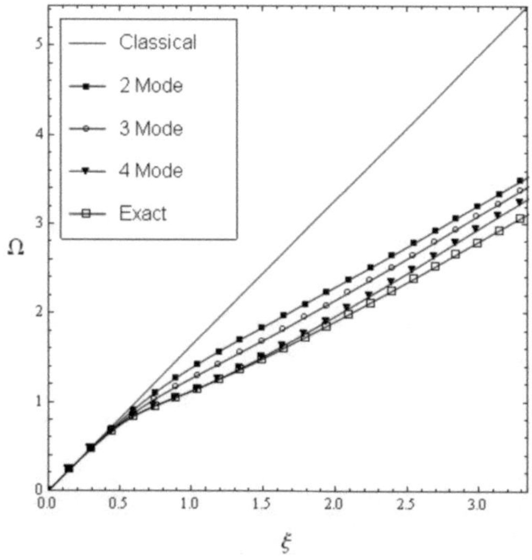

Fig. 8. First branches of the two, three, four mode models, and the exact solution.

6. Conclusion

In this article, a generalised theory for the derivation of approximate theories describing the longitudinal vibration of elastic bars has been proposed. The models outlined in this article represent a family of one dimensional hyperbolic differential equations, since all $u_k = u_k(x,t)$. An infinite number of these approximate theories have been introduced and the general procedure for derivation of the differential equations and boundary conditions for all the models considered has been exposed.

The approximate theories have been categorised as "unimode" or "multimode", and "plane cross sectional" or "non plane cross sectional" theories, based on the representation for longitudinal and lateral displacements (1)-(2). The classical, Rayleigh-Love and Rayleigh-Bishop models are all "unimode", "plane cross sectional" theories. Both the Mindlin-Hermann and the three mode models are "multimode" theories. The Mindlin-Hermann model is a "plane cross sectional" theory, whereas the three-mode model is a "non plane cross sectional" theory. All models subsequent to the three-mode model (four-mode, five-mode, etc) are also "multimode", "non plane cross sectional" theories.

The orthogonality conditions have been found for the corresponding multimodal models which substantially simplify construction of the solution in terms of Green functions. The solution procedure for the Mindlin-Herrmann model has been presented, using the Fourier method. Using the method of two orthogonalities (presented here), it is possible to obtain the solution for all models considered in this article.

Finally, it has been shown that the accuracy of the approximate models discussed in this article approach that of the exact theory with increasing number of modes, based on a comparison of the frequency spectra with that of the exact Pochhammer-Chree frequency equation.

7. References

Achenbach, J.D. (2005). *Wave Propagation in Elastic Solids*, Elsevier Science, ISBN 978-0-7204-0325-1, Amsterdam.

Bishop, R.E.D. (1952). Longitudinal Waves in Beams. *Aeronautical Quarterly*, Vol. 3, No. 2, 280-293.

Fedotov, I.A., Polyanin, A.D. & Shatalov, M.Yu. (2007). Theory of Free and Forced Vibrations of a Rigid Rod Based on the Rayleigh Model. *Doklady Physics*, Vol. 52, No. 11, 607-612, ISSN 1028-3358.

Fedotov, I., Shatalov, M., Tenkam, H.M. & Marais, J. (2009). Comparison of Classical and Modern Theories of Longitudinal Wave Propagation in Elastic Rods, *Proceedings of the 16th International Conference of Sound and Vibration*, Krakow, Poland, 5 - 9 July, 2009.

Fedotov, I., Shatalov, M.A, Fedotova, T. & Tenkam, H.M. (2010). Method of Multiple Orthogonalities for Vibration Problems, *Current Themes in Engineering science 2009: Selected Presentations at the World Congress on Engineering 2009, AIP Conference Proceedings*, Vol. 1220, 43-58, ISBN 978-0-7354-0766-4, American Institute of Physics.

Fung, Y.C. & Tong, P. (2001). *Classical and Computational Solid Mechanics*, World Scientific, ISBN 978-981-02-3912-1, Singapore.

Gai, Y., Fedotov, I. & Shatalov, M. (2007). Analysis of a Rayleigh-Bishop Model For a Thick Bar, *Proceedings of the 2006 IEEE International Ultrasonics Symposium*, 1915-1917, ISBN 1-4244-0201-8, Vancouver, Canada, 2 - 6 October, 2006, Institute of Electrical and Electronics Engineers.

Graff, K.F. (1991). *Wave Motion in Elastic Solids*, Dover Publications, ISBN 978-0-486-66745-6, New York.

Grigoljuk, E.I. & Selezov, I.T. (1973). *Mechanics of Solid Deformed Bodies, Vol. 5, Non-classical Theories of Rods, Plates and Shells*, Nauka, Moscow. (In Russian).

Love, A.E.H. (2009). *A Treatise on the Mathematical Theory of Elasticity*, 2nd (1906) Edition, BiblioLife, ISBN 978-1-113-22366-1.

Mindlin, R.D. & McNiven, H.D. (1960). Axially symmetric waves in elastics rods. *Journal of Applied Mechanics*, Vol. 27, 145-151, ISSN 00218936.

Porubov, A.V. (2003). *Amplification of Nonlinear Strain Waves in Solids*, World Scientific, ISBN 978-981-238-326-3, Singapore.

Rayleigh, J.W.S. (1945). *Theory of sound*, Vol I, Dover Publications, ISBN 978-0-486-60292-3, New York.

Zachmanoglou, E.C. & Volterra, E. (1958). An Engineering Theory of Longitudinal Wave Propagation in Cylindrical Elastic Rods, *Proceedings of the 3rd US National Congress on Applied Mechanics*, 239-245, Providence, Rhode Island, New York, 1958.

11

A Multiphysics Analysis of Aluminum Welding Flux Composition Optimization Methods

Joseph I. Achebo
Department of Production Engineering, University of Benin
Nigeria

1. Introduction

Manufacturing and mass production have been the main factors propelling the drive towards innovation and technological advancement. The principal substance in materials science that has driven this technological drive is metal, and of all the metals, Aluminum is of inestemable value. Welding is the main bane of manufacturing. It is the process used to join two or more pieces of metals permanently together. Aluminum welding, which is the main target of this research, is particularly dependent on the utilization of a suitable welding flux to achieve excellent results. Aluminum is ubiquitous in application and is of great relevance in nearly all fields of technological development and research, invariably, the same applies to its welding flux. Fluxes are invaluable because they facilitate the removal of the Tenacious Aluminum Hydrated Oxide layer (AlOH) which is always found on Aluminum surfaces which have been exposed to atmospheric oxygen. If this Aluminum oxide layer is not removed before or during welding, its chemical constituents, unless reduced to trace amounts, will act as impurities that would significantly compromise the quality of the weld. It is therefore important to understand the characteristics, the chemical composition, morphological personality, and the weld adaptability of Aluminum and its alloys; in general, a multiphysical approach. All geared towards the realization of an optimal flux composition for Aluminum fluxes.

In this chapter, the physics of Aluminum flux composition development process is studied applying several optimization models. To improve on the quality of the welding processes, new ways of developing and optimizing welding fluxes are being investigated with focus on statistical quality control. However, Jackson (1973) was of the opinion that the complex welding technology prevalent in the 1970's demands an understanding of the formulation, manufacture, performance and use of welding fluxes. This statement still holds true even today. He emphasized that the technology leading to proper flux formulation has been little understood. Natalie et al, (1986) said that new engineering requirements demand innovative approaches to the formulation and manufacture of a welding flux. They also observed that the need for higher quality finished metal products, for applications requiring both higher strength and toughness, demands better control of the weld metal composition in the aftermath of any welding using fluxes.

In recent years, mechanical properties such as strength or ductility have been in higher demand in engineering projects, as components are designed to carry even heavier loads.

Welds of equivalent strength are required to sustain the maintainability and reliability of the continuous use of such materials. Chai & Eagar (1983) said that the ultimate goal of any weld is the production of a deposit with properties which meet or exceed those of the baseplate.
Each chemical constituent element of a flux has been found by other investigators to influence the quality of the weld, even perhaps increasing the strength of the resulting welds (Achebo & Ibhadode, 2008). Boniszewski (1979) recognized that there are several formulated flux/coatings compositions. The composition selected depends on its utility. Achebo & Ibhadode (2009) observed that various manufacturers have produced different flux compositions depending on the weld strengths they intend to achieve; this being the criterion for developing their own unique flux compositions.
An Aluminum welding flux composition is comprised mainly of fluoride and chloride salts. In principle, the real advantage fluoride salts possess is that they are non-hygroscopic, making it quite possible to produce a flux consisting of the fluoride salts only. Chloride salts on the other hand have an affinity for atmospheric oxygen, making them hygroscopic. However, although the fluoride salts are a very vital and effective constituent, the utility of fluoride salts is somewhat inhibited. Firstly, by their relatively high melting point (being higher than 900°C), and secondly, by their diminished ability to completely dissolve the Aluminum oxide layer on their own. The interaction of the fluoride salts with atmospheric oxygen and moisture found within the weld environment (in the form of vapour), could cause the evolution of harmful gases such as Aluminum Fluoride (AlF), and Hydrogen Fluoride (HF). These gases are highly carcinogenic. This is the main reason fluoride salts' inclusion as one of the flux constituent elements, is in perpetually smaller proportion to other additives. Jackson (1973) wrote that Calcium Fluoride (CaF_2) for instance would usually make up only about 5% to 7% of the composition. However, according to him, this proportion could be in even larger quantities for special purpose fluxes, servicing a niche market. Utigard et al (1998) said that fluoride salts could be up to 20% by weight. The application and use of such fluoride heavy fluxes must however to be balanced against the health risks involved.
Chloride salts are a virtually safe constituent elements and could be applied generously. The majority of the chloride salts of alkali and alkali earth elements have a melting point lower than 800°C and consequently they melt in the stage of formation of the droplet, ensuring sufficient shielding of the slag. The chlorides of Potassium (K), Sodium (Na), Lithium (Li), and Calcium (Ca), are hygroscopic. Chlorides salts exhibit the same property as fluorides but to a much lesser extent being in the same active element group. Their stability in dissolving AlOH can be predicted from the simplistic concept of electro-negativity series theory (Utigard et al, 1998). The reason fluorides and chlorides of potassium, sodium and calcium are used to dissolve the AIOH is explained by the Gibbs Energy of Formation, as well as the Electro-Negativity Series Theory. Utigard et al, (1998) suggest in their work that as the stability of the compound increases with an increasing negative value of the Gibbs energy formation, the thermodynamic stability decreases, in the order of, fluorides > chlorides > oxides > suffides > phosphates > nitrates > carbonates.
This explains why a compound containing oxides can only be removed / or dissolved by fluoride and chloride compounds. From the Gibbs energy of formation, fluoride is more effective than chloride in removing oxides, i.e. fluorides are more stable than the corresponding elements; chloride > oxide > sulfide (Utigard et al, 1998).
In the electro-negativity series, the metal elements are in the order: Li, K, Na, Ca, Mg, Al, Zn, Fe, Pb, H, Cu, Hg, Ag, Au. The more reactive metals are lithium, potassium, sodium,

calcium and magnesium. The reactive metals are Aluminum, Zinc, Iron and the less reactive metals are lead, copper, mercury, silver, and gold (Holderness & Lambert, 1982). The compounds within these three groups described above (i.e, more reactive metals, reactive metals and less reactive metals) can be substituted for one another, that is, in a particular group any element can be substituted for the other, if their individual effects, when used as flux material, are not significantly different from each other. Since these elements are surface active elements within the same group, they are likely to achieve vastly similar results or effects.

As a general rule, the higher the difference in electronegativity between any two elements, the greater the bond strength and stability of any compound made up of these two elements. This means that any metal higher up in the series will displace from its salts any metal below it. The greater the gap separating the metals in the series, the more readily will the displacement take place (Holderness & Lambert, 1982).

Therefore, only Li, K, Na, Ca and Mg can displace Al, but since K, Na, Ca and Mg are the more reactive metals, they are the elements that effectively displace Aluminum considering the Gibbs energy of formation. Fluoride and chloride compounds of K, Na, Ca and Mg can effectively dissolve AIOH.

From the series, it is shown that all metals higher in the series than hydrogen displace it. Therefore, the metals high up in the series being K, Na, Ca and Mg would most effectively displace hydrogen from the molten weld pool. In general the higher metals in the series oxidize readily. They float to the top to form slag to protect the weld bead from contact with the environment (thus preventing oxidation and re-oxidation). Utigard et al (1998) were of the opinion that although chloride salts strip Aluminum of its oxide and assists in the coalescence of Aluminum, the interfacial tension between Aluminum and chloride based melts does not change with the addition of chlorides or with the variation in the composition of chloride salts. On the other hand, the addition of fluorides decreases the interfacial tension to various extents due to the absorption of Na and K at the interface. Further research carried out explains that the combination with chloride salt reduces its melting point (eutectic) but the addition of fluoride salt further reduces the melting temperature (ternary eutectic). A low melting point is important since it improves the fluidity of the flux and forms a thin layer on the melt surface. Lincoln Electric Foundation wrote that low melting point components in the molten weld metal are forced to the center of the joint during solidification since they are the last to solidify.

In this study, the multiphysical examination explains the displacement of a constituent element by a superior or more active element. The mechanical property of ductility and strength is here applied as a standard to determine flux compositions. Optimization methods such as Hadamard Matrix design and Taguchi experimental design methods alongside with the Expert evaluation method were also used in this study to develop optimum flux compositions. The efficiencies of these methods were compared and analyzed.

2. The Hadamard matrix design for four variables

The two level multivariate factorial design generated from the Hadamard matrices, was formulated by Jacques Hadamard, a French mathematician, in 1893. He has shown the applicability of these matrices to most two level experimental designs; where a two level experimental design is a design that operates in a range of values within a low level and a high level. Two level multivariate resolution IV Hadamard matrix design is a two level, four

variable experimental design; each of the four variables has a high level and a low level (Diamond, 1989). All designs (regardless of numbers of compositions or variables), where all the main effects of the compositions and groups of interactions between the variables that constitute the flux compositions are known and computed, can be estimated. The model as illustrated hereunder is used to obtain an optimum flux composition amongst a wide range of existing flux compositions.
The Aluminum welding flux composition used for this study is as expressed in Table 1

Flux Material Designation	Constituent Element (% by weight)
A LiCl	25 - 30 at most 35
B NaCl	30 - 45
C KCl	30 - 40
D CaF_2	5 – 10

Table 1. Aluminum Welding Flux Chemical Composition

The Hadamard matrix design layout for four variables is shown in Table 2

Flux No	0	A 1	B 2	C 3	CD -AB 4	AD -BC 5	D ABC 6	BD -AC 7	Treatment comninations
1	+	+	−	−	+	−	+	+	ad
2	+	+	+	−	−	+	−	+	ab
3	+	+	+	+	−	−	+	−	abcd
4	+	−	+	+	+	−	−	+	bc
5	+	+	−	+	+	+	−	−	ac
6	+	−	+	−	+	+	+	−	bd
7	+	−	−	+	−	+	+	+	cd
8	+	−	−	−	−	−	−	−	(1)

Table 2. Hadamard Matrix Design For Four Variables (Diamond, 1989)

The main flux variables A, B, C and D were extracted from Table 2 and the flux composition ranges in Table 1 were used to fill the matrices of the extracted variables noting that (+) signifies a high value of the flux composition ranges and (-) signifies a low level of the composition ranges; the fourth variable D being considered first in the formulation process. The other variables A, B and C are filled in the first three columns and the column reserved for the D variable is left blank. Bearing in mind that the condition of this formulation process states that each composition or trial must add up to 100% by weight, to make a complete composition. Then variables A, B and C are added up and the remaining value to sum it up to 100% by weight is entered on the D column if that value falls within the range or limits set for variable D as specified in Table 1. However, if the value is above or below the range, it would be skipped (Diamond, 1989) as shown in Tables 3 – 5

Flux No	A	B	C	D	
1	30	30	30	10	(1)
2	30	45	30	–	
3	30	45	40	–	
4	25	45	40	–	
5	30	30	40	–	
6	25	45	30	–	
7	25	30	40	5	(2)
8	25	30	30	–	

Table 3. Step 1: Considering Variable D, CaF_2 (5 – 10%)

Flux No	A	B	C	D	
1	30	30	30	10	(1)
2	30	45	–	5	
3	30	45	–	10	
4	25	45	–	5	
5	30	30	35	5	(3)
6	25	45	–	10	
7	25	30	35	10	(4)
8	25	30	40	5	(2)

Table 4. Step 2: Considering Variable C, KCl (30 – 40%)

Flux No	A	B	C	D	
1	30	30	30	10	(1)
2	30	35	30	5	(5)
3	30	–	40	10	
4	25	30	40	5	(2)
5	30	–	40	5	
6	25	35	30	10	(6)
7	25	–	40	10	
8	25	40	30	5	(7)

Table 5. Step 3: Considering Variable B, NaCl (30 – 45%)

Flux No	A	B	C	D	
1	30	30	30	10	(1)
2	–	45	30	5	
3	–	45	40	10	
4	–	45	40	5	
5	25	30	40	5	(2)
6	–	45	30	10	
7	–	30	40	10	
8	35	30	30	5	(8)

Table 6. Step 4: Considering Variable A, L_iCl (25 – 30%)

The summary of the eight (8) newly formulated welding flux chemical compositions based on the given flux composition ranges in Table 1 and extracted from the procedures conducted in Tables 3 – 6 is shown in Table 7.

Flux No.	LiCl	NaCl	KCl	CaF_2
1	30	30	30	10
2	25	30	40	5
3	30	30	35	5
4	25	30	35	10
5	30	35	30	5
6	25	35	30	10
7	25	40	30	5
8	35	30	30	5

Table 7. Eight newly formulated chemical compositions (% by wt)

Flux No.	UTS MPa
1	293
2	302
3	262
4	296
5	303
6	296
7	254
8	243

Table 8. The average UTS Results of the Weld Metals made by the Eight Newly formulated fluxes.

Each treatment combination (i.e. flux composition) was used to make five weld deposits which were machined into the standard dimension required to make the samples needed to conduct tensile tests in accordance with the Federal Test Method Standard No. 151 Metals Test methods. The average ultimate tensile strength (UTS) results were recorded as shown in Table 8.

The main variables defining the constituent elements of the flux material have been obtained. Here since the UTS has been determined for each flux combination. The next step is to determine the effect of these main variables on weld strength.

Flux No.	A	B	C	D
1	+293	-293	-293	+293
2	+302	+302	-302	-302
3	+262	+262	+262	+262
4	-296	+296	+296	-296
5	+303	-303	+303	-303
6	-296	+296	-296	+296
7	-254	-254	+254	+254
8	-243	-243	-243	-243
$\sum X_{high} - \sum X_{low}$	71	63	-19	-39

Table 9. Effects of flux composition on weld strength (UTS)

The mean effects of the main variables are determined as follows:

$$\bar{X}A_{high} - \bar{X}A_{low} = \frac{71}{4} = 17.75$$

$$\bar{X}B_{high} - \bar{X}B_{low} = \frac{63}{4} = 15.75$$

$$\bar{X}C_{high} - \bar{X}C_{low} = \frac{-19}{4} = -4.75$$

$$\bar{X}D_{high} - \bar{X}D_{low} = \frac{-39}{4} = -9.75$$

Having obtained the mean above, the estimates of the variances of the contrast are estimated as is expressed in Table 10

The variances of contrast 5, 6 and 7 are estimated as follows:

$$S_i^2 = \frac{\left[\sum(\text{Column sign})(\text{Test result})\right]^2}{T} \tag{1}$$

Where T is the number of flux compositions of the experiments = 8 and i represents the contrast numbers (in this case i = 5, 6 and 7). Applying Eq (1).

Flux No	Contrast 5 CD - AB	Contrast 6 AD - BC	Contrast 7 BD - AC
1	+293	-293	+293
2	-302	+302	+302
3	-262	-262	-262
4	+296	-296	+296
5	+303	+303	-303
6	+296	+296	-296
7	-254	+254	+254
8	-243	-243	-243
$\sum\left(X_{high} - X_{low}\right)$	127	61	41

Table 10. Estimates of the variance of the contrasts

$$S_5^2 = \frac{(127)^2}{8} = 2016.125$$

$$S_6^2 = \frac{(61)^2}{8} = 465.125$$

$$S_7^2 = \frac{(41)^2}{8} = 210.125$$

The average of variances of contrast 5, 6, and 7 are estimated from the equation

$$S_{avg}^2 = \frac{\sum^{i} S_i^2}{j}$$ with j degrees of freedom

j = N – 1 degrees of freedom. N is the number of flux elements = 4.

$$S_{avg}^2 = \frac{2016.125 + 465.125 + 210.125}{3}$$

= 897.125

Whereas, the standard deviation is the square root of the average variance of contrasts 5, 6 and 7. This is obtained as is expressed as follows

$$S = \sqrt{897.125} = 29.95$$

2.1 Test criterion determination

At chosen values of 3 degrees of freedom, ϕ; where $a = 0.05$ at 95% confidence level, $t_\beta = 2.35$ (t_β is obtained from probability points of t-distribution single sided table when σ^2 is unknown). Since N_{high} = N_{low} = 4 and S = 29.95, substituting values into the selection criterion, as expressed hereunder, is a standardized equation for selecting the chemical composition constituent elements.

$$\left|\overline{X}_{high}-\overline{X}_{low}\right|^{*}=t_{\beta}S\sqrt{\frac{1}{N_{high}}+\frac{1}{N_{low}}} \tag{2}$$

$= 2.35(29.95)\sqrt{\frac{1}{4}+\frac{1}{4}}$
= 2.35(29.95) x 0.7071 = 49.77

2.2 Conditions for making decision

A low value is desirable if the mean effect is positive, the low level (μ low) is better. If the mean effect is negative, the high level (μ high) is better, that is,
If $\left(\overline{X}_{high}-\overline{X}_{low}\right)$ is negative and $\left|\overline{X}_{high}-\overline{X}_{low}\right|>\left|\overline{X}_{high}-\overline{X}_{low}\right|^{*}$ accept that μ high is better than μ low
If $\left(\overline{X}_{high}-\overline{X}_{low}\right)$ is positive and greater than $\left|\overline{X}_{high}-\overline{X}_{low}\right|^{*}$, accept that μ low is better than μ high
* signifies the standard selection criterion

2.3 Selection test

The selection test is done by comparing the average mean effect of the main variables determined from Table 9 with the mean effect of the standard selection (*) for the variables under study as it relates to variables A, B, C and D below

$$\left(\left|\overline{X}A_{high}-\overline{X}A_{low}\right|=17.75\right)<\left(\left|\overline{X}_{high}-\overline{X}_{low}\right|^{*}=49.77\right)$$

From the above, and subject to the conditions for making decision criteria, μA_{high} is better than μA_{low}. Therefore high A is acceptable.

$$\left(\left|\overline{X}B_{high}-\overline{X}B_{low}\right|=15.75\right)<\left(\left|\overline{X}_{high}-\overline{X}_{low}\right|^{*}=49.77\right)$$

From the above and subject to the conditions for making decision criteria, μB_{high} is better than μB_{low}. Therefore high B is acceptable.

$$\left(\left|\overline{X}C_{high}-\overline{X}C_{low}\right|=-4.75\right)<\left(\left|\overline{X}_{high}-\overline{X}_{low}\right|^{*}=49.77\right)$$

From the above and subject to the conditions for making decision criteria, μC_{low} is better than μC_{high}. Therefore low C is acceptable

$$\left(\left|\overline{X}D_{high}-\overline{X}D_{low}\right|=-9.75\right)<\left(\left|\overline{X}_{high}-\overline{X}_{low}\right|^{*}=49.77\right)$$

From the above and subject to the conditions for making decision criteria, μD_{low} is better than μD_{high}. Therefore low D is acceptable

2.4 Decision

From the conditions for making the decision described above and considering the selection test as is also stated above, it is deduced that the best combination of the variables

statistically derived is as follows: high A, high B, low C and low D, which is A = 30%, B = 45%, C = 30% and D = 5%. The sum of these percentages by weight adds up to 110%. However, being that percentages need to be rounded up to portions per hundred, a novel approach has to be introduced for this combination to add up to 100% by weight.
This novel approach is stated thus: in the case where certain elements that constitute a flux composition possess a high percent by weight or proportion, the average value should be determined. Values below that average value should be considered to be of the lower range, and those above it, should be considered to be of the higher range, within the initially specified range of values as reflected in Table 1. The iteration is done in such a way that the 100% by weight threshold value is not exceeded. This approach was adopted to arrive at the best or optimum combination of A = 27.5%, B = 37.5%, C = 30% and D = 5% (27.5%LiCl, 37.5%NaCl, 30%KCl and 5%CaF_2).This combination was used to conduct a welding process and the weld deposits were prepared to suit the standard tensile test specimen which were subjected to tensile test and an average UTS of 316 MPa was obtained. This test confirms the reliability of the applied model.

3. Taguchi method

The Taguchi methods are statistical methods developed by Genichi Taguchi to improve the quality of manufactured goods. Dr. Genichi Taguchi was born in Japan in 1924, and has displayed a keen interest in quality management in general. He has developed and promoted a philosophy and methodology for continuous quality improvement in products and processes. His methods have also been successfully applied to engineering experimentation. The Taguchi method can show how Statistical Design of Experiments (SDOE or DOE) can help industrial engineers design and manufacture products that are both of high quality and low cost (Antony & Antony, 2001). According to Antony & Antony (2001), DOE is a powerful statistical technique for determining the optimal factor settings of a process and thereby achieving improved process performance, reduced process variability and improved manufacturability of products and processes. Taguchi understood that excessive variation lay at the root of poor manufactured quality and that reacting to individual items inside and outside specification was counterproductive. Taguchi realized that the best opportunity to eliminate variation is during the design of a product and its manufacturing process. Esme (2009) wrote that the Taguchi method uses a special design of orthogonal arrays to study the entire process parameters with only a small number of experiments. Using an orthogonal array to design the experiment could help the designers to study the influence of multiple controllable factors on the average of quality characteristics and the variations, in a fast and economic way, while using a signal - to - noise ratio to analyze the experimental data that could help the designers of the product or the manufacturer to easily find out the optimal parametric combinations. A loss function is defined to calculate the deviation between the experimental value and the desired value. The loss function is further transformed into signal - to - noise (S/N) ratio. The statistical analysis of variance (ANOVA) is performed to see which process parameters are statistically significant. The Taguchi method is illustrated herein-under to predict the optimum combination of Aluminum welding flux.
From the layout in Table 1, an $L_8(2^4)$ orthogonal array which has 7 degrees of freedom was applied. In this case eight experimental procedures are conducted when using L_8 orthogonal array. The corresponding experimental layout is as expressed in Table 11.

Experiment Number	Flux constituent element levels			
	LiCl A	NaCl B	KCl C	CaF_2 D
1	1	1	1	1
2	1	1	2	2
3	1	2	1	2
4	1	2	2	1
5	2	1	1	2
6	2	1	2	1
7	2	2	1	1
8	2	2	2	2

Table 11. Experimental Layout using $L_8(2^4)$ Orthogonal Array

In this case, 1 represents the low level of the flux range values present in Table 1, whereas 2 represents the high level. Using the flux combinations in Table 11 to make five weld deposits for each flux combination which were subjected to tensile tests, the average ultimate tensile strength (UTS) test results for the eight flux combinations are shown in Table 12.

Flux Number	Average Ultimate Tensile Strength (UTS) in MPa
1	247
2	262
3	268
4	304
5	298
6	235
7	304
8	268

Table 12. Experimental Results for the Ultimate Tensile Strength (UTS) Test

Since the UTS of these weld deposits fall within the values reported in other literature (Achebo & Ibhadode, 2008), therefore the larger the UTS, the better the weld quality. The loss function of the larger the better quality characteristics is applied here as expressed in Eq(3).

$$L_f = \left(\frac{1}{n} \sum_{k=1}^{n} \frac{1}{y_i^2} \right) \quad (3)$$

And the S/N ratio, η_j is

$$\eta_j = -10 \log L_f \quad (4)$$

The η_j values for each UTS test result, y_i, in Table 12, were determined using Eqs (3) - (4) and the corresponding S/N ratios there from are presented in Table 13

Flux Number	S/N Ratio db
1	47.71
2	48.37
3	48.56
4	49.66
5	49.48
6	47.42
7	49.66
8	48.56

Table 13. S/N Ratios for the UTS Results

Categorizing the values in Table 13 into their various flux constituent elements and levels. Table 14 is created there from.

Designation	Flux constituent Elements	S/N Ratio dB		Total mean	Maximum – Minimum
		Level 1	Level 2		
A	LiCl	48.57	48.78*	48.68	0.21
B	NaCl	48.24	49.11*		0.87
C	KCl	48.85*	48.50		0.35
D	CaF_2	48.61	48.74*		0.13

* is the selected optimum level for the larger-the-better criterion

Table 14. Summary of S/N Ratios of different flux combinations.

From Table 14, the optimum flux composition is derived as A_2 B_2 C_1 D_2. This composition is clearly specified as 30% LiCl, 45% NaCl, 30% KCl and 10% CaF_2 .These values combined is greater than 100% by weight. When the novel approach was applied, the composition was refined to 27% LiCl, 37% NaCl, 30%KCl and 6%CaF_2.

In Table 14, a parameter with larger difference implies a high influence to weldability as its level is changed (Kim & Lee, 2009). In this study, parameter B has the largest difference. The levels with these differences are shown in Fig. 1. Fig. 1 shows the S/N ratio graph where the dash line is the value of the total mean of the S/N ratio. Esme (2005) was of the opinion that percent contribution indicates the relative power of a factor to reduce variation. For a factor with a high percent contribution, a small variation will have a great influence on the performance.

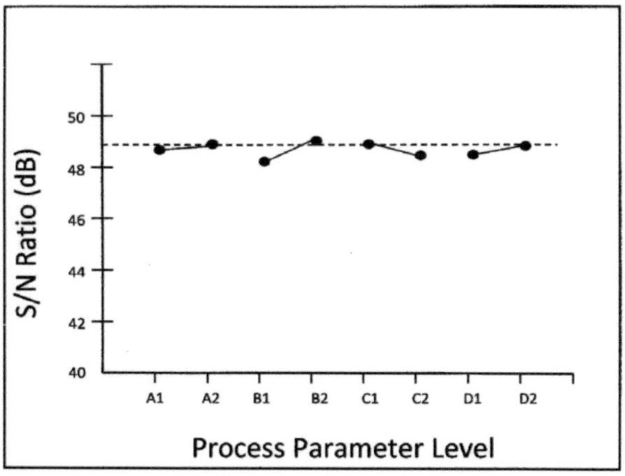

Fig. 1. S/N Ratio Graph

Table 15 shows the ANOVA results of the S/N Ratios in Table 14. Equations (5-7) were used to derive the sum of squares. Berginc et al (2006) proposed Eqs (5) and (6).

$$SS_1 = \sum_{i=1}^{N} y_i^2 - CF \tag{5}$$

$$CF = \frac{T_s^2}{N} \tag{6}$$

Where
T_s = the sum of all results
N = the number of results
CF = correction factor
Whereas, Scheaffer & McClave (1982) proposed Eqs (7), which was used to determine the sum of squares for each of the flux elements.

$$SSE = TSS - SST = \sum_{i=1}^{N} \left(y_i - \bar{y} \right)^2 \tag{7}$$

Parameter	*Process Parameter*	*Degree of Freedom*	*Sum of Squares*	*Variance*	*F Ratio*	*Contribution Percentage*
A	*LiCl*	1	0.02	0.02	0.01	0.38
B	*NaCl*	1	0.35	0.35	0.22	6.72
C	*KCl*	1	0.06	0.06	0.04	1.15
D	*CaF_2*	1	0.01	0.01	0.01	0.19
Error		3	4.77	1.59	–	91.55
Total		7	5.21	–	–	100.00

Table 15. ANOVA Results for the S/N Ratio containing Optimum Flux Combinations

In Table 15, NaCl was found to be the major factor affecting Aluminum flux composition (6.72%), followed by KCl (1.15%), whereas, LiCl and CaF_2 have lower values of 0.38% and 0.19% .

3.1 Confirmation test

The confirmation test is to validate the findings of this research work. The optimum formulation is used to make weld deposits that were subjected to the determination of the tensile property of the weldments. Here, the S/N ratio is a powerful variable for measuring performance characteristics. It has to be predicted to verify the improvement of the performance characteristics.

The predicted S/N ratio η applying the optimal combination or levels is determined using Eq(8).

$$\eta = \eta_m + \sum_{i=1}^{n} (\bar{\eta} - \eta_m) \tag{8}$$

Where η_m is the total mean of S/N ratio, $\bar{\eta}$ is the mean of S/N ratio at the optimal level, and n is the number of main welding parameters that significantly affect performance. The application of Eq (8) is illustrated as follows:

For $A_2\ B_2\ C_1\ D_2$

$$\begin{aligned} \text{For } A_2 &: \bar{\eta}_i - \eta_m = 48.78 - 48.68 = 0.10 \\ B_2 &: \bar{\eta}_i - \eta_m = 49.11 - 48.68 = 0.43 \\ C_1 &: \bar{\eta}_i - \eta_m = 48.85 - 48.68 = 0.17 \\ D_2 &: \bar{\eta}_i - \eta_m = 48.74 - 48.68 = 0.06 \end{aligned}$$

$$\sum_{i=1}^{n} \left(\bar{\eta}_i - \eta_m \right) = 0.76$$

$$\eta = \eta_m + \sum_{i=1}^{n} (\bar{\eta}_i - \eta_m) = 48.68 + 0.76 = 49.44$$

The existing flux combination used for welding processes has the formulation $A_1\ B_1\ C_2\ D_1$

$$\begin{aligned} \text{For } A_1 &: \bar{\eta}_i - \eta_m = 48.57 - 48.68 = -0.11 \\ B_1 &: \bar{\eta}_i - \eta_m = 48.24 - 48.68 = -0.44 \\ C_2 &: \bar{\eta}_i - \eta_m = 48.50 - 48.68 = -0.18 \\ D_1 &: \bar{\eta}_i - \eta_m = 48.61 - 48.68 = -0.07 \end{aligned}$$

$$-0.80$$

$$\eta = \eta_m + \sum_{i=1}^{n} (\bar{\eta}_i - \eta_m) = 48.68 - 0.80 = 47.88$$

The same procedure was carried out for A_2 B_2 C_1 D_2 produced from experimental methods. The increase in S/N ratio shows that there are greater amounts of the same alloying elements in the weld chemical composition than that contained in the weld deposit made by the predicted process parameter. Its predicted S/N ratio is also presented in Table 16.
The results of experimental confirmation using optimal welding parameters and comparing it with predicted process are shown in Table 16.

Process Factors	Initial Process Parameter	Optimum Process Parameters		Inprovement In S/N Ratio
		Prediction	Experiment	
Flux Composition	$A_1B_1C_2D_1$	$A_2B_2C_1D_2$	$A_2B_2C_1D_2$	1.62
UTS (MPa)	296	316	320	
S/N dB	47.88	49.44	49.50	

Table 16. Confirmation Experimental Test Results

The improvement in S/N ratio from the initial welding parameter to the optimal welding parameter is 1.62 dB and the UTS increased by 1.08 times. Therefore the UTS is significantly improved by using the Taguchi method.

4. Expert evaluation method

The expert evaluation method was applied by Nikitina (2004) and further applied by Achebo (2009) for developing new flux compositions based on the shear stress of the weld metal. Using this method, Experts in the field of welding were used; five Engineers who are welders, each with at least 15 years working experience; three independent welders with at least 25 years welding experience; and two University Professors of Manufacturing Engineering with exceptional welding experience for over 10 years. These were employed to evaluate the technological performance of the newly developed fluxes. The combined skill of the experts was taken into consideration by the coefficient δ equal to 2 and 1 which is a 10 point scale, where 2 represents the weld of highest quality and 1 represents the weld with the lowest quality (Nikitina (2004); Achebo (2009)). In this study, the Expert evaluation method is used to develop new welding fluxes as illustrated in Tables (17 - 20).
In order, to implement this expert evaluation method, it demands that Table 1 be rearranged, and this in turn produced Table 17.

	Factor	Variation Level			Variation Range
		Main	Lower	Upper	
X_1	LiCl	27.5	25	30	2.5
X_2	NaCl	37.5	30	45	7.5
X_3	KCl	35	30	40	5
X_4	CaF_2	7.5	5	10	2.5

Table 17. Chemical Composition arrangement of Aluminum welding flux elements

Using the derived flux composition in Table 7 the expert evaluation scores based on the scale of 1 – 10 were itemized and this lead to the generation of Table 18.

Flux No	Average Evaluation scores of Experts
1	5.8
2	6.8
3	4.6
4	6
5	8.4
6	6.8
7	4.6
8	5.2

Table 18. Expert Evaluation of Flux Composition constituent Elements

The experts were asked to make the individual assessments of the performance and characteristics of the Eight flux compositions based on their UTS, with their average values listed in Table 8. Table 19 shows the Expert evaluation of the quality of the flux weldments based on UTS.

Number of Experts	Scores made by Experts								T_i	δ_i
	1	2	3	4	5	6	7	8		
1	5	8	4	5	9	5	3	4	5	1.4
2	7	7	5	8	8	8	4	2	5	1.7
3	4	5	4	7	8	6	6	4	5	1.2
4	6	6	4	4	8	7	5	5	6	1.5
5	7	8	6	6	9	8	5	6	5	2
$\sum_{i=1}^{n} x_{ij}\delta_j$	46.7	54.1	36.9	47.0	65.8	54.3	35.0	33.3	$\left[\sum_{i=1}^{n} x_{ij}\delta_i\right]_{Average}$	$= 46.64$
R	4	6	3	5	8	7	2	1		
γ	0.06	7.46	9.74	0.36	19.16	7.66	1.64	13.34		
γ_j^2	$3.60\text{x}10^{-3}$	55.65	94.88	0.13	367.11	58.68	135.49	177.96	$\sum \gamma_j^2 = 889.90$	
	5.8	6.8	4.6	6.0	8.4	6.8	4.6	5.2		

Table 19. Expert Evaluation of the Quality of the flux weldments based on UTS

To evaluate the extent of the correlation between the scores and the individual expert assessments, the rank correlation coefficient (concordation) was applied.

$$W = \frac{12m\sum_{i=1}^{n}\gamma_i^2}{\left[m\left(n^3-n\right)-\sum_{i=1}^{m}T_i^2\right]\left(\sum_{i=1}^{m}\delta_i\right)^2} \tag{9}$$

Where

$$\sum_{j=1}^{n}\gamma^2 = \sum_{j=1}^{n}\left[\sum_{i=1}^{m} a_{ij}\delta_i - \frac{\sum_{j=1}^{n}\sum_{i=1}^{n} x_{ij}\delta_i}{n}\right]^2 \tag{10}$$

$$T_i = \left(\sum t_i\right)$$

And t_i = number of repetitions of each score in the ith series, n is the number of flux compositions, m is the number of experts.
Substituting the corresponding values into Eq(9), gives

$$W = \frac{12 \times 5 \times 889.90}{\left[5\left(8^3 - 8\right) - 26^2\right](7.8)^2} = 0.48$$

The significance of the concordation coefficient was calculated using the criterion equation in Eq(11)

$$\chi^2_{cal} = m(n-1)W \tag{11}$$

$$\chi^2_{cal} = 5(8-1)0.48 = 16.8$$

Since the tabulated volume $\chi^2_{table}(0.05,7) = 14.1$, which is lower than the calculated value, it is concluded that the expert evaluation scores are in agreement.
Multiple regression analysis in the excel Microsoft package was used to analysis the flux composition, elements in Table 7 and the independent variable, y_i which is the average scores of the expert evaluation process shown in Table 18, to be as follows:

$$y = 6.54 - 0.035\underset{1}{\overline{\beta}} + 0.007\underset{2}{\beta} + 0.000\underset{3}{\beta} + 0.041\underset{4}{\beta} \tag{12}$$

This regression analysis can also be derived manually from the least square method which suggests that

$$\overline{y} = \underset{1}{\overline{\beta}} + \underset{1}{\overline{\beta}}x_1 + \underset{2}{\overline{\beta}}x_2 + \underset{3}{\overline{\beta}}x_3 + \underset{4}{\overline{\beta}}x_4 \tag{13}$$

And the sum of square error, SSE is represented by

$$SSE = \sum_{i=1}^{n}\left(y_i - \overline{y}\right)^2 \tag{14}$$

Where β_i is the independent variables representing the flux constituent elements i = 1, 2, 3 and 4
Substituting Eq(13) into Eq(14)

$$SSE = \left(y_i - \overline{\beta}_0 - \overline{\beta}_1 x_1 - \overline{\beta}_2 x_2 - \overline{\beta}_3 x_3 - \overline{\beta}_4 x_4 \right)^2 \qquad (15)$$

Differentiating Eq (15) with respect to $\overline{\beta_1}$, the following is obtained

$$\frac{\partial(SSE)}{\partial \overline{\beta}_1} = -2\sum_{i=1}^{n} x_1 \left(y_i - \overline{\beta}_0 - \overline{\beta}_1 x_1 - \overline{\beta}_2 x_2 - \overline{\beta}_3 x_3 - \overline{\beta}_4 x_4 \right) = 0$$

Differential analysis were also done for

$$\frac{\partial(SSE)}{\partial \overline{\beta}_2}, \frac{\partial(SSE)}{\partial \overline{\beta}_3} \text{ and } \frac{\partial(SSE)}{\partial \overline{\beta}_4}$$

And values for $\overline{\beta}_1$, $\overline{\beta}_2$, $\overline{\beta}_3$ and $\overline{\beta}_4$ were arranged in a matrix form. Quadratic equations were formed from the matrix layout. This enabled the determination of the independent variables which lead to the generation of Eq(12).
This model lead to the development of new flux compositions as shown in Table 20

Factor	$\overline{\beta_1}$	$\overline{\beta_2}$	$\overline{\beta_3}$	$\overline{\beta_4}$
k_i	-0.04	0.01	0.00	0.04
l_j	2.50	7.50	5.00	2,50
$k_i l_j$	-0.09	0.08	0.00	0.10
Composition by wt				
Step	-0.03	0.03	-	0.03
Zero level	27.50	37.50	35.00	7.50
	27.47	37.53	35.00	7.53
	27.44	37.56	35.00	7.56
	27.41	37.59	35.00	7.59
	:	:	:	:
	:	:	:	:
	:	:	:	:
	25.00	40.02	35.00	10.01

Table 20. Flux Development Process

After this tedious process, 74 new flux compositions emerged. The best combination of the lot, and the one which had the optimum combination was the one with the following element proportion of 28.2% L_iCl, 38.6% NaCl, 35% KCl and 8.6% CaF_2. This conclusion was arrived at on the basis of possessing the highest UTS of 298 MPa amongst the lot. This flux composition was over a 100% by weight. Therefore the flux composition was then further subjected to a novel approach elucidated above in the Hadamard Matrix Method. A new flux composition of 25.4% LiCl, 35% NaCl, 33% KCl and 6.6% CaF_2 was generated with an impressive UTS of 308 MPa.

5. Discussion of results

Three methods for developing flux combinations and compositions were investigated. These were the Hadamard Multivariate Chemical Composition Model, the Taguchi Method, and the Expert Evaluation Method. From the findings, the Hadamard Multivariate model was capable of generating several flux compositions and integrating the effects of one variable on another variable (the interactions), in the process of determining the optimum composition. Using this method the optimum composition was determined to be 30% L_iCl, 45% NaCl, 30% KCl and 5% CaF_2. This composition value is above 100%. However, applying the novel approach elucidated above will lead to a rearrangement of the percentages of the flux elements of the new composition, being the following: 27.5% L_iCl, 37.5% NaCl, 30% KCl and 8.5% CaF_2. However from the several compositions generated applying this novel method, this new flux composition gave the highest value of UTS of 316 MPa which is within the range of reported values in other literature (Achebo and Ibhadode, 2008).

The Taguchi method was also applied to determine the optimum flux composition, which gave a composition of 30% L_iCl, 45% NaCl, 30% KCl and 10% CaF_2, but having applied this novel method, a composition of 27% L_iCl, 37% NaCl, 30% KCl and 6% CaF_2 was derived. The derived flux composition weld deposit gave an UTS of 320 MPa.

Further investigation was done using the Expert evaluation method. In this case, the expert evaluation skills based on the performance of the flux compositions generated by other optimization methods were used to further generate new flux compositions. The generated flux composition using this method was 28.2% L_iCl, 38.6% NaCl, 35% KCl and 8.6% CaF_2, with the application of the above stated novel method, the composition that emerged was 25.4% L_iCl, 35% NaCl, 33% KCl and 6.6% CaF_2 with an UTS of 308 MPa.

Having considered the optimum compositions above, the flux compositions formulated and used by other researchers were investigated. Varley (1970) in his book suggested a typical flux composition for Aluminum welding as 30%NaCl, 28%KCl, 26%L_iCl and 16%NaF, Glizmaneko & Yevseyer gave some values for Aluminum flux composition in the range of 19-45%NaCl, 29-51%KCl, 9-15% L_iCl and 7-10%NaF. Davies (1984) gave the range of 0-30%L_iCl, 0.6%KCl, NaCl-the remainder and 5-15%KF. Manfredi et al (1997) gave a flux composition of 70%NaCl, 28%KCl and 2%CaF_2, whereas Utigard et al (1998) used a flux composition of 47.5%NaCl, 47.5%KCl and 5%Fluoride salts. Other investigators who did the tensile test of their Aluminum fluxed weld metals, had the UTS test results in the range of 298 - 434MPa (Shah, et al (1992); Ellis (1996)). Padmanabham et al (2007) had a UTS test result of a range of 255 - 334MPa and Achebo & Ibhadode (2008) had a weld metal whose UTS was 310MPa. Weston investigated the weldments of Aluminum alloys 2219 and 5083 and found their UTS to be 270MPa and 297MPa respectively. Yoon (1996) also investigated the tensile properties of Aluminum alloy 6061 and found its UTS to be 200MPa. Palmer et al (2006) investigated the tensile properties of Aluminum alloy 6061-T6 and found its UTS to be 310MPa while their investigation on 6061-0 alloy showed a corresponding value of 117MPa.

From the values above, it can be seen that the optimum flux composition constituent elements derived by applying the Hadamard Matrix design method, Taguchi optimization method and the Expert evaluation method fall within the range of values formulated by other investigators. The same applies to their UTS values. This therefore confirms that the three methods considered in this study are very effective and are recommended for application depending on any researcher's needs.

6. Conclusion

In this study, several processes for the selection of flux composition elements in their various proportions, have been demonstrated. Three optimization methods were used to generate new flux compositions. A novel approach was applied to round off the sum of the percentage by weight of the flux constituent elements to 100%. The Hadamard multivariate method and the Taguchi method were less complex and easier to apply. These two methods developed optimum flux compositions which eventually gave the highest UTS values within their various groups. The difference between these two methods however, is that the Hadamard method actually considers the interactions between the elements that constitute the composition. However, very many flux compositions, with rather wide ranging differences tend to be produced, these would usually require a significant number of weld tests over a rather long period of time for the researcher to narrow the entire process down to an optimum flux. The Taguchi method is also very adaptable and maneuverable in terms of how diverse constituent elements could be researched simultaneously. The drawback however is that the Taguchi method has received scathing criticism and is not a well trusted method in certain quarters in general. It is best to apply the Taguchi method in consonance with another method to improve its credibility. The expert evaluation method, on the other hand, has the advantage that it does not generate initial flux compositions. It utilizes the assessments made by experts who have had considerable work experience in the field of welding and with good academic background. These assessments were used to generate new flux compositions whose welds were subjected to tensile tests to determine their UTS. This property was seen as a measure of performance, in terms of weld quality, ductility, strength and weldability. It was observed however that the expert evaluation method seems to be very cumbersome. It is also prone to the inevitability of human error. However when it is applied in certain cases which lean towards real quality control and marketing, it is the most ideal. Conclusively, a multiphysical approach in applying these methods has been successfully demonstrated to generate an optimum flux composition; and the relevance of the use of any of these methods, or a combination of the three, would depend on the aim of the research the investigators intend to carry out.

7. References

Achebo J.I & Ibhadode, A.O.A. (2008), Development of a New Flux for Aluminum Gas Welding; *Advanced Material Research*, Vols. 44/46 (Trans Tech Publications, Switzerland). p.677-684.

Achebo J.I. (2009), Development of Compositions of Aluminum Welding Fluxes, using Statistical Method. *International Multi conference of Engineeers and Computer Scientists, Hong Kong, 18-20 March*, p.1876.

Achebo J.I & Ibhadode, A.O.A. (2009), Determination of Optimum Welding Flux Composition Using the Bend Strength Test Technique; *Advanced Material Research*, Vols. 62/64 (Trans Tech Publications, Switzerland). p.393-397.

Antony, J & Antony, F. J. (2001) Teaching the Taguchi Method to Industrial Engineers, *Work Study*, MCB University Press, Vol. 50, No. 4, p.141- 149 (ISSN 0043-8022).

Berginc, B; Kampus, Z & Sustarsic, B. (2006) The Use of Taguchi Approach to Determine the Influence of Injection Moulding Parameters on the Properties of Green Parts,

Journal of Achievements in Materials and Manufacturing Engineering, vol. 15, Issue 1 - 2, p.66.

Boniszewski T (1979) Manual Metal Arc Welding. *Metallurgist and Materials Technologist*, Vol.11 No.10. p.567-574; Vol.11. No.11. p.640-644; Vol. 11. No.12. p.697-705

Chai, C.S. & Eagar, T.W.(1983) Prediction of weld-metal composition during flux-shielded welding, *Journal of Materials for Energy Systems*. American Society for Metals, Vol. 5, No. 3, December, p.160-164

Davies, A.C. (1984) *Welding Science*, Prentice Hall publication, UK. p.55

Diamond, W. J. (1989) *Practical Experimental Design for Engineers and Scientists*, 2nd Ed. Van Nostrand Reinhold, New York, p.89 - 123, 296 - 306.

Ellis, M.B.D (1996). Fusion Welding of Aluminum Lithium Alloys *Welding & Metal Fabrication*, Vol. 2. p.55-60.

Esme, U. (2009) Application of Taguchi Method for the Optimization of Resistance Spot Welding Process, *The Arabian Journal for Science and Engineering*, Vol. 34, No. 2B, p.519 - 528

Glizmaneko, D. & Yevseyer, G. (undated) *Gas Welding and Cutting*, Peace Publishers, Moscow, p.180

Holderness, A. & Lambert, J. (1982) *A New Certificate Chemistry*. 6th Edition, Heinemann Publishers, Ibadan,

Jackson, C.E. (1973) 'Fluxes and Slags in Welding' *Welding Research Council* Bulletins No.190, p.25-57.

Kim H. R. & Lee, K. Y.(2009) Application of Taguchi Method to Hybrid Welding Conditions of Aluminum Alloy, *Journal of Scientific & Industrial Research*, Vol. 68, p.296 - 300

Manfredi, O; Wulh, W. & Bohlinger, I. (1997) 'Characterizing the Physical and Chemical Properties of Aluminum Dross' *JOM*, November, p.48

Natalie, C. A.; Olson, D. L. & Blander, M. (1986) 'Physical and Chemical Behaviour of Welding Fluxes' *Annual Review of Materials Science*, Vol.16, p.389 - 413, August

Nikitina, E. V. (2004) 'Development of the Composition of Electrode Coatings for Welding Aluminum Alloys Using the Expert Evaluation Method', *Welding International*, Vol. 18(4), 307 - 310.

Padmanabham, G; Schaper, M; Pandey, S. & Simmchen, E (2007)'Tensile and Fracture Behavior of Pulsed Gas Metal Arc Welded Al - Cu - Li' *Welding Journal*, Vol. 86, No. 6, p.147-s - 160-s, June

Palmer, T. A; Elmer, J. W; Brasher, D; Butler, D. & Riddle, R. (2006) Development of an Explosive Welding Process for Producing High - Strength Welds between Niobium and 6061-T651 Aluminum' *Welding Journal*, Vol. 85, No.11, p.252-s - 263-s,

Scheaffer, R. L. & McClave, J. T. (1982) *Statistics for Engineers*, Duxbury Press, Boston, p.239 - 355.

Shad, S.R. Wittig, J.E., & Hahn, G.T.(1992) Microstructural Analysis of a High Strength Al-Cu-Li (Weldalite 049).Alloy Weld. *Proceedings of the 3rd International Conference on Trends in Welding Research*, Gatlinburg, Tenn. .

The James F. Lincoln Arc Welding Foundation; Weld Cracking:An Excerpt from Fabricators' and Erectors'Guide to Welded Steel Construction; Information available on http://www.treatrade.hr/pdf/DM/weldcracking.pdf

Utigard, T. A.; Friesen, K,; Roy, R. R.; Lim, J.; Silny, A. & Dupuis, C. (1998) 'The Properties and Uses of Fluxes in Molten Aluminum Processing' *JOM*, November, p.38

Varley, P.C. (1970) *The Technology of Aluminum and its Alloys*: Newnes- Butterworths, London p.78

Weston, J. (2001) *Laser Welding of Aluminum* Alloys. PhD Thesis, Department of Materials Science and Metallurgy, University of Cambridge, p.142

Yoon, J. W. (1996) *Laser Welding of Aluminum Alloys.* , Department of Materials Science and Metallurgy, University of Cambridge

12

Estimation of Space Air Change Rates and CO_2 Generation Rates for Mechanically-Ventilated Buildings

Xiaoshu Lu, Tao Lu and Martti Viljanen
Department of Structural Engineering and Building Technology,
Aalto University School of Science and Technology
Finland

1. Introduction

It is well known that people spend 80-90% of their life time indoors. At the same time, pollution levels of indoors can be much higher than outdoor levels. Not surprisingly, the term 'sick building syndrome' (SBS) has been used to describe situations where occupants experience acute health and comfort effects that are related to poor air in buildings (Clements-Croome, 2000). It is an increasingly common health problem which has been acknowledged as a recognizable disease by the World Health Organization (Redlich et al., 1997, Akimenko et al., 1986).

Since its recognition in 1986, many efforts have been put to try to identify the causes to eliminate SBS. The causes may involve various factors. Mainly, it is thought to be a direct outcome of poor indoor air quality (IAQ) (Clements-Croome, 2004). In most cases ventilation system is found to be at the heart of the problem as well as high carbon dioxide (CO_2) levels (Redlich et al., 1997). Since 70's energy crisis, buildings have been tried to build with tight envelopes and highly rely on mechanical ventilation so as to reduce energy cost. Due to tight envelopes, a big portion of energy contributes to ventilation. In most cases SBS occurs in mechanically-ventilated and commercial buildings, although it may occur in other buildings such as apartment buildings. It has been estimated that up to 30% of refurbished buildings and a significant number of new buildings suffer from SBS (Sykes, 1988). However, the solutions to SBS are difficult to implement by the complexity of ventilation system and the competing needs of energy saving.

Hence the issue about ventilation efficiency is getting more and more people's attention. It is useful to evaluate ventilation in order to assess IAQ and energy cost. A number of techniques are available to perform such evaluations. Among them, the measurement and analysis of CO_2 concentrations to evaluate specific aspects of IAQ and ventilation is most emphasized. CO_2 is a common air constituent but it may cause some heath problems when its concentration level is very high. Normally CO_2 is not considered as a causal factor in human health responses. However, in recent literalities, it has been reported that there is a statistically significant association of mucous membrane (dry eyes, sore throat, nose congestion, sneezing) and lower respiratory related symptoms (tight chest, short breath, cough and wheeze) with increasing CO_2 levels above outdoor levels (Erdmann & Apte,

2004). Elevated levels may cause headaches and changes in respiratory patterns (Environment Australia, 2001). Although no hard evidences have shown direct causal link between indoor CO_2 level and the above symptoms, indoor CO_2 level should be concerned regarding human health risk. Because occupants are the main source of indoor CO_2, indoor CO_2 levels become an indicator to the adequacy of ventilation relative to indoor occupant density and metabolic activity. In order to keep a good IAQ, indoor CO_2 concentration must be reduced to a certain level. Therefore, CO_2 is often used as a surrogate to test IAQ and ventilation efficiency.

Many works contributed to use indoor CO_2 concentration to evaluate IAQ and ventilation. Nabinger et al. (Nabinger et al., 1994) monitored ventilation rates with the tracer gas decay technique and indoor CO_2 levels for two years in an office building. Their aims were to assess the operation and performance of the ventilation system and to investigate the relationship between indoor CO_2 levels and air change rates. However, the assessment was done for a whole building without detaining individual rooms. Lawrence and Braun (lawrence & Braun, 2007) used parameter estimation methods to estimate CO_2 source generations and system flow parameters, such as supply flow rate and overall room ventilation effectiveness. They examined different parameter estimation methods from simulated data and the best-performed method was applied to field results. Their goal was to evaluate cost savings for demand-controlled ventilation (DCV) system for commercial buildings. Wong and Mui (Wong & Mui, 2008) developed a transient ventilation model based on occupant load. Similar as Lawrence's work (lawrence & Braun, 2007), they used optimization method to determine model parameters from a year-round occupant load survey. Their interest was also energy saving. Miller et al. (Miller et al., 1997) used nonlinear least-squares minimization and tracer gas decay technique to determine interzonal airflow rates in a two-zone building. But they didn't apply their method to filed measurement. Other similar works have been done by Honma (Honma, 1975), O'Neill and Crawford (O'Neil & Crawford, 1990) and Okuyama (Okuyama, 1990).

Despite extensive studies, there is sparse information available regarding the use of field measured CO_2 concentrations to estimate ventilation rates (i.e. space air change rates) and CO_2 generation rates for a particular space, such as office room, in commercial buildings. Particularly there lacks a simple and handy method for estimating space air change rates and CO_2 generation rates for a particular space with indoor CO_2 concentrations. A strong limitation of the existing models in the literature is either they focus on the effect of ventilation over a whole building without considering particular spaces or they are too complicated for practical use. A big number of field measured data are required in these models to determine several model parameters, such as ventilation effectiveness, ventilation rate, exfiltration rate, occupant-load ratio and so on. Therefore, their interests lie mainly with overall and long-term efforts - energy saving. This is understandable, but it is generally not practical as it does not provide any information relevant to indoor air for a particular space, and hence cannot serve as some kind of guidance from which a good IAQ can be derived. In addition, in the above models, ventilation rates are mostly determined using the tracer gas technique. Although the tracer gas technique is powerful, in practice the technique is not easy to implement and in some way is not economical (Nabinger et al., 1994).

In this paper, we develop a new method to estimate space air change rates and transient CO_2 generation rates for an individual space in commercial buildings using field measured CO_2 concentrations. The new approach adopts powerful parameter estimation method and

Maximum Likelihood Estimation (MLE) (Blocker, 2002), providing maximum convenience and high speed in predicting space air change rates with good accuracy. With MLE, the model enables us to use obtained space air change rates for further estimating CO_2 generation rates in a great confidence.

Additionally, a novel coupled-method is presented for predicting transient CO_2 generation rates. Traditionally, transient CO_2 generation rates are directly computed by solving mass balance equation of CO_2. In our coupled-method, we combine the traditional method and equilibrium analysis to estimate CO_2 generation rates. The coupled-method provides a simple and reliable method as an alternative to traditional methods. Importantly, the method proposed in this study also works well for general commercial buildings and other mechanically-ventilated buildings as the school building represents a common case for commercial buildings. The objectives of this study are:

- to develop a concise method to estimate space air change rate during a working day by directly applying field measured CO_2 concentrations from a particular and mechanically-ventilated space. Furthermore, the method should be able to be easily adapted for some complex ventilation systems, where ventilation rate (i.e. space air change rate) is not constant, e.g. variable air volume (VAV) and demand-controlled ventilation (DCV) systems;
- to propose a novel method for further predicting transient CO_2 generation rates during the day;
- to examine MLE's suitability in terms of ventilation rate prediction. MLE is widely used in a great range of fields, but rarely seen in predicting ventilation rates.

Overall, the method should be simple, economical and universal, and can be used as supplement tool to evaluate IAQ and ventilation efficiency for a particular space.

2. Methodology

Nowadays, except some spaces where occupants vary with time and are the main heat load and main pollutant source (e.g. conference rooms, assembly halls, classrooms, etc.), constant air volume (CAV) system is still primary way to ventilate spaces in commercial and residential buildings because of its simplicity and convenience. Moreover, a summary of data from mechanically ventilated commercial buildings suggests that for a given room in the building, the air is well mixed, although there are differences in the age of air in different rooms (Frisk et al., 1991). Therefore, the method discussed in this paper focuses on spaces with nearly constant air change rates and well-mixed indoor air. But the method can be easily adapted for time-varying ventilation systems, such as variable air volume (VAV) and demand-controlled ventilation (DCV) systems. In Section 4.1.1, we will offer an introduction about the application of the method in time-varying ventilation systems. For a well-mixed and mechanically-ventilated space, the mass balance of CO_2 concentration can be expressed as:

$$V\frac{dC}{dt} = Q(C_o(t) - C(t)) + G(t) \tag{1}$$

where

V = space volume,

$C(t)$ = indoor CO_2 concentration at time t,

Q = volumetric airflow rate into (and out of) the space,

$C_o(t)$ = supply CO_2 concentration,
$G(t)$ = CO_2 generation rate in the space at time t.

The space with the mechanical ventilation system normally experiences infiltration when the ventilation is on, namely, the return airflow rate is slightly over the supply airflow rate to avoid any moisture damage to the building structures (for example most buildings in Finland) (D2 Finnish Code of Building Regulations, 2003). Therefore, the return airflow rate can be assumed to be the sum of the supply airflow rate and infiltration. If a well-mixed condition for the space is assumed and the space is served by 100% outdoor air, which is common phenomenon in Finnish buildings, the mass balance of CO_2, Eq. (1) does not change by including infiltration. In such setting, Q becomes the return airflow rate in Eq. (1). However, if the space is not served by 100% outdoor air and the infiltration cannot be ignored, Eq. (1) has to be extended by including infiltration and outdoor CO_2 concentration. Calculation procedures may be more tedious, but the model is not principally different from Eq. (1). In this study, Eq. (1) is sufficient for our investigated building, in which rooms are served by 100% outdoor air. Furthermore, the above arguments are also applicable to those commercial buildings whose spaces experience exfiltration rather than infiltration.

In practice, whether the space experiences exfiltration or infiltration, its rate is quite small compared with the supply or the return airflow rate in commercial buildings when the ventilation is on. Therefore, sometimes we can ignore it for simplicity in some commercial buildings when the ventilation is on. Note: Eq. (1) is used for the estimation of space air change rate, which may include not only outside but also recirculated air in supply air. In Finland, most rooms/spaces in commercial buildings are served by 100% fresh air and the recirculation of indoor air is in general not taken as a way to save energy due to concerns on IAQ. If the space is supplied by mixed air, the percent outdoor air intake has to be known before applying Eq. (1) to estimate the air change rate of fresh air.

If we assume Q, $C_o(t)$ and $G(t)$ are constant, Eq. (1) can be solved as follows:

$$C(t) = C_o + \frac{G}{Q} + (C(0) - C_o - \frac{G}{Q})e^{-It} \tag{2}$$

where

$C(0)$ = indoor CO_2 concentration at time 0,
I = Q/V, space air change rate.

When CO_2 generation rate G is zero, Eq. (2) can be expressed as:

$$C(t) = C_o + (C(0) - C_o)e^{-It} \tag{3}$$

The obtained Eq. (3) is the fundamental model to estimate space air change rate in this study. If CO_2 generation rate is constant for a sufficient time, the last term on the right side of Eq. (2) converges to zero, and the airflow rate can be expressed as:

$$Q = \frac{G}{(C_{eq} - C_o)} \tag{4}$$

where C_{eq} is equal to $C_o + \frac{G}{Q}$ and called the *equilibrium* CO_2 *concentration*. Eq. (4) is often used to estimate airflow rate (i.e. space air change rate) if an equilibrium of CO_2 concentration is reached. This method is called *equilibrium analysis*. The time required to reach equilibrium state mainly depends on air change rate. It takes about three hours to reach 95% of the equilibrium CO_2 concentration at 0.75 ach if the CO_2 generation rate is 0.0052 L/s (approximately one person's CO_2 generation rate in office work) and the outside and initial CO_2 concentrations are 400 ppm for an 80 m^3 space. In the same condition at 2.5 ach, it takes 35 minutes to reach 95% of its equilibrium value.

Furthermore, we split the working (i.e. occupied) period of a working day into *occupied working period* when staff is present and *unoccupied working period* when staff has left for home with the 'on' ventilation system. In our case, the ventilation system will remain 'on' and continue working for the duration after staff has left the office, much like a delay off timer. The space air change rate in the *occupied working* period can be evaluated through that of the rate in the *unoccupied working* period based on the assumption of an approximate constant air change rate for the occupied period of a working day as discussed previously. The space air change rate for an *unoccupied working period* is relatively easier to estimate as the CO_2 generation rate is zero. Therefore, we can take Eq. (3) as the governing equation of CO_2 concentration for an *unoccupied working period*. Note: Eq. (3) is derived based on the assumption that supply CO_2 concentration is stable, such as the case of spaces served by 100% outdoor air. If supple CO_2 concentration is unstable (e.g. mixed supple air), the measurement of supple CO_2 concentration has to be required.

2.1 Estimating space air change rate by Maximum Likelihood Estimation

For the determination of the model parameters from such measurements, such as the space air change rate from measured indoor CO_2 concentrations, we adopted Maximum Likelihood Estimation (MLE). Very often, such determination of the model parameters is executed through least squares fit (IEEE, 2000). The method fails when some assumptions (independent, symmetrically distributed error) are violated. More methods include χ^2 fits, binned likelihood fits, average calculation, and linear regression. In general, MLE is the most powerful one (Blocker, 2002). The idea behind it is to determine the parameters that maximize the probability (likelihood) of the sample or experimental data.

Supposing α is a vector of parameters to be estimated and $\{d_n\}$ is a set of sample or experimental data points, Bayes theorem gives

$$p(\alpha \mid \{d_n\}) = \frac{p(\{d_n\} \mid \alpha) p(\alpha)}{p(\{d_n\})} \tag{5}$$

What MLE tries to do is to maximize $p(\alpha \mid \{d_n\})$ to get the best estimation of parameters (i.e. α) from $\{d_n\}$. Because $p(\{d_n\})$ is not a function of the parameters and normally a range of possible values for the parameters (i.e. α) is known, $p(\{d_n\})$ and $p(\alpha)$ are left out of the equation. So only $p(\{d_n\} \mid \alpha)$ needs to be dealt with. Note that $\{ d_n \}$ can be expressed in terms of

$$d(n)=f(n, \alpha)+\varepsilon_n \tag{6}$$

with ε_n being the measurement error and $f(n,\alpha)$ the true model. The error ε_n often trends to normal distribution:

$$p(\varepsilon_n) = \frac{1}{\sqrt{2\pi\sigma^2}} \exp\left[-\frac{\varepsilon_n^2}{2\sigma^2} \right] \tag{7}$$

where σ^2 is the variance of the measurement errors and assumed to be independent of the time. The secret to finding the probability of a data set (i.e. $\{ d_n \}$) is to have a model for the measured fluctuations in the data; i.e. the noise. Therefore,

$$p(\{d_n\} \mid \alpha) = p(\varepsilon_n) = \frac{1}{\sqrt{2\pi\sigma^2}} \exp(-\frac{(d(n) - f(n,\alpha))^2}{2\sigma^2}) \tag{8}$$

Commonly, the data set at each measurement point are statistically independent, so are the measured errors. Therefore, $p(\{d_n\} \mid \alpha)$ can be rewritten as

$$p(\{d_n\} \mid \alpha) = p(d_1 \mid \alpha) p(d_2 \mid \alpha) p(d_3 \mid \alpha) .... p(d_n \mid \alpha) = \prod_n p(d_n \mid \alpha) \tag{9}$$

Since the logarithm of a function is the maximum when the function is the maximum, the logarithm of the probability is preferred for the sake of convenience. The logarithm of $p(\{d_i\} \mid \alpha)$ is given by

$$\log p(\{d_n\} \mid \alpha) = \sum_n \log p(d_n \mid \alpha) \tag{10}$$

In order to maximize $p(\alpha \mid \{d_i\})$, MLE only needs to maximize Eq. (10), namely to solve the set of equations

$$\frac{\partial \log p(\{d_n\} \mid \alpha)}{\partial \alpha_i} = 0, \qquad i = 1,2,3...... , \tag{11}$$

subject to the usual constraints that the second derivatives be negative. The set of equations in Eq. (11) are called *Maximum Likelihood Equations.*
Substituting Eq. (8) into Eq. (10), we obtain

$$\log p(\{d_n\} \mid \alpha) = -\sum_n \frac{(d_n - f(n,\alpha))^2}{2\sigma^2} - 0.5 \sum_n \log 2\pi\sigma^2 \tag{12}$$

If the variance σ^2 is not a function of α, we just need to maximize the first sum in Eq. (12) in order to maximize Eq. (10). If the variance σ^2 is a function of α and/or n, all terms in Eq. (12) need to be kept. In our study, we assume the variance σ^2 of measurement errors to be constant but not a function of parameters. Hence Eq. (3) can be re-expressed as

$$f(n,\alpha) = C(n) = (C(0) - \alpha_0) \exp(-\alpha_1 n \Delta t) + \alpha_0 \tag{13}$$

where α_0 and α_1 are two unknown parameters, supply CO_2 concentration and space air changer rate respectively, and Δt is the time interval for each measurement count. Substituting Eqs. (12) and (13) into Eq. (11), the MLE equations are obtained as:

$$\frac{\partial \log p(\{d_n\} \mid \alpha)}{\partial \alpha_0} = \frac{1}{\sigma^2} \sum_n (1 - \exp(-\alpha_1 n \Delta t)) \left[d_n - (C(0) - \alpha_0) \exp(-\alpha_1 n \Delta t) - \alpha_0 \right] = 0 \tag{14}$$

$$\frac{\partial \log p(\{d_n\} \mid \alpha)}{\partial \alpha_1} = -\frac{(C(0) - \alpha_0)\Delta t}{\sigma^2} \sum_n n \exp(-\alpha_1 n \Delta t) \left[d_n - (C(0) - \alpha_0) \exp(-\alpha_1 n \Delta t) - \alpha_0 \right] = 0 \tag{15}$$

Solving these two equations, Eqs. (14) and (15), simultaneously allows for the estimation of the space air change rate (i.e. α_1) and supply CO_2 concentration (i.e. α_0) for a working day. MATLAB can be employed to obtain the solutions. Residuals are often used to examine the general and specific fit between the data and the model which are the differences between the observed and the predicted values:

$$\varepsilon_n = d(n) - f(n,\alpha) \tag{16}$$

Both the sum and the mean of the residuals of a correct model should be equal/or near to zero. In addition, the residual plot of a correct model should show no any trend and pattern and all residual points should scatter randomly. In this study, the residuals of the model fit were examined.

As previously mentioned, in practice MLE is often implemented through least squares fit. But unlike conventional least square method, MLE is more flexible and powerful by taking measurement errors into account, which can avoid any highly-biased result. MLE gives the answer with some probabilistic sense; i.e. the answer obtained from MLE is probably the best we can get, knowing what we know. In addition, if the variance of measurement errors is known, it is possible to use MLE procedure to estimate parameter errors. Taking space air change rate as example, we possibly can use MLE procedure to report not only expected value (i.e. space air change rate) but also a prediction interval for space air change rate with a certain confidence, meaning that the expected air change will fall within the predicted interval with a certain confidence (e.g. 95% confidence). Prediction interval provides more knowledgeable information on space air change rate. About how to estimate predict interval is out of the scope of this study, we will reserve it for our future work.

2.2 Estimating CO_2 generation rates

Theoretically, the obtained space air change rate by MLE (i.e. solving Eqs. (14) and (15)) can be used to estimate transient CO_2 generation rates by solving Eq. (1) where the derivative of indoor CO_2 concentration needs to be calculated. However, in practice, the derivative of indoor CO_2 concentration cannot be solved analytically. Numerical differentiation is often employed which is very unstable and inevitably produces errors and amplifies noise errors from the measurements. Moreover, the supply CO_2 concentration is often unknown. When all of these factors come together, Eq. (1) cannot be used alone. We will provide a solution for such problem in Section 3.2.2.

In our study, the supply CO_2 concentrations were not measured but estimated using MLE (i.e. solving Eqs. (14) and (15)). For a short period, supply CO_2 concentrations don't change much which can be considered as constant. However, for a long period, the supply CO_2 concentrations may have significant changes. Sometimes, morning and evening supply CO_2 concentrations can have up to 40 ppm difference or even more. That means actual supply CO_2 concentrations at other times of a working day, particularly at morning times, may have significant differences from the estimated supply CO_2 concentration. In order to account for these changes, we tried to compute the upper and lower bounds of indoor CO_2 generation rates when solving Eq. (1). In general, the supply CO_2 concentration ranges from 370 ppm to 420 ppm in buildings in Finland, but this range may change. Derivatives of indoor CO_2 concentrations were calculated using Stirling numerical differentiation (Lu, 2003, Bennett, 1996, Kunz, 1975).

The proposed method (i.e. solving Eqs. (14) and (15)) was first implemented and tested thorough simulated data and then applied to field site data.

3. Simulated data

All data were generated from Eq. (2) with five-minute intervals. Two cases were simulated with constant space air change rates and supply CO_2 concentrations:

Case 1: The ventilation rate is 0.7 ach and supply CO_2 400 ppm;

Case 2: The ventilation rate is 2.5 ach and supply CO_2 400 ppm.

The duration of the simulated indoor CO_2 concentrations for each case was four days with the following noise variance settings for each day: (day 1) constant variance=1; (day 2) constant variance=4; (day 3) constant variance=9; and (day 4) variable variances. Noise component was generated by a random number generator via a normal distribution. Fig. 1 displays the typical simulated indoor CO_2 concentrations for one day.

Hence, a total of eight day's simulated data were tested. The space air change rate is evaluated in the *unoccupied working* period (see Fig. 1) and then applied to the *occupied working period* to compute CO_2 generation rates as presented previously. Sections 3.1 and 3.2 will present the comparison results and discussions.

3.1 Results for space air change rates

Table 1 shows the results of the estimated space air change rates during *unoccupied working periods*, and Table 2 the model performances.

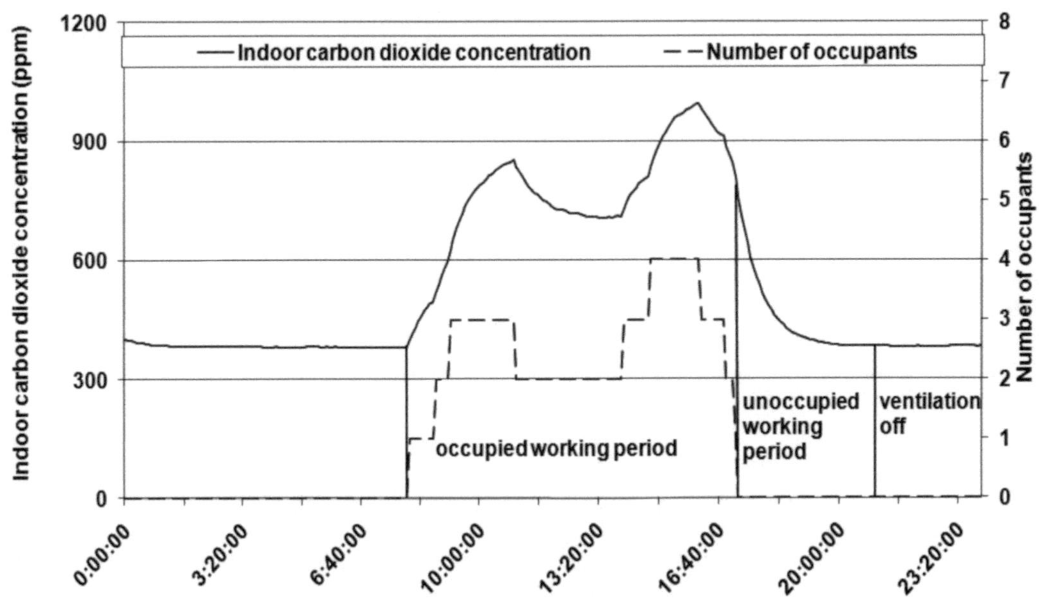

Fig. 1. Indoor CO_2 concentrations for a typical working day in an office.

In Table 1, the variances for variable noise were generated based on ±1.5% accuracy range with 95% confidence (e.g. standard deviation = 3.75 =500*1.5%/2 for the simulated indoor CO_2 concentration of 500 ppm). Table 1 also demonstrates that even though Eqs. (14) and (15) are derived under the assumption of constant variances, both equations work well for variable noise variances as long as noise variances are not very big. An increase in noise variances does not seem to have an effect on the results, as all the estimated space air change rates are close to the true values. However, an increase of the fitting error is observed in Table 2 with increased noise variances or variable noise variances, which implies that big noise variances can cause instabilities in estimated results of space air change rates. Due to space limitations, we only show here the comparison results for the cases with the largest variance of 9. Fig. 2 displays the fitting results of CO_2 concentrations based on the estimated space air change rates from MLE, and Fig. 3 the corresponding residuals.

Case	Parameter	Actual	Maximum Likelihood Estimation (MLE)			
			$\sigma^2=1$[c]	$\sigma^2=4$[c]	$\sigma^2=9$[c]	σ^2 is variable[d]
Case 1	α_0 (ppm)[a]	400	399.96	404.8	402.2	406.1
	α_1 (ach)[b]	0.7	0.704	0.718	0.728	0.733
Case 2	α_0 (ppm)[a]	400	400.3	399.6	400.9	399.9
	α_1(ach)[b]	2.5	2.5	2.45	2.55	2.61

[a] Supply CO_2 concentration, see Eq. (13)

[b] Space air change rate, see Eq. (13)

[c] Constant noise variance.

[d] Variable noise variance computed by $(\frac{(CO_2 * 1.5\%}{2})^2$. 1.5% is accuracy range for simulated CO_2 concentrations with 95% confidence.

Table 1. Estimated space air change rates for Case 1 and Case 2

Figs. 2 and 3 indicate a good fit of the model (i.e. Eq. (13)) to the simulated data. All residual plots in Fig. 3 show no pattern and trend. These results prove that in theoretical level the proposed model is suitable for the estimation of space air change rate which is near constant during the whole working period.

Case	Noise Variance	MSE (mean squared error)	R^2 (coefficient of determination)
Case 1	$\sigma^2=1$	1.16	1
	$\sigma^2=4$	1.88	1
	$\sigma^2=9$	10.3	0.997
	σ^2 is variable	12.46	0.997
Case 2	$\sigma^2=1$	1.16	0.998
	$\sigma^2=4$	6.13	0.992
	$\sigma^2=9$	4.59	0.994
	σ^2 is variable	7.61	0.996

Table 2. Model performances for simulated data

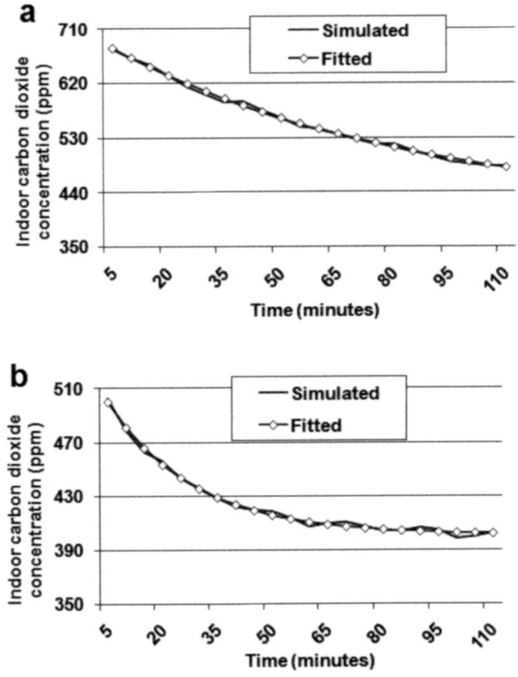

Fig. 2. Simulated and fitted indoor CO_2 concentrations during unoccupied working periods: (a) Case 1 (σ^2=9). (b) Case 2 (σ^2=9).

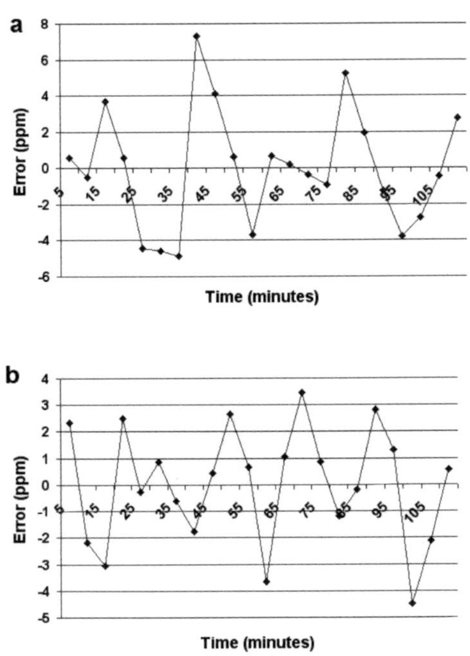

Fig. 3. Residuals for the CO_2 concentration fittings: (a) Case 1 (σ^2=9). (b) Case 2 (σ^2=9).

3.2 Results for CO_2 generation rates

3.2.1 Difficulties with estimation of CO_2 generation rates

For measured indoor CO_2 concentrations in which analytical derivatives are not available, numerical methods by finite difference approximation are probably the only choice. However, all the numerical differentiation is unstable due to the growth of round-off error especially for the noise contaminated data which further amplifies the measurement errors (Anderssen & Bloomfield, 1974, Burden & Faires, 1993) as demonstrated in Fig. 4 for Case 1 using Stirling numerical differentiation. Fig. 4 illustrates that the CO_2 generation rates oscillate with increasing noise. When the noise variance reaches 9, the CO_2 concentrations jump to the highest value 0.0083 L/s and drop to the lowest value 0.0032 l/s vs. the actual value 0.0052 L/s, resulting in instability. We need to develop a new strategy with regard to such problem.

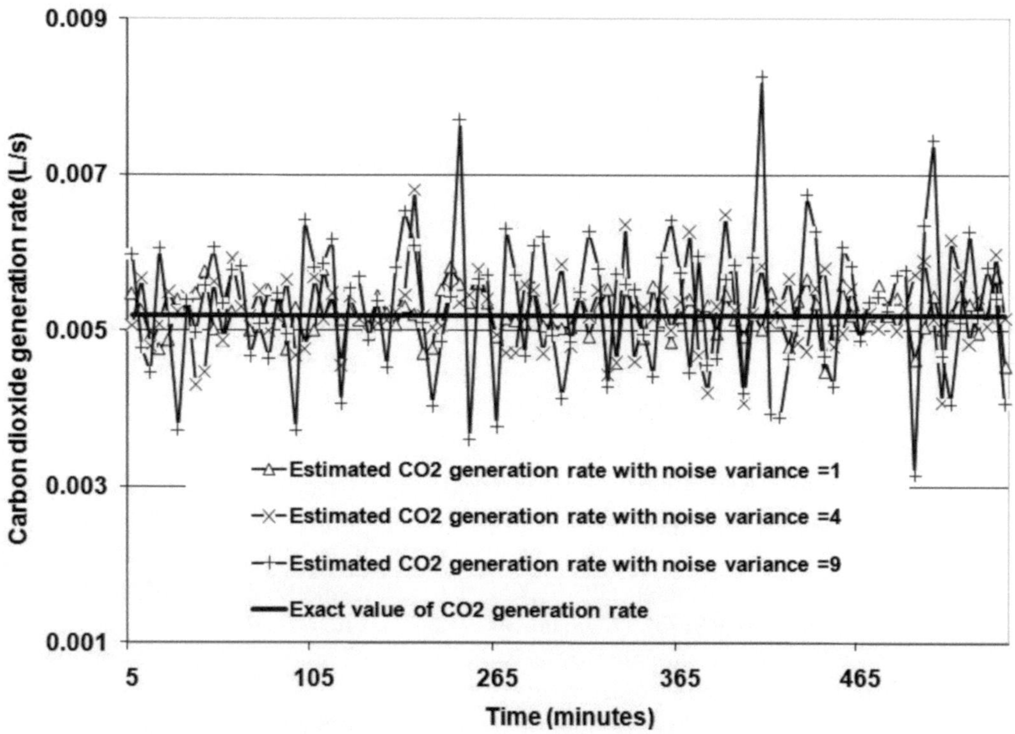

Fig. 4. Predicted CO_2 generation rates for Case 1 using Stirling numerical differentiation.

3.2.2 New strategy for estimation of CO_2 generation rates

Instead of directly estimating the CO_2 generation rates, we opted to evaluate the number of occupants. In fact, almost all ventilation regulations were stipulated based on the number of occupants. Another benefit of knowing the number of occupants is that it can somehow compensate for the losses from calculation errors. Taking Case 1 as an example (see Fig. 4), due to computation errors, the outcome can be as high as 0.0083 L/s vs. actual value, 0.0052 L/s. If we knew that the number of occupants was one, we could immediately obtain the corresponding CO_2 generation rate of 0.0052 L/s for an average-sized adult in office work. The new method is described with the following four steps:

Step 1. compute derivatives of all measured CO_2 concentrations for a range of supply CO_2 concentrations. In other words, we set the lower and upper bounds for the supply CO_2 concentrations and calculate the corresponding bounds for CO_2 generation rates. For instance, in this study, the supply CO_2 concentrations are normally between 370 ppm and 420 ppm which are then set as the lower and upper bounds respectively to compute the corresponding bounds for CO_2 generation rates. However, due to the errors of numerical round-off and measurement as well as the error from the estimated space air change rate, the actual CO_2 generation rates may fall outside the computed range. Nevertheless, the obtained range at least gives us some picture about the CO_2 generation rate at that point;

Step 2. identify significant jumps and drops from the measured CO_2 concentrations. In this study, we consider 10 plus ppm jump or drop as significant change. However, one significant jump or drop does not mean that the number of occupants has a change. Further analysis on derivatives of the measured CO_2 concentrations needs to be done. This is followed by Step 3;

Step 3. analyze derivatives of all measured CO_2 concentrations (i.e. CO_2 generation rates) at the jumped or dropped point as well as subsequent points;

Step 4. finally, further confirm the obtained possible numbers of occupants by computing the value of the equilibrium CO_2 concentration. This step mainly targets the complex in estimating the number of occupants described in Step 2.

To gain some insight into practical problems, we use one example from a field measurement to illustrate the above four steps.

Example 1: Suppose seven continuous measured points (indoor CO_2 concentrations, ppm) are

$$\begin{matrix} P_1 & P_2 & P_3 & P_4 & P_5 & P_6 & P_7 \\ 503\text{->} & 510\text{->} & 526\text{->} & 562\text{->} & 579.6\text{->} & 579.2\text{->} & 578.8 \end{matrix}$$

Step 1. we set 380 ppm and 460 ppm as the lower and upper bounds for the supply CO_2 concentrations, and use these bounds to compute CO_2 generation rates for all points. We obtain:

DP_1 (0.0047, 0.0099), DP_2 (0.0057, 0.01), DP_3 (0.017, 0.02), DP_4 (0.0148, 0.02), DP_5 (0.0123, 0.0175), DP_6 (0.0073, 0.0125), DP_7 (0.0077, 0.013).

The first value in each parenthesis is the lower bound for CO_2 generation rate (L/s) at that point and the second one the upper bound;

Step 2. From these seven points, we identify three significant jumps: P_3, P_4 and P_5;

Step 3. We analyze P_3, P_4 and P_5 as well as their subsequent points: P_6 and P_7. From the results in Step 1, we can get the following guesses if we assume n as the number of occupants after the jumps:

for P_3, $3 \le n \le 4$ for the lower bound, $3 \le n \le 4$ for the upper bound,
for P_4, $2 \le n \le 3$ for the lower bound, $3 \le n \le 4$ for the upper bound,
for P_5, $2 \le n \le 3$ for the lower bound, $3 \le n \le 4$ for the upper bound,
for P_6, $1 \le n \le 2$ for the lower bound, $2 \le n \le 3$ for the upper bound,
for P_7, $1 \le n \le 2$ for the lower bound, $2 \le n \le 3$ for the upper bound,

where we assume that one person's CO_2 generation rate is 0.0052 L/s;

Step 4. Judging from P_3, P_4, and P_5, the number of occupants is more likely three while from P_6 and P_7 is close to two. But, due to no significant drop between P_5 and P_6, the number of occupants at P_5 should be the same as at P_6. In addition, because the computed ranges of CO_2 generation rates at P_3, P_4 and P_5 are close, the number of occupants should be unchanged from P_3 to P_5. Now we can confirm that the number has changed at P_3. The possible number after P_3 is two or three based on the computed CO_2 generation rates at P_3, P_4, P_5, P_6 and P_7. If we assume that the space air change rate is 2.92 ach for an 80 m^3 space, the lowest equilibrium CO_2 concentration for three occupants will be 610.411 ppm = $370+3*0.0052*10^3*3600/(2.92*80)$ which is significantly bigger than P_5, P_6 and P_7. If the number of occupants were three, CO_2 concentrations should have gone up continuously after jumps. However, actually CO_2 concentrations trend to be steady instead. So we can conclude that the number of occupants after jumps is two.

The above example shows how to estimate the numbers of occupants in this study. The proposed method is original. However, keep in mind that the proposed method is only applicable for the spaces where activity levels are relatively stable and occupants are present for long enough time, such as office room, lecture room, conference rooms and so on. In these spaces, minimum requirements of outdoor air per person are explicitly indicated by industry standards or building codes, therefore knowing the number of occupants is significant in order to fulfill minimum requirements of outdoor air for spaces. As for spaces where activity levels (occupants) change considerably with time, such as sporting halls, swimming pools and so on, it isn't recommended to use the proposed method to estimate the number of occupants, instead direct calculation of CO_2 generation rates from Eq. (1) is probably better way to evaluate occupants. Section 4.1.2 presents the results by applying this method to our field measurement. Section 4.1.1 provides results of estimations of space air changes rates using the method discussed in Section 2.1. The CO_2 generation rate for a typical office occupant in Finland is 0.0052 L/s.

4. Experimental data

The field measurement was set up in an office (27.45 x 2.93 m^3, on the third floor) in a three-storey school building. The mechanical ventilation is supplied (100% outdoor air) in daytime on working day from 6:10 a.m. to 8:00 p.m. and shut down during nighttime, weekends, and public holidays. Three persons, two males and one female, work at the office regularly and the design airflow rate is around 200 plus m^3/h (2.5 ach). In addition to indoor CO_2 concentrations, the pressure differences between the return air vent and room were also measured. Fig. 5 shows the office's layout as well as the measurement location. The measurement was categorized based on two stages. At the first stage (22.9.2008 – 28.9.2008), the existing ventilation system was examined. At the second stage (13.10.2008-19.10.2008), the ventilation system was reconfigured by blocking some holes at the supply and return air vents, aiming at reducing airflow rates. Finally, ten day's measurement data were obtained except for weekends. However, due to unexpected long working hours of the occupants which were beyond 8 p.m., there were no *unoccupied working periods* available for several days. Finally, five day's data were obtained which are displayed in Fig. 6. All data were measured within 5 min interval. The measurements show that the pressure differences, an important indicator to airflow rate, were almost constant for all working hours each day despite small fluctuations. This implies that space air change rates on each working day are near constant.

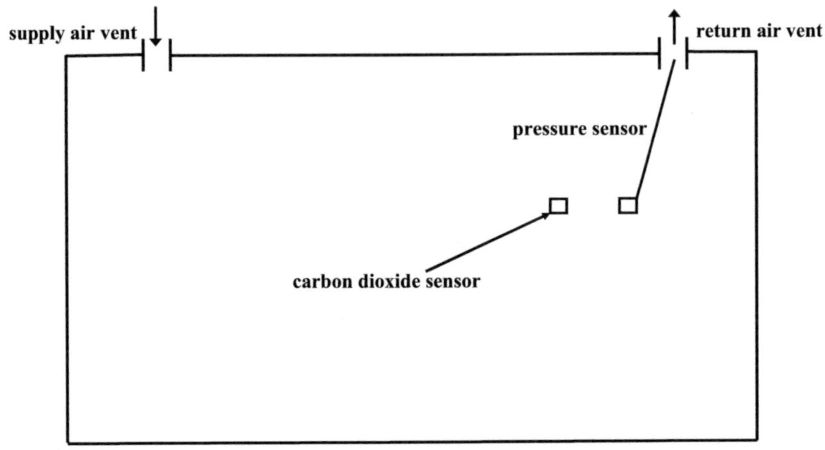

Fig. 5. The plan layout of the office.

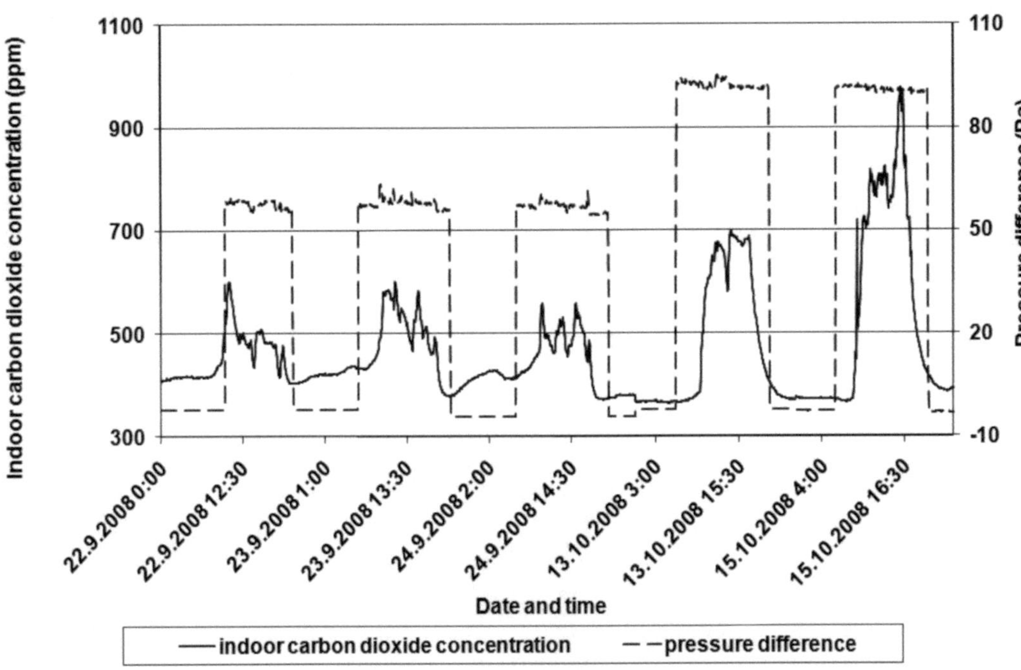

Fig. 6. Measured indoor CO_2 concentration and pressure difference between the return air vent and room.

4.1 Results and discussion

4.1.1 Results and discussion for space air change rates

Although we have measured pressure differences between the return air vent and space, there was no direct measurement available for airflow rate due to technical difficulties. Most literatures summarize the relationship between airflow rate and pressure difference across an opening as the following empirical formula (Feustel, 1999, Awbi, 2003):

$$Q = C(\Delta P)^n \tag{17}$$

where

Q = airflow rate, m^3/s,

ΔP = pressure difference across the opening, Pa,

C = a constant value depending on the opening's geometry effects,

n = flow exponent.

Eq. (17) is called powerlaw relationship also. Theoretically, the value of the flow exponent should lie between 0.5 and 1.0. The values are close to 0.5 for large openings and near 0.65 for small crack-like openings. Supply and return air vents can be regarded as large openings. Note the 'unknown' value C is not essential for evaluating airflow rate if we use the following Eq. (18) based on Eq. (17)

$$\frac{Q_1}{Q_2} = (\frac{\Delta P_1}{\Delta P_2})^n \tag{18}$$

However, we need an extra equilibrium analysis, Eq. (4), as a supplement tool to evaluate and analyze results. Fortunately, on 22.9.2008 and 13.10.2008, one person was present in the office for a long time which allowed reaching near-equilibrium. Table 3 illustrates the measurement situations during the period when the measures were taken.

On 22.9.2008, only one person worked in the office for nearly the whole afternoon with a number of visitors for less-than-five-minute visit during 14:05 – 15:35 when the indoor CO_2 concentrations (about 500 ppm) were higher than the average 481 ppm obtained at a near-equilibrium state during 15:40 – 17:20. The near-equilibrium was judged from the measured CO_2 concentration shown in Table 3 as no noticeable change was monitored within the period. It is worth mentioning that the person has been out shortly enough during the time 15:40 – 17:20 which allowed us to quantify the lower bound of CO_2 concentrations at near-equilibrium stage on a shorter time scale. The actual equilibrium CO_2 concentration value should lie between 478 ppm and 483 ppm. We took the average value, 481 ppm, as the equilibrium concentration value. The CO_2 generation rate for this person was estimated as 0.0052 L/s based on his size.

Similarly, the near-equilibrium was observed at an even longer period of 14:25-17:00 on 13.10.2008. The indoor CO_2 concentrations fluctuated around 680 ppm (almost unnoticeable) at the near-equilibrium state. The actual equilibrium value should be between 670 ppm and 690 ppm, we took the average value, 681 ppm, as the equilibrium concentration value. Again, Eq. (4) was used for the equilibrium analysis. Tables 4 and 5 show the estimated space air change rate results from the equilibrium analysis and MLE on 22.9.2008 and 13.10.2008 as well as comparisons with other days.

When proceeding MLE for one working day, we used only the measured CO_2 concentrations during *unoccupied working period*. The outliers in the measurement data were discarded since they can result in biased estimates and wrong conclusions (Boslaugh & Watters, 2008). The fitting results for five day's *unoccupied working periods* are shown in Fig. 7 and Fig. 8, and their residuals are presented in Fig. 9 and Fig. 10.

Essentially we evaluated space air change rates from MLE by: 1) the equilibrium analysis and 2) pressure differences based on the powerlaw relationship (i.e. Eq. (18)). In other words, if the pressure differences are close in all periods, nearly the same estimated space air change rates result no matter what methods we employ, namely MLE or equilibrium analysis. Table 4 verifies this assertion. On 22.9.2008, 23.9.2008 and 24.9.2008, all periods have close pressure differences, the space air change rates estimated from MLE present nearness to those from the equilibrium analysis. Table 5 shows similar results for 13.10.2008 and 15.10.2008.

It is worth mentioning that Tables 4 and 5 also present somewhat violations against the powerlaw relationship. For instance, the space air change rate with 91-Pa pressure difference (13.10.2008) should be greater than that with 90-Pa pressure difference. However, Table 5 shows reserve results on 13.10.2008 and 15.10.2008. Such violations are quite natural in practice due to the calculation and measurement errors as well as underestimated equilibrium CO_2 concentrations. Those errors are ignorable. Additionally, numbers after one decimal place are meaningless in terms of mechanical ventilation.

Date	Time	CO_2 concentration	The number of occupants
22.9.2008	9:55 – 13:40	From 526 ppm to 495 ppm	Ranging from 3 to 1
	13:45 – 14:00	Lunch break. From 488 ppm to 435 ppm	0
	14:05 – 15:35	From 435 ppm to 495 ppm	1 at most times, but there were some short-time visitors, less than five minutes
	15:40 – 17:20	From 488 ppm to 479 ppm. Near constant. The average is 481 ppm	1
	17:25-	Decaying	0
13.10.2008	9:40-13:15	From 386 ppm to 659 ppm	Ranging from 2 to 1
	13:15-13:40	Lunch break. From 659 ppm to 581 ppm	0
	13:50-14:20	From 581 ppm to 695 ppm	Ranging from 2 to 1
	14:25-17:00	From 688.4 ppm to 688.2 ppm. Stable and near constant despite of small fluctuation. The average is 680 ppm	1
	17:05-	Decaying	0

Table 3. Situations about indoor CO_2 concentration changes for 22.9.2008 and 13.10.2008

Date	Method	Space air change rate (α_1, ach)	Supply CO_2 concentration (α_0, ppm)	Pressure difference (Pa)[a]
22.9.2008	Equilibrium analysis	2.93	401[b]	58
	MLE	2.92	401[b]	56
23.9.2008	MLE	2.94	378[b]	56
24.9.2008	MLE	2.92	370[b]	55

[a] This is average pressure difference between the space and return air vent for the estimated period
[b] Supply CO_2 concentration estimated by MLE

Table 4. Space air change rates estimated from equilibrium analysis and Maximum Likelihood Estimation (MLE) on 22.9.2008, 23.9.2008 and 24.9.2008

Date	Method	Space air change rate (α_1, ach)	Supply CO_2 concentration (α_0, ppm)	Pressure difference (Pa)
13.10.2008	Equilibrium analysis	0.77	378	92
	MLE	0.74	378	91
15.10.2008	MLE	0.76	387	90

Table 5. Space air change rates estimated from equilibrium analysis and Maximum Likelihood Estimation (MLE) on 13.10.2008 and 15.10.2008

Table 6 illustrates excellent model performances from MLE for all five days. Figs. 7 and 8 demonstrate good fittings between the measured and estimated indoor CO_2 concentrations, and the residuals in Figs. 9 and 10 shows no trend and pattern. In practical applications, the following cases often make the parameter assessment methods more difficult to use:

1. A large number of parameters. This could lead to multiple solutions.
2. Inadequate governing equation. If the governing equation cannot model well the actual condition in a physical means, the parameter method could perform bad and the resulting parameters may have misleading interpretations.

In our study, there are only two parameters (i.e. space air change rate and the supply CO_2 concentration), and the range of supply CO_2 concentrations is often known. In practice, the range of supply CO_2 concentration can be narrowed by observation. Most importantly, the governing equation Eq. (1) in this study well reflects the physical reality as a well-mixed indoor air is a widely accepted assumption for an office with mechanical ventilation (Fisk et al., 1991). Therefore, satisfactory results were obtained which demonstrated the suitability of the governing equation. As such, the computational load was small and convergence took few seconds in our calculation. All these show that the proposed method is substantially simpler and faster than most traditional methods. In summary, the space air change rates estimated from MLE are accurate and the proposed method is simple and fast.

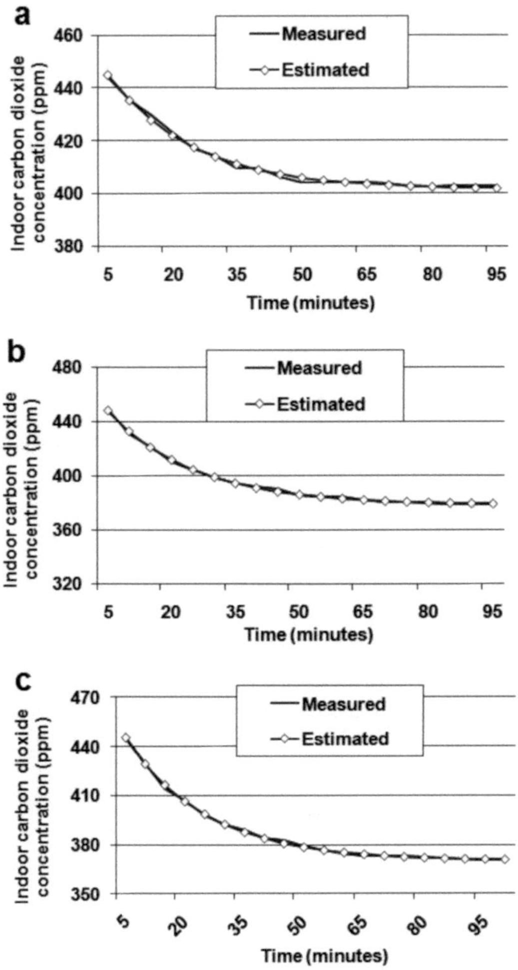

Fig. 7. Measured and estimated indoor CO_2 concentrations for unoccupied working periods on: (a) 22.9.2008, (b) 23.9.2008 and (c) 24.9.2008.

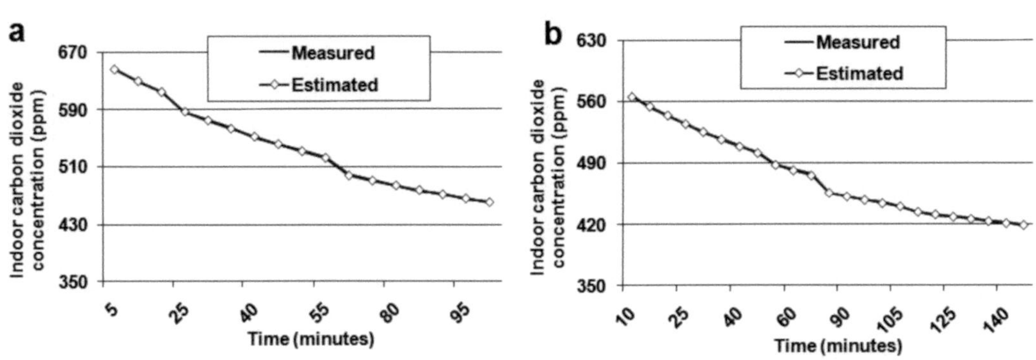

Fig. 8. Measured and estimated indoor CO_2 concentrations for unoccupied working periods on: (a) 13.10.2008 and (b) 15.10.2008.

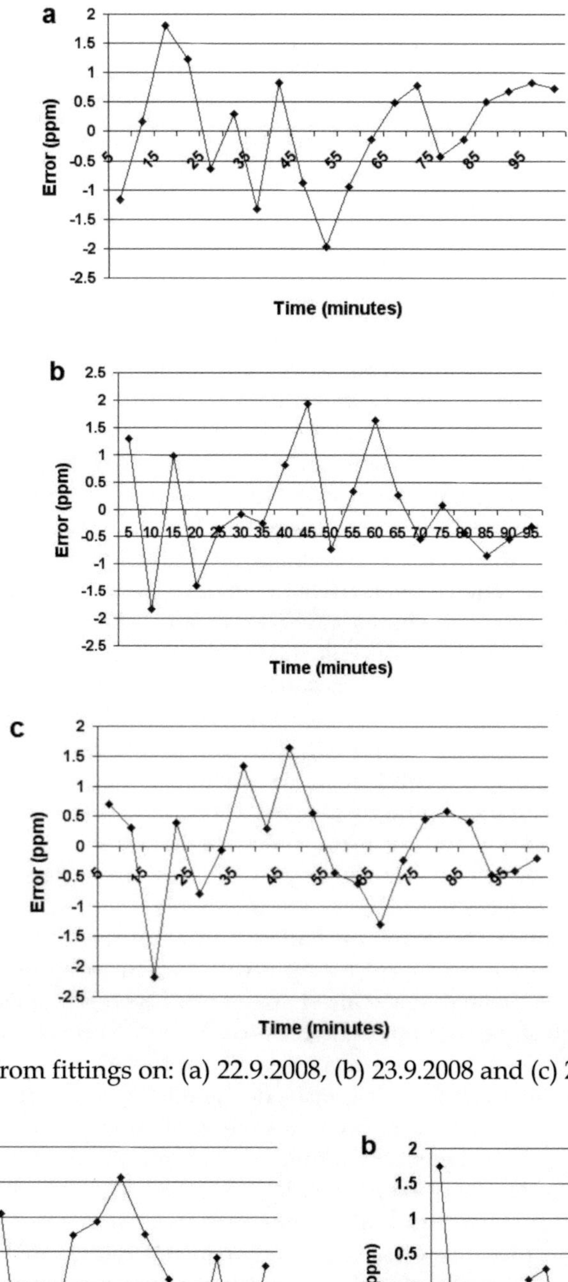

Fig. 9. Residuals from fittings on: (a) 22.9.2008, (b) 23.9.2008 and (c) 24.9.2008.

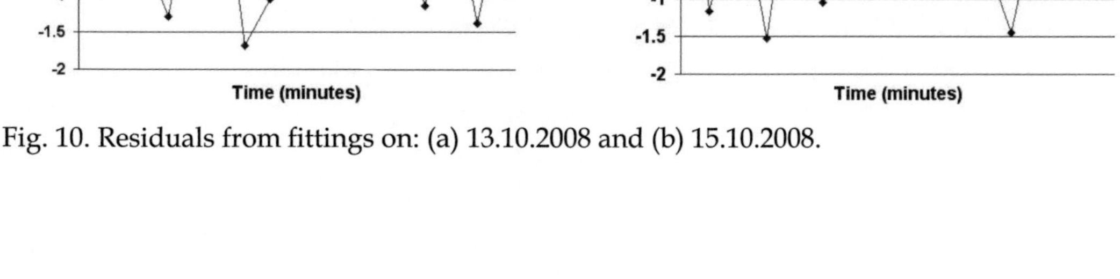

Fig. 10. Residuals from fittings on: (a) 13.10.2008 and (b) 15.10.2008.

Date	MSE (mean squared error)	R^2 (coefficient of determination)
22.9.2008	0.95	1
23.9.2008	0.92	0.998
24.9.2008	0.63	0.998
13.10.2008	0.98	1
15.10.2008	0.82	1

Table 6. Model performances for experimental data

The proposed MLE method works more efficiently with spaces having big space air changes. These spaces, such as office rooms, lecture rooms, and alike, often have high demands on IAQ. But, as for the spaces with large volumes and small air changes rates (e.g. sporting halls), because air movements are slow sometimes sensors cannot catch changes of CO_2 concentrations within one or even more measurement intervals provided intervals are rather small. In this case, the measurement interval needs to be set a big value in order to avoid any form of stair-like curve from measured CO_2 concentrations, which obviously would bring big trouble for the estimation of space air change rate using MLE. The above assertion was verified by our later works. After this study, the proposed MLE method was further applied to estimate space air change rates for several sports halls. All these halls are served by full ventilation in daytime and half in nighttime, and space air change rates are small (<0.7). The first round of measurements started with small interval: 1 min. The graphs of measured CO_2 concentrations from the first round showed that there were many stairs existing in curves for *unoccupied working periods*, meaning that CO_2 concentrations remained the same within one interval (i.e. 1 min) or more during the decay due to small space air change rates and large volumes. Although the proposed MLE method still worked in this complex and difficult condition, fitting errors were so big that we cannot trust results. Actually estimated space air rates were near actual ones. Later on, the new round of measurements were conducted and the measurement interval was enlarged to 15 min. Measured CO_2 concentrations therefore presented continuously and smoothly decaying trends for *unoccupied working periods*, and fitting errors turned to be reduced significantly and become very small. Estimated space air changes rates were quite close to actual ones and trusted as a result. All these show that the propose MLE method can work well in some complex conditions as long as the measurement is well conducted.

In addition, although the method was primarily designed for constant air volume (CAV) system, it is easy to switch the method to time-varying ventilation system, such as demand-controlled ventilation (DCV) systems or variable air volume (VAV) system. But, as for a time-varying ventilation system, it is very difficult to estimate space air change rates only by measurements of indoor CO_2 concentrations. Some extra measurements must be needed. In most cases, we often take pressure differences between the return air vent and space as supplemental measurements due to technical simplicity in implementation. In order to proceed the estimation, some reference pressure difference between return air vent and space must be set first. This reference value can be selected randomly, such as 8 Pa. or 10 Pa. Moreover, Eq. (13) also has to be changed accordingly as followed:

$$f(n, a) = C(n) = (C(n-1) - \alpha_0)\exp(-\alpha_{ref}\sqrt{\frac{\Delta P_n}{\Delta P_{ref}}}\Delta t) + \alpha_0 \quad (19)$$

where

α_0 = supply CO_2 concentration for *unoccupied working period,*

ΔP_{ref} = reference pressure difference between the return air vent and space,

α_{ref} = space air change rate corresponding to ΔP_{ref},

ΔP_n = pressure difference between the return air vent and space at measurement count, n.

Note that in the above equation we apply the powerlaw relationship (i.e. Eq. (18)) to account for changes of space air change rates. Therefore, Eqs. (14) and (15) are modified as follows:

$$\frac{\partial \log p(\{d_n\}\mid\alpha)}{\partial \alpha_0} = \frac{1}{\sigma^2}\sum_n (1-\exp(-\alpha_{ref}\sqrt{\frac{\Delta P_n}{\Delta P_{ref}}}\Delta t))\left[d_n - (C(n-1)-\alpha_0)\exp(-\alpha_{ref}\sqrt{\frac{\Delta P_n}{\Delta P_{ref}}}\Delta t) - \alpha_0\right] = 0 \quad (20)$$

$$\frac{\partial \log p(\{d_n\}\mid\alpha)}{\partial \alpha_{ref}} = \dots$$
$$-\frac{\Delta t}{\sigma^2}\sum_n (C(n-1)-\alpha_0)\sqrt{\frac{\Delta P_n}{\Delta P_{ref}}}\exp(-\alpha_{ref}\sqrt{\frac{\Delta P_n}{\Delta P_{ref}}}\Delta t)\left[d_n - (C(n-1)-\alpha_0)\exp(-\alpha_{ref}\sqrt{\frac{\Delta P_n}{\Delta P_{ref}}}\Delta t) - \alpha_0\right] = 0 \quad (21)$$

Solve Eqs. (20) and (21) to estimate the space air change rate corresponding to the reference pressure difference and supply CO_2 concentration for *unoccupied working period.* And then take the reference pressure difference, $\Delta P_{ref,}$ and estimated corresponding space air change rate, $\alpha_{ref,}$ as reference values to estimate the space air change rate at any time step using the powerlaw relationship (i.e. Eq. (18)). For instance, assume that:

- reference pressure difference between return air vent and space = 8 Pa,
- space air change rate estimated from Eqs. (20) and (21) for the reference pressure difference = 1 ach,
- measured pressure difference at some time step = 50 Pa.

Hence we take 1 ach and 8 Pa as reference values to approximate the space air change rate at that time step as: 2.5 ach=1 * (50/8)^0.5 (see Eq. (18)). Clearly, our method is also applicable for time-varying ventilation system.

4.1.2 Results and discussion for CO_2 generation rates

We used the method described in Section 3.2.2 (four-step method) to estimate the number of occupants, and then compared the results with records from diaries. The diaries recorded the numbers of occupants. For short-time visitors with less than 5-minute stay, they were not recorded in diaries. Because diaries are incomplete for 13.10.2008 and 15.10.2008, here we just present the results for 22.9.2008, 23.9.2008 and 24.9.2008, totally three days in Fig. 11. Fig. 11 illustrates that even if the number of occupants didn't change, the indoor CO_2 concentrations could vary and sometimes show a decaying trend. In addition to the occupants and space air change rates, indoor CO_2 concentrations can be influenced by other factors, such as the supply CO_2 concentrations, short-time visitors and particularly changes on CO_2 generation rates. Activities have great influences on human CO_2 generation rates. When a person sits for long time, his CO_2 generation rate will turn to decrease steadily due to his fatigue, which results in a decaying trend of indoor CO_2 concentrations even if the number of occupants is unchanged.

Hence a significant change on indoor CO_2 concentrations does not necessarily mean a change on the number of occupants. For example, on 23.9.2008, one significant change from 461 ppm to 484.2 ppm was observed, which seemed to be associated the change of occupants. However, with the developed model we evaluated that the number of the occupants was the same as before. Therefore, the changes might due to the occupant's activity. Indeed, an informal request from the person revealed that he actually did a little excise so as to alleviate the tiredness from the long-time work. Human activity does have a great impact on CO_2 generation rate, and sometimes misleads our judgments on the number of occupants. The developed model can correctly estimate the number of the occupants in such complicated case.

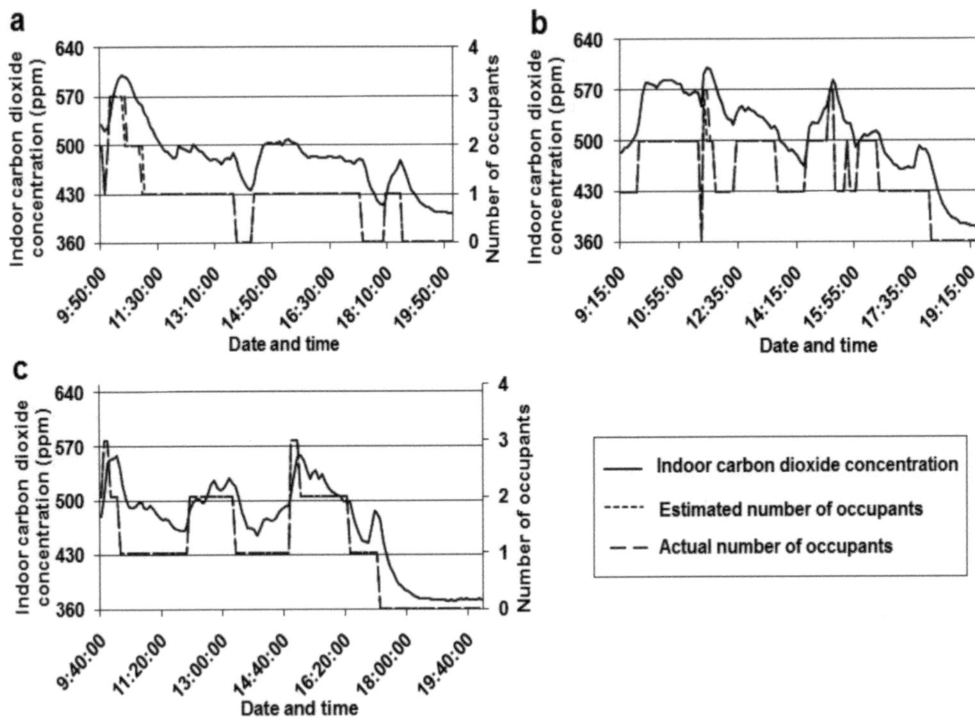

Fig. 11. The estimated and recorded numbers of occupants vs. measured indoor CO_2 concentrations on: (a) 22.9.2008, (b) 23.9.2008 and (c) 24.9.2008.

5. Conclusions

A simple and efficient model based on Maximum Likelihood Estimation (MLE) was developed to estimate space air change rates for an individual space in the commercial building. The results were verified by experimental measurements. The residuals from experimental results showed no trend and pattern, and all fittings between estimated and measured were satisfactory with at least 0.998 coefficient of determination (R^2). In addition, the estimated space air change rates were applied further to predict the numbers of occupants (see Fig. 11). The predicted numbers of occupants were the same as the actual numbers recorded in diaries. Moreover, the paper also shows the possibility that the model can be adapted for estimating time-varying space air change rates, which are common cases in demand-controlled ventilation (DCV) and variable air volume (VAV) systems. The methodology in the paper presents three new features which improve upon the current literature:

1. Bridging the gap between the Maximum Likelihood Estimation (MLE) and its application in estimating space air change rate. We estimated space air rates through MLE from a simplified mass balance equation of CO_2 concentration on the basis of ventilation schedule.
2. Estimating the number of occupants by coupling the traditional method and equilibrium analysis. In the traditional method, transient CO_2 generation rate is computed by solving the mass balance equation of CO_2 concentration. In this study, we combined the traditional method and equilibrium analysis to estimate the number of occupants.
3. Identifying a potential of the MLE method for evaluating time-varying space air change rates.

It is worth mentioning that the proposed model is based on the assumption of a well-mixed ventilated space, this restriction is chosen for convenience but can easily be relaxed. The model can be extended to more complicated configurations such as non-well-mixed space by changing the governing equations of CO_2 concentration (i.e. Eq. (3)) accordingly. A limitation of the model is that it relies on the *unoccupied working period* of a working day for estimating the space air change rate. If the *unoccupied working period* is too short or there is no *unoccupied working period* at all, the model will lose its ability in estimating the corresponding space air change rate. In our future work, we will tackle the above-mentioned limitation. One possibility is to use some global optimization method, such as genetic algorithm, to estimate the space air change rate and CO_2 generation rates during the whole occupied period. In addition, we will also extend our work to more complicated cases such as non-well-mixed and large spaces.

6. Acknowledgement

We are grateful to the Academy of Finland for financial support.

7. References

Akimenko, VV., Anderson, I., Lebovitze, MD. & Lindvall, T. (1986). The sick building syndrome, In: *Indoor Air, Vol. 6. Evaluations and Conclusions for Health Sciences and Technology,* Berglund et al., 97-97, Swedish Council for Building Research, Stockholm

Anderssen, RS. & Bloomfield, P. (1974). Numerical differentiation procedures for non-exact data. *Numerische Mathematik,* Vol., 22, No., 3, 157-182, ISSN: 0945-3245

Awbi, HW. (2003). Ventilation of Buildings, E& FN Spon, ISBN: 0415270561, London

Bennett, JS., Feigley, CE., Underhill, DW., Drane, W., Payne, TA., Stewart, PA., Herrick, RF., Utterback, DF. & Hayes, RB. (1996). Estimating the contribution of individual work tasks to room concentration: method applied to embalming, *American Industrial Hygiene Association Journal,* Vol., 57, 599–609, ISSN: 1542-8117

Blocker, C. (2002). *Maximum Likelihood Primer,* Lecture note

Boslaugh, S. & Watters PA. (2008). *Statistics in a Nutshell: A Desktop Quick Reference,* OReilly, ISBN-10: 0596510497, USA

Burden, RL. & Faires, JD. (1993). *Numerical Analysis,* PWS, ISBN-10: 0534407617, Boston

Clements-Croome, D. (2000). *Creating the Productive Workplace,* Taylor &Francis, ISBN-10: 0415351383, London

Clements-Croome, D. (2004). *Intelligent Buildings: Design, management and Operation,* Thomas Telford, ISBN-10: 0727732668, London

D2 Finnish Code of Building Regulations. (2003). *Indoor Climate and Ventilation of Buildings,* Ministry of the Environment, Helsinki

Environment Australia. (2001). *State of Knowledge Report: Air Toxics and Indoor Air Quality in Australia,* Department of the Environment and Heritage, ISBN: 0642547394, Australia

Erdmann, CA. & Apte, MG. (2004). Mucous membrane and lower respiratory building related symptoms in relation to indoor carbon dioxide concentrations in the 100-building BASE dataset, *Indoor Air,* Vol., 14, 127-134, ISSN: 1600-0668

Feustel, HE. (1999). COMIS-an international multizone air-flow and contaminant transport Model, *Energy and Buildings,* Vol., 3, 3-18, ISSN: 0378-7788

Fisk, WJ., Faulkner, D. & Prill, RJ. (1991). Air Exchange Effectiveness of Conventionaland and Task Ventilation for Offices, In: *Report LBL_31652,* Lawrence Berkeley Laboratory Berkeley, CA, USA

Honma, H. (1975). Ventilation of dwellings and its disturbances, In: *Fabo Grafiska,* Stockholm

IEEE. (2000). *IEEE Standard for Terminology and Test Methods for Analog-to Digital Converters,* The Institute of Electrical and Electronics Engineers (IEEE Std 1241-2000), ISBN: 0-7381-2724-8, New York

Kunz, KS. (1975). *Numerical analysis,* McGraw-Hill, ISBN-10: 0070356300, New York

Lawrence, TM. & Braun, JE. (2007). A methodology for estimating occupant CO_2 source generation rates from measurements in small commercial buildings, *Building and Environment,* Vol., 42, 623-639, ISSN: 0360-1323

Lu, XS. (2003). Estimation of indoor moisture generation rate from measurement in Buildings, *Building and Environment,* Vol., 38, No., 5, 665-675, ISSN: 0360-1323

Miller, SL., Leiserson, K. & Nazaroff, WW. (1997). Nonlinear least-squares minimization applied to tracer gas decay for determining airflow rates in a two-zone building, *Indoor Air* , Vol., 7, 64-75, ISSN: 1600-0668

Nabinger, SJ., Persily, AK. & Dols, WS. (1994). A study of ventilation and carbon dioxide in an office building, *ASHRAE Transaction,* Vol., 100, No., 2, 1264-73, ISSN: 0001-2502

Okuyama, H. (1990). System identification theory of the thermal network model and an application for multi-chamber airflow measurement, *Building and environment,* Vol., 25, 349-363, ISSN: 0360-1323

O'Neill, PJ. & Crawford, RP. (1990). Multizone flow analysis and zone selection using a new pulsed tracer gas technique. *Proceedings of Progress and Trends in Air Infiltration and ventilation Research. Vol. 1, 127-156,* Finland, Sept., 1989

Redlich, CA., Sparer J.& Cullen, MR.(1997). Sick-building syndrome, *Lancet;* Vol., 349, No., 9057, 1013-1016, ISSN: 0140-6736

Sykes, JM. (1988). Sick Building Syndrome: A Review, In: Specialist Inspector Reports No. 10, Health and Safety Executive, Technology Division, London

Wong, LT. & Mui, KW. (2008). A transient ventilation demand model for air-conditioned offices, *Applied Energy* , Vol., 85, 545-554, ISSN: 0306-2619

13

Decontamination of Solid and Powder Foodstuffs using DIC Technology

Tamara Allaf[1], Colette Besombes[2],
Ismail Mih[1], Laurent Lefevre[1] and Karim Allaf[2]
[1]*ABCAR-DIC Process Cie, Department of Valorizing Innovative Processes, 40 rue Chef de Baie, 17000 La Rochelle,*
[2]*University of La Rochelle– Laboratory Transfer Phenomena and Instantaneity in Agroindustry and Building LEPTIAB – Pole Science and Technology. Av. Michel Crépeau 17042 La Rochelle Cedex 01, France*

1. Introduction

1.1 Generalities

Micro-organisms correspond to a multitude of living organisms. Indeed, may be considered as micro-organisms: bacteria, yeast, fungi, protozoa, micro-algae, prions. As for viruses, belonging to micro-organisms is still debated, since some scientists consider them more as "objects" than living organisms. Pathogenic microorganisms are harmful to humans. Their destruction is completely required to adapt the processes to inhibit their proliferation.

It is important to note that many microorganisms has two forms: a "vegetative" form in which the microorganisms is present when the environmental conditions are favorable for its development and a "spore" form which appears when these conditions become unfavorable. The microorganisms have hence the particularity to "wrap" themselves with a sort of protective "shell". The “spore” forms are thus much less sensitive to potential unfavorable environmental situation. The destruction of these germs is generally carried out in two stages: the first aims to trigger the spores' germination and the second takes place destroying the germinated spores. If germination is incomplete germs inactivation will then be incomplete and will lead to final product partially treated but still infected. These microorganisms are present in our environment and can be found in our diet.

Decontamination techniques must also take into account the very strong ability of microorganisms to adapt themselves rapidly to their enviroment. Thus, the microorganisms that suffered sub-lethal stress factor can develop new resistance mechanisms (Hill et al., 2002; Lou & Yousef, 1997; Rajkovic et al., 2009; Rowan, 1999). This evolution is usually not abrupt but more gradual. (Rajkovic et al., 2009).

Safety standards become a shared concern increasingly limiting food market access. Facing this constraint, the food industry has only two solutions:

1. limiting the contamination of raw materials and probably during the manufacturing process,
2. applying final appropriate technologies to reduce microbial load.

Indeed, the precautionary measures settled in various manufacturing processes to acquire healthy foods are in no way sufficient to fully guard against various sources of microbiological contamination. On the one hand, the possibility of clean production processes (microbiologically speaking) is never perfect and the need to include a specific decontamination step is a vital reality, even in the most developed countries. On the other hand, the food industry must also provide products with high nutritional, gustative, etc. quality while remaining "natural". On various industrial and traditional handwork levels, these operations have two seemingly contradictory objectives:

1. a relevant microbial destruction and
2. the best biochemical, nutritional, sensory… preservation.

The need for a specific optimization for each case is hence highly needed. There are so many constraints related to the need of a good decontamination operation in terms of technical performances (microorganism's destruction efficiency, energy consumption…) and great preservation of product attributes and quality.

1.2 Issues of some decontamination techniques

Early techniques of microorganisms destruction were established on the use of temperature, with different levels of temperature and different treatment time: pasteurization (temperature between 62 and 88°C) sterilization (temperature above 100°C) and canning (temperature around 121°C).

Pasteurization destroys a significant fraction of the microbial load. However, products that undergo this process require special storage conditions. In fact, these products still contain germs capable of multiplying. If they are placed under favourable environmental conditions to their multiplication, the products will then quickly become unfit for human consumption.

Sterilization has been used for a long time in order to inactivate microorganisms (Hope, 1901; Kim et al., 2007). Unfortunately these heat treatments have very negative effects on nutritional, gustative, etc. qualities, (Jo et al., 2003).

Furthermore, the use of thermal shock (positive or negative) poorly controlled may lead to increase resistance to subsequent decontamination techniques. (Nevarez et al., 2010) have studied the case of Penicillium glabrum; (Chang et al., 2009), Cronobacter sakazakii; (Lin & Chou, 2004) and Listeria monocytogenes. (Broadbent & Lin, 1999) have studied application to increase the germs preservation *(Lactococcus lactis)* used as processing assessment.

Although relatively effective, conventional steam treatments often require a long period of rising and fall edges in temperature and a great temperature gradient, in other words a lack of homogeneity, which naturally affect the qualities of the end product.

The use of specific gases such as ethylene oxide or propylene oxide has long been practiced at room temperature. Nevertheless, standards are more and more stringent mainly regarding residual molecules introduced into the treated product. They hence tend to be completely banned such as ethylene oxide that has been prohibited in France since 1990.

The various processing operations applied to liquid or pumpable products are, somehow, more easily achievable.

An obvious statement can now be established in the decontamination field: after a great and long activity of studying, investing and optimizing the broadest possible range of technologies, several new types of treatment have been realized successfully. However, the heat treatment remains the major industrial operation adopted to destroy microorganisms in liquids mainly as UHT (e.g.: ohmic heating) (Lewis & Heppell, 2002).

Microorganism destruction in solid faces several types of difficulties. The heat transfer or radiation penetration phenomena are more difficult to achieve. Heat or radiation treatments are almost impossible to be uniform. This is even more difficult since solids must be often processed in bulk. Dried food products as solid (spices, herbs, onions, garlic ...) or powder (flour ...) are known for their high microbial load sometimes coupled to a presence of insects, often because of their traditional way of production including harvesting, drying, grinding, storage, etc. Very few remediation technologies have been suggested to adapt to this type of products.

Although relatively effective, conventional steam treatments often require a long period of rising and fall edges in temperature, a great temperature gradient and in other words a lack of homogeneity, which naturally is capable to harm the qualities of the end product. The use of specific gases such as ethylene oxide or propylene oxide has long been practiced at room temperature. Nevertheless, standards are more and more stringent mainly regarding residual chemical molecules introduced into the treated product. They hence tend to be completely banned such as ethylene oxide that has been prohibited in France since 1990.

The ionization by nuclear gamma irradiation has for a very long time and for many solid and/or powders foodstuffs emerged as the best decontamination treatment (Fan et al., 2003; Molins, 2001; WHO, 1988; R.A. Molins et al., 2001). This treatment has proven to be highly effective and very convenient since the product can be treated in its airtight packaging away from any recontamination. γ irradiation has been employed for the decontamination and/or sterilization of dehydrated vegetables, fruits, seasonings and animal foods, and to prolong the storage period (Chwla et al., 2003; Fu et al., 2000; Mahrour et al., 2003). The dose to deliver to food depends on the desired effect: "low" dose irradiations (50-150 Gy) don't decontaminate and are used to only inhibit sprouting of potatoes and onions. Food sterilization (e.g.: pre-cooked meals) requires much higher doses (10-50 kGy). (Thomas et al., 2008) irradiation dose of 7 kGy can be effective to control microbial growth in black tea and in extending their shelf life without any significant deterioration of quality constituents. This technology enables food processors to deliver larger amounts of high quality tea with extended shelf life.

Nevertheless some negative impacts of such treatment are possible. Because of the radiation energy, ionization can remove electrons from atoms and break molecular bonds leading then to the formation of highly reactive free radicals. New molecules could thus appear in the food as a result of chemical recombination. Irradiation of lipids causes the formation of cyclobutanones whose toxicity is well known. Although works are needed to identify these chemicals toxicity, studies done in 1950/1960 have revealed very disturbing effects including chromosomal damage.

Radiation can also induce the loss or the degradation of amino acids and vitamins (including A, B1, B6, B12, C, E, K, PP and folic acid) depending on the dose and the radiosensitivity of molecules. High dose irradiation kills bacteria but does not affect the toxins previously produced. However, these toxins are often responsible for many foodborne illnesses. Alternatively, such irradiation eliminates all micro-organisms in food, including those with useful features. Finally, some authors highlight the risk of a particular mutation induced by irradiation in insects and bacteria. In addition to these scientific and technical aspects and despite a big marketing effort developed by the concerned industry to attest the safety of irradiation (proved only for doses up to 10 kGy), ionizing radiation suffers from a very bad public opinion due to the confusion between radiation and radioactivity. Consumer rejection has been strengthened especially since the mandatory labelling in 2001 of all products processed by ionizing radiation. This set of elements and the relatively high equipment cost explain its very low approval.

The World Health Organization (WHO) expert committee on the wholesomeness of food irradiation agreed with the food and drug administration (CAC, 2003) that foods subjected to low dosages (10 kGy) of γ irradiation are safe and do not require toxicological testing (WHO, 1981; FDA, 2005; WHO, 1988). γ irradiation can extend the shelf life of treated foods without inducing the formation of any radionuclide in food products. (Lacroix & Quattara, 2000).
High Pressure Processing HPP treatment is generally considered to:

1. affect bacterial cell membranes and impair their permeability and ion exchange, but also
2. but also to inactivate some of the enzymes vital for survival and reproduction of bacterial cells (Cheftel, 1995; Hoover et al., 1989; Considine et al., 2008; Yaldagard et al., 2008).

Through HPP treatment, microorganisms undergo different range of resistance, with some strains being more resistant than others (Alpas et al., 1998; Chung & Yousef, 2008).
The inactivation of spores by HPP compared to efficiency in vegetative cells, is less efficient and requires higher pressures and higher temperatures (Heinz & Knorr, 2005 and references therein).
Bacterial spores were set up to survive up to 1200 MPa at room temperature (Zhang & Mittal, 2008 and references therein). Besides they compiled a review with data details showing that there can be significant variations in the requirements of high pressure and temperature among different bacterial spore species and also among strains of the same species. For a successful inactivation of spores, the optimization of the HPP conditions or the combination with other treatments and agents may be needed.
The use of a specific heat treatment similar to UHT in the case of solid or powder foods may be a necessary and indispensable solution. The needs of a very rapid heating and an instant cooling have been noticed through the use of an instant controlled treatment: the DIC.
Indeed, during over twenty-two years (since 1988), the LMTAI (Laboratory Mastering of Technologies for AgroIndustry) has managed to develop a specific research activity about the impact of the instantaneous pressure drop on cells structure and biological structures. This work, in addition to its apparent scientific interest, had an obvious technological impact. Saturated or superheated steam injection, at controlled pressure reaching a level of seven or eight bars of absolute pressure applied to products put initially under vacuum, implies a very rapid heating done mainly by condensation on the inner surface of the product. The definition of a limiting thickness can achieve this step in less than three seconds. The heating time is completely controlled by introducing a new stage in vacuum (around 5 kPa of absolute pressure), abruptly established (in less than 1/10th second i.e. a decompression rate of more than 50 MPa s^{-1}).
Thanks to the autovaporization the product temperature drops immediately to reach very low levels, necessarily lower than the equilibrium temperature of the water (which is in our case 33°C).
Other versions of this process consist in achieving proper heating by hot air, contact with hot plates, microwaves... possibly coupled with vibration or mechanical mixing for a more uniform treatment. The application of the instant pressure drop towards vacuum generates an instant cooling by autovaporizing a part of the product water.
Such treatment reflects perfectly the heat treatment required by the UHT process usually applied to liquids. However, studies conducted by the LMTAI (Debs-Louka et al., 1999) have proven efficiency twice as high. It was then possible to prove that after applying the DIC, the action of the instant pressure drop was not confined to the only impact of abrupt

cooling. A thermo-mechanical effect that may lead to the microorganism cells explosion (spores or vegetative forms) also occurs.

The higher the amount of "steam" generated within the cell and the smaller the pressure drop time, the more efficient the mechanical effect. Besides water, further molecules could be considered. The choice of the molecule is closely related to the importance of its possible mechanical action. This must be due to the extent of the difference between the initial and final pressures and the rate of pressure drop itself.

The use of carbon dioxide has been studied because of its high relative dissolution capacity during a high pressure stage. For each fluid used the most important point was its capacity to generate a force capable of breaking and even cracking the cell walls.

Therefore various industrial applications have been obviously established. The most immediate consisted in the definition of thermo-mechanical destruction of microorganisms while maintaining as well as possible, the various contents on the agro-food quality (texture, flavor, vitamins, protein activities, etc.). At the initial LMTAI (Allaf et al. 1998; Debs-Louka et al., 1999; Debs-Louka 2000) research lies in the definition of the various impacts of operations and determination of their main phases of intervention. The couple "temperature-time" will establish the level of decontamination. Quantifying the impact on various quality parameters can lead to the establishment of a multidimensional optimization generally very relevant.

Other researches, carried out subsequently by the company ABCAR-DIC process, have identified areas of treatment different from those initially planned. Application sectors are dramatically widening. Various studies have been made on many solids and powders, such as fruits, vegetables, meat and seafood, algae and microalgae, spices, ginger, etc.

In the case of this operation, the impact of the number of pressure drops towards vacuum has been quantified. The effect of decontamination by DIC has therefore been optimized according to various constraints related to: the product and its requirements in terms of quality, the microorganisms that we seek to eliminate and those that we want to preserve.

DIC specificity is related to the ability to define the degree of decontamination across the triumvirate "temperature-time-number of pressure drops" instead of the conventional torque "temperature-time". The impact of such possibility is immediate in terms of quality control of the finished product.

This work results from the identification and analysis of a new thermo-mechanical process of destruction of microorganisms, mainly valid for solid or powder products. DIC can advantageously substitute conventional processes in this field where many new treatments, such as radiation (γ, ultraviolet, acoustic...) or mechanical (UHP, ultra-sound), have had, when achievable, only very restrictive applications.

The efficiency of the instant controlled pressure drop DIC developed as microbial inactivation system was studied, analyzed, and optimized. This chapter aims to illustrate the main impact of saturated steam instant controlled pressure drop STEAM-DIC per se. Its double impact as heating and explosion effects allowed it to be very relevant in terms of industrial operation capable to intervene in both decontamination and preservation of functional, nutritional, and sensorial quality, in a large domain of very heat fragile foodstuffs. The study of the second version of this operation had, as objective, to reduce even more the thermal impact by inserting numerous pressure-drops maintaining the same temperature level and the total treatment time range. As the main functional and sensorial properties as well as the nutritional contents closely depend only on the processing temperature and the treatment time, such pressure drops normally intervened to improve the decontamination effect, while maintaining quality. It was even possible to improve some functional quality by increasing the specific surface area. By inserting numerous pressure drops, the Multi-Cycle DIC treatment was studied for expanding the granule, creating internal pores, preserving the quality while implying more decontaminating effect.

1.3 The DIC and its application fields

The DIC Détente Instantanée Contôlée, French for Instant Controlled Pressure-Drop, is based on the principles of thermodynamics of instantaneity. It started in 1988 by the fundamental study on the expansion through alveolation and has targeted several industrial applications in response to issues of control and quality improvement, coupled with reduced energy costs. They are various operations studied such as steaming, extraction, drying, and sterilization. The approach has always involved the integration of phenomena of instantaneity to intensify the elementary processes of transfer. Several industrial projects have been developed, the first one in 1993. Several patents have been filed since 1993, (Allaf et al., 1993) and more than twenty Phd thesis have treated the subject from different angles.

1.3.1 Waterlogged wood

This application has been patented (Allaf et al., 1997). Archaeological investigations often renew pieces of wood having spent long periods in water (mostly seawater). Once emerged, and as they gradually lose water (dehydration), they deteriorate very quickly. The DIC treatment can stop these degradations.

1.3.2 Rice steaming

The results of this application have been prepared following several thesis and research works (Duong Thai, 2003). The DIC treatment is presented as an operation of pre-drying just after harvesting or otherwise as part of a treatment for rice steaming. In both cases, the DIC-rice has many advantages compared to the conventional method:

1. a time of particularly low heat treatment (30 seconds instead of 40 to 60 minutes with conventional drying),
2. a 2-hour drying instead of 8 hours without any tempering period and a higher quality end product,
3. a better performance (a percentage of broken rice generally less than 3% instead of 15% to 35% for conventional methods).

1.3.3 Sterilization

Three patents protect this application (Allaf et al., 1994; Allaf et al., 1998; Allaf et al., 1999). DIC treatment eliminates micro-organisms (even spore forms) through two main mechanisms: a particularly well controlled heat treatment and mechanical stress on the micro-organisms caused by the instant pressure-drop that lead to their explosion.

1.3.4 Drying and texturing

Both applications are very often associated, although we can approach one without the other. In the case of coupling the two processes, applications studied have been numerous on vegetables, fruits, fish, meat products... DIC treatment causes an expansion in response to the mechanical stress due to the autovaporisation by instant pressure drop, leading to a good textured, porous once the operation is performed near the glass transition. The final drying step is generally carried out by conventional hot air or TPG (Total Pressure Gradient).

1.3.5 Drying by TPG (Total Pressure Gradient)

This is another version of the DIC-drying. The autovaporization is used as a step of removing a certain amount of water, so a succession of pressure cycles followed by a pressure-drop towards vacuum will intensify dramatically the drying since it brings the solution to the paradox of (Al Haddad et al., 2008).

1.3.6 Volatile molecules extraction

Through the autovaporization of volatile compounds, the DIC technology allows removing a big part of essential oils present in the plant (aromatic herbs, fruits, flowers...). By assuring a Multi- DIC-Cycles, the complete extraction is generally carried out in some minutes (2-4 min), with low energy and low added water consumption.

1.3.7 Non-Volatile molecules extraction (solvent extraction)

The expansion of the solid matrix through the DIC treatment can act on the solvent extraction. Indeed, such a treatment implies increasing the porosity and the specific surface area of the treated plant. Therefore it subsequently allows the solvent to easily enter the matter and hence extract the requested material. DIC texturing is considered as a solvent extraction pretreatment, which generates a dramatic decrease of extraction time of non-volatile compounds.

2. Material and methods

2.1 Raw materials: Powders

Trials were carried out on various varieties of seaweeds, skim milk "low heat" powder manufactured at the INRA of Rennes, France (Research Laboratory of Dairy Technology), which was artificially contaminated by ASR spores and vegetative forms. Table 1 shows the initial chemical composition. Before treating by DIC, powder humidity is controlled from 4% to 22% dry basis depending on the spray-drying conditions (air temperature, speed of flow and humidity content).

Some seaweed industrial amounts from SETALG Co and microalgae powders such as spirulina were STEAM-DIC treated just after a first stage of drying (hot air drying, spray-drying, freeze-drying).

Sample N°	Powder				Spray-Drying Temperature	
	Casein	Whey protein	H_2O	a_w		
	concentration ($g.kg^{-1}$)		(%)		T_{inlet} (°C)	T_{outlet} (°C)
H_1	250.1	66.8	6.0	0.34	140	64
H_2	246.2	65.9	7.5	0.41	110	47

Table 1. Physical and chemical characterization of classical spray-dried skim milk powder

2.2 Treatment equipment

Fig. 1 shows the operational protocol used in different trials. The experimental set-up has been largely described (Allaf et al., 1989, 1992, 1993a, 1993b). It comprises three main parts (Fig. 2):

The processing vessel (1), where steam or gas pressure may be established up to 1 MPa.
The vacuum system, which is mainly a vacuum tank (2) with a volume 100/150 times greater than the processing reactor, and an adequate vacuum pump capable of reaching and keeping the vacuum level constant at 5±0.1 kPa in all our experiments just before dropping the pressure.
An abrupt pneumatic valve (3) that assures the connection/separation between the vacuum tank and the processing vessel. It can be opened in less than 0.2 second, which ensures the "instant" pressure drop within the reactor.

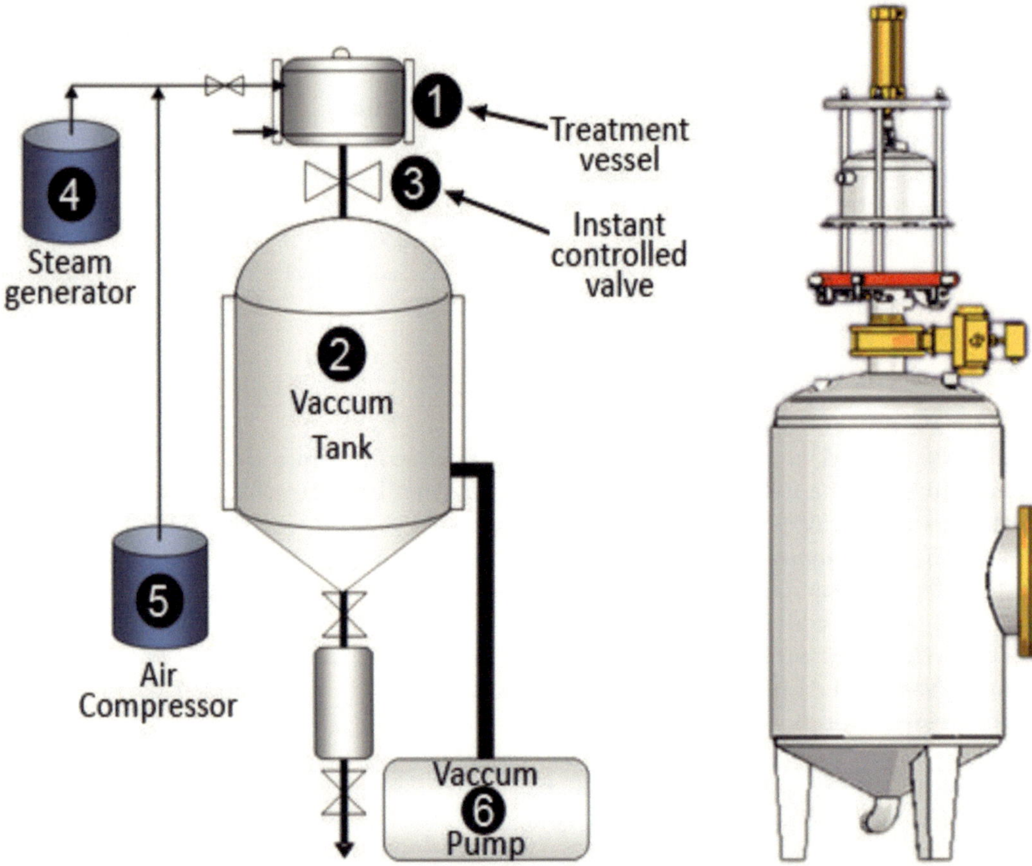

Fig. 1. Schematic presentation of DIC reactor: 1- treatment vessel; 2- vacuum tank with double Jacket as condensers; 3- controlled instant pressure drop valve; 4- steam generator; 5- air compressor; 6- water ring vacuum pump

Samples of approximately 60 g of powders are first placed in the DIC treatment vessel. The treatment consists in setting up a first vacuum stage, then injecting gas at a predefined pressure and maintaining it for a predefined time; the gas we use is compressed air in the case of Multi-Cycle DIC and saturated steam in the case of STEAM-DIC. By abruptly dropping the pressure ($\Delta P/\Delta t$ > 0.5 $MPa.s^{-1}$) towards vacuum, instant autovaporization occurs, inducing texturing and "instant" cooling of the treated material (Figure 2). Similar system was used at industrial scale. It is a 150 L processing treatment and 25 m3 as vacuum tank. Scaling up studies allowed us to adopt the same DIC processing parameter values to reach the same results.

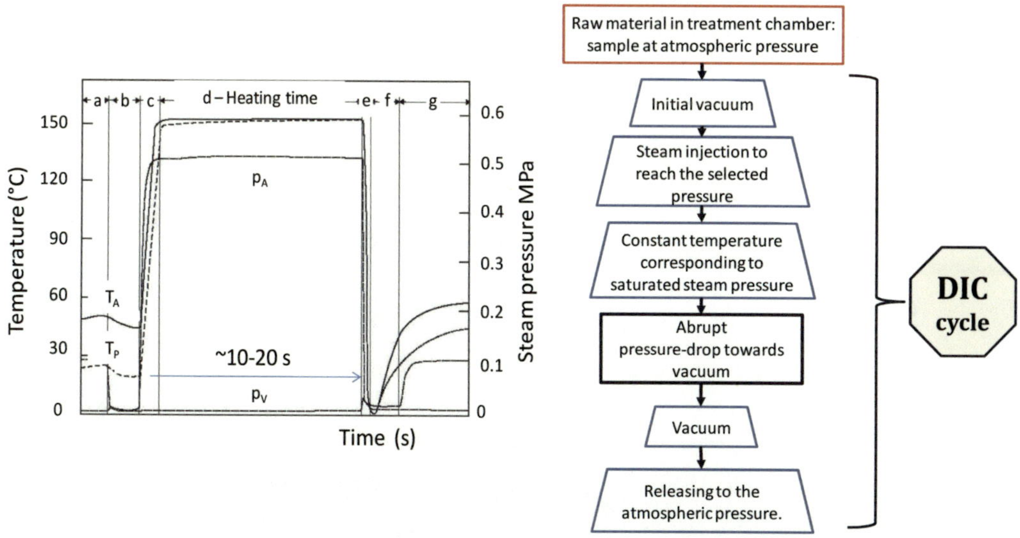

Fig. 2. Temperature and pressure history of a STEAM-DIC processing cycle. P_A is the steam pressure in autoclave, P_V pressure in vacuum tank, T_A temperature in autoclave, T_P temperature of product: (a) sample at atmospheric pressure; (b) initial vacuum; (c) saturated steam injection to reach the selected pressure; (d) constant temperature corresponding to saturated steam pressure; (e) abrupt pressure drop towards vacuum; (f) vacuum; (g) releasing to the atmospheric pressure.

In the Multi-Cycle DIC treatments, products were directly heated up to 155°C through a heating plate whose temperature was defined at various levels depending on an adequate experimental design. To intensify the cooling process of the powder surface, airflow was introduced and released towards vacuum, till reaching the high pressure level.

In some cases, a final drying stage had to intervene after DIC treatment. It usually was a convective drying carried out in an independent drier with a stream of dry air at 50°C in order not to modify the decontamination state; the dried samples were then recovered and ready for microorganism characterization.

In order to achieve a relevant experiment study on the impact of various operating parameters and optimize the DIC treatment, a five-level Central Composite Rotatable Experimental Design method was adopted. In the STEAM-DIC, two DIC operating parameters were studied: steam pressure (P), and processing time (t), while keeping the other operating parameters constant. Other three operating parameters were studied in the case of Multi-Cycle DIC: the heating plate temperature (T), the total processing time (t), and the number of cycles, (keeping the other operating parameters constant). In both cases, the experiments were run at random to minimize the effects of unexpected variability of responses due to unrelated factors. Experiments of DIC treatment were then carried out using the operating conditions described in Tables 2 and 3.

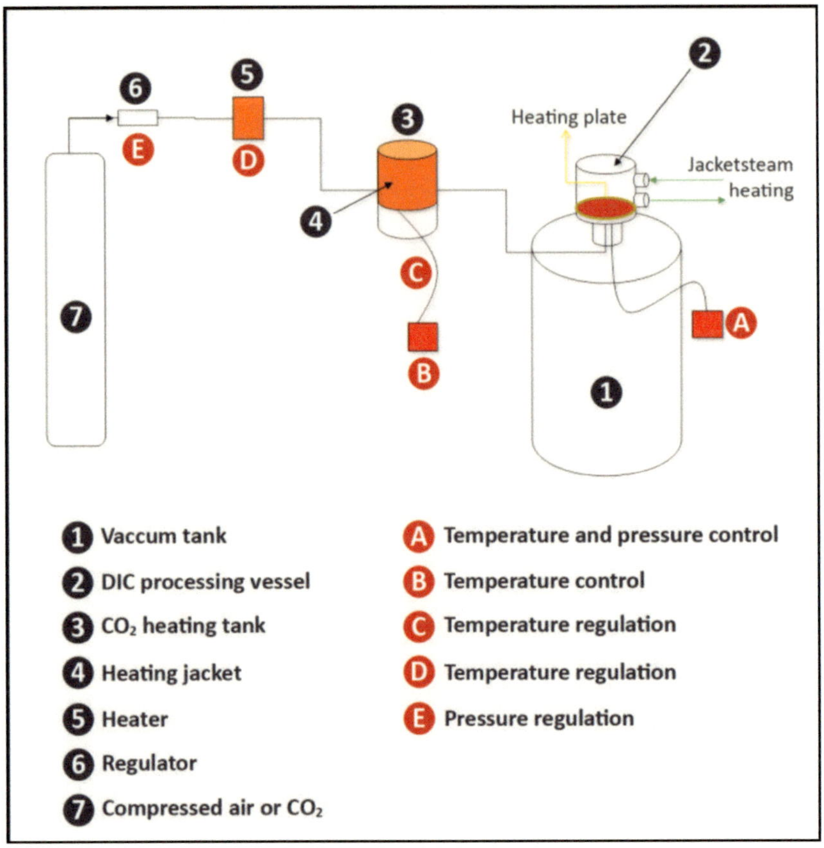

Fig. 3. Schematic presentation of Multi-Cycle DIC reactor

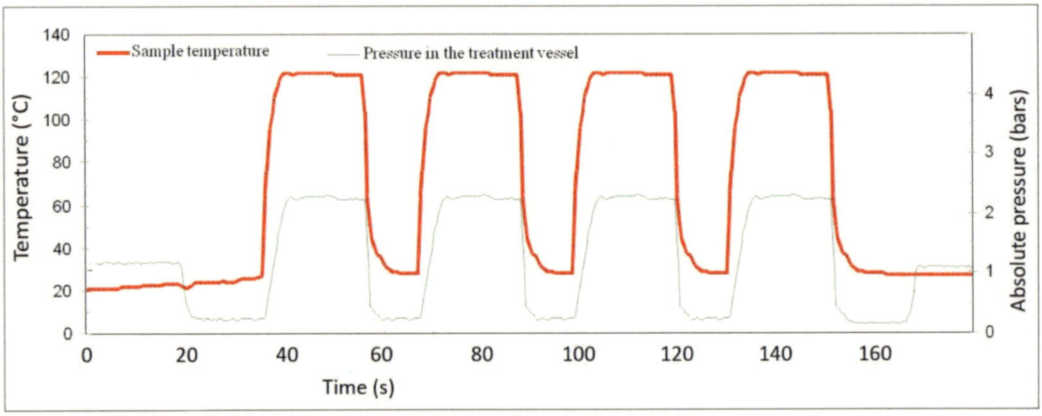

Fig. 4. Temperature and pressure history of a Multi-Cycle DIC. P_{atm} is the atmospheric pressure in the treatment vessel, P_{Vac} pressure vacuum level, P Processing pressure

The statistical treatment leading to Pareto Chart, main trends, surface responses, empirical model and R^2 were determined through the analysis design procedure of Statgraphic Plus software for Windows (1994-4.1 version- Levallois-Perret, France).

Trials N°	Saturated steam Pressure (MPa)	Total treatment time (s)
1	0.44±0.02	40±2
2	0.3±0.02	12±2
3	0.2±0.02	60±2
4	0.3±0.02	40±2
5	0.4±0.02	60±2
6	0.3±0.02	68±2
7	0.3±0.02	40±2
8	0.16±0.02	40±2
9	0.3±0.02	40±2
10	0.2±0.02	20±2
11	0.4±0.02	20±2
12	0.3±0.02	40±2

Table 2. Experimental design of decontamination of spirulina powder by STEAM-DIC treatment.

Trial n°	Heating plate temperature T (°C)	Total heating time (min)	Number of cycles
1	125	5	6
2	125	5	6
3	116	6	4
4	140	5	6
5	125	7	6
6	110	5	6
7	134	4	4
8	125	5	10
9	116	6	8
10	116	4	8
11	125	5	6
12	125	5	6
13	134	6	4
14	125	5	6
15	125	5	6
16	125	3	6
17	134	4	8
18	116	4	4
19	134	6	8
20	125	5	6
21	125	5	6
22	125	5	2

Table 3. Experimental design of Multi-Cycle DIC treatment of a mixture of spray-dried skim milk powder.

2.3 Assessment protocol

2.3.1 General assessment

Water content, expressed as % dry matter (g water/100 g dray basis), was determined by the desiccation method in a Mettler Toledo LP-16 Infrared Dryer/Moisture Analyzer with Mettler Toledo PE360 Balance - Bishop International Akron, OH, USA LP16 balance. The measurement of water content by calibration with a drying oven at 105°C during 24 hours was carried out two times: just before DIC treatment and after final drying to generally be expressed in g H_2O/100 g of dry matter.

2.3.2 Enumeration of living microorganisms.

The main enumeration of living microorganisms was achieved at the "Laboratoire d'Analyses Sèvres ATlantique (LASAT)" for measuring total flora, faecal coli, Salmonella, Clostirdium P B., Cereus, Yeast/Mold, Staph Aureus, ASR spores…

3. Results and discussion

3.1 Physical characterization

Whatever the type of treatment may be, the bulk density of skim milk powder is significantly influenced by either air or steam pressures depending on the two versions of DIC-decontamination. Color, expansion ratio, porosity, as well as functional properties were quantified, thus contributing to the optimization of the process. Furthermore, industries participating to the present study or those adopting the STEAM-DIC in their manufacturing process, were able to define the processing parameters to get the best preservation of total quality.

3.2 STEAM-DIC decontamination; case of spirulina

Points		Efficiency of Decontamination Ratio
STEAM-DIC DECONTAMINATION	1	100%
	2	88%
	3	100%
	4	100%
	5	100%
	6	100%
	7	100%
	8	97%
	9	100%
	10	96%
	11	100%
	12	100%
Low-temperature (30°C) Multi-Cycle DIC		98%
Freeze-Drying		19%

Table 4. Decontamination ratio for different Steam-DIC samples (see Table 2.) in comparison with low-temperature (30°C) Multi-Cycles DIC and freeze-drying

Trials of raw Spirulina do not necessarily have the same microbial load. In order to compare the effect of each process on the quality of the final product depending on the initial microbial load of raw material, we calculated the decreasing ratio of this load using the following formula:

$$\text{Efficiency of decontamination ratio} = \frac{(\text{Initial microbiological charge} - \text{final microbiological charge})}{\text{Initial microbiological charge}} (\%)$$

Although the spray-drying air flow temperature is high, the final product microbiological charges are normally greater than that of non processed raw material. This is due to a product temperature during drying very close to the ideal temperature for the growth of microorganisms. Meanwhile, freeze-drying did not imply any detectable decontamination, while, the STEAM-DIC treatment did give very relevant results, with a decreasing ratio systematically higher than 87%; some STEAM-DIC treated spirulina could be considered as sterile, with 100% as a decreasing ratio. The statistical study of the experimental design provided the following results:

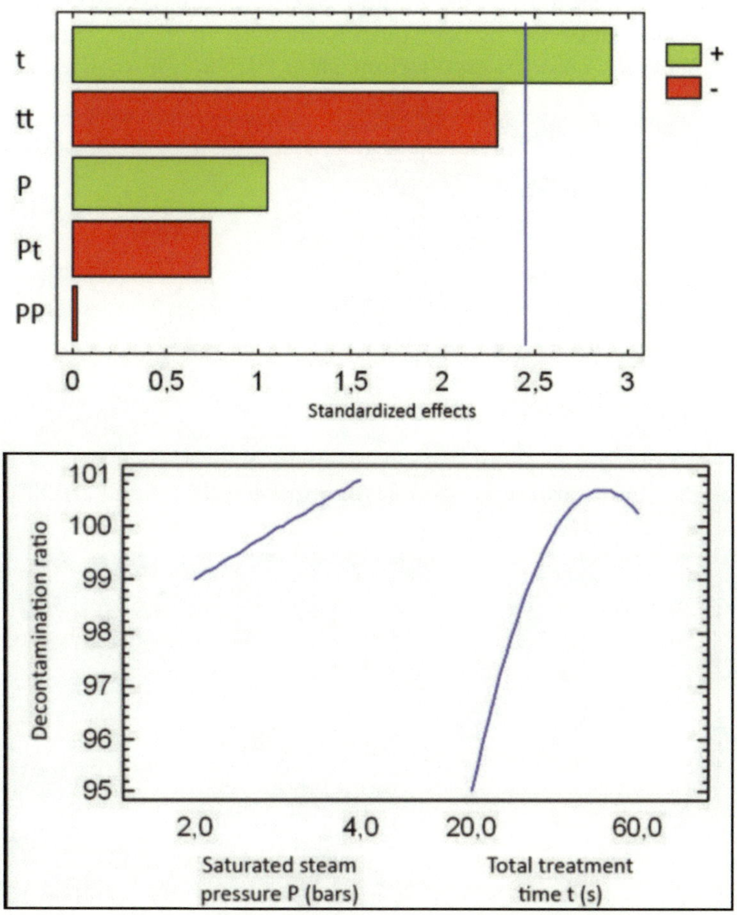

Fig. 4. Statistical treatment of experimental design of STEAM-DIC decontamination of spirulina.

Both operating parameters, total processing time and saturated steam pressure, have a positive influence on lowering the microbial load. The influence of processing time is the most significant because of its large range used during this study.
By observing the absolute level of the microbial load of mesophilic flora, one can note that different Steam-DIC products have less than 100 UFC/g product.
Finally, the Multi-Cycle DIC process used as low temperature drying (30°C), allowed to notably reducing the microbiological load.

3.3 Analysis of Multi-Cycle DIC decontamination

Analysis of Multi-Cycle DIC decontamination was studied in the case of skim milk powder on the two aspects of vegetative and spore impacts. The results obtained with progressive decompression $\Delta P/\Delta t$=50 kPa s^{-1} (Debs-Louka, 1999) demonstrated that decontamination ratio could improve versus temperature and time, but also versus the number of cycles. This impact was observed with spores as well as with vegetative forms. Overall, Multi-Cycle DIC decontaminating powder has an impact through the pressure drops because a possible explosion of such microorganism cells. Debs-Louka et al. (1999) observed such an explosion in the case of steam-explosion. In this operation, the decompression rate $\Delta P/\Delta t$ is presented as the principal factor since the system quickly evolves from an initial non-equilibrium thermodynamic state towards an equilibrium state very far from the starting situation.

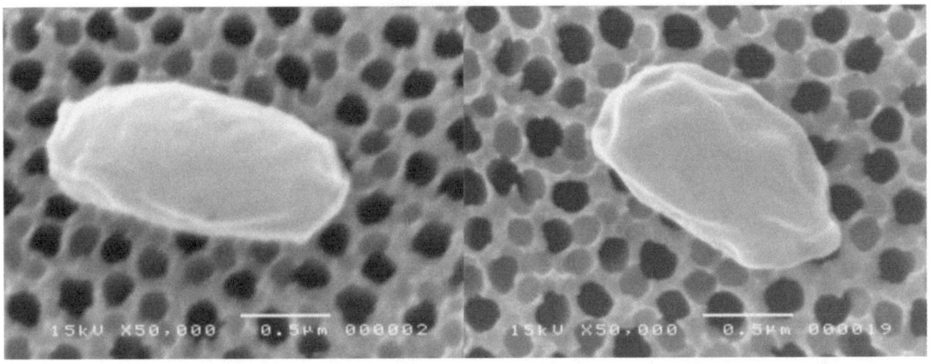

Fig. 5. Spores de Bacillus stearothermophilus: (a) untreated (b) treated at 130°C and 30 s

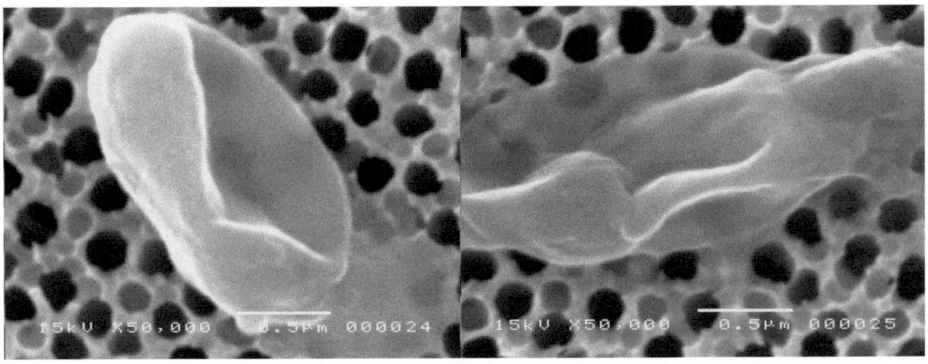

Fig. 6. Spores de Bacillus stearothermophilus treated by STEAM-DIC at 130°C and 30 s with instant pressure drop till vacuum at decompression $\Delta P/\Delta t$ = 3 MPa s^{-1} (Debs-Louka , 1999)

As experiments in this work were undertaken with an instant release of pressure ($\Delta P/\Delta t > 5$ MPa s^{-1}), from high temperature towards the equilibrium temperature of water/vapor at 5 kPa, the operation was carried out in the "explosion conditions" defined by Lin et al. (1991, 1992[a]). In the cases we adopted, only 0.2 s were necessary to reach the complete vacuum stage from 0.6 MPa ($\Delta P/\Delta t = 3$ MPa s^{-1}) in the processing vessel. No explosion effect was observed when we adopted the same treatment conditions but with 12 s as a decompression time ($\Delta P/\Delta t = 50$ kPa s^{-1}).
Statistical carried out on the results concerning the inhibition of vegetative form:

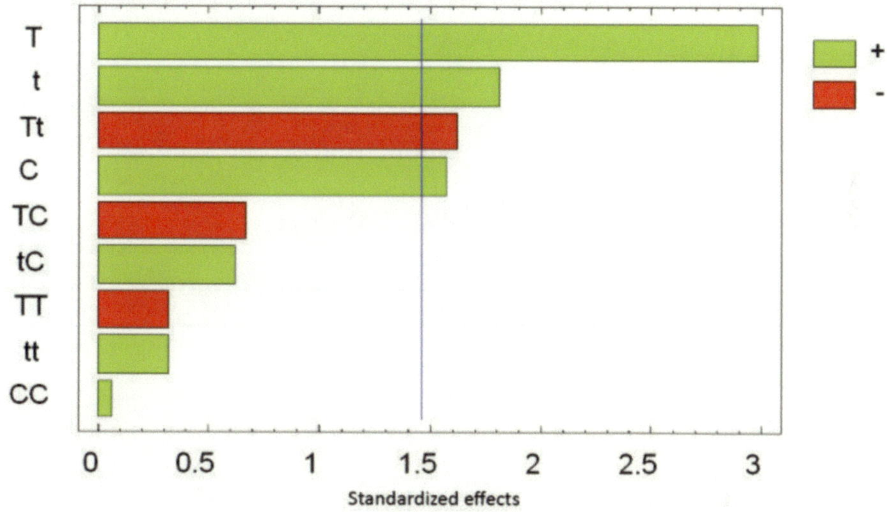

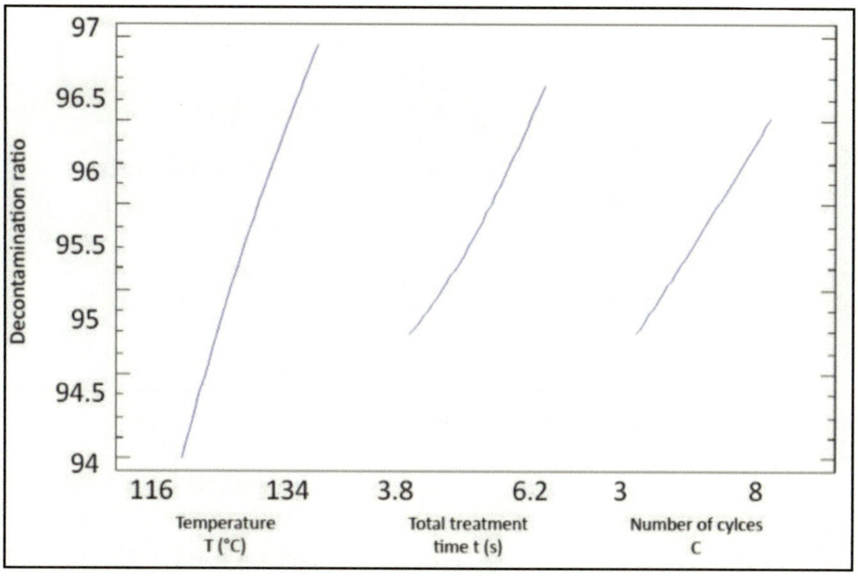

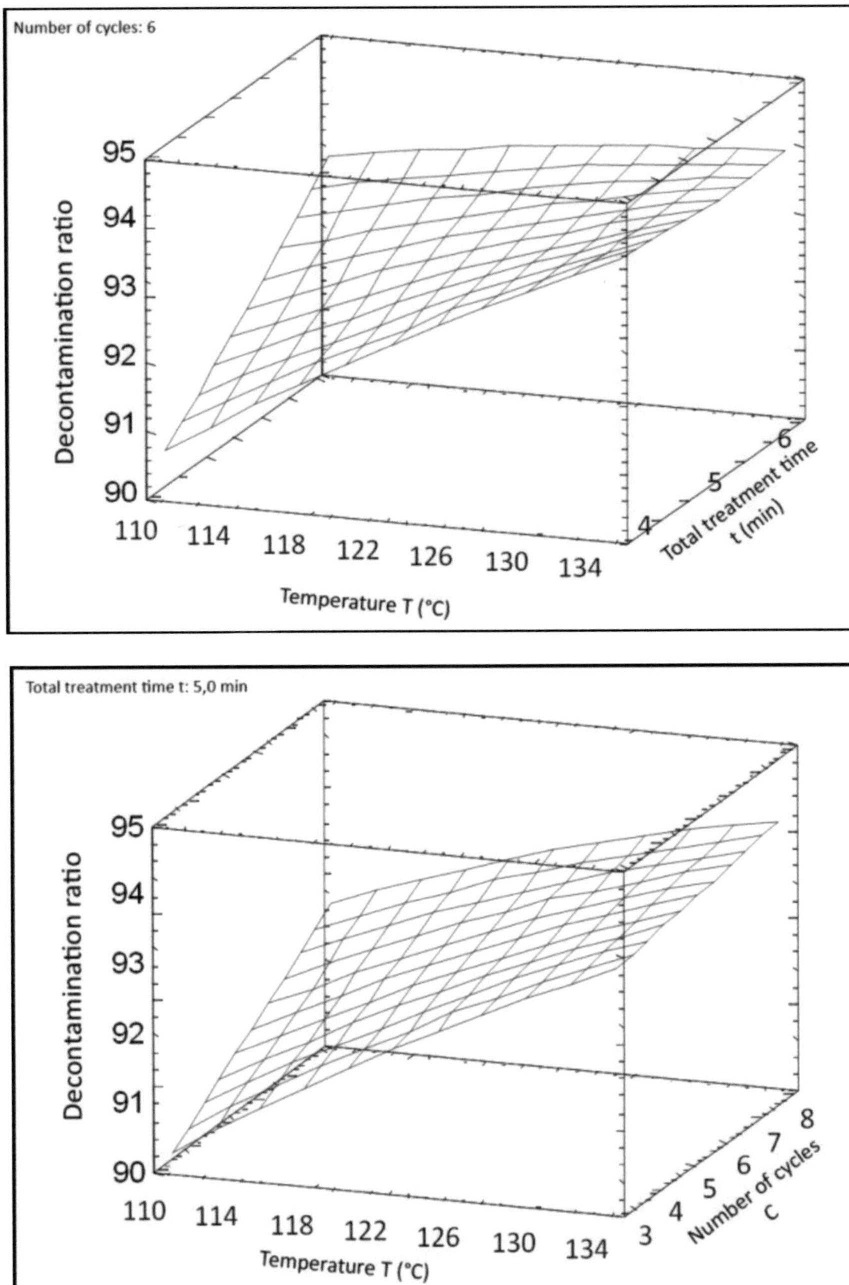

Fig. 7. Pareto Chart, trends of main effects and response surfaces of pressing temperature T (°C), total thermal treatment time t (s), and number of cycles C as Multi-Cycle DIC operating parameters from five-level central composite rotatable RSM experimental design in the case of ASR vegetative forms

In the case of Multi-Cycle DIC, the effects of various processing parameters on decontamination showed that the processing temperature was the most relevant parameter, whereas the total thermal treatment time (t) and the number of cycles (C) have non negligible impacts. It is worth noting that the higher T, t and C, the higher the direct Multi-Cycle DIC decontamination impact.

It was then possible to establish an empirical model of the MC-DIC decontamination ratio of ASR vegetative versus the DIC processing parameters. The R^2 value (R^2 = 60.2%) directly proved that such a study would have to be carried out with more precise experiment measurements.

$$Decontamination - ratio - of - vegetative - ASR = -806{,}293 + 8.07574T + 73.0524t + 13.716C - \\ - 0.0119666T^2 - 0{,}641782 * Tt - 0.131539TC + 0.666216t^2 + 0.907552tC + 0.0269125C^2$$

Each processing parameters has an effect, including the number of cycles C; this last coupled with temperature, and treatment time can define the highest decontamination rate. The specificity of C is due to its positive impact in terms of preservation of quality, whereas t and T normally imply an inevitable degradation.

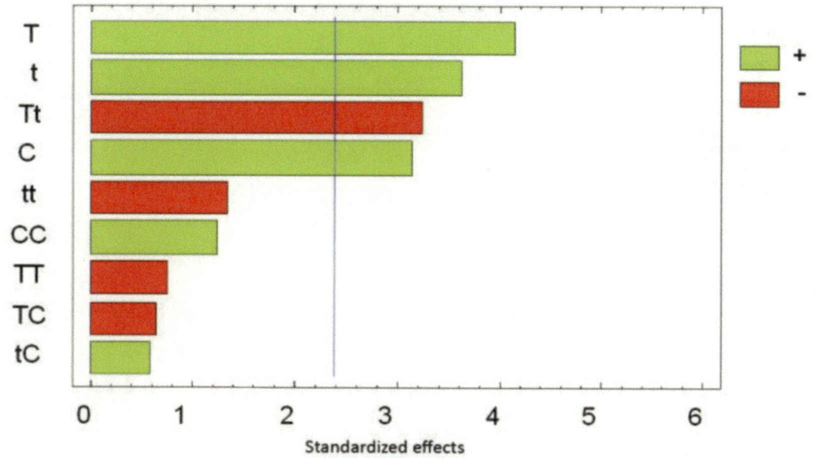

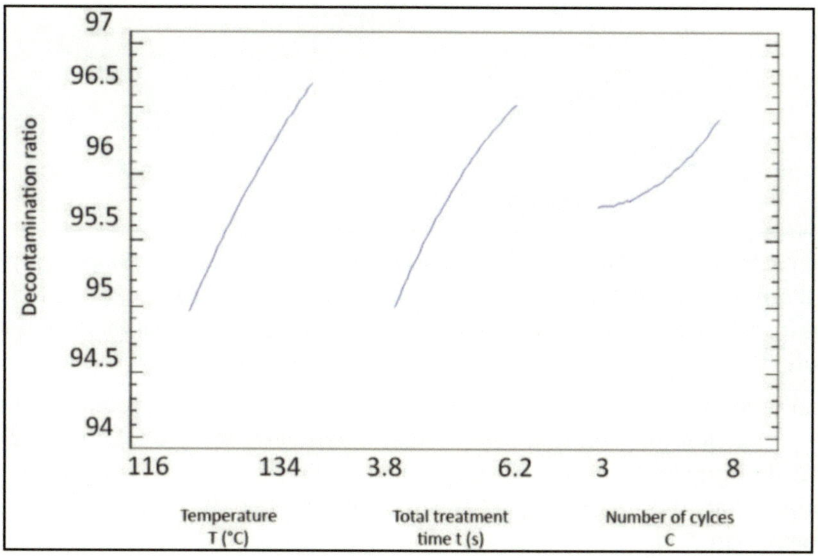

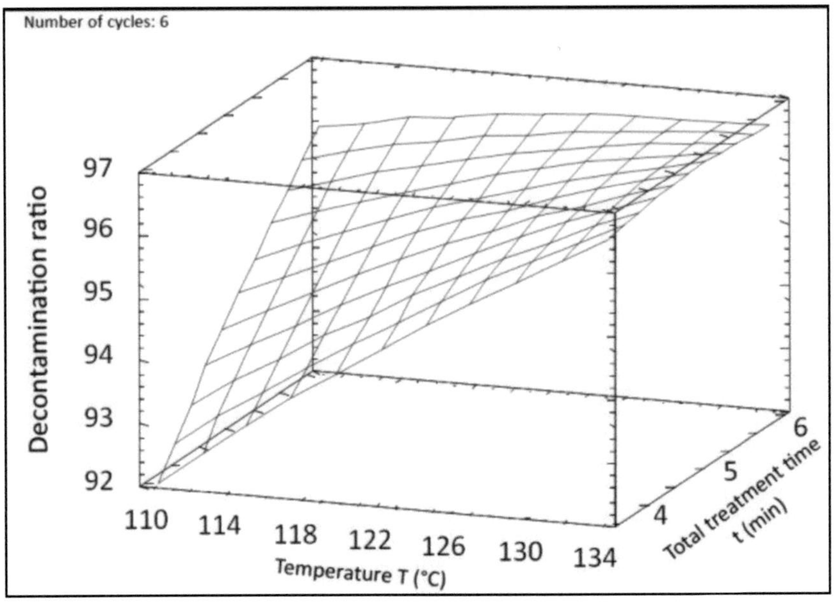

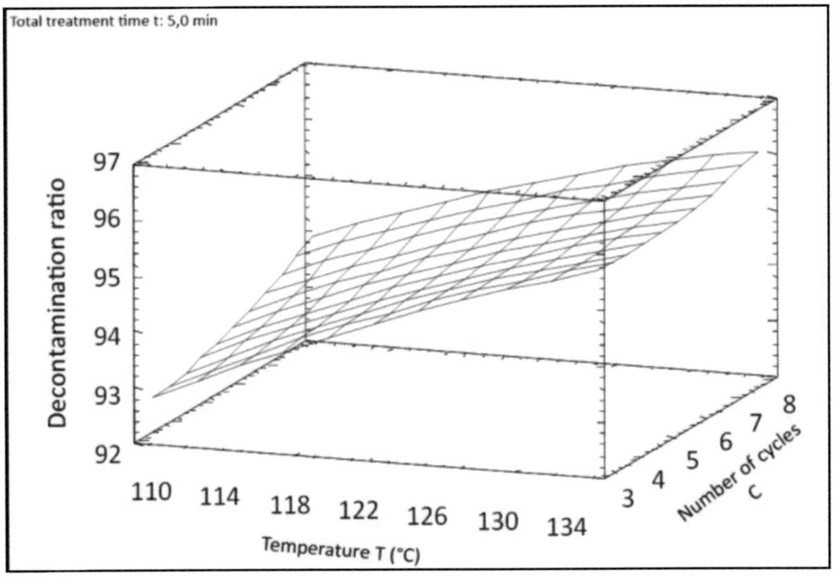

Fig. 8. Pareto Chart, trends of main effects and response surfaces of pressing temperature T (°C), total thermal treatment time t (s), and number of cycles C as Multi-Cycle DIC operating parameters from five-level central composite rotatable RSM experimental design in the case of ASR spores

With the aim to inhibit ASR spores, the results issued from various Multi-Cycle DIC processing parameters showed that the processing temperature, the total thermal treatment time (t) and the number of cycles (C) were all with non negligible impacts. Here too, it is worth noting that the higher T, t and C, the higher the direct Multi-Cycle DIC decontamination impact.

It was then possible to establish decontamination ratio of ASR vegetative versus the DIC processing parameters. The R^2 value (R^2 = 76.77%) of empirical model of the Multi-Cycle DIC directly proved the relatively good impact of such a model, however this study has to be carried out with more precise experiment measurements.

$$\text{Decontamination - ratio - of - spores - ASR} = 1365.23 + 13.4322T + 162.997t + 6{,}23863C - 0{,}023054T^2 - 1{,}09387Tt - 0{,}101794TC - 1.97197t^2 + 0{,}667969tC + 0{,}45166C^2$$

The impact of the number of cycles C as processing parameter has a specific impact because this parameter would normally have positive effect or no impact on preservation of quality, whereas t and T normally imply an inevitable degradation.

4. Conclusion

The aim of this work was to study and define more precisely the instant controlled pressure-drop DIC technology as a very relevant decontamination process which has been used since twenty years for inhibiting spores and vegetative forms more specifically in the cases of thermally sensitive dried solids and powders. The two versions of one-cycle saturated-steam (STEAM-DIC) and Multi-cycle air DIC used in this work were both relevant in the cases of thermal sensitive products (seaweed, microalgae, skim powder…). The coupled mechanical and thermal impacts allowed us to obtain high decontamination levels, differently and relevantly defined in order to perfectly master the final product quality. DIC technology as an innovative technique has been designed and developed at industrial scale by ABCAR-DIC Process more especially for decontamination of various products such as seaweeds, herbs, mushroom... and different industrial sectors. DIC reactors are currently operating at laboratory, semi-industrial and industrial fields. Thus, there are several models of infrastructure with features and abilities. (Besombes et al. 2010) could calculate the energy consumption to be 0.110 kWh per kg and per cycle.

5. References

Al Haddad, M., Mounir, S., Sobolik, V. & Allaf K.(2008). Fruits and vegetables drying combining hot air, DIC technology and microwaves. *IJFE International Journal of Food Engineering*, Vol. 4, Issue 6, Article 9.

Allaf, K., Debs-Louka,E., Louka, N., Cochet, N. & Abraham, G. (1994). *Procédé de réduction ou d'élimination d'organismes ou micro-organismes, de pasteurisation et/ou de stérilisation et installation pour la mise en œuvre d'un tel procédé*. Demande de French Patent n° 94/14832 du 09/12/1994.

Allaf, K., Cioffi, F., Rezzoug, S., Contento, M.P., Louka, N. & Sanya, E. (1997). *Procédé de traitement en vue de sécher, conserver, préserver, restaurer ou consolider le bois naturel, détérioré ou gorgé d'eau, et installation pour la mise en œuvre d'un tel procédé*. Brevet français issu de la demande FR n°97/14513 en date du 19/11/97.

Allaf, K., Debs-Louka, E., Louka, N. & Abraham, G. (1998). *Procédé de réduction ou d'élimination d'organismes, de microorganismes, de pasteurisation et de stérilisation des produits solides en morceaux ou pulvérulents et installation pour la mise en œuvre d'un tel procédé*. Demande de Brevet français N°98/02032 du 19/02/98.

Allaf, K., Louka, N., Bouvier, J. M., Parent, F. & Forget M. (1993).*Procédé de traitement de produits biologiques et installation pour la mise en œuvre d'un tel procédé*. Brevet français issu de la demande n° FR 93/09728 du 6 Août 1993 - délivré le 13/10/95 et publié sous le n° F2708419 en date du 10/02/95.

Allaf, K., Louka, N., Maache-Rezzoug, Z., Rezzoug, S.-A., Debs-Louka, E., Habba, A. & G. Abraham. (1999). *Procédé de traitement thermique, thermo-mécanique, hydro-thermique et hydro-thermo-mécanique de produits divers solides ou pulvérulents, pâteux, liquides ou mélange de liquides, applications de ce procédé et installation pour la mise en œuvre de ce procédé*. Brevet français issu de la demande N° FR 98/11106 du 04/09/98 sous priorité de la demande française N° 98/02032 du 19/02/98 publiée le 20 Août 1999 sous le n° 2 774 911.

Alpas, H., Kalchayanand, N., Bozoglu, F. & Ray, B. (1998). Interaction of pressure, time and temperature of pressurization on viability loss of Listeria innocua. *World Journal of Microbiology & Biotechnology*, Vol. 14, (251–253).

Besombes, C. Berka-Zougali, B. Allaf, K. 2010. Instant Controlled Pressure Drop Extraction of Lavandin Essential Oils: Fundamentals and Experimental studies. *Journal of Chromatography A*, Volume 1217, Issue 44, 29 October 2010, Pages 6807-6815.

Broadbent, J. R. & Lin, C. (1999). Effect of Heat Shock or Cold Shock Treatment on the Resistance of *Lactococcus lactis* to Freezing and Lyophilization. *Cryobiology*, Vol. 39, (88–102).

CAC (2003). *Codex general standard for irradiated foods*. CODEX STAN 106–1983, Rev. 1-2003.

Chang, C.-H., Chiang, M.-L. & Chou, C.-C. (2009). The effect of temperature and length of heat shock treatment on the thermal tolerance and cell leakage of *Cronobacter sakazakii* BCRC 13988. *International Journal of Food Microbiology*, Vol. 134, (184–189).

Cheftel, J.C. (1995). Review: High-pressure, microbial inactivation and food preservation. *Food Science and Technology International*, Vol. 1, (75–90).

Chung, Y.K. & Yousef, A.E. (2008). Inactivation of barotolerant strains of *Listeria monocytogenes* and *Escherichia coli* O157:H7 by ultra high pressure and tertbutylhydroquinone combination. *Journal of Microbiology*, Vol. 46, (289–294).

Chwla, S. P., Kim, D. H., Jo, C., Lee, J. W., Song, H. P., & Byun, M. W. (2003). Effect of γ irradiation on the survival of pathogens in Kwamegi, a traditional Korean semidried sea food. *Journal of Food Protection*, Vol. 66, No 11, (2093–2096).

Considine, K.M., Kelly, A.L., Fitzgerald, G.F., Hill, C. & Sleator, R.D. (2008). High-pressure processing – effects on microbial food safety and food quality. *Fems Microbiology Letters*, Vol. 281, (1–9).

Debs-Louka, E. (2000). *Microorganisms destruction by controlled thermal mechanical process in solid or powdery products. Application on spices and aromatic herbs* . Ph Dissertation. Université de La Rochelle.

Debs-Louka, E., Louka, N., Abraham, G., Chabot, V. & Allaf, K. (1999). Effect of Compressed Carbon Dioxide on Microbial Cell Viability. *Applied and environmental microbiology*, Vol. 65, No. 2, (626–631).

Duong Thai, C. (2003). *Etude de l'application du procédé hydro-thermique dans le traitement de différents types de riz : procédé d'étuvage et micro-expansion par détente instantanée contrôlée et impact sur les propriétés fonctionnelles*. Ph Dissertation. Université de La Rochelle.

Fan, X., Niemira, B. A., & Sokorai, K. J. B. (2003). Sensorial, nutritional and microbiological quality of fresh cilantro leaves as influenced by ionizing radiation and storage. *Food Research International*, Vol. 36, (713–719).

FDA (2005). *Irradiation in the production, processing and handling of food.* Federal Register, 70(157), 48057–48073.

Fu, J., Shen, W., Bao, J., & Chen, Q. (2000). The decontamination effects of γ irradiation on the edible gelatin. *Radiation Physics and Chemistry*, Vol. 57, (345–348).

Heinz, V. & Knorr, D. (2005). High pressure assisted heating as a method for sterilizing foods. In: Barbosa-Cánovas, G.V., Tapia, M.S., Cano, M.P., Belloso, O.M. & Martinez, A. (Eds.), *Novel food processing technologies*. Marcel Dekker, New York, USA.

Hill, C., Cotter, P.D., Sleator, R.D. & Gahan, C.G.M. (2002). Bacterial stress response in *Listeria monocytogenes*: jumping the hurdles imposed by minimal processing. *International Dairy Journal,* Vol. 12, (273–283).

Hoover, D.G., Metrick, C., Papineau, A.M., Farkas, D.F. & Knorr, D. (1989). Biological effects of high hydrostatic pressure on food microorganisms. *Food Technology,* Vol. 43, (99–107).

Hope, E. W. (1901). Sterilisation and pasteurisation v. tubercle-free herds, & c. *The Lancet,* Vol. 158, Issue 4065, (July 1901), (197-198).

Jo, C., Kim, D. H., Shin, M. G., Kang, I. J. & Byun, M. W. (2003). Irradiation effect on bulgogi sauce for making commercial Korean traditional meat product, bulgogi. *Radiation Physics and Chemistry*, Vol. 68, (851–856).

Kim, S. R., Rhee, M. S., Kim, B. C., Lee, H. & Kim, K. H. (2007). Modeling of the inactivation of Salmonella typhimurium by supercritical carbon dioxide in physiological saline and phosphate-buffered saline. *Journal of Microbiological Methods*, Vol. 70, (131–141).

Lacroix, M. & Quattara, B. (2000). Combined industrial processes with irradiation to assure innocuity and preservation of food products - a review. *Food Research International,* Vol. 33, (719–724).

Lewis, M.J. & Heppell, N. (2000). *Continuous thermal processing of foods – Pasteurization and UHT Sterilization* , Aspen Food Engineering Series, Maryland, USA, ISBN 0-8342-1259-5.

Lin, Y.-D. & Chou C.-H. (2004). Effect of heat shock on thermal tolerance and susceptibility of *Listeria monocytogenes* to other environmental stresses. *Food Microbiology,* Vol. 21, (605–610).

Lou, Y.Q. & Yousef, A.E. (1997). Adaptation to sublethal environmental stresses protects *Listeria monocytogenes* against lethal preservation factors. *Applied and Environmental Microbiology,* Vol. 63, (1252–1255).

Mahrour, A., Caillet, S., Nketsa-Tabiri, J., & Lacroix, M. (2003). Microbial and sensory quality of marinated and irradiated chicken. *Journal of Food Protection,* Vol. 66, No 11, (2156–2159).

Molins, R. A. (Ed.). (2001). *Food irradiation principles and applications.* New York: Wiley-Interscience.

Molins, R.A., Motarjemi, Y. & Käferstein, F.K. (2001). Irradiation : a critical control point in ensuring the microbiological safety of raw foods. *Food Control,* Vol. 12, (347-356).

Nevarez, L., Vasseur, V., Debaets, S., Barbier, & G. (2010). Use of response surface methodology to optimise environmental stress conditions on *Penicillium glabrum*, a food spoilage mould. *Fungal biology,* Vol. 114, (490-497).

Rajkovic, A., Smigic, N., Uyttendaele, M., Medic, H., De Zutter, L., Devlieghere, F. (2009). Resistance of *Listeria monocytogenes, Escherichia coli* O157 :H7 and *Campylobacter jejuni* after exposure to repetitive cycles of mild bactericidal treatments. *Food microbiology*, Vol. 26, (889-895).

Rowan, N.J. (1999). Evidence that inimical food-preservationbarriers altermicrobial resistance, cell morphology and virulence. *Trends in Food Science & Technology*, Vol. 10, (261–270).

Thomas, J., Senthilkumar, R.S., Raj Kumar, R., Mandal, A.K.A. & Muraleedharan N. Induction of gamma irradiation for decontamination and to increase the storage stability of black teas. *Food Chemistry*, Vol. 106, Issue 1, (January 2008), (180-184).

WHO (1981). *Wholesomeness of irradiated food*: report of a Joint FAO/ IAEA/WHO expert committee. In World Health Organization technical report series 659 (pp. 36). Geneva, Switzerland: World Health Organization.

WHO (1988). Food irradiation - a technique for preserving and improving the safety of food. Geneva, Switzerland: World Health Organization.

Yaldagard, M., Mortazavi, S.A. & Tabatabaie, F. (2008). The principles of ultra high pressure technology and its application in food processing/preservation: a review of microbiological and quality aspects. *African Journal of Biotechnology*, Vol. 7, (2739–2767).

Zhang, H. & Mittal, G.S. (2008). Effects of high-pressure processing (HPP) on bacterial spores: an overview. *Food Reviews International*, Vol. 24, (330–351).

Part 3

Electrical Engineering and Applications

14

Dynamic Analysis of a DC-DC Multiplier Converter

J. C. Mayo-Maldonado, R. Salas-Cabrera, J. C. Rosas-Caro, H. Cisneros-Villegas, M. Gomez-Garcia, E. N.Salas-Cabrera, R. Castillo-Gutierrez and O. Ruiz-Martinez
Instituto Tecnologico de Ciudad Madero
Ciudad Madero, Mexico

1. Introduction

Renewable energy generation systems bring the promise of providing green energy which is highly desirable for decreasing global warming. Therefore, renewable energy systems are gaining attention among researchers.

In terms of power electronics, several challenges are emerging with the advent of the green energy generation systems. The first issue is that renewable energy power sources such as Photo-Voltaic PV panels, fuel cells and some wind turbine generators provide a low level dc voltage. This voltage must be boosted and then inverted in order to be connected to the grid. Since the level of the output voltage of these power sources depends on the weather conditions, there should be a method to control the generated voltage.

Other types of green energy power sources such as AC machine based wind generators provide a low level ac voltage with amplitude and frequency depending on the wind speed. A common method to deal with the generated ac voltaje is to rectify it, then a DC-DC converter is used to boost it. Once the boosted DC voltage is controlled, it may feed an electric load under some operating range or it may be inverted for connecting it to the grid.

This is a scenario of increased interest in DC-DC converters with high conversion ratios. Several converters have been proposed R. D. Middlebrook (1988), D. Maksimovic et al. (1991), B. Axelrod et al. (2008), Zhou Dongyan (1999), Leyva-Ramos J (et al 2009), however all of them are complex compared with conventional single-switch converters. Some desirable features of those converters are a high conversion ratio without the use of extreme duty cycles and a transformer-less topology that allows the use of high switching frequency providing high efficiency.

One of the recently proposed converters is the multiplier boost converter (MBC) which is also known as multilevel boost converter Rosas-Caro J.C. et al (2010), Rosas-Caro J.C. et al (2008), Rosas-Caro J.C. et al (2008), Mayo-Maldonado J.C. et al (2010). This topology combines the traditional single-switch boost converter with a Cockcroft-Walton voltage multiplier. Fig. 1 shows the Nx DC-DC Multiplier Boost Converter (Nx MBC). The nomenclature Nx is associated with the number of capacitors at the output of the converter. The main advantages of the MBC are (i) high voltage gain without the use of extreme duty cycles and transformer-less, (ii) self balancing, in other words the multiplier converter maintains the voltage of the capacitors at the output equal to each other, (iii) the structure is very simple and only one switch is required.

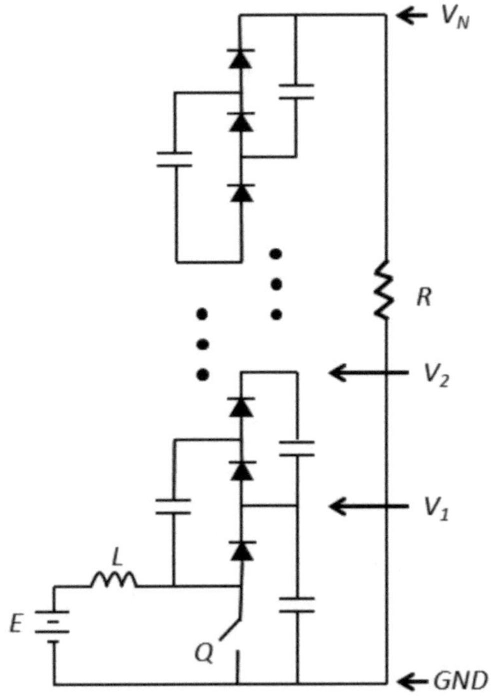

Nx MBC

Fig. 1. Electrical diagram of the Nx Multiplier Boost Converter.

There are several contributions in this paper. Since the MBC is a recently proposed topology its dynamic behavior has not been studied deeply. We propose both a full order nonlinear dynamic model and a reduced order nonlinear dynamic model for the MBC. In addition, a new controller for the MBC is obtained by utilizing the differential geometry theory, A. Isidori (1995). In particular, input-output feedback linearization is employed to control the inductor current. In our approach, the output voltage is indirectly controlled by defining a reference for the inductor current. The controller is derived by using the proposed reduced order model. The stability of the zero dynamics of the closed loop system is analyzed. Experimental results of the closed loop implementation are also presented.

Previous works present different models for other boost converters. In Morales-Saldana J.A. et al (2007), authors propose both nonlinear and average linear models for a quadratic boost converter. In Bo Yin et al. (2009), authors propose a single-input-single-output model for an AC-DC boost converter; the model is similar to the model of the conventional DC-DC boost converter.

Different control techniques for power electronics devices can be found in the literature. In Hebertt Sira-Ramirez et al. (2006), a wide series of control techniques are presented for well known power electronics converters, including the conventional DC-DC boost converter. In Leyva-Ramos J (et al 2009), authors present experimental results of the implementation of a current-mode control for the quadratic boost converter. In Gensior A. et al. (2009), authors present some current controllers for three-phase boost rectifiers.

2. Modeling of the DC-DC Multiplier Boost Converter

In this section we will be presenting both the full order nonlinear dynamic model and a reduced order nonlinear dynamic model for the MBC. The proposed models are obtained from the equivalent circuits depending on the commutation states of the converter. The derived reduced order model is able to define an approximate dynamics for the MBC containing any number of levels without modifying the order of the dynamic model. This feature provides several advantages for control design and implementation.

2.1 Full order modeling

Let us consider the electrical diagram in Fig. 2 that depicts a 2x MBC. This converter has 2 capacitors at the output (C_1 and C_2). For this particular converter the number N is equal to 2. In this section V_3 is a notation related to a voltage across a capacitor that is not at the output of the MBC. In addition, let us define an input $u = \{1, 0\}$ associated with the commutation states of the switch.

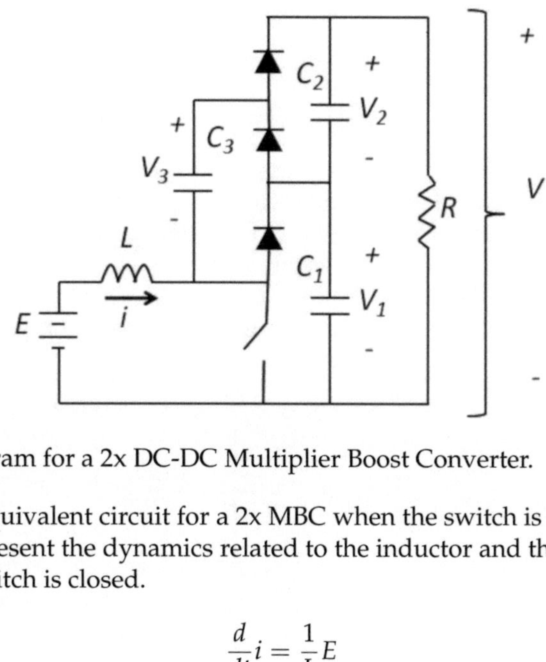

Fig. 2. Electrical diagram for a 2x DC-DC Multiplier Boost Converter.

Figure 3 shows the equivalent circuit for a 2x MBC when the switch is closed, this is $u = 1$. Equations (1)-(4) represent the dynamics related to the inductor and the $N+1$ capacitors of a 2x MBC when the switch is closed.

$$\frac{d}{dt}i = \frac{1}{L}E \tag{1}$$

$$\frac{d}{dt}V_1 = -\frac{1}{(C_1+C_3)R}V_1 - \frac{1}{(C_1+C_3)R}V_2 - \lambda_1(t) \tag{2}$$

$$\frac{d}{dt}V_2 = -\frac{1}{C_2R}V_1 - \frac{1}{C_2R}V_2 \tag{3}$$

$$\frac{d}{dt}V_3 = -\frac{1}{(C_1+C_3)R}V_1 - \frac{1}{(C_1+C_3)R}V_2 + \lambda_1(t) \tag{4}$$

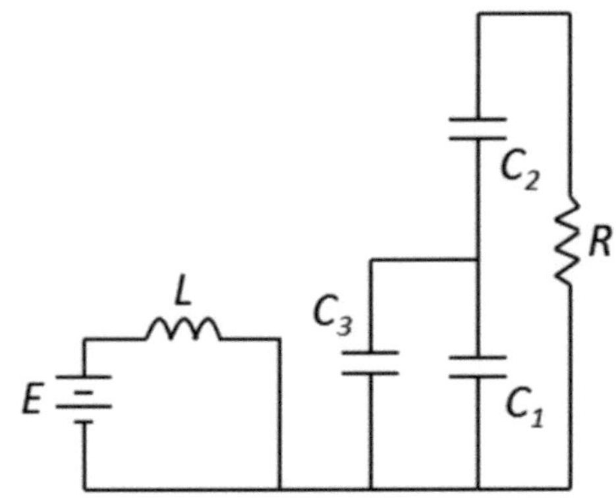

Fig. 3. Equivalent circuit for a 2x DC-DC Multiplier Boost Converter when the switch is closed.

In equation (2) and (4), function $\lambda_1(t)$ represents a very fast transient that occurs when capacitors C_1 and C_3 are connected in parallel (see Fig. 3). Function $\lambda_1(t)$ is given by the following equation

$$\lambda_1(t) = \frac{V_1 - V_3}{R_G C_1}$$

where R_G is a very small resistance. If it is assumed that the resistances of the diodes and capacitors are neglected then the value of R_G tends to be zero.
As voltages across capacitors C_1 and C_3 tend to be equal, the function $\lambda_1(t)$ approximates to zero. Therefore, $\lambda_1(t)$ defines the dynamics in which C_3 obtains energy from C_1 when the switch is closed. The rest of the terms of the state equations (1)-(4) produce slower transients. Figure 4 shows the equivalent circuit when the switch is opened, this is $u = 0$.

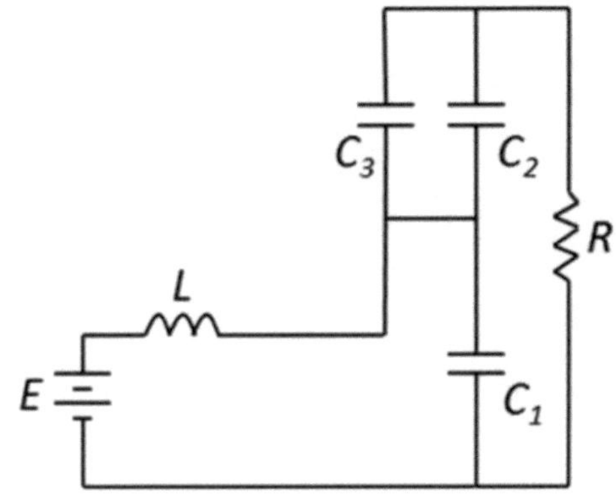

Fig. 4. Equivalent circuit for a 2x DC-DC Multiplier Boost Converter when the switch is opened.

Equations (5)-(8) represent the dynamics of the converter when the switch is opened.

$$\frac{d}{dt}i = -\frac{V_1}{L} + \frac{1}{L}E \tag{5}$$

$$\frac{d}{dt}V_1 = \frac{i}{C_1} - \frac{1}{C_1R}V_1 - \frac{1}{C_1R}V_2 \tag{6}$$

$$\frac{d}{dt}V_2 = -\frac{1}{(C_1+C_2)R}V_1 - \frac{1}{(C_1+C_2)R}V_2 + \lambda_2(t) \tag{7}$$

$$\frac{d}{dt}V_3 = -\frac{1}{(C_1+C_3)R}V_1 - \frac{1}{(C_1+C_3)R}V_2 - \lambda_2(t) \tag{8}$$

State equations associated with the voltages across capacitors C_2 and C_3 have a term denoted by $\lambda_2(t)$. This function defines a transient similar to the one defined by $\lambda_1(t)$ when capacitors C_1 and C_3 were connected in parallel. The function $\lambda_2(t)$ can be expressed as

$$\lambda_2(t) = \frac{V3 - V_2}{R_G C_3}$$

Therefore, when the switch is closed, C_3 obtains energy from C_1, this task is represented by $\lambda_1(t)$. On the other hand, when the switch is opened, C_3 transfers energy to C_2, this is represented by $\lambda_2(t)$. It is possible to conclude that capacitor C_3 works as the circuital vehicle that transports energy from capacitor C_1 to capacitor C_2. In general, there are always $N-1$ capacitors transferring energy to the capacitors at the output. Let us consider the inductor current as the output of the dynamic system, this is

$$h(x) = \begin{bmatrix}1 & 0 & 0 & 0\end{bmatrix}\begin{bmatrix}i & V_1 & V_2 & V_3\end{bmatrix}^T = i \tag{9}$$

The selection of this variable as an output will be explained as the controller is derived in Section 3. The full order nonlinear dynamic model is composed by state equations (1)-(8) and the output equation in (9). When more levels are added to the circuit (see Fig. 1), the number of equations increases as well, however the system has always the same circuital structure. It is clear that the dimension of the state space increases when more capacitors are added. However, it is possible to make use of the voltage balancing feature of the MBC and obtain a reduced order model. This model should be able to approximate the dynamics of the system having any number of levels..

2.2 Reduced order modeling

For the purpose of reducing the order of the system, let us consider Fig. 5 and Fig.6 They depict the equivalent circuits for a 2x MBC when $u = 1$, and $u = 0$. They correspond to Fig. 3 and Fig. 4, respectively.

By employing basic principles and setting $C = C_1 = C_2 = C_3$, the equivalent capacitors become $C_{eq1} = 2C$ and $C_{eq2} = C$. In addition, the voltage across each capacitor at the output will be considered as the output voltage divided by the number of levels at the output (V/N). This assumption is supported by the voltage balancing feature of the MBC which was firstly presented in Rosas-Caro J.C. et al (2008). In Mayo-Maldonado J.C. et al (2010), an example of the dynamic traces of the capacitors at the output is presented. In terms of equations we have

$$V_1 \cong V_2 \cong \frac{V}{2} \tag{10}$$

where V denotes the output voltage. If there is any number of levels we may write

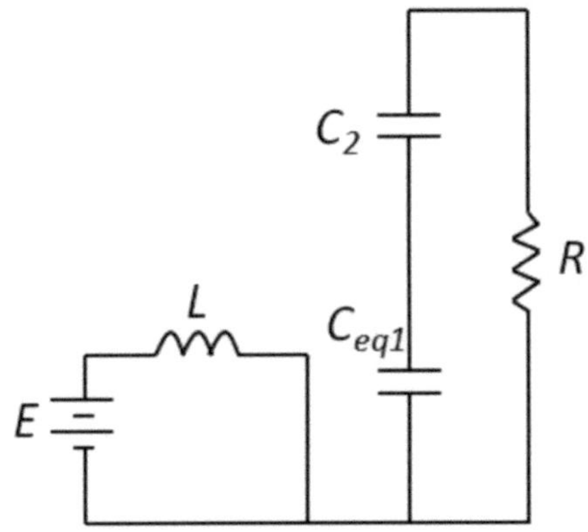

u=1

Fig. 5. Equivalent Circuit with u=1 and equivalent capacitances for the 2x MBC.

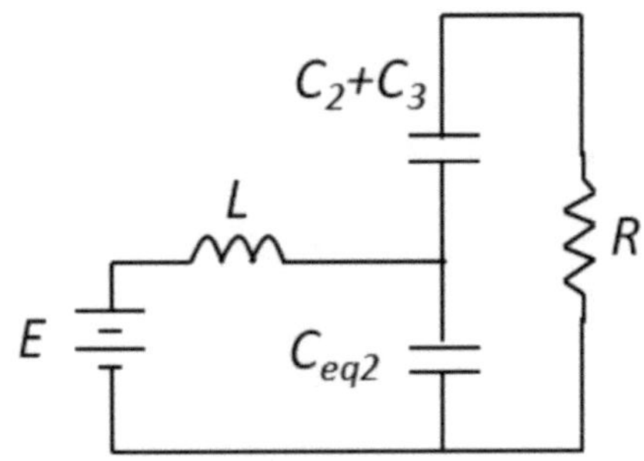

u=0

Fig. 6. Equivalent Circuit with u=0 and equivalent capacitances for the 2x MBC.

$$V_1 \cong V_2 \cong V_3 \cong ... \cong V_N \cong \frac{V}{N} \tag{11}$$

Employing the equivalent circuit shown in Fig. 5 and using equation (11) the dynamics for inductor current and the output voltage can be written as

$$L\frac{d}{dt}i = E \tag{12}$$

$$C_{eq1}\frac{d}{dt}V = -\frac{N}{R}V \tag{13}$$

It is clear that expressions (12)-(13) are valid when the switch is closed. On the other hand, based on the equivalent circuit in Fig. 6 and using equation (11), the dynamics of the system is defined as

$$L\frac{d}{dt}i = -\frac{V}{N} + E \tag{14}$$

$$C_{eq2}\frac{d}{dt}V = i - \frac{N}{R}V \tag{15}$$

Equations (14)-(15) are valid when the switch is opened. Expressions (12)-(15) may be written into a more compact form that is valid for both commutation states $u = \{1, 0\}$. This is

$$L\frac{d}{dt}i = -(1-u)\frac{V}{N} + E \tag{16}$$

$$[C_{eq1}u + (1-u)C_{eq2}]\frac{d}{dt}V = (1-u)i - \frac{N}{R}V \tag{17}$$

Average models are frequently employed for defining average feedback control laws in power electronics converters, Hebertt Sira-Ramirez et al. (2006). These models represent average currents and voltages. From equations (16) and (17) and considering u_{av} as the average input, we may write

$$L\frac{d}{dt}i = -(1-u_{av})\frac{V}{N} + E \tag{18}$$

$$[C_{eq1}u_{av} + (1-u_{av})C_{eq2}]\frac{d}{dt}V = (1-u_{av})i - \frac{N}{R}V \tag{19}$$

where the average input denoted by u_{av} is actually the duty cycle of the switch. Let us denote the inductor current i as x_1, the output voltage V as x_2 and $C_{eq1}u_{av} + (1-u_{av})C_{eq2}$ as $C(t)$. This capacitance denoted by $C(t)$ may be considered as a time-varying parameter. Equations (18) and (19) now become

$$L\frac{d}{dt}x_1 = -\frac{x_2}{N} + \frac{x_2}{N}u_{av} + E \tag{20}$$

$$C(t)\frac{d}{dt}x_2 = x_1 - x_1u_{av} - \frac{Nx_2}{R} \tag{21}$$

Using equations (20) and (21) and employing the inductor current as the output to be controlled, the reduced order nonlinear dynamic model for the MBC may be expressed as

$$\frac{d}{dt}x = f(x) + g(x)u_{av}$$

$$y = h(x) \tag{22}$$

where

$$f(x) = \begin{bmatrix} -\frac{x_2}{NL} + \frac{E}{L} \\ \frac{x_1}{C(t)} - \frac{Nx_2}{RC(t)} \end{bmatrix}; g(x) = \begin{bmatrix} \frac{x_2}{NL} \\ -\frac{x_1}{C(t)} \end{bmatrix}$$

$$h(x) = x_1; x = \begin{bmatrix} x_1 & x_2 \end{bmatrix}^T$$

Equation (22) represents the reduced order average nonlinear dynamic model for the Nx MBC containing an arbitrary number of levels. Figures 7 and 8 show the comparison between the full order model and the reduced order model. These simulations are performed for the 2x MBC. The simulation of the full order model is carried out using the Synopsys Saber software and employing the electrical diagram of the 2x MBC, while the simulation of the reduced order model is obtained by using the MATLAB software to solve equation (22). The parameters involved in this simulation are $L = 250\,\mu$H, $C = C_1 = C_2 = C_3 = 220\,\mu$F, $N = 2$, $E = 40$ volts, $R = 50\,\Omega$, and $u_{av} = 0.6$.

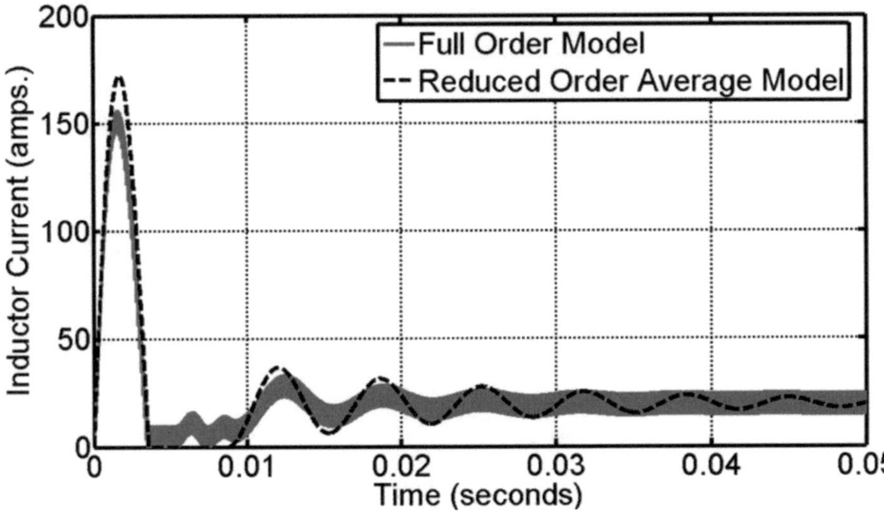

Fig. 7. Comparison between the reduced order average model and the full order model for the 2x MBC.

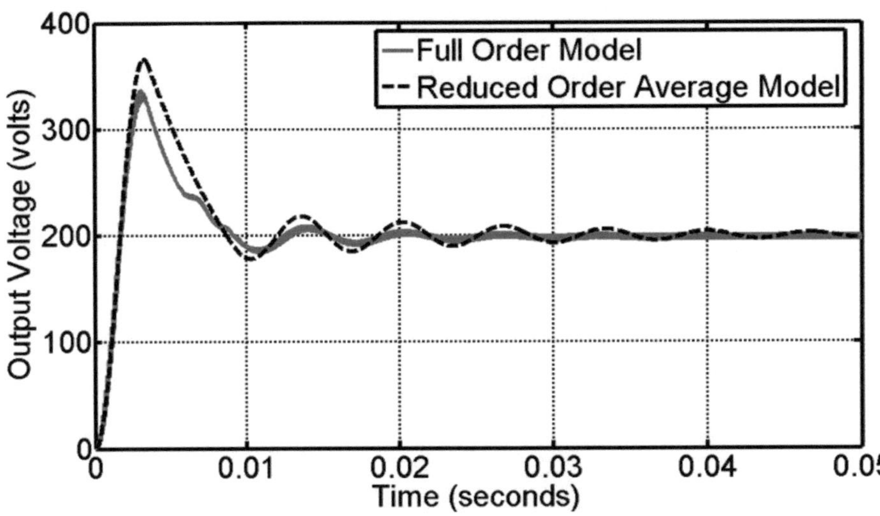

Fig. 8. Comparison between the reduced order average model and the full order model for the 2x MBC.

3. Control law

In this section, a controller based on the input-output feedback linearization theory, A. Isidori (1995), is defined for a MBC having an arbitrary number of levels N. This controller is derived by utilizing the reduced order model in (22) . Employing the input-output feedback linearization technique, the following input can be considered

$$u_{av} = \frac{1}{L_g L_f^{r-1} h(x)} [-L_f^r h(x) + v]$$

Where r is the relative degree of the system, A. Isidori (1995), and it is obtained from

$$L_g L_f^{i-1} h(x) = 0; i = 1, 2, ..., r-1.$$

$$L_g L_f^{r-1} h(x) \neq 0$$

since

$$L_g h(x) = \frac{\partial h(x)}{\partial x} g(x) = \begin{bmatrix} 1 & 0 \end{bmatrix} \begin{bmatrix} \frac{x_2}{NL} \\ -\frac{x_1}{C(t)} \end{bmatrix} = \frac{x_2}{NL} \neq 0$$

system in (22) has a relative degree equal to 1 providing that $x_2 \neq 0$. Therefore, the input may be written as, A. Isidori (1995),

$$u_{av} = \frac{v - L_f h(x)}{L_g h(x)} \tag{23}$$

where

$$L_f h(x) = \frac{\partial h(x)}{\partial x} f(x) = -\frac{x_2}{NL} + \frac{E}{L}$$

$$L_g h(x) = \frac{\partial h(x)}{\partial x} g(x) = \frac{x_2}{NL}$$

By substituting the input (23) into (22), the state equation corresponding to the inductor current x_1 is transformed into a linear form, this is

$$\frac{d}{dt} x_1 = v \tag{24}$$

In addition, parametric uncertainty will be addressed by using an integrator, this is

$$\frac{d}{dt} x_I = x_1 - i_{ref} \tag{25}$$

Then, a standard state feedback for the linear subsystem composed by (24)-(25) is defined as follow

$$v = -k_1 x_I - k_2 x_1 \tag{26}$$

In this particular case, the poles of the linear subsystem were proposed by considering a desired time constant for the closed loop system. The proposed poles are

$$s_{1,2} = \begin{bmatrix} -1500 & -1501 \end{bmatrix}$$

Employing the pole placement technique, Hebertt Sira-Ramirez et al. (2006), the following gains are calculated

$$\begin{bmatrix} k_1 & k_2 \end{bmatrix} = \begin{bmatrix} 2.2515x10^6 & 3001) \end{bmatrix}$$

It is clear that the stability of the equilibrium point associated with the subsystem defined by (24) and (25) is guaranteed by selecting adequate gains of the standard linear state feedback in (26). On the other hand, the stability of the equilibrium point of the subsystem defined by the second state equation in (22) may be verified by analyzing the zero dynamics of that subsystem, A. Isidori (1995). In order to analyze the zero dynamics, let us assume that $v = 0$ and $x_1(0) = i_ref = 0$. Under these conditions, it is clear that $x_1(t) = 0$ for all t. The input u_{av} can be rewritten now as

$$u_{av} = \frac{-L_f h(x)}{L_g h(x)} = \frac{\frac{x_2}{NL} - \frac{E}{L}}{\frac{x_2}{NL}} \tag{27}$$

Considering $x_1(t) = 0$ and using (27), the second equation in (22) now becomes

$$\frac{d}{dt}x_2 = -\frac{Nx_2}{RC(t)} \tag{28}$$

Let us consider the following Lyapunov function

$$V(x_2) = \frac{1}{2}x_2^2$$

its derivative is given by

$$\dot{V}(x_2) = x_2\left[-\frac{Nx_2}{RC(t)}\right] = -\frac{Nx_2^2}{RC(t)}$$

On the other hand, substituting C_{eq1} and C_{eq2} into the expression for $C(t)$, we obtain

$$C(t) = Cu_{av} + C$$

From a practical standpoint, the duty cycle is defined in the range $(0, 1)$. This is $0 < u_{av} < 1$. Therefore $C(t) > 0$. Since parameters N, R and $C(t)$ are strictly positive, the derivative $V(x_2)$ is negative definite. Therefore the zero dynamics of the MBC is stable at $x_2 = i_{ref}$.

4. Experimental results

As it was established earlier, the output voltage is indirectly controlled by defining a reference for the inductor current in terms of the desired output voltage. The expression that relates both variables is derived by carrying out a steady state analysis of the dynamic model in (22), i.e.

$$i_{ref} = \frac{V_{ref}^2}{RE} \tag{29}$$

where V_{ref} denotes the desired output voltage.

The implementation of the control law is carried out by employing RTAI-Lab, R. Bucher et al. (2008), as a Linux based real-time platform and a NI PCI-6024E data acquisition board. Fig. 9 depicts the Linux-based real time program of the implemented controller.

The parameters involved in the implementation are: $L = 250\,\mu H$, $C = C_1 = C_2 = C_3 = 222.2\,\mu F$, $N = 2$, $E = 30$ volts, $R = 230\,\Omega$ and $V_{ref} = 150$ volts.

Figure 10 shows the experimental and simulated traces of the output voltage. It is important to note that since power losses in some electronic devices (diodes, transistor) are not included in the model defined by (22), the actual experimental measured output voltage is slightly smaller than the desired one.

Another experiment was designed for the purpose of showing a DC-DC multiplier boost converter in a wind energy generation system. Figure 11 shows the diagram of the wind energy conversion system. In this case, we consider a resistance as an electric load that is

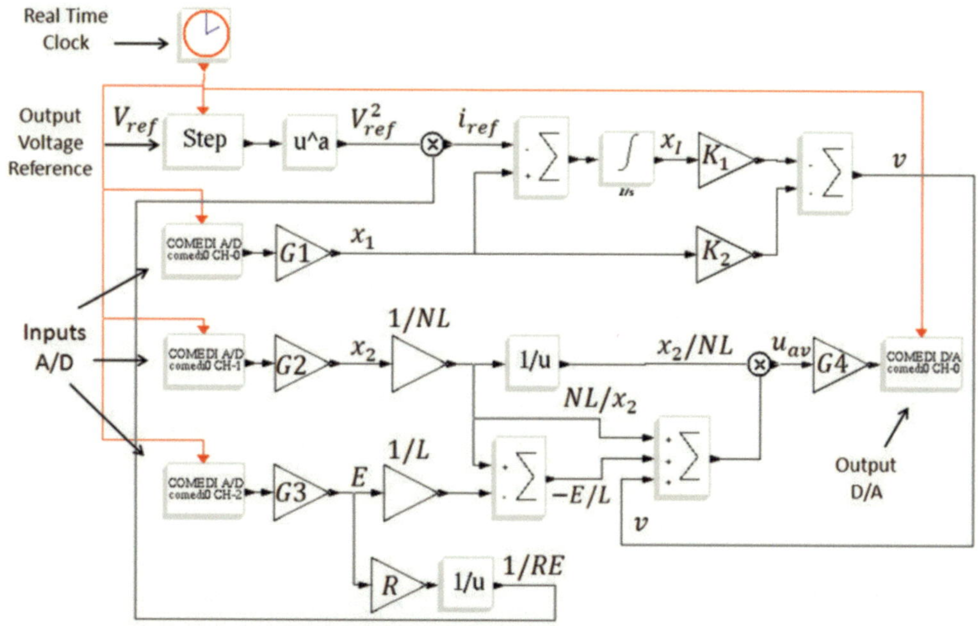

Fig. 9. Real time program of the implemented controller in RTAI-Lab.

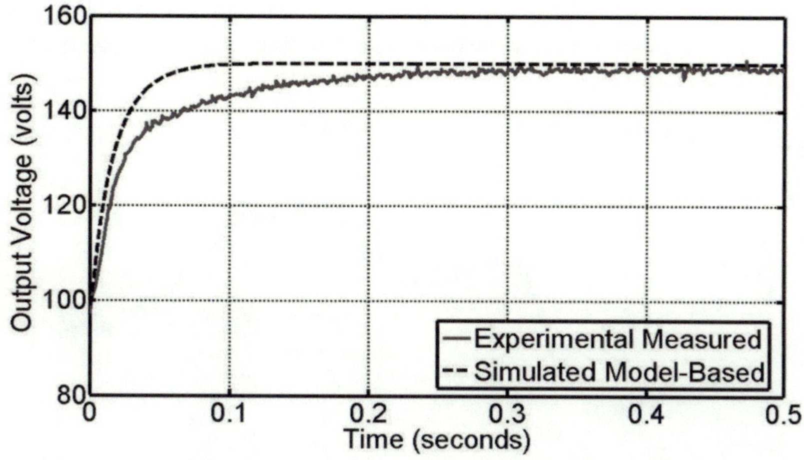

Fig. 10. Transient traces of the experimental measured and simulated model-based output voltage.

fed with a constant DC voltage. A variable speed wind turbine which is directly coupled to a permament magnet synchronous generator is employed. As the wind speed changes, the generator speed changes as well. The result is a variable amplitude and variable frequency output voltage. In order to deal with this situation, the AC voltage is rectified by employing a standard uncontrolled AC-DC converter. Then, for the purpose of providing a constant DC voltage at the load terminals, a Nx MBC is included. It is important to note that this application works for a particular operation range. In other words, if the wind speed reaches very low or very high levels, the wind turbine may show an unstable behavior. In order to avoid this situation, the electric load that is depicted in Fig. 11 may be replaced by a grid connected inverter. A feature of the grid connected inverter is that the energy extracted from the wind energy generation system can be defined depending on the wind speed.

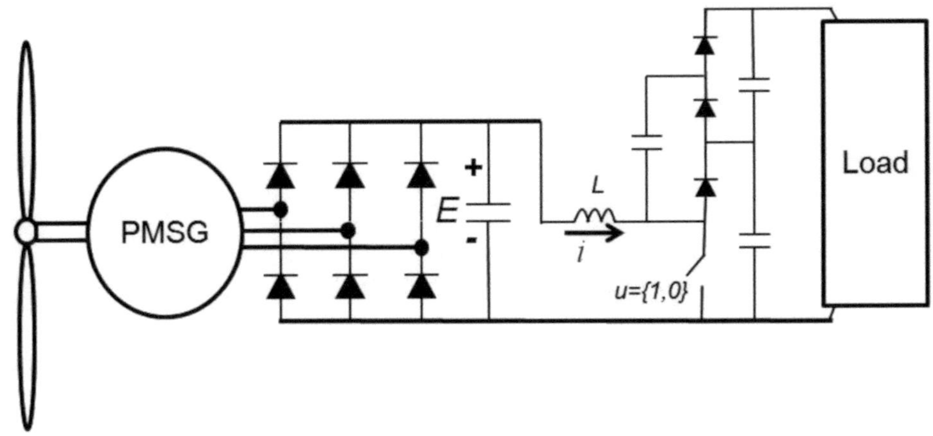

Fig. 11. Wind Energy Conversion System.

In the previous test the input voltage E is constant. In this new test, the input voltage E is varied as it is shown in Fig. 12. According to expression (29) the set point for the inductor current i_{ref} is calculated (in real time) as the input voltage E is varied. Figure 13 shows the experimental measured inductor current. The resulting experimental measured output voltage is depicted in Figure 14.

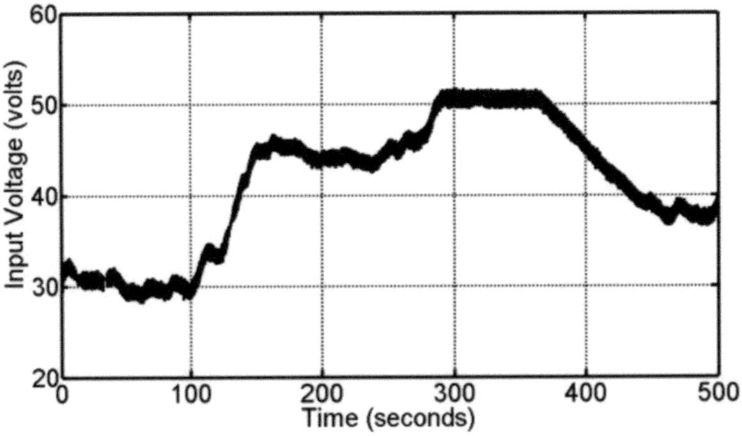

Fig. 12. Experimental input voltage E.

5. Conclusions

This work presents the state space modeling of a DC-DC Multiplier Boost Converter. Full and reduced order nonlinear models for the Nx MBC are proposed. A second order model is able to define an approximate dynamics for the Nx MBC having any number of levels. A

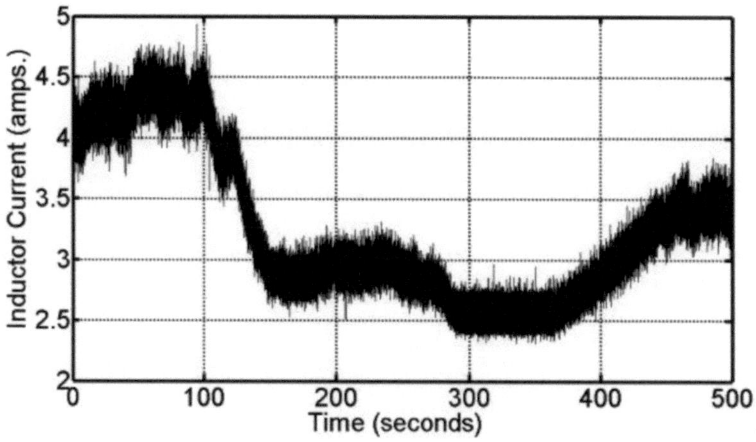

Fig. 13. Experimental inductor current when variations of the input voltage appear.

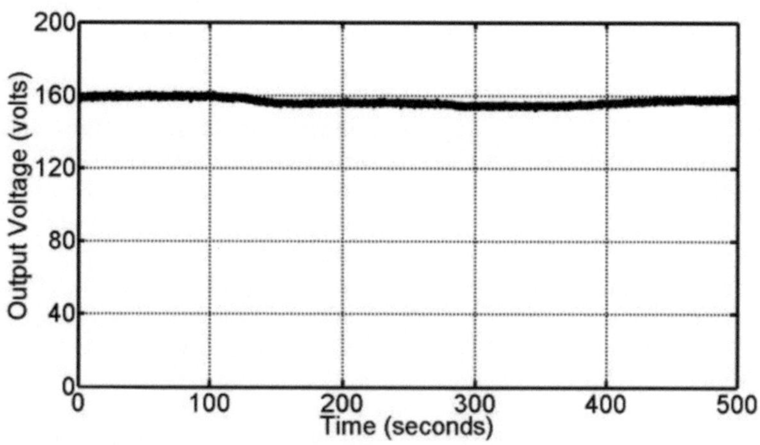

Fig. 14. Experimental measured output voltage when variations of the input voltage appear.

good agreement is obtained when comparing the full order and the reduced order models. In addition, the output voltage is indirectly controlled by using a control law based on the input-output feedback linearization technique. The controller is derived using the reduced order model of the Nx MBC. Excellent experimental results are shown for a 2x MBC. In future works, a controller for the Nx MBC having higher number of levels will be implemented by using the reduced order model derived in this paper.

6. References

R. D. Middlebrook, "Transformerless DC-to-DC converters with large conversion ratios". *IEEE Trans. Power Electronics*, vol. 3, Issue 4, pp. 484-488. Oct. 1988.

D. Maksimovic; S. Cuk, "Switching converters with wide DC conversion range". *IEEE Trans. Power Electronics*, vol. 6, Issue 1, pp. 151-157. Jan. 1991.

B. Axelrod; Y. Berkovich, A. Ioinovici, "Switched-Capacitor/Switched-Inductor Structures for Getting Transformerless Hybrid DC-DC PWM Converters". *IEEE Trans. Circuits and Systems I*, vol. 55, Issue 2, pp. 687-696, March 2008.

Zhou Dongyan, A. Pietkiewicz, S. Cuk, "A three-switch high-voltage converter". *IEEE Transactions on Power Electronics*, Volume 14, Issue 1, pp. 177-183. Jan. 1999.

Leyva-Ramos, J.; Ortiz-Lopez, M.G.; Diaz-Saldierna, L.H.; Morales-Saldana, J.A. "Switching regulator using a quadratic boost converter for wide DC conversion ratios". *IET Power Electronics*. vol. 2, Issue 5, pp. 605-613, Sept. 2009.

Rosas-Caro, J.C.; Ramirez, J.M.; Peng, F.Z.; Valderrabano, A.; , "A DC-DC multilevel boost converter," *Power Electronics, IET*, vol.3, no.1, pp.129-137, Jan. 2010.

Rosas-Caro, J.C.; Ramirez, J.M.; Garcia-Vite, P.M.; , "Novel DC-DC Multilevel Boost Converter," *Power Electronics Specialists Conference, 2008. PESC 2008. IEEE*, pp. 2146-2151, Jun. 2008.

Rosas-Caro, J.C.; Ramirez, J.M.; Valderrabano, A.; , "Voltage balancing in DC/DC multilevel boost converters," *Power Symposium, 2008. NAPS '08. 40th North American*. Sept. 2008.

Mayo-Maldonado J. C., Salas-Cabrera R., Cisneros-Villegas H., Gomez-Garcia M., Salas-Cabrera E. N., Castillo-Gutierrez R., Ruiz-Martinez O.; , "Modeling and Control of a DC-DC
Multilevel Boost Converter," *Proceedings of the World Congress on Engineering and Computer Science 2010*, Vol II, San Francisco, USA. Oct. 2010.

A. Isidori. Nonlinear Control Systems. *Springer*, 3rd edition, 1995.

Morales-Saldana, J.A.; Galarza-Quirino, R.; Leyva-Ramos, J.; Carbajal-Gutierrez, E.E.; Ortiz-Lopez, M.G.; , "Multiloop controller design for a quadratic boost converter," *Electric Power Applications, IET* , vol.1, no.3, pp.362-367, May 2007.

Bo Yin; Oruganti, R.; Panda, S.K.; Bhat, A.K.S.; , "A Simple Single-Input-Single-Output (SISO) Model for a Three-Phase PWM Rectifier," *Power Electronics, IEEE Transactions on*, vol.24, no.3, pp. 620-631, March 2009.

Hebertt Sira-Ramirez and Ramon Silva-Ortigoza. "Control Design Techniques in Power Electronics Devices". *Springer*. 2006.

Gensior, A.; Sira-Ramirez, H.; Rudolph, J.; Guldner, H.; , "On Some Nonlinear Current Controllers for Three-Phase Boost Rectifiers," *Industrial Electronics, IEEE Transactions on*, vol.56, no.2, pp. 360-370, Feb. 2009.

R. Bucher, S. Mannori and T. Netter. RTAI-Lab tutorial: Scilab, Comedi and real-time control. 2008.

15

Computation Time Efficient Models of DC-to-DC Converters for Multi-Domain Simulations

Johannes V. Gragger
AIT Austrian Institute of Technology GmbH, Mobility Department
Austria

1. Introduction

In this work power electronic models for DC-to-DC converters, suitable for multi-domain simulations, are presented. Loss calculations in complex electromechanical systems are the main application of the proposed models. Using the proposed power electronic models, the overall efficiency and energy consumption of complex electromechanical systems (e.g. in modern vehicle concepts) working in many different operation points can be simulated with reasonable efforts.
Energy balance is guaranteed and linear temperature dependence of on-resistances, knee voltages and switching losses is considered. Therefore, the modeling approach allows a consistent calculation of the energy flow (electrical, mechanical, thermal, etc.). A detailed outline of the analytical approach used for three DC-to-DC converter models is given. Buck (fig. 1), boost (fig. 2) and buck-boost converter models (fig. 3) with consideration of switching and conduction losses are described.

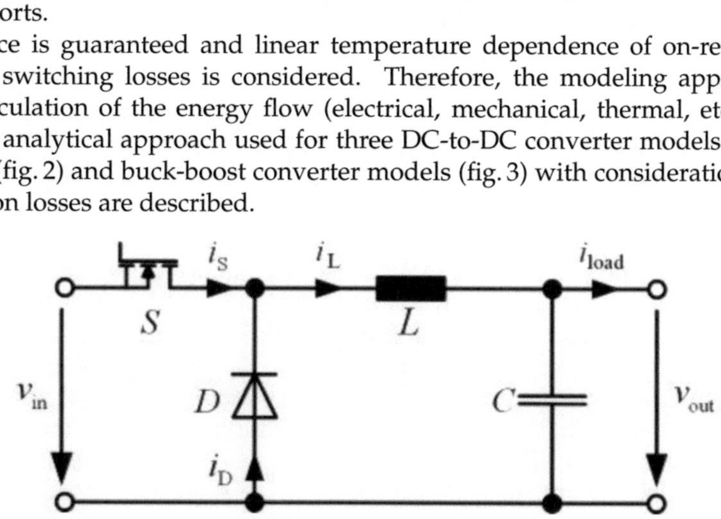

Fig. 1. Topology of a buck converter.

2. System design using multi-domain simulation

The development of complex electromechanical systems (e.g. systems in HEVs, EVs, processing plants, power stations, etc.) is very challenging because of the huge number of interacting components. When specifying the core components, the interactions of all components have to be taken into account. These interactions are difficult to overlook if the total number of components is high. In many cases such complex systems are verified through very cost intensive prototyping. For systems in processing plants, etc. the design

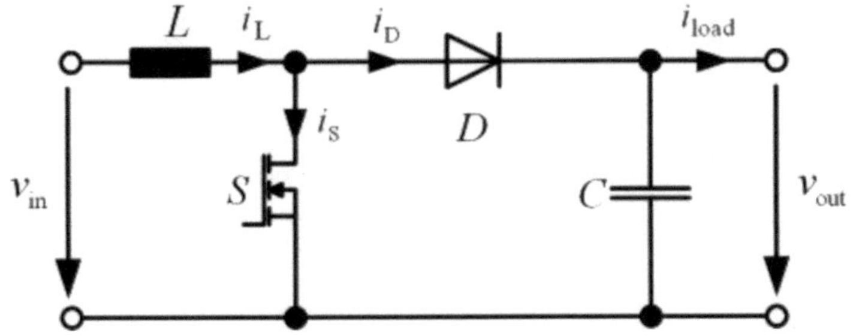

Fig. 2. Topology of a boost converter.

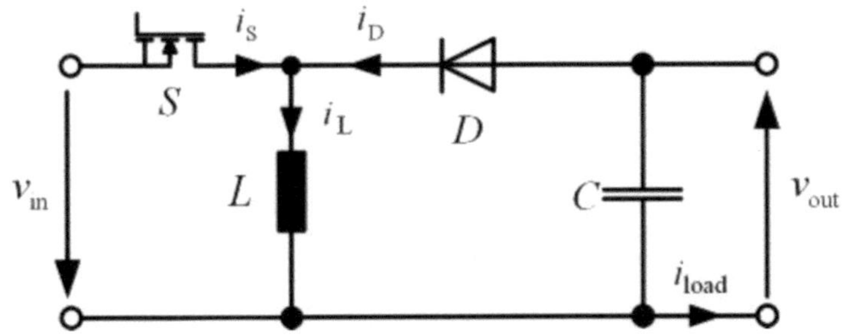

Fig. 3. Topology of a buck-boost converter.

verification is even more difficult. Utilizing computer aided design tools to improve the design process has become state-of-the-art. However, many of the simulation tools that are widely used in industry are specialized in the analysis of individual aspects of the development of electromechanical systems. Some of these aspects are control design, electric circuit design and thermodynamics. A simulation tool applicable for the support of the design process of electromechanical systems should allow the simulation engineer to choose which physical effects he or she wants to consider in the simulation. Therefore, a simulation tool utilizing an open programming standard is more desirable than a proprietary tool. In this work the practical implementation of the proposed power electronic models is done with Modelica using the Dymola software platform.
Figure 4 shows the simulation of a battery powered air conditioning system (for heavy duty vehicles) written in Modelica. The compressor is driven by an induction machine with an integrated inverter and a control system. In order to generate an appropriate DC-link voltage for the inverter, the battery voltage gets boosted by a two-stage boost converter. Mechanical, electrical and thermal effects are considered in the model as shown in fig. 4. It can be used for choosing the core components of the air conditioning system and for calculating the overall system efficiency of the electrical components.

3. Object oriented modeling with Modelica

All models presented in this work have been implemented using Modelica. Modelica is an open programming standard and supports object orientation and multi-domain modeling. In Fritzson (2004) is described how to utilize Modelica to create models of any kind of physical object or device that can be described by algebraic equations and ordinary differential equations. Typical examples for such physical objects are electric components such as resistors, inductors, capacitors, semiconductors, etc. and mechanical components such as

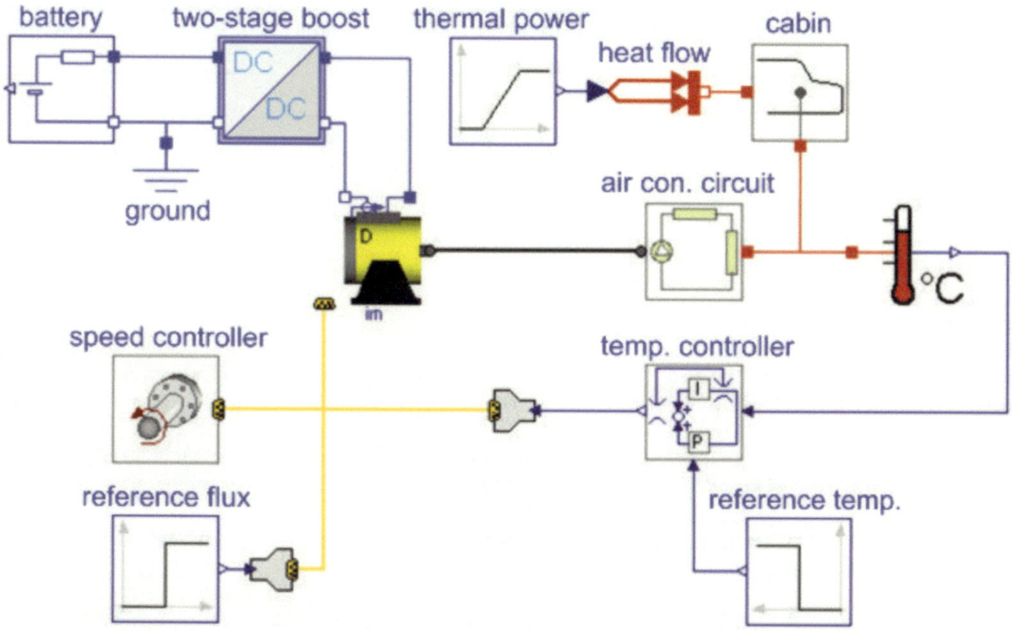

Fig. 4. Simulation of a battery powered air conditioning system for calculating the energy consumption.

masses, springs, inertias, etc. Once programmed, Modelica models can be connected to form more complex models in nested structures. Due to the principle of object orientation it is easy to change the level of detail in a model by simply exchanging certain elementary models. For example, in the simulation of an electric drive the inverter model calculating switching events can be easily replaced with an inverter model only considering averaged voltage and current signals and power balance between input and output, as shown in Gragger et al. (2006).
Multi-domain simulation models written in Modelica are platform independent and therefore can be simulated by using any software that provides suitable solvers for the mathematical system described in Modelica syntax.

4. Challenges of simulating power electronic components in multi-domain simulations

For the efficient utilization of multi-domain simulation software, it is of high importance to have fast simulation models of power electronic components on hand. Especially in simulations of electromechanical systems such as in fig. 4 it is crucial to limit the processing effort to a minimum. Many times such electromechanical systems contain power electronic subsystems such as rectifiers, inverters, DC-to-DC converters, balancing systems (for energy sources), etc. When simulating these power electronic devices together with the other electrical and mechanical components of the application, computing the quantities of the power electronic models requires a large share of the available processing power if switching events are calculated in the power electronic models. Simulation models including power electronic devices with switching frequencies around 100 kHz require at least four calculation points within simulation times of around 10 μs for calculating the switching events. However, if the energy flow in an electromechanical system has to be investigated by simulation, it is

Algorithm 1 Pseudo code of DC-to-DC converter models for calculating switching events in CICM.

```
Model:
BuckConverter, BoostConverter, BuckBoostConverter
Parameter:
L, C, R_S, R_L, R_D, V_D, f_s
Real variables:
v_in, v_out, i_S, i_L, i_D, i_load, t, d
Boolean variables:
s_control
Equations:
if (s_control = true),
consider equations corresponding to the equivalent circuit with the MOSFET in
conducting state and the freewheeling diode in blocking state
else
consider equations corresponding to the equivalent circuit with the MOSFET in
blocking state and the freewheeling diode in conducting state
```

not necessary to calculate the switching events in the power electronic model as long as the relevant losses are considered.

5. Conventional models calculating switching events

It is widely accepted that power electronic circuits can be modeled with semiconductor models, that have a discrete blocking state and a discrete conducting state. This means that the respective semiconductor model has a very large off-resistance, a very low on-resistance and a knee voltage, if applicable (e.g. in diodes and IGBTs). Such semiconductor models are implemented with if-clauses and change their state at every switching event. Consequently, the entire circuit changes whenever one or more semiconductors change their states. Many simulation tools calculate the behavior of power electronic circuits using this approach or a similar one. This causes a considerable processing effort. The pseudo code in alg. 1 can be used to implement models with discrete states of the circuits shown in fig. 1 – fig. 3. Usually switching losses are not considered in such models. However, the approach for the calculation of switching losses described in subsection 6.2 can also be applied to conventional models calculating switching events.

6. Averaged models with consideration of power balance

Converter models, built with the approach described in section 5, require a lot of processing time because the signal changes caused by switching events get calculated. If the calculation of switching events can be omitted the simulation time can be decreased significantly. Using the method of system averaging described by Cuk & Middlebrook (1978) it is possible to derive converter models without the calculation of switching events. In this work the general approach of system averaging is applied to the three DC-to-DC converter topologies shown in fig. 1 – fig. 3. For the calculation of the conduction losses in the averaged models presented in this work the ohmic contributions of the storage inductors R_L, the on-resistances of the MOSFETs R_S, and the on-resistances R_D and knee voltages V_D of the freewheeling diodes are considered. The presented models are valid for converter operation in continuous inductor current conduction mode (CICM).

6.1 Output voltage and conduction losses

In order to build an averaged model that considers power balance, a relation for the output voltage has to be found. For the buck converter the averaged output voltage can be found by

$$\begin{aligned}\overline{v}_{\mathtt{out,buck}} &= d(v_{\mathtt{in}} - \bar{i}_{\mathrm{L}} R_{\mathrm{S}} + \bar{i}_{\mathrm{L}} R_{\mathrm{D}} + V_{\mathrm{D}}) - \\ &- (\bar{i}_{\mathrm{L}} R_{\mathrm{L}} + \bar{i}_{\mathrm{L}} R_{\mathrm{D}} + V_{\mathrm{D}})\end{aligned} \tag{1}$$

whereas for the boost converter,

$$\begin{aligned}\overline{v}_{\mathtt{out,boost}} &= \frac{-v_{\mathtt{in}} + \bar{i}_{\mathrm{L}} R_{\mathrm{L}} + \bar{i}_{\mathrm{L}} R_{\mathrm{D}} + V_{\mathrm{D}}}{d-1} - \\ &- \frac{d(\bar{i}_{\mathrm{L}} R_{\mathrm{D}} + V_{\mathrm{D}} - \bar{i}_{\mathrm{L}} R_{\mathrm{S}})}{d-1}\end{aligned} \tag{2}$$

and for the buck-boost converter,

$$\begin{aligned}\overline{v}_{\mathtt{out,buck-boost}} &= \frac{\bar{i}_{\mathrm{L}} R_{\mathrm{D}} + V_{\mathrm{D}} + \bar{i}_{\mathrm{L}} R_{\mathrm{L}}}{d-1} - \\ &- \frac{d(v_{\mathtt{in}} - \bar{i}_{\mathrm{L}} R_{\mathrm{S}} + \bar{i}_{\mathrm{L}} R_{\mathrm{D}} + V_{\mathrm{D}})}{d-1}\end{aligned} \tag{3}$$

where $\overline{v}_{\mathtt{out}}$ is the average value of the output voltage, $v_{\mathtt{in}}$ stands for the input voltage, $\bar{i}_{\mathrm{L}}$ represents the average value of the inductor current, and d is the duty ratio of the converter. For calculating the conduction losses in the semiconductors and the storage inductors of the DC-to-DC converters a relation for the RMS values of the currents through the MOSFETs $I_{\mathrm{S},\mathtt{rms}}$, the freewheeling diodes $I_{\mathrm{D},\mathtt{rms}}$, and the storage inductors $I_{\mathrm{L},\mathtt{rms}}$ must be known. Assuming that the waveforms of the currents through the storage inductors are very close to a triangular shape (This is true for any of the presented DC-to-DC converter topologies designed with reasonable efficiency.) it is possible to derive

$$I_{\mathrm{S},\mathtt{rms}} = \sqrt{d\left[I_{\mathrm{L},\mathtt{min}}^2 + I_{\mathrm{L},\mathtt{min}}\Delta I_{\mathrm{L}} + \frac{\Delta I_{\mathrm{L}}^2}{3}\right]} \tag{4}$$

$$I_{\mathrm{D},\mathtt{rms}} = \sqrt{(1-d)\left[I_{\mathrm{L},\mathtt{max}}^2 - I_{\mathrm{L},\mathtt{max}}\Delta I_{\mathrm{L}} + \frac{\Delta I_{\mathrm{L}}^2}{3}\right]} \tag{5}$$

and

$$I_{\mathrm{L},\mathtt{rms}} = \sqrt{I_{\mathrm{S},\mathtt{rms}}^2 + I_{\mathrm{D},\mathtt{rms}}^2} \tag{6}$$

where

$$I_{\mathrm{L},\mathtt{min}} = \bar{i}_{\mathrm{L}} - \frac{\Delta I_{\mathrm{L}}}{2} \tag{7}$$

and

$$I_{\mathrm{L},\mathtt{max}} = \bar{i}_{\mathrm{L}} + \frac{\Delta I_{\mathrm{L}}}{2}. \tag{8}$$

(4) - (8) hold for all three described converter topologies. Though the relations for the averaged inductor current and the inductor current ripple depend on the converter topology. The averaged inductor current in the buck converter can be found by

$$\bar{i}_{\mathrm{L,buck}} = \bar{i}_{\mathtt{load}} \tag{9}$$

whereas in the boost converter

$$\bar{i}_{\mathrm{L,boost}} = \frac{\bar{i}_{\mathtt{load}}}{1-d} \tag{10}$$

and in the buck-boost converter

$$\bar{i}_{\mathrm{L,buck-boost}} = \frac{\bar{i}_{\mathtt{load}}}{1-d} \tag{11}$$

where $\bar{i}_{\mathtt{load}}$ is the average value of the load current.
The relations for the inductor current ripples in the three converters can be expressed by

$$\Delta I_{\mathrm{L,buck}} = \frac{\bar{v}_{\mathrm{out}} + \bar{i}_{\mathrm{L}} R_{\mathrm{D}} + V_{\mathrm{D}} + \bar{i}_{\mathrm{L}} R_{\mathrm{L}}}{L} (1-d) T_{\mathtt{switch}} \tag{12}$$

$$\Delta I_{\mathrm{L,boost}} = \frac{v_{\mathtt{in}} - \bar{i}_{\mathrm{L}} R_{\mathrm{L}} - \bar{i}_{\mathrm{L}} R_{\mathrm{S}}}{L} d T_{\mathtt{switch}} \tag{13}$$

$$\Delta I_{\mathrm{L,buck-boost}} = \frac{v_{\mathtt{in}} - \bar{i}_{\mathrm{L}} R_{\mathrm{L}} - \bar{i}_{\mathrm{L}} R_{\mathrm{S}}}{L} d T_{\mathtt{switch}} \tag{14}$$

where L is the storage inductance and $T_{\mathtt{switch}} = \frac{1}{f_{\mathtt{switch}}}$ is the switching period.
The averaged input currents of the three converters can be calculated by

$$\bar{i}_{\mathtt{in}} = \frac{P_{\mathrm{out}} + P_{\mathrm{con}} + P_{\mathtt{switch}}}{v_{\mathtt{in}}} \tag{15}$$

with

$$P_{\mathrm{out}} = \bar{v}_{\mathrm{out}} \cdot \bar{i}_{\mathtt{load}} \tag{16}$$

and

$$P_{\mathrm{con}} = R_{\mathrm{S}} I_{\mathrm{S,rms}}^2 + R_{\mathrm{D}} I_{\mathrm{D,rms}}^2 + V_{\mathrm{D}} \bar{i}_{\mathrm{D}} + R_{\mathrm{L}} I_{\mathrm{L,rms}}^2 \tag{17}$$

where P_{con} are the total conduction losses and $P_{\mathtt{switch}}$ are the total switching losses (calculated in subsection 6.2 by (21)). As the input voltage and the load current can be determined by simulating the respective converter model together with an appropriate voltage source model and load model, all quantities of the power balance are known.

6.2 Switching losses

The calculation of detailed voltage and current waveforms in a semiconductor during the transition from the blocking state to the conducting state and vice versa, caused by parasitic capacitances and inductances, takes a lot of processing time if differential equations are used to describe the waveforms during switching. Aubard et al. (2002) proposed a detailed dynamic model based on physical analysis of charge locations, that is too complex for multi-domain simulation. For models using piecewise, linear approximations such as presented by Eberle et al. (2008), many parameters must be known with good accuracy. Drofenik & Kolar (2005) presented a straight forward method to calculate switching losses

with polynomial approximation. This method is used (with small adaptations for MOSFET DC-to-DC converters) for the switching loss calculation in this work.
If the switching times are not used in a semiconductor model, it is possible to calculate the switching losses at various operation points using known switching loss characteristics (for the MOSFET and the freewheeling diode) together with the currents commutating between the MOSFET and the freewheeling diode $i_{\mathtt{switch\,on}}$ and $i_{\mathtt{switch\,off}}$, the blocking voltage $v_{\mathtt{blocking}}$, and the switching frequency $f_{\mathtt{switch}}$. It is most practicable to generate the coefficients of the switching loss characteristics (a_{n}, b_{n} and c_{n}) from measurements of a ready made device at different commutating currents $i_{\mathtt{ref,switch\,on}}$ and $i_{\mathtt{ref,switch\,off}}$. This is necessary because the switching losses are heavily dependent on the specific MOSFET-diode combination, the layout of the PCB and the gate resistance of the MOSFET. The model can be further improved if two switching loss characteristics (e.g. $a_{\mathrm{n,50°C}}$ and $a_{\mathrm{n,120°C}}$) can be generated from measurements at two different temperatures so that junction temperature dependence can be considered too. By measuring three operation points in a converter the quadratic switching loss characteristics

$$P_{\mathtt{S,switch\,on}}(i_{\mathtt{S,switch\,on}}) = a_1 i_{\mathtt{S,switch\,on}} + a_2 i^2_{\mathtt{S,switch\,on}} \tag{18}$$

$$P_{\mathtt{S,switch\,off}}(i_{\mathtt{S,switch\,off}}) = b_1 i_{\mathtt{S,switch\,off}} + b_2 i^2_{\mathtt{S,switch\,off}} \tag{19}$$

$$P_{\mathtt{D,switch\,off}}(i_{\mathtt{D,switch\,off}}) = c_1 i_{\mathtt{D,switch\,off}} + c_2 i^2_{\mathtt{D,switch\,off}} \tag{20}$$

that specify the current dependence at a given switching frequency $f_{\mathtt{ref,switch}}$ and blocking voltage $v_{\mathtt{ref,blocking}}$ can be generated. The switching losses in the converter can be calculated from

$$\begin{aligned} P_{\mathtt{switch}} = & \frac{f_{\mathtt{switch}}}{f_{\mathtt{ref,switch}}} \frac{v_{\mathtt{blocking}}}{v_{\mathtt{ref,blocking}}} [P_{\mathtt{S,switch\,on}}(i_{\mathtt{S,switch\,on}}) + \\ & + P_{\mathtt{S,switch\,off}}(i_{\mathtt{S,switch\,off}}) + P_{\mathtt{D,switch\,off}}(i_{\mathtt{D,switch\,off}})] \end{aligned} \tag{21}$$

with the commutating currents found by

$$i_{\mathtt{S,switch\,on}} = I_{\mathtt{L,min}} \tag{22}$$

$$i_{\mathtt{S,switch\,off}} = I_{\mathtt{L,max}} \tag{23}$$

$$i_{\mathtt{D,switch\,off}} = i_{\mathtt{S,switch\,on}} \tag{24}$$

where the minimum and maximum value of the inductor current ripple $I_{\mathtt{L,min}}$ and $I_{\mathtt{L,max}}$ is given by (7) and (8) with the specific relations for each converter taken from (9) – (14). The different blocking voltages for the three converters are

$$v_{\mathtt{blocking,buck}} = v_{\mathtt{in,buck}} \tag{25}$$

$$v_{\mathtt{blocking,boost}} = \overline{v}_{\mathtt{out,boost}} \tag{26}$$

$$v_{\mathtt{blocking,buck-boost}} = v_{\mathtt{in,buck-boost}} + \overline{v}_{\mathtt{out,buck-boost}} \tag{27}$$

where $\overline{v}_{\mathtt{out,boost}}$ and $\overline{v}_{\mathtt{out,buck-boost}}$ can be found by (2) and (3). From an analytical point of view, in (25) – (27) some very small voltage drops across the MOSFET and the freewheeling diode in on-state are neglected. However, in DC-to-DC converters with proper design and reasonable efficiency these voltage drops are very small compared to the input and output voltages.

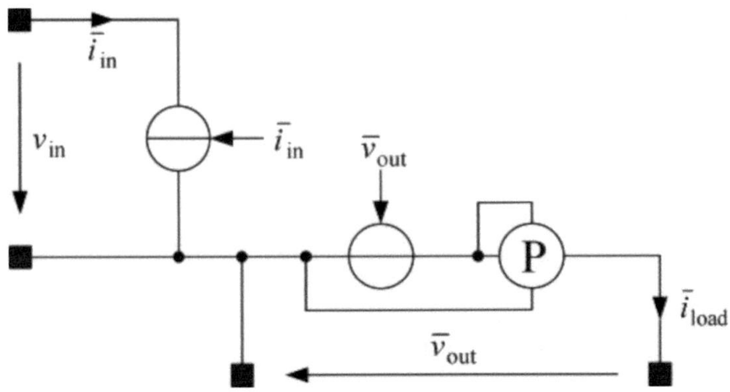

Fig. 5. Scheme of the averaged model of a DC-to-DC converter.

6.3 Temperature dependence

On-resistances and knee voltages in semiconductors as well as the ohmic contribution of the storage inductance change significantly when the junction temperature increases. Also switching losses are temperature dependent. Therefore it is useful to implement temperature dependence by linear or polynomial approximation (depending on the number of reference points). In this work linear temperature dependence is implemented for the on-resistance of the MOSFET and the freewheeling diode, the knee voltage of the freewheeling diode, the ohmic contribution of the storage inductance and for the reference points defining the current dependence of the switching losses. In a multi-domain simulation the presented loss models can be connected to thermal-network models of the converters. In such way it is possible to determine the thermal behavior of the converters by simulation.

6.4 Implementation of the averaged models

The basic scheme of the averaged model of a DC-to-DC converter, such as in fig. 1 – 3, is shown in fig. 5. The model of the energy source (e.g. a battery model) has to be connected to the two pins of the input side of the converter to define v_{in} and the model of the load (e.g. a DC-motor model) has to be connected to the output pins to close the circuit so that a current $\bar{i}_{load}$ can flow. The output voltage is generated by the controlled voltage source where $\bar{v}_{out}$ is calculated through the converter-specific relation among (1) – (3) and the input current is generated by the controlled current source where $\bar{i}_{in}$ can be found by (15).

7. Simulation and comparison

For the verification of the proposed models the simulation results of a voltage controlled buck converter modeled with the calculation of switching events (as in section 5), indicated as model 1, and modeled as an averaged system (as in section 6), indicated as model 2 are compared. The buck converter in the two models operates with a switching frequency of 50 kHz and a maximum output power of 120 W. The storage inductance is 300 μH and the buffer capacity is 200 μF.

In fig. 6 and 7 screen shots of model 1 and model 2 are shown. It can be seen in fig. 7 that the capacitor at the input of the converter is not modeled. This is because in model 2 the mean value of the input current gets calculated instead of the actual pulsed input current calculated in model 1.

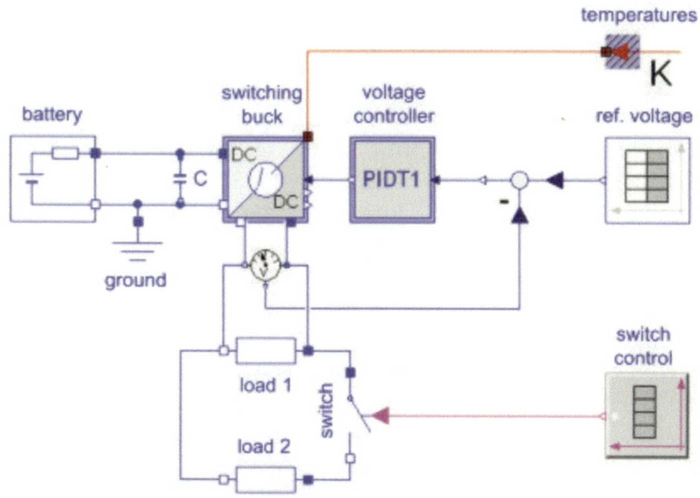

Fig. 6. Model of a voltage controlled buck converter with calculation of switching events (model 1).

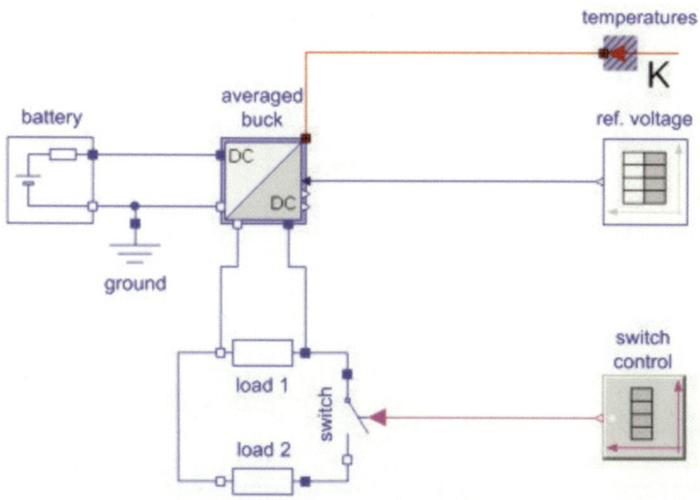

Fig. 7. Averaged model of a voltage controlled buck converter (model 2).

Furthermore, there is no linear voltage controller modeled in fig. 7 because in model 2 only steady states of the converter are calculated. Therefore, an inverse model of (1) for the calculation of the duty cycle is sufficient. This inverse model is implemented directly in the buck converter model. Instead of the differential equations of a controller only an algebraic equation has to be solved.

Both models were processed on a conventional personal computer with a 2.4 GHz dual core CPU (However, only a single core was used for processing.) and 3.0 GB RAM. The simulation of model 1 takes 2.89 s CPU time whereas the simulation of model 2 takes only 15 ms. This shows that the processing of model 2 is significantly faster than the processing of model 1.

Some simulation results of model 1 and model 2 are shown in fig. 8 – 10. A reference voltage step of 20 % and a load increase of 100 % are simulated with both models. The voltage step occurs between time 0.01 s and time 0.03 s, and the load increases after the switch between the two equal load resistances closes at time 0.05 s.
In fig. 8 the influence of the converter input current on the battery voltage can be observed. The output voltage waveforms match in steady state. (The ripple of the output voltage of model 1 is too small to be recognized.) During changes of the operation point the influence of the voltage controller and the transient behavior of the converter can be seen in the output voltage of model 1. These transient effects appear also in the current and power signals of model 1 in fig. 9 and 10. In the input current and inductor current waveforms of model 1 the switching of the converter becomes obvious. Please note, that in fig. 10 the signals of model 1 are mean values averaged over a switching period $T_{\mathtt{switch}}$.
The mean value of any steady state voltage or current signal of model 2 matches the corresponding signal in model 1. Consequently, also the steady state results of the input power, and the total converter losses match. Therefore, model 1 and model 2 have an equivalent steady state behavior.

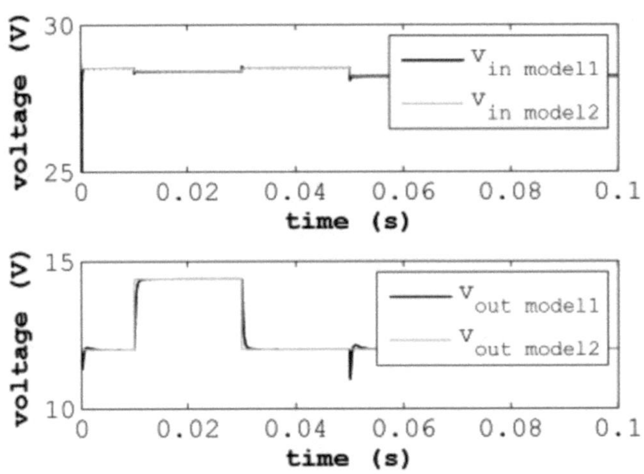

Fig. 8. Voltage waveforms in model 1 and model 2. Input voltages (top); Output voltages (bottom).

8. Conclusion

A computation time efficient method using system averaging and polynomial approximation for modeling three DC-to-DC converters with consideration of temperature dependent conduction and switching losses is described and implemented. The models are developed for multi-domain simulations of electromechanical systems. These simulations are used to investigate system efficiency taking electrical, mechanical and thermal effects into account while assuring power balance. The simulation results of two voltage controlled buck converter models are presented and compared. Voltages and currents calculated with the

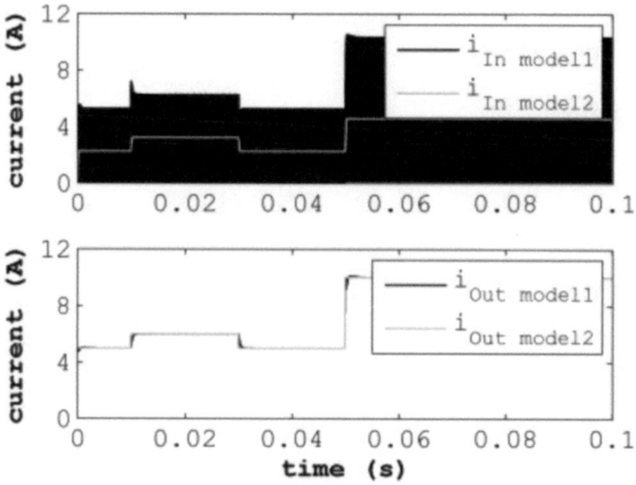

Fig. 9. Current waveforms in model 1 and model 2. Input currents (top); Output currents (bottom).

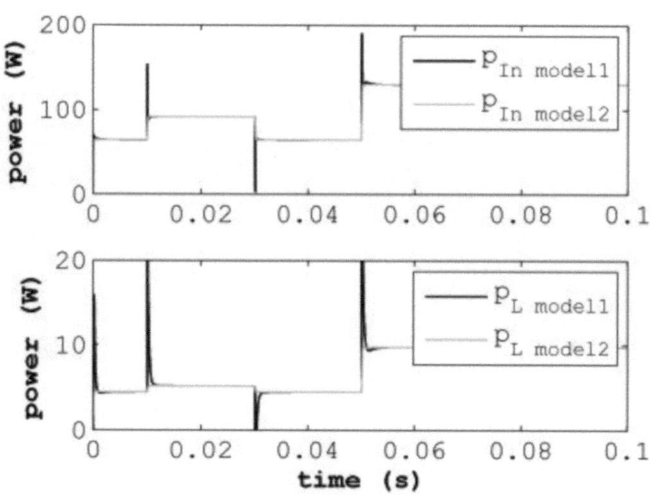

Fig. 10. Power in model 1 and model 2. The signals of model 1 are mean values. Input power (top); Total converter losses (bottom).

averaged model (model 2) match the respective mean values of the conventional model (model 1) in steady state.
A comparison of the CPU times of the two presented simulations shows that the proposed averaged models can be processed significantly faster than conventional models describing semiconductors with discrete states.

9. Acknowledgment

The author would like to thank Claus-Jürgen Fenz and Markus Einhorn for proof reading this work.

10. References

Aubard, L., Verneau, G., Crebier, J., Schaeffer, C. & Avenas, Y. (2002). Power MOSFET switching waveforms: An empirical model based on a physical analysis of charge locations, *The 33rd Annual Power Electronics Specialists Conference, IEEE PESC* 3: 1305–1310.

Cuk, S. & Middlebrook, R. D. (1978). Modeling, analysis and design of switching converters, *NASA CR-135174* .

Drofenik, U. & Kolar, J. (2005). A general scheme for calculating switching- and conduction-losses of power semiconductors in numerical circuit simulations of power electronic systems, *The 7th International Power Electronics Conference, IPEC* .

Eberle, W., Zhang, Z., Liu, Y.-F. & Sen, P. (2008). A simple switching loss model for buck voltage regulators with current source drive, *The 39th Annual Power Electronics Specialists Conference, IEEE PESC* pp. 3780–3786.

Fritzson, P. (2004). *Principles of Object-Oriented Modeling and Simulation with Modelica 2.1*, Wiley-Interscience.

Gragger, J. V., Giuliani, H., Kral, C., Bäuml, T., Kapeller, H. & Pirker, F. (2006). The SmartElectricDrives Library – Powerful models for fast simulations of electric drives, *The 5th International Modelica Conference* pp. 571–577.

16

How to Prove Period-Doubling Bifurcations Existence for Systems of any Dimension - Applications in Electronics and Thermal Field

Céline Gauthier-Quémard
ESIEE-Amiens
France

1. Introduction

When a stable period-k cycle ($k \geq 1$) loses its stability varying one of its parameters μ from a particular value $\mu = \mu_0$ and when a stable period-$2k$ cycle appears at $\mu = \mu_0$, then we generally have a period-doubling bifurcation.
The variation of this system parameter μ in a larger interval can highlight this phenomenon several times: this is called a cascade of period-doubling bifurcations.
Figure 1 represents bifurcation diagrams and illustrates this type of bifurcations.

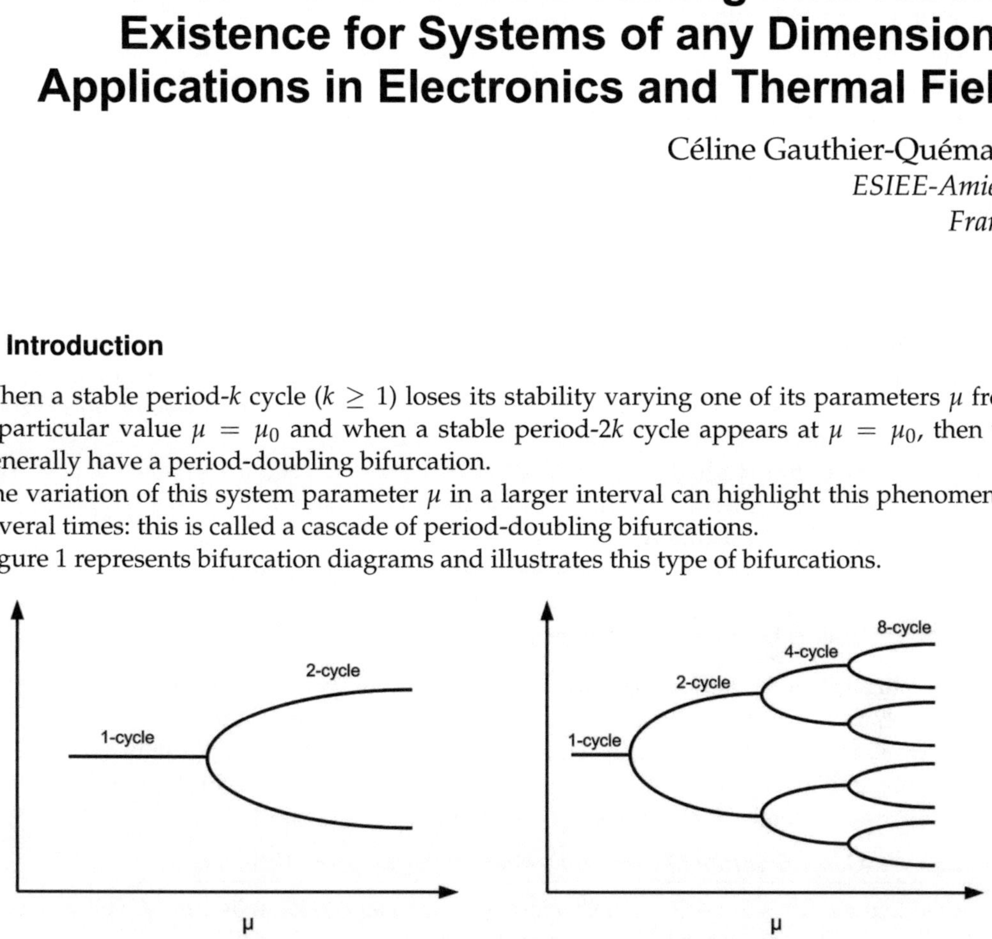

Fig. 1. Illustration of a period-doubling bifurcation with the crossing of a period-1 cycle to a period-2 cycle (on the left) and of a period-doubling bifurcations cascade (on the right).

We can observe this phenomenon in many fields like:

- medicine: onset of a heart attack, epilepsy, neural network... (Aihara et al., 1998), (Smith & Cohen, 1984)
- demography: evolution of animal populations considering for example prey and predator populations (Holmes et al., 1994), (Murray, 1989),
- stock market study (Gleick, 1991),
- sociology: human behaviors study...
- mechanics: system oscillations... (Chung et al., 2003)

In this chapter, we focus on two applications: one in the thermal field with a thermostat with an anticipative resistance (Cébron, 2000) and the second in electronics with a DC/DC converter (Zhusubaliyev & Mosekilde, 2003).
Besides the fact that the bifurcations study allows to know the system behavior, it presents other advantages. Indeed, it can be a useful way to study the system robustness with respect to incertitudes related to the estimation of parameters. It can detect the apparition of chaos. Moreover, bifurcations study can become a practical tool to detect the more influential parameters on the system and so to know what parameter requires an accurate estimates of its value. So, for example, it can save time and money on some costly experiments.
Many authors have already studied period-doubling bifurcations (Baker & Gollub, 1990), (Demazure, 1989), (Guckenheimer & Holmes, 1991), (Kuznetsov, 2004), (Robinson, 1999), (Zhusubaliyev & Mosekilde, 2003)... but most of the time, they focus on one-dimensional systems or they have limited their work to numerical and graphical studies with a bifurcation diagram. So, the theoretical proof of the existence of period-doubling bifurcations for systems of any dimension N, $N \geq 1$, was lacking.
Therefore, here, using some indices given in an exercise in (Robinson, 1999) and following work begun in (Quémard, 2007a), we propose a generalization to any dimension N, $N \geq 1$, of the period-doubling bifurcation theorem. This result is introduced in (Robinson, 1999) for only one-dimensional systems. A proof is also proposed.
Then, we present the studied particular class of hybrid dynamical systems whose two industrial applications (thermostat with an anticipative resistance and DC/DC converter) are chosen to apply this new theorem.
Finally, we conclude this chapter giving some prospects for the future.

2. Period-doubling bifurcation theorem

2.1 Generalization of the period-doubling bifurcation theorem to systems of any dimension

We propose in this paragraph the generalization to any dimension N, $N \geq 1$, of the period-doubling bifurcation theorem. This result was initially found in (Robinson, 1999) for only one-dimensional systems. To do this, we use some indices given in (Robinson, 1999) in an exercise and we complete the work initially realized in (Quémard, 2007a).

Theorem 2.1 (*Generalization of the period-doubling bifurcation theorem*)

Assume that $f : \mathbb{R}^N \times \mathbb{R} \to \mathbb{R}^N$ is a C^r-class ($r \geq 3$) function. We will write $f_\mu(x) = f(x, \mu)$. We assume that f satisfies the following conditions:

1. *The point x_0 is a fixed point of f_μ for the parameter value $\mu = \mu_0$ i.e. $f(x_0, \mu_0) = f_{\mu_0}(x_0) = x_0$.*
2. *The Jacobian matrix of f_{μ_0} at x_0 that is noted $Df_{\mu_0}(x_0)$ has for eigenvalues $\lambda_1(\mu_0) = -1$ and $\lambda_j(\mu_0)$, $j = 2, ..., N$ with $|\lambda_j(\mu_0)| \neq 1$.*

   Let v^1 be a right eigenvector of $Df_{\mu_0}(x_0)$ associated to eigenvalue $\lambda_1(\mu_0)$. We set $V =< v^1 >$. Let v^2,...,v^N be the $N-1$ vectors which form a basis of V', direct sum of the characteristic subspaces (on the right) of $Df_{\mu_0}(x_0)$ different than V. So, we have in particular $V \oplus V' = \mathbb{R}^N$.
3. *Let $x(\mu)$ be the curve of f_μ fixed points near $x(\mu_0)$. We note $\lambda_j(\mu)$, $j = 1, ..., N$, the eigenvalues of the matrix composed of the first partial derivatives of f_μ with respect to*

$x, \partial_x f_\mu(x(\mu))$. We have:

$$\alpha = \frac{d}{d\mu}\lambda_1(\mu)|_{\mu_0} \neq 0.$$

4. Let:

$$\beta = \tfrac{1}{3!}w^1 D^3 f_{\mu_0}(x_0)(v^1,v^1,v^1) + \tfrac{1}{4}w^1 D^2 f_{\mu_0}(x_0)(v^1,(Df_{\mu_0} + Id_{\mathbb{R}^N})U)$$
$$+\tfrac{1}{4}w^1 D^2 f_{\mu_0}(x_0)(v^1, D^2 f_{\mu_0}(x_0)(v^1,v^1)) \neq 0,$$

with:

$$U = \begin{pmatrix} 0 \\ -\left[(\Pi D f_{\mu_0}(x_0)\,(v^2\ldots v^N))^2 - Id_{V'}\right]^{-1}\Pi(Df_{\mu_0}(x_0) + Id_{\mathbb{R}^N})D^2 f_{\mu_0}(x_0)(v^1,v^1) \end{pmatrix},$$

and Π which corresponds to the projection of $\mathbb{R}^N$ on $V' =< v^2...v^N >$ in parallel to $V =< v^1 >$,

Then, there is a period-doubling bifurcation at (x_0, μ_0). More specificially, there is a differentiable curve of fixed points $x(\mu)$, passing through x_0 at μ_0 such that stability of the fixed point changes at μ_0 (depends on α sign). Moreover, there is also a differentiable curve γ passing through (x_0, μ_0) such that $\gamma \backslash (x_0, \mu_0)$ is the union of period-2 orbits. The curve is tangent to $< v^1 > \times \{\mu_0\}$ at (x_0, μ_0) so γ is the graph of a function of x, $\mu = m(x)$ with $m'(x_0) = 0$ and $m''(x_0) = \frac{-2\beta}{\alpha} \neq 0$. Finally period-2 cycles are on one side of $\mu = \mu_0$ and their stability depends on β sign.

Remark 2.2

When parameter μ is fixed at μ_0, function f_{μ_0} only depends on x. So, we can note $Df_{\mu_0}(x)$ and we call this matrix, jacobian matrix of f_{μ_0}. Nevertheless, if μ is not fixed, we note $\partial_x f_\mu(x)$ and call this matrix, matrix of the first derivatives of f_μ with respect to x.

2.2 Theorem proof

2.2.1 Existence of $x(\mu)$, curve of fixed points of f_μ crossing through x_0 at μ_0

We set
$$t : \begin{array}{ccc} \mathbb{R}^N \times \mathbb{R} & \longrightarrow & \mathbb{R}^N \\ (x,\mu) & \longmapsto & f(x,\mu) - x. \end{array}$$

Function t is clearly a C^r-class function ($r \geq 3$) on $\mathbb{R}^N \times \mathbb{R}$. Moreover, we have $t(x_0, \mu_0) = 0$ and $\det(\partial_x t(x_0, \mu_0)) \neq 0$ since, by assumption, $Df_{\mu_0}(x_0)$ has not 1 as eigenvalue.
So, we can apply the implicit functions theorem *i.e.* we can solve $t(x, \mu) = 0$ in x near (x_0, μ_0) that gives the existence of $x(\mu)$, fixed points curve of f_μ near μ_0 with, in particular, $x(\mu_0) = x_0$.

2.2.2 Study of the fixed points stability near μ_0

To work on this part, we have to introduce some notations. Let $v^1(\mu)$ be a right eigenvector of $\partial_x f_\mu(x(\mu))$ associated to eigenvalue $\lambda_1(\mu)$ and with $v^1 = v^1(\mu_0)$ associated to $\lambda_1 = \lambda_1(\mu_0) = -1$. Then, we set $V(\mu) =< v^1(\mu) >$ and $V'(\mu)$ the direct sum of the characteristic sub-spaces of $\partial_x f_\mu(x(\mu))$ different than $V(\mu)$.
Let $\mathcal{B}'_\mu = (v^2(\mu), \ldots, v^N(\mu))$ be a basis of $V'(\mu)$. As we have $\mathbb{R}^N = V(\mu) \bigoplus V'(\mu)$, $\mathcal{B}_\mu = (v^1(\mu), \ldots, v^N(\mu))$ is a basis of $\mathbb{R}^N$. Finally, let $\Pi(\mu)$ be the projection on $V'(\mu)$ in parallel to

$V(\mu)$. When all those elements are applied at μ_0, we will just note the name of the element without parenthesis (for example, $V(\mu_0) = V$).
Firstly, we need to compute the matrix of $\partial_x f_\mu(x(\mu))$ in basis $\mathcal{B}_\mu$. To do this, we set $\{w^j\}_{j=1,\ldots,N}$ the dual basis of $\{v^j\}_{j=1,\ldots,N}$ such that $w^j v^i = \begin{cases} 1 \text{ if } i = j \\ 0 \text{ otherwise.} \end{cases}$
So, here, $w^1(\mu)$ represents a left eigenvector of $\partial_x f_\mu(x(\mu))$ associated to $\lambda_1(\mu)$ and $w^1(\mu) \in V'(\mu)^\perp$. We have:

$$\partial_x f_{\mu\mathcal{B}_\mu}(x(\mu)) = \mathrm{Mat}_{\mathcal{B}_\mu}(\partial_x f_\mu(x(\mu))) = \begin{pmatrix} w^1(\mu) \\ \vdots \\ w^N(\mu) \end{pmatrix} \partial_x f_\mu(x(\mu)) \left(v^1(\mu) \ldots v^N(\mu) \right)$$

$$= \begin{pmatrix} \lambda_1(\mu)\ 0 & \ldots & 0 \\ 0 & & \\ \vdots & \mathrm{Mat}_{\mathcal{B}'_\mu}(\Pi(\mu) D f_\mu(x(\mu))) & \\ 0 & & \end{pmatrix}.$$

Then, we call $x_{0_\mathcal{B}}$ the column matrix of vector $x_0 = x(\mu_0)$ written in basis $\mathcal{B} = \mathcal{B}_{\mu_0}$ with $x_{0_\mathcal{B}} = (x^1_{0_\mathcal{B}}, \ldots, x^N_{0_\mathcal{B}})^T = (w^1 \ldots w^N)^T x_0$ and $x_{\mathcal{B}_\mu}(\mu)$ the column matrix of vector $x(\mu)$ written in basis $\mathcal{B}_\mu$ with $x_{\mathcal{B}_\mu}(\mu) = (x^1_{\mathcal{B}_\mu}(\mu), \ldots, x^N_{\mathcal{B}_\mu}(\mu))^T = (w^1(\mu) \ldots w^N(\mu))^T x(\mu)$ where x_0 and $x(\mu)$ are considered relatively to the canonical basis.
Similarly, we note $f_{\mu\mathcal{B}_\mu} = \left(f^1_{\mu\mathcal{B}_\mu} \cdots f^N_{\mu\mathcal{B}_\mu} \right)^T = (w^1(\mu) \ldots w^N(\mu))^T f_\mu$ the column matrix of vector $f_\mu = (f^1_\mu \ldots f^N_\mu)^T$ written in basis $\mathcal{B}_\mu$.
Now, we define the following function Ψ :

$$\begin{aligned} \Psi : \mathbb{R}^N \times \mathbb{R} &\longrightarrow \mathbb{R}^{N-1} \\ (x, \mu) &\longmapsto \Pi(\mu)(f^2_\mu(x) - x), \end{aligned} \tag{1}$$

where $f^2_\mu = f_\mu \circ f_\mu$. We have near $\mu = \mu_0$, $\Psi(x(\mu), \mu) = 0$ since, by assumption, $x(\mu)$ is a fixed point of f_μ near μ_0. Moreover:

$$\frac{\partial \Psi}{\partial x^2_{\mathcal{B}_\mu} \ldots x^N_{\mathcal{B}_\mu}}(x(\mu), \mu) = \Pi(\mu) \left[\left(\frac{\partial f_{\mu\mathcal{B}_\mu}}{\partial x^1_{\mathcal{B}_\mu} \ldots x^N_{\mathcal{B}_\mu}}(x(\mu)) \right)_{\mathcal{B}_\mu} \left(\frac{\partial f_{\mu\mathcal{B}_\mu}}{\partial x^2_{\mathcal{B}_\mu} \ldots x^N_{\mathcal{B}_\mu}}(x(\mu)) \right)_{\mathcal{B}_\mu} - \begin{pmatrix} 0 \ldots 0 \\ I_{N-1} \end{pmatrix}_{\mathcal{B}_\mu} \right]$$

$$= \left(\frac{\partial f^2_{\mu\mathcal{B}_\mu} \cdots f^N_{\mu\mathcal{B}_\mu}}{\partial x^2_{\mathcal{B}_\mu} \cdots x^N_{\mathcal{B}_\mu}}(x(\mu)) \right)^2_{\mathcal{B}'_\mu} - Id_{V'(\mu)}. \tag{2}$$

Since $|\lambda_j(\mu_0)| \neq 1\ \forall j \geq 2$, we can conclude that, near μ_0, $\frac{\partial \Psi}{\partial x^2_{\mathcal{B}_\mu} \ldots x^N_{\mathcal{B}_\mu}}(x(\mu), \mu)$ is an invertible matrix. Thus, for a fixed μ near μ_0, we can apply the implicit functions theorem near $x(\mu)$ and we can solve $\Psi(x, \mu) = 0$ in terms of $x^1_{\mathcal{B}_\mu}$ *i.e.* there exists a function φ_μ,

defined near $x^1_{\mathcal{B}_\mu}$ such that $\varphi_{\mu_{\mathcal{B}'_\mu}}(x^1_{\mathcal{B}_\mu}) = (x^2_{\mathcal{B}_\mu} \dots x^N_{\mathcal{B}_\mu})^T = (\varphi^2_{\mu_{\mathcal{B}'_\mu}}(x^1_{\mathcal{B}_\mu}) \dots \varphi^N_{\mu_{\mathcal{B}'_\mu}}(x^1_{\mathcal{B}_\mu}))^T$ with $\Psi((x^1_{\mathcal{B}_\mu}, \varphi_{\mu_{\mathcal{B}'_\mu}}(x^1_{\mathcal{B}_\mu}))_{\mathcal{B}_\mu}, \mu) = 0$.
Derivating Ψ with respect to $x^1_{\mathcal{B}_\mu}$, we have:

$$\frac{\partial \Psi}{\partial x^1_{\mathcal{B}_\mu}}(x,\mu) + \frac{\partial \Psi}{\partial x^2_{\mathcal{B}_\mu} \dots x^N_{\mathcal{B}_\mu}}(x,\mu)\frac{\partial \varphi_\mu}{\partial x^1_{\mathcal{B}_\mu}}(x^1_{\mathcal{B}_\mu}) = 0 \text{ at } x = (x^1_{\mathcal{B}_\mu}, \varphi_{\mu_{\mathcal{B}'_\mu}}(x^1_{\mathcal{B}_\mu}))_{\mathcal{B}_\mu}.$$

Thus, using the form of the $\partial_x f_\mu(x(\mu))$ matrix in basis $\mathcal{B}_\mu$, we obtain:

$$\frac{\partial \Psi}{\partial x^1_{\mathcal{B}_\mu}}(x(\mu),\mu) = \Pi(\mu)\left[\left(\partial_x f_{\mu_{\mathcal{B}_\mu}}(x(\mu))\frac{\partial f_{\mu_{\mathcal{B}_\mu}}}{\partial x^1_{\mathcal{B}_\mu}}(x(\mu)) - \begin{pmatrix}1\\0\\\vdots\\0\end{pmatrix}\right)\right]_{\mathcal{B}_\mu} = 0_{V'}$$

and since $\frac{\partial \Psi}{\partial x^2_{\mathcal{B}_\mu}\dots x^N_{\mathcal{B}_\mu}}(x(\mu),\mu)$ is invertible near μ_0, we conclude that $\frac{\partial \varphi_\mu}{\partial x^1_{\mathcal{B}_\mu}}(x^1_{\mathcal{B}_\mu}(\mu)) = 0_{V'}$.
Thereafter, in order to obtain 0 as a fixed point near all μ, we introduce, in the basis $\mathcal{B}_\mu$, the following function ϕ_μ near $(0,\mu_0)$:

$$\phi_\mu(y) = \begin{pmatrix} x^1_{\mathcal{B}_\mu}(\mu) + y \\ \varphi_\mu(x^1_{\mathcal{B}_\mu}(\mu) + y) \end{pmatrix}_{\mathcal{B}_\mu} \quad \text{with} \quad \begin{cases} \phi_\mu(0) = x(\mu) \\ \frac{\partial \phi_\mu}{\partial y}(0) = v^1(\mu). \end{cases}$$

Then, we introduce $g(y,\mu) = w^1(\mu)\left[f_\mu(\phi_\mu(y)) - \phi_\mu(y)\right]$. We have $g(0,\mu) = w^1(\mu)\left[f_\mu(x(\mu)) - x(\mu)\right] = 0$ since $x(\mu)$ is a fixed point of f_μ and $\phi_\mu(0) = x(\mu)$.
Since $\frac{\partial g}{\partial y}(0,\mu) = w^1(\mu)[\partial_x f_\mu(x(\mu)) - I_{\mathbb{R}^N}]\frac{\partial \phi_\mu}{\partial y}(0) = \lambda_1(\mu) - 1$, the calculation of $\frac{\partial g^2}{\partial \mu \partial y}(0,\mu)$ permits us to study the stability change of the fixed points along the fixed points curve. We have near μ_0: $\frac{\partial^2 g}{\partial \mu \partial y}(0,\mu) = \frac{d\lambda_1}{d\mu}(\mu) \neq 0$ by the third condition of the theorem.
Conclusion: the sign of $\alpha = \frac{d\lambda_1}{d\mu}(\mu_0)$ determines which side of the plan $\mu = \mu_0$ the fixed point will be attractive or repulsive.

2.2.3 Existence of a differentiable curve γ passing through (x_0, μ_0) such that $\gamma \backslash (x_0, \mu_0)$ is the union of period-2 cycles

We set $h(y,\mu) = w^1(\mu)\left[f^2_\mu(\phi_\mu(y)) - \phi_\mu(y)\right]$.
We have $h(0,\mu) = w^1(\mu)\left[f_\mu \circ f_\mu(x(\mu)) - x(\mu)\right] = 0$. Here, we search y not null, solution of $h(y,\mu) = 0$ which will give us a fixed point $\phi_\mu(y)$ different than $\phi_\mu(0) = x(\mu)$ for f^2_μ. To do this, we introduce:

$$M(y,\mu) = \begin{cases} \frac{h(y,\mu)}{y} \text{ if } y \neq 0 \\ \lim_{y \to 0} \frac{h(y,\mu)}{y} = \frac{\partial h}{\partial y}(0,\mu) \text{ if } y = 0. \end{cases}$$

We compute $M(0,\mu) = \frac{\partial h}{\partial y}(0,\mu) = w^1(\mu)\left[(\partial_x f_\mu(x(\mu)))^2 - Id_{\mathbb{R}^N}\right]\frac{\partial \phi_\mu}{\partial y}(0) = \lambda_1^2(\mu) - 1$. So, $M(0,\mu_0) = 0$.

Then, we compute $M_\mu(0,\mu_0) = \frac{\partial M}{\partial \mu}(0,\mu_0)$:

$$M_\mu(0,\mu_0) = 2\frac{d\lambda_1}{d\mu}(\mu_0)\lambda_1(\mu_0) = -2\alpha \neq 0 \text{ (third theorem condition).}$$

Thus, we can apply the implicit functions theorem and we obtain the existence of a differentiable function $\mu = m(y)$ (whose curve is noted γ, $\mu_0 = m(0)$) such that $M(y, m(y)) = 0$ near $(0,\mu_0)$. Then, $\phi_{m(y)}(y)$ is a period-2 fixed point of f_μ.

2.2.4 Calculation of $m'(0)$

Differentiating function M, we have:

$$M_y(0,\mu_0) + M_\mu(0,\mu_0)m'(0) = 0 \Rightarrow m'(0) = -\frac{M_y(0,\mu_0)}{M_\mu(0,\mu_0)}.$$

We know $M_\mu(0,\mu_0) = -2\alpha$ so it remains to compute $M_y(0,\mu_0) = \frac{\partial M}{\partial y}(0,\mu_0) = \lim_{y\to 0} \frac{h(y,\mu_0)}{y^2}$. A limited development of h near $y = 0$ gives:

$$h(y,\mu_0) = h(0,\mu_0) + \frac{\partial h}{\partial y}(0,\mu_0)y + \frac{1}{2!}\frac{\partial^2 h}{\partial y^2}(0,\mu_0)y^2 + \mathcal{O}(y^3),$$

and permits us to conclude $M_y(0,\mu_0) = \frac{1}{2}\frac{\partial^2 h}{\partial y^2}(0,\mu_0)$. Moreover, derivating twice function h with respect to y, we obtain at $y = 0$, $\mu = \mu_0$:

$$\begin{aligned}&\tfrac{\partial^2 h}{\partial y^2}(0,\mu_0) = w^1 \tfrac{\partial}{\partial y}\left[Df_{\mu_0}(f_{\mu_0}(\phi_{\mu_0}(y)))\right]|_{y=0} Df_{\mu_0}(x_0)v^1 \\ &+ w^1 Df_{\mu_0}(x_0)\tfrac{\partial}{\partial y}\left[Df_{\mu_0}(\phi_{\mu_0}(y))\right]|_{y=0}v^1 + w^1(Df_{\mu_0}(x_0))^2\tfrac{\partial^2\phi_{\mu_0}}{\partial y^2}(0) - w^1\tfrac{\partial^2\phi_{\mu_0}}{\partial y^2}(0).\end{aligned}$$

Since $w^1(Df_{\mu_0}(x_0))^2\frac{\partial^2\phi_{\mu_0}}{\partial y^2}(0) - w^1\frac{\partial^2\phi_{\mu_0}}{\partial y^2}(0) = 0$ (because $w^1 Df_{\mu_0}(x_0) = -w^1$) and:

$$\begin{aligned}&w^1 \tfrac{\partial}{\partial y}\left[Df_{\mu_0}(f_{\mu_0}(\phi_{\mu_0}(y)))\right]|_{y=0} Df_{\mu_0}(x_0)v^1 + w^1 Df_{\mu_0}(x_0)\tfrac{\partial}{\partial y}\left[Df_{\mu_0}(\phi_{\mu_0}(y))\right]|_{y=0}v^1 \\ &= -w^1 D^2 f_{\mu_0}(x_0)(Df_{\mu_0}(x_0)v^1, v^1) - w^1 D^2 f_{\mu_0}(x_0)(v^1, v^1) = 0,\end{aligned}$$

we obtain $\frac{\partial^2 h}{\partial y^2}(0,\mu_0) = 0$ and we finally conclude that $M_y(0,\mu_0) = 0$, so $m'(0) = 0$. Therefore, γ is tangent to $< v^1 > \times \{\mu_0\}$ at (x_0,μ_0).

2.2.5 Calculation of $m''(0)$

As $\mu = m(y) = m(0) + m'(0)y + \frac{1}{2}m''(0)y^2 + \mathcal{O}(y^3) = \mu_0 + \frac{1}{2}m''(0)y^2 + \mathcal{O}(y^3)$, we know that a sufficient condition to have γ on only one side of $\mu = \mu_0$ is that $m''(0) \neq 0$.
To compute $m''(0)$, by differentiating twice function M, we obtain:

$$M_{yy}(y,m(y)) + 2M_{\mu y}(y,m(y))m'(y) + M_{\mu\mu}(y,m(y))(m'(y))^2 + M_\mu(y,m(y))m''(y) = 0.$$

Evaluating this equation at $y = 0$ and using $m'(0) = 0$, we have:

$$m''(0) = -\frac{M_{yy}(0,\mu_0)}{M_\mu(0,\mu_0)}.$$

As we know $M_\mu(0,\mu_0) = -2\alpha$, it remains to compute $M_{yy}(0,\mu_0) = \frac{1}{3}\frac{\partial^3 h}{\partial y^3}(0,\mu_0)$ (we have used a limited development of h to order three near $y = 0$). We already know:

$$\begin{cases} \frac{\partial h}{\partial y}(y,\mu_0) = w^1 R(y,\mu_0)\frac{\partial \phi_{\mu_0}}{\partial y}(y) \\ \frac{\partial^2 h}{\partial y^2}(y,\mu_0) = w^1 \frac{\partial R}{\partial y}(y,\mu_0)\frac{\partial \phi_{\mu_0}}{\partial y}(y) + w^1 R(y,\mu_0)\frac{\partial^2 \phi_{\mu_0}}{\partial y^2}(y), \end{cases}$$

with $R(y,\mu_0) = Df_{\mu_0}(f_{\mu_0}(\phi_{\mu_0}(y)))Df_{\mu_0}(\phi_{\mu_0}(y)) - Id_{\mathbb{R}^N}$.
Then, derivating $\frac{\partial^2 h}{\partial y^2}(y,\mu_0)$ with respect to y and applying it at $y = 0$, we obtain:

$$\frac{\partial^3 h}{\partial y^3}(0,\mu_0) = w^1 \frac{\partial^2 R}{\partial y^2}(0,\mu_0)\frac{\partial \phi_{\mu_0}}{\partial y}(0) + 2w^1 \frac{\partial R}{\partial y}(0,\mu_0)\frac{\partial^2 \phi_{\mu_0}}{\partial y^2}(0) + w^1 R(0,\mu_0)\frac{\partial^3 \phi_{\mu_0}}{\partial y^3}(0). \quad (3)$$

In order to alleviate notations, we study each term of $\frac{\partial^3 h}{\partial y^3}(0,\mu_0)$ separately.
• For the first element, we have:

$$w^1 \frac{\partial^2 R}{\partial y^2}(0,\mu_0)v^1 = w^1 \frac{\partial}{\partial y}\left[D^2 f_{\mu_0}(f_{\mu_0}(\phi_{\mu_0}(y)))\left(Df_{\mu_0}(\phi_{\mu_0}(y))\frac{\partial \phi_{\mu_0}}{\partial y}(y), Df_{\mu_0}(\phi_{\mu_0}(y))v^1\right)\right]$$
$$+w^1 \frac{\partial}{\partial y}\left[Df_{\mu_0}(f_{\mu_0}(\phi_{\mu_0}(y)))D^2 f_{\mu_0}(\phi_{\mu_0}(y))\left(\frac{\partial \phi_{\mu_0}}{\partial y}(y), v^1\right)\right],$$

with the convention for all function f and all vectors u_1 and $u_2 \in \mathbb{R}^N$:
$D^2 f(x)(u_1,u_2) = D^2 f(x)(u_2,u_1) = \sum_{i,j}\frac{\partial^2 f}{\partial x^i \partial x^j}(x)u_1^i u_2^j$.
So, after some calculations and simplifications, we obtain:

$$w^1 \frac{\partial^2 R}{\partial y^2}(0,\mu_0)v^1 = -2w^1 D^3 f_{\mu_0}(x_0)\left(v^1,v^1,v^1\right) - 3w^1 D^2 f_{\mu_0}(x_0)\left(v^1, D^2 f_{\mu_0}(x_0)\left(v^1,v^1\right)\right)$$
$$-w^1 D^2 f_{\mu_0}(x_0)\left(v^1, (Df_{\mu_0}(x_0) + Id_{\mathbb{R}^N})\frac{\partial^2 \phi_{\mu_0}}{\partial y^2}(0)\right).$$

• Then, we study the second term of (3) and we finally have:

$$w^1 \frac{\partial R}{\partial y}(0,\mu_0)\frac{\partial^2 \phi_{\mu_0}}{\partial y^2}(0) = -w^1 D^2 f_{\mu_0}(x_0)\left(v^1, Df_{\mu_0}(x_0)\frac{\partial^2 \phi_{\mu_0}}{\partial y^2}(0)\right) - w^1 D^2 f_{\mu_0}(x_0)\left(v^1, \frac{\partial^2 \phi_{\mu_0}}{\partial y^2}(0)\right).$$

• Finally, the last term of (3) gives:

$$w^1 R(0,\mu_0)\frac{\partial^3 \phi_{\mu_0}}{\partial y^3}(0) = w^1((Df_{\mu_0}(x_0))^2 - 1)\frac{\partial^3 \phi_{\mu_0}}{\partial y^3}(0) = w^1 \frac{\partial^3 \phi_{\mu_0}}{\partial y^3}(0) - w^1 \frac{\partial^3 \phi_{\mu_0}}{\partial y^3}(0) = 0,$$

since $w^1\left(Df_{\mu_0}(x_0)\right)^2 = w^1$.

From this, we can conclude:

$$\frac{\partial^3 h}{\partial y^3}(0,\mu_0) = -2w^1 D^3 f_{\mu_0}(x_0)\left(v^1,v^1,v^1\right) - 3w^1 D^2 f_{\mu_0}(x_0)\left(v^1, D^2 f_{\mu_0}(x_0)\left(v^1,v^1\right)\right)$$
$$-3w^1 D^2 f_{\mu_0}(x_0)\left(v^1, (Df_{\mu_0}(x_0) + Id_{\mathbb{R}^N})\frac{\partial^2 \phi_{\mu_0}}{\partial y^2}(0)\right).$$

Now, it remains to find a relation between $\frac{\partial^2 \phi_{\mu_0}}{\partial y^2}(0)$ and $f_{\mu_0}(x_0)$ in order that $M_{yy}(0,\mu_0)$ be only a function of $f_{\mu_0}(x_0)$. To do this, we differentiate again function Ψ defined by (1) with respect to $x^1_{\mathcal{B}_\mu}$. We obtain:

$$\frac{\partial^2 \Psi}{\partial x^{1^2}_{\mathcal{B}_\mu}}(x,\mu) + 2\frac{\partial^2 \Psi}{\partial x^1_{\mathcal{B}_\mu}\partial x^2_{\mathcal{B}_\mu}\ldots x^N_{\mathcal{B}_\mu}}(x,\mu)\frac{\partial \varphi_\mu}{\partial x^1_{\mathcal{B}_\mu}}(x^1_{\mathcal{B}_\mu}) + \frac{\partial^2 \Psi}{(\partial x^2_{\mathcal{B}_\mu}\ldots x^N_{\mathcal{B}_\mu})^2}(x,\mu)\left(\frac{\partial \varphi_\mu}{\partial x^1_{\mathcal{B}_\mu}}(x^1_{\mathcal{B}_\mu})\right)^2$$
$$+\frac{\partial \Psi}{\partial x^2_{\mathcal{B}_\mu}\ldots x^N_{\mathcal{B}_\mu}}(x,\mu)\frac{\partial^2 \varphi_\mu}{\partial x^{1^2}_{\mathcal{B}_\mu}}(x^1_{\mathcal{B}_\mu}) = 0, \quad (4)$$

at x which satisfies $\Psi(x,\mu) = 0$ *i.e.* $x = (x^1_{\mathcal{B}_\mu}, \varphi_{\mu_{\mathcal{B}'_\mu}}(x^1_{\mathcal{B}_\mu}))_{\mathcal{B}_\mu}$.
Applied at (x_0,μ_0), relation (4) becomes:

$$\frac{\partial^2 \Psi}{\partial x^{1^2}_{\mathcal{B}}}(x_0,\mu_0) + \frac{\partial \Psi}{\partial x^2_{\mathcal{B}}\ldots x^N_{\mathcal{B}}}(x_0,\mu_0)\frac{\partial^2 \varphi_{\mu_0}}{\partial x^{1^2}_{\mathcal{B}}}(x^1_{0_\mathcal{B}}) = 0.$$

As $\frac{\partial \Psi}{\partial x^2_{\mathcal{B}}\ldots x^N_{\mathcal{B}}}(x_0,\mu_0)$ given by (2) is an invertible matrix, it remains to compute $\frac{\partial^2 \Psi}{\partial x^{1^2}_{\mathcal{B}}}(x_0,\mu_0)$. We have:

$$\frac{\partial^2 \Psi}{\partial x^{1^2}_{\mathcal{B}}}(x_0,\mu_0) = \Pi\left[D^2 f_{\mu_0}(x_0)\left(\frac{\partial f_{\mu_0}}{\partial x^1_{\mathcal{B}}}(x_0), \frac{\partial f_{\mu_0}}{\partial x^1_{\mathcal{B}}}(x_0)\right) + Df_{\mu_0}(x_0)\frac{\partial^2 f_{\mu_0}}{\partial x^{1^2}_{\mathcal{B}}}(x_0)\right]$$
$$= \Pi\left[\left(Df_{\mu_0}(x_0) + Id_{\mathbb{R}^N}\right) D^2 f_{\mu_0}(x_0)(v^1,v^1)\right]$$

since by definition, $\frac{\partial^2 f_{\mu_0}}{\partial x^{1^2}_{\mathcal{B}}}(x_0) = D^2 f_{\mu_0}(x_0)(v^1,v^1)$.
Finally, all these calculations lead to write:

$$\frac{\partial^2 \varphi_{\mu_0}}{\partial x^{1^2}_{\mathcal{B}}}(x^1_{0_\mathcal{B}}) = -\left[\left(\Pi Df_{\mu_0}(x_0)(v^2\ldots v^N)\right)^2 - Id_{V'}\right]^{-1} \Pi\left(Df_{\mu_0}(x_0) + Id_{\mathbb{R}^N}\right) D^2 f_{\mu_0}(x_0)(v^1,v^1).$$

Thus, we obtain $\frac{\partial^2 \phi_{\mu_0}}{\partial y^2}(0)$ as a function of $f_{\mu_0}(x_0)$ since $\frac{\partial^2 \phi_{\mu_0}}{\partial y^2}(0) = \begin{pmatrix} 0 \\ \frac{\partial^2 \varphi_{\mu_0}}{\partial x^{1^2}_{\mathcal{B}}}(x^1_{0_\mathcal{B}}) \end{pmatrix}_{\mathcal{B}}$.

We can conclude that $\frac{\partial^3 h}{\partial y^3}(0,\mu_0) = 3M_{yy}(0,\mu_0) = -12\beta \neq 0$ (fourth assumption of the theorem) so $m''(0) = -\frac{-4\beta}{-2\alpha} = -2\frac{\beta}{\alpha} \neq 0$. This confirms that γ, curve of period-2 fixed points, is on one side of $\mu = \mu_0$.

2.2.6 Stability study of period-2 cycles

To study the stability of the period-2 cycles, we study function $\frac{\partial h}{\partial y}(y, m(y))$ near $y = 0$ ($\mu = \mu_0$). To do this, we give the limited development of $\frac{\partial h}{\partial y}(y, m(y))$ near 0:

$$\frac{\partial h}{\partial y}(y, m(y)) = \frac{\partial h}{\partial y}(0, \mu_0) + \frac{\partial^2 h}{\partial y^2}(0, \mu_0)y + \frac{\partial^2 h}{\partial \mu \partial y}(0, \mu_0)(\mu - \mu_0)$$

$$+\frac{1}{2!}\frac{\partial^3 h}{\partial y^3}(0, \mu_0)y^2 + \mathcal{O}(y^3) + \mathcal{O}((\mu - \mu_0)^2) + \mathcal{O}(y^2(\mu - \mu_0)).$$

We know $\frac{\partial h}{\partial y}(0, \mu_0) = 0$, $\frac{\partial^2 h}{\partial y^2}(0, \mu_0) = 0$, $\frac{\partial^2 h}{\partial \mu \partial y}(0, \mu_0) = -2\alpha$ and $\frac{\partial^3 h}{\partial y^3}(0, \mu_0) = 3M_{yy}(0, \mu_0) = -12\beta$.
Moreover, we have:

$$\frac{\partial^2 h}{\partial \mu \partial y}(0, \mu_0)(m(y) - m(0)) = M_\mu(0, \mu_0)(\frac{1}{2}m''(0)y^2 + \mathcal{O}(y^3)) = 2\beta y^2 + \mathcal{O}(y^3)).$$

Finally, we find $\frac{\partial h}{\partial y}(y, m(y)) = -4\beta y^2 + \mathcal{O}(y^3))$. This confirms that the stability of period-2 cycles depends ont the β sign. This completes the proof of the theorem.

3. Presentation of the studied particular class of hybrid dynamical systems

3.1 General presentation

We consider the following hybrid dynamical system (h.d.s.) of order N, $N \geq 1$:

$$\begin{cases} \dot{X}(t) = A\big(q(\xi(t))\big)X(t) + V\big(q(\xi(t))\big), \\ \xi(t) = cst - WX(t), \end{cases} \tag{5}$$

where A is a stable square matrix of order N, V and X are column matrices of order N and W is a row matrix of order N, all these matrices having real entries. Moreover, cst is a real constant. We suppose that X and so ξ are continuous.
In this model, the discrete variable is q which can take two values u_1, u_2 according to ξ which follows a hysteresis phenomenon described by figure 2.

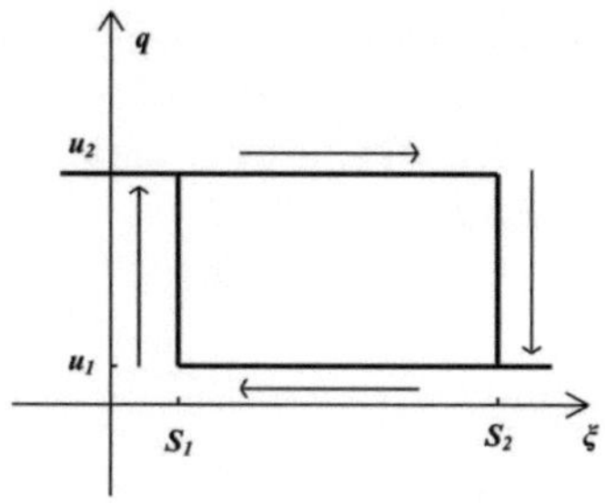

Fig. 2. Hysteresis phenomenon followed by discrete variable q.

If ξ reaches its lower threshold S_1 by decreasing value then q changes its value from u_1 to u_2. Similarly, if ξ reaches its upper threshold S_2 by increasing value then q changes its value from

u_2 to u_1. In those conditions, multifunction $q(\xi)$ is explicitly given by:

$$\begin{cases} q(\xi(t)) = u_1 \text{ if } \xi(t^-) = S_2 \text{ and } q(\xi(t^-)) = u_2 \\ q(\xi(t)) = u_2 \text{ if } \xi(t^-) = S_1 \text{ and } q(\xi(t^-)) = u_1 \\ q(\xi(t)) = q(\xi(t^-)) \text{ otherwise.} \end{cases} \tag{6}$$

In the first two cases, t is called switching time and so, S_1 and S_2 are respectively called lower and upper switching thresholds.
A lot of applications of many fields and of all dimensions belong to this h.d.s. class. In this paper, we will study two of these applications:

- the first of dimension three: a thermostat with an anticipative resistance,
- the second of dimension four: a DC/DC converter.

3.2 Application 1: thermostat with an anticipative resistance

The first considered application is the one of a thermostat wtih an anticipative resistance which controls a convector located in the same room (Cébron, 2000). The thermal processus is given by figure 3 (on the left). We note x, y and z (in K) the temperatures respectively of the

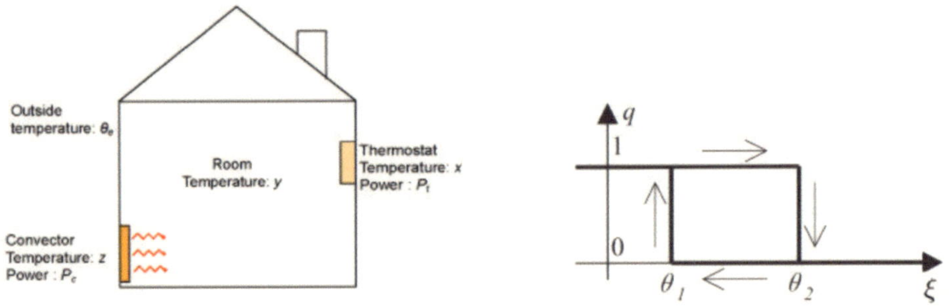

Fig. 3. thermal processus (on the left) and hysteresis phenomenon (on the right).

thermostat, of the room and of the convector. The functioning principle of such a thermostat is the following: powers of the thermostat P_t and of the convector P_c (in W) are active when $q = 1$ and inactive when $q = 0$. If initially $q = 1$, as P_t is active, the desired temperature is reached firstly by the thermostat temperature before the room temperature that makes q changes its value from 1 to 0. Thus, the introduction of the anticipative resistance reduces the amplitude of y. This presents an interest of energy saving.
The Fourier law and a power assessment (Saccadura, 1998) give the following differential system of dimension three with the same form than (5):

$$\begin{cases} \dot{X}(t) = AX(t) + q(\xi(t))B + C, \\ \xi(t) = LX(t), \end{cases}$$

where:

$$A = \begin{pmatrix} -a & a & 0 \\ e & -(b+d+e) & b \\ 0 & c & -c \end{pmatrix}, B = \begin{pmatrix} p_t \\ 0 \\ p_c \end{pmatrix}, C = \begin{pmatrix} 0 \\ d.\theta_e \\ 0 \end{pmatrix}, L = \begin{pmatrix} 1 \\ 0 \\ 0 \end{pmatrix}^T,$$

and

$$a = \frac{1}{m_t C_t R_t},\ b = \frac{1}{m_p C_p R_c},\ c = \frac{1}{m_c C_c R_c},\ d = \frac{1}{m_p C_p R_m},\ e = \frac{1}{m_p C_p R_t},\ p_t = \frac{P_t}{m_t C_t},\ p_c = \frac{P_c}{m_c C_c}.$$

Coefficients R_t, R_c, R_m (in $K.W^{-1}$) are thermal resistances, C_t, C_p, C_c (in $J.kg^{-1}.K^{-1}$) are heat capacities and m_t, m_p, m_c (in kg) are masses according to indices t, p, c and m which respectively represent the thermostat, the convector, the room and the house wall. Moreover, θ_e (in K) corresponds to the outside temperature.
Here, the discrete variable q follows the hysteresis phenomenon described in figure 3 where $u_1 = 0$, $u_2 = 1$, $S_1 = \theta_1$ and $S_2 = \theta_2$.

3.3 Application 2: DC/DC converter

The second studied application is the one of a DC/DC converter (Zhusubaliyev & Mosekilde, 2003), (Lim & Hamill, 1999). The electrical equivalent circuit is given by figure 4. This circuit

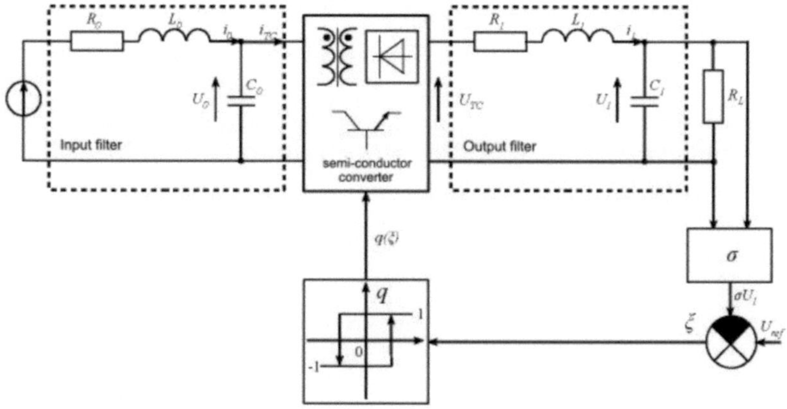

Fig. 4. Electrical equivalent circuit of a DC/DC converter.

includes a converter DC voltage generator and two filters LC (input and output). The output voltage of the circuit, given by σU_1, $0 < \sigma < 1$, with σ the sensor gain, will be compared to the reference signal U_{ref} (in V). The difference of these two quantities, noted $\xi = U_{\text{ref}} - \sigma U_1$, called deviation signal, is applied to the relay element with hysteresis in order to form square pulses to control the converter switching elements. Here, $u_1 = -1$, $u_2 = 1$, $S_1 = -\chi_0$, $S_2 = \chi_0$. Thus, electronical laws give the following differential system of order four which takes the form of (5):

$$\begin{cases} \dot{X} = A(q(\xi(t)))X(t) + V, \\ \xi(t) = U_{\text{ref}} - UX(t), \end{cases}$$

where:

$$A(q) = \begin{pmatrix} -\eta & -\eta & 0 & 0 \\ \gamma & 0 & -\frac{\gamma}{2}(1+q) & 0 \\ 0 & \frac{\mu}{2}(1+q) & -\nu & -\mu \\ 0 & 0 & \frac{\lambda}{\alpha} & -\frac{\lambda}{\beta} \end{pmatrix},\ V = \begin{pmatrix} \eta\Omega \\ 0 \\ 0 \\ 0 \end{pmatrix},\ U = \begin{pmatrix} 0 \\ 0 \\ 0 \\ \sigma E^* \end{pmatrix}^T,$$

with $\eta = \frac{R_0}{L_0}$, $\Omega = \frac{E_0}{E^*}$, $\gamma = \frac{1}{C_0 R_0}$, $\mu = \frac{R_0}{L_1}$, $\nu = \frac{R_1}{L_1}$, $\lambda = \frac{1}{C_1 R^*}$, $\beta = \frac{R_L}{R^*}$, $\alpha = \frac{R_0}{R^*}$ where R^* is a normalization resistance taken equal to 1. Moreover, $x_1 = \frac{R_0 i_0}{E^*}$, $x_2 = \frac{U_0}{E^*}$, $x_3 = \frac{R_0 i_1}{E^*}$, $x_4 = \frac{U_1}{E^*}$, where E^* is a voltage which permits us to work with dimensionless variables and is equal to 1 here.

Coefficients L_0 and L_1 (in H) are the inductances, C_0 and C_1 (in F) are capacities, R_0, R_1 and R_L (in Ω) are losses in the inductances, R_c is th load resistor. Moreover, i_0 and i_1 (in A) are currents in the inductance coils. Values U_0 and U_1 (in V) are voltages on the condensers of capacities C_0 and C_1 respectively according to indices 0 and 1. These indices respectively represent the elements of the input filter and of the output filter. Finally, E_0 is the input voltage.

3.4 Determination of period-k cycles equations ($k \geq 1$)

In this paragraph, we remain the results established in (Quémard et al., 2005), (Quémard et al., 2006), (Quémard, 2007b).

From general system (5), as we have $\xi(t_n) = S_1$ or S_2 (t_n is the n-th switching time if it exists), the trajectory follows a cycle by construction. So, it is rather natural to study the limit cycles existence for the general system. Moreover, the existence of such cycles for those non linear systems has already been proved in (Zhusubaliyev & Mosekilde, 2003), (Girard, 2003) for example.

Let t_0 be an initial given time and $t_1 < t_2 < ... < t_n < t_{n+1} < ...$ the increasing suite of successive switching times on $[t_0, +\infty[$, necessarily distincts because the definition of $q(\xi(t))$ implies $\xi(t_n) \neq \xi(t_{n-1})$.

To simplify notations, we set $q_n = q(\xi(t_n))$ and we have $q(\xi(t)) = q_n$ on $[t_n, t_{n+1}[$. Similarly, we set $\xi_n = \xi(t_n)$, $A_n = A(q_n)$, $V_n = V(q_n)$. A classical integration of (5) gives on interval $[t_n, t_{n+1}[$:

$$X(t) = e^{(t-t_n)A_n}\Gamma_n - A_n^{-1}V_n, \tag{7}$$

where $\Gamma_n \in \mathbb{R}^N$ correspond to the integration constants, functions of n.

Thus, introducing notation $\sigma_n = t_n - t_{n-1} > 0$, $n \geq 1$ and considering the continuity assumption at t_n, we obtain:

$$\begin{cases} \Gamma_n = e^{\sigma_n A_{n-1}}\Gamma_{n-1} + A_n^{-1}V_n - A_{n-1}^{-1}V_{n-1}, \forall n \geq 1 \\ \Gamma_0 = X(t_0) + A_0^{-1}V_0. \end{cases} \tag{8}$$

Then, we set $\forall n \geq 1$, $\xi_n = f(S_1, S_2, q_{n-1}, q_n)$ (f function from $\mathbb{R}^4$ to $\mathbb{R}$ in order to have $\xi_n = S_1$ or S_2 according to the hysteresis variable q). By definition, we also can write $\forall n \geq 1$, $\xi_n = cst - WX(t_n) = cst - W(\Gamma_n - A_n^{-1}V_n)$. So, combining those two expressions for ξ_n, we finally obtain:

$$\forall n \geq 1, cst - W(\Gamma_n - A_n^{-1}V_n) - f(S_1, S_2, q_{n-1}, q_n) = 0. \tag{9}$$

Resolution of system (5), (6) with unknowns $X(t)$, $(t_n)_{n\in\mathbb{N}}$ is equivalent to the one of system (8), (6) with unknowns $(\Gamma_n)_{n\geq 1}$, $(\sigma_n)_{n\geq 1}$. Nevertheless, it is very difficult to explicitly solve this system with theoretical way (Jaulin et al., 2001), (Zhusubaliyev & Mosekilde, 2003) so we content ourselves with a numerical resolution.

Moreover, such globally non linear systems can admit zero, one or more solutions (Quémard et al., 2006), (Quémard, 2007b), (Quémard, 2009) that implies the existence of period-k cycles ($k \geq 1$). To determine equations of those cycles, we introduce for all suite $(U_n)_{n\in\mathbb{N}}$ the

following notation $U_n^i = U_{2kn+i}$, $n \geq 0$, for $i = 1, ..., 2k$ with $k \in \mathbb{N}^*$ which corresponds to the cycle period.
Thus, the suite of successive switching times is noted $(\sigma_n^1, \sigma_n^2, \ldots, \sigma_n^{2k-1}, \sigma_n^{2k})_{n\in\mathbb{N}}$ and the one of the successive integration constants is noted $(\Gamma_n^1, \Gamma_n^2, \ldots, \Gamma_n^{2k-1}, \Gamma_n^{2k})_{n\in\mathbb{N}}$. We set $R_n = (\sigma_n^1, \Gamma_n^1, \ldots, \sigma_n^{2k}, \Gamma_n^{2k})$. We suppose that R_n has a limit $R = (\sigma^1, \Gamma^1, \ldots, \sigma^{2k}, \Gamma^{2k})$. In those conditions, at R, system of equations (8), (9) is equivalent to system $H(R, R) = 0, \forall n \geq 0$ where $H = (H_1, \ldots, H_{4k})^T$ is a function defined for $i = 1, ..., 2k$ by:

$$\begin{cases} H_i(R,R) = \Gamma^i - e^{\sigma^i A_{i-1}}\Gamma^{i-1} - A_i^{-1}V_i + A_{i-1}^{-1}V_{i-1} = 0, \\ H_{2k+i}(R,R) = cst - W(\Gamma^i - A_i^{-1}V_i) - f(S_1, S_2, q_{i-1}, q_i) = 0, \end{cases} \tag{10}$$

with index $i = 0$ if i is even and $i = 1$ if i is odd. Moreover, $\Gamma_n^0 = \Gamma_n^{2k}$.
From each $2k$ first equations H_i, $i = 1, ..., 2k$ of (10) and using the first remaining $2k - 1$ equations, we can determine by recurrence an expression of Γ^i, $i = 1, ..., 2k$ which becomes a function of σ^i, $i = 1, ..., 2k$. Then, replacing Γ^i, $i = 1, ..., 2k$ with this expression in the last $2k$ equations H_{2k+i}, $i = 1, ..., 2k$, of system (10), we can obtain, for $i = 1, ..., 2k$, the following system of $2k$ equations F_i for $2k$ unknowns σ^i, $i = 1, ..., 2k$:

$$\begin{aligned} F_i = &-W((I_N - \textstyle\prod_{m=1}^{2k} D_{(i-m+1)\mathrm{mod}(2k)})^{-1}(I_N + \sum_{j=1}^{2k-1}(-1)^j(\prod_{l=1}^{2k-j} D_{(i-l+1)\mathrm{mod}(2k)})) \\ &(A_i^{-1}V_i - A_{i-1}^{-1}V_{i-1}) - A_i^{-1}V_i) - f(S_1, S_2, q_{i-1}, q_i) + cst = 0. \end{aligned} \tag{11}$$

with $D_m = e^{\sigma^m A_{m-1}}$, $m = 1, \ldots, 2k$ and setting $D_0 = D_{2k}$.
This system represents the period-k cycle equations ($k \geq 1$) and it will be solved numerically for the two considered applications either with the formal calculus (*Maple*) and the interval analysis (*Proj2D*) or with a classical Newton algorithm (*Matlab*). If we apply system (11) to the application of the thermostat, we have, for example, for a period-2 cycle and after setting $K_1 = F_1 - F_4$, $K_2 = F_3 - F_2$, $K_3 = F_2 - F_4$, $K_4 = F_1$, the following equivalent system:

$$\begin{cases} K_1(\sigma^1,\sigma^2,\sigma^3,\sigma^4) = L(I_N - e^{(\sigma^1+\sigma^2+\sigma^3+\sigma^4)A})^{-1}(I_N - e^{\sigma^1 A}) \\ (I_N - e^{\sigma^4 A} + e^{(\sigma^3+\sigma^4)A} - e^{(\sigma^2+\sigma^3+\sigma^4)A})A^{-1}B + \Delta\theta = 0 \\ K_2(\sigma^1,\sigma^2,\sigma^3,\sigma^4) = L(I_N - e^{(\sigma^1+\sigma^2+\sigma^3+\sigma^4)A})^{-1}(I_N - e^{\sigma^3 A}) \\ (I_N - e^{\sigma^2 A} + e^{(\sigma^1+\sigma^2)A} - e^{(\sigma^1+\sigma^2+\sigma^4)A})A^{-1}B + \Delta\theta = 0 \\ K_3(\sigma^1,\sigma^2,\sigma^3,\sigma^4) = L(I_N - e^{(\sigma^1+\sigma^2+\sigma^3+\sigma^4)A})^{-1}(e^{\sigma^2 A}(I_N - e^{\sigma^1 A} + e^{(\sigma^1+\sigma^4)A}) \\ -e^{\sigma^4 A}(I_N - e^{\sigma^3 A} + e^{(\sigma^2+\sigma^3)A}))A^{-1}B = 0 \\ K_4(\sigma^1,\sigma^2,\sigma^3,\sigma^4) = \Delta q_1 L(I_N - e^{(\sigma^1+\sigma^2+\sigma^3+\sigma^4)A})^{-1}(I_N - e^{\sigma^1 A} + e^{(\sigma^1+\sigma^4)A} \\ -e^{(\sigma^1+\sigma^3+\sigma^4)A})A^{-1}B - (1-q_0)LA^{-1}B - LA^{-1}C - (1-q_0)\theta_1 - q_0\theta_2 = 0. \end{cases} \tag{12}$$

Similarly, wo have for the electronical application the following system for period-2 cycle equations:

$$\begin{cases} K_1(\sigma^1,\sigma^2,\sigma^3,\sigma^4) = U_{ref} - U((I_N - e^{\sigma^1 A_0}e^{\sigma^4 A_1}e^{\sigma^3 A_0}e^{\sigma^2 A_1})^{-1} \\ (I_N - e^{\sigma^1 A_0} + e^{\sigma^1 A_0}e^{\sigma^4 A_1} - e^{\sigma^1 A_0}e^{\sigma^4 A_1}e^{\sigma^3 A_2})(A_1^{-1} - A_0^{-1})V - A_1^{-1}V) - \frac{1}{2}(q_1 - q_0)\chi_0 = 0, \\ K_2(\sigma^1,\sigma^2,\sigma^3,\sigma^4) = U_{ref} - U((I_N - e^{\sigma^2 A_1}e^{\sigma^1 A_0}e^{\sigma^4 A_1}e^{\sigma^3 A_0})^{-1} \\ (I_N - e^{\sigma^2 A_1} + e^{\sigma^2 A_1}e^{\sigma^1 A_0} - e^{\sigma^2 A_1}e^{\sigma^1 A_0}e^{\sigma^4 A_1})(A_0^{-1} - A_1^{-1})V - A_0^{-1}V) - \frac{1}{2}(q_0 - q_1)\chi_0 = 0, \\ K_3(\sigma^1,\sigma^2,\sigma^3,\sigma^4) = U_{ref} - U((I_N - e^{\sigma^3 A_0}e^{\sigma^2 A_1}e^{\sigma^1 A_0}e^{\sigma^4 A_1})^{-1} \\ (I_N - e^{\sigma^3 A_0} + e^{\sigma^3 A_0}e^{\sigma^2 A_1} - e^{\sigma^3 A_0}e^{\sigma^2 A_1}e^{\sigma^1 A_0})(A_1^{-1} - A_0^{-1})V - A_1^{-1}V) - \frac{1}{2}(q_1 - q_0)\chi_0 = 0, \\ K_4(\sigma^1,\sigma^2,\sigma^3,\sigma^4) = U_{ref} - U((I_N - e^{\sigma^4 A_1}e^{\sigma^3 A_0}e^{\sigma^2 A_1}e^{\sigma^1 A_0})^{-1} \\ (I_N - e^{\sigma^4 A_1} + e^{\sigma^4 A_1}e^{\sigma^3 A_0} - e^{\sigma^4 A_1}e^{\sigma^3 A_0}e^{\sigma^2 A_1})(A_0^{-1} - A_1^{-1})V - A_0^{-1}V) - \frac{1}{2}(q_0 - q_1)\chi_0 = 0. \end{cases} \tag{13}$$

3.5 Hybrid Poincaré application

Function f of theorem 2.1 will be the hybrid Poincaré application for our two applications. So, we have to introduce this function for the general system (5) (see (Quémard et al., 2005)).
To do this, we firstly consider the following different ways to write $\xi(t_n) = \xi_n$ given by this system:

$$\begin{cases} \xi_n = f(S_1, S_2, q_{n-1}, q_n), \\ \xi_n = cst - WX(t_n^-) = cst - W(e^{\sigma_n A_{n-1}}\Gamma_{n-1} - A_{n-1}^{-1}V_{n-1}) \end{cases}$$

and that gives:

$$cst - W(e^{\sigma_n A_{n-1}}\Gamma_{n-1} - A_{n-1}^{-1}V_{n-1}) - f(S_1, S_2, q_{n-1}, q_n) = 0. \tag{14}$$

Duration σ_n, $n \geq 1$, implicitly given by equation (14), defines for $n \geq 1$ a function Ψ_{q_n} of Γ_{n-1} such that:

$$\sigma_n = \psi_{q_n}(\Gamma_{n-1}), \quad \forall n \geq 1. \tag{15}$$

Moreover, equation (8), introduced in the last paragraph, defines for $n \geq 1$ a function g_{q_n} of σ_n and of Γ_{n-1} *i.e.*:

$$\Gamma_n = g_{q_n}(\sigma_n, \Gamma_{n-1}), \quad \forall n \geq 1. \tag{16}$$

Then, we set:

$$\begin{cases} \forall n \geq 1, \quad G_{q_n}(.) = g_{q_n}(\psi_{q_n}(.), .), \\ \forall n \geq 2, \quad h_{q_n} = G_{q_n} \circ G_{q_{n-1}}(.). \end{cases} \tag{17}$$

Since $q_n = q_0$ if n is even and $q_n = q_1$ if n is odd, we obtain $h_{q_n} = h_{q_0}$ if n is even and $h_{q_n} = h_{q_1}$ if n is odd ($n \geq 1$). We note:

$$h : \mathbb{R}^N \longrightarrow \mathbb{R}^N$$
$$\Gamma \longmapsto \begin{cases} h_{q_0}(\Gamma) \text{ if } n \text{ is even} \\ h_{q_1}(\Gamma) \text{ if } n \text{ is odd.} \end{cases} \tag{18}$$

Function h defined by (18) corresponds to the hybrid Poincaré application associated to the studied h.d.s. Period-1 cycles are built from fixed points Γ^2 for h_{q_0} and Γ^1 for h_{q_1}. Period-2 cycles correspond to a 2-periodic point Γ^4 (or Γ^2) for h_{q_0} and Γ^1 (or Γ^3) for h_{q_1} characterized by $h_{q_0}(\Gamma^4) = \Gamma^2$, $h_{q_1}(\Gamma^1) = \Gamma^3$ and $h_{q_0} \circ h_{q_0}(\Gamma^4) = h_{q_0}^2(\Gamma^4) = \Gamma^4$, $h_{q_1} \circ h_{q_1}(\Gamma^1) = h_{q_1}^2 = \Gamma^1$.

4. Theorem application to the thermostat

For this application to the thermostat presented in section 3, we decide to vary parameter $\mu = R_c$ which corresponds to the convector resistance and we choose for other parameters, fixed values given in table 1.

R_t	R_m	Q_t	Q_c	Q_p	P_t	P_c	θ_e	θ_1	θ_2
1.5	1	50	800	5000	0.8	50	281	293	294

Table 1. Numerical values to illustrate a period-doubling bifurcation for the thermostat.

To plot the bifurcation diagram given by figure 5, we use *Matlab* and for each value of parameter R_c, we solve system (12) with a classical Newton algorithm. Then, we plot the corresponding values of σ^2 and σ^4 (we could have chosen σ^1 and σ^3). If σ^2 and σ^4 have the same values then, the Newton algorithm tends to a period-1 cycle. Otherwise, it tends to a period-2 cycle. It is from value $R_c = R_{c_0} \simeq 1.5453923$ that σ^2 and σ^4 begin to take different

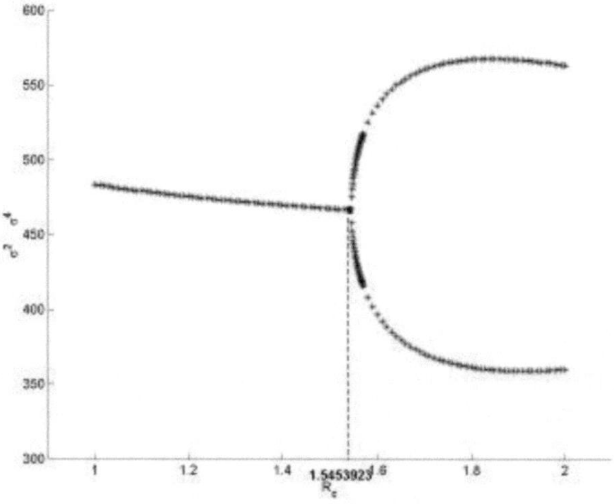

Fig. 5. Bifurcation diagram for the thermostat.

numerical values. For $R_c \leq R_{c_0}$, the Newton algorithm tends to a period-1 cycle and for $R_c > R_{c_0}$, it tends to a period-2 cycle. Figure 6 illustrates this phenomenon.
Before verifying the four conditions of theorem 2.1, we need to compute numerical values for σ^i and Γ^i, $i = 1, 2$ at $R_c = R_{c_0}$. From system (12), we obtain values of σ^i and from these values, we can compute the ones of Γ^i which can be written as a function of σ^i. We obtain $\sigma^1 \simeq 144.473853$, $\sigma^2 \simeq 466.851260$, $\Gamma^1 = (15.172083 \quad 1.049091 \quad -3.221174)^T$, $\Gamma^2 = (-47.749927 \quad -1.221632 \quad 8.971559)^T$.

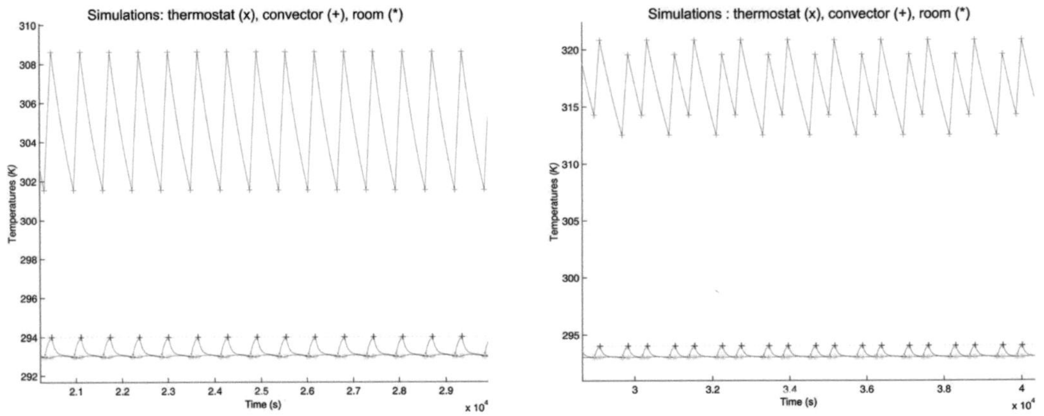

Fig. 6. Period-1 cycle for $R_c \leq R_{c_0}$ (on the left) and period-2 cycle for $R_c > R_{c_0}$ (on the right).

Now, we can begin to apply theorem 2.1 to the adapted Poincaré application h_{q_n} associated to the thermostat which is explicitly given by:

$$h_{q_n} : \mathbb{R}^N \times \mathbb{R} \longrightarrow \mathbb{R}^N$$
$$(\Gamma_{n-2}, R_c) \longmapsto \begin{cases} h_{q_0}(\Gamma^2_{n-1}, R_c) = h_{q_{0R_c}}(\Gamma^2_{n-1}) \text{ if } n \text{ is even} \\ h_{q_1}(\Gamma^1_{n-1}, R_c) = h_{q_{1R_c}}(\Gamma^1_{n-1}) \text{ if } n \text{ is odd.} \end{cases}$$

Here, we restrict our study to the case n even (the case n odd giving the same results). Let us verify the four assumptions of theorem 2.1.

• **First assumption:**

We have built the Poincaré application in order to have Γ^2 as a fixed point of h_{q_0}. So, $h_{q_{0R_{c0}}}(\Gamma^2) = G_{q_{0R_{c0}}} \circ G_{q_{1R_{c0}}}(\Gamma^2) = G_{q_{0R_{c0}}}(\Gamma^1) = \Gamma^2$ and the first assumption is satisfied.

• **Second assumption:**

Here, we can omit parameter R_c since it is fixed and so, does not affect the result. Then, the Poincaré application becomes a function only of Γ^2_{n-1}. Thus, we can write $Dh_{q_0}(\Gamma^2) = \partial_{\Gamma^2_{n-1}} h_{q_{0R_{c0}}}(\Gamma^2)$ the Jacobian matrix of h_{q_0}.

We need to give the expression of the Jacobian matrix Dh_{q_0} so, since it will be also used for the electronical application, we will compute it in the general way. We note $h_{q_n}(\Gamma_{n-2}) = G_{q_n} \circ G_{q_{n-1}}(\Gamma_{n-2})$. Therefore, the Jacobian matrix Dh_{q_n} is given by:

$$\begin{aligned} Dh_{q_n}(\Gamma_{n-2}) &= DG_{q_n}(G_{q_{n-1}}(\Gamma_{n-2}))DG_{q_{n-1}}(\Gamma_{n-2}) \\ &= DG_{q_n}(\Gamma_{n-1})DG_{q_{n-1}}(\Gamma_{n-2}). \end{aligned} \tag{19}$$

>From definition (17) of G_{q_n}, we have:

$$DG_{q_n}(\Gamma_{n-1}) = \frac{\partial g_{q_n}}{\partial \sigma_n}(\sigma_n, \Gamma_{n-1})\frac{\partial \psi_{q_n}}{\partial \Gamma_{n-1}}(\Gamma_{n-1}) + \frac{\partial g_{q_n}}{\partial \Gamma_{n-1}}(\sigma_n, \Gamma_{n-1}). \tag{20}$$

We easily obtain $\frac{\partial g_{q_n}}{\partial \sigma_n}(\sigma_n, \Gamma_{n-1})$ and $\frac{\partial g_{q_n}}{\partial \Gamma_{n-1}}(\sigma_n, \Gamma_{n-1})$ derivating the second member of equation (8) respectively with respect to σ_n and Γ_{n-1}:

$$\begin{cases} \frac{\partial g_{q_n}}{\partial \sigma_n}(\sigma_n, \Gamma_{n-1}) = A_{n-1} e^{\sigma_n A_{n-1}} \Gamma_{n-1} \\ \frac{\partial g_{q_n}}{\partial \Gamma_{n-1}}(\sigma_n, \Gamma_{n-1}) = e^{\sigma_n A_{n-1}}. \end{cases}$$

Moreover, the calculus of $\frac{\partial \psi_{q_n}}{\partial \Gamma_{n-1}}(\Gamma_{n-1})$ is obtained differentiating implicit equation given by (14) with respect to Γ_{n-1} with $\sigma_n = \Psi_{q_n}(\Gamma_{n-1})$ and gives:

$$-WA_{n-1} e^{\sigma_n A_{n-1}} \Gamma_{n-1} \frac{\partial \psi_{q_n}}{\partial \Gamma_{n-1}}(\Gamma_{n-1}) - W e^{\sigma_n A_{n-1}} = 0.$$

If $-WA_{n-1} e^{\sigma_n A_{n-1}} \Gamma_{n-1} \neq 0$ that we assume, we can deduce:

$$\frac{\partial \psi_{q_n}}{\partial \Gamma_{n-1}}(\Gamma_{n-1}) = \frac{-W e^{\sigma_n A_{n-1}}}{WA_{n-1} e^{\sigma_n A_{n-1}} \Gamma_{n-1}}. \tag{21}$$

Finally, we can write:

$$DG_{q_n}(\Gamma_{n-1}) = \left(I_N - \frac{A_{n-1} e^{\sigma_n A_{n-1}} \Gamma_{n-1} W}{WA_{n-1} e^{\sigma_n A_{n-1}} \Gamma_{n-1}} \right) e^{\sigma_n A_{n-1}}, \tag{22}$$

and we deduce the expression of $Dh_{q_n}(\Gamma_{n-2})$ with (19).
For the first application of the thermostat, we choose an eigenvectors basis and relatively to this basis, we obtain:

$$Dh_{q_0}(\Gamma^2) = \left(I_3 - \frac{A e^{\sigma^2 A} \Gamma^1 L}{LA e^{\sigma^2 A} \Gamma^1} \right) e^{\sigma^2 A} \left(I_3 - \frac{A e^{\sigma^1 A} \Gamma^2 L}{LA e^{\sigma^1 A} \Gamma^2} \right) e^{\sigma^1 A}.$$

Numerically, we have:

$$Dh_{q_0}(\Gamma^2) \simeq \begin{pmatrix} -1.8419626299 & 0.4499899352 & -0.8182826401 \\ -0.0011184622 & 0.0097398043 & 0.0174088456 \\ 1.8430810922 & -0.4597297396 & 0.8008737945 \end{pmatrix},$$

which has three eigenvalues $\lambda_1 = -1, \quad \lambda_2 = 0, \quad \lambda_3 \simeq -0.031348$. One is equal to -1 and the others respect $|\lambda_i| \neq 1, i = 2, 3$ so the second assumption of the theorem is verified.

• **Third assumption:** If we reason like in the theorem proof, we have, since $Dh_{q_0}(\Gamma^2)$ has not 1 as eigenvalue, $x_f(R_c)$, curve of fixed points exists with, in particular, $x_f(R_{c_0}) = \Gamma^2$.
Matrix of the first derivatives of $h_{q_{0_{R_c}}}$ with respect to Γ^2_{n-1} at $x_f(R_c)$ takes the following form $\forall n \geq 1$:

$$\partial_{\Gamma^2_{n-1}} h_{q_{0_{R_c}}}(x_f(R_c)) = \left(\frac{\partial h^i_{q_{0_{R_c}}}}{\partial \Gamma^{2j}_{n-1}}(x_f(R_c)) \right)_{i,j=1,\ldots,3} = \begin{pmatrix} a_1 & a_2 & a_3 \\ b_1 & b_2 & b_3 \\ c_1 & c_2 & c_3 \end{pmatrix}, \tag{23}$$

where $\Gamma^{2j}_{n-1}, j = 1,\ldots,3$ represents the j-th component of vector Γ^2_{n-1} and $h^i_{q_{0R_c}}, i = 1,\ldots,3$ is the i-th component of $h_{q_{0R_c}}$.
So, to find eigenvalues of $\partial_{\Gamma^2_{n-1}} h_{q_{0R_c}}(x_f(R_c))$, we have to solve equation $\det(\partial_{\Gamma^2_{n-1}} h_{q_{0R_c}}(x_f(R_c)) - zI_3) = 0$.
Moreover, firstly, we can remark, from equation (9), that we have $-WD\Gamma_n = 0$ *i.e.* $-WDG_{q_n}(\Gamma_{n-1}) = 0$ by definition of G_{q_n}. This means that $-W$ is a left eigenvector of $DG_{q_n}(\Gamma_{n-1})$ associated to eigenvalue 0 and so, 0 is always an eigenvalue for $Dh_{q_n}(\Gamma_{n-2})$ *i.e.* $\det(\partial_{\Gamma^2_{n-1}} h_{q_{0R_c}}(x_f(R_c)) = 0$.
Taking into account this remark, we know that to compute the two other eigenvalues, it remains to solve the following equation:

$$-\lambda^2 + \lambda.\mathrm{Tr}(\partial_{\Gamma^2_{n-1}} h_{q_{0R_c}}(x_f(R_c))) - \mathrm{Tr}(\mathrm{com}(\partial_{\Gamma^2_{n-1}} h_{q_{0R_c}}(x_f(R_c)))) = 0, \tag{24}$$

where $\mathrm{com}(M)$ corresponds to the comatrix of M for any square matrix M and with:

$$\begin{cases} \mathrm{Tr}(\partial_{\Gamma^2_{n-1}} h_{q_{0R_c}}(x_f(R_c))) = a_1 + b_2 + c_3, \\ \mathrm{Tr}(\mathrm{com}(\partial_{\Gamma^2_{n-1}} h_{q_{0R_c}}(x_f(R_c)))) = b_2c_3 - b_3c_2 + a_1c_3 - a_3c_1 + a_1b_2 - a_2b_1. \end{cases}$$

If $\lambda_1(R_c)$ (with $\lambda_1(R_{c_0}) = -1$) is an eigenvalue of $\partial_{\Gamma^2_{n-1}} h_{q_{0R_c}}(x_f(R_c))$, then $\lambda_1(R_c)$ verifies equation (24). Thus, derivating this obtained equation with respect to parameter R_c and then, applying it at $R_c = R_{c_0}$, we obtain:

$$-2\lambda_1'(R_{c_0})\lambda_1(R_{c_0}) + \lambda_1'(R_{c_0})\mathrm{Tr}(\partial_{\Gamma^2_{n-1}} h_{q_{0R_{c0}}}(\Gamma^2)) + \lambda_1(R_{c_0})\frac{\partial}{\partial R_c}(\mathrm{Tr}(\partial_{\Gamma^2_{n-1}} h_{q_{0R_c}}(x_f(R_c))))_{|R_c=R_{c0}}$$

$$-\frac{\partial}{\partial R_c}(\mathrm{Tr}(\mathrm{com}(\partial_{\Gamma^2_{n-1}} h_{q_{0R_c}}(x_f(R_c)))))_{|R_c=R_{c0}} = 0.$$

Thus, we finally obtain an expression for $\lambda_1'(R_{c_0}) = \frac{d\lambda_1}{dR_c}(R_{c_0})$:

$$\lambda_1'(R_{c_0}) = \frac{\frac{\partial}{\partial R_c}\left(\mathrm{Tr}(\partial_{\Gamma^2_{n-1}} h_{q_{0R_c}}(x_f(R_c))) + \mathrm{Tr}(\mathrm{com}(\partial_{\Gamma^2_{n-1}} h_{q_{0R_c}}(x_f(R_c))))\right)_{|R_c=R_{c0}}}{\left(2 + \mathrm{Tr}(\partial_{\Gamma^2_{n-1}} h_{q_{0R_{c0}}}(\Gamma^2))\right)}.$$

Therefore, we developp all computations and applying them to our numerical values, we finally obtain:

$$\lambda_1'(R_{c_0}) = \frac{d\lambda_1}{dR_c}(R_{c_0}) \simeq 16.9072 \neq 0,$$

that satisfies the third assumption of theorem 2.1.

• **Fourth assumption:**

To verify the last assumption of theorem 2.1, we have to compute β. As for the second assumption, we can omit R_c in all expressions because it does not affect the result.
To compute β, we need the calculation of the second and third derivatives of $h^i_{q_0}$, $i = 1,...,3$. They have been obtained applying the formula of the n-th derivatives of a function composition with several variables (we do not explicit them here since it is very long and without a big interest).

Moreover, for the second assumption, we have proved that $Dh_{q_0}(\Gamma^2)$ has three different eigenvalues noted λ_i, $i = 1, ..., 3$. So, we choose a basis a right eigenvectors of $Dh_{q_0}(\Gamma^2)$ noted $(v^1 \quad v^2 \quad v^3)$ such that v^i is associated to λ_i, $i = 1, ..., 3$ with, in particular, v^1 associated to -1. We numerically have:

$$v^1 \simeq \begin{pmatrix} 1 \\ 0.018670 \\ -1.018670 \end{pmatrix}, v^2 \simeq \begin{pmatrix} 1.037479 - 0.297064i \\ 0.811752 - 0.232431i \\ -1.849231 + 0.529494i \end{pmatrix}, v^3 \simeq \begin{pmatrix} 0.870614 - 0.066942i \\ 1.816933 - 0.139705i \\ -0.960593 + 0.073860i \end{pmatrix}.$$

Similarly, we take as a dual basis $\{w^j\}_{j=1,...,3}$ of $\{v^j\}_{j=1,...,3}$ the left eigenvectors of matrix $Dh_{q_0}(\Gamma^2, R_{c_0})$ associated to λ_i, $i = 1, ..., 3$ such that $w^i v^j = 1$ if $i = j$ and $w^i v^j = 0$ otherwise. We numerically obtain:

$$w^1 \simeq \begin{pmatrix} 1.885527 \\ -0.448237 \\ 0.861079 \end{pmatrix}, w^2 \simeq \begin{pmatrix} -1.237960 - 0.354468i \\ -0.049794 - 0.014257i \\ -1.216183 - 0.348232i \end{pmatrix}, w^3 \simeq \begin{pmatrix} 0.575651 + 0.044262i \\ 0.575651 + 0.044262i \\ 0.575651 + 0.044262i \end{pmatrix}.$$

Thus, the computation of β becomes possible and numerically gives:

$$\beta \simeq 0.7049 \neq 0,$$

that verifies the fourth and last assumption of theorem 2.1.

• **Conclusion:** These four assumptions theoretically prove, with the period-doubling bifurcation thereom, that there exists at $R_c \simeq R_{c_0} \simeq 1.5453923$ a period-doubling bifurcation which highlights the loss of stability of the stable period-1 cycle and the emergence of a stable period-2 cycle. It confirms that we had graphically seen.

5. Theorem application to the DC/DC converter

Other authors (Zhusubaliyev & Mosekilde, 2003), (Lim & Hamill, 1999) were interested in the problem of period-doubling bifurcations for this electronical application. However, they often study the phenomenon only using bifurcation diagrams.

Here, we propose a theoretical proof but firstly, we can also propose a bifurcation diagram to highlight the crossing of a period-1 cycle to a period-2 cycle with the variation of one parameter.

We choose the fixed following numerical values in table 2 and L_0 is the variable parameter. To plot the bifurcation diagram given by figure 7, we use the same method than the

R_1	R_0	R_L	L_1	C_0	C_1	U_{ref}	σ	χ_0	E_0
2	5	80	0.09	3.10^{-6}	2.10^{-5}	2.4	0.1	0.25	200

Table 2. Numerical values to illustrate a period-doubling bifurcation for the DC/DC converter.

one use for the thermostat solving system (13) with a Newton algorithm for each value of L_0. It is from value $L_0 \simeq L_{0_0} \simeq 0.1888073$ that σ^2 and σ^4 begin to take different values. Figure 8 illustrates that, for $L_0 \leq L_{0_0}$, the Newton algorithm tends to a period-1 cycle and for $L_0 > L_{0_0}$, it tends to a period-2 cycle. As for the thermal application, we need to compute values of σ^i and Γ^i, $i = 1,2$ at $L_0 = L_{0_0}$. It is done with a Newton algorithm and system (13) to obtain σ^i and the integration constants Γ^i,

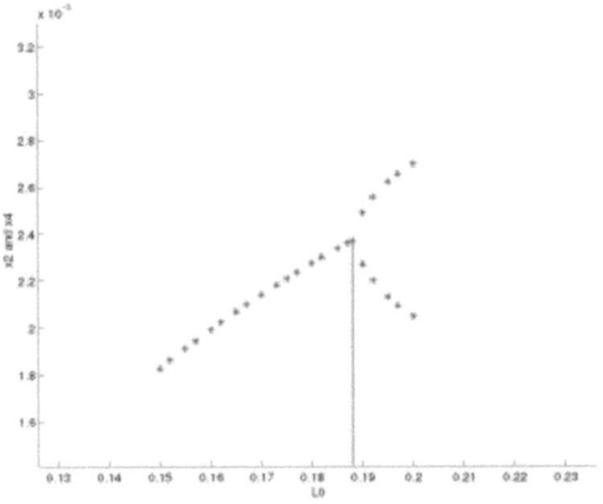

Fig. 7. Bifurcation diagram for the DC/DC converter.

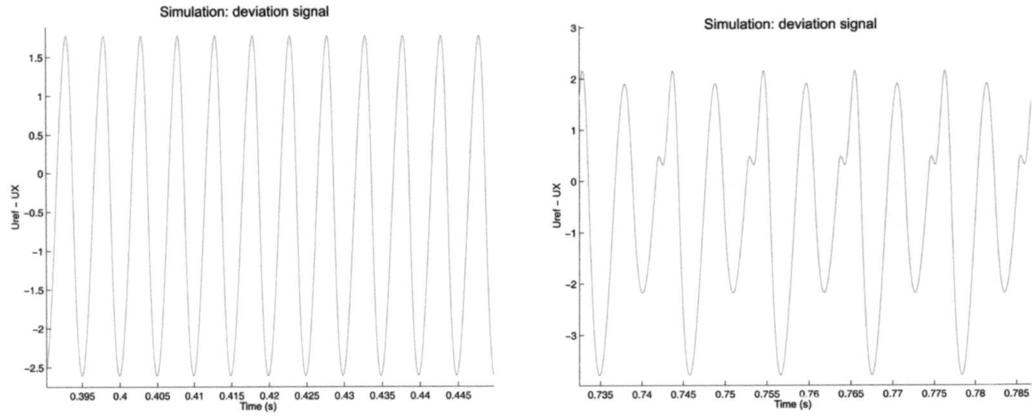

Fig. 8. Period-1 cycle for $L_0 \leq L_{0_0}$ (on the left) and period-2 cycle for $L_0 > L_{0_0}$ (one the right).

$i = 1, 2$ are computed from the obtained values of σ^i since we have seen that they are only functions of σ^i. We numerically obtain: $\sigma^1 \simeq 0.0030227$, $\sigma^2 \simeq 0.0023804$, $\Gamma^1 \simeq (7.690 + 1.156i \quad -54.176 - 386.422i \quad 6.199 + 3.877i \quad -81.201 - 55.029i)^T$, $\Gamma^2 \simeq (-2.266 + 0.742i \quad -38.350 + 113.344i \quad -3.090 + 0.286i \quad 13.250 + 39.466i)^T$.
Thus, we verify the four assumptions of theorem 2.1 using the Poncaré application $h_{q_{0_{L_0}}}$ (we obtain the same results for $h_{q_{1_{L_0}}}$) associated to our DC/DC converter.

• **First assumption:**

The first assumption is clearly staisfied by construction of the Poincaré application associated to our system.

• **Second assumption:**

As for the thermal application, for this assumption, parameter L_0 is fixed to L_{0_0} so does not affect the result. Thus, the Poincaré application can be considered as a function of Γ^2_{n-1}. With numerical values of table 2, of σ^i and of Γ^i, $i = 1, 2$, we numerically compute the Jacobian matrix of h_{q_0} at Γ^2 and L_{0_0} and we obtain:

$$Dh_{q_0}(\Gamma^2) \simeq \begin{pmatrix} -0.3194-0.2921i & 0.0048-0.0027i & 0.1451-0.0027i & 0.0165-0.0074i \\ 12.0276+6.8908i & -0.3194+0.2921i & 8.0084+9.1076i & 0.0673+1.1643i \\ 0.49640+0.1299i & 0.0091+0.0046i & -0.3067-0.0494i & -0.0126-0.0194i \\ 4.2869-5.3865i & 0.1065-0.0865i & -2.2699+3.4955i & -0.3067+0.4939i \end{pmatrix}.$$

This matrix has four different eigenvalues $\lambda_1 = -1$, $\lambda_2 = 0$, $\lambda_3 \simeq 0.079202$ and $\lambda_4 \simeq -0.331416$. One of this value is equal to -1 and the others verify $|\lambda_i| \neq 1$, $i = 2,3,4$ so the second assumption is satisfied.

• Third assumption:

Let $x_f(L_0)$ be the curve of the fixed-point of $h_{q0_{L_0}}$. The matrix of the first derivatives of $h_{q0_{L_0}}$ with respect to Γ^2_{n-1} at $x_f(L_0)$ can be written for the DC/DC converter:

$$\partial_{\Gamma^2_{n-1}} h_{q0_{L_0}}(x_f(L_0)) = \left(\frac{\partial h^i_{q0_{L_0}}}{\partial \Gamma^{2j}_{n-1}}(x_f(L_0)) \right)_{i,j=1,\dots,4} = \begin{pmatrix} a_1 & a_2 & a_3 & a_4 \\ b_1 & b_2 & b_3 & b_4 \\ c_1 & c_2 & c_3 & c_4 \\ d_1 & d_2 & d_3 & d_4 \end{pmatrix}.$$

Then, to compute $\lambda_1'(L_{0_0}) = \frac{d\lambda_1}{dL_0}(L_{0_0})$, we use the same method than the one explained for the thermostat. We develop equation $\det(\partial_{\Gamma^2_{n-1}} h_{q0_{L_0}}(x_f(L_0)) - \lambda I_4) = 0$ and we simplify it using the fact that 0 is always an eigenvalue of $\partial_{\Gamma^2_{n-1}} h_{q0_{L_0}}(x_f(L_0))$. Then, assuming that $\lambda_1(L_0)$ is an eigenvalue of $\partial_{\Gamma^2_{n-1}} h_{q0_{L_0}}(x_f(L_0))$ with $\lambda_1(L_{0_0}) = -1$, we obtain at L_{0_0}:

$$\lambda_1'(L_{0_0}) = \frac{\frac{\partial}{\partial L_0}\left(\mathrm{Tr}(\partial_{\Gamma^2_{n-1}} h_{q0_{L_0}}(x_f(L_0))) + M_1(L_0) + \mathrm{Tr}(\mathrm{com}(\partial_{\Gamma^2_{n-1}} h_{q0_{L_0}}(x_f(L_0)))) \right)_{|L_0=L_{0_0}}}{(3+2\mathrm{Tr}(\partial_{\Gamma^2_{n-1}} h_{q0_{L_{0_0}}}(\Gamma^2)) + M_1(L_{0_0}))},$$

where

$$\begin{cases} \mathrm{Tr}(\partial_{\Gamma^2_{n-1}} h_{q0_{L_0}}(x_f(L_0))) = a_1 + b_2 + c_3 + d_4, \\ M_1(L_0) = a_1b_2 - a_2b_1 + a_1c_3 - a_3c_1 + a_1d_4 - a_4d_1 + b_2c_3 - b_3c_2 + b_2d_4 - b_4d_2 + c_3d_4 - c_4d_3, \\ \mathrm{Tr}(\mathrm{com}(\partial_{\Gamma^2_{n-1}} h_{q0_{L_0}}(x_f(L_0)))) = a_1b_2c_3 + a_1b_2d_4 + a_1c_3d_4 + b_2c_3d_4 + b_3c_4d_2 + b_4c_2d_3 + a_2b_4d_1 \\ +a_3b_1c_2 + a_3c_4d_1 + a_4b_1d_2 + a_4c_1d_3 + a_2b_3c_1 - a_1b_4d_2 - a_1c_4d_3 - a_1b_3c_2 - b_2c_4d_3 - b_3c_2d_4 \\ -b_4c_3d_2 - a_3c_1d_4 - a_4b_2d_1 - a_4c_3d_1 - a_3b_2c_1 - a_2b_1c_3 - a_2b_1d_4. \end{cases}$$

We do not detail calculations here since they are the same than the one for the thermostat with index i which varies from 1 to 4. We finally numerically obtain:

$$\lambda_1'(L_{0_0}) \simeq 376.77 + 48.85i \neq 0,$$

that satisfies the third assumption of theorem 2.1.

• Fourth assumption:

To verify the last assumption of theorem 2.1, we have to compute β. To do this, we need to know the first, the second and the third derivatives of h_{q_0} with respect to Γ^2_{n-1}. They are obtained using our knowledge of the derivatives of a function composition with various variables.

Thus, it remains to give a right and a left eigenvectors basis of $Dh_{q_{0_{L_{0_0}}}}(\Gamma^2)$. For the right eigenvectors basis, we choose $(v^1 \quad v^2 \quad v^3 \quad v^4)$ with v^i associated to λ_i, $i = 1, ..., 4$ with, in particular, $\lambda_1 = -1$. We numerically choose:

$$v^1 \simeq \begin{pmatrix} 1 \\ -11.442836 + 48.851737i \\ -0.426519 - 1.349074i \\ -18.867917 - 2.085051i \end{pmatrix}, v^2 \simeq \begin{pmatrix} 0.5166742 - 0.78824872i \\ 17.01036378 + 44.12314420i \\ 0.65810329 - 0.22792681i \\ 9.27738581 + 1.11320087i \end{pmatrix}$$

$$v^3 \simeq \begin{pmatrix} 0.01119889 - 0.01608901i \\ 0.52509800 + 0.08316542i \\ 0.01236110 + 0.00503187i \\ 0.12880400 - 0.12438117i \end{pmatrix}, v^4 \simeq \begin{pmatrix} 0.01627771 - 0.18549512i \\ 2.81524460 + 8.90855146i \\ 0.05802415 + 0.01511695i \\ 0.50027614 - 0.62998584i \end{pmatrix}.$$

Identically, we take as a dual basis $\{w^j\}_{j=1,...,4}$ of $\{v^j\}_{j=1,...,4}$ the left eigenvectors of $Dh_{q_{0_{L_{0_0}}}}(\Gamma^2)$ associated to eigenvalues λ_i, $i = 1, ..., 4$ such that $w^i v^j = 1$ if $i = j$ and $w^i v^j = 0$ otherwise. We numerically have:

$$w^1 \simeq \begin{pmatrix} -6.00780496 + 3.31230746i \\ -0.10257727 - 0.09040793i \\ -0.65155347 - 1.40122597i \\ -0.10158624 + 0.05428312i \end{pmatrix}, w^2 \simeq \begin{pmatrix} 0 \\ 0 \\ 0.45187014 + 0.88898172i \\ 0.04698337 - 0.05759709i \end{pmatrix},$$

$$w^3 \simeq \begin{pmatrix} -0.15269597 - 0.97827008i \\ -0.007293202 - 0.01833645i \\ 0.44704526 + 0.83019484i \\ -0.026511494 + 0.06508790i \end{pmatrix}, w^4 \simeq \begin{pmatrix} 50.68797524 - 15.97723598i \\ 1.02351719 + 0.27277622i \\ 0.82854165 - 35.60644916i \\ -0.93039774 + 2.48628517i \end{pmatrix}.$$

We conclude $\beta \simeq 0.076 - 0.13i \neq 0$, that satisfies the last assumption.

• **Conclusion:**

The fourth assumptions of theorem 2.1 being satisfied, so, the theorem of period-doubling bifurcation can be applied and theoretically prove the existence of a period-doubling bifurcation at $L_0 = L_{0_0}$. It confirms the observations made on the bifurcation diagram of figure 7.

6. Conclusion

We have presented a new tool to theoretically prove the existence of a period-doubling bifurcation for a particular value of the parameters. This is a generalization of the period-doubling bifurcation theorem of systems of any dimension N, $N \geq 1$.

This result has been applied to two applications of industrial interest and of two different dimensions: the one of dimension three with the thermostat with an anticipative resistance and the second in dimension four with the DC/DC converter. This work has confirmed the observations graphically made on the bifurcation diagrams.

Such a bifurcation can appear from three-dimensional systems for the studied h.d.s. class. Indeed, in dimension one, as zero is the single eigenvalue of the Jacobian matrix Dh_{q_n}, we can directly conclude that there is not exist a bifurcation. Moreover, in dimension two, in (Quémard, 2007a), we have proved that the two eigenvalues of the Jacobian matrix Dh_{q_n} are 0 and $\exp((A_1 + A_2)(\sigma^1 + \sigma^2))$ where A_1 and A_2 are the diagonal elements of matrix A written in an eigenvectors basis and with $A_1 < 0$, $A_2 < 0$. So, since $\sigma^1 > 0$ and $\sigma^2 > 0$, in dimension two, Dh_{q_n} has two eigenvalues which belong to the open unit disk. Thus, there is no such bifurcation in dimension two.

Finally, in this paper, we have directly chosen numerical values for which there exists this type of bifurcation but sometimes, it is very difficult to find them. So, it would be very interesting to find a method which permits to quickly obtain those values. To do this, for exemple in dimension three, we can firstly use a graphical method varying two parameters and solving the period-2 cycle equations system with a Newton algorithm for each value of those parameters. Then, we plot, with two different colors, the corresponding points depending whether the algorithm converges to a period-1 cycle or to a period-2 cycle. It is not very precise but it can give an interval containing searched values. Then, to refine these values, we should build a system with three equations for three unknowns σ^1, σ^2 and the parameter which varies. This system could be solved with a Broyden algorithm for example taking initial values belonging to the obtained interval to ensure the algorithm convergence. From $\det(\partial_{\Gamma^2_{n-1}} h_{q_0}(\Gamma^2) - zI_3) = 0$ and knowing that 0 and -1 are two solutions at the bifurcation point, we could obtain the first equation. Then, from system (11) applied for period-1 cycles, we can obtain the two others considering the varying parameter as the third variable. This could be a future research work.

7. References

Aihara, K., Takabe, T. & Toyoda, M. (1998). Chaotic Neural Networks, *Physics Letters A* 144: 333–340.

Baker, G.-L. & Gollub, J.-P. (1990). *Chaotic dynamics an introduction*, 2nd edn, Cambridge University Press.

Cébron, B. (2000). *Commande de systèmes dynamiques hybrides*, PhD thesis, LISA, Université d'Angers,.

Chung, K., Chan, C. & Xu, J. (2003). An efficient method for switching branches of period-doubling bifurcations of strongly non-linear autonomous oscillators with many degrees of freedom, *Journal of Sound and Vibration* 267: 787–808.

Demazure, M. (1989). *Catastrophes et bifurcations*, Ellipses.

Girard, A. (2003). Computation and Stability Analysis of Limit Cycles in Piecewise Linear Hybrid Systems, *ADHS'2003 [Proc. of IFAC Conf.]*.

Gleick, J. (1991). *La théorie du chaos*, Champs Flammarion.

Guckenheimer, J. & Holmes, P.-J. (1991). *Nonlinear Oscillations, Dynamical Systems, and Bifurcations of Vector Fields*, 3rd edn, Springer.

Holmes, E., Lewis, M., Banks, J. & Veit, R. (1994). Partial differential equations in ecology: spatial interactions and population dynamics, *Physics Letters A* 75: 17–29.

Jaulin, L., Kieffer, M., Didrit, . & Walter, E. (2001). *Applied Interval Analysis with Examples in Parameter and State Estimation*, Springer-Verlag.

Kuznetsov, Y. (2004). *Elements of Applied Bifurcation Theory*, Springer.

Lim, Y. & Hamill, D. (1999). Problems of computing Lyapunov exponents in power electronics, *International Symposium on Circuits and Systems, Orlando FL* 5: 297–301.

Murray, J. (1989). *Mathematical biology*, Springer.

Quémard, C. (2007a). *Analyse et optimisation d'une classe particulière de systèmes dynamiques hybrides à commutations autonomes*, PhD thesis, LISA, Université d'Angers,.

Quémard, C. (2007b). Analysis of a Class of Hybrid Dynamical Systems with Hysteresis Phenomenon, *NumAn (Numerical Analysis, Kalamata)*.

Quémard, C. (2009). Switchings Conditions Study for a Particular Class of Hybrid Dynamical Systems, *WCE (London)*.

Quémard, C., Jolly, J.-C. & Ferrier, J.-L. (2005). Search for Cycles in Piecewise Linear Hybrid Dynamical Systems with Autonomous Switchings. Application to a Thermal Device, *IMACS'2005 World Congress (Paris)*.

Quémard, C., Jolly, J.-C. & Ferrier, J.-L. (2006). Search for Period-2 Cycles in a Class of Hybrid Dynamical Systems with Autonomous Switchings. Application to a Thermal Device, *ADHS'2006 (Alghero)*.

Robinson, C. (1999). *Dynamical Systems*, 2nd edn, CRC Press.

Saccadura, J.-F. (1998). *Initiation aux transferts thermiques*, Lavoisier.

Smith, J. & Cohen, R. (1984). Simple Finite-Element Model Accounts for Wide Range of Cardiac Dysrhythmias, *National Academy of Sciences of the United States of America* 81: 233–237.

Zhusubaliyev, Z. & Mosekilde, E. (2003). *Bifurcations and Chaos in Piecewise-Smooth Dynamical Systems*, Vol. 44 of *Nonlinear Science*, World Scientific.

Part 4

Advances in Applied Modeling

17

Geometry-Induced Transport Properties of Two Dimensional Networks

Zbigniew Domański
Institute of Mathematics, Czestochowa University of Technology, Poland

1. Introduction

This work analyses, in a general way, how the geometry of a network influences the transport of a hypothetical fluid through the network's channels. Here, it is the geometry of the network that matters even though the network and fluid bear broad interpretations ranging from a liquid passing through channel space of a filter, electrons moving inside circuits, bits flying between servers to a suburban highways crowded by cars.

The geometrical properties of networks have attracted much attention due to the progress in the field of computer science, mathematical biology, statistical physics and technology. A lot of systems operate as a two-dimensional network and numerous devices are constructed in a planar fashion. Examples are grids of processors, radar arrays, wireless sensor networks, as well as a wide range of micromechanical devices. Especially, the microfluidic systems are built with the use of methods borrowed from the semiconductor industry. Such systems generally employ the fabrication of highly ordered microscale structures. Also a migration of voids in almost jammed granulates in an example worth to mention in this context since the void-position rearrangement resembles the sliding block puzzles.

Theoretical models related to a given problem are useful if they help researches to explain observed facts and enable them to predict the system's behaviour beyond the experiments already conducted. The complexity of a real system frequently prevents constructing a model, in which all the observed characteristics can be accurately captured. Instead of constructing a model to acquire all the details, and in consequence building the model which is complicated and analytically untreatable, it is possible to formulate a rather rude, but statistically correct, description of the transport phenomena which obeys averaged characteristics. The premise of statistical modelling of a network flow phenomena is the graph theory with the fundamental equivalence between the maximum flow and minimal cost circulation and the cost-capacity scaling. Thus, the populations of transporting-network, appropriate for such statistical analysis, and based on graph theory may provide valuable information about the effectiveness of the network topology.

2. Mathematical modelling

2.1 Technological and physical ingredients

Physical and technological constituents of the network employed in mass and/or current transport cover waste range of size scale. If the transport occurs inside the channels, one can find huge oil installations with macroscopic pipes as well as small nano-fabricated channels transporting countable sets of molecules (Austin, 2007). Such nano-scale transport primarily exists in the world of biology where the nanofluidic channels present in living organisms deliver nutrients into cells and evacuate waste from cells.

A class of artificially fabricated systems can even organize particles' transport in a network-like manner with no material-channel-structure inside it, as is the case of systems sorting in an optical lattice (MacDonald et. al., 2003) or the Maragoni flows induced in thin liquid films for the purpose of microfluidic manipulations. In this latter case such devices as channels, filters or pumps are completely virtual. They have no physical structure and do their job by localized variation in surface tension due to the presence of heat sources suspended above the liquid surface (Basu & Gianchandani, 2008).

Here, we pay special attention to microfluidic devices. They are constructed in a planar fashion (Chou, 1999) and typically comprise at least two flat substrate layers that are mated together to define the channel networks. Channel intersections may exist in a number of formats, including cross intersections, "T" intersections, or other structures whereby two channels are in fluid communication (Han, 2008). Due to the small dimension of channels the flow of the fluid through a microfluidic channel is characterized by the Reynolds number of the order less than 10. In this regime the flow is predominantly laminar and thus molecules can be transported in a relatively predictable manner through the microchannel.

2.2 Network geometry

Numerous channel arrangements forming networks are applied in technology. Besides random or ad hoc arrangements an important class of networks, with dedicated channel architecture, is employed in microelectronic and microfluidic devices. Especially, the ordered-channel-space networks are interesting from the theoretical point of view and also because of their applicability in filters.

These networks have channel spaces built around the lattices known in the literature as Archimedean and the Laves lattices (Grünbaum & Shepard, 1986). For a given Archimedean lattices all its nodes play the same role thus, from the mathematical point of view, all the Archimedean lattices are the infinite transitive planar graphs. They divide the plane into regions, called faces, that are regular polygons. There exist exactly 11 Archimedean lattices. Three of them: the triangular, square and hexagonal lattices are built with only one type of face whereas the remaining eight lattices need more than one type of face. The former lattices belong to the regular tessellations of the plane and the latter ones are called semiregular lattices.

Another important group of lattices contains dual lattices of the Archimedean ones. The given lattice G can be mapped onto its dual lattice DG in such a way that the center of every face of G is a vertex in DG, and two vertices in DG are adjacent only if the corresponding faces in G share an edge. The square lattice is self-dual, and the triangular and hexagonal lattices are mutual duals. The dual lattices of the semiregular lattices form the family called Laves lattices. Finally, there are 19 possible regular arrangements of channel spaces.

The lattices are labeled according to the way they are drawn (Grünbaum & Shepard, 1986). Starting from a given vertex, the consecutive faces are listed by the number of edges in the face, e.g. a square lattice is labeled as (4, 4, 4, 4) or equivalently as (4^4). Consequently, the triangular and hexagonal lattices are (3^6) and (6^3), respectively. Other, frequently encountered lattices are (3, 6, 3, 6) – called Kagomé lattice and its dual *D*(3, 6, 3, 6) - known as Necker Cube lattice.

In some ways these 5 lattices serve as an ensemble representative to study conduction problems in two dimension. They form pairs of mutually dual lattices and also share some local properties as e.g. the coordination number *z* being the number of edges with a common vertex. One of the most interesting lattices in two dimension is the Kagomé lattice. Each its vertex touches a triangle, hexagon, triangle, and a hexagon. Moreover the vertices of this lattice correspond to the edges of the hexagonal lattice, which in turn is the dual of a triangular lattice. The Kagomé lattice is also related to the square lattice, they have the same value, $z = 4$, of the coordination number. Besides the above mentioned lattices, in this paper we have also analyzed other tiling, namely ($3, 12^2$), ($4, 8^2$), $D(4, 8^2)$, ($3^3, 4^2$), and $D(3^3, 4^2)$. Some of these lattices are presented in Fig. 1.

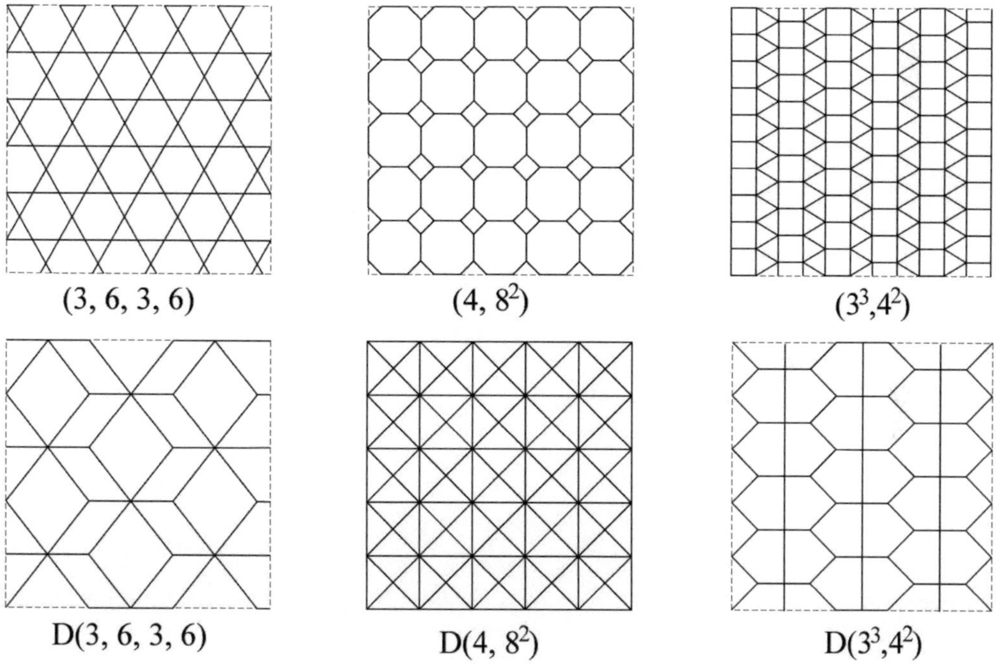

Fig. 1. Examples of Archimedean and Laves lattices.

2.3 Distribution of distance

Many questions considered in recently published papers lead to a problem of analysis of properties of random walk path and end-to-end distances distributions on regular networks. Examples are: the optimal shape of a city (Bender et al., 2004), properties of polymers on directed lattices (Janse van Rensburg, 2003) or quantum localization problems in the context of a network model of disordered superconductors embedded on the Manhattan lattice (Beamond et al., 2003). In the field of computer science an important problem concerns the allocation of processors to parallel tasks in a grid of a large number of processors. This problem relays on the nontrivial correlation between the sum of the pair-wise distances between the processors allocated to a given task and the time required to complete the task (Leung et al., 2002).

The common question of the above mentioned problems is how many pairs of points separated by a given number q of steps can be found in a bounded region of a two-dimensional lattice. Such number q is referred to as the so-called Manhattan distance. For a square lattice the Manhattan distance is defined as the sum of the horizontal and the vertical distances. Similarly, for a given lattice we can define the Manhattan distance as the sum of the distances along directions parallel to the edges of the lattice, see Fig. 2.

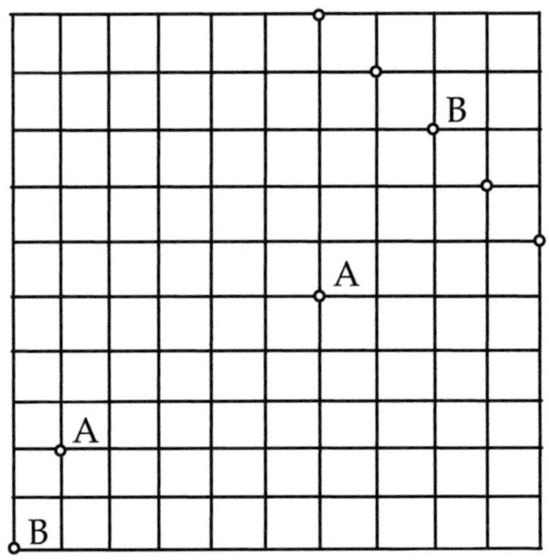

Fig. 2. A-A and B-B are pairs of points on a square lattice with $N = 11$. The Manhattan distances $q(A,A) < N$ and $N < q(B,B) < 2N - 2$.

First, we consider the square lattice. From the Fig. 2 it is easy to see that the number of two-point segments A-A separated by a given length q measured in steps a = 1, is equals to:

$$2 \times \sum_{j=0}^{j=q-1} (N - q + j) \cdot (N - j) \tag{1}$$

Multiplication by 2 comes from the segments obtained by counterclockwise rotation of the A-A segments. The number of B-B segments is equals to

$$2 \times \sum_{j=1}^{j=p+1} j \cdot (p - j + 2) \quad \text{with} \quad q = 2 \cdot (N - 1) - p \tag{2}$$

where an auxiliary quantity $q = 0,1,\ldots,N-2$ measures the distance between the right end of B-B segment and the upper right corner of the square. From Eqs. (1-2) we obtain the following expression for the number Δ_S of distances q in the square:

$$\Delta_S = \begin{cases} 2N(N-q)q + (q-1)q(q+1)/3 & \text{for} \quad q = 1,2,\ldots,N-1, \\ (2N-q-1)(2N-q)(2N-q+1)/3 & \text{for} \quad q = N,N+1,\ldots,2N-2. \end{cases} \tag{3}$$

With the help of normalization condition

$$\sum_{q=1}^{q=2N-2} \Delta_S(q) = \frac{1}{2}N^2\left(N^2-1\right) \tag{4}$$

the Eq. (3) can be written in the form of the probability distribution function for the discrete sets of distances $x_q = q/N$ in the unit square with the step $1/N$. In the limit of $N \to \infty$ we get the following probability density function of Manhattan distances inside the unit square:

$$D_S = \begin{cases} 4x(1-x)+\frac{2}{3}x^3 & \text{for} \quad 0 < x \le 1, \\ \frac{2}{3}(2-x)^3 & \text{for} \quad 1 < x \le 2. \end{cases} \tag{5}$$

In a similar way we derive the formulas corresponding to the distance distribution inside an equilateral triangle:

$$\Delta_T = \frac{2}{3}q(N-q)(N-q+1) \quad \text{for} \quad q = 1,2,\ldots,N-1 \tag{6}$$

and

$$D_T = 12x\left(1-x^2\right) \quad \text{for} \quad 0 \le x \le 1. \tag{7}$$

Subscripts S and T are for square and triangular geometries, respectively.
In a bounded regions of a given lattice its function $\Delta(q)$, referred to numbers of distances, depends on the shape and the size of this region. However, the corresponding probability density functions yield an intrinsic characteristic of the lattice symmetry i. e., the density of steps, a hypothetical walker would have to invest, in order to move along the trajectory lying on a dense grid with this lattice connectivity.
Probability density functions (5) and (7) enable us to calculate the moments $\int_{\Re} x^k D(x)dx$ of the corresponding distributions:

$$m_S^{(k)} = \frac{2^{k+6}-8(k+5)}{(k+1)(k+2)(k+3)(k+4)}, \tag{8}$$

$$m_T^{(k)} = \frac{36}{(k+2)(k+4)}. \tag{9}$$

Thus, in the case of the square, the moments diverge, $m_s^{(k)} \to \infty$ with $k \to \infty$, and they asymptotically decay for the triangle $m_T^{(k)} \to 0$. On a different approach, for the square lattice, the same mean value of the distance $m_s^{(1)} = 2/3$, was obtained in (Bender et al., 2004). The quantity $m_s^{(1)}$ is important in certain physical and computational problems. For example in physics and in optimization theory $m_s^{(1)}$ determines the statistical properties of complicated chains of interactions among objects located on complex networks. It also yields a valuable information needed for estimating the optimal path in the travelling salesman problem (TSP).

It is interesting to note that Eqs. (5) and (7) give the distribution of distances between two consecutive steps of a random walker allowed to jump to any point within the unit square or unit triangle, whereas the distribution of distances between this walker and a given corner of its walking area is equal to:

$$\begin{aligned} d_S &= 1-\left|1-x\right| \quad \text{for} \quad 0 \le x \le 2, \\ d_T &= x \quad\quad\quad\quad \text{for} \quad 0 \le x \le 1. \end{aligned} \tag{10}$$

for the square and the triangular lattices, respectively.
This contribution focuses on geometry but the knowledge of the number of Manhattan distances in a particular lattice can be useful for studying many quantities of physical and technological importance.

2.4 Percolation phase transition

Percolation theory is a concept which merges connectivity and transport in complex networks. The mathematical constituent of percolation deals with the connectivity regarded as the possibility to find an accessible route between the terminal nodes of a given network. The physical side of percolation relies on the possibility to pass an amount of transported medium through this accessible route.
Percolation theory was invented in late fifties of the last century in order to explain the fluid behaviour in a porous material with randomly clogged channels (Broadbent & Hammersley, 1957). Consider a network with two terminals, a source and sink, and assume that only a fraction of the channels is accessible to transport. If this part of conducting channel is spanned between the source and the sink then the network is in the conducting phase with nonzero conductibility (Chubynsky & Thorpe, 2005). If the fraction of channels, available for a medium flow, is not sufficient to connect these two reservoirs the flow conductance vanishes and the network becomes locked. This threshold fraction of working channels for which the network enters the non-conducting phase is called the percolation threshold and this phase change is known as the percolation transition. If instead of blocked channels we consider the non-transporting nodes of the lattice then we deal with the so-called site percolation. Here we are mainly interested in the case of non-transporting channels so we will evoke the bond percolation transition at the bond percolation threshold.

3. Efficiency of media transfer through networks with different geometries

The problem we consider here is the conductibility of the networks with different channel-network geometries. Assume that a hypothetic flow of particles transported by fluid is operated by the network whose channels are arranged according to the edges of a given lattice. We apply the network flow language. In this framework, all channels are characterized by their capacitances C. These capacitances are quenched random variables governed by a uniform probability distribution defined in the range [0, 1] to assure $C = 0$ for the clogged channel and $C = 1$ for the fully opened channel.
We define the filter's effective conductibility as follows

$$\phi(C_1, C_2, \ldots, C_n) = \frac{1}{\Phi_0}\Phi(C_1, C_2, \ldots, C_n) \tag{11}$$

where $\Phi(C_1, C_2, \ldots, C_n)$ is the flux transmitted by the filter whose channels have restricted possibilities to maintain the flow and $\Phi_0(C_1 = 1, C_2 = 1, \ldots, C_n = 1)$.
Equation (11) permits to compare the performance of different lattice geometries in their job as a potential transporting network. We have computed the average values of ϕ for an ample set of values of length (L_X) and width (L_Y) of our 10 networks. As an example, in Fig. 4 we present ϕ for the square lattice. We have found that for all lattices ϕ has the following form:

$$\phi(L_X, L_Y) = \left(a_1 + a_2 / L_X^{\delta}\right)\tan^{-1}\left[\psi(L_X)\cdot L_Y\right], \tag{12}$$

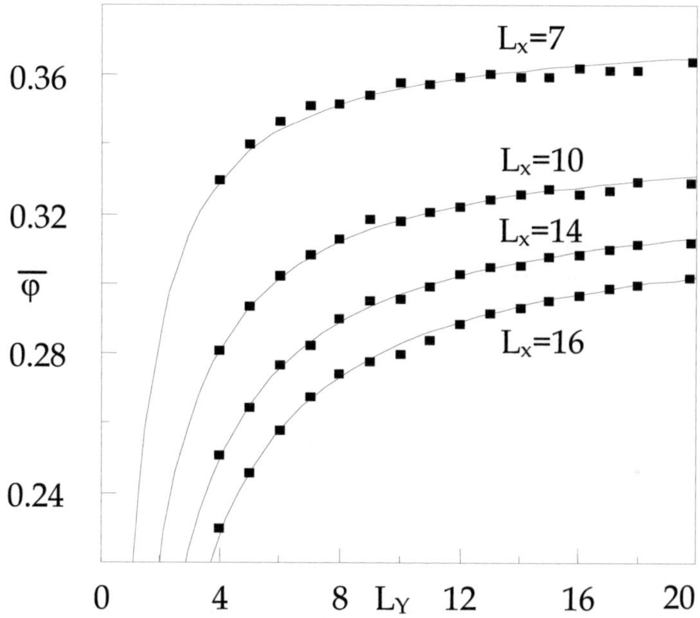

Fig. 4. Average filter's effective conductibility, defined by (11), computed for different values of length (L_X) and width (L_Y) of the square lattice. The lines are drawn using (12) and they are only visual guides.

where: a_1, a_2, δ are the parameters and ψ is the function, all dependent on the lattice symmetry.
Since the limiting form of (12) is equal to

$$\phi(L_X \gg 1, L_Y \gg 1) \approx \frac{\pi}{2} a_1 \tag{13}$$

therefore, the effective conductibility of sufficiently long and wide network is characterized mainly by the value of a_1. This one-parameter characteristics permits us to estimate how two-dimensional networks are resistant to clogging. For the square, Kagomé and hexagonal lattices a_1 takes the values: 0.237, 0.1722 and 0.1604, respectively. Thus, the square lattice is much more robust then e.g., Kagomé lattice even though both these lattices share the same value of the coordination number $z = 4$, and so their local channel arrangements are similar.

4. Size-exclusion separations

Network models can serve as a bridge between a simplified yet physically founded microscopic description of flow and its macroscopic properties observed in daily experiments. Among the applications worth to mention there is the control of ground water contaminant transport and production from oil reservoirs. These applications concern so-called large scale phenomena, i.e. phenomena involving an ample volume of liquid. On the other side of the length scale there is a class of flow phenomena related to micro- or even nano-scale flows through highly integrated microfluidic devices (Han et. al., 2008). In this work we are concerned mainly with these micro-flows problems.

Depth filtration is a process for cleaning a fluid from undesirable molecules by passing it through a porous medium. The filtration is effective if both, the area available for trapping of suspended particles and the time of chemical reactions are sufficient to mechanically arrest or chemically transform the harmful molecules (Hampton & Savage, 1993; Datta & Redner, 1998; Redner & Datta, 2000).

The connectivity of the medium is modelled by a network model. We consider a hypothetic flow of particles transported by fluid through the network of channels arranged according to the positions of the edges of the chosen lattice. All channels are characterized by their radii r which are quenched random variables governed by a given probability distribution. This distribution will be specified later.

In order to analyze the filter clogging process we employ a cellular automata model with the following rules (Lee & Koplik, 1996; Lee & Koplik, 1999):

- Fluid and a particle of a radius R enter the filter and flow inside it due to an external pressure gradient.
- The particle can move through the channel without difficulty if $r > R$, otherwise it would be trapped inside a channel and this channel becomes inaccessible for other particles.
- At an end-node of the channel, the particle has to choose a channel out of the accessible channels for movement.
- If at this node there is no accessible channel to flow the particle is retained in the channel. Otherwise, if the radius of the chosen channel $r' > R$ the particle moves to the next node.
- The movement of the particle is continued until either the particle is captured or leaves the filter.
- Each channel blockage causes a small reduction in the filter permeability and eventually the filter becomes clogged.

The cellular automata approach constitutes the effective tool for numerical computations of particles transfer. For the filter blockage investigation a minimalist description requires two assumptions:

- injected particles are identical spheres with the radius R,
- the channel radius is drawn from a discrete two-point probability distribution function, whereas $P(r > R) = p$ is the only model parameter.

Thus, the channel space is represented by a network of interconnected, wide (W) and narrow (N), cylindrical pipes (Fig. 5). Fluid containing suspended particles flows through the filter according to the previously stated rules.

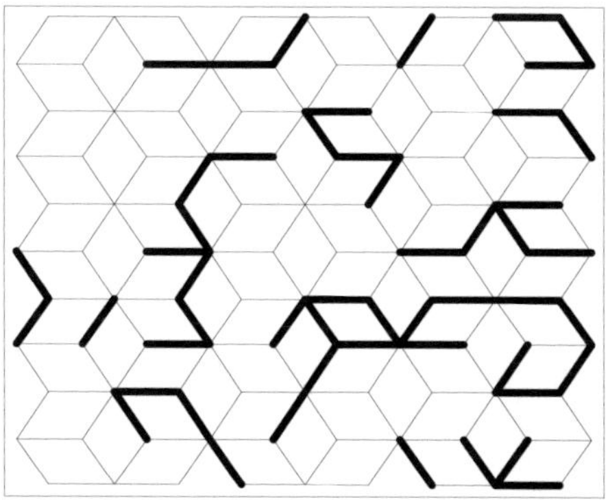

Fig. 5. Examples of two-dimensional model filters: N channels – thin lines, W channels – thick lines. Fluid with suspended particles is injected on the left side of the filter - exits the right side.

We present the results of the numerical simulations of the above specified filter. Every time step particles enter the filter - one particle per each accessible entry channel - we count the time t required for the filter to clog. For each analyzed geometry and for several values of p from the range $[0.05, p_c]$ we performed 10^3 simulations and then we have built empirical distributions of the clogging time t. Here p_c is the fraction of W channel for which the network lost its filtering capability. It is because of sufficiently high p values that there exits a statistically significant number of trajectories formed only by W channels and spanned between input and output of the filter.

Our simulations yield a common observation (Baran, 2007; Domanski et. al., 2010a): the average time required for the filter to clog can be nicely fitted as:

$$\bar{t} \approx \tan\left[\pi p / (2p_c)\right] \tag{14}$$

where the values of p_c are in excellent agreement with the bond percolation thresholds of the analyzed networks (see Table 1). Fig. 6 shows $\bar{t}$ as a function of p for selected lattices, 3 lattices out of 10 lattices we have analyzed.

Lattice	Bond percolation threshold p_c
(3^6) triangular	0.3473
(4^4) square	0.5000
(6^3) hexagonal	0.6527
(3, 6, 3, 6)	0.5244
D(3, 6, 3, 6)	0.4756
(4, 8^2)	0.6768
D(4, 8^2)	0.2322
(3^3, 4^2)	0.4196
D(3^3, 4^2)	0.5831
(3, 12^2)	0.7404

Table 1. Bond percolation thresholds and coordination numbers for networks analysed in this work.

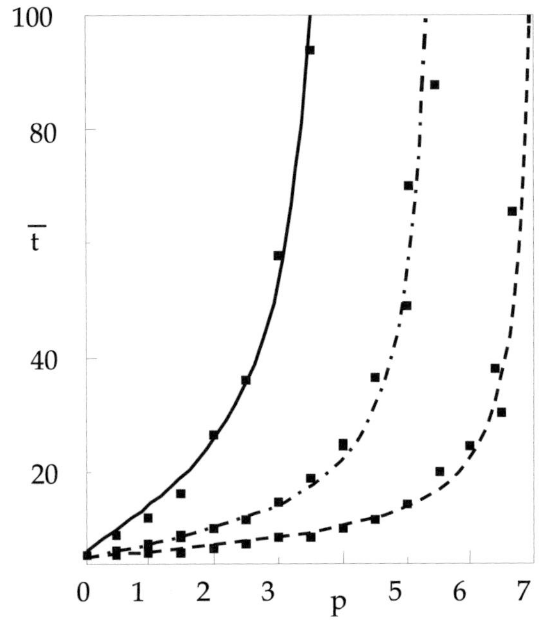

Fig. 6. Average clogging time for regular lattices: solid line, triangular lattice; dashed line, square lattice; dash-dotted line, hexagonal lattice. The lines are drawn using (14) and they are only visual guides.

5. Failure propagation

The accumulation of fatigue is an irreversible damage process causing the progressive destruction of the system components. In mechanical systems, metal fatigue occurs when a repetitive load induces strongly fluctuating strains on the metal. The formation of a fatigue fracture is initiated by the local microcracks, which grow when the local stress exceeds the threshold strength of the material. At some concentration, microcracks start to act coherently to enhance the local stress and induce more failures. The formation of secondary failures eventually stops and the system can be loaded again. The successive loading is repeated until the system breaks due to the avalanche of failures.

The knowledge of the fracture evolution up to the global rupture and its effective description are important for the analysis of the mechanical behaviour of the systems in response to the applied loads. From the theoretical point of view the understanding of the complexity of the rupture process has advanced due to the use of lattice models. An example of great importance is the family of transfer load models, especially the Fibre Bundle Model (FBM) (Alava et al. 2006; Moreno et al., 2000; Gomez et al., 1998). In the FBM a set of elements (fibres) is located in the nodes of the supporting lattice and the element-strength-thresholds are drawn from a given probability distribution. After an element has failed, its load has to be transferred to the other intact elements. Two extreme cases are: the global load sharing (GLS) - the load is equally shared by the remaining elements and the local load sharing (LLS) - only the neighbouring elements suffer from the increased load.

Here we employ an alternative approach - the extra load is equally redistributed among the elements lying inside the Voronoi regions (Ocabe et al., 1998) generated by a group of elements destroyed in subsequent intervals of time. We call this load transfer rule as Voronoi load sharing (VLS) (Domanski & Derda, 2010b). This kind of load transfer merges the GLS and the LLS approach concepts.

Our discussion is motivated by recent uniaxial tensile experiments on nanoscale materials that confirm substantial strength increase via the size reduction of the sample (Brinckmann et al., 2008). The mechanical properties of a nanometer-sized sample of a given material are considerably superior compared to these of its macro-sized specimen.

Especially studies on arrays of free-standing nanopillars, see Fig. 7, subjected to uniaxial microcompression reveal the potential applicability of nanopillars as components for the fabrication of micro- and nano-electromechanical systems, micro-actuators or optoelectronic devices (Greer et al., 2009). Thus, it is worth to analyse the failure progress in such systems of nanoscale pillars subjected to cyclic longitudinal stress.

For this purpose we apply the FBM. We simulate failure by stepwise accumulation of the destructed pillars and compute the number of time-steps elapsed until the array of pillars collapses.

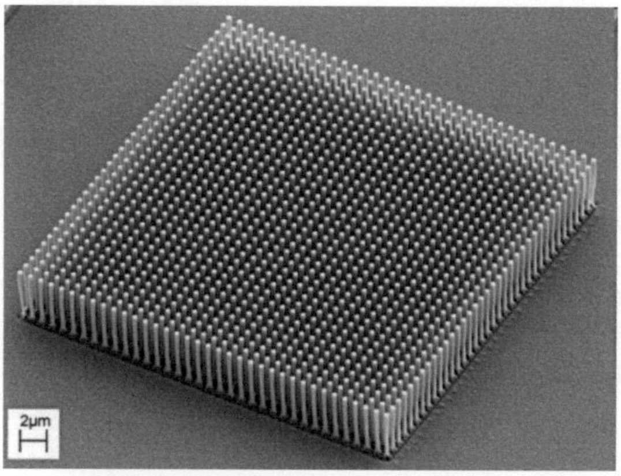

Fig. 7. An example of nanoscale pillars: a 36x36 nanopillar array. Pillar diameter=280 nm, height=4 µm. Source: http://nanotechweb.org/cws/article/tech/37573

In order to illustrate the failure propagation we map the array of nanopillars onto the surface with two-valued height function $h_m(\tau)$:

$$h_m(\tau) = \begin{cases} 1 & \text{if} \quad \text{the node } m \text{ is occupied by the intact pillar,} \\ 0 & \text{otherwise} \end{cases} \tag{15}$$

Within this mapping the dynamics of the model can be seen as a rough surface evolving between two flat states: starting with an initially flat specimen we apply the load, thus the pillars start to be destroyed and after the last pillars fail the surface becomes flat. Fig. 2 illustrates such surface for some time τ.

Thus, the way the number of crushed pillars changes under the load can be characterised by the surface width, defined as

$$W^2(\tau) = N^{-1} \sum_{1 \le m \le N} \left[h_m(\tau) - \langle h(\tau) \rangle \right]^2 \tag{16}$$

where $\langle h(\tau)\rangle$ is the average height over different sites at time τ.
We realised numerically the dynamic formation of the rough surface for two system $N \approx 10^4$. Calculations have been done for three types of lattice, namely for hexagonal, square and triangular symmetries.

Fig. 8. An example of rough surface with two-valued height function defined by (14). Illustration for the set of nanopillars on the square lattice.

A common observation resulting from our simulations is that the damage spreading depends strongly on the load transfer rules. The geometry of lattice is irrelevant for the GLS scheme. In this case we obtained almost equal mean values of time steps of the damaging process for different lattice geometries. For the LLS scheme the damage process is the fastest for a triangular lattice and the slowest for a hexagonal lattice, so the greater number of neighbours the faster the damage process. Similarly to the GLS, for the VLS rule the damaging process lasts almost the same number of time steps irrespective of lattice geometry.

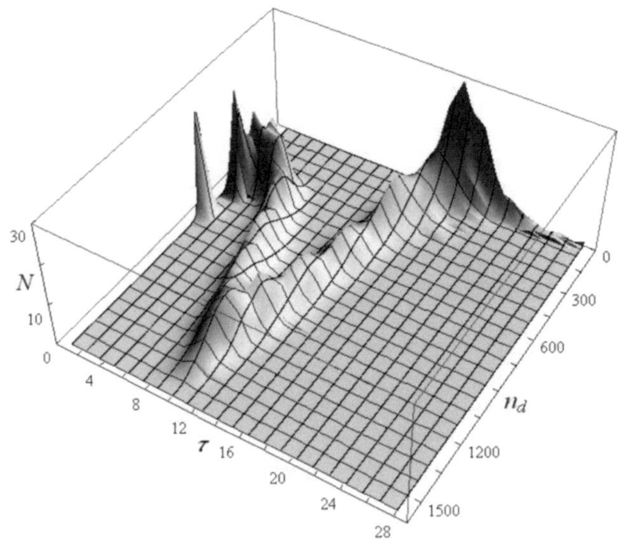

Fig. 9. Distribution of the number of damaged elements n_d vs. τ with the VLS rule. Here, $N = 100 \times 100$ and the averages are taken over 10^3 samples.

In general the damage process is the fastest for the GLS scheme and the slowest for the LLS scheme. The VLS rule yields results intermediate between these extreme cases. The distribution of the number of damaged elements n_d as a function of time, computed within the VLS scheme is presented in Fig. 9 and Fig. 10 shows the evolution of the mean number of damaged pillars computed according to the LLS rule.

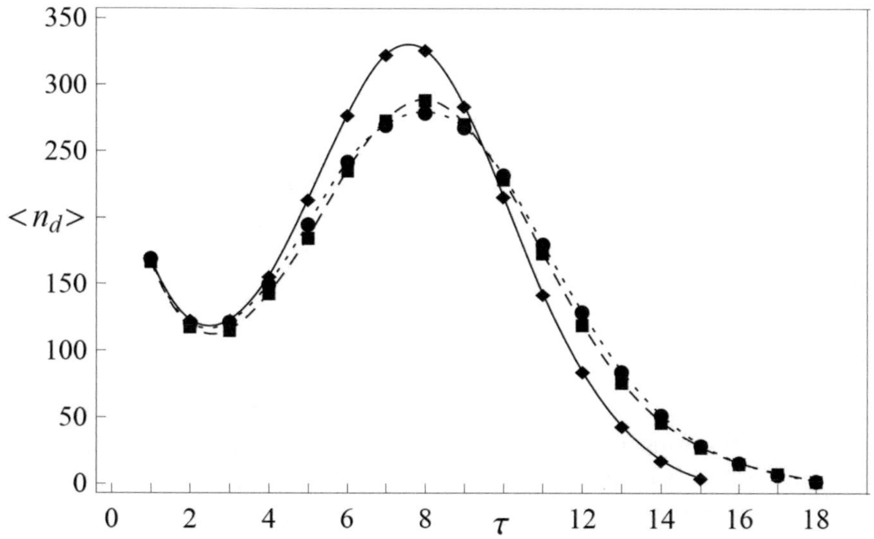

Fig. 10. Evolution of the average number of damaged elements $\langle n_d \rangle$ with the LLS rule. Comparison of lattices: hexagonal (circle), square (square), triangular (diamond). The number of pillars $N \approx 10^4$ and the averages are taken over 10^4 samples.

6. Conclusion

In this paper we have discussed transport properties of two-dimensional networks. We exploit two extreme pictures: a cellular automata microscopic-like picture and a completely statistical approach to an operating network considered as the network supporting the flow trough a collection of randomly conducting channels. Even though the cellular automata rules are too simple to capture the detailed interactions in the real system this approach enables us to see how the system becomes damaged. Also the network flow concept is useful to study the interplay between geometry and transport properties of ordered lattices. Its main advantage relays on a very simple representation of the inner structure yet keeping a bridge between the conductibility, the geometry (lattice's symmetry, coordination number) and the statistical global property (bond percolation threshold).

We have also derived the distributions of distances and probability density functions for the Manhattan distance related to the following tessellations of the plane: square, triangular, hexagonal and Kagomé. These functions are polynomials of at most the third degree in the lattice-node-concentrations. The probability density functions of two-dimensional lattices give the probability weight of class q containing pairs of points with given distance q. Thus, they may contain valuable information related to the directed walk models, such as Dyck or Motzkin (Orlandini & Whittington, 2004).

An interesting subclass of the transportation problem, not directly discussed in this contribution, concerns the transport in the environments that evolve in time (Harrison & Zwanzig, 1985). Each pair of the neighbouring nodes is connected by a channel, which can be conducting or blocked and the state of the channel changes in time. An example is a network of chemically active channels that capture undesired molecules. Ones the molecules are trapped by channel-binding-centres the channel itself becomes inactive during the chemical reaction needed to convert the molecules. Keeping fixed the portion of conducting channels the evolving environment reorganises their positions. The conductibility of the network in such circumstances differs from that one corresponding to the static partition of gradually clogging channels. Appropriate models of transport in the changing environment deal with so-called dynamic (or stirred) percolation (Kutner & Kehr, 1983).
Even though dynamically percolated networks have not been analysed here our efficiency analysis and cellular automata approaches are also applicable in such case. Problems concerning the effective conductibility of two-dimensional lattices with evolving bond-activities will be addressed in prospective works.

7. References

Alava, M., J., Nukala, P., K. & Zapperi, S. (2006). Statistical models of fracture, *Advances in Physics*, Vol. 55, Issue 3&4 (May 2006) 349-476, ISSN: 1460-6976

Austin, R. H. (2007). Nanofluidics: a fork in the nano-road, *Nature Nanotechnology*, Vol. 2, No. 2 (February 2007) 79-80, ISSN: 1748-3387

Baran, B. (2007). Ph. D. Thesis, Czestochowa University of Technology, unpublished

Basu, A. S. & Gianchandani, Y. (2008). Virtual microfluidic traps, filters, channels and pumps using Marangoni Flows, *Journal of Micromechechanics and Mocroengineering*, Vol. 18, No. 11 (November 2008) 115031

Bender, C., M., Bender, M., A., Demaine, E., D. & Fekete, S., P. (2004), What is the optimal shape of a city?, *Journal of Phys. A: Math. Gen.*, Vol. 37, Issue 1 (January 2004), 147-159, ISSN: 0305-4470

Beamond, E., J., Owczarek, A., L. & Cardy, J. (2003). Quantum and classical localizations and the Manhattan lattice, *Journal of Phys. A: Math. Gen.*, Vol. 36, Issue 41 (October 2003), 10251-10267, ISSN: 0305-4470

Brinckmann, S., Kim, J.-Y., Greer, J., R. (2008). Fundamental differences in mechanical behaviour between two types of crystals at the nanoscale, *Phys. Rev. Letters*, Vol. 100, Issue 15, (April 2008), 155502, ISSN: 0031-9007

Broadbent, S., R. & Hammersley, J., M. (1957). Percolation processes, I. Crystals and mazes, *Math. Proc. Cambridge Philos. Soc.*, Vol. 53, Issue 3, (July 1957), 629-641, ISSN: 0305-0041

Chou, C-F., et al. (1999). Sorting by diffusion: An asymmetric obstacle course for continuous molecular separation, *Proc. Natl. Acad. Sci. United States Am.*, Vol. 96, No. 24, (November 1999) 13762-13765, ISSN: 0027-8424

Chubynsky, M., V. & Thorpe, M. F. (2005). Mean-field conductivity in a certain class of networks, *Phys. Review E*, Vol. 71, (May 2005), 56105, ISSN: 1539-375

Datta, S. & Redner, S. (1998). Gradient clogging in depth filtration, *Phys. Rev. E*, Vol. 58, No. 2, (August 1998), R1203-R1206, ISSN: 1539-37

Domanski, Z., Baran, B., Ciesielski, M. (2010a). Resistance to clogging of fluid microfilters, *Proceedings of the World Congress on Engineering 2010*, ISBN: 978-988-17012-0-6, San Francisco, October 2010, Newswood Ltd. International Association of Engineers, Honk Kong

Domanski, Z. & Derda, T. (2010b) Voronoi tessellation description of fatigue load transfer within the fibre bundle model of two dimensional fracture, will appear in Materials Science, ISSN: 1068-820X

Gomez, J., B., Moreno, Y., Pacheco, A., F. (1998). Probabilistic approach to time-dependent load-transfer models of fracture, *Phys. Rev. E*, Vol. 58, No. 2, (August 1998), 1528-1532, ISSN: 1539-375

Grünbaum, B. & Shepard, G. (1986). *Tilings and Patterns*, Freeman W. H., New York

Greer, J., R., Jang, D., Kim., J.-Y., Burek, M., J. (2009). Emergence of new mechanical functionality in materials via size reduction, *Adv. Functional Materials*, Vol. 19, Issue 18, (September 2009), 2880-2886, Online ISSN: 1616-3028

Hampton, J., H. & Savage, S., B. (1993). Computer modelling of filter pressing and clogging in a random tube network, *Chemical Engineering Science*, Vol. 48, No. 9, (1993) 1601-1611

Han, J.; Fu, J. & Schoch, R. (2008). Molecular sieving using nanofilters: past, present and future. *Lab on a Chip*, Vol. 8, No. 1, (January 2008) 23-33, ISSN:1473-0197

Harrison, A., K., Zwanzig, R. (1985), Transport on a dynamically disordered lattice, Phys. Rev. A, Vol. 32, Issue 2 (August 1085), 1072-1075, ISSN: 1050-2947

Jense van Rensburg, E., J. (2003). Statistical mechanics of directed models of polymer in the square lattice, *Journal of Phys. A: Math. Gen.*, Vol. 36, Number 15 (April 2003), R11-R61, ISSN: 0305-4470

Kutner, R. & Kehr, K., W. (1983), Diffusion in concentrated lattice gases IV. Diffusion coefficient of tracer particle with differnt jump rate, *Philos. Mag. A*, Vol. 48, Issue 2 (August 1983), 199-213,ISSN: 0141-8610

Lee, J. & Koplik, J. (1996). Simple model for deep bed filtration, *Phys. Rev. E*, Vol. 54, No. 4, (October 1996), 4011-4020, ISSN: 1539-375

Lee, J. & Koplik, J. (1999). Microscopic motion of particles flowing through a porous medium, *Phys. of Fluids*, Vol. 11, Issue 1, (January 1999), 76-87, ISSN: 1070-6631

Leung, V., J., Esther, M., A., Bender, M., A., Bunde, D., Johnston, J., Lal, A., Mitchell, J., S., B., Phillips, C. & Seiden, S., S. (2002). Processor allocation on Cplant: Achieving general processor locality using one-dimensional allocation strategies, *Proceedings of the 4th IEEE International Conference on Cluster Computing*, 296-304, ISBN: 0-7695-1745-5, Chicago, September 2002, Wiley-Computer Society Press

MacDonald, M., P., Spalding, G., C. & Dholakia, K. (2003), Microfluidic sorting in an optical lattice, *Nature*, Vol. 426, (November 2003), 421-424, ISSN: 0028-0836

Moreno, Y., Gomez, J., B., Pacheco, A., F. (2000). Fracture and second-order phase transitions, *Phys. Rev. Letters*, Vol. 85, Issue 14, (October, 2000), 2865-2868, ISSN: 0031-9007

Ocabe, A., Boots, B., Sugihara, K. & Chiu, N., S. (1998). Spatial tessellations: Concepts and applications of Voronoi diagrams, John Wiley & Sons, England 1992, ISBN: 978-0-471-98635-5

Orlandini, E. & Whittington, S., G. (2004), Pulling a polymer at an interface: directed walk model, *Journal of Phys. A: Math. Gen.*, Vol. 37, Number 20 (May 2004), 5305-5314, ISSN: 0305-4470

Redner, S & Datta, S. (2000). Clogging time of a filter, *Phys. Rev. Letters*, Vol. 84, Issue 26, (June 2000), 6018-6021, ISSN: 0031-9007

18

New Approach to a Tourist Navigation System that Promotes Interaction with Environment

Yoshio Nakatani[1], Ken Tanaka[2] and Kanako Ichikawa[3]
[1]*College of Information Science and Engineering, Ritsumeikan University, 1-1-1, Noji-Higashi, Kusatsu, Shiga 525-8577. e-mail: nakatani@is.ritsumei. ac.jp*
[2]*Graduate School of Science and Engineering, Ritsumeikan University, 1-1-1, Noji-Higashi, Kusatsu, Shiga 525-8577. e-mail: cc007056@ed.ritsumei. ac.jp*
[3]*Quality Innovation Center, Honda Motor Co.,Ltd., Hagadai, Haga-Machi, Haga-gun, Tochigi, 321-3325. e-mail: kanako_ichikawa@hm.honda.co.jp*
Japan

1. Introduction

As an ITS (Intelligent Transport Systems) field, a tourist navigation system (TNS) is being developed to support transportation in sightseeing areas. Most tourist navigation systems fundamentally adhere to the concept of a car navigation system. They clearly calculate and propose the optimal route in terms of time and distance from the current location to the destination. This type of system is very convenient for tourists who do not have much time for a sightseeing stroll. However, some tourists enjoy the process to the destination by straying from the direct route. From our experience, in the case of a TNS which clearly shows the shortest optimal route, this often changes a sightseeing stroll into an act of tracing the recommended route. To enjoy strolling and the landscape, it is important to enjoy casual walking and not be tied down by a predetermined route unless we lose the relationship between the destination and the current position.
This study proposes a tourist navigation system that haphazardly encourages tourists in finding routes and sightseeing spots without providing detailed route information [1]. We discuss the concept of sightseeing, which is the background of design and construction of the system. In planning sightseeing, users of the system use the icons to specify the spots, and draw routes freehand on the digital map system. When they start sightseeing, the digital map is not displayed on the mobile computer, and they can only refer to spot icons, freehand routes and the real-time location data from the GPS system. Not providing the detailed route is expected to create accidental encounters. We report experiment results using the system in Nara city, a traditional sightseeing city in Japan, and introduce the new approach that we are trying.

2. Sightseeing and tourist navigation system

2.1 Current status of tourist navigation systems

Existing TNSs and services include the personal navigation system P-Tour [2] and the Raku-Raku scheduler provided by NAVIT [3]. Tourists can visit multiple sightseeing spots they want to see in the order of their choice under a time constraint (schedule function) and obtain an optimum route in accordance with their schedule. These systems accurately adhere to a concept of car navigation systems. That is, these systems are designed to lead people to the destination with the minimum lost.

Tarumi et al. [4] performed an open experiment where they overlapped virtual space on the map displayed on mobile phones to guide tourists in sightseeing areas. They reported that the system was evaluated differently by age and gender. Twenties or younger were highly evaluated the informative screen design and women preferred photos. The most important finding in this experiment was that some subjects did not appreciate the system because it provided the same information as the travel brochures and advertising signs. This means the system should provide new information or opportunities to meet new things.

2.2 Experience with tourist navigation systems

We participated in an open experiment of a TNS to understand the current status for tourist support, and we investigated the current status of guideboards for tourists.

2.2.1 Nara prefecture tourist navigation experiment

We participated in Nara's autonomous mobile support project performed by the Ministry of Land, Infrastructure, Transport and Tourism and Nara prefecture in autumn 2006 [5]. Nara city is the ancient capital in the 8th century. More than 35 millions of tourists visit to this traditional city. This experiment provided information service using ubiquitous technology for smooth transport and enhancing the appeal of sightseeing areas aiming at the 1,300th anniversary (2010) of the change of the national capital to Nara.

The experiment provided a route from the Kintetsu Nara railway station to the Todai-ji temple, the biggest wooden building in the world, and information about sightseeing areas, shops, public restrooms, and resting-places from a PDA (Personal Digital Assistant). We could move about with the PDA, obtaining information from IC tags on guideboards and area information for current positions through the wireless (Bluetooth) communication system (Figure 1). For route guidance, spoken commands and instructions on a terminal screen were provided at turning points. Usage of the PDA, and experiment area maps were printed on an A4 paper.

Fig. 1. System usage to download the sightseeing information.

Eight students participated in the experiment. Opinions after the experiment are shown below. Some students admired the PDA:

1. We could walk listening to voice navigation without watching the screen.
2. One group enjoyed the PDA display.

Others were critical of the PDA:

3. We could obtain detailed route information from the PDA. However, it is difficult to walk while watching the screen.
4. We tended to aim at the next radio spot (Figure 1). We could not enjoy how the street looked as we walked.
5. For audio assist, we had to listen to unnecessary information before necessary information.
6. If a person is familiar with the area, it is enough to listen to the person's explanation (The PDA did not provide additional information.).
7. We could not obtain information that was not part of the specified route.

2.2.2 Current status of tourist navigation system

The TNS that we investigated provided the shortest route to the destination. Of course, TNSs are designed to provide detailed information about both sightseeing spots and purpose determined spots (i.e., restaurants, facilities) along the route. However, the information imposes preconditions for tracing the route proposed by the system. The TNS has the same concept as car navigation in terms of a system-driven tourist guide.

Social psychology proposes two travel patterns: "place-name driven" sightseeing and "purpose-driven" sightseeing [6]. Existing goal-oriented navigation is useful for place-name driven sightseeing (i.e., place-name oriented sightseeing). However, for people who enjoy strolling, this kind of system does not lead to smart shops not in guidebooks. It does not provide opportunities for walking into labyrinthian alleys through a trial-and-error process and feeling excitement in their doing so. When using the PDA, they cannot find something new or feel the atmosphere of an area. We realized that enjoying assimilation into an area was required to enjoy strolling.

2.3 Field investigation

2.3.1 Investigation of guideboards

In order to enjoy strolling, equipment and social devices are required to support strolling at a site. We investigated the distribution of sightseeing guideboards in a sightseeing area. We investigated around Yasaka shrine in Kyoto. This area is one of the most popular sightseeing spots in Kyoto and many tourists sightsee there on foot. There are many narrow streets and tourists easily get lost.

We found 56 guideboards. Of these guideboards, 29 were sketched maps, 17 were simple directional signs and 10 were standard maps. We observed many tourists who pointed out the destination on a guideboard, asked a route to a volunteer guide, and are strolling with paper maps (Figure 2).

To classify the purposes of using guideboards, analysis was carried out on a conversation within a tourist group and their behavior, such as pointing fingers and looking around. We analyzed 15 groups.

Tourists used guideboards as follows:

1. Checking current position.

2. Considering a subsequent route after that (planning)
3. Checking the direction of the destination

Fig. 2. Example of using a guideboard.

These maps had various scale sizes and different illustrations. Installers included the city, local towns, individuals and stores. The maps showed travel direction, north direction or destination, and they were inconsistent. Tourists reflected on a route by comparing maps. However because some maps were blocked by bicycles parked in front of them, we could not approach some of the maps. Some maps could not be read because the characters on the wooden board had been drawn using felt pens and the texts had faded so they were illegible. On the surface, we assumed that these complications would bother the sightseeing. However, we discovered that our initial assumption was not entirely true. When several individuals were strolling, they discussed how to interpret maps and check their location. Their behaviors were unexpectedly impressive, and we confirmed those behaviors could increase the excitement of sightseeing.

2.3.2 Confirmatory experiment for sightseeing behavior

We investigated enjoyment in sightseeing behavior and determining destination in Nara. The subjects were eight individuals including university students with a GPS. We asked four pairs to sightsee starting from JR Nara station and complete their sightseeing within two hours. After completion, we checked their routes using GPS data. Additionally, we asked the subjects to illustrate their routes. We questioned why they stayed at some places for a certain period of time and what the most impressive sites were.

The subjects found routes by searching the surroundings for landmarks, such as many trees, a pagoda, and a residential area, for their destination. They reported "The main street has to be bustling, so we walked to the direction people and shops are increasing in number" and "The five-storied pagoda is located on a hill, so we tried to find tall trees between trees."

They also reported "We found an interesting spot in the approaching route and we did not much time, so we stopped when we returned" and "We made haste in the approaching route and played with deer when we backed." Thus, in approaching a route, they behaved in a destination-oriented manner due to time constraints. In the return route, they flexibly stopped at a spot they noticed during their approach route when they were under time pressure. In listening to the subjects after their sightseeing, the places they stopped and the objects and spots they saw by chance came up in conversation. Judging from route selections and the recollections of the subjects, they seemed to be interested in chance factors.

The subjects were asked to draw route maps. Most subjects emphasized the spots that impressed them in the route maps. Sightseeing spots were emphasized by adding place names and illustrations. Figure 3 shows a map drawn by a subject. Interesting spots on the route had impressed the subjects. They did not understand other spots in as detailed and accurate a manner.

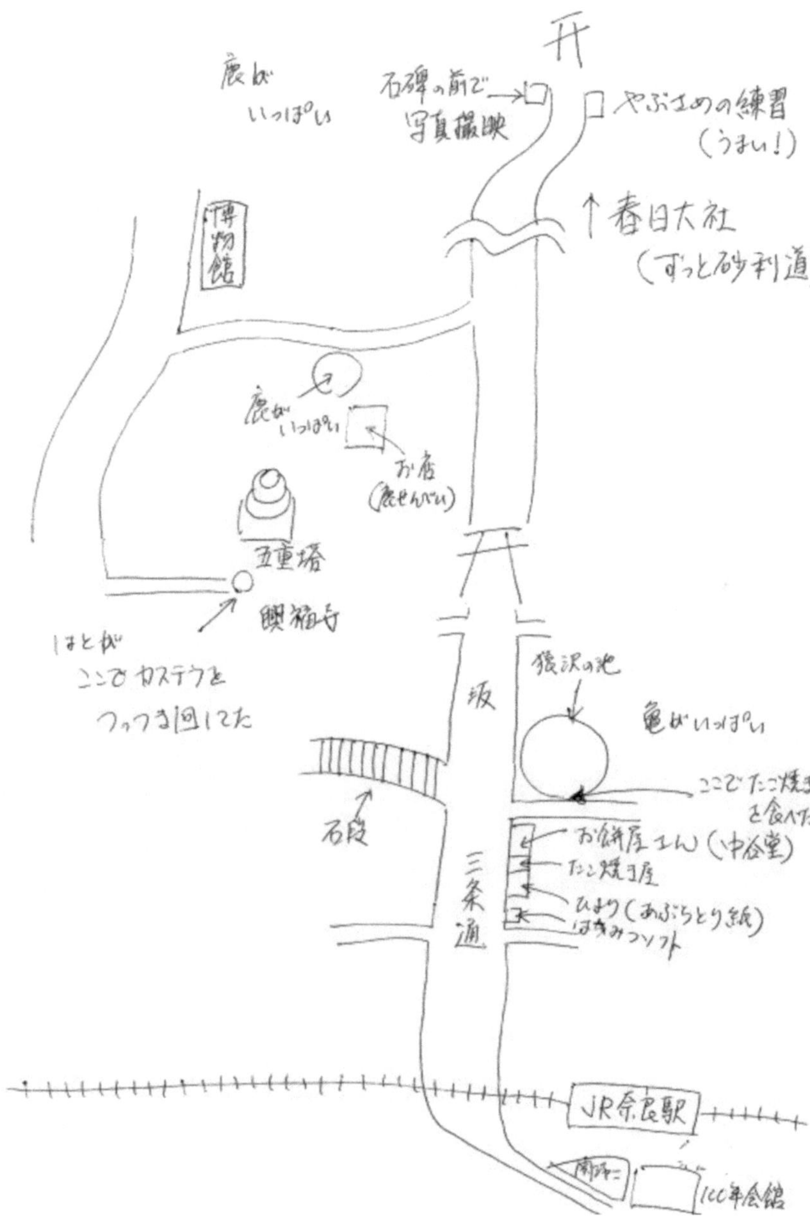

Fig. 3. Example of a constructed route map.

3. Support of sightseeing area image construction

3.1 Approach of this study

Based on our analysis shown above, we tried in this study to provide chance factors for strolling by utilizing an image of the sightseeing area. Accidental events are an important factor for play, which corresponds to "casualness" proposed by R. Caillois, a famous researcher of play [7]. Conditions in which users can play are developed by the system creating a situation that is likely to generate casualness. At this moment, users do not "play with the system." The system generates a situation in which users "play with the environment." Nishimura described "Space owned by the situation that surrounds me" in "Phenomenology of play" [8]. Playing with the environment generates a state for "playing with the situation." Further, it generates casualness.

3.2 System configuration

Figure 4 shows the configuration of the prototype system. The system is roughly divided into a sightseeing area image forming system before the actual sightseeing and a transportation support system on the day of sightseeing.

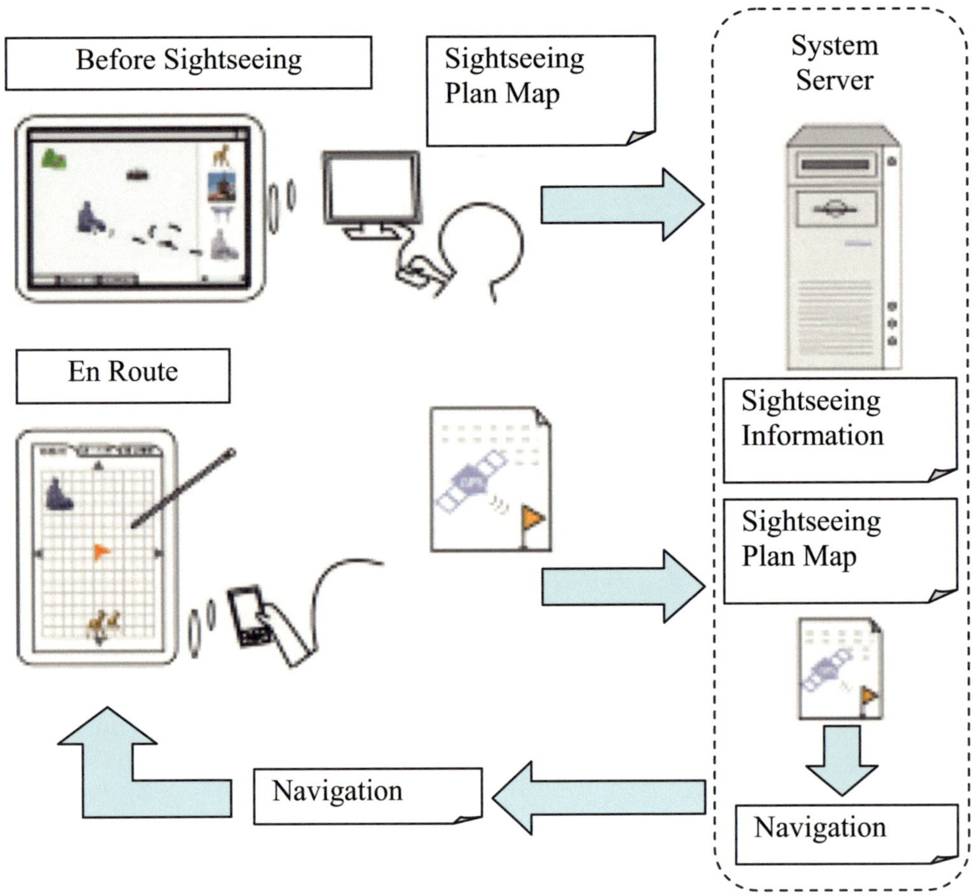

Fig. 4. System architecture

At first, the system prepares sightseeing information for the area to be visited on the system server in XML format. In the figure, the file is named the "sightseeing information" file. Then, users describe the sightseeing plan (spots to be visited and route) on the electronic map with the destination icon (and explanation) and a freehand route line based on sightseeing information file, guidebooks, magazines and information on the Web to save as the "sightseeing plan map."

On the sightseeing day, users move about with a GPS. At this moment, no map is displayed. Sightseers are provided with the position data file obtained from the GPS on the sightseeing map file. Only the icons to be visited, the freehand route and current position information obtained from GPS are provided.

3.3 Sightseeing area image forming system

In this study, users themselves prepared a sightseeing plan map before sightseeing to create an image of the sightseeing plan. Tourists have images of sightseeing areas as a mental map. Therefore, even if they see an ambiguous map on the day of sightseeing, they have sense of direction and can guess about facilities at the spot. They can avoid a situation where they become completely disoriented and cannot at all enjoy sightseeing. Additionally, images of appropriate levels of detail will make tourists lose touch with the realities in the sightseeing areas to promote play in the situation.

For the expression method, sightseeing image icons were prepared. Tourists were asked to put images of the sightseeing spots to be visited on the electronic map (Figure 5). The result is stored in the "sightseeing plan map" file on the server.

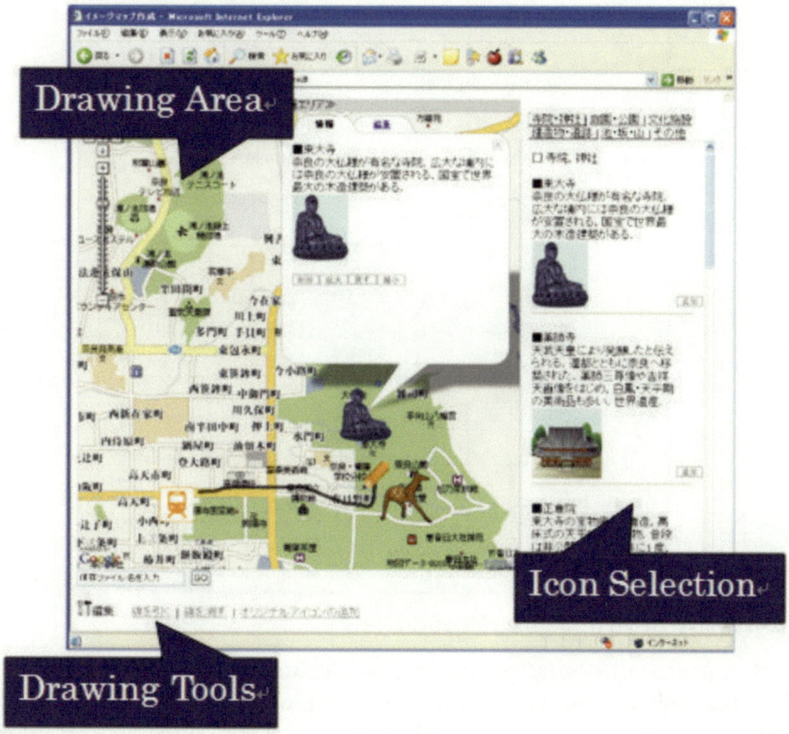

Fig. 5. A screen image of the image building system.

We prepared specific icons for major sightseeing spots. However, common icons, such as parks, temples, and shrines, were used for other spots.
Users set their degree of interest and length of stay for each sightseeing spot as a guideline of interest information and action plan. The size of icons was determined depending on the degree of interest of users. Users could input text about the contents in which they were interested at each sightseeing spot. This text may express expectations that users had before sightseeing.
After inputting sightseeing spots, users drew a freehand route by including the order and route with a mouse on the map. Before drawing, users were explained that the route was changeable and could deviate in some degree from the roads.
Types and positions of icons, descriptive text and freehand route plan of sightseeing spots were recorded in an XML file as a sightseeing plan map.

3.4 Transport support system

During the actual sightseeing, users moved while referring to the sightseeing plan they had prepared in advance using the PDA.

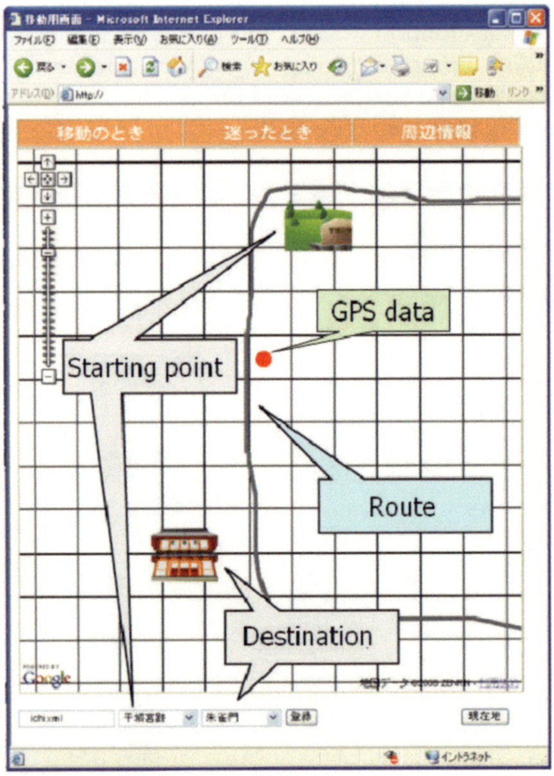

Fig. 6. A screen image of an on-site navigation.

At first, users specified the starting point and destination. By doing so, the scale was automatically changed so that two icons were displayed at a time on the screen. It is supposed that scale changes the difficulty in tracing the route, which contributes to creation of random chance. Scale size could be changed during sightseeing.

On the mobile screen, the map displayed during planning was not displayed to effectively utilize ambiguity of the image. Only the sightseeing plan prepared by users was displayed (Figure 6). Additionally, users could use information about the current position obtained by GPS data and a straight line connecting the starting point to the current position as direction information. That is, during sightseeing, users could refer to only the relative positional relationship for the sightseeing spot to be visited, the freehand route plan and the current position indicating the deviation from route plan. However, a map was displayed when users were lost.

Users could use only limited, outlined information on the PDA. Therefore, they were always conscious of the route plan and their current position. If the current position deviated from the route plan or users were ordered to turn in accordance with the route plan, they needed to stop looking at the PDA and check their surroundings to confirm their location and find the direction to take. Doing this, users selected a street they did not plan, found interesting streets and facilities, and asked people for directions. They created encounters in the sightseeing areas that could not be obtained from guidebooks. Our basic concept for tourist navigation was that too much information was not necessarily good and going as planned (expectation) was not always good. Chance encounter is important. Limiting information promotes interaction with the environment, and generates unexpected encounters with something new. Casual encounters are remembered as impressive events.

4. Evaluation of the system

We prepared a system for Nara city to verify this approach on a trial basis. We selected Nara city because it is a location for historical sightseeing with an environment suited for strolling. Sightseeing spots and historical streets are preserved in a relatively narrow space in which tourists can walk. Round trips on foot are possible. A Sony VAIO type U was used for the PDA (Figure 7).

Fig. 7. An example of system utilization.

The subjects were nine individuals (male: 7, female: 2). They were divided into three groups (five individuals, two, and two) (Table 1) and strolled.

	Group 1	Group 2	Group 3
Number of persons	5	2	2
Spots to be visited	2	3	4
Nara sightseeing experience	Insufficient	Rather insufficient	Sufficient

Table 1. Experimental subjects

We explained to the subjects to make a walking sightseeing plan of two or three hours with your friends in Nara. After this explanation, we asked them to prepare a sightseeing plan sheet, sightsee using the system and answer a questionnaire after the experiment as an assignment. The experiment was performed in January 2008.

4.1 Preparation of map

Three groups drew different types of sightseeing plan map according to their characteristics. They enjoyed drawing maps well. We confirmed from interviews that they had concrete images of sightseeing areas.
Group 1: This group knew little about the geography in Nara, and decided to visit Todai-ji temple and Sanjo street. They traced the streets to carefully prepare a route (Figure 8 (a)). They really did not want to lose their way.
Group 2: This group selected the same area as Group 2, but they did not select Todai-ji temple but selected minor three spots as Sanjo street, Nara-machi old town and Ukimi-do temple (Figure 8 (b)). This area is smaller than that of Group 1. They linked three spots with a rough route, almost ignoring streets. On the other hand, group members enjoyed putting various icons, such as the restaurant and gift shop, on a map.
Group 3: This group knew Nara well, and selected a less popular western side area of Nara station. They selected four spots (Figure 8 (c)). Among them, three spots were not prepared in the system. This shows specificity of Group 3. The line drawn traced almost all the streets. However, the line was parallel to the street in some places, showing ambiguity.
Three maps in Figure 8 have the same scale.

(a) Plan map of Group 1

(b) Plan map of Group 2

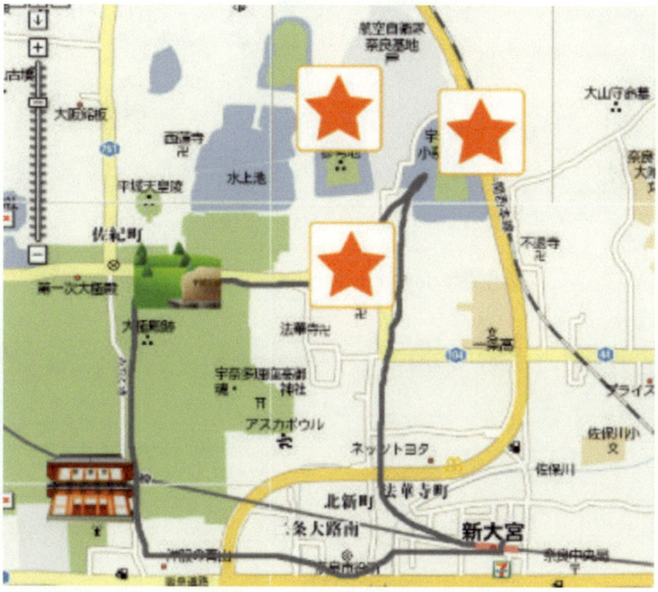

(c) Plan map of Group 3

Fig. 8. Plan maps.

4.2 Situation of movement

Groups 1 and 2 referred mainly to this system as the information source during walking. Purposes of use included confirmation of the current position and destination, and reference for registered plan information. Groups 1 and 2 used the PDA when they had discussions.

Their questionnaire after the experiment indicated the following: "We required the distance to the destination." Group 3 rarely used the PDA because the system was frequently down and the group memorized the route when they made the map.

Group 1: Only one route was different from the plan. The group traced the route almost as planned (Figure 9 (a)). They said "The system requires shortcut display function." They did target-oriented sightseeing.

Group 2: The group's strategy was to walk on the main street. Group members moved roughly as planned (Figure 9 (b)). They turned back once because the street had disappeared around Ukimi-do. This is because the planned route was not accurate. They changed the order of their going to the various tourist spots on the sightseeing day and flexibly selected the routes.

(a) Transportation log of Group 1

(b) Transportation log of Group 2

(c) Transportation log of Group 3

Fig. 9. Transportation logs.

Group 3: Before reaching the first destination, group members looked at a guideboard beside the road. They were interested in an unscheduled spot and spent approximately 30 minutes at the spot (Figure 9 (c)). The distance became 500m longer than the planned distance. This group changed the route largely because they were interested in a country road.
Figure 10 shows an example of system utilization.

Fig. 10. Example of system utilization.

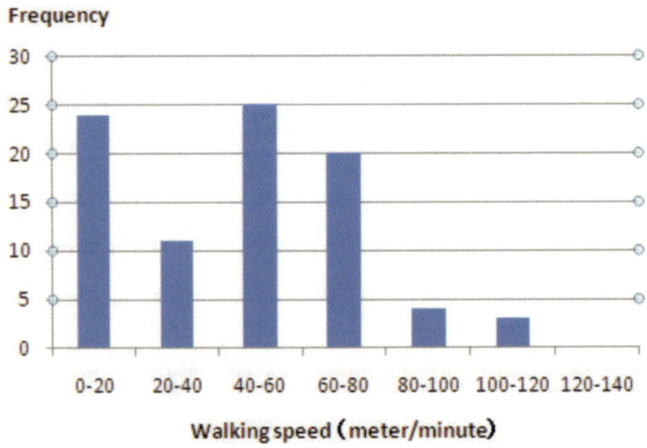

(a) Walking speed of Group 1

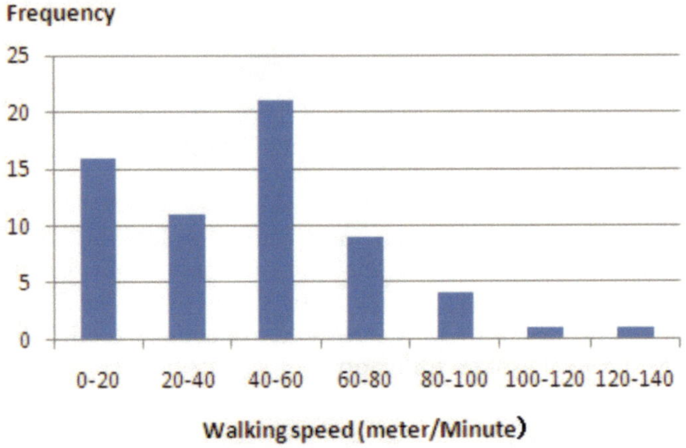

(b) Walking speed of Group 2

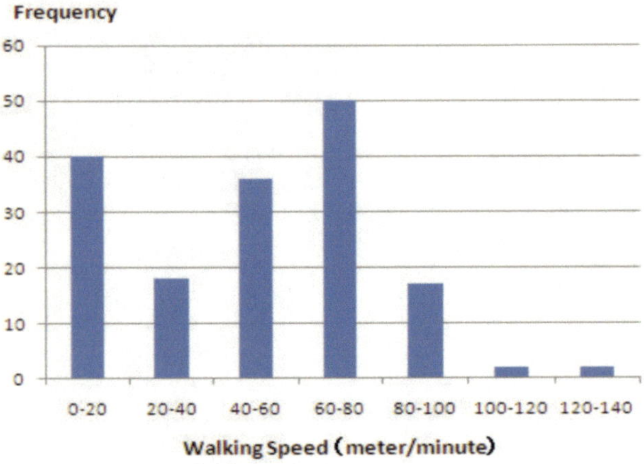

(c) Walking speed of Group 3

Fig. 11. Walking speed of three groups.

4.3 Ambiguity of planned route and movement

The ratio of the original route the groups actually traced was calculated as "relevance ratio" to investigate the correlation between ambiguity of the map and the route actually taken (Table 2).

	Group 1	Group 2	Group 3
Planned route length (km)	5.9	3.5	5.6
Concordant distance (km)	5.3	1.5	4.0
Relevance rate (%)	89.8	42.9	71.4

Table 2. The distance actually walked in the plan.

The relevance rate of group 1 and 3 is high. The relevance rate of group 2 was less than 50% showing significant difference from the other groups. The planned route of group 2 was rougher than the other groups. This may have facilitated their changing routes.
Figure 11 shows the distribution of walking speed of each group. Walking speed per minute was calculated based on the GPS data. For walking speed (brisk walking: 80m /min as a reference), groups 1 and 2 stopped walking (0-20m/min) and walked slowly (20-60m/min) more frequently than group 3. Especially, group 2 showed this tendency. This is because planned route was ambiguous and they walked and checked their surroundings.
As shown above, it was suggested that ambiguity of the planned route promoted selection of an unplanned route and reduced waking speed.

4.4 Creation of contingency

The ratio of the unplanned route to the entire movement distance was calculated as the rate of deviation (Table 3).

	Group 1	Group 2	Group 3
Total movement distance (km)	5.9	3.6	7.2
Unplanned distance (km)	0.6	2.1	3.2
Rate of deviation (%)	10.2	58.3	44.4

Table 3. Ratio of distance from the plan.

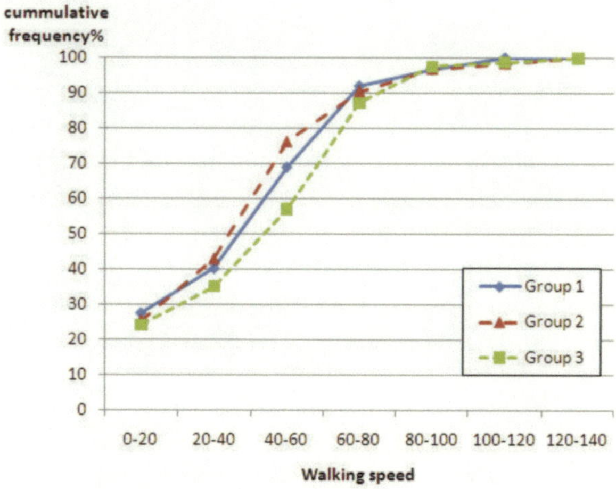

Fig. 12. Cummulative walking speed of three groups.

(a) Places where subjects stayed: Group 1

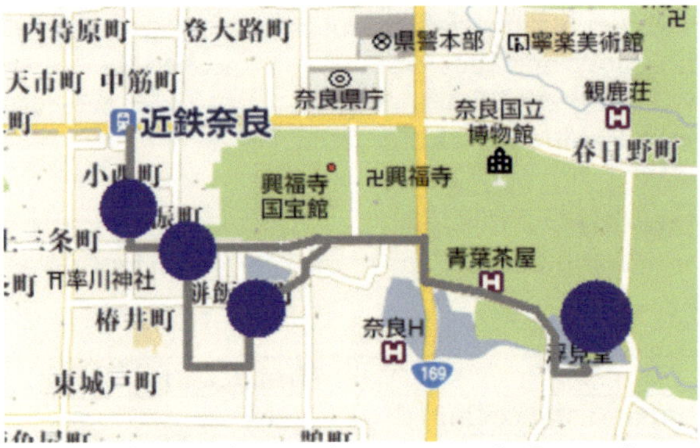

(b) Places where subjects stayed: Group 2

(c) Places where subjects stayed: Group 3

Fig. 13. Places where subjects stayed for more than 3 minutes.

Group 1 prepared a rigorously planned route that rarely showed behavior in looking for an unplanned route. The rate of deviation was lowest (approximately 10%). For group 2, the walking distance was short and the relevance rate was low. Therefore, the rate of deviation was highest (approximately 58%). The rate of deviation for group 3 was also high. The group followed the planned route. However, group members added destinations on site and passed an unplanned street at some point. Therefore, movement distance was longer than planned.

Figure 12 compares the cumulative rate of walking speed of each group. Slow movement speed spots (0-40m/min) were analyzed for each group in Figure 13.

Group 1 stopped for 10 minutes at the starting point. In these 10 minutes, group members started the system and decided their sightseeing strategy. They rarely stayed long on a spot.

Group 2 stopped during the movement. Group members took pictures of the scenery and posters. They seemed to enjoy strolling as they moved.

Group 3 stopped for approximately 10 minutes when the system was down. Other than the 10-minute stop, the group did not stop. Group members did their sightseeing while they walked.

Group 2 was an only group who stayed more than 3 minutes during the movement. On these points, they enjoyed buying and eating Japanese sweets at a shop which they came across, and enjoyed being surprised to accidentally find that a temple could be seen from an unexpected point.

As shown above, the group that prepared an ambiguous map during the planning enjoyed the casualness (change of route, stopping midway on the route, etc.).

4.5 Discussions

After the experiment, all subjects were asked to answer a questionnaire which included items as follows:

1. Was route planning easy?
2. Did your sightseeing plan map match your own image?
3. How did you feel when you could not be provided detailed route information?
4. Under what situation did you use the system?
5. Did you have any strategy for movement?
6. What kind of additional functions do you want?
7. Other feedback

According to the results of the questionnaire, all groups had difficulty in making a route plan. This is because the subjects were difficult to know the actual situation of the route and to decide an appropriate route to be selected. One subject answered that altitude data were required to estimate the fatigue level and to decide how many spots to visit.

On the other hand, all group members answered that they enjoyed making a route plan and that the map was satisfactory corresponding to the interest and knowledge level of each group.

An interesting thing is that all members enjoyed having got lost. They have troubles in finding routes in daily lives. In a sense, they felt as participating in a game which was provided by the system. Of course, they reported that finding new things during lost was very fascinating and exciting. This is anticipated efficacy of this system. This is a kind of "benefit of inconvenience" which was proposed by Kawakami et al. [9].

Some members of Group 1 said, said, "We need distance information to the destination" and "We require information about shortcuts." These requests went against the concept of this system. Group 1 did not know the detailed geographical knowledge about the area and felt anxious if they could lose their way without the detailed route information. The level of unfamiliarity to the area has to be considered when the detailed information is hidden. Some tactics or know-how of orienteering could be useful support. When Group 2 got lost around Ukimi-do, they tried to find the landscape which best matched their image of the destination. This could be a clue of supporting unfamiliar tourists.

5. Conclusion

We proposed a TNS that did not provide detailed route information. We evaluated the system in Nara city. The system was relatively highly evaluated. However, some subjects said, "We need distance information to the destination" and "We require information about shortcuts." The requests went against the concept of this system. When tourists use a TNS, they tend to depend on the system. Finding a route by itself is difficult and requires tactics or know-how of orienteering. We need to further study this issue in the next step. Now we are investigating a framework which helps tourists with only photographs of landmarks on a route and other framework which completely hides a map except the limited number of landmarks, such as post offices, schools, and drug stores. Some photographs are taken from the opposite direction of travel. Thus far, photographs are very effective to navigate people by making them look around the environment. Even familiar people to an area found new routes and shops, which made them excited.

6. References

Yoshio Nakatani, Ken Tanaka and Kanako Ichikawa, A Tourist Navigation System That Does NOT Provide Route Maps, *Lecture Notes in Engineering and Computer Science: Proceedings of The World Congress on Engineering and Computer Science 2009*, WCECS 2009, 20-22 October, 2009, San Francisco, USA, pp.1264-1269.

A. Maruyama, N. Shibata, Y. Murata, K. Yasumoto and M. Ito, "P-TOUR: A Personal Navigation System," *Proc. the 11th World Congress on ITS*, 2004, 18-22 October, Nagoya, Japan, pp. 18–21.

NAVIT, Raku-Raku scheduler, http://www17.pos.to/~navit/hp/mannavi/scheduler01.html. (in Japanese)

H. Tarumi, et al., "Open experiments of mobile sightseeing support systems with shared virtual worlds," *Proc. 2006 ACM SIGCHI Intl. Conf.* Advances in Computer Entertainment Technology, 2006 (DVD).

Ministry of Land, Infrastructure, Transport and Tourism and Nara prefecture, "Nara Prefecture Autonomous Mobile Support Experiment," http:// www.pref.nara.jp/doroi/jiritsu/. (in Japanese)

K. Oguchi, *Social Psychology of Sightseeing*, Tokyo: Kitaoji-Shobo, 2006. (in Japanese)

R. Caillois, *Man, Play, and Games* (translated from the French by Meyer Barash), Urbana : University of Illinois Press, 2001.

K. Nishimura, *Phenomenology of play*, Tokyo: Keiso-Shobo, 1989. (in Japanese)

H. Kawakami, et al., "System Design Based on Benefit of Inconvenience and Emotion," *Proc. ICCAS-SICE 2009*, 18-21 August, 2009, Fukuoka, Japan, pp.1184-1188.

19

Logistic Operating Curves in Theory and Practice

Peter Nyhuis and Matthias Schmidt
Institute of Production Systems and Logistics,
Leibniz Universitaet Hannover
Germany

1. Introduction

The Competitiveness of a company is determined by its ability to adjust its product offerings and performance to the changing market needs and its capability to realize the existing potentials in purchasing, production and distribution. Therefore, the long-term survivability of a company is measured by target values like relative competitive position, growth in sales, increase in productivity and the return on equity. At the same time, delivery reliability and delivery time have established themselves as equivalent buying criteria alongside product quality and price (Enslow, 2006; Hon, 2005; Wildemann, 2007;). High delivery reliability and short delivery times for companies demand high schedule reliability and short throughput times in production (Kim and Duffie, 2005). In order to manufacture efficient under such conditions, it is necessary to generate a high logistic performance and to minimise logistic costs simultaneously (figure 1) (Wiendahl, 1997).

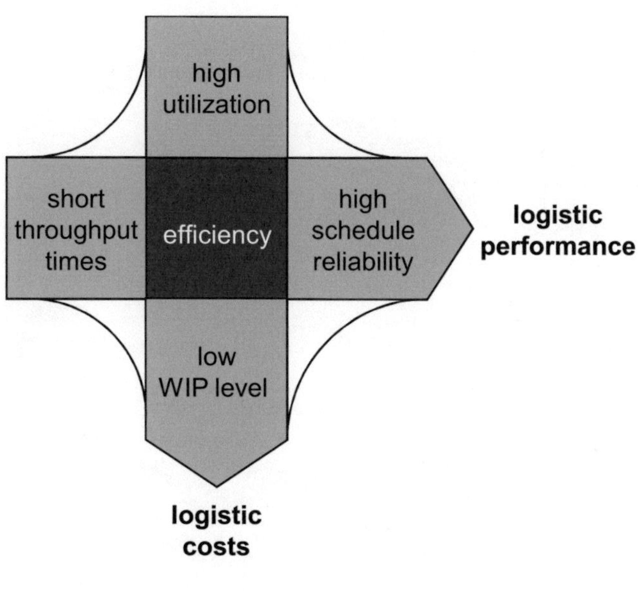

Fig. 1. Objectives of Production Logistics.

The logistic performance is defined by short throughput times and high schedule reliability. The logistic costs depend on low WIP levels in production and high utilisation of operational resources.

2. Challenges for production management

The above mentioned production logistics objectives short throughput times, high schedule reliability, low WIP level and high machine utilisation can not be reached simultaneously because the objectives show a conflicting orientation (figure 2). This fact is known as the scheduling dilemma (Hopp and Spearman, 2000; Gutenberg, 1951). For example, it is not possible to maximise the utilisation of a work system and to minimise throughput times simultaneously. On the one hand a high utilisation of work systems calls for high WIP levels in order to prevent interruptions to the materials flow during production. On the other hand high WIP levels lead to long throughput times because of long material queues at work station. That means that the aim of high machine utilisation in conjunction with short throughput times cannot be achieved. In addition, long throughput times increase the likelihood of orders queuing at work systems being swapped around. The result is a decrease in the schedule reliability within the production. Several authors have pointed out that the challenge for managers therefore is not to "optimise" a certain logistic objective, but rather to find a rational trade-off between satisfactory levels of performance of all the conflicting objectives (Hopp and Spearman, 2000; Schuh, 2006; Schönsleben, 2004). In order to overcome the scheduling dilemma, certain work systems and production areas must be positioned in the field of conflict between the production logistics objectives. To do this, it is necessary to map the relationships between the effects of these different objectives and to describe the behaviour of the logistic system. The Logistic Production Operating Curves outlined in figure 2 provide a suitable approach. These curves describe the utilisation and the throughput times depending on the WIP level.

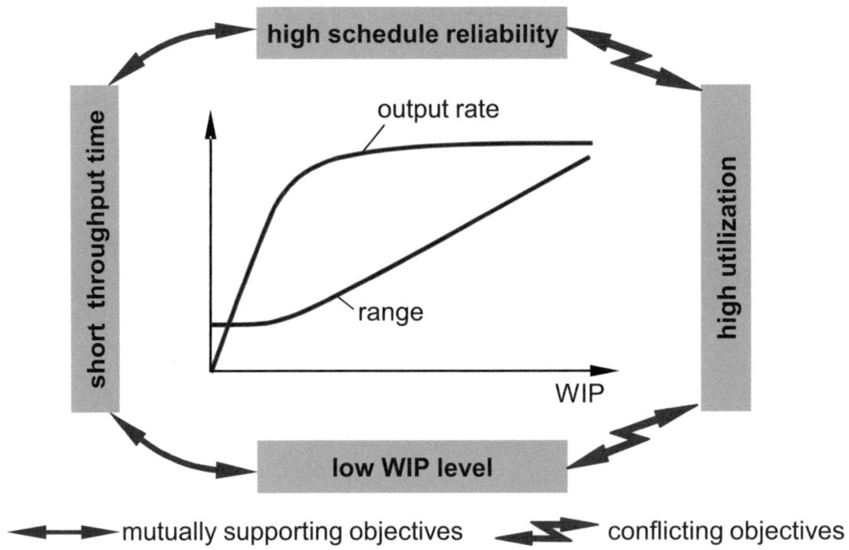

Fig. 2. Scheduling Dilemma and Logistic Production Operating Curves.

Both research and industrial practice use various methods to model the described relationships. Popular methods are the queuing theory from the field of operations research, simulation and the Theory of Logistic Operating Curves developed at the Institute of Production Systems and Logistics (IFA). Figure 3 shows a qualitative comparison of the modelling methods by the criteria illustration quality and implementation efforts as well as the extension in industrial practice.

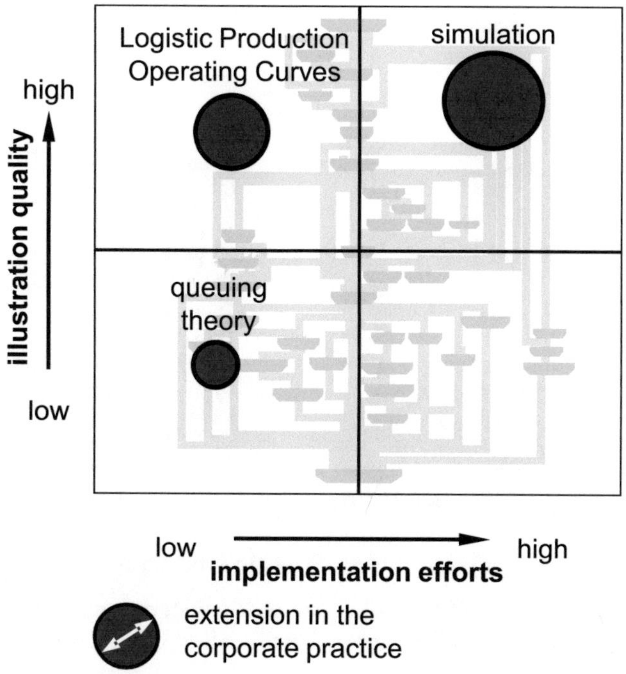

Fig. 3. Illustration Quality and Implementation Efforts of Different Modelling Methods.

Both the queuing theory and the Logistic Production Operating Curves require low illustration efforts while a high illustration quality can only be provided by the simulation and the Logistic Production Operating Curves, which both are widespread in industrial practice. Therefore, the queuing theory and simulation are often not entirely suitable for modelling logistic relationships, especially for the description of real production contexts (Nyhuis et al., 2005).

3. Derivation of the Logistic Production Operating Curves

The Logistic Production Operating Curves reduce the complexity and the cost of modelling the behaviour of logistic systems. Thus, they create a way of positioning a work system or a production area in the field of conflict between the logistic objectives. This chapter shows the derivation of the Logistic Production Operating Curves (Nyhuis and Wiendahl, 2009). Firstly, equations are developed for assumed ideal production conditions and result in ideal Logistic Production Operating Curves. Secondly, the ideal curves are adapted to real production processes. Thirdly, the validation of the Logistic Production Operating Curves is presented.

3.1 Logistic Production Operating Curves

The development of the ideal Logistic Production Operating Curves requires to define an ideal production process. In this process, a single work system is considered. The utilisation of this work system is about 100% and the WIP level is at its minimum. This originates in the fact that a new order is fed to the work system whenever a completed order leaves it. Accordingly, no order has to wait for processing and no interruptions to the materials flow occur in the production process. The resulting throughput diagram is shown on the left in figure 4.

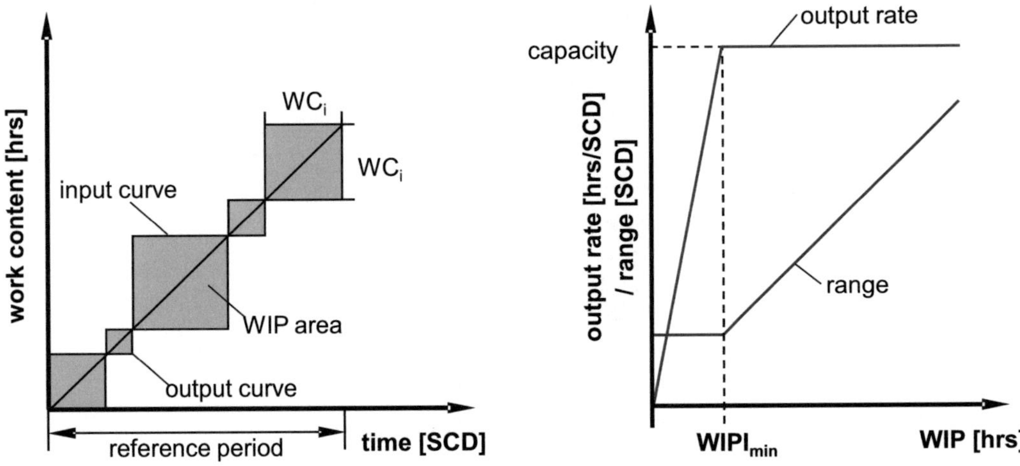

Fig. 4. Ideal Throughput Diagram and Ideal Logistic Production Operating Curves.

In the ideal process, the mean WIP level at the work system is governed exclusively by the work content (order times) and their scatter. This is called the ideal minimum WIP level:

$$WIPI_{min} = WC_m \cdot (1+WC_v^2). \quad (1)$$

$WIPI_{min}$ ideal minimum WIP level [hrs]
WC_m mean work content [hrs]
WC_v variation coefficient for work content [-]
[Note: hrs = hours]

The upper limit to the output rate of the work system is defined by the maximum possible output rate. This is described by the restrictive capacity factors operational and personnel resources:

$$ROUT_{max} = \min (CAP_{mc}, CAP_{op}) \quad (2)$$

$ROUT_{max}$ maximum possible output rate [hrs/SCD]
CAP_{mc} available machine capacity [hrs/SCD]
CAP_{op} available operator capacity [hrs/SCD]
[Note: SCD = shop calendar day]

The ratio of mean WIP level to mean output rate corresponds to the mean range of the WIP level. This relationship is designated the funnel equation:

$$R_m = WIP_m / ROUT_m \quad (3)$$

R_m mean range [SCD]
WIP_m mean WIP level [hrs]
$ROUT_m$ mean output rate [hrs/SCD]

The ideal Production Operating Curves, shown on the right in figure 4, can be derived from the ideal minimum WIP level and the maximum possible output rate. The Logistic Operating Curve of the output rate of a work system describes how the mean output rate varies with respect to the mean WIP level. In the ideal process, full utilisation of the work system and hence also the maximum possible output rate is achieved with the ideal minimum WIP level. A further increase in the WIP level does not bring about any increase in the output rate. And below the ideal minimum WIP level, the output rate drops in proportion to the WIP level until both values reach zero. The Logistic Operating Curve of the range can be calculated from the output rate operating curve with the help of the funnel equation. Above the ideal minimum WIP level, the range increases in proportion to the WIP level. Below the ideal minimum WIP level, the mean range corresponds to the minimum range which is due to mean order work content.

3.2 Real Production Operating Curves

Ideal process conditions do not occur in practice. However, a simulation carried out at the IFA showed that although the ideal Logistic Production Operating Curves do not represent real process conditions they provide a suitable framework. The simulation covered eight simulation experiments with the mean WIP level as the only changing variable (figure 5).

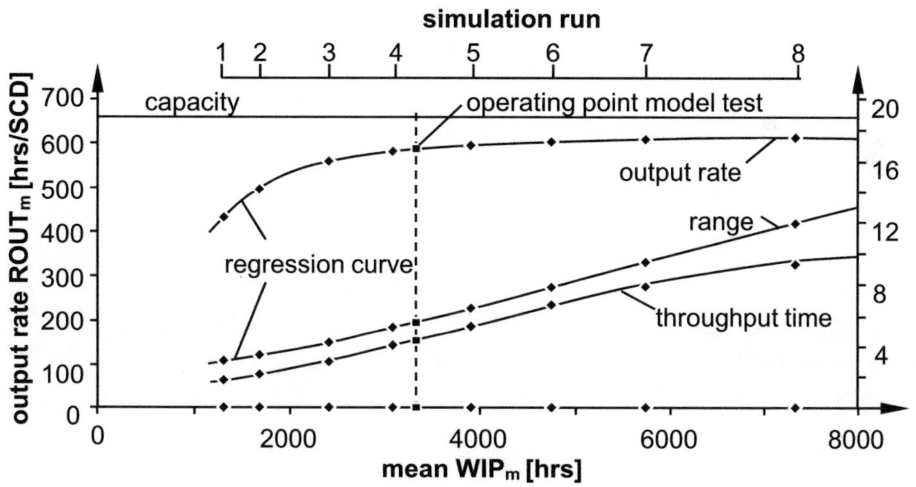

Fig. 5. Simulated Logistic Production Operating Curves.

The simulated operating states show clearly that the Logistic Production Operating Curves do not exhibit a defined break point under real process conditions. Instead, we see a smooth transition from the full machine utilisation zone of the operating curve (stable output, in this case WIP level approximately 5000 h) to the under-utilised zone.

In order to be able to model real process conditions with minimum effort but adequate accuracy, we require a mathematical description of the real Logistic Production Operating Curves. An approximation equation was developed for the mathematical description based on an approximation of the parameterised C_{Norm} function:

$$x = x(t) = t \text{ and } y = y(t) = -(1 - t^c)^{1/c} \quad (4)$$

x variable [-]
t running variable [-]
y variable [-]
C C_{Norm} parameter [-]

The parameterised C_{Norm} function has been transformed into the approximation equation in four steps. The four transformation steps required are shown in figure 6. Firstly, the set of equations (see formula 4) is translated by the value one in the positive y-direction. The second transformation step stretches the set of equations in the y-direction such that the maximum value y_1 of the curve corresponds to the maximum possible output rate. The third transformation step shears the set of equations in the x direction.

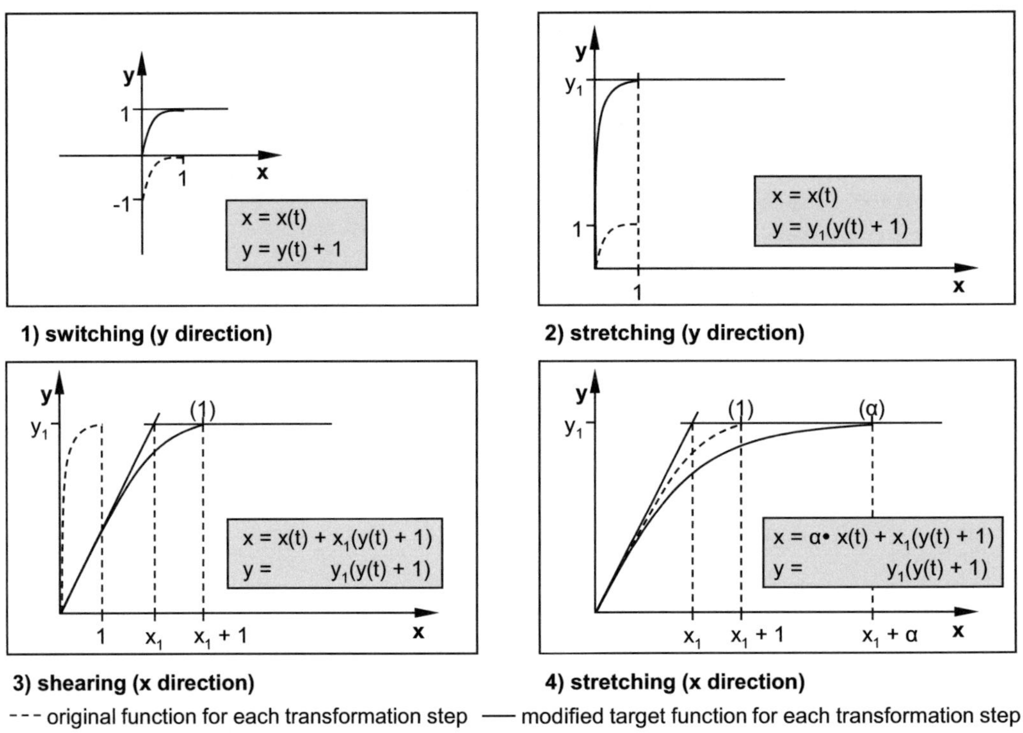

Fig. 6. Transformation of the C_{Norm} Function.

The ideal Logistic Operating Curve of the output rate characterised by the ideal minimum WIP level now forms the system of coordinates for the real Production Operating Curves. The fourth transformation step stretches the curve by the stretch factor α_1 in the x direction. Replacing the variables x and y by the mean WIP level and the mean output rate respectively as well as the variables x_1 and y_1 by the ideal minimum WIP level and the maximum output rate respectively enables the transformed set of equations to be converted into the following set of equations. This describes the real Logistic Production Operating Curves of the output rate:

$$\mathrm{WIP_m}(t) = \mathrm{WIPI_{min}} \cdot (1 - (1 - t^c)^{1/c} + \mathrm{WIPI_{min}} \cdot \alpha 1 \cdot t \quad (5)$$

$$ROUT_m(t) = ROUT_{max} \cdot (1-(1-t^c)^{1/c} \quad (6)$$

$WIP_m(t)$	mean WIP level (as a function of t) [hrs]
t	running variable [-]
$WIPI_{min}$	ideal minimum WIP level [hrs]
C	C_{Norm} value [-] (default value C = 0,25)
α_1	stretch factor [-] (default value $\alpha_1 = 10$)
$ROUT_m(t)$	mean output rate (as a function of t) [hrs/SCD]
$ROUT_{max}$	maximum output rate [hrs/SCD]

A pair of values for the mean WIP level and the mean output rate can be calculated for a given ideal minimum WIP level and maximum possible output rate for every value of t ($0 \geq t \geq 1$). The combination of several such pairs of values results in the Logistic Operating Curve of the output rate. This curve can now be converted into the Logistic Production Operating Curve of the range with the help of the funnel equation (see formula 3).

The parameters of the approximation equations deduced, which describe the Logistic Production Operating Curves, take into account a series of production logistics factors (figure 7). These are included in the parameters for ideal minimum WIP level, maximum possible output rate and stretch factor α_1. The batch size of the orders, the individual processing times for the products and the setup time necessary for the work systems are included in the calculation of the ideal minimum WIP level. In addition, by extending the scope of the study we can also include transport times and minimum inter-operation times (e.g. due to technological restrictions). The maximum possible output rate is mainly limited by the capacity of the work system. Furthermore, faults that reduce capacity, the level of

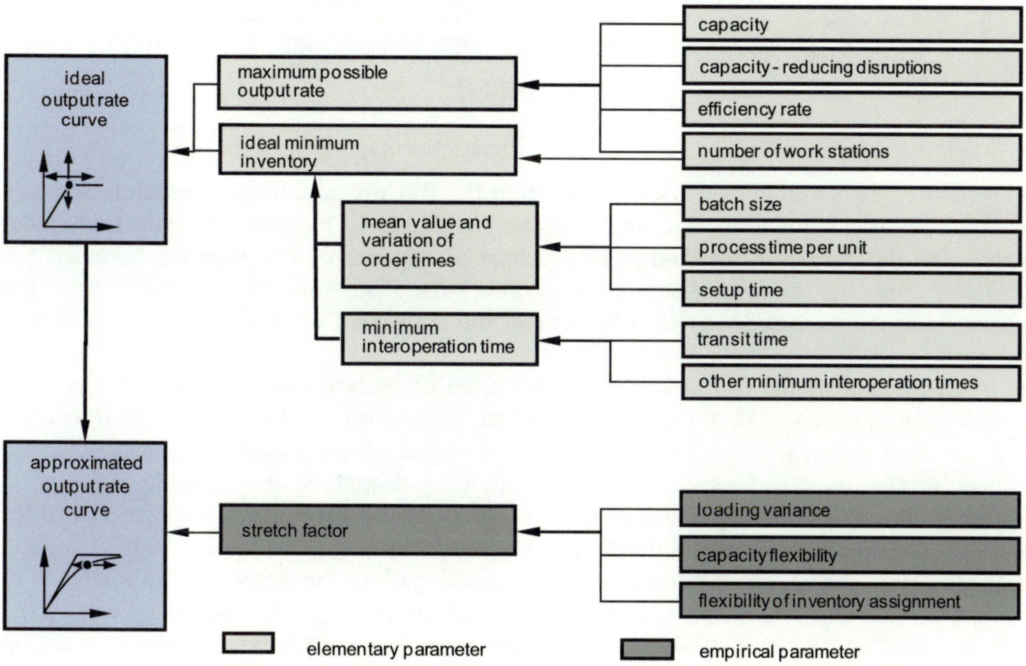

Fig. 7. Parameters of Logistic Production Operating Curves.

performance and, lastly, the number of work systems determine the maximum possible output rate. The stretch factor α_1, which until now could only be calculated empirically, is essentially determined by the capacity flexibility available on the one hand and the scatter of the workload on the other.

3.3 Validating the Real Production Operating Curves

The Logistic Production Operating Curves describe the relationships between the effects of the logistic performance measures of a work system for constant order time and capacity structures. As different WIP levels for a work system are hardly feasible in practice for identical order time and capacity structures, the real Production Operating Curves are validated by means of simulations (fig. 8).

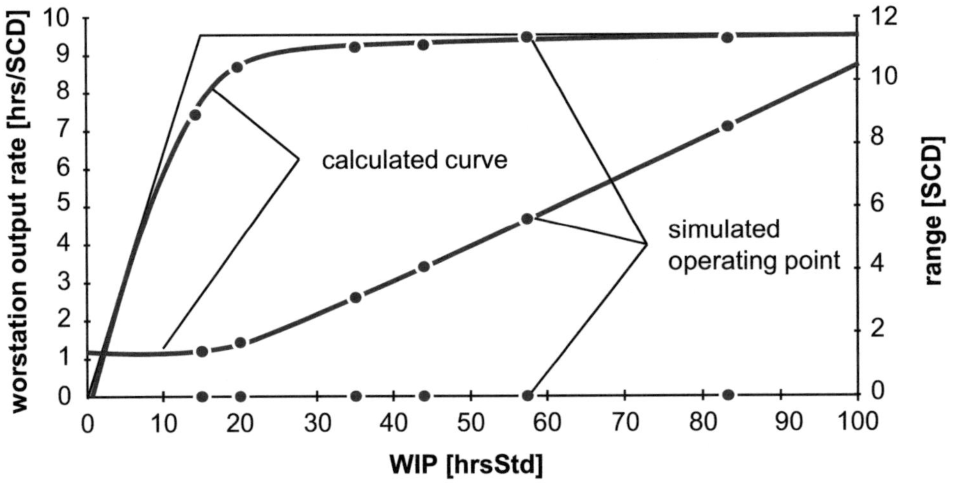

Fig. 8. Simulation based Validation of Logistic Production Operating Curves.

The results of the simulation work carried out at the IFA reveal a high correlation between the result of the simulation and the Logistic Production Operating Curves calculated. Analyses of the deviation resulted in an average divergence of less than 2% between the calculated and the simulated operating conditions. The simulations prove that the mathematical model describes the behaviour of the simulated work system with sufficient accuracy.

The mathematical model of the Logistic Production Operating Curves was developed for practical applications and therefore additional validation under industrial operating conditions was necessary. The practical trials carried out exhibit a high correlation with the findings of the model. Therefore, the mathematical model of the Logistic Production Operating Curves has been proved as suitable for practical application. The procedure for validating the model by means of practical trials is as follows.

Feedback data from a work system was evaluated within the scope of the analyses of throughput time and WIP level. The operating condition of the work system is given by the analysis, and this result is subsequently compared with a calculated Logistic Production Operating Curve which initially uses a default value (α_1 = 10) for the stretch factor α_1. If a comparison of the operating condition and the calculated Production Operating Curve does not reveal any significant differences with respect to possible machine utilisation losses due to WIP level, the parameterising of the model can be regarded as suitable. If this is not the case, the stretch factor α_1 must be modified. Only in those cases with very high WIP levels it is impossible to check the parameters in this way. However, this limitation does not usually represent a problem in practice because in these cases the options for reducing the WIP level are obvious.

3.4 Normalized Logistic Production Operating Curves

For a number of problems it is helpful to normalize reference parameters in order to be able to draw conclusions that are independent of the system specific conditions or to compare different work systems with the help of the Logistic Production Operating Curves. In order to do so it is necessary to determine appropriate reference values for such normalisations. It seems obvious that for the output rate and WIP level they can be based on the ideal operating state and thus expressed as a relative parameter.

In our discussion about Output Rate Operating Curves we already conducted a similar type of normalization, using the definition of the mean WIP dependent utilization U_m as a ratio of $ROUT_m$ to $ROUT_{max}$. In order to describe a relative WIP level, the mean WIP is set in relation to $WIPI_{min}$.

Fig. 9 shows the normalized Logistic Production Operating Curves, where α_1 = 10. The graph describes how a change in the WIP impacts the utilization of the workstation, independent of the existing work content structures and the workstation's capacity. It shows, for example, that the WIP dependent loss of utilization is approximately 17% when the mean WIP corresponds to WIP_{min}. If the WIP is tripled the loss of utilization is reduced to approximately 1%.

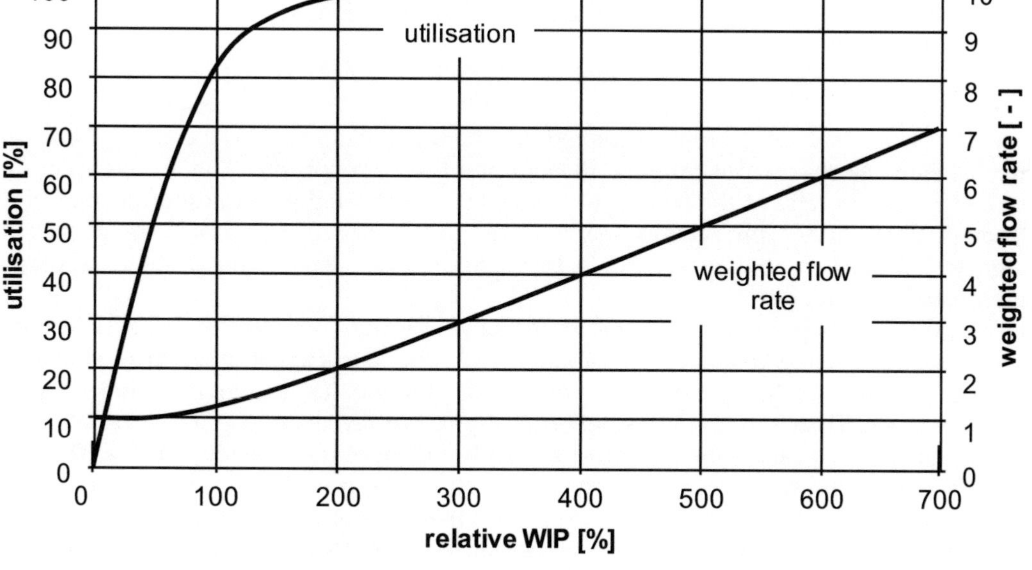

Fig. 9. Normalised Logistic Production Operating Curves.

A relative measure of the throughput time is the flow rate. If, in analogy to the Funnel Formula the relative WIP is set in relation to the utilization we obtain the mean weighted flow rate as a normalized parameter for the range. This can also be calculated through the ratio of range to minimum range.

4. Practical Applications of Logistic Production Operating Curves

Logistic Production Operating Curves enable the logistic controlling of production processes. They are applicable in different industries. Specially developed control methods such as the Bottleneck Oriented Logistic Analysis make it possible to evaluate and improve existing production processes by describing them qualitatively and quantitatively, from a logistic perspective (Nyhuis and Wiendahl, 2009; Nyhuis and Penz, 1995). The specific causes of problems can then be localised and presented in the form of cause-and-effect relationships. Furthermore, the existing logistic potentials for improvement as well as the possible measures for developing them can be demonstrated and evaluated.

The basis of production control is the structured analysis of production processing data. The logistic analysis of this data is based on a well delineated, but complex problem. 'Well delineated' means here that there is enough data to extensively document the problem. The problem's complexity is for example due to the interactions between the workstations or because a number of related but partially contradicting objectives have to be simultaneously considered. The production processing data can be aggregated into key figures, such as a workstations mean WIP or output rate. They thus first provide information about the workstation's logistic behaviour.

Demonstrating the practical applications of the Logistic Production Operating Curves an excerpt of a Bottle-neck Oriented Logistic Analysis accomplished at a manufacturer of printed circuit boards is given. The target of the analysis was on the one hand a reduction of the order throughput times and on the other hand a reduction of the WIP. The left side of figure 10 shows a section of the material flow diagram for the observed manufacturer. Here, we can see that the workstation "resist coating" is a key station, because most of the material flow lines pass this workstation.

The right side of figure 10 shows a logistic portfolio. It illustrates that on the one hand the workstation "resist coating" runs at a very high WIP level. This comparison is made by the use of the normalised Logistic Production Operating Curves. On the other hand this workstation shows an outstanding throughput time proportion. The throughput time proportion is the ratio of the sum of the workstation´s throughput times to the sum of the through times of the production analysed. So the workstation "resist coating" has the highest influence on the production's throughput times. Therefore, this workstation is examined in detail.

Firstly, the order's processing behaviour on the workstation "resist coating" is determined and visualized using a throughput diagram (figure 11). The output curve shows the outgoing orders' accumulated work content during the investigation period. It has a constant slope. Therefore, the workstation's output rate reveals no significant fluctuations. The input curve visualises the accumulated work content of the incoming orders. The input curve's slope indicates certain fluctuations, which can be traced back to the workstation's varying load. The WIP level on the workstation therefore also oscillates, because it results from the difference between the in- and output. By using the previously determined key figures together with the throughput diagram the behaviour of the workstation's logistic system can be evaluated.

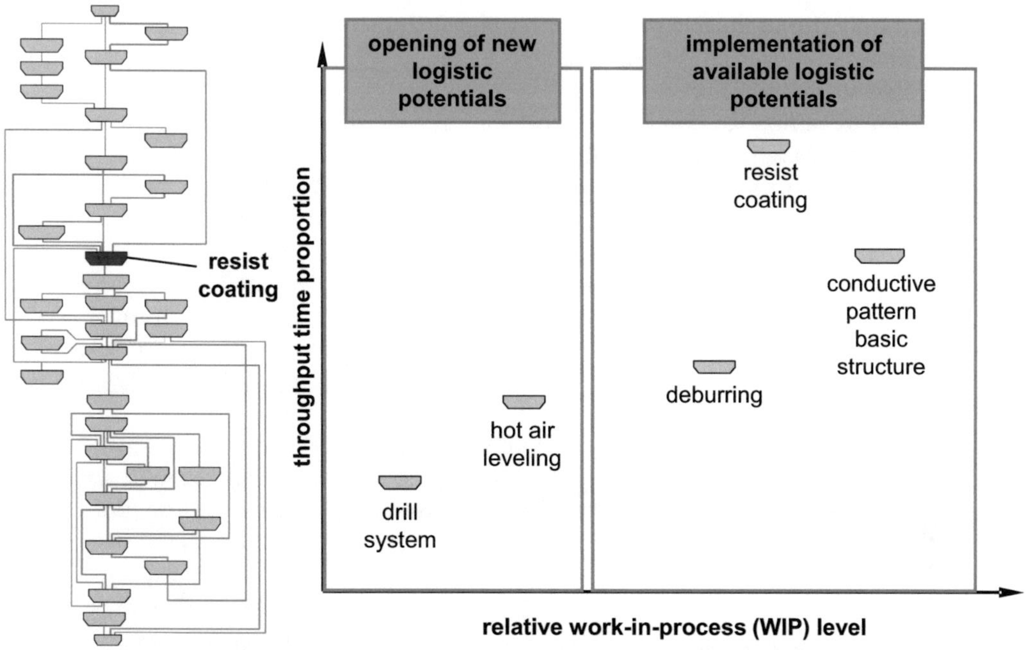

Fig. 10. Material Flow Diagram and Logistic Portfolio.

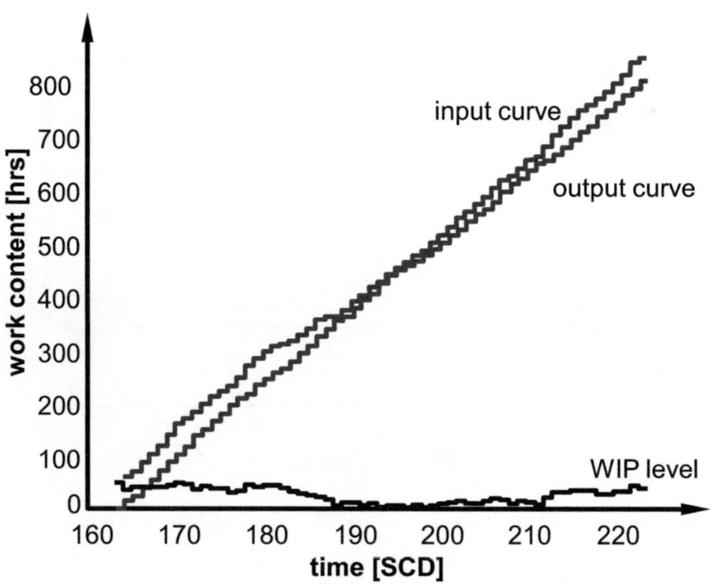

Fig. 11. Throughput Diagram of the Work Station Resist.

To identify logistic potential for improvement the relationships between the logistic objectives must be described. Therefore, the Logistic Production Operating Curves are used (figure 12). The calculated operating point is located well into the overload operating state and the WIP level on the workstation is very high. The output rate is therefore high, but there are also long throughput times. Reducing the WIP by approximately 22 hours would make it possible to reduce the throughput time by ca. 75% (from 2 SCD down to 0.5 SCD), without notable output rate losses.

As can be seen in figure 10, due to the workstation's central role reducing the WIP and therefore also the throughput time would affect the entire manufacturing process. In order to reduce the WIP of the workstation, the company could introduce measures that temporarily increase the output rate either through over-time or additional shifts. In total the capacity needs to be increased by 20 hours. This would be possible because the resist coating workstation had worked up until now with an output rate of 13.4 hours per shop calendar day. This however influences the work-stations downstream, which then have to ensure that the resulting additional load is processed through capacitive measures. Otherwise, the WIP problem is only transferred to the following workstations (Nyhuis and Penz, 1995).

Another approach to lowering the WIP on the resist coating workstation is to limit the load by temporarily restricting the order input. This has to be controlled through the order release. Here, it has to be considered that the disruption of the material flow at the input could lead to a loss of output on the workstations located upstream the resist coating station.

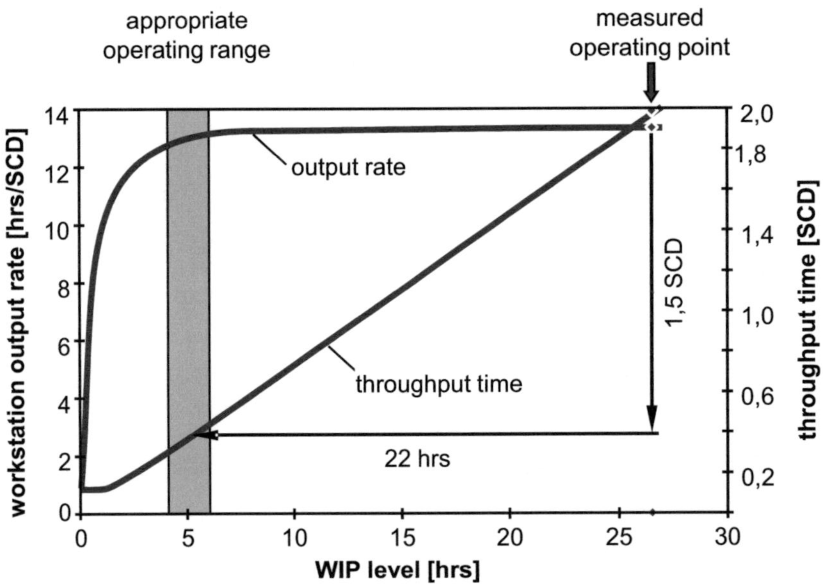

Fig. 12. Logistic Production Operating Curves of the Work Station Resist Coating.

5. Derivation of the Schedule Adherence Operating Curve

The measures described above will reduce the production´s throughput times as well as the scatter of the throughput times. To be able to estimate the impact on the schedule adherence of production analysed which directly determines the delivery reliability, the Schedule Adherence Operating Curve was developed at the Institute of Production Systems and Logistics recently. To clarify the derivation of this model figure 13 illustrates a simulated histogram of a production´s output date deviation which is weighed with the order value during a reference period of one year.

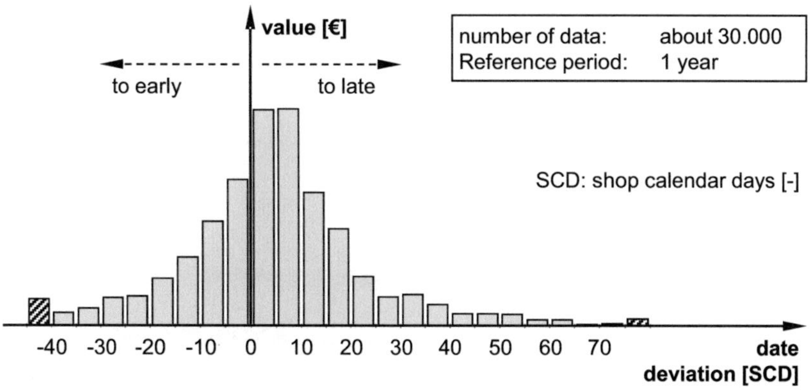

Fig. 13. Typical Distribution of a Production´s Date Deviation.

The classes of the date deviations are plotted on the x-axis. The y-axis reflects the order value of a class. It is typical for such a distribution to be similar to a normal distribution. The weighted average is just under 5 SCD and a standard deviation is about 20 SCD. The grey striped bars on the left and right edge of the histogram represent all orders with a date deviation of less than 40 SCD and more than 75 SCD, respectively. As a result, there is an intolerable date situation as a result of the broad scattering of date deviation and the high number of orders delayed. This has a significant impact on the supply of internal and external customers and thus the delivery reliability. Overall, only about one-third of the orders are completed on time. The other orders leave production stage late. A higher schedule adherence can be achieved with an increased stock of finished orders. To determine this stock and to explain the connection between the mean weighted schedule adherence and the stock of finished orders depending on the distribution of the date deviation, the distribution of figure 13 should be considered in more detail. Therefore, the value weighted distribution of the date deviation is illustrated in the upper part of figure 14 again. This illustrates that a delivery time buffer, which is defined as a buffer time between the target finishing date and the target delivering date of the orders to the customer, is a key control variable in the field of tension between a high schedule adherence and a low level of stock of finished orders.

In the lower part of figure 14, the order values of the individual date deviation classes of the upper part are cumulated in a graph. It shows the part of orders which will be finished on time (before or on the target finishing date plus a defined delivery time buffer). This value corresponds to the weighted schedule adherence. In the case of a buffer with an assumed time of 0 SCD, the weighted schedule adherence is 35%. But orders which are completed on time generate stock, because the majority of them are finished before the target finishing date (dark grey bars in histogram). In order to weight this stock with the time period of early completion, the stock area of the finished orders will be determined by calculating the integral below the curve of the cumulated value from negative infinity to a determined delivery time buffer of 0 BKT. In case a, the stock area of the finished orders has a value of 1,700 million € · SCD.

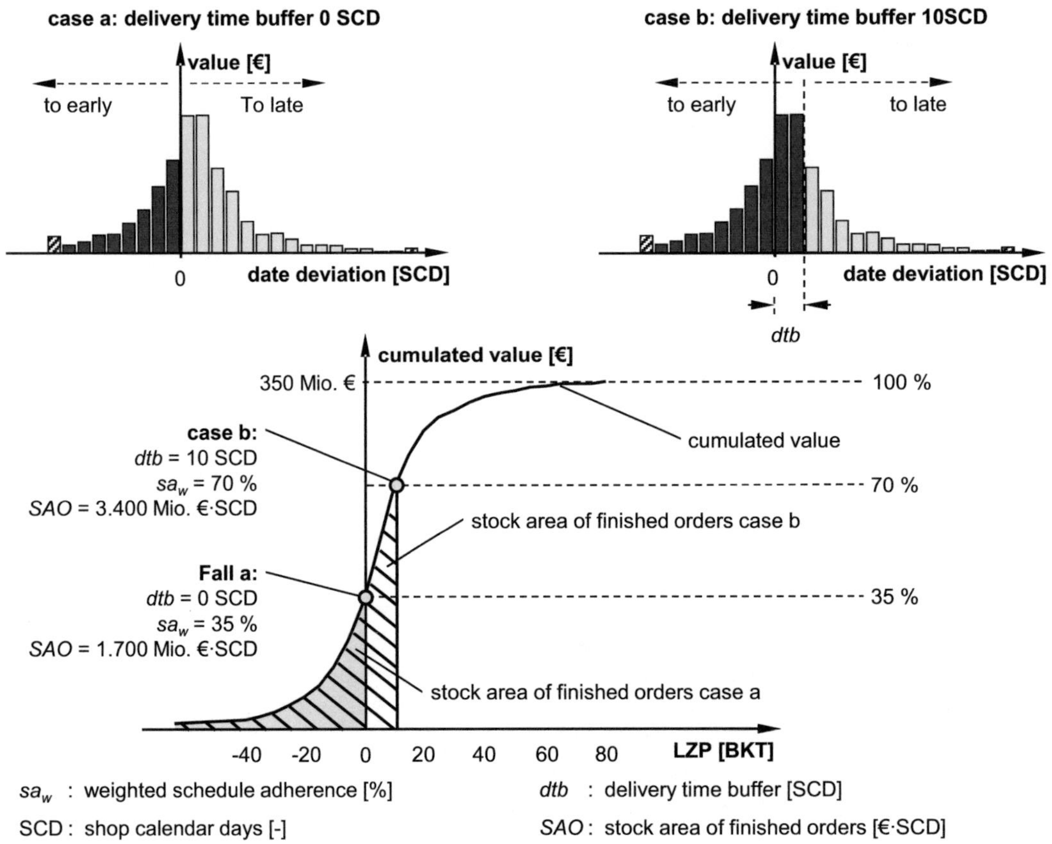

Fig. 14. Delivery Time Buffer as a Key Control Variable.

In case b, a delivery time buffer of 10 BKT is set exemplarily. The corresponding histogram in the upper part represents that a lot more orders leave the production stage without delay using the delivery time buffer (dark grey bars). The curve of the cumulated value in the lower part of figure 14 shows a weighted schedule adherence of 70%. The stock area of finished orders is approximately 3,400 million € · SCD.

However, the stock area of finished orders is not sufficient to compare different schedule adherence scenarios with a similar order structure in terms of their values and their date deviations, because the stock area of finished orders depends on the selected reference period. Therefore, the mean stock level of finished orders can be calculated by dividing the stock area of finished orders by the selected reference period. To develop this knowledge into an effect model the upper part of figure 15 shows three curves of the cumulated value with different delivery time buffers and corresponding stock areas.

Case a shows an assumed delivery time buffer of 0 SCD. The result is a low schedule adherence and a small stock area of finished orders. Case b represents a larger delivery time buffer. Accordingly, we find the values of the schedule adherence and the stock area of finished orders in a middle range. In case c, the delivery time buffer is adopted generously. The schedule adherence is close to 100%, which is the result of a large stock area of finished orders.

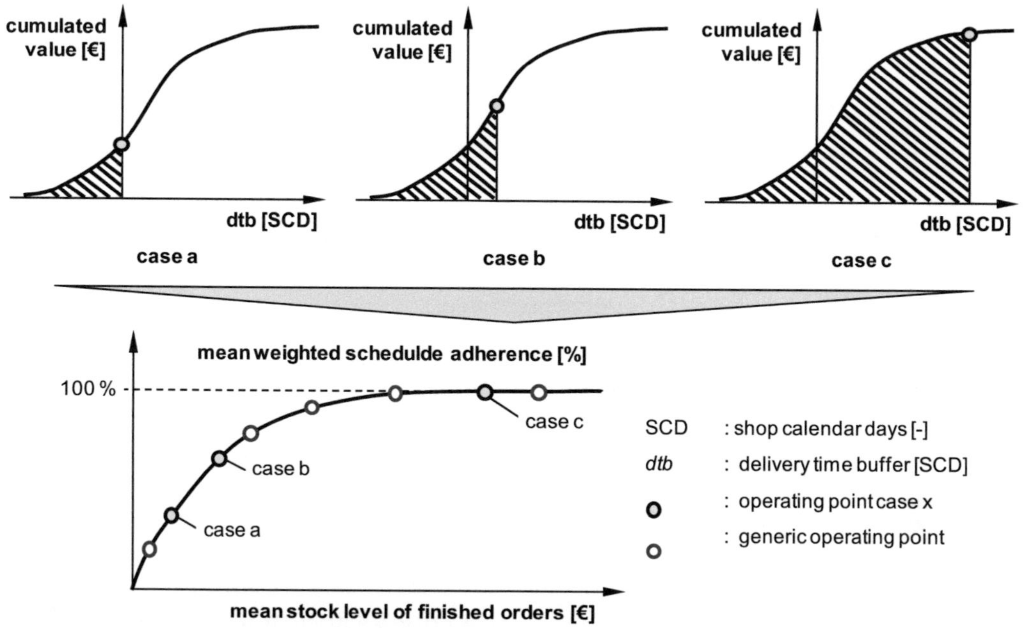

Fig. 15. Qualitative Derivation of the Schedule Adherence Operating Curve.

The respective stock level of finished orders is calculated for the cases a, b and c. In the lower part of figure 15 the case-specific schedule adherence is confronted with the corresponding mean stock level of finished orders and illustrated in one chart. The grey rimmed points with white filling present generic operating points which might be generated by a modification of the delivery time buffer. If a large number of such pairs of values is plotted in a graph, the result is the Schedule Adherence Operating Curve.

This kind of modelling ensures the independence of the Schedule Adherence Operating Curve from the kind of statistic distribution of the date deviation. Now, it is possible to position a production stage in the field of tension between high schedule adherence and a low stock level of finished goods. Figure 16 shows this exemplarily. It is possible to calculate the stock of finished orders which is needed to ensure a target schedule adherence. The Schedule Adherence Operating Curve shows that an assumed schedule adherence of 95% can be achieved by a mean stock level of finished goods of S_1. To position the production stage on this operating point, the delivery time buffer is the key control variable. This variable has to be considered critically because in practice, a delivery time buffer is connected with an earlier release of production orders. Thus, in principle, the planned throughput time will be increased which directly extends the delivery time to the customer. It is also possible that the so-called vicious cycle of production planning and control is triggered (Plossl 1973; Wiendahl 2008).

The Schedule Adherence Operating Curve can be used to determine potentials which result from structural changes. For this purpose a mathematical description of this Operating Curve is required. The formula is based on an approximate equation. It is assumed that the distribution of order values over the output date deviation after the implementation of measures that cause the structural changes especially regarding the throughput times is similar to a normal distribution. This function is determined by the mean value and the standard deviation of the distribution as well as by the variable date deviation (Kühlmeyer 2001).

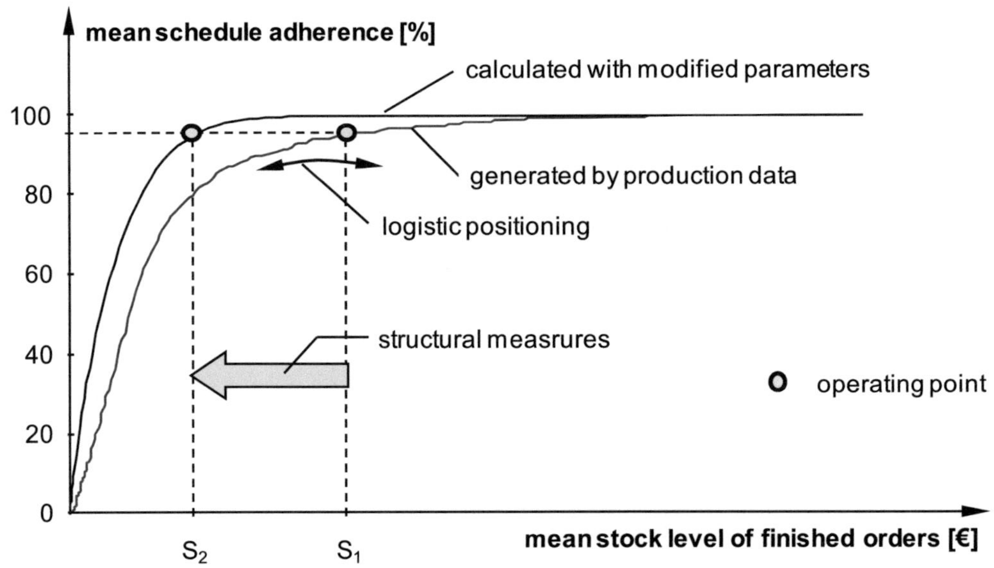

Fig. 16. Schedule Adherence Operating Curve.

$$vo(dd;\mu;\sigma) = OUT \cdot \frac{1}{\sigma\sqrt{2\Pi}} \cdot e^{\frac{(dd-\mu)^2}{2\sigma^2}} \tag{7}$$

vo(dd;μ;σ)	value of orders with a specific date deviation [€]
dd	date deviation [SCD]
μ	mean value of the date deviation [SCD]
σ	standard deviation of the date deviation [SCD]
OUT	output in the reference period [€]

The integral of this function from negative infinity up to the assumed delivery time buffer allows the estimation of the value of orders which leave the production stage on time.

$$voo(dtb;\mu;\sigma) = OUT \cdot \frac{1}{\sigma\sqrt{2\Pi}} \cdot \int_{-\infty}^{dtb} e^{\frac{(dd-\mu)^2}{2\sigma^2}} \, ddd \tag{8}$$

voo(dtb;μ;σ)	value of orders finished on time [€]
dtb	delivery time buffer [SCD]

The mean weighted schedule adherence is calculated by dividing this value by the output in the reference period.

$$sa_{mw}(dtb;\mu;\sigma) = \frac{1}{\sigma\sqrt{2\Pi}} \cdot \int_{-\infty}^{dtb} e^{\frac{(dd-\mu)^2}{2\sigma^2}} \, ddd \tag{9}$$

sa_{mw}(dd;μ;σ)	mean weighted schedule adherence [-]

Calculating the integral of equation 8 again determines the stock area of finished orders. The mean stock level of finished orders is the result of the division of the stock area of finished orders by the reference period.

$$sfo_m(dtb;\mu;\sigma) = \frac{OUT}{rp}\frac{1}{\sigma\sqrt{2\Pi}} \cdot \int_{-\infty}^{dtb}\int_{-\infty}^{dtb} e^{\frac{(dd-\mu)^2}{2\sigma^2}} ddd \cdot ddd \tag{10}$$

$sfo_m(dd;\mu;\sigma)$ mean stock level of finished orders [€]

rp reference period [SCD]

The Schedule Adherence Operating Curve can be described in parameterized form by equations 9 and 10. Mainly, the calculated Schedule Adherence Operating Curve is applied to represent potentials, which result from structural changes within the production stage and lead to a change of the behaviour of the throughout times and consequently the date deviation.

Next to the generated curve, figure 16 represents a Schedule Adherence Operating Curve which is calculated according to equation 9 and 10. A changed behaviour of the date deviation has a direct effect on the parameters of the Operating Curve (mean value and standard deviation of date deviation). If the company is able to realise measures in a way to reduce the scatter of the output date deviation, the form of the Schedule Adherence Operating Curve is influenced directly. Consequently, this opens new potentials to be realized. Figure 16 shows that now, in order to realise the target schedule adherence of 95% only the mean stock level of finished orders S_2 is required. This stock level can be adjusted by a corresponding lower delivery time buffer.

Only few data is necessary to establish the Schedule Adherence Operating Curve: the order number, the output date deviation of the order and a weighted value. An evaluation of the order with their monetary values seems to be the most meaningful evaluation parameter, because the stock cost caused can be estimated directly through it. In principle, other parameters like weight could also be considered. The Schedule Adherence Operating Curve provides a simple possibility to estimate potentials regarding the stock of finished orders and the mean weighted schedule adherence, which affects directly the logistical performance towards the customer.

6. Practical Alication of the Sedule Aerence Operating Curve

To discuss the practical Application of the Schedule Adherence Operating Curve we concentrate on the analysed production stage of the manufacturer of printed circuit boards again (see chapter 4). Figure 17 shows the output date deviation of the production stage.

The mean delay is 4.5 SCD and the scatter of the date deviation is close to 10 SCD. The result is low schedule adherence. This can also be seen in figure 18. The actual operating point shows a date adherence of 34% with a delivery time buffer of 0 SCD causing a mean stock level of finished orders of 59.100 €.

To reach the target date adherence of 95% by increasing the delivery time buffer up to 15 SCD a mean stock level of 590,000 € is required (measure 1). If the scatter of the output date deviation can be reduced to about 5 SCD by measures described in chapter 4 it is possible to realise the target date adherence with a delivery time buffer of 5 SCD. This will lead to a mean stock level of finished orders of 240,000 €.

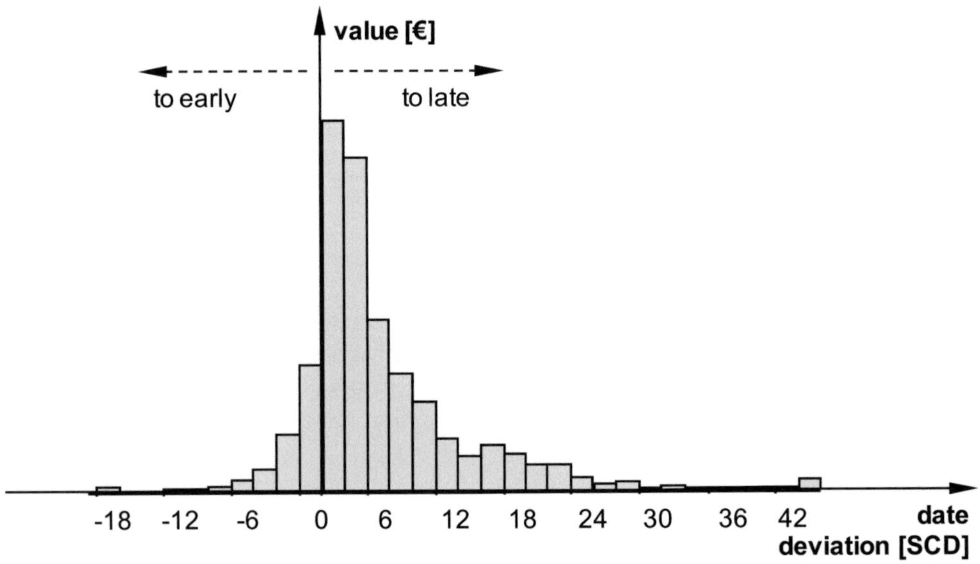

Fig. 17. Output Date Deviation of the Productions Stage.

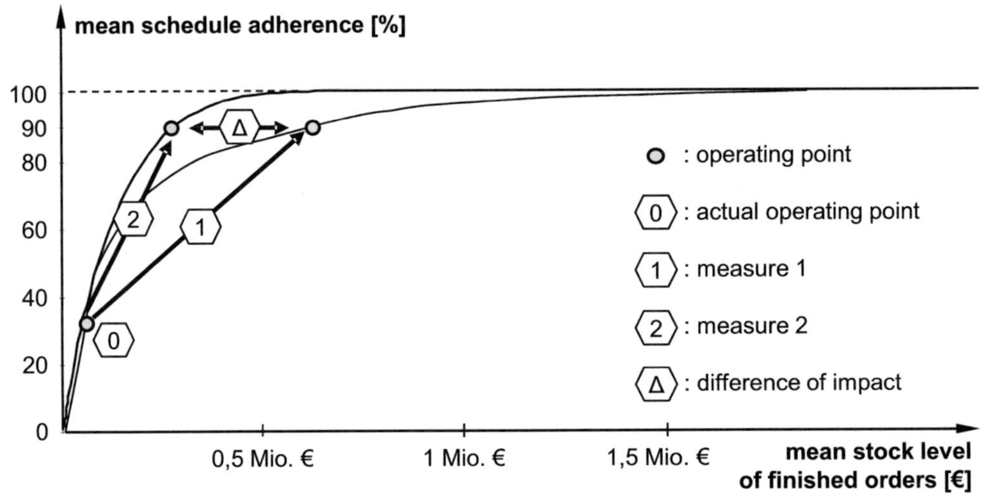

Fig. 18. Output Date Deviation of the Productions Stage.

7. Conclusions

A main challenge of production management is the logistic positioning in the field of tension between the logistic objectives utilization, throughput time, delivery reliability and WIP. These contradicting logistic objectives form what is commonly known as the 'Dilemma of Operations Planning'. In order to make the Dilemma of Operations Planning controllable, it is necessary to position the target operating points amidst the 'field of tension' created by these competing logistic objectives. This is possible with the help of the Logistic Operating Curves. Therefore, this paper showed the derivation of the Logistic Production Operating

Curves and the Schedule Adherence Operating Curve. These models are thus an ideal foundation for supporting and monitoring a company's processing reliability and capability and can be drawn upon when evaluating the process during production controls.

An example of a practical application of the Logistic Operating Curves was given in the paper. The industrial application was conducted in a printed circuit boards manufacturing. For this manufacturing potentials were shown on the one hand of reducing throughput times and WIP without a significant loss of output rate and on the other hand of increasing the date adherence with a tolerable mean stock level of finished orders. Further practical applications are summarized by Nyhuis (Nyhuis, 2007).

The principle of mapping the relationships of the effects between the production logistics performance measures by means of the Logistic Operating Curves technique was transferred to other areas of industrial production. For example the Logistic Operating Curves for inventory processes map the mean stock holding time and the mean delivery delay for a product or group of products in relation to the mean inventory level (Lutz, 2002; Gläßner, 1995; Schmidt and Wriggers, 2008).

Altogether the IFA wants to establish a comprehensive Logistic Operating Curves Theory which enables a model-based description of all production logistics performance measures. This theory provides an easy-to-use method for companies with any type of manufacturing organisation.

8. References

Enslow, B. (2006). *Best Practices in International Logistic*, Aberdeen Group, Boston

Gläßner, J. (1995). *Modellgestütztes Controlling der Beschaffungslogistischen Prozesskette*, Leibniz University Hannover, Hanover

Gutenberg, E. (1951). *Grundlagen der Betriebswirtschaftslehre*, Springer, Berlin

Hon, K. K. B. (2005). Perfomance and Evaluation of Manufacturing Systems. *Annals of the CIRP*, Vol. 54, No. 2, 675-690

Hopp, W. J., Spearman, M. L. (2000). *Factory Physics, Foundations of Manufacturing Management*, Irwin/McGraw-Hill, New York

Kim, J. H., Duffie, N. A. (2005). Design and Analysis of Closed-Loop Capacity Control for a Multi-Workstation Production System. *Annals of the CIRP*, Vol. 54, Mo. 1, 455-458.

Kühlmeyer, M.: *Statistische Auswertungsmethoden für Ingenieure*. Springer, Berlin et al., 2001.

Lutz, S. (2002). *Kennliniengestütztes Lagermanagement*, Leibniz University Hannover, Hanover

Nyhuis, P., von Cieminski, G., Fischer, A. (2005). Applying Simulation and Analytical Models for Logistic Performance Prediction. *Annals of the CIRP*, Vol. 54, No. 1, 417-422

Nyhuis, P., Wiendahl, H.-P. (2009). *Fundamentals of Production Logistics*. Springer, Berlin

Nyhuis, P., Penz, T. (1995). Bottleneck-oriented Logistic Analysis as a Basis for Business Reengineering, In: *Reengineering the Enterprise*, Browne, J., O'Sullivan, D. (Ed), Chapman & Hall, London

Nyhuis, P. (2007). Practical Applications of Logistic Operating Curves. *Annals of the CIRP*, Vol. 56, No. 1, 483-486

Plossl, G. W.: *Manufacturing Control – The Last Frontier for Profits*. Reston Publishing Company, Reston, 1973.

Schmidt, M., Wriggers, F. S. (2008) Logistische Modellierung von Lagerprozessen, In: *Beiträge zu einer Theorie der Logistik,* Nyhuis, P. (Ed.), 139-155, Springer, Berlin

Schönsleben, P. (2004). *Integral Logistics Management,* 2nd edition, St Lucie Press, Boca Raton

Schuh, G. (2006). *Produktionsplanung und Steuerung,* 3rd edition, Springer, Berlin

Wiendahl, H.-P. (1997). *Fertigungsregelung: Logistische Beherrschung von Fertigungsabläufen auf Basis des Trichtermodells,* Carl Hanser, München

Wiendahl, H.-P.: *Betriebsorganisation für Ingenieure.* 6th edition, Hanser, München, Wien, 2008.

Wildemann, H. (2007). *Logistik-Chek,* 5th edition, TCW, Munich

20

Lütkenhöner's „Intensity Dependence of Auditory Responses": An Instructional Example in How Not To Do Computational Neurobiology

Lance Nizami
Independent Research Scholar
USA

1. Introduction

In „Threshold and beyond: modeling the intensity dependence of auditory responses" (*JARO* 9, 2008, pp. 102-121), Dr. Bernd Lütkenhöner introduces us to a puzzle, namely, that responses to stimuli of low intensity appear to climb as the logarithm of the intensity, contrary to the expectation that they be linear with intensity. Towards solving that puzzle, Dr. Lütkenhöner has produced the latest in a long line of attempts by various authors to model „the gross response of the population of auditory nerve fibers" in response to a pure tone (Lütkenhöner, p. 102). From his model, Dr. Lütkenhöner predicts linearity with intensity at low intensities, changing to linearity with log-intensity at higher stimulus intensities.

The present author is one of those who have contributed to this particular field of modeling (Nizami & Schneider, 1997; Nizami 2001, 2002, 2005a, 2005b), and was intrigued by what new insights Dr. Lütkenhöner might have to offer. However, substantial omissions and mistakes were found, which greatly reduce the value of Dr. Lütkenhöner's contribution. In particular, Lütkenhöner omits to mention the many earlier contributions towards modelling the firing of the whole auditory nerve or some portion thereof, so that his model escapes comparison to those of others. His computations use data taken from a variety of species, whose firing-rate characteristics are known to differ, such that his computations may describe no real species at all. Further, Dr. Lütkenhöner's equations do not account for the known variance of dynamic range across neurons, a crucial component of any model of mass neural firing. Indeed, he encourages the use of a discredited equation that cannot actually account for dynamic range variation, while ignoring a proven equation than can. Lütkenhöner also perpetuates the absurd notion of an infinitely low detection threshold for auditory stimuli. Finally, Lütkenhöner's derivations provide an equation of a form known to arise from circular logic. All of these errors are incontrovertible and render Dr. Lütkenhöner's work null and void. Altogether, Lütkenhöner's errors serve as a warning to those who attempt to compute the average neuronal response available from a mass of responding neurons, but serve the larger purpose of illustrating the folly of accepting conventional wisdom and frequently-cited papers on face value without delving deeply enough into the literature to achieve a professional understanding of a problem.

2. The Lütkenhöner model and its predecessors

2.1 Averaging of neuronal firing rates

The average firing rate of a pool of related neurons has historically been taken as the „signal" that represents the outside world. That notion has been reinforced, for example, by recent cortical recordings which imply the use of „a code that is robust to perturbations, such as a rate code in which it is the average firing rate over large populations of neurons that carries information" (London et al., 2010). But on average, no two neurons produce the same plot of firing rate as a function of the intensity of a given type of stimulus. To find the average firing rate of a *pool* of neurons, then, it is first necessary to find a rate-level function containing parameters which can be varied in order to represent the rate-vs.-intensity plot for individual neurons. Once such an equation is found, the „average" neuronal response available from a mass of responding neurons can be obtained either by averaging modeled firing rates across neurons, or by analytically solving for the average of the actual equations. Dr. Lütkenhöner uses both methods. However, he omits any mention of earlier efforts, as if none exist.

2.2 The pioneering work of Schiaffino

In fact, averaging of stimulus-evoked firing of primary afferent sensory neurons has a long and rich history. The literature on hearing, in particular, shows progressive refinement over the years (Schiaffino, 1957; Barducci, 1961; Siebert, 1965; McGill & Goldberg, 1968; Goldstein, 1974; Howes, 1974, 1979; Lachs et al., 1984; Delgutte, 1987; Viemeister, 1988; Winslow & Sachs, 1988; Nizami & Schneider, 1997; Nizami, 2005b). That literature is worthy of a brief recapitulation. Schiaffino's model (1957) set the stage for all subsequent models. Ironically, Schiaffino did not rely upon properties of neuronal firing per se, which were not well-known at the time. Rather, he relied upon psychophysical results, as follows. He assumed that the absolute detection threshold for an auditory stimulus corresponded to the excitation of a single primary afferent auditory neuron, and that each psychophysical just-noticeable intensity increase corresponded to the firing of another neuron, such that the number of neurons activated by an increase of one unit of auditory intensity was the inverse of the size of the just-noticeable intensity increase. (Such cavalier assumptions would not, of course, be made today.) The just-noticeable intensity increase was known as a function of stimulus intensity for particular circumstances (and has since been found for stimuli of various durations and spectra), and so Schiaffino integrated its inverse with respect to intensity, obtaining the growth of the number of active fibers as a function of the stimulus intensity. He noted that squaring that quantity gave a curve congruent to psychophysical loudness curves established by psychologists. Note well Schiaffino's assumption (now quite unorthodox) that each neuron's contribution to loudness was the same. That assumption would not be made by subsequent others, once experimentalists had established that the firing rates of auditory primary afferents were themselves a monotonically increasing function of stimulus intensity. Nonethless, by using mathematical integration to infer the growth of loudness from neuronal activity, Schiaffino laid the groundwork for all subsequent models of the dependence of loudness upon primary afferent firing. The above describes only the basics of Schaiffino's work. Barducci (1961) extended it to other frequencies by adding an arbitrary parameter to the number of active neurons.

Since Schiaffino's time it has become well-established that single primary afferent auditory neurons in all species studied can be characterized by four properties: their spontaneous rate in the absence of any stimuli, their saturation (maximum) rate beyond which rate cannot increase regardless of stimulus intensity, their threshold intensity at which firing rate (on average) increases beyond spontaneous rate, and their dynamic range, defined as the intensity range between threshold intensity and saturation intensity. There is a different, psychophysical dynamic range for the whole animal. As noted by Lawrence (1965, p. 159), „The [psychophysical] dynamic range expreses the extent of rising intensities over which hearing takes place, but the upper limit is difficult to define". Lawrence (1965) describes the upper limit as that intensity at which the sensation of loudness mingles with the sensation of feeling. That limit appears to be constant despite the fact that the threshold for detection of auditory stimuli (the absolute detection threshold) varies with the frequency of a pure tone (Licklider, 1951/1966). Lawrence (1965, p. 161) notes that Licklider's paper implies human psychophysical dynamic ranges of 90 decibels for 100 Hz tones and for 10,000 Hz tones, and 120 decibels for 1,000 Hz tones.

2.3 The dynamic range problem

These ranges are an object of puzzlement, for the following reasons. Humans are not used for studying the properties of the primary afferent auditory neurons. On the contrary, the mammal whose peripheral auditory neurons we know best is the cat. Individual primary afferent auditory neurons of the cat, which leave the periphery by way of the 8th (auditory) nerve, typically have a range from threshold to saturation of only 14-40 decibels (e.g. Kiang et al., 1965). Thus, theories of neuronal function that hope to capture the full behavioral range of hearing in the cat (and by extension, in man) have to stipulate how neurons of such limited dynamic range can encode intensity over the full behavioral range. One approach has been to assume that auditory stimulus intensity is proportional to activity in the whole auditory nerve (e.g., Schiaffino, 1957; Barducci, 1961; McGill & Goldberg, 1968; Goldstein, 1974; Howes, 1974, 1979; Lachs et al., 1984). The general argument for this type of model is as follows for a pure tone. As the tone intensity increases from the absolute psychophysical (behavioral) detection threshold for the tone, neurons serving the region of the hearing organ (the organ of Corti) at and nearby the locus of its maximum physical displacement increase their rate of firing voltage spikes until they reach their saturation firing rate. However, as the tone's intensity increases still further, there is a lateral spread of the tone-evoked physical movement of the organ of Corti, such that neurons adjacent to the point of maximal physical displacement are recruited (e.g., Howes, 1974, based on Katsuki et al., 1962; Pfeiffer & Kim, 1975). Thus, increasing the tone's intensity means an increase in the firing rate of neurons that are already responding, and an increase in the number of responding neurons (see Whitfield, 1967). The total number of voltage spikes elicited by the stimulus will therefore continue to increase, in such „whole-nerve" models, because the zone of significant physical displacement of the organ of Corti will continue to widen as the tone's intensity rises.

There is evidence, however, that a wide range of intensity can be encoded under conditions that prohibit the recruitment of unsaturated neurons. That is, Viemeister (1983) used a high-intensity notched masking noise to potentially saturate the firing rates of neurons that were most responsive to tones below 6,000 Hz and above 14,000 Hz, thus eliminating the possibility that such neurons could contribute to encoding intensity changes for tones below 6,000 Hz or above 14,000 Hz. Human subjects were required to discriminate intensity changes in a noise whose spectrum of component frequencies spanned the range of 6,000-14,000 Hz. The subjects were able to do so, suggesting that spread of excitation beyond the 6,000-14,000 Hz band was unnecessary for the growth of loudness of the 6,000-14,000 band of noise. One way in which this could happen is for neurons within any limited contiguous span of the organ of Corti to have different firing thresholds and/or different neuronal dynamic ranges. Such a simple system may be realized, for example, in some species of moths, for which there are only two primary auditory afferents, having different thresholds but similar dynamic ranges, which therefore partially overlap (e.g., Perez & Coro, 1985). There is other psychoacoustic evidence which suggests that a small region surrounding the point of maximal stimulus-driven physical displacement on the organ of Corti can encode a large dynamic range. For example, Hellman (1974) found that using a masking noise to presumably remove the neural firing contributions of neurons of greatest sensitivity above 250 Hz does not prevent the normal growth of the loudness of a 250 Hz tone. Thus, any model of pooled neuronal firing must be resticted to a limited portion of the organ of Corti.

2.4 What species for Lütkenhöner?

The most sophisticated model of pooled neuronal firing is that of Nizami and Schneider (1997). It was concerned with the firing of the neurons serving a limited region of the organ of Corti centered on the point of maximal displacement for an 8,000 Hz tone in the cat. The Nizami and Schneider model will be described below in the course of examining Lütkenhöner's model. However, there is already one glaring difference between Dr. Lütkenhöner's model and the others cited here, a difference which arises early in Lütkenhöner's paper. That is, that all of the other models are specific to particular species (usually the cat; but see for example Howes, 1974, for the macaque), whereas Lütkenhöner fails to state what species his computations apply to, as if they apply to all. In practice, he bases his computations upon a hodgepodge of data taken from cats, guinea pigs, and alligator lizards, species whose firing-rate characteristics are well known to substantially differ.

3. Problems with the Lütkenhöner model: dynamic ranges of afferents

Dr. Lütkenhöner focuses his derivations on the average neuronal firing behavior near threshold. However, his various mathematical summations fail to account for the known difference in the distributions of thresholds and of dynamic ranges of the individual afferents. Those variabilities significantly affect average rate-level behavior (see Nizami & Schneider, 1997, and its predecessors listed above). In turn, rate-level behavior affects discriminability, as quantified in Signal Detection Theory models (e.g. Nizami & Schneider, 1997; Nizami 2003, 2005a, 2005b). Hence, threshold and dynamic range affect discriminability, making them of paramount importance. Regarding thresholds, Lütkenhöner states that "there is insufficient information about the true sensitivity distribution of the auditory neurons" (Lütkenhöner, p. 116). However, the distribution of thresholds across primary auditory afferents is well-characterized for the cat (reviewed in Nizami & Schneider, 1997), guinea pig, macaque (e.g., Katsuki et al., 1962), and several other mammals. The distribution of dynamic ranges across neurons is also well-characterized for primary auditory afferents (see the review in Nizami & Schneider, 1997, for the cat). Thus Lütkenhöner has failed to incorporate important data that is readily available.

4. Problems with the Lütkenhöner model: an equation having a fixed dynamic range

Let us examine if and how dynamic range actually appears in Lütkenhöner's formulation. We might expect dynamic range to be defined in terms of the discriminability afforded by a neuron's rate-level relation. In fact, that has been done just once (Nizami, 2005a). In the remainder of the literature, dynamic range was quantified as the difference between a threshold intensity for evoked firing, and an intensity at which firing rate saturates. Those dynamic-range endpoints have in turn been defined in terms of the neuron's minimum (i.e. actual spontaneous) firing rate R_{min} spikes/s and its maximum (i.e. actual „saturation") firing rate R_{max} spikes/s, according to variations on any of four different schemes (reviewed in Nizami, 2002).[1] Indeed, such measurement schemes led originally to the conclusion that dynamic ranges vary significantly from neuron to neuron (e.g., Evans & Palmer, 1980).

Ironically, those same schemes prevent Dr. Lütkenhöner's model from ever accounting for differences in dynamic range, and that is important, because a model that cannot account for differences in dynamic range cannot ultimately provide a good fit to rate-intensity data from the neuron, in which case any forthcoming „average neural response" will be inaccurate. Consider the following. Lütkenhöner's chosen rate-level function was a personal customization of the rate-level function chosen by Sachs and Abbas (1974) to describe the response of single primary auditory afferents in cats exposed to pure tones. The latter equation belongs to a class of equations called saturating power functions. With R being spike firing rate, P being RMS (root-mean-square) sound-pressure-level, and k and α being positive parameters that can be obtained by regression on actual rate-level data, the saturating power functions take the form

$$R(P) = R_{\max} \frac{\left(P/P_0\right)^{\alpha}}{\left(P/P_0\right)^{\alpha} + k} . \tag{1}$$

Because intensity I is proportional to P^2, intensity can be used in place of P without loss of generality. Now, the above equation can be inverted, producing sound-pressure-level P as a function of firing rate. From there, it is easily proven that for a fixed α, the equation R(P) represents *a fixed dynamic range* (Nizami, 2002). That fixed range can be expressed by formulae, according to whichever of the four popular dynamic-range schemes was used *(ibid.)*.

One solution to this problem of an inadvertantly constant dynamic range in rate-intensity equations is to allow dynamic range to vary, by building it into a rate-intensity equation as a parameter. Such a parameter is not present in earlier equations for auditory single-unit

---

[1] Those schemes depend upon arbitrarily-chosen parameters a and b, where $0 < a,b < 50$, as follows. In Scheme 1, threshold firing rate is $\frac{a}{100}\left(R_{\max} - R_{\min}\right)$ and saturation firing rate is $\left(1-\frac{b}{100}\right)\left(R_{\max} - R_{\min}\right)$. In contrast, Scheme 2 uses $\frac{a}{100}\left(R_{\max} - R_{\min}\right)+R_{\min}$ and $\left(1-\frac{b}{100}\right)\left(R_{\max} - R_{\min}\right)+R_{\min}$ respectively; Scheme 3 uses $R_{\min}\left(1+\frac{a}{100}\right)$ and $R_{\max}\left(1-\frac{b}{100}\right)$; and finally, Scheme 4 uses $R_{\max}\frac{a}{100}$ and $R_{\max}\left(1-\frac{b}{100}\right)$. Schemes 1 and 4 have obvious problems; Scheme 2 is the most popular one (see Nizami, 2002).

firing rate (e.g., Schiaffino, 1957; Barducci, 1961; McGill & Goldberg, 1968; Goldstein, 1974; Howes, 1974; Sachs & Abbas, 1974; Lachs et al., 1984; Sachs et al., 1989; Yates et al., 1990). However, Nizami and Schneider (1997) presented such an equation:

$$r(x;\, \varepsilon, \lambda, r_{max}, r_S) = \frac{r_{max} - r_S}{1 + \left(\dfrac{100 - c}{c}\right)^{1-\left[2\left(\frac{x - \varepsilon}{\lambda}\right)\right]}} . \tag{2}$$

where x = intensity in decibels SPL,
ε = threshold for stimulus-evoked firing, in decibels SPL,
λ = dynamic range in decibels,
r_{max} = saturation firing rate in spikes/s,
r_S = spontaneous firing rate in spikes/s.

The actual derivation of Eq. 2 appeared later (Nizami, 2001, 2002). Equation 2 describes a symmetric, sigmoidal (S-shaped) plot. Equation 2 incorporates two assumptions: first, that the neuron's firing rate „at threshold" is characterized by

$$r(x = \varepsilon) = \frac{c}{100}\left(r_{max} - r_S\right) + r_S, \tag{3}$$

and second, that the neuron's saturation firing rate obeys

$$r(x = \varepsilon + \lambda) = \frac{100 - c}{100}\left(r_{max} - r_S\right) + r_S \tag{4}$$

(Footnote 1, Scheme 2, with a = b = „c"), all for c = 2. Equation 2 fits typical rate-intensity plots quite well (see Nizami, 2002, 2005a) using c = 2, with the parameter values obtained through least-squares fitting of equation to data being very close to those estimated [through observation] by the persons who obtained the rate-intensity data in the first place. Indeed, fitted and estimated values mutually diverge more when using other possible values of c, namely c = 1, c = 5, or c = 10 (Nizami, 2002).

In a broad variety of species, *including those that Dr. Lütkenhöner uses as sources of data*, there are a greater or lesser percentage of the examined primary afferent auditory neurons whose rate-intensity plots do not follow a sigmoid. Instead, the plots show a fairly sharp mid-way bend to a shallower slope, presumably followed by eventual saturation beyond the highest stimulus intensities (90-95 decibels sound-pressure-level [SPL}) that were employed (e.g., Sachs & Abbas, 1974; Palmer & Evans, 1979; Sachs et al., 1980; Winter et al., 1990; Ohlemiller et al., 1991; Temchin & Moushegian, 1992; Richter et al., 1995; Koppl & Yates, 1999; Plontke et al., 1999; Yates et al., 2000; Imaizumi & Pollack, 2001). These neurons acquired the name „sloping-saturating". Nizami and Schneider (1997) found that sloping-saturating rate-intensity plots were fitted well by the equation

$$\begin{aligned} r_{SS}(x;\, \varepsilon, \lambda_1, \lambda_2, r_{max}, r_S) &= \gamma \cdot r(x;\, \varepsilon, \lambda_1, r_{max}, r_S) \\ &\quad + (1-\gamma) \cdot r(x;\, \varepsilon, \lambda_2, r_{max}, r_S) \end{aligned} \tag{5}$$

where γ is a fitted parameter. Equation 5 has six fitted parameters, but for the cat we can set the spontaneous rate to zero, reducing the number of fitted parameters to five. Yates produced an equation in six parameters which Yates and others fitted to sloping-saturating plots (e.g., Yates, 1990; Richter et al., 1995; Koppl & Yates, 1999; Yates et al., 2000), but Eq. 5 fits more closely to the bend in the plot, as can be seen by comparing the work of Yates et al. to the fit of Eq. 5 (see for example Nizami & Schneider, 1997; Imaizumi & Pollack, 2001; Nizami, 2002, 2005a). The same goes for the Sachs et al. (1989) equation in five parameters. Equation 5 is not meant to represent any underlying mechanics, unlike the Sachs and Abbas (1974) equation used by Dr. Lütkenhöner, and its successors, the equations of Sachs et al. (1989) and of Yates et al. (1990). All of those equations in fact encapsulate an alleged relation of the shape of the sloping-saturating firing-rate plot to the plot of the intensity-dependence of the mechanical vibration of the organ of Corti, a relation proven illusory (e.g., Palmer & Evans, 1979; Palmer & Evans, 1980). Also, Equation 5 does show saturation (levelling off) at sound pressure levels that lie beyond the range of the data. Earlier models of collected neuronal firing rates (Schiaffino, 1957; Barducci, 1961; McGill & Goldberg, 1968; Goldstein, 1974; Howes, 1974; Lachs et al., 1984; Delgutte, 1987; Viemeister, 1988; Winslow & Sachs, 1988) did not account for neurons whose rate-intensity plots are sloping-saturating.

Equations 2 and 5 can help us determine the rate-intensity relation for an „average" neuron, as follows. Given a mass of primary afferent auditory neurons, the threshold, dynamic range, spontaneous firing rate, and saturation firing rate will vary from neuron to neuron. That variability can be quantified by measuring those characteristics over a large sample of neurons. The characteristics form probability density functions. If the neuronal characteristics appear to be mutually independent of each other - which can be ascertained by plotting one against another and looking for correlations - then the mean firing rate of an ensemble of neurons having sigmoidal rate-intensity plots is given by

$$\int_{\min(\varepsilon)}^{\max(\varepsilon)} \int_{\min(\lambda)}^{\max(\lambda)} \int_{\min(r_{max})}^{\max(r_{max})} \int_{\min(r_s)}^{\max(r_s)} \left[r(x;\varepsilon,\lambda,r_{max},r_S) \cdot p(\varepsilon)\cdot p(\lambda)\cdot p(r_{max})\cdot p(r_S)\right] \, dr_S \, dr_{max} \, d\lambda \, d\varepsilon \tag{6}$$

where $p(\varepsilon)$ = *probability density function for* threshold,

$p(\lambda)$ = *probability density function for* dynamic range,

$p(r_{max})$ = *probability density function for* saturation firing rate,

$p(r_S)$ = *probability density function for* spontaneous firing rate.

A similar expression applies for sloping-saturating neurons. Equation 6 might be solvable analytically, but if not, it can easily be integrated numerically (see Nizami & Schneider, 1997). This method offers greater comprehensiveness than merely averaging firing rates over a few „representative" neurons, as was done elsewhere (e.g., Siebert, 1965; Goldstein, 1974; Howes, 1974; Viemeister, 1983; Winslow & Sachs, 1988).

The point is that there were neuronal rate-intensity equations, and the methodology of how to use them to obtain „average" rate-intensity functions for pools of neurons, that were available to Dr. Lütkenhöner and that could have been used to account for empirical variability in threshold and dynamic range. But these investigative tools were not used, or even mentioned, by Lütkenhöner.

5. Problems with the Lütkenhöner model: infinitely low threshold

Dr. Lütkenhöner's model encourages the continuing needless use of the inflexible saturating-power-function. But that is not all. Lütkenhöner's model also perpetuates an outdated notion, as follows. Lütkenhöner cites Swets (1961) and states that „In accordance with signal detection theory, the model denies the existence of a threshold" (Lütkenhöner, p. 102). This act of denial was considered so important that it was mentioned in Lütkenhöner's abstract. But the notion of no threshold is counterintuitive. Lütkenhöner's use of it compels a reexamination of his source, the paper of Swets (1961). Swets' paper was a review of Signal Detection Theory (here denoted SDT) as it was laid down at the time, including the key SDT concept of the „ideal observer". Swets noted that in a typical psychophysical detection task, the listener decides whether a Signal is present, or only a background Noise, based upon the ratio of the likelihood of Signal+Noise to the likelihood of Noise alone. That likelihood ratio obeys two distributions - one for Signal+Noise and one for Noise - and the listener places their hypothetical decision-making criterion somewhere along that likelihood-ratio continuum. An infinitely low threshold is possible, but only because the theoretical distributions involved have infinitely long tails.

Regarding threshold, Swets (1961) reviewed the successful application of SDT to data from Yes/No, second choice, and rating experiments, in the context of what that success meant for five threshold models „concerning the processes underlying these data" (Swets, p. 175). Swets' words were often unclear, and his analysis was long and complicated and defies brief synopsis. His conclusions were hardly firm; in fact, Swets was oddly equivocal. He first noted that one of the models that he examined fit none of the data, that two of the models fit some of the data, that another of the models could not be evaluated at all using the data, and finally that one of the models fit all of the data, but that SDT did too. In conclusion, Swets stated that „The outcome is that, as far as we know, there may be a sensory threshold" (p. 176). He then started his next paragraph with „On the other hand, the existence of a sensory threshold has not been demonstrated" (*ibid.*). This turnabout seems especially odd in light of some shortcomings of SDT that were noted by Swets, in particular that „the human observer, of course, performs less well than does the ideal observer in the great majority of detection tasks, if not in all" (p. 172). That finding has been replicated many times over; for intensity discriminability, for example, see deBoer (1966), Raab and Goldberg (1975), Schacknow and Raab (1976), Green and Swets (1988), Bernstein and Raab (1990), Buus (1990), Nizami and Schneider (1997), and Nizami (2005b), among others. In sum, Swets (1961) did not produce compelling evidence of an infinitely low threshold, thus leaving no reason to reject the notion, as expressed by Hellman and Zwislocki (1961, p. 687), that "The threshold of audibility is a natural boundary condition which cannot be eliminated".

6. Problems with the Lütkenhöner model: a function containing a circular argument

Dr. Lütkenhöner's derivations lead to one mathematical case, presented on p. 112 of his paper, which resembles an equation by Zwislocki (1965). Lütkenhöner's version was obtained by „an appropriate normalization of both the intensity and the loudness scale" (Lütkenhöner, p. 112). Lütkenhöner notes this equation's similarity to several of his own equations for the normalized auditory firing rate. Unfortunately, as revealed in a recent proceeding (Nizami, 2009), Zwislocki's original equation was based upon circular reasoning. Hence circular reasoning may also underlie Lütkenhöner's equations as well. It may be worthwhile, for the reader's benefit, to briefly reiterate the problems with the Zwislocki derivation, as follows.

Experiments led to the notion that the loudness of an auditory stimulus at its absolute detection threshold is not zero, contrary to traditional assumptions (e.g., Buus et al., 1998; Buus & Florentine, 2001). Nonzero threshold loudness was predicted from theory by Zwislocki (1965), and by Moore et al. (1997) in an update of Zwislocki's paper. The Moore et al. loudness equation actually appears in a modern standard for loudness, ANSI Standard S3.4-2007.

6.1 Zwislocki's (1965) derivation

Zwislocki (1965) used L to represent loudness and P to represent RMS pressure amplitude. Zwislocki proposed that for a physiologically normal listener attending to a single pure tone of intensity > 50 dB SPL, loudness obeys $L = K\,P^{2\theta}$ where $\theta > 0$. The parameter K is found by curvefitting of empirical loudnesses (obtained through magnitude estimation procedures) to the loudness equation. At "sufficiently high sound-pressure levels" P (Zwislocki, p. 84), but for stimuli whose spectra still lie within the critical band f to f+CB, Zwislocki proposed that

$$L = K \left(\sum_{f}^{f+CB} P^2 \right)^{\theta} . \tag{7}$$

For a pure tone S („S" indicating „signal") centered frequency-wise in a noise band N, $L = K\,(P_S^{\,2} + P_N^{\,2})^{\theta}$. Here the P's represent „effective" tone or noise pressures, „effective" because the vibrations of the organ of Corti which are tone-evoked or noise-evoked will physically interfere with each other. Zwislocki then made a bold move: noting that listeners can selectively ignore noise, Zwislocki imagined the loudness of the tone-in-noise as the total loudness minus the noise loudness. The noise loudness was described as $L_N = K\,P_N^{\,2\theta}$ so that tone loudness was $L_S = K\,[(P_S^{\,2} + P_N^{\,2})^{\theta} - P_N^{\,2\theta}]$. Once again, Zwislocki imagined a total stimulus spectrum lying within one single critical band, so that other critical bands contribute nothing to the loudness.

Zwislocki proceeded to assume that there was a „physiological noise" which behaved like a physical masking noise, one that the listener could *not* ignore. Zwislocki attributed the existence of an absolute detection threshold to that physiological noise. Representing that internal noise using the subscript NI, Zwislocki then imagined the total Noise sound pressure, $P_N^{\,2}$, to be the sum of the internal-noise sound pressure and the external-noise sound pressure, altogether $P_N^{\,2} = (P_{NI} + P_{NE})^2 = P_{NI}^{\,2} + P_{NE}^{\,2}$. Zwislocki failed to note that the term $2\,P_{NI}\,P_{NE}$ is zero when, presumably, P_{NI} and P_{NE} are independently drawn from zero-mean Gaussian distributions (see for example Green, 1960, or deBoer, 1966).

According to Zwislocki (1965), then, the total loudness of a pure tone embedded in noise is

$$L = K\left[\left(P_S^2 + P_{NI}^2 + P_{NE}^2\right)^{\theta} - \left(P_{NI}^2 + P_{NE}^2\right)^{\theta} \right]. \tag{8}$$

Without the external noise, tone loudness is

$$L = K\left[\left(P_S^2 + P_{NI}^2\right)^{\theta} - \left(P_{NI}^2\right)^{\theta} \right]. \tag{9}$$

Zwislocki then calculated the power of the external noise that would be equivalent to that of the imagined internal physiological noise. Using T to denote tone threshold, $P_S = P_T$ at the tone's absolute detection threshold *in quiet*. Then Zwislocki declared that $P_{NI}{}^2 = 2.5\ P_T{}^2$. No proof was provided for that equality. In the absence of external noise, then, $L_S = K\ [(P_S{}^2 + 2.5\ P_T{}^2)^\theta - (2.5\ P_T{}^2)^\theta]$, so that $L_S = K\ [(3.5\ P_T{}^2)^\theta - (2.5\ P_T{}^2)^\theta]$ at the tone's absolute detection threshold. Thus, according to Zwislocki, the tone has nonzero loudness at its absolute detection threshold in quiet.

Zwislocki's conclusion depended crucially upon including P_{NI}^2 in the subtracted term in Eq. (3). It allows zero tone loudness when there is no tone ($P_S^2 = 0$). In so doing, Zwislocki violates his own assumption that the „physiological noise" cannot be ignored by the listener. If that assumption is held to, then the internal noise cannot be included in the subtracted term. However, Zwislocki acted as if internal noise was a kind of *external* noise that appeared only when the tone appeared. Zwislocki's approach is truly extraordinary. Effectively, Zwislocki's pure tone carries a noise of fixed energy that masks the tone's own energy, creating an absolute detection threshold.

If this point is not yet clear, consider an expansion of $L_S = K\ [(P_S{}^2 + P_{NI}{}^2)^\theta - P_{NI}{}^{2\theta}]$ in a binomial series:

$$L = K\left(\begin{array}{l} P_{NI}^{2\theta} + \theta P_{NI}^{2\cdot(\theta-1)}P^2 + \dfrac{\theta\cdot(\theta-1)}{2!}P_{NI}^{2\cdot(\theta-2)}P_S^{2\cdot(2)} \\ + \dfrac{\theta(\theta-1)(\theta-2)}{3!}P_{NI}^{2\cdot(\theta-3)}P_S^{2\cdot(3)} + \ \ldots\ - P_{NI}^{2\theta} \end{array}\right)$$

$$= K\left(\begin{array}{l} \theta P_{NI}^{2\cdot(\theta-1)}P^2 + \dfrac{\theta(\theta-1)}{2!}P_{NI}^{2\cdot(\theta-2)}P_S^{2\cdot(2)} \\ + \dfrac{\theta(\theta-1)(\theta-2)}{3!}P_{NI}^{2\cdot(\theta-3)}P_S^{2\cdot(3)} + \ \ldots \end{array}\right). \tag{10}$$

The tone and internal-noise pressure components are clearly inseparable.

In sum, Zwislocki (1965) imposed an absolute detection threshold upon a pure tone (and hence incorporated a threshold tone loudness) by making an „internal" noise inseparable from overall loudness. That is, in an act of patent circular logic, Zwislocki *assumed* a nonzero tone loudness at tone-detection threshold.

6.2 The Moore et al. (1997) derivation

In 1997, Moore et al. published an updated version of Zwislocki's book chapter. Their model concerned the loudness of stimuli per equivalent rectangular bandwidth (ERB), their own version of Zwislocki's critical band. Moore et al. called it the „specific" loudness, denoted N′. The specific loudness was imagined as a function of a stimulus-evoked internal excitation E (in power units). As done by Zwislocki (1965), the tone was called „signal", hence the tone-evoked excitation was E_{SIG}. Similarly, the peak excitation from a pure tone „at absolute threshold" was called E_{THRQ}. Omitting several steps, the specific loudness for a pure tone in the absence of an external masking noise was

$$N' = C\left(\frac{2E_{SIG}}{E_{SIG} + E_{THRQ}}\right)^{1.5}\left[\left(GE_{SIG} + A\right)^\theta - A^\theta\right]. \tag{11}$$

„At threshold" $E_{SIG} = E_{THRQ}$ and hence $N'_{THRESHOLD} = C\ [(\ GE_{THRQ} + A\ )^{\alpha} - A^{\alpha}\ ]$, which exceeds zero. Thus Moore et al., like Zwislocki, concluded that a pure tone in quiet has nonzero loudness at absolute detection threshold.

Note the remarkable similarity of Eq. 11 to Eq. 9, Zwislocki's (1965) equation for tone loudness in quiet. This similarity suggests that Moore et al. followed the same circular logic that was used by Zwislocki. After all, Moore et al.'s paper was patterned after Zwislocki's. Their „loudness per ERB" is equivalent to Zwislocki's loudness for the spectrum falling within a critical band; that is, Moore et al. and Zwislocki sought to quantify the same thing. Both Moore et al. and Zwislocki assumed power laws for loudness. Moore et al. effectively adopted Zwislocki's „internal noise", a noise that is ignorable but somehow not ignorable, making tone loudness equal to zero when the tone is absent but inducing nonzero tone loudness „at threshold" when the tone is present. Overall, then, Moore et al. assumed, rather than proved, nonzero tone loudness at the tone's absolute detection threshold.

6.3 The origin of the error

What is the ultimate origin of the circular logic used by Zwislocki (1965) and Moore et al. (1997)? The answer is not obvious. In seeking an answer, we might note that Zwislocki (1965) and Moore et al. (1997) started with a particular assumption, that is, that there is such a thing as a constant „threshold loudness". However, two phenomena suggest that such an approach is spurious. First, magnitude estimates of loudness are distributed rather than constant (e.g., Stevens, 1956; McGill, 1960; Hellman & Zwislocki, 1963; Luce & Mo, 1965; Poulton, 1984; Hellman & Meiselman, 1988). There is thus an „average loudness", rather than a constant loudness, for a given intensity of any particular stimulus. Similarly, absolute detection threshold itself is operationally defined probabilistically, using psychometric functions which illustrate the percentage of the time that a stimulus is heard as a function of the stimulus intensity. Thus there is no fixed stimulus „at threshold".

7. Conclusions

Dr. Lütkenhöner's computations of the average neuronal response available from the mass of responding auditory primary afferents fails to account for two crucial factors, the across-neuron variability of threshold and of dynamic range. Attempts to incorporate dynamic-range variability would fail irregardless, because dynamic range cannot be incorporated as a variable in the saturating power function that Lütkenhöner uses; that equation has a fixed dynamic range. There is an equation in the auditory literature that incorporates dynamic range as a parameter, but Lütkenhöner ignores that equation. Further, Dr. Lütkenhöner perpetuates the outdated notion of an infinitely low detection threshold. Finally, he notes the similarity of his equations to an equation used by Zwislocki (1965), but the latter equation arose from circular logic, implying that Lütkenhöner's equations also arise from circular logic. These errors are by no means trivial and do not appear to be correctable within Dr. Lütkenhöner's computational framework. They cast serious doubt on the accuracy of his computations and stand as a warning to the computational neurobiologist who seeks to further understand the progression of massed neuronal firing rate with intensity. The errors comitted by Lütkenhöner also highlight the need for very careful choices of the equations used to describe single-neuron firing rates. More broadly, Lütkenhöner's mistakes derived from using equations and concepts which are outdated but which remain prominent simply because they have been cited many times in the literature.

Unfortunately, as this critique of Dr. Lütkenhöner's work illustrates, popularity is not a substitute for correctness.

8. Acknowledgements

Professor Claire S. Barnes of Emory University provided valuable insights during the proofreading of this paper. Thanks also to the editorial staff of INTECH for their patient proofreading and especially to Prof. Katarina Lovrecic for her courteous correspondence.

9. References

ANSI Standard S3.4-2007, *American National Standard- Procedure for the Computation of Loudness of Steady Sounds*, Acoustical Society of America, Melville, NY, USA.

Barducci, I. (1961). Loudness function and differential sensitivity of intensity, *Proceedings of the 3rd International Congress on Acoustics, Vol. 1*, pp. 86-88, ASIN B000UG1GM0, Stuttgart, Germany, 1959, Elsevier, New York.

Bernstein, R.S. & Raab, D.H. (1990). The effects of bandwidth on the detectability of narrow- and wideband signals, *Journal of the Acoustical Society of America*, 88, 5, 2115-2125, ISSN 0001-4966.

Buus, S. (1990). Level discrimination of frozen and random noise, *Journal of the Acoustical Society of America*, 87, 6, 2643-2654, ISSN 0001-4966.

Buus, S. & Florentine, M. (2001). Growth of loudness in listeners with cochlear hearing losses: recruitment reconsidered, *Journal of the Association for Research in Otolaryngology*, 3, 2, 120-139, ISSN 1525-3961.

Buus, S., Musch, H. & Florentine, M. (1998). On loudness at threshold, *Journal of the Acoustical Society of America*, 104, 1, 399-410, ISSN 0001-4966.

deBoer, E. (1966). Intensity discrimination of fluctuating signals, *Journal of the Acoustical Society of America*, 40, 3, 552-560, ISSN 0001-4966.

Delgutte, B. (1987). Peripheral auditory processing of speech information: implications from a physiological study of intensity discrimination, In: *The Psychophysics of Speech Perception*, M.E.H. Schouten (Ed.), pp. 333-353, Dordrecht, ISBN 902473536X, Nijhoff, Holland.

Evans, E.F. & Palmer, A.R. (1980). Relationship between the dynamic range of cochlear nerve fibres and their spontaneous activity, *Experimental Brain Research*, 40, 1, 115-118, ISSN 0014-4819.

Goldstein, J.L. (1974). Is the power law simply related to the driven spike response rate from the whole auditory nerve?, In: *Sensation and Measurement*, H.R. Moskowitz, B. Scharf & J.C. Stevens (Eds.), pp. 223-229, D. Reidel Pub. Co., Dordrecht-Holland, ISBN 9027704740, Boston, MA, USA.

Green, D.M. (1960). Auditory detection of a noise signal, *Journal of the Acoustical Society of America*, 32, 1, 121-131, ISSN 0001-4966.

Green, D.M. & Swets, J.A. (1988). *Signal Detection Theory and Psychophysics*, Peninsula Publishing, ISBN 0-932146-23-6, Los Altos, CA, USA.

Hellman, R.P. (1974). Effect of spread of excitation on the loudness function at 250 Hz, In: *Sensation and Measurement*, H.R. Moskowitz, B. Scharf & J.C. Stevens (Eds.), pp. 241-249, D. Reidel Pub. Co., Dordrecht-Holland, ISBN 9027704740, Boston, MA, USA.

Hellman, R.P. & Meiselman, C.H. (1988). Prediction of individual loudness exponents from cross-modality matching, *Journal of Speech & Hearing Research,* 31, 4, 605-615, ISSN 0022-4685.

Hellman, R.P. & Zwislocki, J.J. (1961). Some factors affecting the estimation of loudness, *Journal of the Acoustical Society of America*, 33, 5, 687-694, ISSN 0001-4966.

Hellman, R.P. & Zwislocki, J.J. (1963). Monaural loudness function at 1,000 cps and interaural summation, *Journal of the Acoustical Society of America,* 35, 6, 856-865, ISSN 0001-4966.

Howes, W. (1974). Loudness function derived from data on electrical discharge rates in auditory-nerve fibers, *Acustica*, 30, 5, 247-259, ISSN 0001-7884.

Howes, W. (1979). Loudness of steady sounds - a new theory, *Acustica*, 41, 5, 277-320, ISSN 0001-7884.

Imaizumi, K. & Pollack, G.S. (2001). Neural representation of sound amplitude by functionally different auditory receptors in crickets, *Journal of the Acoustical Society of America*, 109, 3, 1247-1260, ISSN 0001-4966.

Katsuki, Y., Suga, N. & Kanno, Y. (1962). Neural mechanism of the peripheral and central auditory system in monkeys, *Journal of the Acoustical Society of America*, 34, 9B, 1396-1410, ISSN 0001-4966.

Kiang, N.Y.-S., Watanabe, T., Thomas, E.C. & Clark, L.F. (1965). *Discharge Patterns Of Single Fibers In The Cat's Auditory Nerve,* MIT Press, ISBN 0262110164, Cambridge, MA, USA.

Koppl, C. & Yates, G. (1999). Coding of sound pressure in the barn owl's auditory nerve, *Journal of Neuroscience*, 19, 21, 9674-9686, ISSN 0270-6474.

Lachs, G., Al-Shaikh, R., Bi, Q., Saia, R.A. & Teich, M.C. (1984). A neural-counting model based on physiological characteristics of the peripheral auditory system. 5. Application to loudness estimation and intensity discrimination, *IEEE Transactions on Systems Man & Cybernetics*, SMC-14, 6, 819-836, ISSN 0018-9472.

Lawrence, M. (1965). Dynamic range of the cochlear transducer, *Cold Spring Harbor Symposia on Quantitative Biology*, 30, 159-167. ISSN 0091-7451.

Licklider, J.C.R. (1951/1966). Basic correlates of the auditory stimulus, In: *Handbook Of Experimental Psychology*, S.S. Stevens (Ed.), pp. 985-1039, Wiley, ASIN B000H4HIFE, New York, NY, USA.

London, M., Roth, A., Beeren, L., Häusser, M. & Latham, P.E. (2010). Sensitivity to perturbations *in vivo* implies high noise and suggests rate coding in cortex, *Nature*, 466, 7302, 123-127, ISSN 0028-0836.

Luce, R.D. & Mo, S.S. (1965). Magnitude estimation of heaviness and loudness by individual subjects: a test of a probabilistic response theory, *British Journal of Mathematical and Statistical Psychology*, 18, 2, 159-174, ISSN 0007-1102.

Lütkenhöner, B. (2008). Threshold and beyond: modeling the intensity dependence of auditory responses, *Journal of the Association for Research in Otolaryngology*, 9, 1, 102-121, ISSN 1525-3961.

McGill, W. (1960). The slope of the loudness function: a puzzle, In: *Psychological Scaling: Theory and Applications*, H. Gulliksen & S. Messick (Eds.), pp. 67-81, Wiley, ASIN B0000CKP1Q, New York, NY, USA.

McGill, W.J. & Goldberg, J.P. (1968). Pure-tone intensity discrimination and energy detection, *Journal of the Acoustical Society of America*, 44, 2, 576-581, ISSN 0001-4966.

Moore, B.C.J., Glasberg, B.R. & Baer, T. (1997). A model for the prediction of thresholds, loudness, and partial loudness, *Journal of the Audio Engineering Society*, 45, 4, 224-240, ISSN 1549-4950.

Nizami, L. (2001). A rate-level equation that contains the four quantities reported from experiment, and in the units favored by experimentalists, *Abstracts of the Associaiton for Research in Otolaryngology*, 24, 102.

Nizami, L. (2002). Estimating auditory neuronal dynamic range using a fitted function, *Hearing Research*, 167, 1-2, 13-27, ISSN 0378-5955.

Nizami, L. (2003). Afferent response parameters derived from postmasker probe-detection thresholds: „The decay of sensation" revisited, *Hearing Research*, 175, 1-2, 14-35, ISSN 0378-5955.

Nizami, L. (2005a). Dynamic range relations for auditory primary afferents, *Hearing Research*, 208, 1-2, 26-46, ISSN 0378-5955.

Nizami, L. (2005b). Intensity-difference limens predicted from the click-evoked peripheral N_1: the mid-level hump and its implications for intensity encoding, *Mathematical Biosciences*, 197, 1, 15-34, ISSN 0025-5564.

Nizami, L. (2009). An important flaw in American National Standards Institute ANSI S3.4-2007 and why it happened, *World Academy of Science, Engineering, and Technology, Proceedings Vol. 55 (International Conference on Mathematical Biology)*, pp. 689-693, ISSN 2070-3724, Oslo, Norway, July 2009, Open Science Research, Oslo, Norway.

Nizami, L. & Schneider, B.A. (1997). Auditory dynamic range derived from the mean rate-intensity function in the cat, *Mathematical Biosciences*, 141, 1, 1-28, ISSN 0025-5564.

Ohlemiller, K.K., Echteler, S.M. & Siegel, J.H. (1991). Factors that influence rate-versus-intensity relations in single cochlear nerve fibers of the gerbil, *Journal of the Acoustical Society of America*, 90, 1, 274-287, ISSN 0001-4966.

Palmer, A.R. & Evans, E.F. (1979). On the peripheral coding of the level of individual frequency components of complex sounds at high sound levels, In: *Hearing Mechanisms And Speech*, O. Creutzfeld, H. Scheich, & Chr. Schreiner (Eds.), pp. 19-26, Springer-Verlag, ISBN 0387096558, Heidelberg, Germany.

Palmer, A.R. & Evans, E.F. (1980). Cochlear fibre rate-intensity functions: no evidence for basilar membrane nonlinearities, *Hearing Research*, 2, 3-4, 319-326, ISSN 0378-5955.

Perez, M. & Coro, F. (1985). Physiological characteristics of the tympanic organ in noctuoid moths. II. Responses to 45 ms and 5 s acoustic stimuli, *Journal of Comparative Physiology*, 156, 5, 689-696, ISSN 0340-7594.

Pfeiffer, R.R. & Kim, D.O. (1975). Cochlear nerve fiber responses: distribution along the cochlear partition, *Journal of the Acoustical Society of America*, 58, 4, 867-869, ISSN 0001-4966.

Plontke, S.K.-R., Lifshitz, J. & Saunders, J.C. (1999). Distribution of rate-intensity function types in chick cochlear nerve after exposure to intense sound, *Brain Research*, 842, 1, 262-274, ISSN 0006-8993.

Poulton, E.C. (1984). A linear relation between loudness and decibels, *Perception & Psychophysics*, 36, 4, 338-342, ISSN 0031-5117.

Raab, D.H. & Goldberg, I.A. (1975). Auditory intensity discrimination with bursts of reproducible noise, *Journal of the Acoustical Society of America*, 57, 2, 437-447, ISSN 0001-4966.

Richter, C.-P., Heynert, S. & Klinke, R. (1995). Rate-intensity-functions of pigeon auditory primary afferents, *Hearing Research*, 83, 1-2, 19-25, ISSN 0378-5955.

Sachs, M.B. & Abbas, P.J. (1974). Rate versus level functions for auditory-nerve fibers in cats: tone-burst stimuli, *Journal of the Acoustical Society of America*, 56, 6, 1835-1847, ISSN 0001-4966.

Sachs, M.B., Winslow, R.L. & Sokolowski, B.H.A. (1989). A computational model for rate-level functions from cat auditory-nerve fibers, *Hearing Research*, 41, 1, 61-70, ISSN 0378-5955.

Sachs, M.B., Woolf, N.K. & Sinnott, J.M. (1980). Response properties of neurons in the avian auditory system: comparisons with mammalian homologues and consideration of the neural encoding of complex stimuli, In: *Comparative Studies Of Hearing In Vertebrates*, A.N. Popper & R.R. Fay (Eds.), pp. 323-353, Springer-Verlag, ISBN 0387904603, New York, NY, USA.

Schacknow, P. & Raab, D.R. (1976). Noise-intensity discrimination: effects of bandwidth conditions and mode of masker presentation, *Journal of the Acoustical Society of America*, 60, 4, 893-905, ISSN 0001-4966.

Schiaffino, P. (1957). Méthodes objectives de mesure de l'équivalent de référence et de l'affaiblissement équivalent de netteté en téléphonométrie, *Annales des Télécommunications*, 12, 10, 349-358, IDS O1223.

Siebert, W.M. (1965). Some implications of the stochastic behavior of primary auditory neurons, *Kybernetik*, 2, 5, 206-215, ISSN 0023-5946.

Stevens, S.S. (1956). The direct estimation of sensory magnitudes - loudness, *American Journal of Psychology*, 69, 1, 1-25, ISSN 0002-9556.

Swets, J.A. (1961). Is there a sensory threshold?, *Science*, 134, 347, 168-177, ISSN 0036-8075.

Temchin, A.N. & Moushegian, G. (1992). Is avian basilar membrane truly linear?, *Society for Neuroscience Abstracts*, 18, 1190.

Viemeister, N.F. (1983). Auditory intensity discrimination at high frequencies in the presence of noise, *Science*, 221, 4616, 1206-1208, ISSN 0036-8075.

Viemeister, N.F. (1988). Intensity coding and the dynamic range problem, *Hearing Research*, 34, 3, 267-274, ISSN 0378-5955.

Whitfield, I.C. (1967). Coding in the auditory nervous system. *Nature*, 213, 756-760.

Winslow, R.L. & Sachs, M.B. (1988). Single-tone intensity discrimination based on auditory-nerve rate responses in backgrounds of quiet, noise, and with stimulation of the crossed olivocochlear bundle, *Hearing Research*, 35, 2-3, 165-190, ISSN 0378-5955.

Winter, I.M., Robertson, D. & Yates, G.K. (1990). Diversity of characteristic frequency rate-intensity functions in guinea pig auditory nerve fibres, *Hearing Research*, 45, 3, 191-202, ISSN 0378-5955.

Yates, G.K. (1990). Basilar membrane nonlinearity and its influence on auditory nerve rate-intensity functions, *Hearing Research*, 50, 1-2, 145-162, ISSN 0378-5955.

Yates, G.K., Manley, G.A. & Koppl, C. (2000). Rate-intensity functions in the emu auditory nerve, *Journal of the Acoustical Society of America*, 107, 4, 2143-2154, ISSN 0001-4966.

Yates, G.K., Winter, I.M. & Robertson, D. (1990). Basilar membrane nonlinearity determines auditory nerve rate-intensity functions and cochlear dynamic range, *Hearing Research*, 45, 3, 203-220, ISSN 0378-5955.

Zwislocki, J. J. (1965). Analysis of some auditory characteristics, In: *Handbook of Mathematical Psychology, Vol. 3*, R.D. Luce, R.R. Bush & E. Galanter (Eds.), pp. 1-98, Wiley, ASIN B000RFSIFW, New York, NY, USA.

21

A Warning to the Human-Factors Engineer: False Derivations of Riesz's Weber Fraction, Piéron's Law, and Others Within Norwich et al.'s Entropy Theory of Perception

Lance Nizami
Independent Research Scholar
USA

1. Introduction

The Entropy Theory of Perception of Professor K.H. Norwich and various collaborators spans 1975 to 2010. Thirty-five years is a surprisingly long publication life for a mathematical model of perception. Its longevity is no doubt related to its unusual ability to provide derivations, *from pure theory*, of a large cadre of well-established empirical relations of psychophysics, referred to by Norwich et al. as „laws". Norwich et al.'s work involves computational biology, because they always started their derivations using the same base equation, whose utility was justified through curve-fitting to various kinds of empirical data (see Norwich, 1993). Norwich et al. intended the scope of their theory to be vast, and so the present paper focuses on just one particular set of derivations. Few people offer first-principles derivations of natural relations, making such derivations all the more demanding of our attention.

At „Fechner Day 96", the 12th Annual Meeting of the International Society for Psychophysics, W. Wong and K.H. Norwich introduced „Weber fraction and reaction time from the neural entropy". Therein they showcased what appeared to be two long-overdue breakthroughs: the first-principles derivation of Riesz's equation for auditory just-noticeable intensity differences (Riesz, 1928), and the first-principles derivation of Piéron's empirical relation for the minimum time required for a human subject to signal their perception of a newly presented auditory or visual stimulus (Piéron, 1952). The Wong and Norwich breakthroughs were allowed by a „universal model of single-unit sensory receptor action" presented in a previous paper (Norwich & Wong, 1995). The present paper summarizes the latter work, as an introduction to Norwich et al.'s Entropy Theory, and then proceeds to scrutinize the Wong and Norwich (1996) derivations. In so doing, it reveals that, unfortunately, the algebra of Wong and Norwich (1996) conceals hidden assumptions, unjustified simplifications, and outright mistakes, which had not been brought to public attention. The problems prove to be uncorrectable. This is all the more important because several of the derivations produced in Wong and Norwich (1996) were presented again later, in Wong and Figueiredo (2002). The problems with the Wong and Norwich (1996) and Wong and Figueiredo (2002) derivations are instructional, as they illustrate just how easily misleading outcomes can arise in the kind of theory work that underlies computational biology. They also show what happens when models are made which ignore the warning by William of Ockham (c. 1285-1349) that „entities must not be multiplied beyond necessity".

2. The empirical equations for which Wong and Norwich (1996) provided first-principles derivations

Let us briefly review the empirical relations that Wong and Norwich (1996) claim to derive, starting with that of Riesz (1928). First, some crucial experimental details. Riesz's subjects listened to two simultaneous sinusoidal pressure waveforms whose frequencies were sufficiently close to produce an audible oscillating intensity apparently at a single carrier frequency, the well-known phenomenon called „beating". Early experiments by Riesz had revealed that listeners were most sensitive to a frequency of oscillation - the „beat frequency" - of three per second. Therefore, listeners indicated their threshold intensity change, ΔI, for just barely detecting three beats/second, as a function of the base intensities of the component sinusoids. The dependence of beat-detection threshold upon base intensity I was plotted by Riesz, who then fitted an equation to the plot. Riesz's empirical equation was

$$\frac{\Delta I}{I} = S_\infty + \left(S_0 - S_\infty\right)\left(\frac{I_0}{I}\right)^r, \quad \text{where } S_\infty, S_0, I_0, \text{r} > 0. \tag{1}$$

The terms S_∞, S_0, r are empirical constants required to have no physical units, constants for which Riesz supplied approximate empirical relations as a function of tone frequency. The term $(\Delta I)/I$ is well-known in psychophysics as the *Weber fraction*. Eq. 1 will be referred to as Riesz's Weber fraction or, as done in various Entropy Theory papers, as *Riesz's Law*.

Wong and Norwich (1996) (and later Wong and Figueiredo, 2002) also claimed to derive an empirical relation for auditory absolute detection thresholds.[1] Using I_{th} as the threshold stimulus intensity, I_∞ as the detection threshold for a stimulus that is infinitely long (or its equivalent practical duration), t as the actual stimulus duration, and „a" as an empirical constant (whose value may be dependent upon tone frequency), the threshold relation of interest is

$$I_{th} = \frac{I_\infty}{1 - e^{-at}}, \quad \text{where } I_\infty, a > 0. \tag{2}$$

In this equation, „I" refers to physical intensity, not decibels (taking ten times the logarithm to base 10 of I gives decibels). From Eq. 2, Wong and Norwich derived *Bloch's Law*, which states that for short light flashes, the stimulus intensity multiplied by the stimulus duration yields the same brightness, at absolute detection threshold and above: $I \cdot t = \text{constant}$, phrased by Wong and Norwich as $\Delta I \cdot \Delta t = \text{constant}$ (e.g., Brindley, 1952).

[1] Wong and Norwich (1996) attributed the empirical relation to Zwislocki (1960); later Wong and Figueiredo (2002) attributed it to Plomp and Bouman (1959) as well as to Zwislocki (1960). Plomp and Bouman (1959), in turn, noted that the equation had already been published by Feldtkeller and Oetinger (1956).

Wong and Norwich also derived Piéron's empirical relation for reaction time (Piéron, 1952), which is as follows. Using $t_{r,\min}$ as the shortest possible time of reaction, and with empirical constants „A" and „n", *Piéron's Law* is

$$t_r = t_{r,\min} + \frac{A}{I^b}, \quad \text{where } t_{r,\min}, A, b > 0 \tag{3}$$

(Piéron, 1952, pp. 352-353).

In order to understand how Wong and Norwich (1996) derived the preceding psychophysical laws, an earlier paper, Norwich and Wong (1995), had to be consulted. Norwich and Wong (1995) reviewed the basic ideas of the Entropy Theory of Perception, and that summary is reproduced *in brevia* below.

3. Background: The Entropy Theory of Perception

Norwich and Wong (1995) summarized the Entropy Theory of Perception, as follows. They first explained that „All modalities of sensation conduct information from the outside world to the nervous system of the sensating organism" (*ibid.*, p. 84). They also explained that, in crafting the Entropy Theory, „We also utilize Shannon's doctrine that information represents uncertainty or entropy which has been dispelled" (*ibid.*, p. 84). The Shannon in question is Claude Shannon, author of „A mathematical theory of communication" (Shannon, 1948), the paper that launched Information Theory as a major theme within communications science. Norwich and Wong continue: „That is, immediately following the start of a sensory stimulus, the receptor is maximally uncertain about the intensity of its stimulus signal and, hence, has received very little information. As time proceeds, the receptor loses uncertainty (that is, decreases its information theoretical entropy), and, therefore, gains information" (*ibid.*, p. 84). The entropy in question, which Norwich and Wong represented by the symbol H, was then developed by Norwich and Wong from theory and assumptions, synopsized over several pages of algebra that need not be repeated here. Finally, Norwich and Wong introduced „The fundamental assumption of the entropy theory of sensation" (*ibid.*, p. 86), which was „that the impulse frequency F in the primary afferent neuron issuing from a sensory receptor is in direct proportion to the entropy *H*, that is, *F* = *kH*" (*ibid.*, p. 86; original italics). Note that H has no physical units, so that any physical units of F must be those of k. Norwich and Wong then made the implicit assumption that F also represents the sensation experienced by the organism, albeit with a probably different value (and a lack of physical units) for k.

As Norwich and Wong (1995, p. 86) explained, „We take the receptor to be *sampling* its stimulus signal". The number of samples taken was assigned to symbol „m", the „receptor memory", where by conjecture m = αt for some positive constant α. Within the Entropy Theory, it was always understood that $m \ge 0$. Altogether, using the symbol β' to represent „a constant parameter of unknown value but greater than zero" (*ibid.*, p. 87), the sensation F as a function of I, the intensity of a steady stimulus, was given by what Norwich and Wong called the „seminal" equation

$$F = \frac{1}{2} k \ln\left(1 + \frac{\beta' I^n}{t}\right), \quad \text{such that } t \ge t_0, \text{ and } t_0, \beta', n > 0, \tag{4}$$

where t_0 = the time required for one sampling, and β' and n are unknowns.

This equation is identified elsewhere by Norwich and co-authors as the Entropy Equation. Norwich and Wong noted a failing of Eq. 4, viz., it predicts that all sensation disappears over time, i.e. that there is complete adaptation to a maintained stimulus. Empirically, however, sensory adaptation is not always complete. Therefore a maximum value of t, called t_{max}, was proposed which, when substituted into Eq. 4, allows a non-zero asymptotic value of sensation. Norwich and Wong also introduced greater sophistication to their model by changing their equation for m, the number of samples of the stimulus taken by the sensory receptor, as will now be described.

4. A necessary preamble: The Entropy Theory under the „relaxation model" for receptor memory (Norwich & Wong, 1995)

Without providing any physiological rationale, Norwich and Wong (1995) conjectured that

$$\frac{dm}{dt} = -a\left(m - m_{eq}\right), \quad \text{where } m_{eq} = m(\infty), \ a > 0 \tag{5}$$

(Norwich & Wong, 1995, Eq. 24; Wong & Norwich, 1996, Eq. 2). The unknown constant „a" is the same one as in Eq. 2, as will be shown. Norwich and Wong also introduced the unknown constants m_{eq}^0 and q and declared (without proof) that m was a power function of intensity,

$$m_{eq} = m_{eq}^0 I^q \quad \text{where} \quad m_{eq}^0, \ q > 0 \tag{6}$$

(Norwich & Wong 1995, Eq. 28). Note that the superscript 0 is not an exponent. Norwich and Wong then stated, again without proof, that if the receptor memory at the start of a new steady stimulus is called $m(0)$, then

$$m(t) = m(0)\,e^{-at} + m_{eq}\left(1 - e^{-at}\right), \quad \text{where } m(t) \geq 0 \tag{7}$$

(Norwich & Wong, Eq. 25). Norwich and Wong then introduced (without explanation) the constant β''. Altogether, sensation now follows

$$F = \frac{1}{2} k \ln\left(1 + \frac{\beta'' I^n}{m(0)\,e^{-at} + m_{eq}\left(1 - e^{-at}\right)}\right) \tag{8}$$

(Norwich & Wong, Eq. 33), which allows for „cases of successively applied step functions in stimulus intensity" (Norwich & Wong, p. 95).[2] Note that when Eq. 6 for m_{eq} is substituted

[2] β'' appears to have the same meaning and value as β' in Eq. 4, which begs the question of why Norwich and Wong changed the notation. The reader will find that the Entropy Theory papers contain many such confusing changes in notation, none of them apparently needed, and none of them explained.

into Eq. 8, the latter contains 7 unknowns: k, β'' , n, $m(0)$, m_{eq}^{0}, q, and a. Eq. 8 was the major result presented by Norwich and Wong.
Norwich and Wong (1995) noted that „for the case where the receptor is initially de-adapted (or adapted to a very small stimulus)", $m(0) \cong 0$ (*ibid.*, p. 94), so that

$$m(t) = m_{eq}\left(1 - e^{-at}\right), \tag{9}$$

$$\text{where} \quad m_{eq} > 0 \quad \text{and where} \quad \left(1 - e^{-at}\right) \geq 0 \ \text{for} \ t \geq 0$$

(Norwich & Wong, 1995, Eq. 26). Eq. 9 was an element of „our new, generalized entropy equation for the single, step stimulus" (*ibid.*, p. 94),

$$F = \frac{1}{2} k \ln\left(1 + \frac{\beta'' I^{n}}{m_{eq}\left(1 - e^{-at}\right)}\right), \quad \text{where} \quad k,\ \beta'',\ n,\ m_{eq},\ \left(1 - e^{-at}\right) > 0 \tag{10}$$

(Norwich & Wong, 1995, Eq. 27). Here I and t are the physical quantities; all of the other letters represent unknown constants. As time increases, $m \to m_{eq}$ so that F approaches a nonzero limit, as Norwich and Wong (1995) had desired.

5. A missing derivation of the Norwich and Wong (1995) equation for receptor memory

Unfortunately, Norwich and Wong (1995) did not clarify the origin of the equation labeled above as Eq. 7. That equation is clearly crucial to the new Entropy Equation, Eq. 8, so let us try to understand Eq. 7, for example by solving Eq. 5. Some boundary conditions must be presumed, so let us reasonably presume that m has some minimum $m_0 = m(t_0)$ where $t_0 \geq 0$. We obtain

$$\int_{m_0}^{m(t)} \frac{dm}{m - m_{eq}} = -a \int_{t_0}^{t} dt, \qquad \therefore\ m(t) = m_0\, e^{-a\left(t - t_0\right)} + m_{eq}\left(1 - e^{-a\left(t - t_0\right)}\right). \tag{11}$$

Eq. 11 allows $m_{eq} = m(\infty)$, as required from Eq. 5. The term $m_0 = m(t_0)$ will be dealt with below. If the first sample is taken at $t = 0$, such that the minimum number of samples occurs at *t = 0*, then $t_0 = 0$. Eq. 11 then becomes

$$m(t) = m_0\, e^{-at} + m_{eq}\left(1 - e^{-at}\right), \quad t \geq 0, \tag{12}$$

which resembles Eq. 7. (Recall that Norwich and Wong defined t_0 as the time required for one sampling, a definition that was repeated by Wong and Norwich, 1996, p. 432.)

6. The Entropy Equation of Wong and Norwich (1996)

The Norwich and Wong (1995) new, generalized Entropy Equation for the single, step stimulus (Eq. 10) has a problem that has existed from the start of the Entropy Theory

(Norwich, 1975). That is, $F \to \infty$ as $t \to 0$. This problem was finally addressed by Wong and Norwich (1996). Bearing in mind their own conjecture that F is proportional to H, Wong and Norwich rewrote the entropy H by introducing $I(t)$, „an intensity input which may vary with time" (Wong & Norwich, 1996, p. 429), and δI, „an internal signal greater than threshold" (*ibid.*), to give

$$H = \frac{1}{2}\ln\left(1 + \frac{\beta \cdot \left(I(t) + \delta I\right)^p}{m(t)}\right), \quad \textit{where} \;\; \beta,\, \mathrm{t},\, \mathrm{I(t)},\, \delta I,\, \mathrm{p},\, \mathrm{m(t)} \; > 0 \tag{13}$$

(Wong & Norwich, 1996, Eq. 1). Wong and Norwich explained that „ $m(t)$ represents the dynamic memory required to store stimulus samples drawn by the receptor" (Wong & Norwich, 1996, p. 430). The purpose of δI was not explained.

Eq. 13 displayed a number of oddities. For example, Wong and Norwich replaced the exponent n of Eq. 4 with the exponent p. The two are equivalent, but no rationale was offered for the change in notation. Wong and Norwich (1996, p. 429) also made the mysterious statement that Eq. 13 was proposed in Norwich and Wong (1995), where in fact it does not appear. They also made the remarkable declaration that Eq. 13 „is capable of accounting for almost all sensory phenomena, empirical laws, and rules of thumb relating the firing rate of the primary afferent neuron to the intensity and duration of the sensory stimulus" (*ibid.*). Wong and Norwich also declared that Eq. 13 has „five parameters" (*ibid.*). However, a closer look reveals 7 unknowns: β, p, δI, $m_0 = m(t_0)$, m_{eq}^0, q, and a. Finally, the origin of δI was not explained until later, by Wong and Figueiredo (2002). As they noted (*ibid.*, p. ICAD02-2), „ δI is a term that accounts for the non-zero fluctuations at the receptor level in the absence of a signal" (original italics). Adopting δI helps to remove the infinity in H which occurs as $t \to 0$, as will be made apparent in the following explanations.

Wong and Norwich (1996) then dealt with an experimental paradigm in which the subject must „detect a continuous increment in intensity" for which „the initial pedestal of duration τ may be considered much longer than the duration of increment, Δt [*sic*]. Indeed, τ may be made great enough to insure complete neural adaptation" (Wong & Norwich 1996, p. 431; original italics). Without proof, Wong and Norwich presented the relevant solution of Eq. 5,

$$m(t') = (I + \delta I)^q e^{-a(t' - \tau)} + (I + \Delta I + \delta I)^q \left(1 - e^{-a(t' - \tau)}\right), \tag{14}$$

where presumably τ > 0. Comparison of Eq. 14 to Eq. 7 implies that m for the pedestal alone follows

$$m(t) = m_0 e^{-a(t - t_0)} + (I + \delta I)^q \left(1 - e^{-a(t - t_0)}\right), \quad t \ge t_0, \tag{15}$$

and that m_{eq} for the pedestal-plus-increment obeys

$$m_{eq}^0 = 1, \quad m_{eq} = (I + \Delta I + \delta I)^q. \tag{16}$$

7. The derivation of $\Delta I/I$ by Wong and Norwich (1996)

Wong and Norwich (1996) did not explain why they replaced t by $t'-\tau$. It can eventually be understood by following the principal argument offered by Wong and Norwich, that the intensity increment ΔI of duration Δt starting at time τ „can be detected if and only if"

$$H\left(I+\Delta I,\tau+t_0\right)-H\left(I+\Delta I,\tau+\Delta t\right)\geq\Delta H \quad \text{for the interval } \{\tau,\tau+\Delta t\}. \tag{17}$$

Wong and Norwich replaced „≥" by „=" in Eq. 17, and set out to evaluate the resulting equality using Eqs. 13 and 14. Note that Eq. 17 inherently contains 7 parameters whose values are unknown: β, δI, p, $m_0=m\left(t_0\right)$, q, a, and ΔH. Nonetheless, Wong and Norwich (1996) adopted the assumptions that $\Delta H \ll 1$, that $\Delta I \ll \left(I+\delta I\right)$, and that $t_0 \ll \Delta t$. Wong and Norwich consequently used series expansions to first order in ΔH and $\Delta I/\left(I+\delta I\right)$. The series expansion to first order in ΔH was not shown by Wong and Norwich; it gives

$$e^{2\Delta H}\approx 1+2\Delta H. \tag{18}$$

The series expansion to first order in $\Delta I/\left(I+\delta I\right)$ was also not shown by Wong and Norwich; it yields

$$\left(I+\Delta I+\delta I\right)^p=\left(I+\delta I\right)^p\left(1+\frac{\Delta I}{I+\delta I}\right)^p\approx\left(I+\delta I\right)^p\left(1+\frac{p\Delta I}{I+\delta I}\right). \tag{19}$$

The solution to Eq. 17 that was offered by Wong and Norwich was

$$\frac{\Delta I}{I}=\frac{2\Delta H}{q\left(1-e^{-a\Delta t}\right)}\left(1+\frac{\delta I}{I}\right)\left(1+\frac{1}{\beta\left(I+\delta I\right)^n}\right),\quad \textit{where } n=p-q. \tag{20}$$

Note that Wong and Norwich re-introduced the term n, which they first used in Eq. 4 and then had replaced, without explanation, by the letter p. The present n was implied by Wong and Norwich to be a positive number, which will turn out to be very important. Eq. 20 has 6 unknowns - ΔH, q, a, δI, β, and n - and one supplied parameter, Δt. Wong and Norwich then held Δt constant and assumed that $\delta I \ll I$, so that δI can be set to zero, and arrived at

$$\frac{\Delta I}{I}=A\left(1+\frac{B}{I^n}\right) \tag{21}$$

$$\text{where } A=\frac{2\Delta H}{q\left(1-e^{-a\Delta t}\right)},\quad B=\frac{1}{\beta}$$

(Wong & Norwich, 1996, Eq. 11; Wong & Figueiredo, 2002, Eq. 12) which „is identical to the empirical Knudsen-Riesz Weber fraction equation" (Wong & Norwich, 1996, p. 432).
Returning to Eq. 20, when $I\to 0$, such that $\delta I \gg I$ and thus $\delta I/I \gg 1$, Wong and Norwich obtained

$$\frac{\Delta I}{I} = \frac{C}{I}, \tag{22}$$

$$\text{where } C = \frac{2\Delta H \delta I}{q\left(1 - e^{-a\Delta t}\right)}\left(1 + \frac{1}{\beta(\delta I)^n}\right)$$

(Wong & Norwich, 1996, Eq. 12; Wong & Figueiredo, 2002, Eq. 14). Wong and Norwich (1996) claimed that this relation characterizes the empirical Weber fraction „as the pedestal intensity is made smaller and smaller" (*ibid.*, p. 432), a phenomenon said to be „observed by many investigators" (*ibid.*, p. 433; no citations supplied). Eq. 20 can also be rearranged under the assignment *I=0*, giving

$$\Delta I = \frac{I_\infty}{1 - e^{-a\Delta t}}, \tag{23}$$

$$\text{where } I_\infty = \frac{2\Delta H \delta I}{q}\left(1 + \frac{1}{\beta(\delta I)^n}\right)$$

(Wong & Norwich, 1996, Eq. 13; Wong & Figueiredo, 2002, Eq. 15), which Wong and Norwich recognized as Zwislocki's (1960) empirical relation for auditory absolute detection thresholds. (Note that Wong and Norwich implicitly adopted the old but unqualified notion that the absolute detection threshold is a just-noticeable intensity increment.) The reader may note the similarity of the constants C and I_∞; the latter was written out in Wong and Norwich, whereas the former was described only as „a constant" (*ibid.*, p. 433). Eqs. 22 and 23 are in fact the same, a point not made by Wong and Norwich.

Wong and Norwich (1996) then expanded the denominator of Eq. 23 to first order under the assumption that $\Delta t \ll 1/a$, so that Eq. 23 became $\Delta I \cdot \Delta t$=constant. The latter appeared as an unnumbered equation in Wong and Norwich (1996) and as Eq. 16 of Wong and Figueiredo (2002), and was described as Bloch's Law. Of course, under these circumstances, it can only describe threshold phenomena, not above-threshold phenomena also (viz. the original Bloch's Law).

8. A re-derivation of $\Delta I/I$: some disagreements with Wong and Norwich (1996)

We may start with Eq. 17 and attempt to recreate the derivation described by Wong and Norwich. The resulting equation contains 10 elements: the 6 unknowns, ΔH, q, a, δI, β, and p, the 2 supplied parameters t_0 and Δt, the dependent variable $(\Delta I)/I$, and the independent variable I. In order to achieve a solution resembling Eq. 20, a further assumption had to be made that was not mentioned by Wong and Norwich, viz., that $t_0=0$. This reduced the total number of elements from 10 to 9. Altogether, the solution found was

$$\frac{\Delta I}{I} = \frac{2\Delta H}{q\left(1 - e^{-a\Delta t}\right)}\left(1 + \frac{\delta I}{I}\right)\left(1 + \frac{1}{\beta(I + \delta I)^n}\right) \Bigg/ \left(1 - \frac{2\Delta H}{\beta(I + \delta I)^n} - \frac{2p\Delta H}{q\left(1 - e^{-a\Delta t}\right)}\right). \tag{24}$$

Despite the Wong and Norwich assumption that $\Delta H \ll 1$, Eq. 24 can only be reconciled with the Wong and Norwich solution, Eq. 20, if Wong and Norwich had simply chosen to ignore the second and third terms in the denominator on the right-hand-side of Eq. 24. Such a simplification is unjustified, however, because q, a, δI, β, and p (= n+q) remain unknown. This is still a problem even if a range of values was specified for I (which was not done). Values for such unknowns had traditionally been obtained by Norwich and co-authors through fitting of equations to other people's data, but no such parameters were provided by Wong and Norwich. (In any case, curve-fitting is not measurement.)

Let us examine the derivations made by Wong and Norwich, but now using Eq. 24 in its entirety rather than Eq. 20. First, let us hold Δt constant and assume that $\delta I << I$, so that δI can be set to zero. This yields

$$\frac{\Delta I}{I} = A\left(1+\frac{B}{I^n}\right)\Big/\left(1-Ap-\frac{2B\Delta H}{I^n}\right), \tag{25}$$

$$\text{where } A = \frac{2\Delta H}{q\left(1-e^{-a\Delta t}\right)}, \quad B = \frac{1}{\beta}.$$

This is not quite the equation for the „empirical Knudsen-Riesz Weber fraction". To recover that particular equation, the denominator in Eq. 25 would have to be unity alone.

Let us continue to follow the Wong and Norwich derivations. Now, letting $I \to 0$ gives

$$\frac{\Delta I}{I} = \frac{C'}{I}, \tag{26}$$

$$\text{where } C' = \frac{2\Delta H\delta I}{q\left(1-e^{-a\Delta t}\right)}\left(1+\frac{1}{\beta(\delta I)^n}\right)\Big/\left(1-\frac{2\Delta H}{\beta(\delta I)^n}-\frac{2p\Delta H}{q\left(1-e^{-a\Delta t}\right)}\right).$$

Eq. 26 has the same form as Eq. 22, but the C′ of Eq. 26 is not the C of Eq. 22.

We now leave Eq. 26 and return to Eq. 24, in order to continue to follow the Wong and Norwich derivations, and set *I=0*. After some rearrangement, we obtain

$$\Delta I = \frac{K}{L\cdot\left(1-e^{-a\Delta t}\right)-M}, \tag{27}$$

$$\text{where } K = 2\Delta H\cdot\delta I\cdot\left(1+\frac{1}{\beta(\delta I)^n}\right), \quad L = q\left(1-\frac{2\Delta H}{\beta(\delta I)^n}\right), \quad M = 2p\Delta H.$$

This is not quite Zwislocki's (1960) equation for absolute detection thresholds, as Eq. 23 was claimed to be. Note that Eq. 27 is in fact the same as Eq. 26, just as Eq. 23 was the same as Eq. 22.

Finally, continuing from Eq. 27 and following the Wong and Norwich (1996) assumption that $\Delta t << 1/a$, we obtain

$$\Delta I\cdot\left(\Delta t-\frac{M}{aL}\right) = \frac{K}{aL}, \tag{28}$$

which is certainly not Bloch's Law, $\Delta I\cdot\Delta t = \text{constant}$.

9. The derivation of Piéron's Law by Wong and Norwich (1996)

In the Wong and Norwich (1996) derivation of Piéron's Law, they started fresh with Eq. 17, solving it for Δt under the conditions that (1) the pedestal (background) stimulus intensity was zero (I=0), so that the only stimulus intensity was ΔI; (2) ΔH<<1; and (3) δI<<ΔI. However, Wong and Norwich abandoned their earlier approximation $t_0 \approx 0$ (used above), although they did not explain why. They also expanded in "zeroth order" in $\delta I/\Delta I$. Altogether they obtained

$$\Delta t = \Delta t_{\min} \cdot \left(1 + \frac{1}{\zeta \cdot (\Delta I)^n} \right), \tag{29}$$

where $\Delta t_{\min} = \frac{2\Delta H}{a}\left(e^{a t_0} - 1\right)$ and ζ was unspecified.

As before, Wong and Norwich implied that $n = p - q$ is a positive number. When a constant representing physiological motor-response time was added to both sides of Eq. 29, the resulting equation was identified by Wong and Norwich as Piéron's Law for reaction time.

10. A re-derivation of Piéron's Law: some disagreements with Wong and Norwich (1996)

The present author attempted to retrace the Wong and Norwich derivation, starting right back with Eq. 17. It was immediately noted that „a" could only appear as a free parameter under the approximation, not mentioned by Wong and Norwich, that $e^{-a\Delta t} \approx 1 - a\Delta t$. Evaluating Eq. 17 using this approximation, and the approximations outlined by Wong and Norwich, leads to an equation containing 9 elements: the 6 unknowns, ΔH, q, a, δI, β, and p; the supplied parameter t_0; the dependent variable Δt; and the independent variable ΔI,

$$\Delta t = \frac{1}{a}\left(\frac{C_1 \, (\Delta I)^n + C_2}{C_3 (\Delta I)^n + C_4} \right), \tag{30}$$

where

$$C_1 = -\beta(1+2\Delta H)\left(e^{-a t_0} - 1\right) + \beta\left[2\Delta H + \left(e^{-a t_0} - 1\right)(1+2\Delta H)\right]\left(\frac{\delta I}{\Delta I}\right)^q,$$

$$C_2 = \left(\frac{\delta I}{\Delta I}\right)^q \left[\left(e^{-a t_0} - 1\right) - \frac{\left(e^{-a t_0} - 1\right)(1+2\Delta H)}{(\Delta I)^q} + 2\Delta H\left[1 + \left(e^{-a t_0} - 1\right)\right]\left(\frac{\delta I}{\Delta I}\right)^q \right],$$

$$C_3 = \beta\left[1 - \left(\frac{\delta I}{\Delta I}\right)^q\right],$$

$$C_4 = 2\Delta H\left(e^{-a\,t_0} - 1\right) + \left(\frac{\delta I}{\Delta I}\right)^q \left[\begin{matrix}\left(e^{-a\,t_0} - 1\right) - \dfrac{a}{(\Delta I)^q}\left[(1+2\Delta H)\left(2e^{-a\,t_0} - 1\right)\right] \\ +\left(\dfrac{\delta I}{\Delta I}\right)^q \left[2\Delta H\, e^{-a\,t_0}\right]\end{matrix}\right].$$

Eq. 30 is not the same as Eq. 29. If we assume, simply for the sake of exploration, that the term $(\delta I/\Delta I)^q$ is ignorable, then Eq. 30 simplifies to

$$\Delta t = -(1+2\Delta H)\left(e^{-a\,t_0} - 1\right) \Bigg/ \left(a\left[1 + \frac{2\Delta H\left(e^{-a\,t_0} - 1\right)}{\beta(\Delta I)^n}\right]\right). \tag{31}$$

This is still not Eq. 29. Note especially that in Eq. 31, n is in the denominator of a denominator, rendering n overall of opposite sign in Eq. 31 to that in Eq. 29. This difference is crucial; recall that n was defined by Wong and Norwich as being greater than zero, just like the exponent of Piéron's Law (Eq. 3), so that the exponent n in Eq. 29 is a positive number, as required. We can also now see a possible reason why Wong and Norwich abandoned their earlier approximation $t_0 \approx 0$; letting $t_0 = 0$ in Eq. 31 results in $\Delta t = 0$, which would imply instantaneous reactions.

Let us see what happens when we start from Eq. 30 under the assumption that $t_0 = 0$, but that $(\delta I/\Delta I)^q$ is *not* ignorable. Then

$$C_1 = 2\Delta H\beta\left(\frac{\delta I}{\Delta I}\right)^q, \quad C_2 = 2\Delta H\left(\frac{\delta I}{\Delta I}\right)^{2q},$$

$$C_4 = \left(\frac{\delta I}{\Delta I}\right)^q \left[-\frac{a}{(\Delta I)^q}(1+2\Delta H) + \left(\frac{\delta I}{\Delta I}\right)^q (2\Delta H)\right],$$

and Eq. 30 simplifies somewhat to

$$\Delta t = \frac{2\Delta H\left(\dfrac{\delta I}{\Delta I}\right)^q \left[\beta(\Delta I)^n + \left(\dfrac{\delta I}{\Delta I}\right)^q\right]}{a\left(\beta\left[1 - \left(\dfrac{\delta I}{\Delta I}\right)^q\right](\Delta I)^n + \left(\dfrac{\delta I}{\Delta I}\right)^q \left[-\dfrac{a}{(\Delta I)^q}(1+2\Delta H) + \left(\dfrac{\delta I}{\Delta I}\right)^q (2\Delta H)\right]\right)}, \tag{32}$$

which is still not Eq. 29.

It transpires there is indeed a way to obtain an equation of the form of Eq. 29 starting from Eq. 30, but some imagination is needed. Let us make the assumption that led to Eq. 31 – that is, that $(\delta I/\Delta I)^q$ is ignorable – and let us further assume the series approximation

$$\frac{1}{1 + (2\Delta H/\beta)\left(e^{-a\,t_0} - 1\right)(\Delta I)^{-n}} \cong 1 - \frac{(2\Delta H/\beta)\left(e^{-a\,t_0} - 1\right)}{(\Delta I)^n} \tag{33}$$

$$for \quad \left|(2\Delta H/\beta)\left(e^{-a\,t_0}-1\right)(\Delta I)^{-n}\right|<1 .$$

The latter move transforms Eq. 31 to

$$\Delta t = \frac{(1+2\Delta H)\left(1-e^{-a\,t_0}\right)}{a}\left[1 + \frac{2\Delta H\cdot\left(1-e^{-a\,t_0}\right)}{\beta\cdot(\Delta I)^{n}}\right], \tag{34}$$

which looks like Piéron's Law as expressed in Eq. 29 if $\left(1-e^{-a\,t_0}\right)>0$, which is guaranteed from Eq. 9 for any $t_0>0$, and also if $\Delta t_{\min}$ is defined as $(1+2\Delta H)\left(1-e^{-a\,t_0}\right)/a$ and if ζ is defined as $\zeta=\beta\Big/\left[2\Delta H\cdot\left(1-e^{-a\,t_0}\right)\right]$. Wong and Norwich did not mention using the simplification that is shown here in Eq. 33; justifying that simplification would require knowing the values of the 5 unknowns ΔH, q, a, β, and p (=n+q), as well as the value of the supplied parameter t_0, and all relevant values of the independent variable ΔI. Wong and Norwich could not supply that knowledge, but apparently they made the approximation nonetheless.

Finally, the arbitrariness of the above derivation of Piéron's Law can be demonstrated by returning to Eq. 17 and re-simplifying it under some starting assumptions that are similar, and some that are different. That is, let us assume that $e^{-a\Delta t}\approx 1-a\Delta t$, as used above, and also that $\delta I=0$ (the equivalent of the later assumption, used above, that $(\delta I/\Delta I)^q$ is ignorable). Now, instead of following the Wong and Norwich conjecture that $e^{2\Delta H}\approx 1+2\Delta H$ (Eq. 18), made under the unsupported Wong and Norwich assumption ΔH<<1, let us instead make the equally unsupported assumptions that

$$-1<\frac{\beta\cdot(I+\Delta I+\delta I)^{p}}{m(\tau+t_0)},\ \frac{\beta\cdot(I+\Delta I+\delta I)^{p}}{m(\tau+\Delta t)}\le 1$$

so that

$$\ln\left(1 + \frac{\beta\cdot(I+\Delta I+\delta I)^{p}}{m(\tau+t_0)}\right)\cong\frac{\beta\cdot(I+\Delta I+\delta I)^{p}}{m(\tau+t_0)}, \tag{35a}$$

and that

$$\ln\left(1 + \frac{\beta\cdot(I+\Delta I+\delta I)^{p}}{m(\tau+\Delta t)}\right)\cong\frac{\beta\cdot(I+\Delta I+\delta I)^{p}}{m(\tau+\Delta t)}. \tag{35b}$$

After some algebra, and finally letting I=0,

$$\Delta t = -\left(e^{-a\,t_0}-1\right)\Bigg/\left(a\left[1 + \frac{2\Delta H\left(e^{-a\,t_0}-1\right)}{\beta(\Delta I)^{n}}\right]\right). \tag{36}$$

Note that only the lack of the multiplier $1+2\Delta H$ differentiates Eq. 36 from Eq. 31, whose derivation involved a partly different set of assumptions! This exercise should make clear the arbitrariness of the Wong and Norwich derivations.

Altogether, we can fairly say that Wong and Norwich did not actually derive Piéron's Law.

11. Summary

Wong and Norwich (1996) (repeated in Wong and Figueiredo, 2002) proposed an equation in seven unknowns to describe how the information-theoretic *entropy* of sensation will decrease over time for a quiescent sensory receptor suddenly exposed to a step base intensity followed by a superimposed step increment. Hypothetically, the increment can only be detected if the change in sensory entropy over the increment's duration equals or exceeds some minimum entropy change (of unknown size). When the entropy change equals the minimum, such that the intensity increment is just detectable, an equation in six unknowns emerges. Wong and Norwich rearranged that equation, under simplifying assumptions about the magnitudes of some of the unknowns, to give the hypothetical just-detectable intensity increment divided by the base intensity, the so-called Weber fraction. Further simplification from that point yielded an equation resembling an empirical relation proposed by Riesz (1928) for detection of beats. Similar manipulations by Wong and Norwich, but with the base intensity set to zero, gave an equation for the absolute detection threshold as a function of stimulus duration, which resembled an empirical equation of Zwislocki (1960). Simplifying that equation under yet another assumption about the values of the unknowns produced Bloch's Law, which states that stimulus duration multiplied by stimulus intensity is constant at the absolute detection threshold. A yet different set of assumptions about the unknowns was then made, from which Wong and Norwich obtained an equation relating the duration of a just-detectable stimulus to that stimulus' intensity, an equation said to be the empirical relation found by Piéron (1952) for reaction time to a stimulus as a function of stimulus intensity.

The Wong and Norwich (1996) derivations of empirical psychophysical relations from pure theory are remarkable. They deserve re-examination, and so the present author attempted to recreate the Wong and Norwich (1996) derivations. It first proved necessary to return to an earlier paper of theirs, Norwich and Wong (1995), in order to understand the origin of some of the Wong and Norwich (1996) starting equations. Following that, the derivation outlined by Wong and Norwich for the hypothetical Weber fraction was pursued. The Wong and Norwich version of the Weber fraction turns out to be missing two terms, terms that Wong and Norwich presumably ignored, perhaps in the hope that they would be too small to matter. Such a hope is unsupported because the parameters in the extra terms are all unknowns, and one term is intensity-dependent. The extra terms nullify the Wong and Norwich derivations of Riesz's Weber fraction, the Zwislocki relation, and Bloch's Law. Next to be pursued was the Wong and Norwich derivation of Piéron's Law, which relates the duration of a just-detectable stimulus to that stimulus' intensity. An equation eventually emerges whose intensity exponent is of opposite sign to that in Wong and Norwich's equation. The only way to arrive at Piéron's law is through a further unsupported assumption, one that Wong and Norwich did not even mention. Altogether, Wong and Norwich cannot fairly be said to have derived Piéron's Law.

12. Discussion

The Wong and Norwich (1996) derivations hid a number of conceptual problems that have not yet been mentioned because they were independent of the mathematical errors noted so far. Those conceptual problems are substantive and will now be described.

12.1 Hidden assumptions about receptor memory

In retrospect, the Wong and Norwich procedure of substituting Eq. 14 into Eq. 17 under the stimulus increment's starting time $t' = \tau + t_0$ and its finish time $t' = \tau + \Delta t$, followed by the unspoken assumption that $t_0 = 0$, is equivalent to using

$$m(t) = (I + \delta I)^q e^{-at} + (I + \Delta I + \delta I)^q \left(1 - e^{-at}\right) \qquad (37)$$

for the number of samples associated with an increment of duration Δt starting at $t = 0$. Thus the number of samples at $t = 0$ is $(I+\delta I)^q$, which is the equilibrium number of samples for the pedestal stimulus alone, as can be seen by letting $t_0 = 0$ in Eq. 11. Letting $I = 0$, so that there is no pedestal stimulus, the starting number of samples for the increment ΔI is $(\delta I)^q$. This should equal the number that occurs just at the start of a stimulus of intensity ΔI, presented when the receptor is completely unadapted, such that the resting number of samples is zero. Thus $m_0 = m(t_0 = 0)$ from Eq. 9 must equal $(\delta I)^q$, although Wong and Norwich never say so. If the minimum nonzero number of samples is 1, then $(\delta I)^q = 1$, which is a hidden limit that makes δI and q covary. Hence, from Eq. 13, at the instant that a stimulus is applied (t=0) to an unadapted receptor, we have

$$F = kH = \frac{1}{2} k \ln\left(1 + \beta (\delta I)^p\right) . \qquad (38)$$

This initial value of sensation is not mentioned in Wong and Norwich (1996) or in Wong and Figueiredo (2002). F is hence *undefined*, rather than zero or constant, before the application of a stimulus to an unadapted receptor. This is another issue not mentioned in Wong and Norwich (1996) or in Wong and Figueiredo (2002). It seems to imply an extraordinary conclusion: that an unadapted receptor is nonetheless in a perpetual state of adaptation.

There is yet another unmentioned but significant issue. The intensity-dependence of detection thresholds for the kind of amplitude-modulated stimuli used by Riesz (1928) has not proven to be the same as the intensity-dependence of detection thresholds for step stimuli (see for example Wojtczak and Viemeister, 1999). Further, Riesz's modulation-detection thresholds fall monotonically with increase in base intensity. As such, they can be curve-fitted easily by the various versions of the Entropy Equation (above). In contrast, however, detection thresholds for step increments in single-frequency tones (e.g. Nizami et al., 2001, 2002; Nizami, 2006) or increments in auditory clicks (e.g., Nizami, 2005) do not fall monotonically with intensity; rather, they show, to a greater or lesser degree, a „mid-level hump" which cannot be easily fitted by the Entropy Equation.

12.2 Misassignment of stimulus duration as reaction time

In the Wong and Norwich derivation of Piéron's Law, they first defined Δt as the duration of a step in stimulus intensity. They then described it also as a property of a human observer, such as a reaction time! This duality is absurd on its face. Furthermore, the empirical dependence of reaction time upon stimulus intensity is always determined while stimulus duration is held constant, in order to remove duration as a possible confound. Hence Δt, defined as stimulus duration, would not vary. Norwich et al. (1989) presented an earlier derivation of Piéron's Law (repeated in Norwich, 1991) along the same lines as Wong and Norwich (1996), but using Eq. 4 rather than its later and more elaborate version, Eq. 8. The Norwich et al. (1989) derivation, like the later Wong and Norwich (1996) derivation, inappropriately equates reaction time to stimulus duration, and is therefore false.

12.3 The range of data described by the Wong and Norwich „laws"

Having read all that has been noted so far, some readers might still be tempted to believe that Wong and Norwich (1996) had derived psychophysical laws. If so, consider a crucial issue that has been saved for last: the range of data actually covered by the Wong and Norwich derivations. In deriving the Riesz Weber fraction, Wong and Norwich assumed that $\Delta H<<1$, that $\Delta I<<(I+\delta I)$, and that $t_0=0$; they then held Δt constant and assumed that $\delta I<<I$, operationally setting $\delta I=0$. The third of these assumptions was discussed above, and the first assumption has no obvious meaning. The second and fifth assumptions together combine to create the assumption that $\Delta I<<I$, that is, that the Weber fraction is much less than unity. Empirically, however, ΔI in audition can be the same order of magnitude as I and can even exceed I. Under the Wong and Norwich assumption that $\Delta I<<I$, the Weber fraction in decibels, defined as $10 \log_{10}[1+((\Delta I)/I)]$, will approach $10 \log_{10}1$, which is zero. Such infinitely fine auditory discrimination has never been recorded. Therefore, the Riesz Weber fraction derived by Wong and Norwich is unlikely to describe any real data.

The Zwislocki relation for absolute detection threshold was derived under the assumptions that $\Delta H<<1$, that $\Delta I<<(I+\delta I)$, and that $t_0=0$, followed by the stipulation that $I=0$. Letting $\Delta I<<(I+\delta I)$ and then $I=0$ amounts to the assumption that $\Delta I<<\delta I$. For the resulting equation to be Zwislocki's threshold relation, as stated, then δI would have to be well above the absolute detection threshold. That notion was not noted by Wong and Norwich (1996).

The Wong and Norwich (1996) derivation of Bloch's Law continued from their derivation of Zwislocki's relation, under the further assumption that $\Delta t << 1/a$. Recall that „a" (Eq. 7) is an unknown constant said to characterize the rate at which samples build up in the sensory receptor's memory, and that Δt is the duration of the stimulus increment, here, the duration of the just-audible stimulus itself. Because "a" is unknown, there is no way of knowing under what circumstances $\Delta t << 1/a$ is obeyed, or indeed, whether there are any circumstances under which it is obeyed at all. For example, if $1/a$ is on the order of a few milliseconds, as would characterize a fast neuronal process in general, then Δt could well be too brief to represent any empirically detectable stimulus.

The Wong and Norwich derivation of Piéron's Law involved the assumptions that $I = 0$, $\Delta H << 1$, and $\delta I << \Delta I$. Regarding the last assumption, they in fact must have assumed that $\delta I = 0$, as mentioned. They also adopted the hidden assumption that $e^{-a\Delta t} \approx 1 - a\Delta t$. Altogether, then, there are limits upon ΔH, a, and Δt. Further, Wong and Norwich evidently used another hidden assumption, that $\left|(2\Delta H/\beta)\left(e^{-a t_0}-1\right)(\Delta I)^{-n}\right|<1$. Along with the restrictions just mentioned, this places limits also upon β, t_0, n, and ΔI. Such a set of restrictions places mutual limits upon the values of Δt, Δt_{min}, ζ, ΔI, and n in Eq. 29. Piéron himself noted no such limitations (Piéron, 1952).

13. Conclusions

Wong and Norwich (1996) claimed to derive several important psychophysical laws, but in fact they did not. Their derivations involved indisputable mathematical errors. Those errors involved oversimplifications of Wong and Norwich's starting equation, the equation for the change in sensory entropy over the duration of an intensity increment. That equation has seven unknowns, about which a variety of assumptions were made in an effort to simplify the math, assumptions that were not justified by data or by theory. Indeed, one assumption

that was used in deriving Riesz's Weber fraction – that the starting time of an intensity increment was effectively zero - was then reversed in deriving Piéron's Law for reaction time, with no explanation given for the reversal. It turns out that without the reversal, the predicted reaction times are zero – a completely unrealistic situation.
The Wong and Norwich (1996) derivations also involve two serious conceptual errors. First, they made the hidden assumption of a nonzero receptor memory at the instant of the imposition of a stimulus to an unadapted receptor. That assumption is extraordinary, because it implies stimulus-driven neuronal activity in a quiescent receptor. They also made a second extraordinary assumption, viz., that the stimulus duration, a stimulus property, was identifiable with reaction time, an observer property. That assumption alone nullifies the Wong and Norwich derivation of Piéron's Law.
All of these problems remain unresolved, and resolution seems highly unlikely. Indeed, others have expressed profound doubts about the origin and meaning of the Entropy Equation itself, the equation on which Wong and Norwich (1996) ultimately based all of their algebra (e.g. MacRae, 1982; Ward, 1991; Laming, 1994; Ashby, 1995). Profound doubts have also been expressed elsewhere by the present author (Nizami 2008a, 2008b, 2009a, 2009b, 2009c, 2009d, 2009e, 2010).
Regardless, the flaws presently revealed stand alone, as a useful warning about the dangers of using equations in too many unknowns and then attempting to simplify those equations under arbitrary assumptions about the values of those unknowns. To their detriment, Wong and Norwich failed to heed the famous warning by William of Ockham (c. 1285-1349) that „entities must not be multiplied beyond necessity", inadvertently leaving a valuable lesson for the human-factors engineer who must likewise avoid needlessly complicated models of human perception.

14. Acknowledgements

Professor Claire S. Barnes of Emory University provided valuable insights during the proofreading of this paper. Thanks also to the editorial staff of INTECH for their patient proofreading and especially to Prof. Katarina Lovrecic for her courteous correspondence.

15. References

Ashby, F.G. (1995). Resurrecting information theory: Information, Sensation, and Perception by Kenneth H. Norwich, *American Journal of Psychology*, 108, 4, 609-614, ISSN 0002-9556.

Brindley, G.S. (1952). The Bunsen-Roscoe Law for the human eye at very short durations, *Journal of Physiology*, 118, 1, 135-139, ISSN 0022-3751.

Feldtkeller, R. & Oetinger, R. (1956). Die Horbarkeitsgrenzen von Impulsen vershiedener Dauer, *Acustica*, 6, 489-493, ISSN 0001-7884.

Laming, D.R.J. (1994). Review: Information, Sensation, and Perception by K.H. Norwich, *Perception*, 23, 12, 1491-1494, ISSN 0301-0066.

MacRae, A.W. (1982). The magical number fourteen: making a very great deal of none-sense, *Perception & Psychophysics*, 31, 6, 591-593, ISSN 0031-5117.

Nizami, L. (2005). Intensity-difference limens predicted from the click-evoked peripheral N_1: the mid-level hump and its implications for intensity encoding, *Mathematical Biosciences*, 197, 1, 15-34, ISSN 0025-5564.

22

A Model of Adding Relations in Two Levels of a Linking Pin Organization Structure with Two Subordinates

Kiyoshi Sawada
University of Marketing and Distribution Sciences
Japan

1. Introduction

A pyramid organization is a hierarchical structure based on the principle of unity of command (Koontz, 1980) that every member except the top in the organization should have a single immediate superior. On the other hand an organization characterized by System 4 (Likert, 1976) has a structure in which relations between members of the same section are added to the pyramid organization structure. Members of middle layers of System 4 which are both members of the upper units and chiefs of the lower units are called linking pins, and this type of organization is called a linking pin organization. In the linking pin organization there exist relations between each superior and his direct subordinates and those between members which have the same immediate superior.

The linking pin organization structure can be expressed as a structure where every pair of siblings which are nodes which have the same parent in a rooted tree is adjacent, if we let nodes and edges in the structure correspond to members and relations between members in the organization respectively. Then the linking pin organization structure is characterized by the number of subordinates of each member, that is, the number of children of each node and the number of levels in the organization, that is, the height of the rooted tree, and so on (Robbins, 2003; Takahara & Mesarovic, 2003). Moreover, the path between a pair of nodes in the structure is equivalent to the route of communication of information between a pair of members in the organization, and adding edges to the structure is equivalent to forming additional relations other than those between each superior and his direct subordinates and between members which have the same direct subordinate.

The purpose of our study is to obtain an optimal set of additional relations to the linking pin organization such that the communication of information between every member in the organization becomes the most efficient. This means that we obtain a set of additional edges to the structure minimizing the sum of lengths of shortest paths between every pair of all nodes.

We have obtained an optimal depth for a model of adding edges between every pair of nodes with the same depth to a complete K-ary linking pin structure of height $H(H = 2, 3, \ldots)$ where every pair of siblings in a complete K-ary tree of height H is adjacent (Sawada, 2008). A complete K-ary tree is a rooted tree in which all leaves have the same depth and all internal nodes have $K(K = 2, 3, \ldots)$ children (Cormen et al., 2001). Figure 1 shows an example of a complete K-ary linking pin structure of K=2 and H=5. In Fig.1 the value of N expresses the depth of each node.

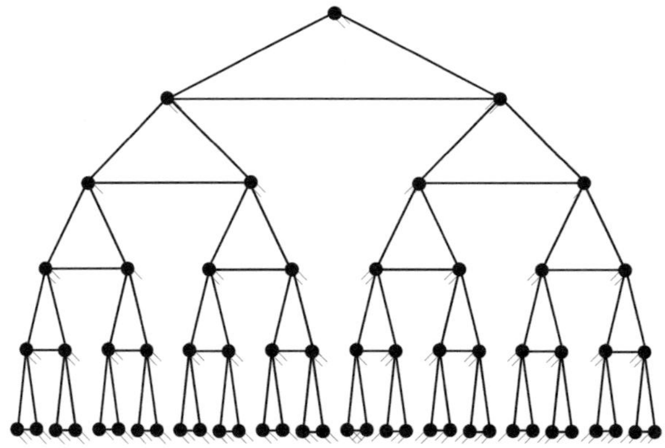

Fig. 1. An example of a complete K-ary linking pin structure of K=2 and H=5

This model gives us an optimal level when we add relations in one level to the organization structure which is a complete K-ary linking pin structure of height H, but this model cannot be applied to adding relations in two or more levels. This chapter expands the above model into the model of adding relations in two levels to the organization structure, which is that of adding edges between every pair of nodes at each depth of two depths to a complete binary (K = 2) linking pin structure of height $H(H = 3, 4, \ldots)$.

If $l_{i,j}$ (= $l_{j,i}$) denotes the distance, which is the number of edges in the shortest path from a node v_i to a node v_j ($i, j = 1, 2, \ldots, 2^{H+1}-1$) in the complete binary linking pin structure of height H, then $\Sigma_{i<j} l_{i,j}$ is the total distance. Furthermore, if $l'_{i,j}$ denotes the distance from v_i to v_j after adding edges in this model, $l_{i,j} - l'_{i,j}$ is called the shortening distance between v_i and v_j, and $\Sigma_{i<j} (l_{i,j} - l'_{i,j})$ is called the *total shortening distance.*

In Section 2 for the model of adding relations in one level we show formulation of a total shortening distance and an optimal depth which maximizes the total shortening distance. In Section 3 for the model of adding relations in two levels we formulate a total shortening distance and obtain an optimal pair of depths which maximizes the total shortening distance.

2. A model of adding relations in one level

This section shows an optimal depth L^* by maximizing the total shortening distance, when edges between every pair of nodes at one depth $L(L = 2, 3, \ldots, H)$ are added to a complete binary linking pin structure of height $H(H = 2, 3, \ldots)$ (Sawada, 2008).

2.1 Formulation of total shortening distance

Let $\sigma_H(L)$ denote the total shortening distance, when we add edges between every pair of nodes with a depth of L.

The total shortening distance $\sigma_H(L)$ can be formulated by adding up the following three sums of shortening distances: (i) the sum of shortening distances between every pair of nodes whose depths are equal to or greater than L, (ii) the sum of shortening distances between every pair of nodes whose depths are less than L and those whose depths are equal to or greater than L and (iii) the sum of shortening distances between every pair of nodes whose depths are less than L.

The sum of shortening distances between every pair of nodes whose depths are equal to or greater than L is given by

$$\alpha_H(L) = \{W(H-L)\}^2 2^L \sum_{i=1}^{L-1} i2^i, \tag{1}$$

where $W(h)$ denotes the number of nodes of a complete binary tree of height $h (h = 0, 1, 2, \dots)$.

The sum of shortening distances between every pair of nodes whose depths are less than L and those whose depths are equal to or greater than L is given by

$$\beta_H(L) = W(H-L)2^{L+1} \sum_{i=1}^{L-2} \sum_{j=1}^{i} j2^j, \tag{2}$$

and the sum of shortening distances between every pair of nodes whose depths are less than L is given by

$$\gamma(L) = 2^L \sum_{i=1}^{L-3} \sum_{j=1}^{i} j(i-j+1)2^j, \tag{3}$$

where we define

$$\sum_{i=1}^{0} \cdot = 0 \tag{4}$$

and

$$\sum_{i=1}^{-1} \cdot = 0. \tag{5}$$

From these equations, the total shortening distance $\sigma_H(L)$ is given by

$$\begin{aligned}\sigma_H(L) &= \alpha_H(L) + \beta_H(L) + \gamma(L) \\ &= \{W(H-L)\}^2 2^L \sum_{i=1}^{L-1} i2^i + W(H-L)2^{L+1} \sum_{i=1}^{L-2} \sum_{j=1}^{i} j2^j + 2^L \sum_{i=1}^{L-3} \sum_{j=1}^{i} j(i-j+1)2^j.\end{aligned} \tag{6}$$

Since the number of nodes of a complete binary tree of height h is

$$W(h) = 2^{h+1} - 1, \tag{7}$$

$\sigma_H(L)$ of Eq.(6) becomes

$$\sigma_H(L) = (L-2)2^{2H+2} + 2^{2H-L+3} - 2^{H+L+3} + (L+1)2^{H+3} + L(L-1)2^L. \tag{8}$$

2.2 An optimal depth L^*

In this subsection, we seek $L = L^*$ which maximizes $\sigma_H(L)$ of Eq.(8).

Let $\Delta\sigma_H(L) \equiv \sigma_H(L+1) - \sigma_H(L)$, so that we have

$$\Delta\sigma_H(L) = 4\left(1-2^{-L}\right)2^{2H} + 8\left(1-2^{L}\right)2^{H} + L(L+3)2^{L} \tag{9}$$

for $L = 2, 3, \ldots, H$-1. Let us define x as

$$x = 2^{H}, \tag{10}$$

then $\Delta\ \sigma_H(L)$ in Eq.(9) becomes

$$\tau_L(x) = 4\left(1-2^{-L}\right)x^2 + 8\left(1-2^{L}\right)x + L(L+3)2^{L} \tag{11}$$

which is a quadratic function of the continuous variable x. By differentiating $\tau_L(x)$ in Eq.(11) with respect to x, we obtain

$$\tau'_L(x) = 8\left(1-2^{-L}\right)x + 8\left(1-2^{L}\right). \tag{12}$$

Since $\tau_L(x)$ is convex downward from

$$4\left(1-2^{-L}\right) > 0, \tag{13}$$

and

$$\tau_L(2^{L+1}) = L(L+3)2^{L} > 0 \tag{14}$$

and

$$\tau'_L(2^{L+1}) = 8\left(2^{L}-1\right) > 0, \tag{15}$$

we have $\tau_L(x) > 0$ for $x \geq 2^{L+1}$. Hence, we have $\Delta\ \sigma_H(L) > 0$ for $H \geq L+1$; that is, $L = 2, 3, \ldots, H$-1.

From the above results, the optimal depth of this model is $L^* = H$.

2.3 Numerical examples

Table 1 shows the optimal depths L^* and the total shortening distances $\sigma_H(L^*)$ in the case of H=2, 3, …, 20.

3. A model of adding relations in two levels

This section obtains an optimal pair of depths $(M, N)^*$ by maximizing the total shortening distance, when edges between every pair of nodes with depth $M(M = 2, 3, \ldots, H-1)$ and those between every pair of nodes with depth $N(N = M+1, M+2, \ldots, H)$ which is greater than M are added to a complete binary linking pin structure of height $H(H = 3, 4, \ldots\ldots)$.

3.1 Formulation of total shortening distance

Using formulation of the model of adding relations in one level shown in Subsection 2.1, we formulate the total shortening distance of the model of adding relations in two levels $S_H(M, N)$.

H	L^*	$\sigma_H(L^*)$
2	2	8
3	3	112
4	4	960
5	5	6528
6	6	38784
7	7	211200
8	8	1083392
9	9	5324800
10	10	25356288
11	11	117878784
12	12	537870336
13	13	2418180096
14	14	10742497280
15	15	47255977984
16	16	206183596032
17	17	893408772096
18	18	3848412856320
19	19	16492941803520
20	20	70369327185920

Table 1. Optimal depths L^* and total shortening distances $\sigma_H(L^*)$

Let V_1 denote the set of nodes whose depths are less than M. Let V_2 denote the set of nodes whose depths are equal to or greater than M and are less than N. Let V_3 denote the set of nodes whose depths are equal to or greater than N.

The sum of shortening distances between every pair of nodes in V_3 is given by

$$A_H(N) = \alpha_H(N) \tag{16}$$

from Eq.(1). The sum of shortening distances between every pair of nodes in V_3 and nodes in V_1 and V_2 is given by

$$B_H(N) = \beta_H(N) \tag{17}$$

from Eq.(2). The sum of shortening distances between every pair of nodes in V_1 is given by

$$C(M) = \gamma(M) \tag{18}$$

from Eq.(3), and the sum of shortening distances between every pair of nodes in V_1 and nodes in V_2 is given by

$$D(M,N) = \beta_{N-1}(M) \tag{19}$$

from Eq.(2). The sum of shortening distances between every pair of nodes in V_2 is formulated as follows.

The sum of shortening distances between every pair of nodes in each linking pin structure whose root is a node with depth M is given by

$$E(M,N) = \gamma(N-M)2^M \tag{20}$$

from Eq.(3). The sum of shortening distances between every pair of nodes in two different linking pin structures whose roots are nodes with depth M is given by summing up $F(M, N)$ and $G(M, N)$. $F(M, N)$ which is the sum of shortening distances by adding edges only between nodes with depth M is given by

$$F(M,N) = \alpha_{N-1}(M) \tag{21}$$

from Eq.(1). $G(M, N)$ which is the sum of additional shortening distances by adding edges between nodes with depth N after adding edges between nodes with depth M is expressed by

$$G(M,N) = \left(2^M - 1\right) \sum_{i=1}^{N-M-2} 2^{N-i} \sum_{j=1}^{N-M-i-1} 2^{N-M-j}(N-M-i-j), \tag{22}$$

where we define

$$\sum_{i=1}^{0} \cdot = 0 \tag{23}$$

and

$$\sum_{i=1}^{-1} \cdot = 0\,. \tag{24}$$

From these equations, the total shortening distances $S_H(M, N)$ is given by

$$\begin{aligned} S_H(M,N) &= A_H(N) + B_H(N) + C(M) + D(M,N) + E(M,N) + F(M,N) + G(M,N) \\ &= \{W(H-N)\}^2 2^N \sum_{i=1}^{N-1} i2^i + W(H-N)2^{N+1} \sum_{i=1}^{N-2}\sum_{j=1}^{i} j2^j \\ &+ 2^M \sum_{i=1}^{M-3}\sum_{j=1}^{i} j(i-j+1)2^j + W(N-M-1)2^{M+1} \sum_{i=1}^{M-2}\sum_{j=1}^{i} j2^j \\ &+ 2^N \sum_{i=1}^{N-M-3}\sum_{j=1}^{i} j(i-j+1)2^j + \{W(N-M-1)\}^2 2^M \sum_{i=1}^{M-1} i2^i \\ &+ \left(2^M - 1\right) \sum_{i=1}^{N-M-2} 2^{N-i} \sum_{j=1}^{N-M-i-1} 2^{N-M-j}(N-M-i-j). \end{aligned} \tag{25}$$

Since the number of nodes of a complete binary tree of height h is

$$W(h) = 2^{h+1} - 1, \tag{26}$$

$S_H(M, N)$ of Eq.(25) becomes

$$\begin{aligned} S_H(M,N) &= (N-2)2^{2H+2} + 2^{2H-N+3} - 2^{H+N+3} + (N+1)2^{H+3} + (N-M)2^{N+M+1} \\ &+ (N-M)(N-M-3)2^N + M(M-1)2^M\,. \end{aligned} \tag{27}$$

3.2 An optimal depth *N** for a fixed value of *M*

In this subsection, we seek $N = N^*$ which maximizes $R_{H,M}(N) = S_H(M, N)$ for a fixed value of $M(M = 2, 3, \ldots, H-1)$.
Let $\Delta R_{H,M}(N) \equiv R_{H,M}(N+1) - R_{H,M}(N)$, so that we have

$$\begin{aligned}\Delta R_{H,M}(N) &= 4\left(1-2^{-N}\right)2^{2H} + 8\left(1-2^{N}\right)2^{H} + (N-M+2)2^{N+M+1} \\ &+\{(N-M)(N-M+1)-4\}2^{N}\end{aligned} \tag{28}$$

for $N = M+1, M+2, \ldots, H-1$. Let us define x as

$$x = 2^H, \tag{29}$$

then $\Delta R_{H,M}(N)$ in Eq.(28) becomes

$$\begin{aligned}T_{M,N}(x) &= 4\left(1-2^{-N}\right)x^2 + 8\left(1-2^{N}\right)x + (N-M+2)2^{N+M+1} \\ &+\{(N-M)(N-M+1)-4\}2^{N}\end{aligned} \tag{30}$$

which is a quadratic function of the continuous variable x. By differentiating $T_{M,N}(x)$ in Eq.(30) with respect to x, we obtain

$$T'_{M,N}(x) = 8\left(1-2^{-N}\right)x + 8\left(1-2^{N}\right). \tag{31}$$

Since $T_{M,N}(x)$ is convex downward from

$$4\left(1-2^{-N}\right) > 0, \tag{32}$$

and

$$T_{M,N}(2^{N+1}) = (N-M)2^{N+M+1} + (N-M)(N-M+1)2^{N} + \left(2^{M}-1\right)2^{N+2} > 0 \tag{33}$$

and

$$T'_{M,N}(2^{N+1}) = 8\left(2^{N}-1\right) > 0, \tag{34}$$

we have $T_{M,N}(x) > 0$ for $x \geq 2^{N+1}$. Hence, we have $\Delta R_{H,M}(N) > 0$ for $H \geq N+1$; that is, $N = M+1, M+2, \ldots, H-1$.
From the above results, the optimal depth N^* for a fixed value of $M(M = 2, 3, \ldots, H-1)$ is $N^* = H$.

3.3 An optimal pair of depths (*M*, *N*)*

In this subsection, we seek $(M, N) = (M, N)^*$ which maximizes $S_H(M, N)$ in Eq.(27).
Let $Q_H(M)$ denote the total shortening distance when $N = H$, so that we have

$$\begin{aligned}Q_H(M) &\equiv S_H(M,H) \\ &= (H-4)2^{2H+2} + (H-M)2^{H+M+1} + (H+2)2^{H+3} + (H-M)(H-M-3)2^{H} \\ &+M(M-1)2^{M}.\end{aligned} \tag{35}$$

Let $\Delta Q_H(M) \equiv Q_H(M+1) - Q_H(M)$, so that we have

$$\Delta Q_H(M) = (H-M-2)\left(2^M-1\right)2^{H+1} + M(M+3)2^M > 0 \tag{36}$$

for M = 2, 3, …, H-2.
From the results in Subsection 3.2 and 3.3, the optimal pair of depths is $(M, N)^* = (H\text{-}1, H)$.

3.4 Numerical examples

Tables 2-19 show the optimal depths N^* for a fixed value of M(M = 2, 3, …, H-1) and the total shortening distances $S_H(M,N^*)$ in the case of H=3, 4, …, 20.

M	N^*	$S_H(M, N^*)$
2	3	120

Table 2. Optimal depth N^* and total shortening distance $S_H(M,N^*)$ in the case of H=3

M	N^*	$S_H(M, N^*)$
2	4	1000
3	4	1040

Table 3. Optimal depths N^* and total shortening distances $S_H(M,N^*)$ in the case of H=4

M	N^*	$S_H(M, N^*)$
2	5	6664
3	5	6896
4	5	7040

Table 4. Optimal depths N^* and total shortening distances $S_H(M,N^*)$ in the case of H=5

M	N^*	$S_H(M, N^*)$
2	6	39176
3	6	39984
4	6	41024
5	6	41472

Table 5. Optimal depths N^* and total shortening distances $S_H(M,N^*)$ in the case of H=6

M	N^*	$S_H(M, N^*)$
2	7	212232
3	7	214576
4	7	218304
5	7	222592
6	7	223872

Table 6. Optimal depths N^* and total shortening distances $S_H(M,N^*)$ in the case of H=7

M	N^*	$S_H(M, N^*)$
2	8	1085960
3	8	1092144
4	8	1103040
5	8	1118848
6	8	1136000
7	8	1139456

Table 7. Optimal depths N^* and total shortening distances $S_H(M,N^*)$ in the case of H=8

M	N^*	$S_H(M, N^*)$
2	9	5330952
3	9	5346352
4	9	5375168
5	9	5421696
6	9	5486464
7	9	5554432
8	9	5563392

Table 8. Optimal depths N^* and total shortening distances $S_H(M,N^*)$ in the case of H=9

M	N^*	$S_H(M, N^*)$
2	10	25370632
3	10	25407536
4	10	25479360
5	10	25602688
6	10	25794432
7	10	26055936
8	10	26324992
9	10	26347520

Table 9. Optimal depths N^* and total shortening distances $S_H(M,N^*)$ in the case of H=10

M	N^*	$S_H(M, N^*)$
2	11	117911560
3	11	117997616
4	11	118169792
5	11	118477440
6	11	118986624
7	11	119764224
8	11	120813568
9	11	121880576
10	11	121935872

Table 10. Optimal depths N^* and total shortening distances $S_H(M,N^*)$ in the case of H=11

M	N^*	$S_H(M, N^*)$
2	12	537944072
3	12	538140720
4	12	538542272
5	12	539280000
6	12	540551040
7	12	542618880
8	12	545748992
9	12	549949440
10	12	554190848
11	12	554323968

Table 11. Optimal depths N^* and total shortening distances $S_H(M,N^*)$ in the case of H=12

M	N^*	$S_H(M, N^*)$
2	13	2418343944
3	13	2418786352
4	13	2419704000
5	13	2421424768
6	13	2424473472
7	13	2429637888
8	13	2437969920
9	13	2450526208
10	13	2467325952
11	13	2484219904
12	13	2484535296

Table 12. Optimal depths N^* and total shortening distances $S_H(M,N^*)$ in the case of H=13

M	N^*	$S_H(M, N^*)$
2	14	10742857736
3	14	10743840816
4	14	10745905344
5	14	10749837952
6	14	10756949888
7	14	10769339648
8	14	10790156288
9	14	10823602176
10	14	10873890816
11	14	10941067264
12	14	11008458752
13	14	11009196032

Table 13. Optimal depths N^* and total shortening distances $S_H(M,N^*)$ in the case of H=14

M	N^*	$S_H(M, N^*)$
2	15	47256764424
3	15	47258927152
4	15	47263514816
5	15	47272362624
6	15	47288616832
7	15	47317521664
8	15	47367469056
9	15	47451049984
10	15	47585060864
11	15	47786323968
12	15	48054943744
13	15	48324050944
14	15	48325754880

Table 14. Optimal depths N^* and total shortening distances $S_H(M,N^*)$ in the case of H=15

M	N^*	$S_H(M, N^*)$
2	16	206185299976
3	16	206190018608
4	16	206200111296
5	16	206219772544
6	16	206256342912
7	16	206322406656
8	16	206438938624
9	16	206639501312
10	16	206974445568
11	16	207510925312
12	16	208316153856
13	16	209390370816
14	16	210465685504
15	16	210469584896

Table 15. Optimal depths N^* and total shortening distances $S_H(M,N^*)$ in the case of H=16

M	N^*	$S_H(M, N^*)$
2	17	893412442120
3	17	893422665776
4	17	893444686016
5	17	893487940224
6	17	893569206144
7	17	893717845248
8	17	893984192512
9	17	894452142080
10	17	895255930880
11	17	896596930560
12	17	898743681024
13	17	901964857344
14	17	906261004288
15	17	910559608832
16	17	910568456192

Table 16. Optimal depths N^* and total shortening distances $S_H(M,N^*)$ in the case of H=17

M	N^*	$S_H(M, N^*)$
2	18	3848420720648
3	18	3848442740784
4	18	3848490451136
5	18	3848584823424
6	18	3848763606912
7	18	3849093911808
8	18	3849693181952
9	18	3850762752000
10	18	3852638185472
11	18	3855856398336
12	18	3861222801408
13	18	3869811376128
14	18	3882696409088
15	18	3899879129088
16	18	3917067321344
17	18	3917087244288

Table 17. Optimal depths N^* and total shortening distances $S_H(M,N^*)$ in the case of H=18

M	N^*	$S_H(M, N^*)$
2	19	16492958580744
3	19	16493005766704
4	19	16493108527296
5	19	16493313000064
6	19	16493703071616
7	19	16494429738240
8	19	16495761438720
9	19	16498167943168
10	19	16502454577152
11	19	16509963563008
12	19	16522842488832
13	19	16544312819712
14	19	16578670067712
15	19	16630210428928
16	19	16698936655872
17	19	16767675006976
18	19	16767719571456

Table 18. Optimal depths N^* and total shortening distances $S_H(M,N^*)$ in the case of H=19

M	N^*	$S_H(M, N^*)$
2	20	70369362837512
3	20	70369463500848
4	20	70369683701952
5	20	70370124104320
6	20	70370969257856
7	20	70372554708224
8	20	70375484438528
9	20	70380832198656
10	20	70390477056000
11	20	70407640281088
12	20	70437690687488
13	20	70489218449408
14	20	70575109013504
15	20	70712543477760
16	20	70918704463872
17	20	71193598099456
18	20	71468518473728
19	20	71468617564160

Table 19. Optimal depths N^* and total shortening distances $S_H(M,N^*)$ in the case of H=20

Table 20 shows the optimal pairs of depths $(M, N)^*$ and the total shortening distances $S_H(M,N)^*$ in the case of H=3, 4, …, 20.

H	$(M, N)^*$	$S_H(M, N)^*$
3	(2, 3)	120
4	(3, 4)	1040
5	(4, 5)	7040
6	(5, 6)	41472
7	(6, 7)	223872
8	(7, 8)	1139456
9	(8, 9)	5563392
10	(9, 10)	26347520
11	(10, 11)	121935872
12	(11, 12)	554323968
13	(12, 13)	2484535296
14	(13, 14)	11009196032
15	(14, 15)	48325754880
16	(15, 16)	210469584896
17	(16, 17)	910568456192
18	(17, 18)	3917087244288
19	(18, 19)	16767719571456
20	(19, 20)	71468617564160

Table 20. Optimal pairs of depths $(M, N)^*$ and total shortening distances $S_H(M,N)^*$

4. Conclusions

This study considered obtaining optimal depths of adding edges to a complete binary linking pin structure where every pair of siblings in a complete binary tree is adjacent maximizing the total shortening distance which is the sum of shortening lengths of shortest paths between every pair of all nodes in the complete binary linking pin structure. This means to obtain optimal levels of adding relations to a linking pin organization structure in which relations between members of the same section are added to the pyramid organization structure such that the communication of information between every member in the organization becomes the most efficient.

For the model of adding edges between every pair of nodes at one depth L to a complete binary linking pin structure of height H, we had already obtained an optimal depth $L^* = H$ in our paper (Sawada, 2008). This result shows that the most efficient way of adding relations between all members in one level is to add relations at the lowest level, irrespective of the number of levels in the organization structure.

This chapter expanded the above model into the model of adding relations in two levels of the organization structure, which is that of adding edges between every pair of nodes with depth M and those between every pair of nodes with depth N which is greater than M to a complete binary linking pin structure of height H. We obtained an optimal pair of depth $(M, N)^* = (H\text{-}1, H)$ which maximizes the total shortening distances. In the case of $H = 5$ illustrated with the example in Fig.1 an optimal pair of depths is $(M, N)^* = (4, 5)$. This result means that the most efficient manner of adding relations between all members in each level of two levels is to add relations at the lowest level and the second lowest level, irrespective of the number of levels in the organization structure.

5. References

Cormen, T. H.; Leiserson, C. E.; Rivest, R. L. & Stein, C. (2001). *Introduction to Algorithms*, 2nd Edition, MIT Press

Koontz, H.; O'Donnell, C. & Weihrich, H. (1980). *Management*, 7th Edition, McGraw-Hill

Likert, R. & Likert, J. G. (1976). *New Ways of Managing Conflict*, McGraw-Hill

Robbins, S. P. (2003). *Essentials of Organizational Behavior*, 7th Edition, Prentice Hall

Sawada, K. & Wilson, R. (2006). Models of adding relations to an organization structure of a complete *K*-ary tree. *European Journal of Operational Research*, Vol.174, pp.1491-1500

Sawada, K. (2008). Adding relations in the same level of a linking pin type organization structure. *IAENG International Journal of Applied Mathematics*, Vol.38, pp.20-25

Takahara, Y. & Mesarovic, M. (2003). *Organization Structure: Cybernetic Systems Foundation*, Kluwer Academic/Plenum Publishers

23

The Multi-Objective Refactoring Set Selection Problem - A Solution Representation Analysis

Camelia Chisăliţă-Creţu
Babeş-Bolyai University
Romania

1. Introduction

Software systems continually change as they evolve to reflect new requirements, but their internal structure tends to decay. Refactoring is a commonly accepted technique to improve the structure of object oriented software. Its aim is to reverse the decaying process in software quality by applying a series of small and behaviour-preserving transformations, each improving a certain aspect of the system (Fowler, 1999). The Multi-Objective Refactoring Set Selection Problem (MORSSP) is the identification problem of the set of refactorings that may be applied to the software entities, such that some specified constraints are kept and several objectives optimized.

This work is organized as follows: The motivation and a possible working scenario for the proposed refactoring selection problem is presented by Section 2. Section 3 reminds the existing work related to the studied domain. The *General Multi-Objective Refactoring Selection Problem* is formally stated by Section 4. Section 5 defines the *Multi-Objective Refactoring Set Selection Problem* as a two conflicting objective problem. The case study used within the research is shortly reminded by Section 6. The evolutionary approach with a proposed weighted objective genetic algorithm and the different solution representations studied are addressed by Section 7. A proposed refactoring strategy together with the input data for the advanced genetic algorithms are presented by Section 8. The results of the pratical experiments for the *entity based* and *refactoring based* solution representations for the multi-objective approach are summarized and analyzed by Section 9. Section 10 lists the conclusions and future research direction of the presented work.

2. Background

2.1 Motivation

Software systems continually change as they evolve to reflect new requirements, but their internal structure tends to decay. Refactoring is a commonly accepted technique to improve the structure of object oriented software (Fowler, 1999; Mens & Tourwe, 2004). Its aim is to reverse the decaying process in software quality by applying a series of small and behaviour-preserving transformations, each improving a certain aspect of the system (Fowler, 1999). While some useful refactorings can be easily identified, it is difficult to determine those refactorings that really improve the internal structure of the program. It is a fact that many

useful refactorings, whilst improving one aspect of the software, make undesirable another one.
Refactorings application is available for almost all object-oriented languages and programming environments. Though, there are still a number of problems to address in order to raise the refactoring automation level.

2.2 Working scenario

Assuming a tool that detects opportunities for refactoring is used (Mens & Tourwe, 2003), it will identify badly structured source code based on code smells (van Emden & Moonen, 2002; Fowler, 1999), metrics (Marinescu, 1998; Simon et al., 2001) or other techniques. The gathered information is used to propose a set of refactorings that can be applied in order to improve the software internal structure. The developer chooses which refactorings he would consider more appropriate to apply, and use a refactoring tool to apply them.
There are several problems that rise up within the considered context. The first one that hits the developer is the large number of refactorings proposed to him, thus the most useful ones to be applied have to be identified.
Another aspect is represented by the possible types of dependencies that may exist between the selected refactorings. It means that applying any of the suggested refactorings may cancel the application of other refactorings that have been already proposed by the developer, but not selected and applied yet.
In (Mens et al., 2007) are presented three kinds of such dependencies: mutual exclusion, sequential dependency, asymmetric conflict. Therefore, the goal is to explore the possibility of identifying the refactorings that optimize some objectives, like costs or impact on software entities. Thus, the developer is helped to decide which refactorings are more appropriate and in which order the transformations must be applied, because of different types of dependencies existing between them.

3. Related work

A closely related previous work is the Next Release Problem (NRP) studied by several authors (Bagnall et al., 2001; Greer & Ruhe, 2004; Zhang et al., 2007), where the goal was to find the most appropriate set of requirements that equilibrate resource constraints to the customer requests, in this way the problem was defined as a constrained optimization problem.
The corresponding refactoring selection problem is an example of a Feature Subset Selection (FSS) search problem. Other FSS problems in previous work on SBSE include the problem of determining good quality predictors in software project cost estimation, studied by Kirsopp et al. (Kirsopp et al., 2002), choosing components to include in different releases of a system, studied by Harman et al. (Harman et al., 2005) and Vescan et al. (Vescan & Pop, 2008).
Previous work on search-based refactoring problems (Bowman et al., 2007; Harman & Tratt, 2007; O'Keefe & O'Cinneide, 2006; Zhang et al., 2007) in SBSE has been concerned with single objective formulations of the problem only. Much of the other existing work on SBSE has tended to consider software engineering problems as single objective optimization problems too. But recent trends show that multi-objective approach has been tackled lately, which appears to be the natural extension of the initial work on SBSE.
Other existing SBSE work that does consider multi-objective formulations of software engineering problems, uses the weighted approach to combine fitness functions for each objective into a single objective function using weighting coefficients to denote the relative importance of each individual fitness function. In the search based refactoring field, Seng

et al. (Seng et al., 2006) and O'Keeffe and O'Cinneide (O'Keefe & O'Cinneide, 2006) apply a weighted multi-objective search, in which several metrics that assess the quality of refactorings are combined into a single objective function. Our approach is similar to those presented in (O'Keefe & O'Cinneide, 2006; Seng et al., 2006) but the difference is the heterogeneity of the weighted fitness functions that are combined together. Thus, we gather up the cost aspect of a refactoring application, the weight of the refactored software entity in the overall system and the effect or impact of the applied transformation upon affected entities as well.

4. General refactoring selection problem

4.1 GMORSP statement

In order to state the *General Multi-Objective Refactoring Selection Problem* (GMORSP) some notion and characteristics have to be defined. Let $SE = \{e_1, \ldots, e_m\}$ be a set of software entities, e.g., a class, an attribute from a class, a method from a class, a formal parameter from a method or a local variable declared in a method implementation. They are considered to be low level components bounded through dependency relations.

A software system SS consists of a software entity set SE together with different types of dependencies between the contained items. A dependency mapping ed is defined as:

$SED = \{\mathbf{u}ses\mathbf{A}ttribute, \mathbf{c}alls\mathbf{M}ethod, \mathbf{s}uper\mathbf{C}lass, \mathbf{a}ssociatedwith\mathbf{C}lass, \mathbf{n}o\mathbf{D}ependency\}$,

$ed : SE \times SE \rightarrow SED$,

$$ed(e_i, e_j) = \begin{cases} \text{uA, if the } \textit{method } e_i \textit{ uses} \text{ the } \textit{attribute } e_j \\ \text{cM, if the } \textit{method } e_i \textit{ calls} \text{ the } \textit{method } e_j \\ \text{sC, if the } \textit{class } e_i \text{ is a } \textit{direct superclass} \text{ for the } \textit{class } e_j \\ \text{aC, if the } \textit{class } e_i \text{ is } \textit{associated} \text{ with the } \textit{class } e_j \\ \text{nD, otherwise} \end{cases}, \quad (1)$$

where $1 \leq i, j \leq m$.

If a *class* e_i, $1 \leq i \leq m$, is an *indirect superclass*, for the *class* e_j, $1 \leq j \leq m$ then $ed(e_i, e_j) = sC*$ and $\exists$ *class* e_k, $1 \leq k \leq m$ such that $ed(e_i, e_k) = sC$, where $1 \leq i \leq m$, $1 \leq j \leq m$. The association relationship between two classes may be expressed as: aggregation, composition or dependency. If a *class* e_i, $1 \leq i \leq m$, has an aggregation relationship with a *class* e_j, $1 \leq j \leq m$, the association multiplicity is nested within the simple class association notation, i.e., $ed(e_i, e_j) = aC*_1^n$.

A set of possible relevant chosen refactorings (Fowler, 1999) that may be applied to different types of software entities of SE is gathered up through $SR = \{r_1, \ldots, r_t\}$. Specific refactorings may be applied to particular types of software entities, i.e., the *RenameMethod* refactoring may be applied to a method entity only, while the *ExtractClass* refactoring has applicability just for classes. Therefore a mapping that sets the applicability for the chosen set of refactorings SR to the set of software entities SE, is defined as:

$ra : SR \times SE \rightarrow \{\mathbf{T}rue, \mathbf{F}alse\}$,

$$ra(r_l, e_i) = \begin{cases} \text{T, if } r_l \text{ may be applied to } e_i \\ \text{F, otherwise} \end{cases}, \quad (2)$$

where $1 \leq l \leq t, 1 \leq i \leq m$.

There are various dependencies between refactorings when they are applied to the same software entity, a mapping emphasizing them being defined by:
$SRD = \{\mathbf{B}efore, \mathbf{A}fter, \mathbf{A}lways\mathbf{B}efore, \mathbf{A}lways\mathbf{A}fter, \mathbf{N}ever, \mathbf{W}henever\}$,
$rd : SR \times SR \times SE \rightarrow SRD$,

$$rd(r_h, r_l, e_i) = \begin{cases} \text{B}, & \text{if } r_h \text{ may be applied to } e_i \text{ only before } r_l, r_h < r_l \\ \text{A}, & \text{if } r_h \text{ may be applied to } e_i \text{ only after } r_l, r_h > r_l \\ \text{AB}, & \text{if } r_h \text{ and } r_l \text{ are both applied to } e_i \text{ and } r_h < r_l \\ \text{AA}, & \text{if } r_h \text{ and } r_l \text{ are both applied to } e_i \text{ and } r_h > r_l \\ \text{N}, & \text{if } r_h \text{ and } r_l \text{ cannot be both applied to } e_i \\ \text{W}, & \text{otherwise, i.e., } r_h \text{ and } r_l \text{ may be both applied to } e_i \end{cases}, \quad (3)$$

where $ra(r_h, e_i) = T, ra(r_l, e_i) = T, 1 \leq h, l \leq t, 1 \leq i \leq m$.

Let $DS = (SE^m, SR^t)$ be the *decision domain* for te GMORSP and $\vec{x} = (e_1, e_2, \ldots, e_m, r_1, r_2, \ldots, r_t)$, $\vec{x} \in DS$ a *decision variable*. The GMORSP is defined by the followings:

- $f_1, f_2, \ldots, f_M$ – M objective functions, where $f_i : DS \rightarrow \mathcal{R}^{m+t}, i = \overline{1,M}$ and $F(\vec{x}) = \{f_1(\vec{x}), \ldots, f_M(\vec{x})\}, \vec{x} \in DS$;
- $g_1, \ldots, g_J$ – J inequality constraints, where $g_j(\vec{x}) \geq 0, j = \overline{1,J}$;
- $h_1, \ldots, h_K$ – K equality constraints, where $g_k(\vec{x}) = 0, k = \overline{1,K}$.

The GMORSP is the problem of finding a decision vector $\vec{x} = (x_1, \ldots, x_{m+t})$ such that:

$$optimize\{F(\vec{x})\} = optimize\{f_1(\vec{x}), \ldots, f_M(\vec{x})\},$$

where $f_i : DS \rightarrow \mathcal{R}^{m+t}, \vec{x} \in DS, g_j(\vec{x}) \geq 0, j = \overline{1,J}, h_k(\vec{x}) = 0, k = \overline{1,K}, i = \overline{1,M}$.
Multi-objective optimization often means optimizing conflicting goals. For the GMORSP formulation there may be the possibility to blend different types of objectives, like: some of them to be maximized and some of them to be minimized.
For those cases where the conflicting objectives exist, they must be converted to meet the optimization problem requirements. Therefore, for an objective f_i, $0 \leq i \leq M$, that needs to be converted, where MAX is the highest value from the objective space of the objective mapping f_i, $0 \leq i \leq M$, $MAX \in \mathcal{R}^{m+t}$, there are two ways to switch to the optimal objective, as:

- $MAX - f_i(\vec{x})$, when MAX can be computed;
- $-f_i(\vec{x})$, when MAX cannot be computed.

4.2 Specific multi-objective refactoring selection problems

In the context of appropriate refactoring selection research domain there are many problems that may be defined as multi-objective optimization problems. Section 5 states the *Multi-Objective Refactoring Set Selection Problem* as a particular refactoring selection problem. A more restraint problem definition for the case when a single refactoring is searched is discussed too, as *Multi-Objective Single Refactoring Selection Problem* in (Chisăliţă-Creţu & Vescan, 2009), (Chisăliţă-Creţu & Vescan, 2009).
Specific conflicting objectives are studied in order to identify the optimal set of refactorings. Therefore, the *refactoring cost* has to be minimized, while the *refactoring impact* on the affected software entities needs to be maximized.

5. The multi-objective refactoring set selection problem

The *Multi-Objective Refactoring Set Selection Problem* (MORSSP) is a special case of refactoring selection problem. Its definition in Chisăliţă-Creţu (2009) follows the *General Multi-Objective Refactoring Selection Problem* (see Section 4). The two compound and conflicting objective functions are defined as the *refactoring cost* and the *refactoring impact* on software entities.
In order to state the *Multi-Objective Refactoring Set Selection Problem* (MORSSP) some notions and characteristics have to be defined.

Input data
Let

$$SE = \{e_1, \ldots, e_m\}$$

be a set of software entities, e.g., a class, an attribute from a class, a method from a class, a formal parameter from a method or a local variable declared in the implementation of a method.
The weight associated with each software entity $e_i, 1 \leq i \leq m$ is kept by the set

$$Weight = \{w_1, \ldots, w_m\},$$

where $w_i \in [0,1]$ and $\sum_{i=1}^{m} w_i = 1$.
The set of possible relevant chosen refactorings Fowler (1999) that may be applied to different types of software entities of SE is

$$SR = \{r_1, \ldots, r_t\}.$$

Dependencies between such transformations when they are applied to the same software entity are expressed by the formula 3 (see Section 4).
The effort involved by each transformation is converted to cost, described by the following function:
$rc : SR \times SE \rightarrow Z,$

$$rc(r_l, e_i) = \begin{cases} > 0, \text{ if } ra(r_l, e_i) = T \\ = 0, \text{ otherwise} \end{cases},$$

where the ra mapping is defined by the formula 2 (see Section 4), $1 \leq l \leq t, 1 \leq i \leq m$.
Changes made to each software entity $e_i, i = \overline{1,m}$, by applying the refactoring $r_l, 1 \leq l \leq t$, are stated and a mapping is defined:
$effect : SR \times SE \rightarrow Z,$

$$effect(r_l, e_i) = \begin{cases} > 0, \text{ if } ra(r_l, e_i) = T \text{ and has the requested effect on } e_i \\ < 0, \text{ if } ra(r_l, e_i) = T; \text{ has } \textit{not} \text{ the requested effect on } e_i \\ = 0, \text{ otherwise} \end{cases},$$

where the ra mapping is defined by the formula 2 (see Section 4), $1 \leq l \leq t, 1 \leq i \leq m$.
The overall effect of applying a refactoring $r_l, 1 \leq l \leq t$, to each software entity $e_i, i = \overline{1,m}$, is defined as it follows:
$res : SR \rightarrow Z,$

$$res(r_l) = \sum_{i=1}^{m} w_i \cdot effect(r_l, e_i),$$

where $1 \leq l \leq t$.

Additional notations

Each refactoring $r_l, l = \overline{1,t}$ may be applied to a subset of software entities, defined as a function:
$re : SR \rightarrow \mathcal{P}(SE)$,

$$re(r_l) = \left\{ e_{l_1}, \ldots, e_{l_q} \mid \text{if } ra(r_l, e_{l_u}) = T, 1 \leq u \leq q, 1 \leq q \leq m \right\},$$

where the ra mapping is defined by the formula 2 (see Section 4), $re(r_l) = SE_{r_l}, SE_{r_l} \in \mathcal{P}(SE) - \emptyset, 1 \leq l \leq t$.

Output data

The MORSSP is the problem of finding a subset of entities named $ESet_l$, $ESet_l \in \mathcal{P}(SE) - \emptyset$ for each refactoring $r_l \in SR, l = \overline{1,t}$ such that:

- the following objectives have to be optimized:
  - the overall refactoring cost is minimized;
  - the overall refactoring impact on software entities is maximized;
- refactoring dependencies constraints defined by the mapping 3 are satisfied.

The solution $S = (ESet_1, \ldots, ESet_t)$ consists of the $ESet_l$ elements for a specific refactorings $r_l, 1 \leq l \leq t$, where $ESet_l \in \mathcal{P}(SE) - \emptyset, 1 \leq l \leq t$.

5.1 Multi-objective optimization problem formulation

The MORSSP optimizes the required cost minimize required cost for the applied refactorings and to maximize the refactoring impact on software entities. Therefore, the multi-objective function $F(\vec{r}) = \{f_1(\vec{r}), f_2(\vec{r})\}$, where $\vec{r} = (r_1, \ldots, r_t)$ is to be optimized, as described below. Current MORSSP treats cost as an objective instead of a constraint, like the refactoring dependencies described by the mapping 3 (see Section 4).
The first objective function minimizes the total cost for the applied refactorings:

$$minimize\{f_1(\vec{r})\} = minimize \left\{ \sum_{l=1}^{t} \sum_{i=1}^{m} rc(r_l, e_i) \right\},$$

where $\vec{r} = (r_1, \ldots, r_t)$.
The second objective function maximizes the total effect of the refactorings applied to software entities, considering the weight of the software entities in the overall system, like:

$$maximize\left\{f_2(\vec{r})\right\} = maximize\left\{ \sum_{l=1}^{t} res(r_l) \right\} = maximize \left\{ \sum_{l=1}^{t} \sum_{i=1}^{m} w_i \cdot effect(r_l, e_i) \right\}, \quad (4)$$

where $\vec{r} = (r_1, \ldots, r_t)$.
The goal is to identify those solutions that compromise the refactorings costs and the overall impact on transformed entities. The objective that does not follow the maximizing approach needs to be converted in a suitable way.
In order to convert the first objective function to a maximization problem in the MORSSP, the total cost is subtracted from MAX, the biggest possible total cost, as it is shown below:

$$maximize\left\{f_1(\vec{r})\right\} = maximize \left\{ MAX - \sum_{l=1}^{t} \sum_{i=1}^{m} rc(r_l, e_i) \right\}, \quad (5)$$

where $\vec{r} = (r_1, \ldots, r_t)$. The overall objective function for MORSSP is defined by:

$$\begin{aligned} &maximize\left\{F(\vec{r})\right\} = maximize\left\{f_1(\vec{r}),\ f_2(\vec{r})\right\} = \\ &= maximize\left\{MAX - \sum_{l=1}^{t}\sum_{i=1}^{m} rc(r_l, e_i),\ \sum_{l=1}^{t}\sum_{i=1}^{m} w_i \cdot effect(r_l, e_i)\right\}, \end{aligned} \tag{6}$$

where $\vec{r} = (r_1, \ldots, r_t)$.

6. Case study: LAN simulation

The proposed algorithm was applied on a simplified version of the *Local Area Network* (LAN) simulation source code, that was presented in (Demeyer et al., 2005). Figure 1 shows the class diagram of the studied source code. It contains 5 classes with 5 attributes and 13 methods, constructors included.

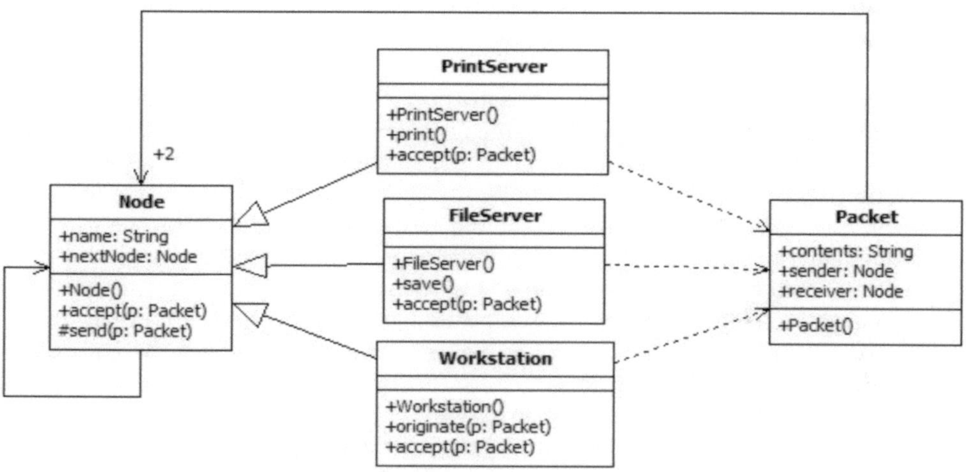

Fig. 1. Class diagram for the LAN Simulation source code

The *LAN Simulation* source code has been successfully used in several introductory programming courses to illustrate and teach good object-oriented design. Moreover, a large number of refactoring domain research papers have used it to present the effect of different refactoring applications.

The *LAN Simulation Problem* is sufficiently simple for illustrative purposes, by covering most of the interesting constructs of the object-oriented programming paradigm, like: inheritance, late binding, super calls, method overriding. While it has been implemented in several object-oriented programming languages, within our research a *Java* implementation is used. The *LAN Simulation* source code has proved its relevance within the research since it follows an incremental development style and it suggests several typical refactorings. Therefore, it is accepted as a suitable example that serves as a basis for different refactoring feasibility studies. The source code version used within our experiments consists of 5 classes: `Packet`, `Node` and its three subclasses `Workstation`, `PrintServer`, and `FileServer`. The `Node` objects are linked together in a token ring network, using the `nextNode` attribute; they can `send` or `accept` a `Packet` object. The `PrintServer`, `FileServer`, and `Workstation` classes refine the behaviour of the `accept` method (and perform a super call) to achieve specific behaviour for printing or saving the `Packet` and avoiding its endless cycling. A `Packet` object can only originate (`sender` attribute) from an `Workstation` object and sequentially visits every `Node` object in the network until it reaches its receiver (`receiver` attribute) that `accepts` the `Packet`, or until it returns to its `sender` workstation, indicating that the `Packet` cannot be delivered. The corresponding initial class diagram is depicted by Figure 1.

Dif□culties. This *LAN Simulation* version has several aspects denoting lack of data hiding and flexibility. The instance variables are visible from outside causing possible unauthorized accesses or changes. Intuitively, shielding the attribute from direct references reduces data coupling. This allows the attribute to change its value without affecting clients using the attribute value. Another issue is related to the small capability of code reuse within the class hierarchy. Generally speaking, generalization may increase code reuse and reduce the impact of changes. Thus, any change is done within a single place and all possible clients remain unchanged.

Solutions. The *EncapsulateField* refactoring can be performed in order to guard the attribute `nextMachine` of the class `Node` from direct access. It results in the introduction of two methods in `Node` class, as: the `getNextNode` method which accesses the attribute and returns its value to the caller and the `setNextNode` method which takes the new value of the attribute as a parameter and updates the attribute. Then, the attribute itself is made `private`.
Generalization degree may be raised by applying the *RenameMethod* refactoring to the `print` method from the `PrintServer` class and to the `save` method from the `FileServer` class to an unique name `process`, while its signature remains unchanged. Then each call of the former methods will be replaced by a call to the corresponding `process` method from the `PrintServer` or `FileServer` classes. The generalization process may go thoroughly. The *PullUpMethod* refactoring may be applied to the `process` methods from the `PrintServer` and `FileServer` classes. This requires the introduction of a new empty body method in the `Node` superclass. By pulling up a method to a base class, its specific behaviour is generalized, making possible for subclasses to reuse and specialize the inherited behaviour.

7. Proposed approach description

The MORSSP is approached here by exploring the various existing refactoring dependencies. Two conflicting objectives are studied, i.e., minimizing the refactoring cost and maximizing the refactoring impact, together with some constraints to be kept, as the refactoring dependencies.
There are several ways to handle a multi-objective optimization problem. The *weighted sum method* (Kim & deWeck, 2005) was adopted to solve the MORSSP. The overall objective function to be maximized $F(\vec{r})$, defined by the formula 6 (see Section 4), is shaped to the weighted sum principle with two objectives to optimize.
Therefore, $maximize\left\{F(\vec{r})\right\} = maximize\left\{f_1(\vec{r}), f_2(\vec{r})\right\}$, is mathematically rewritten to:

$$maximize\left\{F(\vec{r})\right\} = \alpha \cdot f_1(r) + (1-\alpha) \cdot f_2(r),$$

where $0 \leq \alpha \leq 1$ and $\vec{r}$ is the decision variable.

A steady–state evolutionary model is advanced by the proposed evolutionary computation technique (Chisăliţă-Creţu, 2010). Algorithm 1 is the adapted genetic algorithm to the context of the investigated MORSSP, proposed in (Chisăliţă-Creţu, 2009; 2010).

Algorithm 1 the adapted evolutionary algorithm for the MORSSP Chisăliţă-Creţu (2009)

Input:
- SR – the set of refactorings;
- SE – the set of entities;
- rd – the mapping of refactoring dependencies;
- $Weight$ – the set of entity weights;
- rc – the mapping of refactoring costs;
- $effect$ – the mapping of refactoring impact on entities;
- $NumberOfGenerations$ – the number of generations to compute;
- $NumberOfIndividuals$ – the number of individuals within a population;
- $CrossProbability$ – the crossover probability;
- $MutProbability$ – the mutation probability.

Output:
- the solution.

```
Begin
@ Randomly create the initial population P(0);
for t := 1 to NumberOfGenerations do
    for k := 1 to NumberOfIndividuals/2 do
        @Select two individuals p1 and p2 from the current population;
        @OnePointCutCrossover for the parents p1 and p2, obtaining the two offsprings o1
and o2;
        @Mutate the offsprings o1 and o2;
        if (Fitness(o1) < Fitness(o2)) then
            if (Fitness(o1) < the fitness of the worst individual) then
                @Replace the worst individual with o1 in P(t);
            else
                if (Fitness(o2) < the fitness of the worst individual) then
                    @ Replace the worst individual with o2 in P(t);
                end if
            end if
        end if
    end for
end for
@Select the best individual from P(NumberOfGenerations);
End.
```

In a steady-state evolutionary algorithm a single individual from the population is changed at a time. The best chromosome (or a few best chromosomes) is copied to the population in the next generation. Elitism can very rapidly increase performance of GA, because it prevents to lose the best found solution to date.

The proposed genetic algorithm approaches two solution representations for the studied problem. The genetic algorithm that uses a *refactoring-based* solution representation for the

MORSSP is denoted by *RSSGARef*, while the corresponding *entity-based* genetic algorithm is denoted by *RSSGAEnt*.

7.1 Refactoring-based solution representation

For the *RSSGARef* algorithm the solution representation is presented in (Chisăliţă-Creţu, 2009), with the decision vector $\vec{S} = (S_1, \ldots, S_t)$, where $S_l \in \mathcal{P}(SE), 1 \leq l \leq t$, determines the entities that may be transformed using the proposed refactoring set SR. The item S_l on the l-th position of the solution vector represents a set of entities that may be refactored by applying the l-th refactoring from SR, where for each $e_{l_u}, e_{l_u} \in SE_{r_l}, e_{l_u} \in S_l, S_l \in \mathcal{P}(SE), 1 \leq u \leq q, 1 \leq q \leq m, 1 \leq l \leq t$. This means it is possible to apply more than once different refactorings to the same software entity, i.e., distinct gene values from the chromosome may contain the same software entity.

7.1.1 Genetic operators

Crossover and mutation operators are used by this approach, being described in the following.

Crossover operator

A simple one point crossover scheme is used. A crossover point is randomly chosen. All data beyond that point in either parent string is swapped between the two parents.

For instance, if the two parents are:

$parent_1 = [ga[1,7], gb[3,5,10], gc[8], gd[2,3,6,9,12], ge[11], gf[13,4]]$ and

$parent_2 = [g1[4,9,10,12], g2[7], g3[5,8,11], g4[10,11], g5[2,3,12], g6[5,9]]$, for the cutting point 3, the two resulting offsprings are:

$offspring_1 = [ga[1,7], gb[3,5,10], gc[8], g4[10,11], g5[2,3,12], g6[5,9]]$ and

$offspring_2 = [g1[4,9,10,12], g2[7], g3[5,8,11], gd[2,3,6,9,12], ge[11], gf[13,4]]$.

Mutation operator

Mutation operator used here exchanges the value of a gene with another value from the allowed set. Namely, mutation of the i-th gene consists of adding or removing a software entity from the set that denotes the i-th gene.

For example, if the individual to be mutated is

$parent = [ga[1,7], gb[3,5,10], gc[8], gd[2,6,9,12], ge[12], gf[13,4]]$ and if the 5-th gene is to be mutated, the obtained offspring is $offspring = [ga[1,7], gb[3,5,10], gc[8], gd[2,6,9,12], ge[\mathbf{10},12]\ gf[13,4]]$ by adding the 10-th software entity to the 5-th gene.

7.2 Entity-based solution representation

The *RSSGAEnt* algorithm uses the solution representation presented in (Chisăliţă-Creţu, 2009), where the decision vector (chromosome) $\vec{S} = (S_1, \ldots, S_m), S_i \in \mathcal{P}(SR), 1 \leq i \leq m$ determines the refactorings that may be applied in order to transform the proposed set of software entities SE.

The item S_i on the i-th position of the solution vector represents a set of refactorings that may be applied to the i-th software entity from SE, where each entity $e_{l_u} \in S_{r_l}, S_{r_l} \in \mathcal{P}(SR), 1 \leq u \leq q, 1 \leq q \leq m, 1 \leq l \leq t$. It means it is possible to apply more than once the same refactoring to different software entities, i.e., distinct gene values from the chromosome may contain the same refactoring.

7.2.1 Genetic operators

The genetic operators used by the *RSSGAEnt* algorithm are crossover and mutation as described by Section 7.1.1. The *crossover operator* uses a simple one point cut scheme, randomly chosen. All the data beyond the cut point from the parent strings is swapped between the two parents.
The mutation operator used here exchanges the value of a gene with another value from the allowed set. The mutation of the i-th gene consists of adding or removing a refactoring from the set that denotes the i-th gene.

8. Input data

The adapted genetic algorithm proposed in (Chisăliţă-Creţu, 2009; 2010) is applied to a simplified version of the *LAN Simulation* source code (see Section 1). Relevant data about the source code is extracted and the software entity set is defined as: $SE = \{c_1, \ldots, c_5, a_1, \ldots, a_5, m_1, \ldots, m_{13}\}$, $|SE| = 23$. The chosen transformations are refactorings that may be applied to classes, attributes or methods, as: *RenameMethod, ExtractSuperClass, PullUpMethod, MoveMethod, EncapsulateField, AddParameter*. They will form the refactoring set $SR = \{r_1, \ldots, r_6\}$ in the following. The entity weights are gathered within the set $Weight$, that presented by Table 1 , where $\sum_{i=1}^{23} w_i = 1$.
The dependency relationship between refactorings, described by the mapping *rd* and the final impact of each refactoring stated by the *res* mapping are defined by the Table 1. The *res* mapping value computation for each refactoring is based on the weight of each possible affected software entity, as it was defined in Section 5.
Each software entity allows specific refactorings to be applied to, otherwise the cost mapping values are 0. E.g., the r_1, r_3, r_4, r_6 refactorings may be applied to the $m_1, m_4, m_7, m_{10}, m_{13}$ methods. For special methods, i.e., constructors, refactorings like *pullUpMethod* (r_3) and *moveMethod* (r_4) cannot be applied. Here, the cost mapping *rc* is computed as the number of transformations needed in order to apply the refactoring. Therefore, refactoring applications to related entities may have different costs.
Intermediate data for the $effect$ mapping was used to compute the *res* mapping values. The $effect$ mapping values were considered numerical data, denoting an estimated impact of refactoring application, e.g., a software metric assessment.

8.1 Proposed refactoring strategy

A possible refactoring strategy for the *LAN Simulation Problem* is presented below. Based on the *difculties* (see Section 6) presented for the corresponding class hierarchy, three transformation categories may be identified. For each of them several improvement targets that may be achieved through refactoring are defined.

1. *information management* (data hiding, data cohesion):
   (a) control the attribute access (*EncapsulateField* refactoring);
2. *behaviour management* (method definition, method cohesion):
   (a) adapt the method signature to new context (*AddParameter* refactoring);
   (b) increase the expressiveness of a method identifier by changing its name (*RenameMethod* refactoring);
   (c) increase method cohesion within classes (*MoveMethod* and *PullUpMethod* refactorings);
3. *class hierarchy abstraction* (class generalization, class specialization):
   (a) increase the abstraction level within the class hierarchy by generalization (*ExtractSuperClass* refactoring).

(a) Refactoring dependencies (*rd*) and final impact (*res*) of their applying to the entity set (*SE*)

rd	r_1	r_2	r_3	r_4	r_5	r_6
r_1	N		B			AA
r_2		N	B			
r_3	A	A	N	N		
r_4			N	N		
r_5					N	
r_6	AB					N
res	0.4	0.49	0.63	0.56	0.8	0.2

(b) Refactoring costs (*rc*) and their applicability on software entities. The weight for each software entity (*Weight*)

rc	r_1	r_2	r_3	r_4	r_5	r_6	*Weight*
c_1		$\surd/1$					0.1
c_2		$\surd/1$					0.08
c_3		$\surd/2$					0.08
c_4		$\surd/2$					0.07
c_5		$\surd/1$					0.07
a_1					$\surd/4$		0.04
a_2					$\surd/5$		0.03
a_3					$\surd/5$		0.03
a_4					$\surd/5$		0.05
a_5					$\surd/5$		0.05
m_1	$\surd/1$		$\surd/0$	$\surd/0$		$\surd/1$	0.04
m_2	$\surd/3$		$\surd/1$	$\surd/1$		$\surd/3$	0.025
m_3	$\surd/5$		$\surd/1$	$\surd/1$		$\surd/5$	0.025
m_4	$\surd/1$		$\surd/0$	$\surd/0$		$\surd/1$	0.04
m_5	$\surd/1$		$\surd/1$	$\surd/1$		$\surd/1$	0.025
m_6	$\surd/1$		$\surd/1$	$\surd/1$		$\surd/1$	0.025
m_7	$\surd/1$		$\surd/0$	$\surd/0$		$\surd/1$	0.04
m_8	$\surd/2$		$\surd/1$	$\surd/1$		$\surd/2$	0.025
m_9	$\surd/1$		$\surd/1$	$\surd/1$		$\surd/1$	0.025
m_{10}	$\surd/1$		$\surd/0$	$\surd/0$		$\surd/1$	0.04
m_{11}	$\surd/2$		$\surd/1$	$\surd/1$		$\surd/2$	0.025
m_{12}	$\surd/1$		$\surd/1$	$\surd/1$		$\surd/1$	0.025
m_{13}	$\surd/1$		$\surd/0$	$\surd/0$		$\surd/1$	0.04
							$\sum_{i=1}^{23} w_i = 1$

Table 1. Input Data for the *LAN Simulation Problem* case study

9. Practical experiments

The algorithm was run 100 times and the best, worse and average fitness values were recorded. The parameters used by the evolutionary approach were as follows: mutation probability 0.7 and crossover probability 0.7. Different number of generations and of individuals were used: number of generations 10, 50, 100, 200 and number of individuals 20, 50, 100, 200. The following subsections reveal the obtained results for different values of the α parameter: 0.3, 0.5 and 0.7, presented in Chisăliţă-Creţu (2009); Chisăliţă-Creţu (2009) (Chisăliţă-Creţu, 2009; 2010).

9.1 Refactoring-based solution representation experiments

Two types of experiments were run: with equal objective weights and different objectives weights. The equal objective weights uses $\alpha = 0.5$, while the two different weight experiments uses $\alpha = 0.7$ and $\alpha = 0.3$. In the former experiment the refactoring cost has a greater relevance than the refactoring impact, while in the last one, the refactoring impact drives the chromosome competition.

9.1.1 Equal weights ($\alpha = 0.5$)

The current experiment run on the *LAN Simulation Problem* proposes equal weights, i.e., $\alpha = 0.5$, for the studied fitness function Chisăliţă-Creţu (2009); Chisăliţă-Creţu (2009). That is,

$$F(\vec{r}) = 0.5 \cdot f_1(\vec{r}) + 0.5 \cdot f_2(\vec{r}),$$

where $\vec{r} = (r_1, \ldots, r_t)$. Figure 2 presents the 200 generations evolution of the fitness function (best, worse and average) for 20 chromosomes populations (Figure 2(a)) and 200 chromosomes populations (Figure 2(b)).

There is a strong competition among chromosomes in order to breed the best individual. In the 20 individuals populations the competition results in different quality of the best individuals for various runs, from very weak to very good solutions. The 20 individuals populations runs have few very weak solutions, better than 0.25, while all the best chromosomes are good solutions, i.e., all individuals have fitness better than 0.41.

Compared to the former populations, the 200 chromosomes populations breed closer best individuals. The number of good chromosomes is smaller than the one for 20 individuals populations, i.e., 53 chromosome with fitness better than 0.41 only.

The data for the worst chromosomes reveals similar results, since for the 200 individuals populations there is no chromosome with fitness better than 0.25, while for the 20 chromosomes populations there are 12 worst individuals better than 0.25. This situation outlines an intense activity in smaller populations, compared to larger ones, where diversity among individuals reduces the population capability to quickly breed better solutions.

Various runs as number of generations, i.e., 10, 50, 100 and 200 generations, show the improvement of the best chromosome. For the recorded experiments, the best individual for 200 generations was better for 20 chromosomes populations (with a fitness value of 0.4793) than the 200 individuals populations (with a fitness value of just 0.4515). This means in small populations (with fewer individuals) the reduced diversity among chromosomes may induce a harder competition than within large populations (with many chromosomes) where the diversity breeds weaker individuals. As the Figure 2 shows it, after several generations smaller populations produce better individuals (as number and quality) than larger ones, due to the poor populations diversity itself.

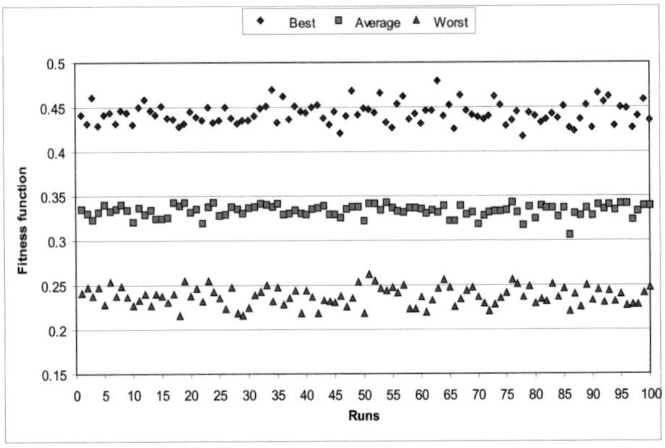

(a) Experiment with 200 generations and 20 individuals

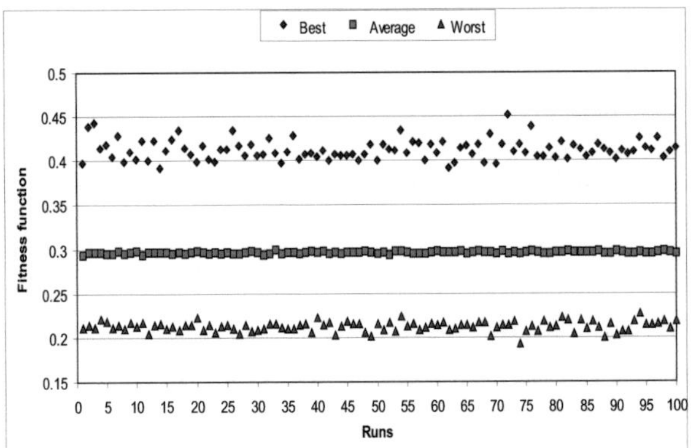

(b) Experiment with 200 generations and 200 individuals

Fig. 2. The evolution of fitness function (best, worse and average) for 20 and 200 individuals with 200 generations, with 11 mutated genes, for $\alpha = 0.5$

The number of chromosomes with fitness value better than 0.41 for the studied populations and generations is captured by Figure 3. It shows that smaller populations with poor diversity among chromosomes involve a harder competition within them and more, the number of eligible chromosomes increases quicker for smaller populations than for the larger ones. Therefore, for the 20 chromosomes populations with 200 generations evolution all 100 runs have shown that the best individuals are better than 0.41, while for 200 individuals populations with 200 generations the number of best chromosomes better than 0.41 is only 53.

Impact on the *LAN simulation* source code

The best individual obtained allows to improve the structure of the class hierarchy. Therefore, a new `Server` class is the base class for `PrintServer` class. Moreover, the signatures of the `print` method from the `PrintServer` class is changed, though the method renaming to `process` identifier was not suggested. Opposite to this, for the `save` method in the `FileServer` class was recommended to change the method name to `process`, while the signature changing was not suggested yet. The two refactorings (*addParameter* and

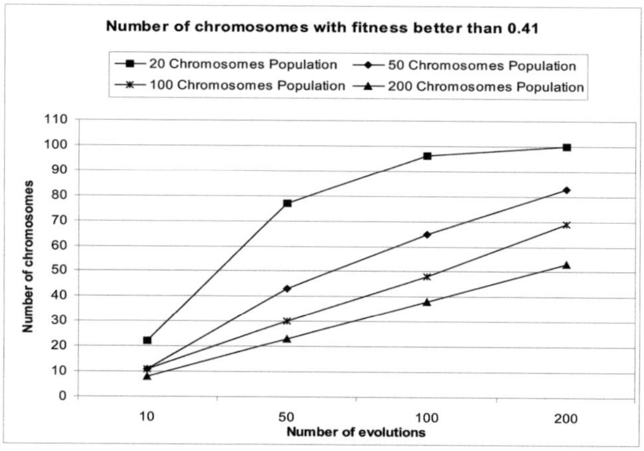

Fig. 3. The evolution of the number of chromosomes with fitness better than 0.41 for the 20, 50, 100 and 200 individual populations, with $\alpha = 0.5$

renameMethod) applied to the `print` and `save` methods would had been ensured their polymorphic behaviour.

The `accept` method is moved to the new `Server` class for the `FileServer` class, though the former was not suggested to be added as a base class of the latter. The correct access to the class fields by encapsulating them within their classes is enabled for three of five class attributes.

The refactoring cost and refactoring impact on software entity have been treated with the same importance within the refactoring process ($\alpha = 0.5$).

The current solution representation allows to apply more than one refactoring to each software entity, i.e., the `print` method from the `PrintServer` class is transformed by two refactorings, as the *AddParameter* and *RenameMethod* refactorings.

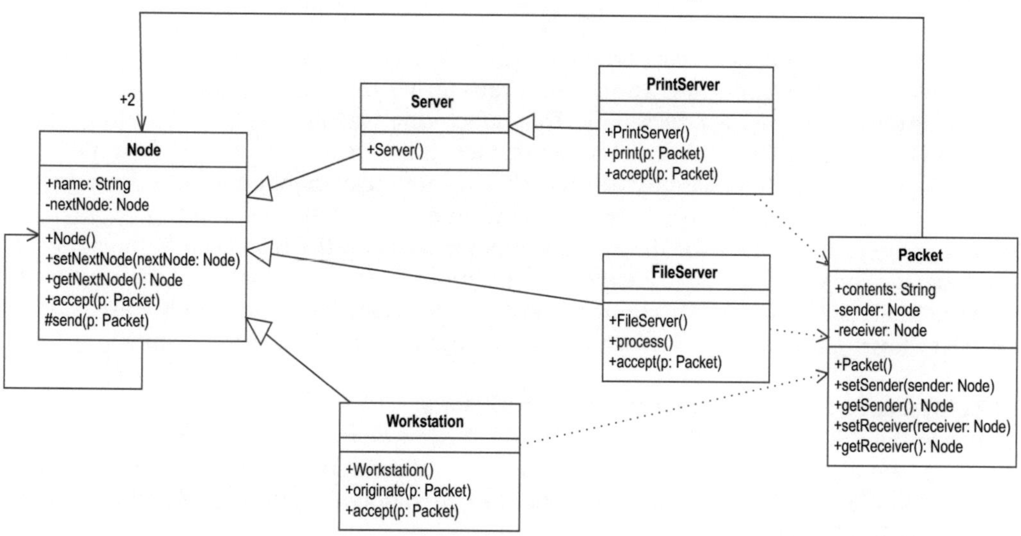

Fig. 4. The class diagram for the *LAN Simulation* source code, after applying the *RSSGARef Algorithm* solution for $\alpha = 0.5$

9.1.2 Discussion on *RSSGARef algorithm* experiments

Current subsection summarizes the results of the proposed *RSSGARef Algorithm* for three different values of the α parameter, i.e., 0.3, 0.5, 0.7, in order to maximize the weighted sum fitness function that optimizes the refactoring cost and the refactoring impact on affected software entities Chisăliţă-Creţu (2009). A chromosome summary of the obtained results for all run experiments as it is presented in Chisăliţă-Creţu (2009); Chisăliţă-Creţu (2009) (Chisăliţă-Creţu, 2009) is given below:

- $\alpha = 0.3$, $bestFitness = 0.33587$ for 20 *chromosomes and* 200 *generations*
  - $bestChrom = [[10, 22, 21, 19, 15], [3, 2], [21, 19, 10, 16, 17, 13, 11, 14, 12], [19, 10, 22, 11, 13, 16], [\varnothing], [21, 22]]$
- $\alpha = 0.5$, $bestFitness = 0.4793$ for 20 *chromosomes and* 200 *generations*
  - $bestChrom = [[20, 13, 19, 11], [1, 2], [15, 10, 20, 17, 19, 13, 12], [12, 11, 15, 14, 21], [6, 8, 9], [22, 12, 18, 17, 13, 14, 15]]$
- $\alpha = 0.7$, $bestFitness = 0.61719$ for 20 *chromosomes and* 200 *generations*
  - $bestChrom = [[20, 16], [3], [15, 18, 14, 21, 16, 13, 22, 10], [20, 10, 22, 16, 17], [\varnothing], [16, 10, 11]]$

The experiment for $\alpha = 0.3$ should identify those refactorings for which the cost has a lower relevance than the overall impact on the applied software entities. But, the best chromosome obtained has the fitness value 0.33587, lower than the best fitness value for the $\alpha = 0.5$ chromosome, i.e., 0.4793. This shows that an unbalanced aggregated fitness function with a higher weight for the overall impact on the applied refactorings, promotes the individuals with a lower cost and small refactorings. Therefore, there are not too many key software entities to be refactored by such an experiment.

The $\alpha = 0.7$ experiment should identify the refactorings for which the cost is more important than the final effect of the applied refactorings. The fitness value for the best chromosome for this experiment is 0.61719, while for the $\alpha = 0.5$ experiment the best fitness value is lower than this one.

The experiment for $\alpha = 0.7$ gets near to the $\alpha = 0.5$ experiment. The data shows similarities for the structure of the obtained best chromosomes for the two experiments. A major difference is represented by the `EncapsulatedField` refactoring that may be applied to the public class attributes from the class hierarchy. This refactoring was not suggested by the solution proposed by the $\alpha = 0.7$ experiment. Moreover, there is a missing link in the same experiment, due to the fact the `AddParameter` refactoring was not recommended for the `save` method from the `FileServer` and the `print` method from the `PrintServer` class.

Balancing the fitness values for the studied experiments and the relevance of the suggested solutions, we consider the $\alpha = 0.5$ experiment is more relevant as quality of the results than the other analyzed experiments. Figure 4 highlights the changes in the class hierarchy for the $\alpha = 0.5$ following the suggested refactorings from the recorded best chromosome.

9.2 Entity-based solution representation experiments

Similar to the *RSSGARef Algorithm*, the *RSSGAEnt Algorithm* was run 100 times and the best, worse and average fitness values were recorded. The algorithm was run for different number of generations and of individuals, as: number of generations 10, 50, 100, 200, and number of individuals 20, 50, 100, 200.

The parameters used by the evolutionary approach were the same as the ones used in the refactoring-based approach, like: mutation probability 0.7 and crossover probability 0.7. The run experiments Chisăliţă-Creţu (2009) have used different values for the α parameter (0.3, 0.5 and 0.7).

9.2.1 Different weights ($\alpha = 0.7$)

One of the different weighted experiments was run for $\alpha = 0.7$, where the cost (*rc* mapping) of the applied refactorings is more important than the implied final effect (*res* function) on the affected software entities Chisăliţă-Creţu (2009).

The results of the this experiment for the 20 individual populations with 50 generations evolution (Figure 5(a)) and 200 chromosome populations with 10 generations evolution (Figure 5(b)) are depicted by the Figure 5 with the fitness function (best, worse and average) values.

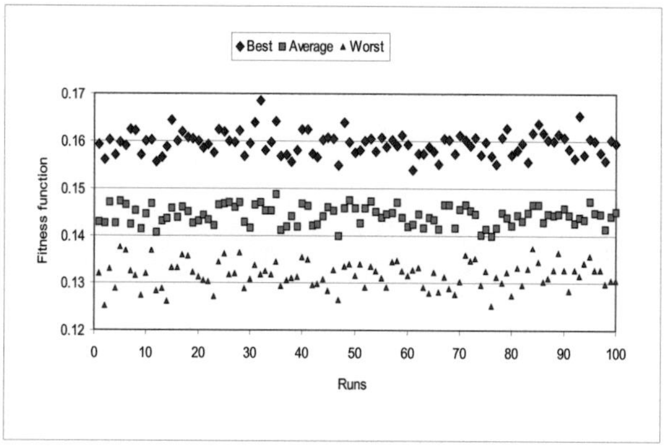

(a) Experiment with 50 generations and 20 individuals

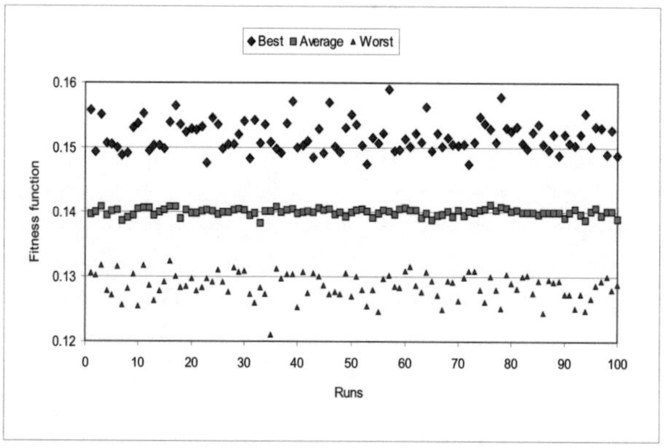

(b) Experiment with 10 generations and 200 individuals

Fig. 5. The evolution of the fitness function (best, worst and average) for 20 and 200 individuals with 50 and 10 generation evolutions, with 11 mutated genes, for $\alpha = 0.7$

The best individual was obtained for a 50 generations run with a 20 chromosomes population with the fitness 0.16862 (with 98 chromosomes with fitness > 0.155), while the greatest fitness value of the 200 chromosomes populations with 10 generations evolution was 0.15901 (11 individuals only with fitness value > 0.155).

The worst individual was recorded for a 200 chromosomes population with a 10 generations evolution with the fitness value 0.121 (72 individuals having the fitness < 0.13), while for the 20 individuals population for a 50 generations evolution the worst chromosome had the fitness value 0.12515 (27 chromosomes with fitness value < 0.13).
The number of chromosomes better than 0.155 for the 20, 50, 100 and 200 individuals populations with 10, 50, 100 and 200 generations is captured by Figure 6. The solutions for the 20 individuals populations for each studied number of evolutions keep their good quality, but the 50, 100 and 200 chromosomes populations carry a more intense chromosome competition compared to previously run experiments.

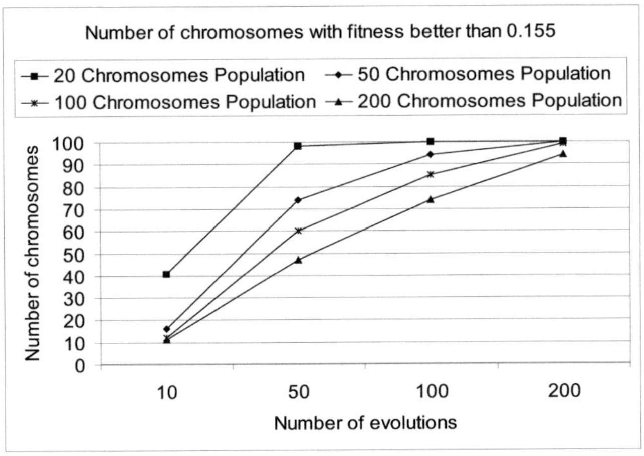

Fig. 6. The evolution of the number of chromosomes with fitness better than 0.155 for the 20, 50, 100 and 200 individuals populations, with $\alpha = 0.7$

Impact on the *LAN simulation* source code
The best chromosome obtained within this experiment suggests several refactorings, but there are some that have to be interpreted by the programmer as well. A new base class for the `PrintServer` and the `FileServer` classes is recorded by the obtained solution. The signature for the `save` method from the `FileServer` class is suggested to be changed by the best chromosome, though the similar change for the `print` method from the `PrintServer` class is not included by the studied best chromosome. The *renameMethod* refactoring was recommended for the `save` method from the `FileServer` class and for the `print` method from the `PrintServer` sibling class yet. Another improvement suggested by the current experiment is to apply the *PullUpMethod* refactoring in order to highlight the polymorphic behaviour of the `accept` method from the `PrintServer` but not for the same method within the `FileServer` class. No appearance of the *EncapsulatedField* refactoring was recorded in order to protect public class attributes from unauthorized access.

9.2.2 Discussion on *RSSGAEnt algorithm* experiments
The results of the proposed *RSSGAEnt Algorithm* for three different values of the α parameter, i.e., 0.3, 0.5, 0.7, in order to maximize the weighted-sum fitness function that optimizes the refactoring cost and the refactoring impact on the affected software entities Chisăliţă-Creţu (2009) are discussed by this section. A best chromosome summary for all run experiments as it is presented in Chisăliţă-Creţu (2009) is given below:

- $\alpha = 0.3$, $bestFitness = 0.19023$ for 20 *chromosomes and* 200 *generations*
  - $bestChrom$ = [[1], [∅], [1], [∅], [1], [4], [∅], [4], [4], [4], [3], [0, 3, 5], [3, 0, 5], [3], [3, 5, 0], [3], [5], [2, 3, 0], [3], [5, 0, 3, 2], [0, 5, 2], [2, 3], [3]]
- $\alpha = 0.5$, $bestFitness = 0.17345$ for 20 *chromosomes and* 200 *generations*
  - $bestChrom$ = [[∅], [1], [1], [1], [1], [4], [∅], [∅], [∅], [4], [0, 2], [2, 0], [0], [5, 2], [5, 3], [2, 5], [2, 0, 3], [0, 3, 2], [5, 0, 3, 2], [3, 2, 5], [3], [3, 0], [3, 5]]
- $\alpha = 0.7$, $bestFitness = 0.16862$ for 20 *chromosomes and* 50 *generations*
  - $bestChrom$ = [[∅], [1], [1], [1], [∅], [∅], [∅], [∅], [∅], [∅], [2, 3], [3, 2, 0], [3], [5, 0, 2], [0, 2], [2, 3], [2], [2, 0, 3], [2, 3], [0, 5, 3, 2], [0, 2, 5], [3, 0], [2, 3, 0]]

The experiment for $\alpha = 0.5$ should identify those refactorings for which the refactoring cost and impact on the applied software entities have the same relevance within the overall maximization problem. Though, this best chromosome is lower than the best fitness value obtained for $\alpha = 0.3$, i.e., 0.19023.

Moreover, the analysis for the obtained best individuals suggests that an unbalanced aggregated fitness function (with a higher weight for the overall impact of the applied refactorings) advances low cost refactorings, bringing a higher benefit for the structure and the quality of the suggested solution.

The refactorings suggested by the $\alpha = 0.5$ experiment are not connected one to another, such that a coherent strategy may be drawn. The main achievement suggested by the analyzed best chromosome of this experiment is related to the *EncapsulateField* refactoring for the public class attributes, not suggested for all five of them yet.

The $\alpha = 0.7$ experiment should identify the refactorings for which the cost is more important than the final effect of the applied refactorings. The fitness value of the best chromosome for this experiment is 0.16862, lower than the $\alpha = 0.5$ experiment best fitness value.

The experiment for $\alpha = 0.7$ gets near to the $\alpha = 0.3$ experiment as quality of the proposed solution. The best chromosome obtained within the former experiment suggests several refactorings, but there are some that have to be interpreted by the programmer. The achieved improvements cover two of the aspects to be improved within the class hierarchy, i.e., common behaviour (refactorings for methods), and class hierarchy abstraction (refactorings for classes). The information hiding aspects by suggesting refactorings for attributes was not recorded at all.

Compared to the other run experiments ($\alpha = 0.5$ and $\alpha = 0.3$) the achievements are more important as quality, though the effective overall fitness value is not the biggest.

The proposed solution by the $\alpha = 0.3$ experiment is more homogeneous, touching all the improvement categories. The drawback of this solutions is the ambiguity in several suggested refactoring sets for behaviour improvement. Therefore, the `save` method from the `FileServer` class and the `print` method from the `PrintServer` class may contain refactorings that belong to different refactoring strategies, i.e., *MoveMethod* and *PullUpMethod* refactorings.

9.3 Results analysis

This section analyzes the proposed solutions for the refactoring-based and entity-based solution representations. Both solution representations identify a set of refactorings for each software entity to which it may be applied to.

The chromosome size within the refactoring-based approach is 6, i.e., the number of possible refactorings to be applied, while the individual for the entity-based approach has 23 genes.

The recommended refactorings proposed by different runs and experiments does not shape a fully homogeneous refactoring strategy for none of the studied solution representations.
The best individual was obtained by the refactoring-based approach (*RSSGARef Algorithm*) was for a 200 generations evolution with 20 chromosomes population, having the fitness value of 0.4793, while by the entity-based approach (*RSSGAEnt Algorithm*) the recorded best chromosome was obtained for 200 generations and 20 individuals, with a fitness value of 0.19023. These solutions may be transposed from a representation to another, which means their structure may be compared and their efficiency assessed.
The idea that emerge from the run experiments was that smaller individual populations produce better individuals (as number, quality, time) than larger ones, that may be caused by the poor diversity within the population itself. Large number of genes of the individual structure induces poor quality to the current entity-based solution representation.
Table 2 summarizes the solutions obtained for the studied solution representation together with the goals reached by each of them. The number of achieved targets is computed based on the recommended refactoring presence within the studied chromosomes genes.

Solution representation	α **value**	**Best chrom.** (pop. size/ no. gen.)	**Best Fitness**	**Execution Time**	**Number of achieved targets (%)**				
					Data *(1a)*	**Method (2)** *(2a)*	*(2b)*	*(2c)*	**Class hierarchy** *(3a)*
Refactoring based	0.5	20c/200g	0.4793	36secs	60	50	50	50	50
	0.3	20c/200g	0.33587	32secs	0	0	0	50	100
	0.7	20c/200g	0.61719	37secs	0	0	50	100	50
Entity based	0.5	20c/200g	0.17345	75secs	40	0	50	100	100
	0.3	20c/200g	0.19023	61secs	80	50	100	100	50
	0.7	20c/50g	0.16862	19secs	0	50	100	100	100

Table 2. The best chromosomes obtained for the refactoring and entity based solution representations, with the α parameter values 0.5, 0.3, and 0.7

10. Conclusions

This work has advanced the evolutionary-based solution approach for the MORSSP. Adapted genetic algorithms have been proposed in order to cope with the multi-objectiveness of the required solution. Two conflicting objectives have been addressed, as to minimize the *refactoring cost* and to maximize the *refactoring impact* on the affected software entities. Different solution representations were studied and the various results of the run experiments were presented and compared.
The main contributions and results of the current work are:

- new genetic algorithms were proposed and different solution representations were studied for the MORSSP;
- adapted genetic operators to the refactoring selection area were tackled;
- a new goal-based assessment strategy for the selected refactorings was proposed in order to analyze and compare different achieved solutions;
- different experiments on the *LAN Simulation Problem* case study were run in order to identify the most appropriate refactoring set for each software entity such that the refactoring cost is minimized and the refactoring impact is maximized.

Further work may be done in the following directions: